KDD-96

KDD–96

Proceedings

Second International Conference on
Knowledge Discovery & Data Mining

Edited by

Evangelos Simoudis
Jiawei Han
& Usama Fayyad

AAAI Press
MENLO PARK • CALIFORNIA

ISBN 1-57735-004-9

Printed on acid-free paper.

Manufactured in the United States of America

Contents

KDD–96 Organization / x

Sponsoring Organizations / xi

Preface / xiii

KDD-96 Regular Papers

Combining Data Mining and Machine Learning

Sharing Learned Models among Remote Database Partitions by Local Meta-Learning / 2

> Philip K. Chan, Florida Institute of Technology and Salvatore J. Stolfo, Columbia University

Combining Data Mining and Machine Learning for Effective User Profiling / 8

> Tom Fawcett and Foster Provost, NYNEX Science and Technology

Local Induction of Decision Trees: Towards Interactive Data Mining / 14

> Truxton Fulton, Simon Kasif, and Steven Salzberg, Johns Hopkins University; David Waltz, NEC Research Institute

Knowledge Discovery in RNA Sequence Families of HIV Using Scalable Computers / 20

> Ivo L. Hofacker, University of Illinois; Martijn A. Huynen, Los Alamos National Laboratory and Santa Fe Institute; Peter F. Stadler, University of Vienna and Santa Fe Institute; Paul E. Stolorz, Jet Propulsion Laboratory, California Institute of Technology

Parallel Halo Finding in N-body Cosmology Simulations / 26

> David W. Pfitzner, Mount Stromlo Observatory, Australia and John K. Salmon, California Institute of Technology

Scalable Exploratory Data Mining of Distributed Geoscientific Data / 32

> Eddie C. Shek, University of California, Los Angeles and Hughes Research Laboratories; Richard R. Muntz, Edmond Mesrobian, and Kenneth Ng, University of California, Los Angeles

Data Mining Applications

Using a Hybrid Neural/Expert System for Data Base Mining in Market Survey Data / 38

> Victor Ciesielski and Gregory Palstra, Royal Melbourne Institute of Technology, Australia

Discovering Knowledge in Commercial Databases Using Modern Heuristic Techniques / 44

> B. de la Iglesia, J. C. W. Debuse, and V. J. Rayward-Smth, University of East Anglia, United Kingdom

KDD for Science Data Analysis: Issues and Examples / 50

> Usama Fayyad, Microsoft Research; David Haussler, University of California, Santa Cruz; and Paul Stolorz, Jet Propulsion Laboratory, California Institute of Technology

Data Mining and Model Simplicity: A Case Study in Diagnosis / 57

> Gregory M. Provan, Rockwell Science Center and Moninder Singh, University of Pennsylvania

Automated Discovery of Medical Expert System Rules from Clinical Databases Based on Rough Sets / 63

> Shusaku Tsumoto and Hiroshi Tanaka, Tokyo Medical and Dental University, Japan

Automated Discovery of Active Motifs in Multiple RNA Secondary Structures / 70

> Jason T. L. Wang, New Jersey Institute of Technology; Bruce A. Shapiro, National Institutes of Health; Dennis Shasha, New York University; Kaizhong Zhang, The University of Western Ontario, Canada; Chia-Yo Chang, New Jersey Institute of Technology

Detecting Early Indicator Cars in an Automotive
Database: A Multi-Strategy Approach / 76

Ruediger Wirth and Thomas P. Reinartz, Daimler-Benz
AG, Germany

Data Mining and Its Applications:
A General Overview

Knowledge Discovery and Data Mining: Towards a
Unifying Framework / 82

Usama Fayyad, Microsoft Research; Gregory Piatetsky-
Shapiro, GTE Laboratories; and Padhraic Smyth,
University of California, Irvine

An Overview of Issues in Developing Industrial Data
Mining and Knowledge Discovery Applications / 89

Gregory Piatetsky-Shapiro, GTE Laboratories; Ron
Brachman, AT&T Reseach; Tom Khabaza, ISL, United
Kingdom; Willi Kloesgen, GMD, Germany; and Evangelos
Simoudis, IBM Almaden Research Center

Decision-Tree and Rule Induction

Linear-Time Rule Induction / 96

Pedro Domingos, University of California, Irvine

Learning from Biased Data Using Mixture Models / 102

A. J. Feelders, Data Distilleries Ltd., The Netherlands

Discovery of Relevant New Features by Generating Non-
Linear Decision Trees / 108

Andreas Ittner, Chemnitz University of Technology and
Michael Schlosser, Fachhochschule Koblenz, Germany

Error-Based and Entropy-Based Discretization of
Continuous Features / 114

Ron Kohavi, Silicon Graphics, Inc. and Mehran Sahami,
Stanford University

Learning, Probability, and Graphical Models

Rethinking the Learning of Belief Network
Probabilities / 120

Ron Musick, Lawrence Livermore National Laboratory

Clustering Using Monte Carlo Cross-Validation / 126

Padhraic Smyth, University of California, Irvine

Harnessing Graphical Structure in Markov Chain Monte
Carlo Learning / 134

Paul E. Stolorz, Jet Propulsion Laboratory, California
Institute of Technology and Philip C. Chew, University of
Pennsylvania

Mining with Noise and Missing Data

Imputation of Missing Data Using Machine Learning
Techniques / 140

Kamakshi Lakshminarayan, Steven A. Harp, Robert
Goldman, and Tariq Samad, Honeywell Technology
Center

Discovering Generalized Episodes Using Minimal
Occurrences / 146

Heikki Mannila and Hannu Toivonen, University of
Helsinki, Finland

Pattern-Oriented Data Mining

Metapattern Generation for Integrated Data Mining /
152

Wei-Min Shen, University of Southern California and
Bing Leng, Inference Corporation

Automated Pattern Mining with a Scale Dimension / 158

Jan M. Zytkow, Wichita State University and Polish
Academy of Sciences, Poland; Robert Zembowicz, Wichita
State University

Prediction and Deviation

A Linear Method for Deviation Detection in Large
Databases / 164

Andreas Arning, IBM German Software Development
Laboratory, Germany; Rakesh Agrawal and Prabhakar
Raghavan, IBM Almaden Research Center

Planning Tasks for Knowledge Discovery in Databases;
Performing Task-Oriented User-Guidance / 170

Robert Engels, University of Karlsruhe, Germany

Predictive Data Mining with Finite Mixtures / 176

Petri Kontkanen, Petri Myllymäki, and Henry Tirri,
University of Helsinki, Finland

An Empirical Test of the Weighted Effect Approach to
Generalized Prediction Using Recursive Neural Nets /
183

Rense Lange, University of Illinois at Springfield

Multiple Uses of Frequent Sets and Condensed Representations: Extended Abstract / 189

Heikki Mannila and Hannu Toivonen, University of Helsinki, Finland

A Comparison of Approaches for Maximizing Business Payoff of Prediction Models / 195

Brij Masand and Gregory Piatetsky-Shapiro, GTE Laboratories

Scalability and Extensibility of Data Mining Systems

Scaling Up the Accuracy of Naive-Bayes Classifiers: A Decision-Tree Hybrid / 202

Ron Kohavi, Silicon Graphics, Inc.

Quakefinder: A Scalable Data Mining System for Detecting Earthquakes from Space / 208

Paul Stolorz and Christopher Dean, Jet Propulsion Laboratory, California Institute of Technology

Extensibility in Data Mining Systems / 214

Stefan Wrobel, Dietrich Wettschereck, Edgar Sommer, and Werner Emde, GMD, FIT.KI, Germany

Spatial, Text and Multimedia Data Mining

Mining Knowledge in Noisy Audio Data / 220

Andrzej Czyzewski, Technical University of Gdansk, Poland

A Density-Based Algorithm for Discovering Clusters in Large Spatial Databases with Noise / 226

Martin Ester, Hans-Peter Kriegel, Jörg Sander, and Xiaowei Xu, University of Munich, Germany

A Method for Reasoning with Structured and Continuous Attributes in the INLEN-2 Multistrategy Knowledge Discovery System / 232

Kenneth A. Kaufman, George Mason University and Ryszard S. Michalski, George Mason University and Polish Academy of Sciences, Poland

Self-Organizing Maps of Document Collections: A New Approach to Interactive Exploration / 238

Krista Lagus, Timo Honkela, Samuel Kaski, and Teuvo Kohonen, Helsinki University of Technology, Finland

Systems for Mining Large Databases

The Quest Data Mining System / 244

Rakesh Agrawal, Manish Mehta, John Shafer, and Ramakrishnan Srikant, IBM Almaden Research Center; Andreas Arning and Toni Bollinger, IBM German Software Development Laboratory, Germany

DBMiner: A System for Mining Knowledge in Large Relational Databases / 250

Jiawei Han, Yongjian Fu, Wei Wang, Jenny Chiang, Wan Gong, Krzystof Koperski, Deyi Li, Yijun Lu, Amynmohamed Rajan, Nebojsa Stefanovic, Betty Xia, and Osmar R. Zaiane, Simon Fraser University, Canada

DataMine: Application Programming Interface and Query Language for Database Mining / 256

Tomasz Imielinski, Aashu Virmani, and Amin Abdulghani, Rutgers University

KDD-96 Technology Spotlight (Concise) Papers

Application of Mathematical Theories

Evaluating the Interestingness of Characteristic Rules / 263

Micheline Kamber, Simon Fraser University and Rajjan Shinghal, Concordia University, Canada

The Field Matching Problem: Algorithms and Applications / 267

Alvaro E. Monge and Charles P. Elkan, University of California, San Diego

Discovering Classification Knowledge in Databases Using Rough Sets / 271

Ning Shan, Wojciech Ziarko, Howard J. Hamilton, and Nick Cercone, University of Regina, Canada

Exceptional Knowledge Discovery in Databases Based on Information Theory / 275

Einoshin Suzuki, Yokohama National University and Masamichi Shimura, Tokyo Institute of Technology, Japan

Interactive Knowledge Discovery from Marketing
Questionnaire Using Simulated Breeding and Inductive
Learning Methods / 279

*Takao Terano, The University of Tsukuba, Tokyo and
Yoko Ishino, The University of Tokyo, Japan*

Representing Discovered Patterns Using Attributed
Hypergraph / 283

*Yang Wang and Andrew K. C. Wong, University of
Waterloo, Canada*

Data Mining: Integration and Application

Developing Tightly-Coupled Data Mining Applications
on a Relational Database System / 287

*Rakesh Agrawal and Kyuseok Shim, IBM Almaden
Research Center*

Mining Entity-Identification Rules for Database
Integration / 291

*M. Ganesh and Jaideep Srivastava, University of
Minnesota; Travis Richardson, Apertus Technologies, Inc.*

Undiscovered Public Knowledge: A Ten-Year
Update / 295

*Don R. Swanson and Neil R. Smalheiser, University
of Chicago*

Genetic Algorithms

A Genetic Algorithm-Based Approach to Data
Mining / 299

*Ian W. Flockhart, Quadstone Ltd. and Nicholas J.
Radcliffe, Quadstone Ltd. and University of Edinburgh,
United Kingdom*

Deriving Queries from Results Using Genetic
Programming / 303

*Tae-Wan Ryu and Christoph F. Eick, University of
Houston*

Mining Association Rules

Maintenance of Discovered Knowledge: A Case in
Multi-Level Association Rules / 307

*David W. Cheung, The University of Hong Kong; Vincent
T. Ng, Hong Kong Polytechnic University; and Benjamin
W. Tam, The University of Hong Kong*

Analysing Binary Associations / 311

*Arno J. Knobbe and Pieter W. Adriaans, Syllogic, The
Netherlands*

Rule Induction and Decision Tree Induction

Growing Simpler Decision Trees to Facilitate Knowledge
Discovery / 315

*Kevin J. Cherkauer and Jude W. Shavlik,
University of Wisconsin*

Efficient Specific-to-General Rule Induction / 319

Pedro Domingos, University of California, Irvine

Data Mining and Tree-Based Optimization / 323

*Robert Grossman, Magnify, Inc. and University of Illinois;
Haim Bodek and Dave Northcutt, Magnify, Inc.; Vince
Poor, Princeton University*

Induction of Condensed Determinations / 327

Pat Langley, Stanford University

SE-Trees Outperform Decision Trees in Noisy
Domains / 331

Ron Rymon, University of Pittsburgh

Learning Limited Dependence Bayesian Classifiers / 335

Mehran Sahami, Stanford University

RITIO - Rule Induction Two In One / 339

*David Urpani, CSIRO; Xindong Wu, Monash University;
and Jim Sykes, Swinburne University of Technology,
Australia*

Spatial, Temporal, and
Multimedia Data Mining

Mining Associations in Text in the Presence of
Background Knowledge / 343

*Ronen Feldman, Bar-Ilan University, Israel and Haym
Hirsh, Rutgers University*

Extraction of Spatial Proximity Patterns by Concept
Generalization / 347

*Edwin M. Knorr and Raymond T. Ng, University of
British Columbia, Canada*

Pattern Discovery in Temporal Databases: A Temporal Logic Approach / 351

    Balaji Padmanabhan and Alexander Tuzhilin, New York University

Special Data Mining Techniques

Exploiting Background Knowledge in Automated Discovery / 355

    John M. Aronis, University of Pittsburgh; Foster J. Provost, NYNEX Science and Technology; and Bruce G. Buchanan, University of Pittsburgh

Data Mining with Sparse and Simplified Interaction Selection / 359

    Gerald Fahner, International Computer Science Institute

Inferring Hierarchical Clustering Structures by Deterministic Annealing / 363

    Thomas Hofmann and Joachim M. Buhmann, Rheinische Friedrich-Wilhelms-Universität, Germany

Static Versus Dynamic Sampling for Data Mining / 367

    George H. John and Pat Langley, Stanford University

Efficient Search for Strong Partial Determinations / 371

    Stefan Kramer and Bernhard Pfahringer, Austrian Research Institute for Artificial Intelligence, Austria

Reverse Engineering Databases for Knowledge Discovery / 375

    Stephen Mc Kearney, Bournemouth University and Huw Roberts, BT Laboratories, United Kingdom

Performing Effective Feature Selection by Investigating the Deep Structure of the Data / 379

    Marco Richeldi and Pier Luca Lanzi, CSELT, Italy

Invited Papers

Harnessing the Human in Knowledge Discovery / 384

    Georges G. Grinstein, University of Massachusetts at Lowell and The MITRE Corporation

Efficient Implementation of Data Cubes Via Materialized Views / 386

    Jeffrey D. Ullman, Stanford University

Index / 389

KDD–96 Organization

KDD-96 Conference Committee

General Conference Chair
   Usama M. Fayyad, Microsoft Research, USA

Program Cochairs
   Jiawei Han, Simon Fraser University, Canada
   Evangelos Simoudis, IBM Almaden Research Center, USA

Publicity Chair
   Padhraic Smyth, University of California, Irvine, USA

Sponsorship Chair
   Gregory Piatetsky-Shapiro, GTE Laboratories, USA

Demo Sessions and Exhibits Chair
   Tej Anand, NCR, USA

KDD-96 Program Committee

Rakesh Agrawal, IBM Almaden Research Center, USA
Tej Anand, NCR, USA
Ron Brachman, AT&T Research, USA
Wray Buntine, Thinkbank, USA
Nick Cercone, University of Regina, Canada
Peter Cheeseman, NASA AMES Research Center, USA
Bruce Croft, University of Massachusetts at Amherst, USA
Stephen G. Eick, Bell Laboratories, USA
Usama Fayyad, Microsoft Research, USA
Dan Geiger, Technion, Israel
Clark Glymour, Carnegie-Mellon University, USA
George Grinstein, University of Lowell, USA
David Hand, Open University, UK
David Heckerman, Microsoft Research, USA
Se June Hong, IBM T. J. Watson Research Center, USA
Tomasz Imielinski, Rutgers University, USA
Larry Jackel, AT&T Research, USA
Larry Kerschberg, George Mason University, USA
Willi Kloesgen, GMD, Germany

David Madigan, University of Washington, USA
Heikki Mannila, University of Helsinki, Finland
Chris Matheus, GTE Laboratories, USA
Sham Navathe, Georgia Institute of Technology, USA
Raymond Ng, University of British Columbia, Canada
Gregory Piatetsky-Shapiro, GTE Laboratories, USA
Daryl Pregibon, AT&T Research, USA
Pat Riddle, Boeing Computer Services, USA
Ted Senator, National Association for Securities Dealers, USA
Wei-Min Shen, University of Southern California, USA
Arno Siebes, CWI, The Netherlands
Avi Silberschatz, AT&T Bell Laboratories, USA
Andrzej Skowron, University of Warsaw, Poland
Steve Smith, Dun and Bradstreet, USA
Padhraic Smyth, University of California, Irvine, USA
Ramakrishnan Srikant, IBM Almaden Research Center, USA
Sal Stolfo, Columbia University, USA
Paul Stolorz, Jet Propulsion Laboratory, USA
Alex Tuzhilin, NYU Stern School, USA
Ramasamy Uthurusamy, General Motors, USA
Xindong Wu, Monash University, Australia
Wojciech Ziarko, University of Regina, Canada
Jan Zytkow, Wichita State University, USA

Auxiliary Reviewers

Chid Apte
David Dowe (KDD-95)
William Frawley
Charles Herman
Jonathan Hosking
Ed Johnson
Randy Kerber
Deyi Li
Edwin Pednault
Barry Rosen
Kyuseok Shim

Sponsoring Organizations

American Association for Artifcial Intelligence

General Motors Corporation

Microsoft Corporation

NASA/Jet Propulsion Laboratory

NCR Corporation

Silicon Graphics Inc.

Preface

As we enter the true digital information era, one of the greatest challenges facing organizations and individuals is how to turn their rapidly expanding data stores into accessible, and actionable knowledge. Digital data sources are ubiquitous, created by a variety of means spanning a spectrum of activities: from a supermarket's electronic scanner, to a bank's automated teller machine, from a credit card reader, to a world wide web server, and the most intricate of technical instruments. While advances on data storage and retrieval continue at a breakneck pace, (several organizations have databases that today contain several hundreds of gigabytes, and in some instances terabytes of online data with millions of rows and hundreds of columns; within two years the multi-terabyte database will be commonplace) the same cannot be asserted about the advances in information and knowledge extraction from large data sets. Only a very small percentage of the captured data is ever converted to actionable knowledge. The traditional approach of a human analyst, intimately familiar with a data set, serving as a conduit between raw data and synthesized knowledge by producing useful analyses and reports, is breaking down.

Responding to this need, researchers from fields such as pattern recognition, statistics, artificial intelligence, very large databases, and visualization in the mid-1980s started developing tools and techniques to discover knowledge from large, complex data stores. These researchers share a set of core issues: representation of discovered knowledge, search complexity, the use of prior knowledge, statistical inference, algorithms that scale to analysis of massive amounts of data both in size and dimensionality, managing uncertainty, and interactive (human-oriented) presentation. What started in 1989 as a workshop aimed at bringing together these research teams, culminated last year into the First International Conference on Knowledge Discovery and Data Mining (KDD-95), which was held in Montreal, Canada, August 20-21, 1995 in conjunction with IJCAI-95 and was attended by over 350 individuals from academia and industry.

The Second International Conference on Knowledge Discovery and Data Mining (KDD-96), held on August 2-4, 1996 in Portland, Oregon, USA, in conjunction with AAAI-96, provides a forum for KDD researchers and practitioners to present their latest work in this field. KDD-96 is a truly international conference. Of the 215 papers received for review 60% came from outside the United States with the following distribution: Australia (12), Austria (1), Belgium (2), Canada (14), Egypt (1), Finland (4), France (10), Germany (15), Hong Kong (2), Ireland (2), Israel (3), Italy (3), Japan (10), Mexico (1), Northern Ireland (3), Poland (5), Singapore (4), Taiwan (1), The Netherlands (6), and UK (10). Only 42 of the submitted papers were accepted for presentation to the conference; an acceptance rate of just under 20%. In addition, 30 papers were accepted for poster presentation. Posters were designated as short papers; each was allocated four pages in the proceedings, and a two-minute presentation as a "technology highlight." The KDD-96 program was further supplemented with five invited speakers and two special sessions each with an associated panel: "KDD and High Performance Computing" and "Systems for Mining Large Databases." The conference closes with a panel entitled "What Have We Discovered?"

Underlying the need to convert their data into actionable knowledge, organizations have started an aggressive effort to deploy KDD applications. Many such applications are now in production in industries such as finance, insurance, retail, telecommunications, health care, astronomy, planetary sciences, biology, etc. As is reported in the press, the early adopters of KDD are reaping significant financial benefits. With the number of knowledge discovery and data warehousing pilot projects doubling every six months, undoubtedly many more KDD applications will be in production by the end of 1996 and beyond. Knowledge discovery and data mining have captured the peoples' imagination. However, oftentimes we find that the excitement and promise offered by KDD is accompanied by high expectations for success that are unreasonable, unjustifiable, and premature. Obviously there is significant risk and exposure to the long term viability of the field by failing to manage expectations. KDD-96 aims at addressing these issues by providing a clear understanding of what represents the state of the art, and the state of practice in each of the various disciplines comprising KDD.

A conference such as this can only succeed as a team effort. We would first like to acknowledge the contributions of the program committee for their reviewing efforts as well as their invaluable input and advice. Our veteran chairs for Publicity (Padhraic Smyth), Corporate Sponsorship (Gregory Piatetsky-Shapiro), and Demonstration Sessions (Tej Anand) have continued the excellent track record they set in KDD-95. We are grateful to our sponsors for their generous support of KDD-96.

Finally, we would like to extend a special appreciation to the American Association for Artificial Intelligence (AAAI) for sponsoring KDD-96, the only conference AAAI has solely sponsored apart from the National Conference on Artificial Intelligence and the Innovative Applications of Artificial Intelligence Conference. We thank the AAAI staff for all their help and especially Annette Eldredge for handling submissions and local arrangements, and Carol Hamilton for her help, advice, and for managing the operations of this conference.

Evangelos Simoudis (IBM) &
Jiawei Han (Simon Fraser University)
Program Committee Cochairs

Usama Fayyad (Microsoft Research)
General Conference Chair

Portland, Oregon, USA, August 2, 1996

KDD–96

Sharing Learned Models among Remote Database Partitions by Local Meta-learning

Philip K. Chan
Computer Science
Florida Institute of Technology
Melbourne, FL 32901
pkc@cs.fit.edu

Salvatore J. Stolfo
Department of Computer Science
Columbia University
New York, NY 10027
sal@cs.columbia.edu

Abstract

We explore the possibility of importing "black-box" models learned over data sources at remote sites to improve models learned over locally available data sources. In this way, we may be able to learn more accurate knowledge from globally available data than would otherwise be possible from partial, locally available data. Proposed meta-learning strategies in our previous work are extended to integrate local and remote models. We also investigate the effect on accuracy performance when data overlap among different sites.

Introduction

Much of the research in inductive learning concentrates on problems with relatively small amounts of data residing at one location. With the coming age of very large network computing, it is likely that orders of magnitude more data in databases at various sites will be available for various learning problems of real world importance. Frequently, local databases represent only a partial view of all the data globally available. For example, in detecting credit card fraud, a bank has information on its credit card transactions, from which it can learn fraud patterns. However, the patterns learned may not represent all of the fraud patterns found in transactions at other banks. That is, a bank might not know a fraud pattern that is prevalent at other banks.

One approach to solving this problem is to merge transactions from all databases into one database and locate all the fraud patterns. It is not uncommon that a bank has millions of credit card transactions; pooling transactions from all banks will create a database of enormous size. Learning fraud patterns from millions of transactions already poses significant efficiency problems; processing transactions gathered from all banks is likely infeasible. In addition, transactions at one bank are proprietary; sharing them with other banks means giving away valuable customer purchasing information. Exchanging transactions might also violate customers' privacy.

Another solution is to share the fraud patterns instead of the transaction data. This approach benefits from a significant reduction of information needed to be merged and processed. Also, proprietary customer transaction information need not be shared. You might now ask that if the data are proprietary, the fraud patterns can also be proprietary. If the patterns are encoded in programs, the executables can be treated as "black boxes." That is, by sharing the black boxes, one doesn't have to worry about giving away valuable and proprietary information. The next question is how we can merge the black boxes.

We adopted the general approach of *meta-learning* (Chan & Stolfo 1993) and developed techniques for coalescing multiple learned models. During meta-learning, the learned models are treated as black boxes so that they can use any representation and can be generated by any inductive learning algorithm. That is, our meta-learning techniques are representation- and algorithm-independent. In this paper we explore the use of meta-learning to improve the accuracy performance of locally learned models by merging them with ones imported from remote sites. That is, at each site, learned models from other sites are also available. Furthermore, we investigate the effects on local accuracy when the local underlying training data overlap with those at remote sites. This situation arises in practice (eg. a person may be a customer at several banks, and/or commit the same credit card fraud at different banks). In this paper we overview the concept of meta-learning and its techniques, followed by a discussion on how meta-learning can improve local learning. We then empirically evaluate local meta-learning and the effect of data replication on performance.

Meta-learning

Given a number of classifiers and their predictions for a particular unlabeled instance, one may combine them by picking the prediction with the largest number of votes. Our approach introduced in (Chan & Stolfo 1993) is to *meta-learn* a set of new classifiers (or *meta-classifiers*) whose training data are based on predictions of a set of underlying base classifiers. Re-

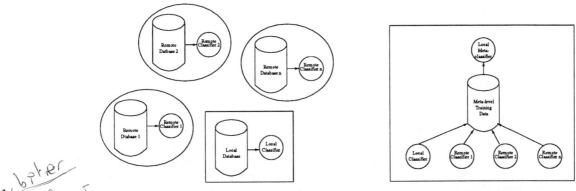

Figure 1: Local meta-learning at a site with three remote sites.

arbiter
to solve
disagreement
between classifiers

sults from (Chan & Stolfo 1995) show that our meta-learning techniques are more effective than voting-based methods.

Our techniques fall into two general categories: the *arbiter* and *combiner* schemes. We distinguish between *base classifiers* and arbiters/combiners as follows. A base classifier is the outcome of applying a learning algorithm directly to "raw" training data. The base classifier is a program that given a test datum provides a prediction of its unknown class. For purposes of this study, we ignore the representation used by the classifier (to preserve the algorithm-independent property). An arbiter or combiner, as described below, is a program generated by a learning algorithm that is trained on the predictions produced by a set of base classifiers and the raw training data. The arbiter/combiner is also a classifier, and hence other arbiters or combiners can be computed from the set of predictions of other arbiters/combiners.

An *arbiter* is learned by some learning algorithm to arbitrate among predictions generated by different base classifiers. That is, its purpose is to provide an alternate and more educated prediction when the base classifiers present diverse predictions. This arbiter, together with an *arbitration rule*, decides a final classification outcome based upon the base predictions. The arbiter is trained from examples that do not have a common prediction among the majority of the base classifiers. More details of this arbiter scheme are in (Chan & Stolfo 1995).

The aim of the *combiner* strategy is to coalesce the predictions from the base classifiers by learning the relationship between these predictions and the correct prediction. For example, a base classifier might consistently make the correct predictions for class c; i.e., when this base classifier predicts class c, it is probably correct regardless of the predictions made by the other base classifiers. In the *combiner* strategy the predictions of the learned base classifiers on the training set form the basis of the meta-learner's training set. A *composition rule*, which varies in different schemes, determines the content of training examples for the meta-learner. The correct classification and predictions from the base classifiers constitute a training example in the *class-combiner* scheme. Attributes of the original example is added in the *class-attr-combiner* scheme. The details of these two schemes appear in (Chan & Stolfo 1995). From these examples, the meta-learner generates a meta-classifier, that we call a *combiner*. In classifying an instance, the base classifiers first generate their predictions. Based on the same composition rule, a new instance is generated from the predictions, which is then classified by the combiner. We note that a combiner computes a prediction that may be entirely different from any proposed by a base classifier, whereas an arbiter chooses one of the predictions from the base classifiers and the arbiter itself.

Local Meta-learning

Our previous work (Chan & Stolfo 1995) assumes a certain degree of "raw" data sharing. As we discussed earlier, situations might arise when data sharing is not feasible, but sharing of "black-box" learned models is possible. In this scenario a local site can "import" classifiers learned at remote sites and use them to improve local learning. The problem we face is how we can take advantage of the imported "black-box" classifiers. Our approach is to treat it as an integration problem and use meta-learning techniques to integrate the collective knowledge of the constituent classifiers.

Since only the local data set, called T_i, is available at site i, we are limited to that data set for meta-learning. A classifier, C_i, is trained from T_i locally and a set of classifiers, C_j where $j \neq i$, is imported from other sites $j, j = 1, .., n$. Using T_i, each C_j then generates predictions P_{ij} and C_i produces P_{ii}. P_{ij} and P_{ii} form the meta-level training set according to the strategies described earlier. That is, the local and remote classifiers are treated as base classifiers in our previous work. Once the meta-level training set is created, the corresponding meta-classifier is learned by applying a local machine learning algorithm to this new training set. Figure 1 depicts the relationship among various classifiers and sites during local meta-learning.

However, the predictions P_{ii} generated by the local classifier C_i on the local training set T_i will be more correct than the predictions, P_{ij}, generated by the remote classifiers because C_i was trained from T_i. As a result, during meta-learning, the trained meta-classifier will be heavily biased towards the local classifier (recall that the remote classifiers were not trained on the local data set T_i). For example, a local nearest-neighbor classifier can predict the local training set perfectly and the meta-learner will ignore all the remote classifiers. That is, we can't use the remote classifiers to improve local learning, which defeats the purpose of importing the remote classifiers.

To resolve this situation, at the local site, we partition T_i into two sets, T_{i1} and T_{i2}, from which classifiers C_{i1} and C_{i2} are trained. C_{i1} then predicts on T_{i2} and C_{i2} on T_{i1}. The union of the two sets of predictions form the predictions for the local classifier (P_{ii}). This method, called 2-fold cross validation partitioning, tries to approximate the behavior of C_i on unseen data. The process of obtaining the predictions P_{ij} from the remote classifiers remains unchanged. Now, during meta-learning, remote classifiers will not be automatically ignored since the local classifier is also judged on "unseen" data. The next section discusses our experimental evaluation of the local meta-learning approach.

Experimental Results

Four inductive learning algorithms were used in our experiments reported here: ID3 (Quinlan 1986), CART (Breiman *et al.* 1984), BAYES (described in (Clark & Niblett 1989)), and CN2 (Clark & Niblett 1989). ID3 and CART are decisions tree learning algorithms and were obtained from NASA Ames Research Center in the IND package (Buntine & Caruana 1991). BAYES is a simple Bayesian learning algorithm. CN2 is a rule learning algorithm and was obtained from Dr. Clark (Boswell 1990).

Four data sets were used in our studies. The DNA splice junction (SJ) data set (courtesy of Towell, Shavlik, and Noordewier (Towell, Shavlik, & Noordewier 1990)) contains sequences of nucleotides and the type of splice junction, if any, at the center of each sequence. *Exon-intron, intron-exon,* and *non-junction* are the three classes in this task. Each sequence has 60 nucleotides with eight different values per nucleotide (four base ones plus four combinations). The data set contains 3,190 training instances. The protein coding region (PCR) data set (courtesy of Craven and Shavlik (Craven & Shavlik 1993)) contains DNA nucleotide sequences and their binary classifications (*coding* or *non-coding*). Each sequence has 15 nucleotides with four different values per nucleotide. The PCR data set has 20,000 sequences. The secondary protein structure data set (SS) (Qian & Sejnowski 1988), courtesy of Qian and Sejnowski, contains sequences of amino acids and the secondary structures at the corresponding positions. There are three structures (*alpha-helix,*

beta-sheet, and coil) and 20 amino acids (21 attributes, including a spacer (Qian & Sejnowski 1988)) in the data. The amino acid sequences were split into shorter sequences of length 13 according to a windowing technique used in (Qian & Sejnowski 1988). The SS data set has 21,625 sequences. The artificial (ART) data set has 10,000 instances randomly generated from a disjunctive boolean expression that has 4 symbolic (26 values) and 4 numeric (1,000 values) variables. A total of 4.6×10^{17} instances are possible.

To simulate the multiple-site scenario, we divided the training set into equi-sized subsets (each subset representing a site) and varied the number of subsets (sites) from 2 to 64. We also ensured that each subset was disjoint but with proportional distribution of examples of each class (i.e., the ratio of examples in each class in the whole data set is preserved). The *arbiter, class-combiner,* and *class-attribute-combiner* strategies were evaluated. The prediction accuracy on a separate test set is our primary comparison measure. The different strategies were run on the above four data sets, each with the above four learning algorithms and the results are plotted in Figure 2. Due to space limitations, only results from two data sets are shown; the rest appears in (Chan 1996). The plotted accuracy is the average accuracy of local meta-classifiers over 10-fold cross-validation runs. In each run, m sites generate m local classifiers and m local meta-classifiers, after "exchanging" all local classifiers. In the following performance graphs, *avg-base* denotes the average accuracy of the local/base classifiers as our standard base line. Statistical significance was measured by using the one-sided t-test with a 90% confidence value.

When compared to the base accuracy, at least one of the three local meta-learning strategies yields significantly higher accuracy in 13 out of the 16 cases (mostly at 4 or more subsets). Local meta-learning still has higher accuracy (not significantly) in 2 of the 3 remaining cases. Larger improvement usually occurs when the size of the local data set is smaller (the number of subsets/sites are larger). In many cases the arbiter strategy improves accuracy more than the two combiner strategies.

While many of the base classifiers drop in accuracy when the data set size gets smaller, some of the meta-learning strategies roughly maintain the same level of accuracy. One apparent example is the arbiter strategy using ID3 as the learner in the Coding Regions data set (top right graph in Figure 2). The arbiter strategy stays above 70% accuracy while the base accuracy drops to below 60%. The arbiter strategy maintains the accuracy in 8 out of 16 cases. For the Coding Regions data set, the arbiter strategy improves local learning by a wide margin using 3 of the 4 learners.

The results obtained here are consistent with those from non-local meta-learning (Chan & Stolfo 1995), where raw data can be shared among sites. Meta-learning improves accuracy in a distributed environment and the arbiter strategy is more effective than the two combiner techniques. Next, we investigate the effects on accuracy of local meta-learning when different sites posses some degree of common data.

Experimental Results on Data Replication

As we discussed previously in the introduction, different sites might have some overlapping data. To simulate this phenomenon, we allow some amount of replication in each partition of data. We prepare each learning task by generating subsets of training data for the local/base classifiers according to the following generative scheme:

1. Starting with N disjoint subsets, randomly choose from any of these sets one example X, distinct from any other previously chosen in a prior iteration.

2. Randomly choose a number r from $1...(N-1)$, i.e. the number of times this example will be replicated.

3. Randomly choose r subsets (not including the subset from which X was drawn) and assign X to those r subsets.

4. Repeat this process until the size of the largest (replicated) subset is reached to some maximum (as a percentage, Δ, of the original training subset size).

In the experiments reported here, Δ ranged from 0% to 40%, with 10% increments. Each set of incremental experimental runs, however, chooses an entirely new distribution of replicated values. No attempt was made to maintain a prior distribution of training data when incrementing the amount of replication. This "shot gun" approach provides us with some sense of a "random learning problem" that we may be faced with in real world scenarios where replication of information is likely inevitable or purposefully orchestrated.

The same experimental setup was used as in the prior experiments. Results for the replicated data scenario using the class-combiner and class-attr-combiner strategies are plotted in Figure 3. Due to space limitations, only 8 of the 32 cases are shown, the rest appears in (Chan 1996). 7 out of 32 cases show significant accuracy improvement when the degree of replication increases; 6 of these 7 cases occur in the Coding Regions data set. 20 out of 32 cases show no significant accuracy changes across all subset sizes and degrees of replication. The remaining 5 cases have some significant accuracy improvement at certain subset sizes.

In summary, the majority does not show significant accuracy improvement when the degree of replication increases. This is contrary to one's intuition since one would expect the accuracy to increase when the local sites have a higher percentage of all the available data combined. That could imply that local meta-learning is quite effective in integrating models from remote sites without the help of replicated data. Our

findings here are consistent with those from non-local meta-learning (Chan & Stolfo 1996).

Concluding Remarks

We have presented techniques for improving local learning by integrating remote classifiers through local meta-learning. Our experimental results suggest local meta-learning techniques, especially the arbiter strategy, can significantly raise the accuracy of the local classifiers. Furthermore, results from our data replication experiments suggest local meta-learning can integrate local and remote classifiers effectively without having a larger share of global data at a local site.

We are currently investigating a simplification process for reducing the complexity of the final meta-learned structures. Some classifiers could be strongly correlated and pruning some of them might not significantly change the performance of the entire structure. Finally, the meta-learning techniques reported in this paper form the basis of a system under development recently granted support by ARPA to learn fraud patterns in network-based financial information systems. The use of locally computed meta-classifiers over inherently distributed datasets of fraudulent transactions will provide an early-warning capability protecting against intruders and information warfare.

Acknowledgements

This work has been partially supported by grants from NSF (IRI-94-13847), NYSSTF, and Citicorp.

References

Boswell, R. 1990. *Manual for CN2 version 6.1*. Turing Institure. Int. Doc. IND: TI/MLT/4.0T/RAB/1.2.

Breiman, L.; Friedman, J. H.; Olshen, R. A.; and Stone, C. J. 1984. *Classification and Regression Trees*. Belmont, CA: Wadsworth.

Buntine, W., and Caruana, R. 1991. *Introduction to IND and Recursive Partitioning*. NASA Ames Research Center.

Chan, P., and Stolfo, S. 1993. Meta-learning for multistrategy and parallel learning. In *Proc. Second Intl. Work. on Multistrategy Learning*, 150–165.

Chan, P., and Stolfo, S. 1995. A comparative evaluation of voting and meta-learning on partitioned data. In *Proc. Twelfth Intl. Conf. Machine Learning*, 90–98.

Chan, P., and Stolfo, S. 1996. Scaling learning by meta-learning over disjoint and partially replicated data. In *Proc. Florida AI Research Symposium*. To appear.

Chan, P. 1996. *An Extensible Meta-Learning Approach for Scalable and Accurate Inductive Learning*. Ph.D. Dissertation, Department of Computer Science, Columbia University, New York, NY. (forthcoming).

Clark, P., and Niblett, T. 1989. The CN2 induction algorithm. *Machine Learning* 3:261–285.

Craven, M., and Shavlik, J. 1993. Learning to represent codons: A challenge problem for constructive induction. In *Proc. IJCAI-93*, 1319–1324.

Qian, N., and Sejnowski, T. 1988. Predicting the secondary structure of globular proteins using neural network models. *J. Mol. Biol.* 202:865–884.

Quinlan, J. R. 1986. Induction of decision trees. *Machine Learning* 1:81–106.

Towell, G.; Shavlik, J.; and Noordewier, M. 1990. Refinement of approximate domain theories by knowledge-based neural networks. In *Proc. AAAI-90*, 861–866.

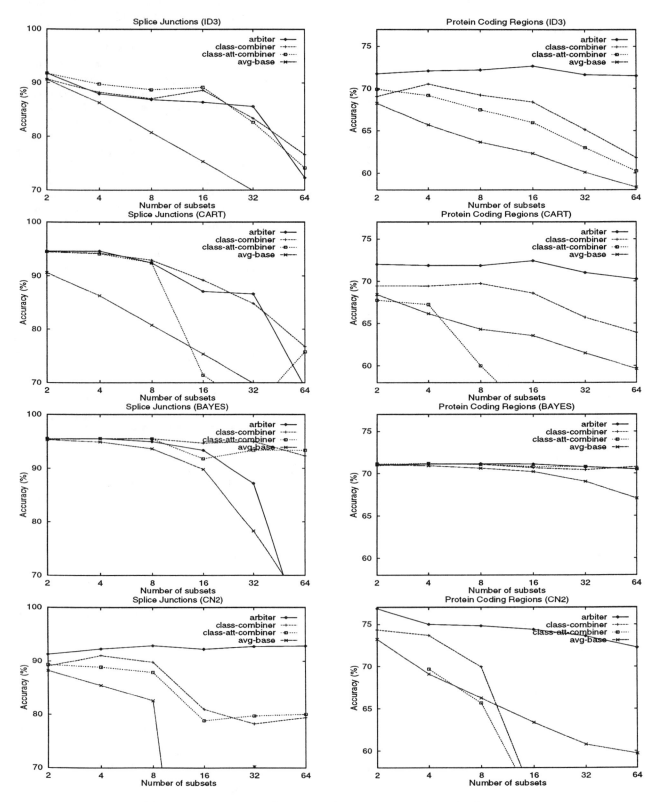

Figure 2: Accuracy for local meta-learning vs number of subsets

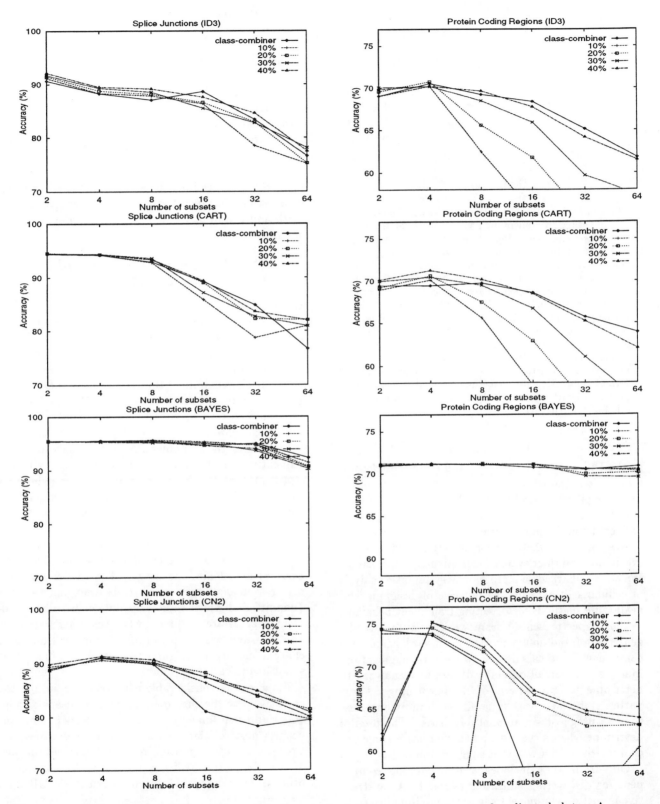

Figure 3: Accuracy for the class-combiner technique trained over varying amounts of replicated data. Δ ranges from 0% to 40%.

Combining Data Mining and Machine Learning for Effective User Profiling

Tom Fawcett and Foster Provost

NYNEX Science and Technology
400 Westchester Avenue
White Plains, New York 10604
{fawcett,foster}@nynexst.com

Abstract

This paper describes the automatic design of methods for detecting fraudulent behavior. Much of the design is accomplished using a series of machine learning methods. In particular, we combine data mining and constructive induction with more standard machine learning techniques to design methods for detecting fraudulent usage of cellular telephones based on profiling customer behavior. Specifically, we use a rule-learning program to uncover indicators of fraudulent behavior from a large database of cellular calls. These indicators are used to create profilers, which then serve as features to a system that combines evidence from multiple profilers to generate high-confidence alarms. Experiments indicate that this automatic approach performs nearly as well as the best hand-tuned methods for detecting fraud.

Introduction

In the United States, cellular fraud costs the telecommunications industry hundreds of millions of dollars per year (Walters & Wilkinson 1994). A specific kind of cellular fraud called *cloning* is particularly expensive and epidemic in major cities throughout the United States. Existing methods for detecting cloning fraud are *ad hoc* and their evaluation is virtually nonexistent. We have embarked on a program of systematic analysis of cellular call data for the purpose of designing and evaluating methods for detecting fraudulent behavior.

This paper presents a framework for automatically generating fraud detectors. The framework has several components, and uses data at two levels of aggregation. Massive numbers of cellular calls are first analyzed to determine general patterns of fraudulent usage. These patterns are then used to profile each individual customer's usage on an account-day basis. The profiles determine when a customer's behavior has become uncharacteristic in a way that suggests fraud.

Our framework includes a data mining component for discovering indicators of fraud. A constructive induction component generates profiling detectors that use the discovered indicators. A final evidence-combining component determines how to combine signals from the profiling detectors to generate alarms. The rest of this paper describes the domain, the framework and the implemented system, the data, and results.

Cellular Cloning Fraud and its Detection

Every cellular phone periodically transmits two unique identification numbers: its *Mobile Identification Number* (MIN) and its *Electronic Serial Number* (ESN). These two numbers are broadcast unencrypted over the airwaves, and can be received, decoded and stored using special equipment that is relatively inexpensive. *Cloning* occurs when a customer's MIN and ESN are programmed into a cellular telephone not belonging to the customer. When this telephone is used, the network sees the customer's MIN and ESN and subsequently bills the usage to the customer. With the stolen MIN and ESN, a cloned phone user (whom we shall call a *bandit*) can make virtually unlimited calls, whose charges are billed to the customer.[1] If the fraudulent usage goes undetected, the customer's next bill will include the corresponding charges. Typically, the customer then calls the cellular service provider (the *carrier*) and denies the usage. The carrier and customer then determine which calls were made by the "bandit" and which were legitimate calls. The fraudulent charges are credited to the customer's account, and measures are taken to prohibit further fraudulent charges, usually by assigning the customer a (new) Personal Identification Number.

Fraud causes considerable inconvenience both to the carrier and to the customer. Fraudulent usage also incurs significant financial losses due to costs of land-line usage (most cellular calls are to non-cellular destinations), costs of congestion in the cellular system, loss of revenue by the crediting process, and costs paid to other cellular companies when a customer's MIN and

---

[1] According to the Cellular Telecommunications Industry Association, MIN-ESN pairs are sold on the streets of major US cities for between $5 and $50 apiece.

ESN are used outside the carrier's home territory.

Cellular carriers therefore have a strong interest in detecting cloning fraud as soon as possible. Standard methods of fraud detection include analyzing call data for overlapping calls (*collisions*), or calls in temporal proximity that could not have been placed by the same user due to geographic dispersion (*velocity checks*) (Davis & Goyal 1993). More sophisticated methods involve profiling user behavior and looking for significant deviations from normal patterns. This paper addresses the automatic design of such methods.

One approach to detecting fraud automatically is to learn a classifier for individual calls. We have not had success using standard machine learning techniques to construct such a classifier. Context is very important: a call that would be unusual for one customer would be typical for another. Furthermore, legitimate subscribers occasionally make isolated calls that look suspicious, so in general decisions of fraud should not be made on the basis of individual calls.

To detect fraud reliably it is necessary to determine the normal behavior of each account with respect to certain indicators, and to determine when that behavior has deviated significantly. Three issues arise:

1. *Which call features are important?* Which features or combinations of features are useful for distinguishing legitimate behavior from fraudulent behavior?

2. *How should profiles be created?* Given an important feature identified in Step 1, how should we characterize the behavior of a subscriber with respect to the feature?

3. *When should alarms be issued?* Given a set of profiling criteria identified in Step 2, how should we combine them to determine when fraud has occurred?

Our goal is to automate the design of user-profiling systems. Each of these issues corresponds to a component of our framework.

The Framework and the DC-1 System

Our system framework is illustrated in Figure 1. The framework uses data mining to discover indicators of fraudulent behavior, and then builds modules to profile each user's behavior with respect to these indicators. The *profilers* capture the typical behavior of an account and, in use, describe how far an account is from this typical behavior. The profilers are combined into a single *detector*, which learns how to detect fraud effectively based on the profiler outputs. When the detector has enough evidence of fraudulent activity on an account, based on the indications of the profilers, it generates an alarm.

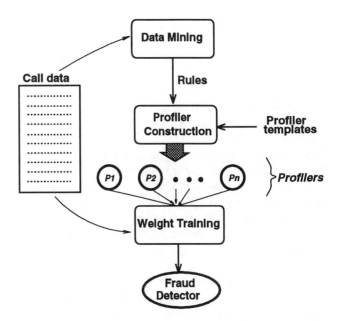

Figure 1: A framework for automatically constructing fraud detectors.

Figure 1 depicts the automatic generation of a fraud detector from a set of data on fraudulent and legitimate calls. The system takes as input a set of *call data*, which are chronological records of the calls made by each subscriber, organized by account. The call data describe individual calls using features such as TIME-OF-DAY, DURATION and CELL-SITE. The constructor also takes as input a set of *profiler templates*, which are the basis for the construction of the individual profilers.

Mining the Call Data

The first stage of detector construction, *data mining*, involves combing through the call data searching for indicators of fraud. In the DC-1 system, the indicators are conjunctive rules discovered by a standard rule-learning program. We use the RL program (Clearwater & Provost 1990), which is similar to other Meta-DENDRAL-style rule learners (Buchanan & Mitchell 1978; Segal & Etzioni 1994). RL searches for rules with certainty factors above a user-defined threshold. The certainty factor we used for these runs was a simple frequency-based probability estimate, corrected for small samples (Quinlan 1987).

The call data are organized by account, and each call record is labeled as fraudulent or legitimate. When RL is applied to an account's calls it produces a set of rules that serve to distinguish, within that account, the fraudulent calls from the legitimate calls. As an example, the following rule would be a relatively good indicator of fraud:

```
(TIME-OF-DAY = NIGHT) AND (LOCATION = BRONX)
                ==> FRAUD
          Certainty factor = 0.89
```

This rule denotes that a call placed at night from The Bronx (a Borough of New York City) is likely to be fraudulent. The `Certainty factor = 0.89` means that, for this account, a call matching this rule has an 89% probability of being fraudulent.

Each account generates a set of such rules. Each rule is recorded along with the account from which it was generated. After all accounts have been processed, a rule selection step is performed, the purpose of which is to derive a general covering set of rules that will serve as fraud indicators.

The set of accounts is traversed again. For each account, the list of rules generated by that account is sorted by the frequency of occurrence in the entire account set. The highest frequency unchosen rule is selected. If an account has been covered already by four chosen rules, it is skipped. The resulting set of rules is used in profiler construction.

Constructing Profilers

The second stage of detector construction, *profiler construction*, generates a set of profilers from the discovered fraud rules. The profiler constructor has a set of templates which are instantiated by rule conditions. The profiler constructor is given a set of rules and a set of templates, and generates a profiler from each rule-template pair. Every profiler has a *Training* step, in which it is trained on typical (non-fraud) account activity; and a *Use* step, in which it describes how far from the typical behavior a current account-day is. For example, a simple profiler template would be:

- **Given:** *Rule conditions* from a fraud rule.

- **Training:** On a daily basis, count the number of calls that satisfy *rule conditions*. Keep track of the maximum as *daily-threshold*.

- **Use:** Given an account-day, output 1 if the number of calls in a day exceeds *daily-threshold*, else output 0.

Assume the Bronx-at-night rule mentioned earlier was used with this template. The resulting instantiated profiler would determine, for a given account, the maximum number of calls made from The Bronx at night in any 24-hour period. In use, this profiler would emit a 1 whenever an account-day exceeded this threshold.

Different kinds of profilers are possible. A *thresholding* profiler yields a binary feature corresponding to whether the user's behavior was above threshold for the given day. A *counting* profiler yields a feature corresponding to its count (*e.g.*, the number of calls from BRONX at NIGHT). A *percentage* profiler yields a feature whose value is between zero and one hundred, representing the percentage of calls in the account-day that satisfy the conditions. Each type of profiler is produced by a different type of profiling template.

Combining Evidence from the Profilers

The third stage of detector construction learns how to combine evidence from the set of profilers generated by the previous stage. For this stage, the outputs of the profilers are used as features to a standard machine learning program. Training is done on account data, and profilers evaluate a complete account-day at a time. In training, the profilers' outputs are presented along with the desired output (the account-day's classification). The evidence combination learns which combinations of profiler outputs indicate fraud with high confidence.

Many training methods for evidence combining are possible. After experimenting with several methods, we chose a simple Linear Threshold Unit (LTU) for our experiments. An LTU is simple and fast, and enables a good first-order judgment of the features' worth.

A feature selection process is used to reduce the number of profilers in the final detector. Some of the rules do not perform well when used in profilers, and some profilers overlap in their fraud detection coverage. We therefore employ a sequential forward selection process (Kittler 1986) which chooses a small set of useful profilers. Empirically, this simplifies the final detector and increases its accuracy.

The Detector

The final output of the constructor is a detector that profiles each user's behavior based on several indicators, and produces an alarm if there is sufficient evidence of fraudulent activity. Figure 2 shows an example of a simple detector evaluating an account-day.

Before being used on an account, the profilers undergo a *profiling period* (usually 30 days) during which they measure unfrauded usage. In our study, these initial 30 account-days were guaranteed free of fraud, but were not otherwise guaranteed to be typical. From this initial profiling period, each profiler measures a characteristic level of activity.

The Data

The call data used for this study are records of cellular calls placed over four months by users in the New York

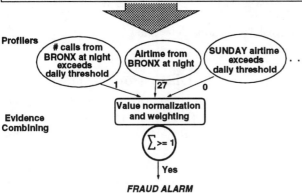

Figure 2: A DC-1 fraud detector processing a single account-day of data.

City area—an area with very high levels of fraud. The calls are labeled as legitimate or fraudulent by cross referencing a database of all calls that were credited as being fraudulent for the same time period. Each call is described by 31 attributes, such as the phone number of the caller, the duration of the call, the geographical origin and destination of the call, and any long-distance carrier used.

The call data were separated carefully into several partitions for data mining, profiler training and testing. Data mining used 610 accounts comprising approximately 350,000 calls.

Once the profilers are generated, the system transforms the raw call data into a series of account-days using the outputs of the profilers as features. Data for the profilers were drawn from a remaining pool of about 2500 accounts. We used randomly selected sets of 5000 account-days for training, and another set of 5000 account-days (drawn from separate accounts) for testing. Each account-day set was chosen to comprise 20% fraud and 80% non-fraud days. An account-day was classified as fraud if five or more minutes of fraudulent usage occurred; days including only one to four minutes of fraudulent usage were discarded.

Results

Data mining generated 3630 rules, each of which applied to two or more accounts. The rule selection process, in which rules are chosen in order of maximum account coverage, yielded a smaller set of 99 rules sufficient to cover the accounts. Each of the 99 rules was used to instantiate two profiler templates, yielding 198 profilers. The final feature selection step reduced this to nine profilers, with which the experiments were performed.

Each detector was run ten times on randomly selected training and testing accounts. Accuracy averages and standard deviations are shown in the leftmost column of Table 1. For comparison, we evaluated DC-1 along with other detection strategies:

- "Alarm on All" represents the policy of alarming on every account every day.

- "Alarm on None" represents the policy of allowing fraud to go completely unchecked. This corresponds to the maximum likelihood classification.

- "Collisions and Velocities" is a detector using two common methods for detecting cloning fraud, mentioned earlier. DC-1 was used to learn a threshold on the number of collision and velocity alarms necessary to generate a fraud alarm.

- The "High Usage" detector generates an alarm on any day in which airtime usage exceeded a threshold. The threshold was found empirically from training data.

- The best individual DC-1 profiler was used as an isolated detector. This experiment was done to determine the additional benefit of combining profilers. The best individual profiler was generated from the rule:

  (TIME-OF-DAY = EVENING) ==> FRAUD

  Data mining had discovered (in 119 accounts) that the sudden appearance of evening calls, in accounts that did not normally make them, was coincident with cloning fraud. The relatively high accuracy of this one profiler reveals that this is a valuable fraud indicator.

- The DC-1 detector incorporates all the profilers chosen by feature selection. We used the weight learning method described earlier to determine the weights for evidence combining.

- The SOTA ("State Of The Art") detector incorporates seven hand-crafted profiling methods that were the best individual detectors identified in a previous

Detector	Accuracy (%)	Cost ($US)	Accuracy at cost (%)
Alarm on All	20	20000	20
Alarm on None	80	18111 ± 961	80
Collisions + Velocities	81 ± .2	16988 ± 685	81 ± .3
High Usage	87 ± .4	6069 ± 280	85 ± 1.1
Best individual DC-1 profiler	88 ± .6	7652 ± 383	85 ± 1
DC-1 detector	91 ± .5	5442 ± 318	89 ± 1.3
State of the Art (SOTA)	94 ± .3	3303 ± 278	94 ± .3

Table 1: A comparison of accuracies and costs of various detectors.

study. Each method profiles an account in a different way and produces a separate alarm. Weights for combining SOTA's alarms were determined by our weight-tuning algorithm.

In this domain, different types of errors have different costs, and a realistic evaluation must take these costs into account. A false positive error (a false alarm) corresponds to wrongly deciding that a customer has been cloned. Based on the cost of a fraud analyst's time, we estimate the cost of a false positive error to be about $5. A false negative error corresponds to letting a frauded account-day go undetected. Rather than using a uniform cost for all false negatives, we estimated a false negative to cost $.40 per minute of fraudulent airtime used on that account-day. This figure is based on the proportion of usage in local and non-local ("roaming") markets, and their corresponding costs.[2]

Because LTU training methods try to minimize errors but not error costs, we employed a second step in training. After training, the LTU's threshold is adjusted to yield minimum error cost on the training set. This adjustment is done by moving the decision threshold from -1 to +1 in increments of .01 and computing the resulting error cost. After the minimum cost on training data is found, the threshold is clamped and the testing data are evaluated. The second column of Table 1 shows the mean and standard deviations of test set costs. The third column, "Accuracy at cost," is the corresponding classification accuracy of the detector when the threshold is set to yield lowest-cost classifications.

---

[2]We have still glossed over some complexity. For a given account, the only false negative fraud days that incur cost to the company are those prior to the *first* true positive alarm. After the fraud is detected, it is terminated. Thus, our analysis overestimates the costs slightly; a more thorough analysis would eliminate such days from the computation.

Discussion

The results in Table 1 demonstrate that DC-1 performs quite well. Though there is room for improvement, the DC-1 detector performs better than all but the hand-coded SOTA detector.

It is surprising that Collisions and Velocity Checks, commonly thought to be reliable indicators of cloning, performed poorly in our experiments. Preliminary analysis suggests that call collisions and velocity alarms may be more common among legitimate calls in our region than is generally believed.

In our experiments, lowest cost classification occurred at an accuracy somewhat lower than optimal. In other words, some classification accuracy could be sacrificed to decrease cost. More sophisticated methods could be used to produce cost sensitive classifiers, which would probably produce better results.

Related Work

Yuhas (1993) and Ezawa and Norton (1995) address the problem of uncollectible debt in telecommunications services. However, neither work deals with characterizing typical customer behavior, so mining the data to derive profiling features is not necessary. Ezawa and Norton's method of evidence combining is much more sophisticated than ours and faces some of the same problems (unequal error costs, skewed class distributions).

Methods that deal with time series are relevant to our work. However, time series analysis (Chatfield 1984; Farnum & Stanton 1989) strives to characterize an entire time series or to forecast future events in the series. Neither ability is directly useful to fraud detection. Hidden Markov Models (Rabiner & Juang 1986) are concerned with distinguishing recurring sequences of states and the transitions between them. However, fraud detection usually only deals with two states (the "frauded" and "un-frauded" states) with a single transition between them. It may be useful to recognize recurring un-frauded states of an account, but this ability is likely peripheral to the detection task.

Conclusions and Future Work

The detection of cellular cloning fraud is a relatively young field. Fraud behavior changes frequently as bandits adapt to detection techniques. A fraud detection system should be adaptive as well. However, in order to build usage profilers we must know which aspects of customers' behavior to profile. Historically, determining such aspects has involved a good deal of manual work, hypothesizing useful features, building profilers and testing them. Determining how to combine them involves much trial-and-error as well.

Our framework automates this process. Results show that the DC-1 detector performs better than the high-usage alarm and the collision/velocity alarm. Even with relatively simple components, DC-1 is able to exploit mined data to produce a detector whose performance approaches that of the state-of-the-art. The SOTA system took several person-months to build. The DC-1 detector took several CPU-hours. Furthermore, DC-1 can be retrained at any time as necessitated by the changing environment.

We believe our framework will be useful in other domains in which typical behavior is to be distinguished from unusual behavior. Prime candidates are similar domains involving fraud, such as credit-card fraud and toll fraud. In credit-card fraud, data mining may identify locations that arise as new hot-beds of fraud. The constructor would then incorporate profilers that notice if a customer begins to charge more than usual from that location.

The DC-1 system is an initial prototype. Further work will develop two aspects of DC-1 in preparation for its deployment. First, we intend to expand the data mining step, particularly to exploit available background knowledge. We believe that there is a good deal of relevant background knowledge (for example, hierarchical geographical knowledge) that can augment the current calling data. Along with this, we hope to be able to characterize and describe the knowledge discovered in our system. Second, we hope to improve the method of combining profilers. We chose an LTU initially because it is simple and fast. A neural network could probably attain higher accuracy for DC-1, possibly matching that of SOTA.

Acknowledgements

We would like to thank Nicholas Arcuri and the Fraud Control department at Bell Atlantic NYNEX Mobile for many useful discussions about cellular fraud and its detection.

References

Buchanan, B. G., and Mitchell, T. M. 1978. Model-directed learning of production rules. In Hayes-Roth, F., ed., *Pattern-directed inference systems*. New York: Academic Press.

Chatfield, C. 1984. *The analysis of time series: An introduction (third edition)*. New York: Chapman and Hall.

Clearwater, S., and Provost, F. 1990. RL4: A tool for knowledge-based induction. In *Proceedings of the Second International IEEE Conference on Tools for Artificial Intelligence*, 24–30. IEEE CS Press.

Davis, A., and Goyal, S. 1993. Management of cellular fraud: Knowledge-based detection, classification and prevention. In *Thirteenth International Conference on Artificial Intelligence, Expert Systems and Natural Language*.

Ezawa, K., and Norton, S. 1995. Knowledge discovery in telecommunication services data using bayesian network models. In Fayyad, U., and Uthurusamy, R., eds., *Proceedings of First International Conference on Knowledge Discovery and Data Mining*, 100–105. Menlo Park, CA: AAAI Press.

Farnum, N., and Stanton, L. 1989. *Quantitative forecasting methods*. Boston, MA: PWS-Kent Publishing Company.

Kittler, J. 1986. Feature selection and extraction. In Fu, K. S., ed., *Handbook of pattern recognition and image processing*. New York: Academic Press. 59–83.

Quinlan, J. R. 1987. Generating production rules from decision trees. In *Proceedings of the Tenth International Joint Conference on Artificial Intelligence*, 304–307. Morgan Kaufmann.

Rabiner, L. R., and Juang, B. H. 1986. An introduction to hidden markov models. *IEEE ASSP Magazine* 3(1):4–16.

Segal, R., and Etzioni, O. 1994. Learning decision lists using homogeneous rules. In *Proceedings of the Twelfth National Conference on Artificial Intelligence*, 619–625. Menlo Park, CA: AAAI Press.

Walters, D., and Wilkinson, W. 1994. Wireless fraud, now and in the future: A view of the problem and some solutions. *Mobile Phone News* 4–7.

Yuhas, B. P. 1993. Toll-fraud detection. In Alspector, J.; Goodman, R.; and Brown, T., eds., *Proceedings of the International Workshop on Applications of Neural Networks to Telecommunications*, 239–244. Hillsdale, NJ: Lawrence Erlbaum Associates.

Local Induction of Decision Trees: Towards Interactive Data Mining

Truxton Fulton[*]
Simon Kasif[*]
Steven Salzberg[*]
David Waltz[†]

Abstract

Decision trees are an important data mining tool with many applications. Like many classification techniques, decision trees process the entire data base in order to produce a generalization of the data that can be used subsequently for classification. Large, complex data bases are not always amenable to such a global approach to generalization. This paper explores several methods for extracting data that is local to a query point, and then using the local data to build generalizations. These adaptively constructed neighborhoods can provide additional information about the query point. Three new algorithms are presented, and experiments using these algorithms are described.

Introduction

For any large, complex body of data, there is often a need to compute summaries and extract generalizations that characterize the data. Data mining research focuses on processing large databases and computing summaries, detecting patterns, and performing automatic classification on new data. For example, modern medical databases contain enormous quantities of patient data, which can provide great value in the treatment of future patients. In order to gain the maximum value from such databases, data mining tools are essential. One popular and successful data mining technique is the decision tree classifier (BFOS84; Qui93; MKS94) which can be used to classify new examples as well as providing a relatively concise description of the database.

In this paper we describe a notion of interactive data mining where we wait for the user to provide a "query" that specifies a neighborhood to be mined. The query is in the form of a specific example from the space of instances in the database. We then produce information that may contain the classification of the point, the confidence in this classification, a summary or a visual display of the local neighborhood around the point, a comparison of this neighborhood with others, or additional local information.

Our approach is also intended to address a statistical problem that is well known in the decision tree research community as *data fragmentation*. This occurs even in very large databases as the tree induction algorithm recursively splits the data into smaller and smaller subsets. Thus at many leaves of a decision tree, very little data is available to make classification decisions. However, given a specific query point, if one can retrieve all the locally relevant instances in the database, then one should be able to build a better classifier.

This paper describes a local approach to building decision trees: first collecting data in the vicinity of a query example, and then building the tree on the fly. The intuition is simply this: when presented with a new example for classification, retrieve a set of relevant examples from the database, and then build a decision tree from those examples. This approach has the potential to circumvent the data fragmentation problem, if the decision is made using sufficient relevant (local) information.

The idea of building local decision trees is similar in spirit to the standard k-nearest neighbor algorithm. Both ideas face an important implementation question, though, which is: how does one decide the appropriate local neighborhood? This problem is addressed in the algorithms described below, each of which approaches it differently. This paper also explores some more sophisticated methods of choosing a neighborhood. For some databases and some domains, the importance of certain features varies from one part of the space to another. For example, the feature "blood pressure" might be of great importance in one part of a medical database, while genetic factors might be most important elsewhere. To capture this notion more formally, we have devised an algorithm that defines an adaptive neighborhood based upon local characteristics of the data. This extends the usual notion of distance and makes it both domain-dependent and query-dependent.

[*]Computer Science Department, Johns Hopkins University, Baltimore, MD 21218. Email: *lastname*@cs.jhu.edu

[†]NEC Research Institute, Princeton, NJ 08540. Email: waltz@research.nj.nec.com

Notation

In this section we give several definitions that are necessary in the algorithm descriptions. For length consideration we will omit formal notation. Let X be a set of instances called the *instance space*. To simplify the presentation we assume that X is the set of points in a multi-dimensional unit square $[0,1]^d$. We are given a very large set of instances D (a subset of X), which is the database of objects. (In machine learning D is often referred to as the training set.) With each instance in D we associate a class label. A typical statistical classification problem is to classify new instances in X that are not contained in D.

Decision trees have been established to be a very useful tool in classification and data mining, where they are used to summarize the database D and produce classification of new examples. Geometrically, a decision tree corresponds to a recursive partitioning of the instance space into mutually disjoint regions. Each region is represented by a leaf node in the tree, and associated with a particular value (C_i) giving the class label of all instances contained in the region. It is important to note that geometrically each leaf label corresponds to a hyperrectangle in X. For simplicity we refer to hyperrectangles as rectangles. We define a *monochromatic* rectangle to be a rectangle that contains only points labelled by the same class label.

Local Induction Algorithms and Memory-Based Reasoning

Local induction algorithms are based on a simple idea. Instead of building a complex statistical model that describes the entire space, we construct a simpler model that describes the space in a particular neighborhood. Local learning is a special case of memory-based reasoning (MBR). Applications of MBR include classification of news articles (MLW92), census data (CMSW92), software agents (MK93), computational biology (YL93; CS93), robotics (AMS95; Atk89; MAS95), computer vision (Ede94), and many other pattern recognition and machine learning applications. Recent work in statistics addresses the issue of adaptive neighborhood to a given query to improve K-nearest neighbour algorithms (HT94; Fri94). See also the very relevant theoretical framework for local learning described in (BV92; VB93).

There are three key steps in local learning and MBR algorithms: 1) Given an instance, retrieve a set of instances in the training set that are relevant to the query; 2) Build a model (e.g, classifier or function approximator) using only retrieved points; 3) Use the model to process the query point (classify it or approximate a function value).

In interactive data mining applications the notion of local learning should be extended to provide both visual and statistical query dependent information. Thus, in a particular local neighborhood two features

may be sufficient to produce a good classification, whereas the entire domain may need a very complex classifier. In many cases the user may care more about query specific accuracy than about an estimate of the accuracy of a global classifier (see below).

Choosing the appropriate local neighborhood around a query point is a difficult task, especially in high dimensional spaces. In this paper we report three new approaches that are primarily designed to complement standard decision tree algorithms in interactive data mining applications. These methods should be most useful when the database is large and when the user is interested in exploring only a small neighborhood around a query point.

Choosing a local neighborhood via nearest neighbors

The simplest approach to local learning with decision trees is simply extracting the k nearest neighbors and constructing a decision tree on these instances. If the neighborhood size is 1, then the decision tree algorithm is equivalent to the 1-nearest neighbor (1-NN) algorithm. If the neighborhood size is N (the full size of the training set), then the algorithm is equivalent to conventional full induction. Nuances in the training set can greatly affect the histogram of accuracy over different values of k between 1 and N. In standard nearest neighbor algorithms the optimal value of K is determined by a specially reserved training set and cross validation techniques. However, it is clear that the best neighborhood size may vary from one query point to another. To make the algorithm more robust, we use a voting scheme as follows. For a given query point, a sequence of k trees is induced using the $1, 2, \ldots, k$ nearest points. These trees then vote on the class of the query point. This is what we call the "local induction voting" (LIV) algorithm. In practice this seems to work well, as shown in the experiments below. The voting method can be implemented in many different ways; in these first experiments we use an ad-hoc method. We weigh the vote of each tree by the number of same-class examples in the leaf that is used to classify the example.

Choosing a local neighborhood via layers of composite rectangles

For the sake of gaining intuition for the algorithm described in this section, assume the target partitioning of the space is actually a decision tree T. Given any query point x it will be contained in some leaf node of T, which is a monochromatic rectangle R. This implies that every other point y in R forms a monochromatic rectangle with x and y at its corners. In other words, all the points in the database D that are contained in the rectangle defined by x and y have the same class label. Next, if we remove all points in R from the database D, we can now form monochromatic rectangles with points that are in regions adjacent to R that

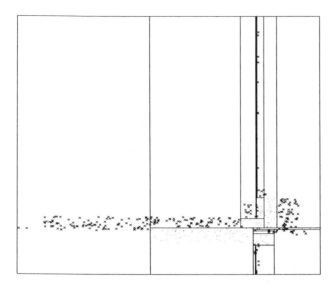

Figure 1: A 2D local decision tree with the local neighborhood defined by two layers of homogeneous rectangles. Only points in the layer one and layer two rectangles are shown, and the local tree is superimposed.

For each query point x

    For each point y_i in the database

        Check if x and y_i form a monochomatic rectangle

        If yes, include y_i in the first layer.

    Remove all points in the first layer.

    Repeat procedure and construct the second layer.

    The neigborhood of x is the set of points in both layers.

    Construct a decision tree on these points.

Figure 2: The multi-layer local decision tree algorithm

are important to the classification of x. We refer to all points in the database that form a monochromatic rectangle with a given query point x as **layer one**. These points are a superset of points in R. Once we remove all points in layer one we can refer to all remaining points that form monochromatic rectangles with a query point as layer two, and so forth. Our algorithm defines the adaptive neighborhood of a query point x as all points in layer one and layer two. The algorithm is given in Figure 2. A two-dimensional example that illustrates this idea geometrically is given in Figure 1.

The algorithm as described in Figure 2 has running time $O(N^2)$, where N is the size of the database. However, it turns out that we can utilize computational geometry techniques to reduce the running time to $O(N \log^{d-1} N)$ obtaining a practical improvement when the dimensionality is small. We provide a very rough sketch of the algorithm for two dimensions be-

low. See (FKSW96) for a complete description. Given a point x we compute the set of monochromatic rectangles that are defined by x and another point in the database. Recall these are the points that we include in the local neighborhood of x. We first sort the points into four quadrants with the query point x defining the origin. We compute the set of monochromatic rectangles separately in each quadrant. Note that the number of non-empty quadrants is bounded by N irrespective of dimensionality. We now determine for each point in the database if it dominates a point of a different class and therefore should be excluded from consideration. (A point (x_1, x_2) dominates another point (y_1, y_2) if $|x_i| > |y_i|$). We call this type of dominance *monochromatic dominance* that extends the standard notion of dominance (PS85). We randomly choose a dimension and project all points on this dimension. We then compute a median on the projected points; the median defines a separator (e.g, vertical line). We recursively solve monocromatic dominance separately for points larger than the median and smaller than the median. We then project all points on the line defined by the median. Finally, by climbing up the line we check for monochromatic dominance of points on the left of the median and the points to the right of the median. The algorithm runs in time $O(N \log N)$.

Choosing a local neighborhood via an adaptive boundary

Our third algorithm was inspired by a method of Hastie and Tibshirani (HT94), who defined a technique for creating an ellipsoidal neighborhood around a query. We have implemented an iterative search for a rectangular neighborhood around a query. Using the obvious greedy algorithm, one would start with a hyperrectangle around the query point and expand outwards until the enclosed region violated some constraint. A reasonable constraint to place on the neighborhood is that it must remain linearly separable; i.e., the examples contained in the rectangle can be classified using a single hyperplane. Once the expansion reaches an obstacle (i.e., a point whose inclusion will violate the constraint), it must limit growth in some dimension. When exploring all possibilities, an obstacle point will create a branch in a search tree. This algorithm is sketched in Figure 3. The size of such a search tree is exponential in the number of dimensions of the feature space, and therefore we experimented with several greedy approximation algorithms (see (FKSW96)).

Experiments

In this section we focus on the performance of the local induction voting algorithm used for several scientific domains: breast cancer diagnosis, star/galaxy classification, and identification of coding regions in DNA. We also performed experiments with the other algorithms using artificial datasets. The "dim" astronomy dataset contains 4192 examples in 14 dimensions with 2 classes

For a given query point
    The initial neighborhood is the query point itself.
    Find a local neighborhood using neighborhood_search().
    Induce a decision tree T upon the local neighborhod.
    Classify query point with T.

Neighborhood_search()
    Expand neighborhood in unblocked dimensions until an obstacle point is reached.
    For each dimensional branch caused by the obstacle point :
        Recursively call neighborhood_search().
    Return the highest scoring neighborhood from among the branches.

Figure 3: The adaptive boundary local induction algorithm

(stars and galaxies) that occur with approximately equal frequency. The human DNA dataset contains approximately 40,000 examples in 6 dimensions with 2 classes (coding and noncoding) which occur with unequal frequency. Each example represents a piece of human DNA that is 162 bases long and comes either from an exon (a coding region, the part of DNA that is used in genes to produce proteins) or from an intron (a noncoding region). Noncoding DNA is about six times more common than coding DNA in this data set (and is at least that common in the human genome), but for the sake of these experiments, two different training sets of size 300 and 5024 were constructed, each containing equal numbers of coding and noncoding regions. The results from the LIV algorithm on these datasets appear in Table 1. The accuracy reported for the DNA data set is the **unweighted** average of the two class accuracies; because of the much higher frequency of noncoding DNA, we did not want to swamp the estimate of accuracy on coding DNA in this average.

In these experiments, the decision tree induction algorithm is implemented using standard axis-parallel splits and information gain as the goodness criterion. This algorithm is thus very similar to Quinlan's C4.5 (Qui93). The decision trees are pruned using standard cost-complexity pruning (BFOS84) with a portion of the training set set aside as a pruning set. The purpose of these experiments is to determine whether local induction voting is an improvement over full induction.

The graphs presented in Figure 4 show overall accuracy as a function of the parameter K. K is the size in training points of the largest local window around the query point. At each point on the abscissa, all window sizes $1, \ldots, K$ contribute their vote to the classification

Data set	num train	num test	FI (%)	LIV (%)
HUMAN DNA	5024	39868	78.2	84.8
HUMAN DNA	300	39868	75.9	77.2
STAR/GALAXY	2500	1692	93.8	95.1
STAR/GALAXY	300	3892	89.7	92.1
BREAST CANCER	500	183	96.3	96.8

Table 1: Comparison of full induction to local induction voting. 20% of the training sets was reserved for pruning. The column labelled FI shows accuracy for full induction. The column labelled LIV shows accuracy for the local induction voting algorithm.

of the query point. In general, accuracy increases and plateaus as K is increased. Accuracy of the decision tree induced upon the full training set is shown as a horizontal rule across each graph. The accuracy of the local induction voting method typically surpasses the accuracy of full induction at a relatively small value of K.

For both of the databases, we experimented with two sizes of training set. The intent of using differently sized training sets was to determine whether local induction was better suited for sparse training sets or for larger training sets.

We used artificial data sets to perform detailed experiments with the multi-layer algorithm and the adaptive neighborhood algorithm. The datasets were generated by creating a random decision tree with approximately 200 nodes in two, four and eight dimensions. We randomly generated 400, 800, and 1600 instances. Each instance was classified using the "true" decision tree. We then used a standard decision tree algorithm, k-NN and the two new methods to classify the same data. Our multi-layer algorithm in two dimensions exhibited similar performance to the standard decision tree algorithm and outperformed k-NN. In four dimensions with 800 points, we obtained better results with the multi-layer algorithm. With 1600 points the results were similar for all methods. We found that the our adaptive neighborhood algorithm is computationally expensive and needs more tuning before it can be used effectively on large datasets.

Local Error Analysis

Another useful data mining tool provided by decision trees (local or global) is error analysis. Figure 5 is a histogram of the numbers of query points close to the decision tree boundaries for the standard algorithm on the star/galaxy data set. For any query, we can compute its bin in the histogram and report our confidence in the prediction basen on the query's distance to the boundary.

Note that the figure also reveals a difference in the distances of correct and incorrect points to a boundary:

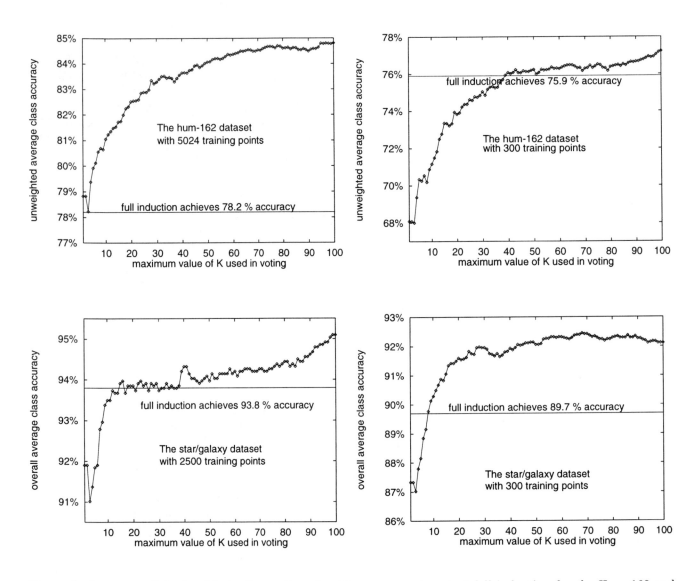

Figure 4: Accuracy of the local induction voting algorithm compared against full induction for the Hum-162 and star/galaxy datasets. The graphs on the left show the performance for large training sets, and on the right for small training sets.

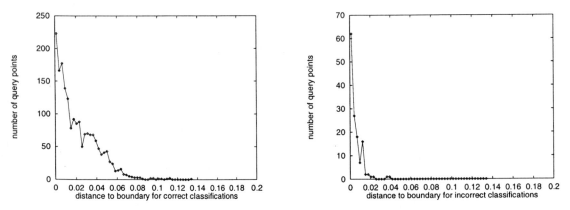

Figure 5: Frequency of distances of query points to the closest decision tree boundary for the star/galaxy dataset.

incorrectly classified points are likely to be much closer than average to a boundary.

Conclusions

In this paper we described three new algorithms for local induction decision trees and reported on some initial experimental data using these techniques. The first algorithm, local induction voting, is the simplest and so far the best in our experiments. The multi-layer composite neighborhood algorithm is more complex, especially in the efficient $O(N \log^{d-1} N)$ version. Its main design goal is to battle data fragmentation and to provide an intuitive feel for the distribution of points in the local region of the query point. For each query point we enumerate all of the monochromatic rectangles that include it. The distribution of these rectangles can be helpful for constructing new confidence measures to use with classifiers. The third method, which created axis-parallel adaptive neighborhoods, has so far shown inferior experimental performance (which is therefore not reported here) and needs further refinement. However, it has an interesting potential for applications where the concept boundaries are locally axis-parallel.

The main drawback of the algorithms reported here is the time to perform a single classification. The running time of local induction voting per query is similar in practice to standard k-NN algorithms and is dominated by the size of the training set. However, in many situations (e.g., medical diagnosis), accuracy is of utmost importance, and it is worth the extra computation to identify the most accurate method.

In high dimensional spaces, using monochromatic rectangles is problematic because most example points do form a monochromatic rectangle with the query point in this case. In this situation, one could use a stricter definition of monochromatic dominance, or one could restrict the rectangle to a limited number of dimensions, possibly based on attributes used by a fully-induced decision tree to classify the query point.

The experiments we performed indicate that local induction voting does outperform full induction in terms of accuracy. The similarity of the graphs of accuracy vs. K in experiments with very different databases indicates that local induction voting is likely to behave similarly for other databases. This makes local induction voting a potentially good candidate for improving classification tools in general.

Acknowledgements

This material is based upon work supported in part by the National Science foundation under Grant Nos. IRI-9116843, IRI-9223591, and IRI-9220960 with equipment support from NSF Grant No. CDA-9421531.

References

Christopher Atkeson, Andrew Moore, and Stefan Schaal. Locally weighted learning. *Artificial Intelligence Review, 1996 (to appear)*.

C. Atkeson. Using local models to control movement. In *Neural Information Processing Systems Conf.*, 1989.

L. Breiman, J. Friedman, R. Olshen, and C. Stone. *Classification and Regression Trees*. Wadsworth Internatl. Group, 1984.

L. Bottou and V. Vapnik. Local learning algorithms. *Neural Computation*, 4:888–900, 1992.

R. Creecy, B. Masand, S. Smith, and D. L. Waltz. Trading MIPS and memory for knowledge engineering. *Communications of the ACM*, 35(8):48–64, 1992.

S. Cost and S. Salzberg. A weighted nearest neighbor algorithm for learning with symbolic features. *Machine Learning*, 10(1):57–78, 1993.

S. Edelman. Representation, similarity and the chorus of prototypes. *Minds and Machines*, 1994.

T. Fulton, S. Kasif, S. Salzberg, and D. Waltz. Local induction of decision trees: Towards interactive data mining. Technical report, Johns Hopkins University, Baltimore, MD 21218, 1996.

J. H. Friedman. Flexible metric nearest neighbor classification. Technical report, Stanford University, Statistics Dept., November 1994.

T. Hastie and R. Tibshirani. Discriminant adaptive nearest neighbor classification. Technical report, Stanford University, Statistics Dept., December 1994.

A. Moore, C. Atkeson, and S. Schaal. Memory-based learning for control. *Artificial Intelligence Review (to appear)*, 1995.

P. Maes and R. Kozierok. Learning interface agents. In *Proc. of the Eleventh National Conf. on Artificial Intelligence*, pages 459–465, Washington, D.C., 1993. MIT Press.

Sreerama K. Murthy, Simon Kasif, and Steven Salzberg. A system for induction of oblique decision trees. *Journal of Artificial Intelligence Research*, 2:1–33, August 1994.

B. Masand, G. Linoff, and D. L. Waltz. Classifying news stories using memory based reasoning. In *Proceedings of the SIGIR*, pages 59–65, 1992.

F. P. Preparata and M. I. Shamos. *Computational Geometry: An Introduction*. Springer-Verlag, New York, NY, 1985.

J. R. Quinlan. *C4.5: Programs for Machine Learning*. Morgan Kaufmann Publishers, San Mateo, CA, 1993.

V. Vapnik and L. Bottou. Local learning algorithms for pattern recognition and dependency estimation. *Neural Computation*, 5:893–909, 1993.

T.-M. Yi and E. Lander. Protein secondary structure prediction using nearest-neighbor methods. *Journal of Molecular Biology*, 232:1117–1129, 1993.

Knowledge Discovery in RNA Sequence Families of HIV Using Scalable Computers

Ivo L. Hofacker
Beckman Institute
University of Illinois
ivo@ks.uiuc.edu

Martijn A. Huynen
Los Alamos National Lab
and Santa Fe Institute
mah@santafe.edu

Peter F. Stadler
University of Vienna
and Santa Fe Institute
stadler@santafe.edu

Paul E. Stolorz
Jet Propulsion Lab
California Inst. of Technology
pauls@aig.jpl.nasa.gov

Abstract

The prediction of RNA secondary structure on the basis of sequence information is an important tool in biosequence analysis. However, it has typically been restricted to molecules containing no more than 4000 nucleotides due to the computational complexity of the underlying dynamic programming algorithm used. We desribe here an approach to RNA sequence analysis based upon scalable computers, which enables molecules containing up to 20,000 nucleotides to be analysed. We apply the approach to investigation of the entire HIV genome, illustrating the power of these methods to perform knowledge discovery by identification of important secondary structure motifs within RNA sequence families.

Introduction

One of the major problems facing computational molecular biology is the fact that sequence information about important macromolecules such as proteins and RNA molecules exists in far greater quantities than information about the three-dimensional structure of these biopolymers. The development and implementation of computational methods capable of predicting structure reliably on the basis of sequence information will provide huge benefits in terms of our understanding of the relationship between sequence and structure. They will also help greatly in tasks such as drug discovery and verification, as well as in the study of molecular evolution. These methods can then be applied to the vast quantities of sequence information at our disposal to discover important motifs and trends within various macromolecules, without having to laboriously and expensively measure the 3D structure of each and every molecule by hand.

It turns out that the full-blown task of three-dimensional structure prediction is much too difficult to be solved with current knowledge and methods. A simpler problem, however, the prediction of secondary structure, is tractable. Functional secondary structures are conserved in evolutionary phylogeny, and they represent a qualitatively important description of the molecules, as documented by their extensive use for the interpretation of molecular evolution data.

The most popular computational approach to the prediction of RNA secondary structure from sequence information is based upon dynamic programming. The main difficulty with this algorithm is the fact that its computational complexity grows as the cubic power of the RNA chain length, and that its memory requirements grow quadratically with chain length. This drawback has limited its use in the past to RNA molecules containing up to a few thousand nucleotides. Unfortunately, many molecules of great biological interest, such as HIV molecules, contain 10,000 or more nucleotides. The genome of HIV is dense with information for the coding of proteins and biologically significant RNA secondary structures. The latter play a role in both the entire genomic HIV-1 sequence and in the separate HIV-1 messenger RNAs which are basically fragments of the entire genome. The total length of HIV-1 (about 9200 bases) makes biochemical analysis of secondary structure of the HIV-1 full genome infeasible. For RNAs of this size computer prediction of the folded structure is the only approach that is available at present.

The goal of this paper is to demonstrate the unique ability of concurrent computers to enable data-mining of families of RNA sequences of the size and scope of HIV, by allowing identification of important motifs. Sequence data-mining problems of this magnitude, requiring secondary structure prediction for a number of long RNA sequences, have never before been tackled because of their severe computational demands. We report the fastest secondary structure predictions ever achieved, and for the largest sequences that have ever been analyzed ($\sim$ 10000 nucleotides). Our results show that concurrency can be applied in this problem domain to allow novel sequence analysis and knowledge discovery on a large scale. Most importantly, massively parallel machines enable not just the prediction of secondary structure for long individual sequences, but also knowledge discovery in the form of comparisons between secondary structures for families of sequences. We have been able to exploit this power to allow the identification of prominent secondary structure motifs within the HIV genome. Our results point the way to a number of new sequence analysis possibilities in the future.

RNA Secondary Structures

RNA structure can be broken down conceptually into a secondary structure and a tertiary structure. The secondary structure is a pattern of complementary base pairings, see Figure 1. The tertiary structure is the three-dimensional configuration of the molecule. As opposed to the protein case, the secondary structure of RNA sequences is well defined; it provides the major set of distance constraints that guide the formation of tertiary structure, and covers the dominant energy contribution to the 3D structure.

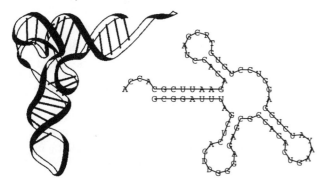

Figure 1: (l.h.s.) The spatial structure of the phenylalanine tRNA form yeast is one of the few known three dimensional RNA structures. (r.h.s.) The secondary structure extracts the most important information about the structure, namely the pattern of base pairings.

A secondary structure of a sequence is a list of base pairs i, j with $i < j$ such that for any two base pairs i, j and k, l with $i \le k$ holds (i) $i = k$ if and only if $j = l$ and (ii) $k < j$ implies $i < k < l < j$. The first condition says that each nucleotide can take part in not more that one base pair, the second condition forbids knots and pseudoknots[1]. Knots and pseudoknots are excluded by the great majority of folding algorithms which are based upon the dynamic programming concept.

A base pair k, l is *interior* to the base pair i, j, if $i < k < l < j$. It is *immediately interior* if there is no base pair p, q such that $i < p < k < l < q < j$. For each base pair i, j the corresponding *loop* is defined as consisting of i, j itself, the base pairs immediately interior to i, j and all unpaired regions connecting these base pairs. The energy of the secondary structure is assumed to be the sum of the energy contributions of

[1] A pseudoknot is a configuration in which a nucleotide that is inside a loop base pairs with a nucleotide outside that loop.

all loops. (Note that two stacked base pairs constitute a loop of size 4; the smallest hairpin loop has three unpaired bases, i.e., size 5 including the base pair.)

Experimental energy parameters are available for the contribution of an individual loop as functions of its size and type (stacked pair, interior loop, bulge, multi-stem loop), of the type of its delimiting base pairs, and partly of the sequence of the unpaired strains (Turner, Sugimoto, & Freier 1988). Inaccuracies in the measured energy parameters, the uncertainties in parameter settings that have been inferred from the few known structures, and most importantly, effects that are not even part of the secondary structure model, limit the predictive power of the algorithms. Nevertheless, local structures can be computed in quite some detail, and a majority of the base pairs is predicted correctly.

A convenient way of displaying the size and distribution of secondary structure elements is the *mountain representation* introduced in (Hogeweg & Hesper 1984). In this representation a base paired to a base downstream is drawn as a step up, a base paired to a base upstream corresponds to step down, and an unpaired base is shown as horizontal line segment, see Figures 2 and 3. The resulting graph looks like a mountain-range where:

Peaks correspond to hairpins. The symmetric slopes represent the stack enclosing the unpaired bases in the hairpin loop, which appear as a plateau.

Plateaus represent unpaired bases. When interrupting sloped regions they indicate bulges or interior loops, depending on whether they occur alone or paired with another plateau on the other side of the mountain at the same height respectively.

Valleys indicate the unpaired regions between the branches of a multi-stem loop or, when their height is zero, they indicate unpaired regions separating the components of secondary structures.

The height of the mountain at sequence position k is simply the number of base pairs that enclose position k; i.e., the number of all base pairs (i, j) for which $i < k$ and $j > k$. The mountain representation allows for straightforward comparison of secondary structures and inspired a convenient algorithm for alignment of secondary structures (Konings & Hogeweg 1989).

In this contribution we shall be interested in the secondary structure of the RNA genomes of a certain class of single-stranded RNA viruses. Lentiviruses such as HIV-1 and HIV-2 are highly complex retroviruses. Their genomes are dense with information for the coding of proteins and biologically significant RNA secondary structures. The latter play a role in both the entire genomic HIV-1 sequence and in the separate HIV-1 messenger RNAs which are basically fragments and combinations of fragments of the entire genome. By predicting the minimum free energy secondary structure of the full length HIV-1 and other known lentiviruses sequences (HIV-2, SIV, CAEV, visna, BIV and EIAV) and their various splicing products, and by comparison of the predicted structures, a first step can be made towards the unravelling of all important secondary structures in lentiviruses.

Elucidation of all the significant secondary structures is necessary for the understanding of the molecular biology of the virus. So far a number of significant secondary structures have been determined that play a role during the various stages of the viral life cycle (see section 4). We expect a high number of undiscovered biologically functional secondary structures to be still present within the various transcripts. A systematic analysis of the 5' end of the HIV genome showed an abundance of functional secondary structures (Baudin *et al.* 1993). Secondary structures further downstream could well be involved in the splicing, regulation of translation of the various mRNAs, or regulation of the stability of the full length sequence and its various splicing products.

Parallel Decomposition Issues and Related Work

Dynamic programming, when applied to RNA folding, requires CPU time that scales roughly as the cubic power of the sequence length, and memory that scales quadratically with sequence length. Even so, sequences such as HIV that are approximately 10000 nucleotides in length still require only on the order of 35 minutes to fold on 256 nodes of the Intel **Delta** supercomputer. The same calculation would require on the order of 60 hours on a high-end workstation.

On the other hand, memory requirements are a severe problem for RNA molecules the size of HIV. The simplest RNA folding calculation, which computes just the single minimum free energy structure, requires of the order of 1 Gigabyte of memory for a sequence of the length of HIV-1. More sophisticated algorithms that compute averages over a larger number of structures near the minimum free energy typically require upwards of 2 Gigabytes. Distributed massively parallel architectures can easily satisfy these memory requirements for viruses such as HIV. These resources are the primary reason that scalable architectures are necessary for performing RNA folding computations on large macromolecules.

As a consequence of the additivity of the energy contributions, the minimum free energy of an RNA sequence can be calculated recursively by dynamic programming (Waterman 1978; Zuker & Sankoff 1984). This method is at the heart of our approach. The basic logic of the folding algorithm is derived from sequence alignment: In fact, folding of RNA can be regarded as a form of alignment of the sequence to itself. The implementation of sequence alignment algorithms on massively parallel architectures in discussed in detail in (Jones 1992).

The algorithm proceeds by calculating energies for every subsequence and can be parallelized very easily: all subsequences with a common length are independent of each other and can therefore be computed concurrently, as in the case of sequence alignment. The major computational difficulty in the case of folding, distinguishing it from standard sequence alignment, is the fact that each entry requires the *explicit* knowledge of a large number data belonging to smaller subsequences.

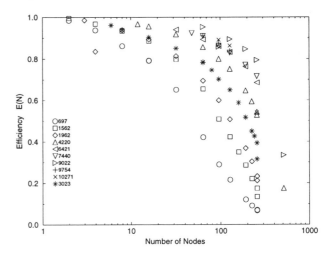

Figure 2: Efficiency of the parallelization versus the number N of nodes for the Touchstone Delta implementation, showing scaling curves for various sequence lengths.

The *efficiency* of the parallelization is measured by $\mathcal{E}(N) := T^*/(Nt)$, where T^* is the (hypothetical) single node execution time, N is as usual the number of nodes used for the calculation and t is real time used for the folding (including the backtracking step). The data in Figure 2 show that we achieve efficiencies of more than 90% when the smallest possible number of nodes is used for the computation.

Knowledge Discovery within the Secondary Structure of Lentiviruses

Retroviruses are viruses that in their life cycle alternate between a single stranded RNA stage and a double stranded DNA stage. The lentiviruses are a subclass of the retroviruses, characterized by long incubation times and a similar genomic organization. The genome of a lentivirus consists of a single RNA molecule with about 7000 to 10000 nucleotides. Almost all of this genome is used for coding for various viral proteins and RNA secondary structures. Below we highlight the role of some of the known functional secondary structures. We then describe the progress we have made towards the discovery of new scientific knowledge by mining information from a number of RNA sequences on massively parallel computers.

The minimum free energy structure was predicted for the 22 available full-length HIV-1 sequences: HIVANT70, HIVBCSG3C, HIVCAM1, HIVD31,

HIVELI, HIVHAN, HIVHXB2R, HIVJRCSF, HIVLAI, HIVMAL, HIVMN, HIVMVP5180, HIVNDK, HIVNL43, HIVNY5CG, HIVOYI, HIVRF, HIVSF2, HIVU455, HIVYU10, HIVYU2, HIVZ2Z6) and for 9 sequences of related lentiviruses: EIAV (equine infectious anemia virus), CAEV (caprine arthritis encephalitis virus), BIV106 (bovine immunodeficiency virus), VLVCG (visna virus), three simian immunodeficiency viruses SIVMM239, SIVMM251 (from macaque) and SIVSYK (from Syke's monkey), and two HIV-2 sequences HIV2BEN and HIV2ST.

The majority of the secondary structures exhibit two distinct domains: whereas the 5' half consists of a large number of fairly small components, the 3' part is a single component (except for a region of about one hundred nucleotides). The boundary between the two structural domains coincides roughly with the end of the *pol* gene.

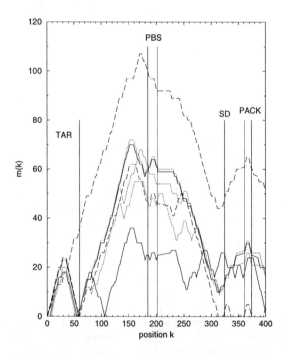

Figure 3: Mountain representation of the secondary structure of the 5' end of seven HIV-1 sequences (HIVLAI, HIVOYI, HIVBCSG3C: dotted line, HIVELI, HIVDNK: dashed line, HIVANT70: solid line, HIVMAL: long-dashed line) The secondary structures were aligned at the sequence level. Although the structures do show considerable variation, some features are conserved: (i) The TAR hairpin structure is present in six out of seven sequences. (ii) The center of the Primer Binding Site (PBS) is always single stranded (sometimes as a hairpin loop, sometimes as an internal loop), thus exposing this part of the sequence for base pairing with the tRNA primer. (iii) The center of the packaging signal (PACK) is always present as a hairpin.

At the 5' end of the viral HIV-1 RNA molecule resides the *trans*-Activating Responsive (TAR) element (Berkhout 1992); binding of the TAT protein to TAR is necessary for high levels of transcription. On the basis of biochemical analysis (Baudin *et al.* 1993) and computer prediction of the 5' end of the genome it is known that the TAR region in HIV-1 forms a single, isolated stem loop structure of about 60 nucleotides with about 20 base pairs interrupted by two bulges. This structure is indeed predicted in the minimum free energy structures of six of the seven sequences in Figure 2. Besides in HIV-1, a functional TAR structure has also been observed in HIV-2 and various SIV types while all other known lentiviruses have a *tat* gene. Although the secondary structure of TAR is strongly conserved within HIV-1, it varies considerably between the various human (HIV-1 and HIV-2) and simian (SIV) lentiviruses, as is also reflected in the minimum free energy foldings. Our analysis shows that CAEV, visna, EIAV and BIV all have a short hairpin structure at their 5' end.

The packaging signal is essential for the packaging of full length genomes into new virion particles. All analyses of its secondary structures are consistent with a short (5 base pairs) hairpin structure that carries a **GGAG** loop (Harrison & Lever 1992). Indeed, this feature is shared by all the sequences in Figure 2. However, the predictions in the literature for the more global secondary structure of this region of the RNA (beyond the 6 base pair hairpin) vary considerably. A large variation in the predicted secondary structures is also present in the minimum free energy structures of the various HIV-1 sequences.

The Primer Binding Site (PBS) at the 5' of the viral genome (Baudin *et al.* 1993) is necessary for the initiation of reverse transcription of the HIV genomic RNA into DNA. It is a sequence of 18 nucleotides that is complementary to the nucleotides at the 3' end of the tRNA with which it base pairs. The tRNA serves as a primer to initiate the reverse transcription of the viral RNA. In absence of the primer, part of the Primer Binding Site is paired to bases outside the PBS. The binding of the primer could therefore lead to a rearrangement of the secondary structure of the 5' end of the molecule. Indeed, such rearrangements were observed up to 69 nucleotides upstream and 72 nucleotides downstream of the PBS after the binding of the primer (Isel *et al.* 1995). Computer prediction of the secondary structure of RNA can play a role in guiding these types of experiments and explaining their results.

Within the *env* gene of lentiviruses resides the Rev response element (RRE). The consensus secondary structure of the RRE in HIV-1 is a multi-stem loop structure consisting of five hairpins supported by a large stem structure (Konings 1992). The interaction of RRE with the Rev protein reduces splicing and increases the transport of unspliced and single-spliced transcripts to the cytoplasm, which is necessary for the

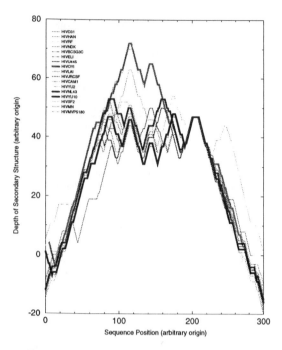

Figure 4: Alignment of the RRE regions of 17 sequences based solely on the minimum free energy secondary structure. The mountain representation reveals the five-fingered motif, the Roman numerals correspond to the numbering of the hairpins in (Dayton, Powell, & Dayton 1989). 5 out of 22 sequences showed a different pattern here. We find three different folding patterns each highlighted by one example. The first one (thick black line) corresponds to the consensus five-fingered motif that is presented in (Konings 1992). The second one (light gray) is present among other in HIVLAI. The third (dark gray) corresponds to the structure proposed (Mann *et al.* 1994).

formation of new virion particles (Malim *et al.* 1989). Figure 33 shows an alignment of the RRE region of 17 out of the 22 HIV-1 sequences based entirely on the predicted secondary structures and without gaps. Most of the secondary structures show the five-fingered hairpin motif. An alternative structure is present in which hairpin III is relatively large and a few of the other hairpins have disappeared from the minimum free energy structure. A comprehensive analysis of the base pairing probabilities in the RRE shows that the hairpins II, IV, and V, as well as the basis of hairpin III are meta-stable in the sense that they allow for different structures with nearly equal probabilities (Huynen *et al.* 1996). This structural versatility within a single sequence is here reflected in the variation in the minimum free energy secondary structure of closely related sequences. Although there is structural versatility in the hairpins, the stem structure on top of which the hairpins are located is generally present in the minimum free energy folding. The comparisons of

the prediction obtained for different, evolutionarily related RNAs can be used to identify local misfoldings in the same way as a comparative analysis can be used to infer the structure from the phylogeny.

Discussion

Our implementation of motif-detection within RNA sequence sequence families on up to 512 nodes of the `Delta` supercomputer demonstrates that massively parallel distributed memory computer architectures are well-suited to the problem of folding the largest RNA sequences available. With sequences comprising several thousand nucleotides, efficiencies above 80% are obtained on partitions of the machine containing about 100 nodes. As the partition size increases beyond 100 nodes the efficiency deteriorates to 20-40%, even for the larger sequences studied. Not surprisingly, the optimal partition sizes are those for which the total available memory on each node is utilized. These results are extremely encouraging. Apart from the insight they provide into the HIV virus itself, they indicate that even longer virus genomes containing up to 30000 nucleotides can be folded on the existing `Delta` architecture, with future scalable machines promising to extend this range even further. One long molecule of special interest is the Ebola virus, which contains roughly 20000 nucleotides.

We have determined the minimum free energy structure of a set of HIV-1, HIV-2, and related lentiviruses. The results show the presence of known secondary structures such as TAR, RRE, and the packaging signal that have been predicted on the basis of biochemical analysis, phylogenetic analysis, and the folding of small fragments of the sequence. In HIV-1 we observe a striking difference between the secondary structures of the first half and the second half of the molecule. Whereas the first 4000 nucleotides form a large number of independent components, the second 5000 nucleotides form a single huge component, on top of which the RRE is located. In general, although some relatively local patterns and the overall pattern with short range interactions in the 5' end and long range interactions at the 3' end appear conserved, there is extensive variation in the secondary structure between the various HIV-1 sequences.

The folding algorithm discussed in this paper predicts only the thermodynamically most stable secondary structure. Under physiological conditions, i.e., at or above room temperature, however, RNA molecules do not take on only the most stable structure, they seem to rapidly change their conformation between structures with similar free energies. A realistic investigation of RNA structures has to account for this fact which is of utmost biological importance. The simplest way to do this is to compute not only the optimal structure but all structures within a certain range of free energies (Waterman & Byers 1985). A more recent algorithm (McCaskill 1990) is capable of computing physically-relevant averages over all possible structures, by calculating an object known as the partition function. From it, the full matrix $P = \{p_{ij}\}$ of base pairing probabilities, which carries the biologically most relevant information about the RNA structure, can be obtained. In fact, a sequential implementation (Hofacker *et al.* 1993) has been ported recently to a `CRAY-Y-MP` and has been successfully applied to analyzing the base pair probabilities of a complete HIV-1 genome (Huynen *et al.* 1996). A comparative analysis of base-pair probabilities of RNA viruses requires an implementation of the partition function algorithm on massively parallel computers. Work in this direction is in progress.

Acknowledgements

This research was performed in part using the facilities of the Center for Advanced Computing Research at Caltech. Access to this facility was provided by the California Institute of Technology. Partial financial support by the Austrian *Fonds zur Förderung der Wissenschaftlichen Forschung*, Proj. No. P 9942 PHY, is gratefully acknowledged. PES acknowledges the support of the Aspen Center for Physics at which part of this research was performed. PES and PFS also thank P. Messina and the hospitality of CACR, where much of the work was conducted. The work was supported by the Los Alamos LDRD program and by the Santa Fe Institute Theoretical Immunology Program through a grant from the Joseph P. and Jeanne M. Sullivan Foundation.

References

Baudin, F.; Marquet, R.; Isel, C.; Darlix, J. L.; Ehresmann, B.; and Ehresmann, C. 1993. Functional sites in the 5' region of human immunodeficiency virus type 1 RNA form defined structural domains. *J. Mol. Biol.* 229:382–397.

Berkhout, B. 1992. Structural features in TAR RNA of human and simian immunodeficiency viruses: a phylogenetic analysis. *Nucl. Acids Res.* 20:27–31.

Dayton, E.; Powell, D. M.; and Dayton, A. I. 1989. Functional analysis of CAR, the target sequence for the Rev protein of HIV-1. *Science* 246:1625–1629.

Harrison, G. P., and Lever, A. M. 1992. The human immunodeficiency virus type 1 packaging signal and major splice donor region have a conserved stable secondary structure. *J. Virology* 66:4144–4153.

Hofacker, I. L.; Fontana, W.; Stadler, P. F.; Bonhoeffer, L. S.; Tacker, M.; and Schuster, P. 1993. `Vienna RNA Package`(public domain software). `ftp://ftp.itc.univie.ac.at/pub/RNA/ViennaRNA-1.03`.

Hogeweg, P., and Hesper, B. 1984. Energy directed folding of RNA sequences. *Nucl. acids res.* 12:67–74.

Huynen, M. A.; Perelson, A. S.; Viera, W. A.; and Stadler, P. F. 1996. Base pairing probabilities in a complete HIV-1 RNA. *J. Comp. Biol.* 3(2):253–274.

Isel, C.; Ehresmann, C.; Keith, G.; Ehresmann, B.; and Marquet, R. 1995. Initiation of reverse transcription of HIV-1: secondary structure of the HIV-1 RNA/tRNA(3Lys) (template/primer). *J. Mol. Biol.* 247:236–250.

Jones, R. 1992. Protein sequence and structure aligments on massively parallel computers. *Int. J. Supercomp. Appl.* 6:138–146.

Konings, D. A. M., and Hogeweg, P. 1989. Pattern analysis of RNA secondary structure similarity and consensus of minimal-energy folding. *J. Mol. Biol.* 207:597–614.

Konings, D. A. M. 1992. Coexistence of multiple codes in messenger RNA molecules. *Comp. & Chem.* 16:153–163.

Malim, M. H.; Hauber, J.; Le, S. Y.; Maizel, J. V.; and Cullen, B. R. 1989. The HIV-1 rev trans-activator acts through a structured target sequence to activate nuclear export of unspliced viral mRNA. *Nature* 338:254–257.

Mann, D. A.; Mikaelian, I.; Zemmel, R. W.; Green, S. M.; Lowe, A. D.; Kimura, T.; Singh, M.; Butler, P. J.; Gait, M. J.; and Karn, J. 1994. A molecular rheostat. Co-operative rev binding to stem I of the rev-response element modulates human immunodeficiency virus type-1 late gene expression. *J.Mol. Biol.* 241:193–207.

McCaskill, J. S. 1990. The equilibrium partition function and base pair binding probabilities for RNA secondary structure. *Biopolymers* 29:1105–1119.

Turner, D. H.; Sugimoto, N.; and Freier, S. 1988. RNA structure prediction. *Annual Review of Biophysics and Biophysical Chemistry* 17:167–192.

Waterman, M. S., and Byers, T. H. 1985. A dynamic programming algorithm to find all solutions in a neighborhood of the optimum. *Math. Biosci.* 77:179–188.

Waterman, M. S. 1978. Secondary structure of single - stranded nucleic acids. *Studies on foundations and combinatorics, Advances in mathematics supplementary studies, Academic Press N.Y.* 1:167 – 212.

Zuker, M., and Sankoff, D. 1984. RNA secondary structures and their prediction. *Bull. Math. Biol.* 46(4):591–621.

Parallel Halo Finding in N-body Cosmology Simulations

David W. Pfitzner
Mount Stromlo Observatory,
PB Weston Creek, Weston ACT 2611 Australia,
dwp@mso.anu.edu.au

John K. Salmon
Center for Advanced Computing Research,
Caltech 206-49, Pasadena, California 91125,
johns@cacr.caltech.edu

Abstract

Cosmological N-body simulations on parallel computers produce large datasets — about five hundred Megabytes at a single output time, or tens of Gigabytes over the course of a simulation. These large datasets require further analysis before they can be compared to astronomical observations. We have implemented two methods for performing *halo finding*, a key part of the knowledge discovery process, on parallel machines. One of these is a parallel implementation of the *friends of friends* (FOF) algorithm, widely used in the field of N-body cosmology. The new *isodensity* (ID) method has been developed to overcome some of the shortcomings of FOF. Both have been implemented on a variety of computer systems, and successfully used to extract halos from simulations with up to 256^3 (or about 16.8 million) particles, which are among the largest N-body cosmology simulations in existence.

Introduction

According to current cosmological theory, most of the mass in the universe (e.g., perhaps 90%) is in the form of so-called *dark matter*, whose only significant interaction is gravitational. During the evolution of the universe, this dark matter forms dense objects, called *halos*, due to gravitational instability. Within these halos, the dark matter is supported against further collapse by random motions. The normal matter in the universe collects at the centers of these halos, where star formation leads to the existence of luminous galaxies and other observable phenomena.

A detailed analytic understanding of the evolution of the dark matter is hampered by the highly nonlinear nature of the problem, and the complexity of the structures formed. Hence numerical methods have become a very important tool for understanding this evolution, and for comparing cosmological theories with astronomical observations. In N-body simulations, the mass in the universe is represented by a set of N discrete particles, which can be interpreted as a Monte Carlo sampling of the (incredibly more numerous) dark matter particles. Simulations with larger N produce more accurate results, because the sampling is more complete. Larger N also gives larger dynamic range, in terms of the range between the smallest and largest scales which can be addressed in a single simulation. This is important, for example, for investigating small-scale structure in simulations with a volume large enough to sample a fair region of the universe (Zurek *et al.* 1994), or for better resolution of substructure in simulations of clusters of galaxies (Carlberg 1994).

Recently, systems with N as large as 256^3 have been simulated on massively parallel computers. These large simulations produce correspondingly large datasets, posing a challenge for analysis, which has traditionally been done on workstations. Practical considerations like available memory, reasonable turnaround time, and a desire to study time-dependent processes make it increasingly desirable for critical data analysis tasks to run on the same parallel machines that performed the simulations. One such task is *halo finding*: identifying all the isolated collections of gravitationally bound particles, i.e., the dark matter halos. Galaxies are believed to form at the centers of these halos, so once they have been found, their distributions and properties can be compared to astronomical observations of galaxies and galaxy clusters.

The halo finding methods discussed here use data at a single output time. Other methods (Couchman & Carlberg 1992; Carlberg 1994; Summers, Davis, & Evrard 1995) use data from several output times, which is expected to be useful since halos should persist as distinct objects over time, apart from processes such as halo formation, merging, and disruption. However finding halos independently at different individual times should be a useful check of the robustness of the method in finding persistent halos, as well as an objective tool to study the evolution of halos.

The methods have been applied to real data sets obtained from cosmological simulations. Table 1 lists the basic parameters of simulations which have been analyzed and will be referred to later. (Note 1 Mpc $= 3.26 \times 10^6$ light years.) Models 2, 3 and 4 are subregions extracted from larger simulations.

In the next section we describe the friends of friends

Model	N	Volume
Model 1	16,777,216	$(100 \text{ Mpc})^3$ cube
Model 2	525,002	$(20 \text{ Mpc})^3$ cube
Model 3	8,599	$\frac{4}{3}\pi \, (10 \text{ Mpc})^3$ sphere
Model 4	1,578,230	$(10 \text{ Mpc})^3$ cube

Table 1: Simulation Parameters

(FOF) halo finding method, and note some shortcomings. This motivates the subsequent description of the new isodensity (ID) method, based on kernel density estimation (McLachlan 1992). Finally we explain how the two methods have been implemented on parallel computers, and present some timing results.

The Friends of Friends Method

In the friends of friends (FOF) method, (Davis *et al.* 1985) one specifies a linking length, h_{link}, and identifies all pairs of particles with a separation of h_{link} or less. Such pairs are designated *friends*, and halos are defined as sets of particles that are connected by one or more friendship relations, i.e., *friends of friends*. The linking length is usefully parameterized as a density, and following (Summers, Davis, & Evrard 1995), we define δ_{min} as the density, divided by the background cosmology density ($\bar{\rho}$), defined by two particles, of average mass, inside a sphere of radius h_{link}.

A second parameter in FOF is the minimum number of particles (N_{min}) in a halo. This is necessary because the particles represent a Monte Carlo sampling of the underlying matter distribution. Because of the essential randomness in the particles' positions, there will be statistical fluctuations in the number of particles in any particular region. Hence it is possible to find groups of friends that do not form persistent objects in the simulation. Obviously, chance associations involving larger numbers of particles are less likely than those involving fewer, so by setting N_{min} sufficiently large one hopes to avoid most of these spurious halos.

Figure 1 show the results of FOF on Model 3, using $N_{min} = 10$, and the left hand panels of figure 2 show the effects of increasing N_{min} to 30. These figures demonstrate two problems with FOF: joining halos together, and poor distinction of small halos from noise. The first problem is that at the center of the cluster, FOF finds one large halo which is clearly composed of at least several distinct halos. This is due to the fact that using FOF, everything in a region where the density is above δ_{min} is joined into a single halo, whether or not the region includes objects which are distinct at some higher density. (This problem was previously noted by (Bertschinger & Gelb 1991).) From the density plots it is seen that there is no value of δ_{min} which will distinguish the halos in the high density region without missing some of the lower density halos.

The second problem is related to N_{min}: The value of $N_{min} = 10$ is seen to be too small, since many of the

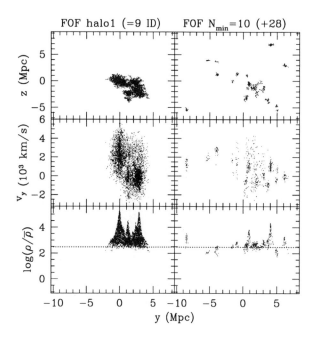

Figure 1: The FOF halo finding results for Model 3. (See text for various details in what follows. The complete model is shown in the left panels of Figure 3.) The upper panels show particle positions, projected into an arbitrary plane; the middle panels show one spatial coordinate and one velocity coordinate; the lower panels show the density (as calculated by ID) against one spatial coordinate. The horizontal line in the lower panels indicates a density of $350 \, \bar{\rho}$, corresponding to the δ_{min} value used for the FOF identification. The panels on the left show the particles in the single most massive halo found by FOF; those on the right show the particles in the other FOF halos, using $N_{min} = 10$.

small halos found have high internal velocity scatter (and hence are not bound), in contrast to others which are clearly distinct, compact objects in velocity space. At a higher N_{min} of 30, most of the spurious halos are rejected, but one remains, and in addition several real (but small) halos have been rejected.

We suggest here a simple improvement to N_{min}: Take as a parameter some minimum number of friends (i.e., direct links), N_{fmin}, and only accept halos which have at least one particle with at least N_{fmin} friends. The advantage of N_{fmin} over N_{min} is that diffuse, relatively low-density linked groups (possibly with many particles), are rejected, while isolated tight clumps (still with at least N_{fmin} particles, but possibly less than N_{min}) are accepted as real halos. The effects of N_{fmin} in Model 3 are shown in the right hand panels of figure 2, using $N_{fmin} = 10$. In this case all of the spurious halos are rejected, and more real halos are accepted than for $N_{min} = 30$.

One could consider alternative criteria for rejecting

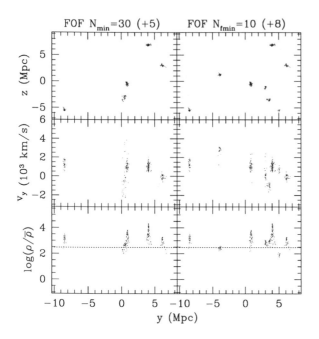

Figure 2: The same as the right hand panels of figure 1, but with alternatives to $N_{min} = 10$: on the left $N_{min} = 30$, and on the right $N_{fmin} = 10$.

spurious halos, such as using actual particle velocities to calculate whether putative halos are gravitationally bound. It is probably most productive to perform these procedures in a later stage of analysis when the halos are actually studied, cataloged, correlated, compared to observational data, etc.

The Isodensity (ID) Method

The main aim of the isodensity (ID) method is to improve on FOF by identifying halos over a wide range of densities, thereby exploiting the full dynamic range available in a simulation. In some respects the method corresponds to applying the FOF method at a range of densities or linking lengths, a course suggested by (Davis *et al.* 1985), but in an integrated and consistent way.

The idea of ID is to calculate a spatial density field defined by the particles, and identify halo centers as local peaks in this field. Isodensity surfaces are then grown around each center, to find those particles belonging to each peak. When the isodensity surfaces of different centers touch at some density, then one instead considers their common isodensity surface. As mentioned regarding FOF, in any local spatial region there will be statistical fluctuations in the number of particles in the region, which will lead to noise in the calculated density field (relative to the hypothetical underlying mass distribution being sampled by the N-body particles). The ID method rejects density peaks which are merely noise peaks by using an estimate of the uncertainty in the calculated density field.

The ID method is related to the DENMAX algorithm (Bertschinger & Gelb 1991; Gelb & Bertschinger 1994), especially in terms of motivation, but differs in most details. (Zurek *et al.* 1994) also use a similar method, but they only consider spherical isodensity surfaces.

The density field calculated from the particles should satisfy two conditions. First, the density should be in some sense spatially continuous, in that nearby particles should generally have similar densities. This condition is necessary for the interpretation of the method in terms of isodensity surfaces. Second, the statistical uncertainty of each estimate must be computable so that chance associations can be reliably rejected.

The density at each particle, ρ_i, is calculated as the sum of the masses, m_j, of the nearest N_{kern} particles, divided by the volume of the sphere enclosing those particles. This is a form of kernel density estimation,

$$\rho_i = \sum_j m_j \, k(r_{ij}, h_i) \tag{1}$$

using the nearest neighbor method to set the kernel smoothing scale, h_i, and a kernel function, k, with uniform density. A variable smoothing scale is important because of the large range in densities present in the simulations. By using the nearest neighbor method with, e.g., $N_{kern} = 24$, the local resolution in the density is tailored to the actual resolution available, in terms of the local number of particles.

The uncertainty in the calculated density can be estimated by assuming that the underlying density distribution is roughly uniform on scales that contain N_{kern} bodies, and that the particle positions are sampled at random from this density field. Then the uncertainty in the density is just due to Poisson noise, and the dispersion, σ, is simply $1/\sqrt{N_{kern}}$ times the density. For non-uniform kernels the situation is more complicated. We have experimented with alternative kernel functions, but find that for the same level of uncertainty in the density field, they are more computationally expensive.

In principle the ID method could use alternative density measures, so long as the requirements of continuity and known uncertainty are satisfied. One possibility is the phase space density: the mass per spatial volume element per velocity volume element. This may be advantageous for cosmology simulations, because low density halos generally have small internal velocities, (e.g., see figure 3) and hence have similar phase space densities to halos with higher spatial density.

The isodensity surfaces are defined implicitly by calculating for each particle a linking length, h_{link}, such that each particle links to precisely N_{link} spatial neighbors. Then, taking all the particles above some density, each group of linked particles (cf FOF), is considered to be surrounded by a single isodensity surface. The value of N_{link} should be large enough that at zero density, all particles are linked together, but not unnecessarily large since this would compromise the spatial resolution of the method. In practice values of 12 to 24 have been used.

We first present a simplified version of the ID method: One first sorts the particles by their density, and then considers each particle in turn in order of density from highest to lowest. Each particle is assigned a halo number, to specify which halo it belongs to. The halo number for each particle is calculated based on the halo numbers of the higher density particles to which it is linked, as follows: If there are no linking particles, the particle is given a new, unused halo number. If the linking particles all have the same halo number, the particle gets that number. Otherwise, the linking particles have different halo numbers. In this case the halos corresponding to those halo numbers are said to overlap at the density of the particle being considered. A new halo number is generated to represent the overlap of those halos, and for future halo linking purposes, particles with those old numbers are taken to have the new halo number, so that the new halo number can in turn participate in overlaps. However the original numbers are recorded so that the previously distinct halos are still identified as such. To keep track of these overlaps, a tree of halo numbers is constructed, where the leaves correspond to the central regions of distinct halos, and the internal nodes correspond to regions, defined by isodensity surfaces, where various halos overlap.

The first modification which is made to this simplified method is to take account of the known uncertainty in the density field to reject noise peaks. If the halo central (peak) density (ρ_c), is less than $n\,\sigma$ above the overlap density (ρ_o), with σ calculated at ρ_o, then the smaller halo is rejected, and joined into the larger halo. The value of n is a parameter of the method; an appropriate value (typically 3 to 4) can be determined by examining test cases (such as Model 3) in detail. The motivation for the above condition is that if it fails, then there is a reasonable probability (although not rigorously defined here) that the peak is a noise peak in some local region with mean density of approximately ρ_o.

A second modification is made to the simple method to improve computational efficiency and facilitate parallelism. Instead of considering each particle in turn in order of density, one makes discrete density cuts, and the particles above each cut are worked on at the same time in a consistent way. The cuts are made so that they are small compared to the uncertainty in the density, so that the consequences of this modification on the results should be small.

Figure 3 show results obtained using ID. In this particular case *all* of the halos found by ID turn out to be real, in terms of their internal velocities (when examined individually). Also, ID distinguishes halos even in the high density central region of the cluster — the single large central halo found by FOF is split into 9

smaller halos by ID. One halo found by FOF (with $N_{fmin} = 10$) is not found by ID; this is because it has fewer particles than $N_{kern} = 24$ used by ID in this case.

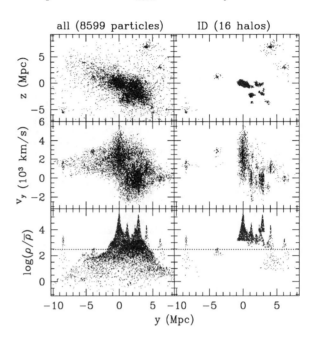

Figure 3: As in in figures 1 and 2. The panels on the left show all the particles; those on the right show the particles in the non-overlapping inner region of each halo found by ID.

In general the results of ID and FOF with $N_{fmin} = 10$ are rather similar, as shown in figure 4. The main noticeable systematic difference is in high density regions, where ID finds more halos. In this case FOF with N_{fmin} actually found more halos in total than ID, again because with the parameters used, FOF can detect halos which have fewer particles.

Implementation

We implement ID as a series of *linking passes* which will be defined shortly. Linking passes are used to calculate the particle kernel scale and linking lengths, then the particle densities, and finally the particle halo numbers. In the last step, successive density cuts are made in which particles without halo numbers are iteratively linked to those with halo numbers, and new halos are identified from local density peaks that pass the noise criterion. With many density cuts and several iterations on each cut, this step involves many individual linking passes, but executes quickly nonetheless because each pass involves relatively few particles.

A linking pass is defined as follows: Given two subsets of the particles, called sinks and sources, then for each sink, one finds all the sources within some distance of that sink, where the distance may depend on the sinks and sources. For each sink and its list of

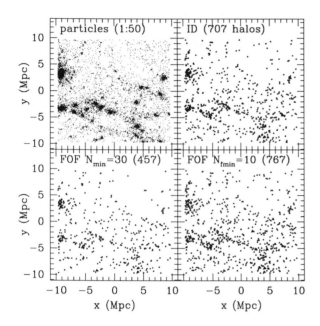

Figure 4: Comparison of particles and halos from ID and FOF (projected into an arbitrary plane). (From Model 2.)

linking sources, some calculations are performed, and information in the sink is updated. Because the density of particles is so irregular, an adaptive oct-tree is used to identify the candidate sources quickly. The neighbor-finding procedure is almost identical to that described in (Warren & Salmon 1995) in the context of smooth particle hydrodynamics (SPH). In fact, a large portion of the code is in a common library which handles all data structure manipulation and explicit communication on message passing parallel architectures. The library was originally designed to implement parallel "Fast" summation algorithms, e.g., (Barnes & Hut 1986) for the computation of gravitational interactions in $O(N \log N)$ time, but the data structures are far more general, as evidenced by this paper. The library distributes the data so that the sinks are uniquely assigned to processors, while read-only copies of the source data are transmitted and stored, on demand, on multiple processors. These two conditions completely eliminate any coherence problems associated with communication and storage and greatly simplify the programming. The libraries (and hence any applications that use them) have been ported to a wide variety of systems including message-passing and shared-memory machines, as well as networks of workstations and uniprocessor systems. In particular, the FOF and ID methods described here have been tested on single and multi-processor SPARC workstations, a 32-node CM-5 at the Australian National University and a 512-node Intel Paragon at Caltech.

Friends of friends can be implemented almost as a

special case of ID, using the number of friends as a measure of density. Other simplifications include not keeping track of halo overlaps or noise estimations. Furthermore, density cuts are not restricted as they are in ID — they can instead be based on efficiency considerations. It is best to minimize the number of distinct density cuts, subject to the condition that for each cut a large fraction of the particles link on the first iteration.

Results

Figure 5 shows the halos found by ID in Model 1. The halo finder ran for approximately 75 minutes on a 512 node Paragon at Caltech, and required over 5 Gigabytes of memory. This computation would have been prohibitively time-consuming on a uniprocessor system – assuming we could have found one with sufficient memory!

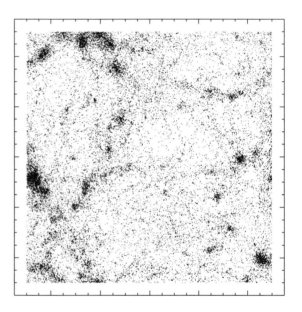

Figure 5: All 29,729 halos from Model 1, as found by ID, projected into an arbitrary plane; the box is 100 Mpc on a side.

Figure 6 shows some additional timing results from halo finding on a Paragon. The density calculation shows very good scaling, with the CPU time per processor, per number of particles on that processor, roughly constant. (The results for the density calculation for model 1 with 512 processors are not available, but are expected to be of the same order.)

The scaling is less good for the step involving density cuts and halo number calculation: when the number of processors is large, increasing the number of processors and keeping the total number of particles fixed does not reduce the time per processor. This is likely due to the

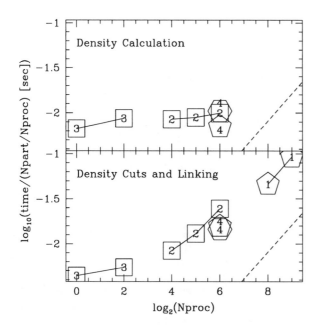

Figure 6: Timing results for the ID method. The *time* is the average CPU time on each processor, *Npart* is the total number of particles, and *Nproc* the number of processors. The different point shapes indicate somewhat different parameters, (for which the results may not be totally comparable), and the numbers correspond to model numbers from table 1 (in particular, different Npart). The dashed line indicates the slope for constant time independent of Nproc.

fact that this part of the method involves many linking passes with relatively few particles in each pass, and the small linking passes parallelize less well than large ones. Hence for this step one should use as few processors as possible, within limits set by memory constraints. In general, halo finding is memory limited rather than CPU-time limited, as are the simulations themselves. Fortunately, the linking passes with the poorest parallel efficiencies require less memory so fewer processors can be used, compared to the density calculation step.

Conclusions

We have presented a new isodensity (ID) algorithm for finding halos in *N*-body cosmology simulations, and described an implementation on parallel computers. This new method has advantages compared to the friends of friends (FOF) algorithm, which has also been implemented in parallel. In particular the ID method robustly finds density peaks even in the high density central regions of clusters. Our tests indicate that these halos are "real" in the sense of being gravitationally bound, persistent objects in the simulation, so the ID method is a genuine knowledge discovery process. The use of a statistical estimate of the uncertainty in density estimation to distinguish real peaks from chance associations is novel and effective, but lacks a firm theoretical foundation.

By implementing these methods on parallel machines we are able to use them to begin the analysis of the massive datasets produced by modern high resolution *N*-body cosmology simulations. This will allow us to address the task of accurately interpreting these simulations, to understand the physical processes involved in the formation and evolution of dark matter halos, and to compare the simulations to astronomical observations.

Acknowledgments

This research was performed in part using a Paragon supercomputer operated by the Center for Advanced Computing Research at Caltech; access to this facility was provided by Caltech. We also acknowledge computing resources provided by the Australian National University Supercomputer Facility. DWP acknowledges support from an Australian Postgraduate Award, and a Caltech Graduate Research Assistantship.

References

Barnes, J. E., and Hut, P. 1986. A hierarchical O(NlogN) force-calculation algorithm. *Nature* 324:446–449.

Bertschinger, E., and Gelb, J. M. 1991. Cosmological N-body simulations. *Computers in Physics* 5:164–179.

Carlberg, R. G. 1994. Velocity bias in clusters. *Astrophysical Journal* 433:468–478.

Couchman, H. M. P., and Carlberg, R. G. 1992. Large-scale structure in a low-bias universe. *Astrophysical Journal* 389:453–463.

Davis, M.; Efstathiou, G.; Frenk, C. S.; and White, S. D. M. 1985. The evolution of large-scale structure in a universe dominated by cold dark matter. *Astrophysical Journal* 292:371–394.

Gelb, J. M., and Bertschinger, E. 1994. Cold dark matter 1: The formation of dark halos. *Astrophysical Journal* 436:467–490.

McLachlan, G. J. 1992. *Discriminant Analysis and Statistical Pattern Recognition*. Wiley series in probability and statistics. Applied probability and statistics. John Wiley & Sons, Inc.

Summers, F. J.; Davis, M.; and Evrard, A. E. 1995. Galaxy tracers and velocity bias. *Astrophysical Journal* 454:1–14.

Warren, M. S., and Salmon, J. K. 1995. A portable, parallel particle program. *Computer Physics Communications* 87:266–290.

Zurek, W. H.; Quinn, P. J.; Salmon, J. K.; and Warren, M. S. 1994. Large scale structure after COBE: Peculiar velocities and correlations of cold dark matter halos. *Astrophysical Journal* 431:559–568.

Scalable Exploratory Data Mining of Distributed Geoscientific Data

Eddie C. Shek[†‡], Richard R. Muntz[†], Edmond Mesrobian[†], and Kenneth Ng[†]

Computer Science Department[†]
University of California
Los Angeles, CA 90024

Information Sciences Laboratory[‡]
Hughes Research Laboratories
Malibu, CA 90265

Abstract

Geoscience studies produce data from various observations, experiments, and simulations at an enormous rate. Exploratory data mining extracts "content information" from massive geoscientific datasets to extract knowledge and provide a compact summary of the dataset. In this paper, we discuss how database query processing and distributed object management techniques can be used to facilitate geoscientific data mining and analysis. Some special requirements of large scale geoscientific data mining that are addressed include geoscientific data modeling, parallel query processing, and heterogeneous distributed data access.

Introduction

A tremendous amount of raw spatio-temporal data is generated as a result of various observations, experiments, and model simulations. For example, NASA EOS expects to produce over 1 TByte of raw data and scientific data products per day by the year 2000, and a 100-year UCLA AGCM simulation (Mechoso *et al.* 1991) running at a resolution of $1° \times 1.25°$ with 57 levels generates approximately 30 TBytes of data when the model's output is written out to the database every 12 simulated hours.

In geoscience studies, a scientist often wants to extract interesting geoscientific phenomena that are not directly observed from the raw datasets. The time-varying location of phenomena reduces the number of variables in the data space while their semantic interpretation makes it more natural for the scientist to hypothesize that there might be some meaning to the classification problem, for example, based on these variables. For example, cyclone tracks, which are the trajectories traveled by low-pressure areas over time, can be extracted from a sea-level pressure dataset by linking observed areas of local pressure minima at successive time steps. Modeled as time-series of polygonal cells on the earth surface, these tracks can be used as content-based indexes that allow efficient access to "interesting" regions in a large geophysical dataset.

There are obvious similarities between geoscientific feature extraction and data mining in business applications (Agrawal & Srikant 1995) (e.g., study stock market trends by correlating the price movements of selected stocks). They both involve sieving through large volumes of isolated events and data to locate salient (spatio-)temporal patterns in the data.

The patterns of interest for business data mining applications are generally simpler and are formed by lists or sets of alpha-numeric data items. On the other hand, a geoscientific feature such as a cyclone track is a complex spatio-temporal object that is derived from massive spatio-temporal datasets through a series of computationally expensive algorithms. Geoscientific feature extraction algorithms are often dependent on complex spatio-temporal definitions of the phenomenon of interest. Scientific data mining is further complicated by the fact that scientists often do not agree on the precise definition of a natural phenomenon, leading them to develop similar but incompatible mining routines.

We cast geoscientific data mining as a database query processing problem in order to take advantage of established automatic query optimization and parallelization techniques to deliver high performance to geoscientific data mining applications. In addition to supporting high performance parallel processing, a query processing system has to support an expressive spatio-temporal data model in order for it to properly handle the diversity and complexity of geoscientific data types.

Motivated by the requirements of geoscientific data mining applications, we are developing an extensible parallel geoscientific query processing system called *Conquest* (Shek, Mesrobian, & Muntz 1996). In this paper, we describe the design of Conquest, concentrating on the features that make it especially suitable for geoscientific data mining, specifically geoscientific data modeling, parallel query processing, and heterogeneous distributed data access. Then we present our experiences with using Conquest in a real-life geoscientific data mining application in which the upward propagation of planetary-scale waves affecting the formation of ozone holes are studied.

Geoscientific Data Modeling

A large scale geoscientific data analysis application often involves the processing and handling of a large variety of spatio-temporal geoscientific data, ranging from multi-dimensional arrays of floating point numbers (e.g., a sea-level pressure dataset) to time series of georeferenced points (e.g., cyclone tracks), and traditional alpha-numeric data.

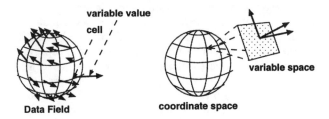

Figure 1: Example Geographic Data Field

A recurring characteristic of these data is that measurements of scientific parameters are recorded over a multi-dimensional, and often spatio-temporal, space. As a result, the central idea of the Conquest data model is that of the *field* (see Figure 1) which associates parameter values with *cells* in a multi-dimensional *coordinate space*. Cells can be of various geometric object types of different dimensionality including points, lines, polygons, and volumes. The type of the cells and hence the coordinate space they lie in are determined by *coordinate attributes*.

Values recorded for cells lie in a multi-dimensional *variable space*. The types of values that can be associated with a cell in the coordinate space of a field is dictated by *variable attributes*. The data type associated with a cell is not limited to simple data types; it can belong to a complex spatio-temporal data type or even be another field.

We refer to a cell and the variable value associated with it as a *cell record*. Not all cells in the coordinate space of a field are associated with variable values. We define a field's *cell coverage* (or simply coverage) to be the set of distinct (but not necessarily disjoint) cells in its coordinate space for which variable values are recorded. Given its cell coverage, the field's *cell mapping* maps each cell in its cell coverage to a value. The cell coverage and cell mapping logically define a field.

Some important semantic properties of data fields are captured in the Conquest data model. For example, the *extent* within the coordinate space in which cells lie and the *regularity* in which cells lie in the coverage strongly influence the choice of storage and index structures. Moreover, cell records in some fields (e.g., time series) have a natural *ordering* which dictate their access patterns.

Geoscientific Algebraic Operators

The Conquest data model defines an algebra which allows algebraic transformation techniques similar to that used in many relational DBMSs to be applied to geoscientific queries. The algebra contains a base set of general purpose logical field data manipulation operators, while users are allowed to introduce operators corresponding to application-specific algorithms. Conquest allows scientists to conveniently express their intentions by functionally combining complex scientific data manipulation operators within the algebra framework. The set of base logical operators supported can be roughly divided into the following classes:

- **Set-Oriented Relational Operators.** We define selection, projection, cartesian product, union, intersection, difference, and join operators similar to their counterparts in the relational algebra. While the logical schema for the result of these operators is well-defined, the resulting field often does not inherit the semantic properties of the input(s). For example, selecting cells in a field based on their variable values (e.g., cells in a regular sea-level pressure field which recorded parameter value greater than 980mb) in general returns a field whose cell coverage is unstructured.

- **Sequence-Oriented Operators.** Many geoscientific data mining applications involve studying the change of time-varying parameters. For example, given a set of cyclone track fields represented as time series of polygonal cyclone extents, we may want to find all cyclone trajectories whose spatial extent shrinks for 3 consecutive days. As a result, we introduce a number of sequence-oriented operators which generate fields by consuming cell records from input fields in sequence, modifying an internal state in the process, and output cell records of the output field.

- **Grouping Operators.** Data analysis applications often involve evaluating aggregate information on collections of related data from a field. We provide several cell record collection operators for collecting related cell records into subfields in preparation for aggregation. The grouping operator associates with each cell in a field's coverage a subfield containing all cells in a *neighborhood*. A nested field is defined as a field in which the values associated with cells in the coverage are fields. The nest operator moves selected coordinate attributes of a field into the variable space. Each cell in the coverage of the resulting field is associated with a field whose coordinate space is composed of the migrated attributes. Nesting a field causes "related" cell records in the original field to be grouped in a cell record, in the resulting field. The unnest operator has the inverse effect of the nest operator.

- **Space Conversion Operators.** We define operators that support the conversion of the format and representation of field data so that differences between data fields from different sources can be reconciliated and then meaningfully compared and correlated. The sample operator derives variable values at a user-specified set of cells in the coordinate space of a field with an interpolation function. By imposing a regular grid on a field, sampling (or gridding) can present a structured view of the data by deriving variable values at regular grid points through interpolation. In addition, a field's cells and their variable values can be changed by applying a mapping function to each cell record. Coordinate attribute mapping can be used to convert one map projection to another, or 'move" cells relative to their current positions by translation or rotation. One use of variable attribute conversion is to perform aggregation on related variable values, after they are collected by grouping operators.

Physical Data Model

A data field is structured in Conquest as a data stream. Conquest uses the cell record as the unit of data passing between physical operators, making it possible to take advantage of the Conquest grouping operators (group, nest and unnest) as a unique mechanism to control the granularity of data communication.

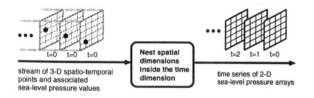

stream of 3-D spatio-temporal points and associated sea-level pressure values

Nest spatial dimensions inside the time dimension

time series of 2-D sea-level pressure arrays

Figure 2: Using the Nesting of a Data Field to Control the Granularity of Data Communication between Conquest Operators

For example, given a regular 3-D floating-point array measuring sea-level pressure on regularly spaced locations on the surface of the earth at regular time intervals, a cell record is a 4-tuple containing the spatio-temporal location and the floating point value recorded at the point. Nesting the spatial coordinate dimensions inside the time dimension causes the same array to be logically viewed as a time series of 2-D spatial array each storing the sea-level pressure values recorded on the earth surface at the corresponding time (see Figure 2). This allows cell records in the array to be implicitly referenced and hence significantly reduces the overhead required to explicitly represent the coordinate of each cell.

Extensible Parallel Query Execution

Parallelization techniques are commonly used to remove bottlenecks in I/O and computation and improve query performance. In particular, Conquest supports pipeline processing, partitioning, and multicasting to improve query performance.

Pipeline processing (or dataflow processing) supports "vertical" inter-operator parallelism in which two connecting operators in a query execution plans are assigned to different processors so that execution of the operators can overlap. Each operator consumes data arriving through a stream from its producer and feeds its output to an output stream until it blocks (e.g., when the stream buffer is full). In addition to its demonstrated effectiveness for traditional set-oriented queries, pipeline parallelism naturally supports stream query processing techniques which take advantage of data ordering to deliver excellent performance for many sequence- or set-oriented scientific queries. The benefit of stream processing is especially obvious when a scientific query is coupled with a visualization routine which consumes query results as they are being generated, allowing visualization to effectively overlap with query evaluation.

Intra-operator parallelization (or partitioned parallelism) is another form of parallelism. It provides opportunities for performance improvement by spreading I/O and computation across multiple processors or storage servers. It is achieved by dividing an input stream or dataset among a set of independent operators, each responsible for processing or retrieving a fragment of the data. In Conquest, a query execution plan fragment can be evaluated by a set of Conquest processes in a process group, each responsible for evaluating the query execution plan fragment on a portion of cell records in the input data stream.

Conquest also allows a data stream to multicast to multiple consumer process groups to provide additional opportunities for I/O and computation to be optimized. In addition, the multicast operator explicitly controls data flow to avoid data being sent too fast from a producer operator and flooding the system when the consumer operators fails to keep pace.

Automatic Query Parallelization

Extensibility is an important requirement of a geoscientific information system. One of the major implications of extensibility to query optimization is that the search space of query execution plans has to be extended as user-defined operators are introduced. As a result, to perform automatic parallelization, the optimizer in an extensible query processing environment has to be able to answer the questions of *whether* an operator in a query execution plan can be parallelized, and if so, *how* it can be parallelized.

The basic approach to achieve intra-operator parallelism for a unary stream operator is to partition the input stream into substreams, each of which is assigned to a copy of the stream operator. To simplify the discussion, we assume that the partitioning is based on time ranges. In order words, each processor is assigned a fragment of the logical input stream and is responsible for producing objects into the output stream for its assigned time range. Finally, the output streams produced by the concurrent copies of the operator are then merged to produce an output stream.

While the complete semantics of a user-defined stream operator cannot be declaratively captured, several aspects of its computation can be characterized and used to aid optimization and parallelization of queries involving the operator. One of the characteristics of a stream operator that can be exploited for parallelization is its *window of relevance* (or simply the window). It is defined as the maximum length of time (in terms the valid time in the input time series) between the arrival of an object and the time it ceases to have an effect on the execution state of the operator. The value of each object in the input stream may have a residual effect on the future execution state of a stream processor. For example, to calculate the monthly average sea-level pressure, an operator has to maintain a running sum of sea-level pressure at each cell on the surface of the earth until the average value is evaluated upon receipt of the last time frame for each month. Since the monthly average sea-level pressure is dependent on the values recorded at all time frames for the month, the window of relevance of the operator that calculates the average monthly sea-level pressure is a month.

The window of relevance is important in determining how an input stream to a stream processor can be partitioned into (overlapping) substreams for parallel execution. Some of the more interesting classes of windows include:

- **Instantaneous.** A simple operator which filters objects in a stream by projecting attributes and/or applying functions to modify attributes is a "trivial" stream operator. It is trivial in the sense that the value of each object in the stream has no effect on the state of execution in the future. In other words, the window of relevance is of zero length, or instantaneous. A logical input stream to this kind of aggregate operator can be partitioned in any way without involving data replication.

- **Known.** There are also operators which require a known time duration of data to be kept in the execution state. For example, an operator that returns, for each time step, the average value for a time-varying attribute during the last week only requires a week's worth of data (or some equivalent derived value) to be maintained by the operator. A one-week window of relevance dictates that for each processor, one week worth of data (in this case, the week before the starting time of the processor's range) has to be replicated at that node.

- **Random but Bounded.** Consider the cyclone tracking operator which consumes a time series of sea-level pressure minima points. Theoretically it has an unpredictable window of relevance. However,

based on our study and domain knowledge from the scientists, we know that cyclone tracks do not last more than 30 days and that the influence of a minima points becomes negligible after a 30-day period. As a result, we can use this application semantics as a "pragma" to the optimizer. The optimizer can than pessimistically parallelize the cyclone tracking operator as if it has a known window of relevance of 30 days.

- **Fixed windows.** The window size alone does not tell the whole story. Consider again the operator calculating monthly average. While the window of relevance for the operator is 1 month, the window is not a "sliding window". Instead, there are a number of disjoint fixed windows along the input stream, each of which starts at the beginning of a month and covers the month. Similar to the case of disjoint fixed windows, it is possible that a stream operator may have a fixed set of overlapping windows. The fixed set of windows present a natural partitioning of the input stream for parallel processing.

In addition to partitioning a data stream along the index dimension (e.g., time dimension for a time series), a data stream can also be partitioned "vertically" into substreams, each containing fragments of the original data objects. For example, a time series of multidimensional arrays can be partitioned into a collection of time series (of the same length as the original) of sub-arrays covering a portion of the original array. A similar classification scheme as that we have described can be used to guide automatic "vertical" partitioning.

Heterogeneous Distributed Data Access

Only a small percentage of the vast amount of archived geoscientific data collected from various sources is ever analyzed. This has partly been due to the unavailability of sufficient storage and bandwidth at reasonable cost, and more importantly because of the difficulties involved in integrating distributed geoscientific datasets managed by various scientific data formats and geoscientific database systems.

Distributed object management technologies merge the notion of location and platform transparency and object-oriented software technology. Emerging standards such as Object Management Group's Common Object Request Broker Architecture (CORBA) (Soley 1992) promise to provide a framework for distributed dataset integration by allowing uniform and convenient access to heterogeneous datasets. In CORBA, each object supports a well-defined interface that can have different implementations. In other words, datasets stored in different repositories can be made available to clients distributed over the network in a consistent manner if they are encapsulated by the same interface.

Conquest supports access to datasets both through a distributed object interface and a repository-specific scanner operator. The reason for this duality is that while convenient, accessing data from distributed objects eliminates opportunities to take advantage of the query capability of data repositories to optimize query evaluation. Some database servers and scientific data format libraries efficiently support some data manipulation and filtering operations. Most notably, indexes can be defined to provide alternative access paths to data and to filtered out unnecessary data internally without having them to be translated for external consumption. In addition, many problems do not fit the stream paradigm (e.g., slab multi-dimensional subarray extraction), and fit better into the storage management subsystem rather than the query execution engine (Graefe 1993). As a result, it is often advantageous to optimize extraction of data from external data sources by pushing operations and filters into the data source to take advantage of efficient processing and reduce the amount of data that needs to be extracted out of the data source.

A description of our proposed approach to optimize access to heterogeneous datasets by taking advantage of the fact that some repositories can efficiently execute some operations can be found in (Shek, Mesrobian, & Muntz 1996). In short, by consulting the data dictionary, a reference to a distributed object in a query execution plan may be mapped to a collection of scan operators to the underlying data repositories for the object. A set of *operator ingestion rules* guide how operators in a query expression can be "pushed" into logical scan operators for execution by the corresponding repository.

Data sources supported by Conquest include files in popular scientific data formats such as HDF (Nat 1993) containing multi-dimensional raster datasets, and extended relational DBMS Postgres which is used as both a storage and an external content-based index server.

Implementations and Experiences

Conquest has been ported to run on massively parallel processor supercomputers (IBM SP1, SP2 and Intel Paragon) as well as workstation farms using the portable message passing library PVM as the inter-process communication mechanism. It has been in use for the past two years at UCLA and JPL for exploratory data analysis and data mining of spatio-temporal phenomena produced by the UCLA and ECMWF Atmospheric General Circulation Models (AGCMs) and satellite-based sensor data such as NCAR's ECMWF Global Basic Surface and Upper Air Advanced Analyses. Previously reported geoscientific data mining activities include the extraction and analysis of cyclonic activity, blocking features, and oceanic warm pools (Stolorz *et al.* 1995).

Upward Energy Propagation

The upward propagation of planetary-scale waves from the troposphere into the stratosphere has a profound effect on the structure of the stratospheric circulation.

Occasionally, the rapid growth and upward propagation of waves during winter in the northern hemisphere can lead to a reversal of the high-latitude stratospheric wind from westerly (i.e., west to east) to easterly. On longer time scales, the weaker upward propagation of the planetary waves in the southern hemisphere leads to a stronger westerly winds than in the northern hemisphere. This results in the formation of a well-defined "ozone hole" each spring over Antartica, while no such ozone hole develops in the Arctic.

To detect upward propagation of wave energy into the stratosphere, we might first compute a measure of the phase difference of a particular component (e.g., zonal wave number 1, the wave with the longest wavelength), at a given latitude, between two pressure levels in the upper troposphere (e.g., 50mb and 500mb levels). Next we locate waves of sufficient strength (amplitude) at the two neighboring pressure levels by computing the first Fourier coefficient of the geopotential height data values measured at these pressure levels.

We implemented the query as a series of Conquest operators which computation can be partitioned along the time dimension for parallel evaluation, i.e., the input datasets can be divided into (equal-size) pieces and processed in parallel. This partitioning is driven by the fact that the window of relevance of the query is instantaneous because no information from an earlier period is needed in order to extract upward wave propagation event at a particular time.

We have performed the study on 3 HDF-based geopotential height datasets on a 4-node Sun workstation network (consisting of SparcStation 10s and SparcStation 20s): a NCAR ECMWF Upper Air Advanced Analyses dataset (14 geopotential levels, 2.5° lat. × 2.5° lon. × 12 hours resolution, from 1985-1994, 2Gbyte), a CSIRO AMIP dataset (6 levels, 3.184° lat. × 5.625° lon. × 6 hours resolution, from 1979-1986, 370Mbyte), and a UCLA AGCM dataset (6 levels, 4° lat. × 5° lon. × 12 hours resolution, from 1980-1989, 330Mbyte). 7304 instances of upward wave propagation events are extracted from the largest NCAR ECMWF Analyses dataset in 8610 seconds with 1 node and in 2430 seconds on 4 nodes. The speedup is not perfect mainly because of the non-even distribution of upward wave propagation events over time (see Figure 3) and that of the computing resources on the heterogeneous collection of computing nodes.

After independent upward wave energy propagation events are extracted, trajectories of such events that persisted for more than 1 day are located. Figure 4 shows the number of upward wave propagation trajectories between 500mb and 50mb levels from the CSIRO AMIP dataset at different latitudes, demonstrating that the frequency of upward wave propagation trajectories decreases as it approaches the equator.

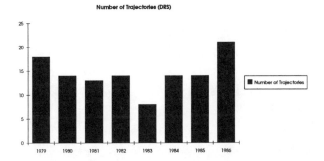

Figure 3: Number of upward wave propagation trajectories between 500mb and 50mb levels extracted from the CSIRO AMIP dataset per year

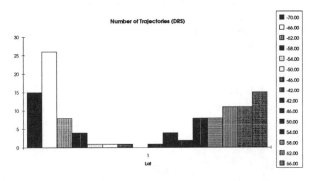

Figure 4: Number of upward wave propagation trajectories between 500mb and 50mb levels at different latitudes extracted from the CSIRO AMIP dataset

Conclusions

Conquest defines a geoscientific data model, and applies distributed and parallel database query processing techniques to handle computationally expensive data mining queries on massive distributed geoscientific datasets. The usefulness of Conquest as a data mining system is demonstrated in a upward energy propagation study in which Gbytes of raw data are digested and summarized into less than 1 Mbyte of energy propagation trajectory information (representing a size reduction of 4 orders of magnitude) which help scientists gain insight into the process of energy propagation and ozone hole formation.

Query optimization in Conquest emphasizes parallelization and optimized data access. This is becasue we realized that the benefit of algebraic transformation (Wolniewicz & Graefe 1993) is limited due to the application-specific nature of scientific operators. Furthermore, it is unclear what the effects of algebraic query expression transformations are on the accuracy of query results since many scientific operators are very sensitive to the accuracy and precision of its inputs; small round-off errors introduced at one point in a query execution plan may snowball as data flows through multiple operators and cause significant error in the result.

OASIS (Mesrobian *et al.* 1996) is a complementary effort to Conquest at UCLA that aims to develop a flexible environment for scientific data analysis, knowledge discovery, visualization, and collaboration. It provides application developers, as well as end-users, the logical abstraction that the environment is simply a set of objects. While the core OASIS services, implemented in Sunsoft's CORBA-compliant NEO, provide users with transparent access to heterogeneous distributed objects without regards for their underlying storage and representation, they do not immediately support parallel processing of data retrieved from these objects. As a result, we are currently reimplementing Conquest as the OASIS distributed query service to exploit distributed object computing technologies to support complex geoscientific query processing.

References

Agrawal, R., and Srikant, R. 1995. Mining sequential patterns. In *Proc. 11th Int'l Conf. on Data Engineering.*

Graefe, G. 1993. Query evaluation techniques for large databases. *ACM Computing Surveys* 25(2):73–170.

Mechoso, C.; Ma, C.; Farrara, J.; and Spahr, J. 1991. Simulations of interannual variability with a coupled atmosphere-ocean general circulation model. In *Proceedings of 5th Conference on Climate Variations.* American Meteorology Society.

Mesrobian, E.; Muntz, R. R.; Shek, E. C.; Nittel, S.; LaRouche, M.; and Kriguer, M. 1996. OASIS: An open architecture scientific information system. In *Proc. of Sixth International Workshop on Research Issues in Data Engineering: Interoperability of Nontraditional Database Systems*, 107–116.

National Center for Supercomputing Applications. 1993. *HDF User's Guide, Version 3.2.*

Shek, E. C.; Mesrobian, E.; and Muntz, R. R. 1996. On heterogeneous distributed geoscientific query processing. In *Proc. of Sixth International Workshop on Research Issues in Data Engineering: Interoperability of Nontraditional Database Systems*, 98–106.

Soley, R. M., ed. 1992. *Object Management Architecture Guide (2nd Edition).* Object Management Group.

Stolorz, P.; Mesrobian, E.; Muntz, R. R.; Shek, E. C.; Santos, J. R.; Yi, J.; Ng, K.; Chien, S. Y.; Nakamura, H.; Mechoso, C. R.; and Farrara, J. D. 1995. Fast spatio-temporal data mining of large geophysical datasets. In *Proc. of First International Conference on Knowledge Discovery and Data Mining*, 300–305.

Wolniewicz, R. H., and Graefe, G. 1993. Algebraic optimization of computations over scientific databases. In *Proc. 19th Int'l Conf. on VLDB.*

Using a Hybrid Neural/Expert System for Data Base Mining in Market Survey Data

Victor Ciesielski and Gregory Palstra

Department of Computer Science
Royal Melbourne Institute of Technology
GPO Box 2476V
Melbourne Vic 3001 Australia
vc@cs.rmit.edu.au

Abstract

This paper describes the application of a hybrid neural/expert system network to the task of finding significant events in a market research data base. Neural networks trained by backward error propagation are used to classify trends in the time series data. A rule system then uses these classifications, knowledge of market research analysis techniques and external events which influence the time series, to infer the significance of the data. The system achieved 86% recall and 100% precision on a test set of 6 months of survey data. This was significantly better than could be achieved by a system using linear regression together with a rule system. Both systems were able to perform analysis of the test data in under 5 minutes. The manual analysis of the same data took a human expert over four working days.

Introduction

Data mining has been described as the process of finding 'nuggets' of information or knowledge in large data bases. Many traditional machine learning approaches are being re-examined for their effectiveness in finding nuggets(Fayyad & Uthurusamy 1995; Piatetsky-Shapiro & Frawley 1991). There is currently no 'universal data base mining engine' and it is unlikely that one will be developed in the foreseeable future. However, what does appear to be within reach is a set of guidelines about what kinds of techniques are good for what kinds of data bases. In this paper we present an approach that we believe will be very useful for data bases of time series data.

A Hybrid Neural/Expert Architecture

It has been well recognized that artificial neural networks and expert systems are complementary in that where one approach is weak the other is strong(Becraft, Lee, & Newell 1991; Ciesielski & Ho 1993). There has been considerable work in devising architectures which realize the benefits of both approaches. One architecture which has had considerable success (Becraft, Lee, & Newell 1991; Ciesielski & Ho 1993;

Scheinmakers & Tourtetzky 1990) involves using network(s) as sub-components of expert systems as suggested by figure 1. Here the feed-forward component of a previously trained network is used to determine values of some of the variables used by the expert system. The network is trained off-line using appropriate examples and the expert system is constructed by an appropriate knowledge engineering process.

This architecture is well suited to problems which have a pattern recognition or classification component and a reasoning component.

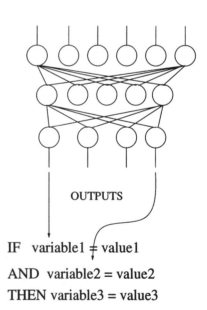

INPUTS

OUTPUTS

IF   variable1 = value1

AND variable2 = value2

THEN variable3 = value3

Figure 1: A Hybrid Neural/Expert Architecture

Goal

The goal of this work was to determine whether a search engine, based on the architecture described above, could be effectively used for finding significant

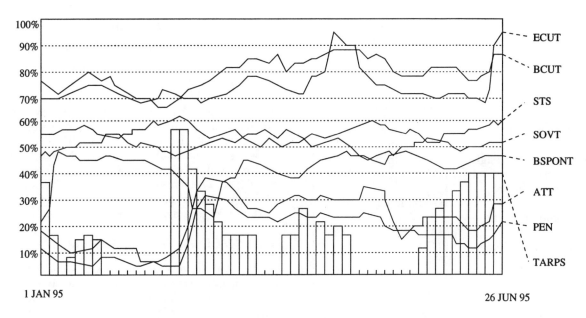

Figure 2: Graphical representation of survey data

Analysis of Market Survey Data

In our domain of market survey data the 'golden nuggets' to be found pertain to whether or not an advertising campaign is effective. Survey data analysts spend long hours analysing graphs of survey data looking for situations where an advertising campaign is not being effective. An analyst may need to look at several hundred graphs a day. Naturally the advertisers want to know about problems as soon as possible so that appropriate action can be taken. A sample of the data on which decisions are based is shown in figure 2. Much of this data comes from surveys carried out at shopping centres where the above data is collected about a product and its main competitors. The variables in the figure are (Sutherland 1993):

Executional cut through (ECUT) How well the advertisement for a product is being recalled amongst the advertising about other products.

Branded cut through (BCUT) How well the advertising for the brand is being recalled.

Attitudinal share (ATT) What brand people are likely to buy next.

Short term share (STS) The last brand bought for this type of product.

Penetration (PEN) Has the person ever bought the product.

Brand Spontaneity (BSPONT) Recall, not recognition, of the brand name.

Share of voice (SOVT) The percentage share of this product's television advertising in relation to its competitors.

Client Advertising (TARPS) The amount of television advertising for a product.

Ad executions (ADEX) The number of advertisements sent to air for the product in one week.

Net message take out (NETMESS)
The percentage of people who derived the intended message from the advertising.

The graph in figure 2 ends at 26-Jun-95. On 27-Jun-95 this data would be examined to determine whether there is a problem. The analyst needs to determine the trends in selected variables prior to 26-Jun-95, consider their inter-relationships and draw a conclusion about the effectiveness of the advertising. Typically the same data will be available for dozens of products causing a 'data flood' problem. Our implementation focuses on finding, as soon as possible, the situations where an advertising campaign is not working. One such result is shown in figure 3. Note that a key aspect of the decision making is the classification of time series segments into the categories shown in table 1.

The data in figure 2 consists of rolling averages, in which the last n data points are averaged to get the value for the current week as follows:

$$p' = \frac{1}{n} \sum_{i=0}^{n-1} p_{current-i}$$

Rolling averages tend to smooth out fluctuations in the survey data, however, if n is too high the variations of interest can be obliterated. A series of preliminary experiments revealed that a 4 week rolling average was

Attribute	Classification	Conf
Executional cut through	SMALL-RISE	67%
Branded cut through	SMALL-RISE	89%
Short term share	FLAT	98%
Attitudinal Share	FLAT	73%
Penetration	BIG-FALL	78%
Unprompted brand awareness	SMALL-RISE	74%
In store promotions	SEQUENCED	
Client advertising	REMAINED	
Share of voice	89%	
Net message take out	40%	
Ad executions	3	
CONCLUSION	AD-MSG-BAD	(67%)

Figure 3: Results of an Analysis

best for this application. Co-incidentally, the analysts believe that 4 weeks is the appropriate time period in which to detect an advertising problem.

The analyst's task is to combine together the shapes and relationships of the curves with other knowledge to determine significance. For example it would be expected that sales of ice creams and soft drinks should rise in a heat wave and that a manufacturer should be alerted if this did not occur. It would be expected that the sales of a product would rise shortly after the commencement of an advertising campaign and an alert should be generated if this did not occur. It is possible for advertising for a product to actually raise the sales of a competitor's product and such situations need to be detected as soon as possible. A particularly tricky and very important aspect of determining advertising effectiveness is the problem of finding 'turning points' as soon as possible. A turning point is a change of trend, from downwards to upwards for example, and is of great importance to an advertiser spending heavily on a television advertisement.

For the purpose of this paper a 'golden nugget' or significant event is a situation where an advertising campaign is not working as expected.

The above examples suggest that the analysis task has a pattern classification component (interpreting the graphs) and a reasoning component (using knowledge of events that affect the time series) and we believed that a major part of it could be automated using a hybrid neural/expert system of the kind described earlier.

Development of the Neural/Expert Search Engine

We developed two neural/expert hybrid systems. Our first system directly used the model suggested in figure 1. A single network was used for all variables and the generated classifications were used by the expert system to determine whether that particular four week period contained a situation that should be reported. This system was unable to detect subtle differences between variables as the experts were doing so we then developed a system with separate networks for each of the eight variables. The performance of this second system was considerably better.

One Network For All Variables

The neural network used was a 4-6-6 network trained by backward error propagation. The six output units corresponded to the categories in table 1. We had successfully used such networks previously for a similar task in an intensive care ventilator monitor(Hayes & Ciesielski 1991).

String	Symbolic Meaning
SRISE	A small rise in the trend
BRISE	A large rise
SFALL	A small fall
BFALL	A large fall
FLAT	No significant change
INCONCLUSIVE	No classification possible

Table 1: Symbolic output from the neural network

The 'INCONCLUSIVE' class was used when the analysts could not place a four week pattern into one of the other five classes. This situation typically arose when there were large fluctuations in values in consecutive weeks. We introduced this class rather than force the experts to select one of the existing classes. Also, some attributes, like 'short term share', approach a threshold which effects the significance of changes in that attribute's value. A jump of four percent in 'short term share' when its value is low may be insignificant, but the same jump, when the attribute's value is close to fifty percent, is a very significant change. This situation does not affect the training of the networks, but does need to be covered in the rule system.

	1-out-of-5	Gaussian-hill
Big Rise	0.0	0.5
Small Rise	1.0	1.0
Flat	0.0	0.5
Small Fall	0.0	0.0
Large Fall	0.0	0.0
Inconclusive	0.0	0.0

Table 2: Output Encodings for 'small-rise'

The training data consisted of 600 four week intervals of survey data classified into the categories shown in table 1. A *1-out-of-5* coding was used. This resulted in rather slow training and an unacceptable error rate. We then adopted a 'Gaussian-hill' approach to coding the outputs(Pomerleau 1991). The coding for 'small rise' is shown in table 2. In this domain 'small rise' is intermediate between 'big rise' and 'flat' and has some of the characteristics of both. This is reflected in the Gaussian-hill encoding. Both training times and accuracy improved significantly (table 3).

	1-out-of-5	Gaussian-hill
6-fold X-validation	74%	80%
Mean Squared Error	0.00043	0.00030
Epochs	3500	2000

Table 3: 1-out-of-5 vs 'Gaussian-hill' output encodings

Separate Network for Each Variable

As testing proceeded, it became clear that we were still not accurately emulating the experts' classifications, with nearly 20% of test cases being incorrectly classified. Analysis of the errors revealed that within some value ranges, several attributes were seldom being classified correctly at all. Further discussion with the analysts revealed that not all attributes were analysed the same way. The same set of points could be interpreted differently, depending on which attribute they were representing. It was clear the use of a single neural network for all attributes would never provide adequate classifications and that a separate network for each variable was needed. Table 4 shows the training statistics for the single network and the average statistics for the eight dedicated neural networks. This group of networks trained at a much faster rate and performed on test cases, with an average error rate of 8%.

	One Network For All Variables	One Network Per Variable
6-fold X-validation	80%	92%
Mean Squared Error	0.00043	0.00030
Epochs	2000	1500

Table 4: Single Neural Network vs Dedicated Neural Networks

The errors that still occur seem to be a direct result of treating the attributes independently. For some attributes, like 'attitudinal share' and 'short term share' it is the relationship between their trends that is the significant factor determining the classification of these attributes. If 'short term share' is classified as flat and 'attitudinal share' is also flat, but is moving very slightly upwards and away from 'short term share',

then 'attitudinal share' should be classified as rising, even though it would normally be classified as 'flat' for such a small rise. However this judgement is very difficult to make on four weeks of data. Longer term relationships are not captured by our current networks. We are currently determining whether the benefits of capturing these relationships are justified by the development costs.

The Expert System

The expert system was developed using the spiral development methodology(Giarratano & Riley 1989). In this approach the system is developed from an initial prototype by successive cycles of knowledge acquisition, coding and evaluation. We commenced the knowledge acquisition using the method of familiar tasks (Hoffman 1987). At this step the key aspects of survey data analysis were identified as was the goal of finding ineffective advertising campaigns. Subsequently we used the method of structured interviews(Hoffman 1987) which involved bi-weekly meetings with the analysts.

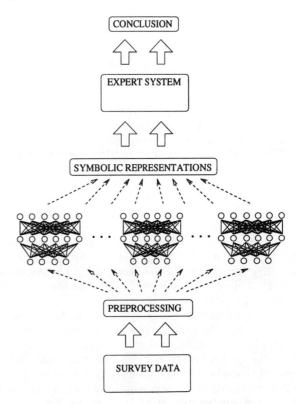

Figure 4: Hybrid System Architecture

The architecture of the developed system is shown in figure 4. The process of consultation involves the user specifying which product and survey data to examine, and the start and end date of the examination period. The hybrid system retrieves the required data from the database and applies the required rolling average. The data is then broken into four-week intervals. The eight attributes from each four-week interval are presented to their respective neural networks for classification. The symbolic representations from the neural networks, and any other facts that are required by the expert system, such as the share of voice value and the state of advertising for the interval, are added to the fact base. The rule interpreter is then invoked and a conclusion is inferred using backward chaining.

Mining Experiments and Results

Our task of finding the significant events in large amounts of survey data is analogous to the information retrieval task of finding relevant documents in a (usually very large) document collection in response to a query. Thus we have used *recall* and *precision*, the standard information retrieval measures(Salton, Allan, & Buckley 1994), to assess system performance. For our purposes recall and precision are:

$$recall = \frac{Number\ of\ significant\ events\ retrieved}{Actual\ number\ of\ significant\ events}$$

$$precision = \frac{Number of\ significant\ events\ retrieved}{Number\ of\ events\ retrieved}$$

In general, there is a tradeoff between recall and precision. For example, requiring a higher recall results in lower precision as attempts to retrieve more significant events also result in the retrieval of more false alarms.

Testing the system presented us with some major problems. We knew from the structured interviews that the analysts were impressed with the system's ability to find significant events. However for a formal evaluation we needed to compare the system's performance with the experts on a significantly large data base. Simply taking chunks of several months of data for a number of products was not really adequate since many of these events are rare and there can be many months between occurrences. Furthermore determining the actual number of significant events in a data set is a very laborious and time consuming process since several analysts need to carefully analyse the data and agree on the significant events.

As a compromise between the need to have a large data base and the very high cost of preparing it we constructed a test set, equivalent to six months of survey data, by splicing a number of significant events (that were not involved in the training phase) into a number of places in an otherwise dull time series. The test data base was equivalent to 104 four week segments. The results are shown as the first line in table 5. The system found 25 out of 29 significant events and none of these events were false positives.

We compared the performance of our hybrid engine with a system containing a linear regression preprocessor in place of the neural network. The regression preprocessor fits a least squares line to the previous four weeks of data. The slope is then classified into

	Recall	Precision
Hybrid System	25/29 (86%)	25/25 (100%)
Expert system with linear regression	21/29 (72%)	20/21 (95%)

Table 5: Recall and precision results neural network and regression systems

the categories shown in table 1. Developing this system required determining optimal thresholds for the five categories of interest. Some of our experiments for doing this are shown in table 6.

Flat	Small Rise	Large Rise	Correct
$0 \leq m < 10$	$10 \leq m < 20$	$20 \geq m$	65%
$0 \leq m < 15$	$15 \leq m < 25$	$25 \geq m$	75%
$0 \leq m < 17$	$17 \leq m < 27$	$27 \geq m$	81%
$0 \leq m < 20$	$20 \leq m < 30$	$30 \geq m$	70%
$0 \leq m < 25$	$25 \leq m < 45$	$45 \geq m$	60%

Table 6: Regression Development

The ranges were determined in a number of knowledge acquisition cycles with the analysts. From table 6 it can be seen that the best gradient range set tested was the third row. The 81% correct classification rate here is virtually the same as the 80% achieved by the single neural network.

The second line of table 5 gives the recall and precision results for this system on the test data base, showing the hybrid system to be clearly superior. The results in the table are perhaps slightly misleading since we have compared a neural system with 8 networks with a regression system containing only a single, global, slope classification for all variables. However the analysts were not willing to repeat the tiresome process of slope determination another 8 times, particularly when they already had a system they were happy with.

While we are not in a position to compare the performance of the hybrid system with the best possible regression system, we can conclude that the development time for the hybrid system is shorter and is much preferred by the analysts. Developing the regression system requires the additional step of determining classification thresholds for the slope (table 7). This requires several iterations of frustrating structured interviews with the experts, since adjusting a threshold to make an improvement in one value typically makes another one worse. We had experienced a similar situation with the development of an intensive care ventilator monitor(Hayes & Ciesielski 1991).

The recall results indicate that the system is currently too strict in its definition of a significant event. In normal operations we would want the system to find all significant events at the cost of a moderate number of false alarms.

Neural/Expert System	Regression/Expert system
1. Collect and Classify Data	1. Collect and Classify Data
2. Train networks	2. Determine prototypical regression line
	3. Search for best thresh-holds
3. Develop rule system	4. Develop rule system
4. Put trained networks into search engine	5. Put thresh-holds into expert system

Table 7: Comparison of development steps

Conclusions

The main goal of this project was to investigate the effectiveness of a hybrid neural/expert system for the task of extracting significant events from market research data. We have developed such a system and evaluated its performance on a significant market survey data base. The hybrid neural/expert system was more accurate than a regression/expert system that could be built within the resource limitations of the project. The system promises considerable improvements in efficiency over the current manual approach. It was able to analyse the test data in under five minutes, whereas the manual analysis of the same data took an expert analyst over four working days. However the system needs some fine tuning before it is ready to be deployed. We particularly need to improve the recall at the expense of the precision, that is we would tolerate a moderate number of false positives to ensure that no significant event is missed.

The key insight that drove the design of the neural/expert search engine was viewing the analysis task as pattern classification followed by symbolic reasoning with domain knowledge. We believe that neural/expert hybrid systems of this kind will be useful for other data bases, particularly data bases of time series.

Acknowledgements

We thank Kingsley Winikoff, Max Sutherland, Roland Seidel and Dale Chant of Marketmind Technologies Pty Ltd for generous contributions of their time and expertise to this work and Angeline Pang for her work on the first prototype.

References

Becraft, W. R.; Lee, P. L.; and Newell, R. B. 1991. Integration of neural networks and expert systems for process fault diagnosis. In *The 12th International Joint Conference on Artificial Intelligence*, volume 2, 824–831. Morgan Kaufman Publishers Inc.

Ciesielski, V., and Ho, T. 1993. The synergistic combination of neural and symbolic computation in the recognition of words degraded by noise. In Rowles, C.; Liu, H.; and Foo, N., eds., *Proceedings of the Sixth Australian Joint Artificial Intelligence Conference*, 131–136. Melbourne: World Scientific.

Fayyad, U., and Uthurusamy, R., eds. 1995. *Proceedings of the First International Conference on Knowledge Discovery and Data Mining (KDD-95)*. Menlo Park, California: AAAI Press.

Giarratano, J., and Riley, G. 1989. *Expert Systems, Principals and Programming*. PWS-Kent Publishing Comapny, Boston.

Hayes, S., and Ciesielski, V. 1991. A comparison of an expert system and a neural network for respiratory system monitoring. Technical Report 92/1, RMIT.

Hoffman, R. R. 1987. The problem of extracting the knowledge of experts from the perspective of experimental psychology. *AI Magazine* 8(2).

Piatetsky-Shapiro, G., and Frawley, W. J., eds. 1991. *Knowledge Discovery in Databases*. Menlo Park, California: AAAI Press and The MIT Press.

Pomerleau, D. A. 1991. Efficient training of artificial neural networks for autonomous navigation. *Neural Computation* 3(1):88–97.

Salton, G.; Allan, J.; and Buckley, C. 1994. Automatic structuring and retrieval of large text files. *Communications of the ACM* 37(2):97–105.

Scheinmakers, J. F., and Tourtetzky, D. S. 1990. Interfacing a neural network with a rule based reasoner for diagnosing mastitis. In Erlbaum, L., ed., *Proceedings of the International Joint Conference on Neural Networks. Volume 2*, 487–490. Morgan Kaufman Publishers Inc.

Sutherland, M. 1993. *Advertising and the Mind of the Consumer, What works, what doesn't and come*. Sydney: Allen and Unwin.

Weiss, S. M., and Kulikowski, C. A. 1991. *Computer Systems That learn*. San Mateo, Ca: Morgan Kaufman.

Discovering knowledge in commercial databases using modern heuristic techniques*

B. de la Iglesia, J.C.W. Debuse and V.J. Rayward-Smith
University of East Anglia
Norwich
NR4 7TJ
UK
{*bli,jcwd,vjrs*} *@sys.uea.ac.uk*

Abstract

In this paper we describe our experiences of using simulated annealing and genetic algorithms to perform data mining for a large financial service sector company. We first explore the requirements that data mining systems must meet to be useful in most real commercial environments. We then look at some of the available data mining techniques, including our own heuristic techniques, and how they perform with respect to those requirements. The results of applying the techniques to two commercial databases are also shown and analysed.

Introduction

Interest by industry in what is known as *Data mining* or *Knowledge Discovery in Databases* has increased dramatically, as companies see more opportunities for exploiting the vast volumes of data they already hold for other purposes. The information extracted from these massive databases can bring very large financial rewards as it is translated into better customer targeting, improved fraud detection, etc.

This interest has been matched by increased research efforts by various research communities including those working in database systems, artificial intelligence, statistics and data visualisation. Each of these communities has an important role to play in the development of data mining as an integrated approach to data analysis. However, it is important to note that data mining techniques must include an element of automated inductive learning to qualify as such, and practical techniques should be developed in the light of lessons learnt from their application to real, commercial databases. Furthermore, some techniques may yield results that can be considered as valid data mining solutions, but do not meet all the requirements of the commercial environment. In this paper we examine those requirements, test the current data mining techniques against them, and present our results and conclusions.

---
*This research was sponsored by the Teaching Company Scheme under grant no. GR/K 39875

Data mining: the complete process

The process of data mining consists of various phases, each encompassing a series of related activities (Limb & Meggs 1994).

• Phase I: The data is prepared, cleansed and studied. Statistical techniques, visualisation and pre-processing can be used in this phase.

• Phase II: We try to construct a model of the data or to extract some interesting patterns that can be applied to characterise new data. The process is one of inductive learning and can take the form of supervised or unsupervised learning. Note that we do not need to construct a total model that characterises each class and each instance of the data; finding any knowledge about a class (or even part of a class) that characterises it may represent clear gains from a commercial point of view.

• Phase III: The usefulness of the characterisation previously built is measured. This might be achieved by using statistical tests or visualisation of the results.

There is a danger of concentrating all the research effort on the second phase, in the belief that this is the most important part of the process. However, it must be understood that each of these phases is important in the overall data mining process, and must be performed to some extent.

The requirements of the commercial environment

We have been performing data mining case studies for a large financial company for some time. The company was already using statistical techniques to analyse their data, which means they had already realised the importance of it. They had a steady supply of good quality data. Our brief was to study the data mining techniques available and their suitability to the company's problems and environment.

When solving business problems, the techniques used to solve those problems and the solutions to the problems should exhibit certain key features that are desirable or necessary, as discussed in (Goonatilake & Treleaven 1995). For our specific problem and environment, the relevant features in order of priority are:

• Automated learning: The need for human intervention should be kept to a minimum. This will ensure that expense associated with human experts is avoided, and also the influence of their often 'subjective' views will not affect the learning process.

• Explanation: The knowledge extracted must be in a form that can be understood and analysed by humans. There are two main reasons for this. First, any decisions in this industry may involve very large amounts of money, and management are not enthusiastic about embracing ideas they cannot understand or analyse for themselves. Second, explanations must often be given to customers when a decision that affects them is reached. This is sometimes a legal requirement.

• Flexibility: This refers to the ability of the technique employed to cope with imprecise, noisy or incomplete information.

• Control: The techniques should allow us to steer the search for knowledge to specific areas, or to conduct a general search. In other words, control of the process must be retained by the user. This will allow us to search for rules describing exceptions. In these cases, the technique is required to produce a rule to describe a minority of records in the database. There are many applications for a technique that can find patterns for exceptions in a database, as this is quite a common occurrence.

• Adaptation: Business is constantly changing. Therefore, a good data mining system should be able to monitor its performance and revise its knowledge as the environment in which it operates changes.

With this set of desirable properties in mind, we examined some techniques in the context of two case studies. As they did not meet all the above requirements, the development of our own data mining tools using heuristic search techniques became necessary.

Choosing suitable techniques according to the requirements of the commercial environment

There are many techniques that can be used for data analysis, and they are increasingly being referred to as data mining techniques. The first division that can be found in the literature (Holsheimer & Siebes 1994) is that of supervised learning (classification) and unsupervised learning (clustering). In this paper we restrict the study to classification techniques. However, as previously discussed, we do not need to create a complete classifier; we are interested in any knowledge that can be used to characterise new data, bearing in mind that the techniques used to extract it should exhibit the key features discussed. In fact, for many problems we are interested in describing specific patterns that apply to a particular class only (for example, describing exceptions).

Under the generic name of classification techniques we find in the literature: neural networks, tree induction, rule induction, statistical classification and modern heuristic techniques. Not all of those are suitable to our comparative study.

Using the set of key features as an initial selector, we can eliminate neural networks from our list of prospective candidate techniques. Neural networks are regarded at present as 'black box' techniques, because they do not provide *explanations* of the knowledge in a form suitable for verification or interpretation by humans, although increasing research efforts are being made in this area.

Tree induction

Tree induction techniques produce decision trees, covering the whole data set, as a result of their classification process. There are two approaches to decision tree construction. The first approach was developed by the machine learning community and includes algorithms such as C4.5 (Quinlan 1993). The second approach is based on statistical theory and includes CART (Breiman *et al.* 1984) and XAID/CHAID methods (Kass 1975). We will examine these tree induction methods separately.

Machine learning methods The trees produced by the most highly developed machine learning algorithms tend to be extremely large for any real commercial database. As Quinlan puts it in (Quinlan 1987),

> Although decision trees generated by these methods are accurate and efficient, they often suffer the disadvantage of excessive complexity and are therefore incomprehensible to experts. It is questionable whether opaque structures of this kind can be described as knowledge, no matter how well they function.

These types of decision trees can therefore be described as black box techniques as well, and as such are not suitable for our problems and environment. The interpretation and validation of these trees by humans is either impossible, depriving the techniques of the 'explanation' feature, or achievable only by a great deal of human intervention, depriving the technique of the 'automated learning' feature.

A further problem of these decision trees is 'overfitting' and 'overspecialising'. This can be observed when a technique produces a model that has a zero error in classifying the training set of data, but much higher error when classifying new cases. Techniques to avoid overfitting exist. Pruning (Quinlan 1993),for example, grows the whole expanded tree and then examine subtrees in a bottom-up fashion, cutting off any branches that are weak. Pruning techniques attempt to produce simplified trees that do not overfit the data, but the trees obtained are often still very large indeed.

Statistical methods The statistical approach to tree induction is implemented in the package KnowledgeSeeker (Biggs, de Ville, & Suen 1991), based upon the CHAID/XAID models. CHAID looks at a categorical variables, and XAID looks at numerical variables.

The difference between the tree building approach used in KnowledgeSeeker, and the machine learning tree building approaches is that the former uses the statistical significance hypothesis testing framework to construct the tree. At each step of growing the tree this significance testing is used first to determine the best attribute to branch on, if any, and also to establish the best way to cluster the values of the partitioning attribute. This means that the branches of the tree, for numerical attributes represent ranges of values, and for categorical variables represent groups of values, that are clustered together according to tests of statistical significance of the various possible groupings. This leads to more compact trees than the binary partitions of numerical attributes and the individual partitions of categorical attributes performed by C4.5, but it is still necessary to analyse them to extract the desired or relevant knowledge.

The main drawback of decision trees is that, even for compact examples, it may not be straightforward to see how each part of the tree, which represents a pattern of knowledge, is performing. For example, if we are trying to explain some exceptions we would have to look at the individual branches of the tree, extract those that have the required outcome and measure their performance. We can do this by interpreting the tree as a set of rules. If we do this, the knowledge extracted will exhibit not only the features automatic learning and explanation, but also the fourth key feature: *control*.

Trees as a set of rules   A decision tree represents a set of decision rules, one for every terminal node in the tree. Most tree induction algorithms convert the tree into a set of rules automatically. However, the set of potential rules in this representation is limited. First, because a tree starts at a root node, all rules must begin with the same feature. Most importantly, the rules must be mutually exclusive. No two rules can be satisfied simultaneously. However, techniques for transforming the trees produced by C4.5 into a set of non-mutually exclusive rules exist (Quinlan 1993).

Rule induction

As the name implies, rule induction algorithms generate rules outright. We will use CN2, one of the best known rule induction algorithms, for the comparison.

We will also use the 1-R algorithm, which extracts rules based on a single attribute, and claims to produce rules of comparable quality to those produced by other methods.

Our heuristic techniques output rules. We have used two different meta heuristics: genetic algorithms and simulated annealing. We are also considering the use of another meta heuristic, tabu search, in the future. Hybrid techniques will also be investigated.

Simple rules, whether they are generated from a tree,

by a rule induction algorithm, or by a meta-heuristic, represent knowledge in a clear and understandable way. They allow us to *control* the search for knowledge and guide it to particular areas by considering only those rules that cover the desired areas.

Classical statistical classification techniques

It is not our intention to compare our techniques to the statistical classification techniques, as we see both approaches as complementary. In our environment we use linear modelling to create models of the data. This would be comparable to a decision tree, or a set of rules that cover each record in the database. The comparison to rules containing isolated patterns would not be straight forward.

We have selected techniques that produce a comparable output, viz rules. We can therefore establish a uniform base for comparison of the three sets of techniques. Furthermore, automatically extracted simple rules will display three of our most important key features: automated learning, explanation and control.

A framework for comparison

Let us assume we have a flat file, D, of d records and that all fields have known values for each $r \in D$. We will refer to these records as *defined records*. Therefore, D consists of a set of records specifying values for the attributes $A_1, A_2, \ldots, A_n$ over the domains $Dom_1, Dom_2, \ldots, Dom_n$, respectively. We are asked to find a rule of the form $\alpha \Rightarrow \beta$ which appears to hold for some records in this database. For simplicity, α, the precondition of the rule can be interpreted as a conjunction of the form

$$(A_{\delta_1} \in v_{\delta_1}) \wedge (A_{\delta_2} \in v_{\delta_2}) \wedge \ldots \wedge (A_{\delta_i} \in v_{\delta_i})$$

with $v_{\delta_1} \subseteq Dom_1, v_{\delta_2} \subseteq Dom_2 \ldots, v_{\delta_i} \subseteq Dom_i$. We can then construct more complex rules with preconditions in Disjunctive Normal Form (DNF) by taking the disjunction of various rules expressed as above to be one rule. The predictive part of the rule, β, can take the form of $(A_j \in v_j)$, where $v_j \subseteq Dom_j$.

We use $\alpha(r)$ to denote that α is true for record r. Associated with any rule $\alpha \Rightarrow \beta$ are three sets of records,

$$A = \{r \mid \alpha(r)\}, \; B = \{r \mid \beta(r)\} \text{ and}$$
$$C = \{r \mid \alpha(r) \wedge \beta(r)\} = A \cap B.$$

We can then define the integer values a, b and c by

$$a = |A|, \; b = |B| \text{ and } c = |C|.$$

Remembering that d denotes the size of the database, one can define various ratios between these values which measure properties of the rule. The two ratios which are of greatest interest for measuring the quality of our rules are as follows:

$$App(\alpha \Rightarrow \beta) = \frac{a}{d} \quad \text{APPLICABILITY}$$
$$Acc(\alpha \Rightarrow \beta) = \frac{c}{a} \quad \text{ACCURACY}$$

Rules that rate highly in both accuracy and applicability are of greatest interest to us.

We can now see that the rules expressed as above can cope with noise. We are currently investigating the use of fuzzy and rough sets within our rules. They can also be adapted to cope with missing information (Rayward-Smith, Debuse, & de la Iglesia 1995). Therefore, they display the third of our features: flexibility.

Case studies

The two databases described in this section contained a collection of information from which rules explaining any patterns of customer behaviour were to be induced. The rules produced, if of sufficiently high quality, have the potential to give the company a significant commercial advantage. Although we have used various algorithms in a commercial environment, we have applied them to this commercial data for research purposes, in order to provide a comparative study.

The databases have 17 and 5 input fields respectively, of type continuous or integer. The single output field in both cases was of Boolean type. Both databases were split at random into separate training and testing sets. For the first problem, the company was interested in finding rules to describe the output 'false'. The second database allowed us to test the performance of the techniques used when mining for *exceptions*, since rules were to be produced for which the output value was 'true'. The proportion of records within the database with such an output value was only 4.31%, yet was of great interest to the client company. An alternative version of the training database which had records with output value 'false' randomly removed until they made up 50% of the database was created. All methods other than our own gave improved performance using this database; the rules produced are tabulated in the results section.

Case study	Database	No. of records	% with target output
1	Original	32,378	70.0
1	Training	16,311	70.3
1	Testing	16,067	69.7
2	Original	37925	4.31
2	Training	18818	4.21
2	Testing	19107	4.41

Genetic algorithms

Genetic algorithms (GAs) are search techniques, designed by John Holland (Holland 1975) in the late 1960s to solve hard optimisation problems.

The GA based approach, using the toolkit GAmeter (Mann, Kapsalis, & Smith 1995), has been previously described in (Rayward-Smith, Debuse, & de la Iglesia 1995). Our measure of quality of the rule which will represent 'fitness' for the genetic algorithm or solution quality for the simulated annealing algorithm is described briefly here.

Rules produced by the data mining packages must maximise c, since this represents the number of records for which the rule fired correctly. The number of records for which the rule fired incorrectly $(a-c)$ must clearly be minimised. We also wish to minimise $(b-c)$, since this represents the number of records for which the rule did not fire. However, the size of b is frequently fixed, since the output value of our rules is a given fixed value. This is the case for many problems, and in particular, for those used in this paper. We therefore wish to maximise $\lambda c - a$.

This allows us to control the type of rule produced using a single parameter. The value of λ determines the generality of rules produced; increasing λ gives greater applicability with reduced accuracy and vice versa.

The output value of rules produced was forced to be 'false' for the first and 'true' for the second case study. The fitness was evaluated using λ values of 1.41 and 12 for the first and second problems respectively. The adequate λ values for each problem were found after some experimentation, and depend upon the required level of accuracy/applicability desired in the rules.

The 'genotype' rules produced by the GA were converted to 'phenotypes', using a simplification process. This simply removed any inequalities within the rule which excluded less than a threshold minimum percentage of the database.

The GA algorithm selected consecutive pairs of parents for mating, using roulette wheel selection with replacement, from a population of size 10. Single point crossover, with 60% probability and a mutation rate of 1%, was used. Offspring were merged into the population using the 'best fit' method, which sequentially replaces the worst solution in the population with the best of the offspring until there is no child better than the next candidate for replacement.

Simulated annealing

Simulated annealing algorithms (Kirkpatrick, Gelatt, & Vecchi 1983), like GAs, are search procedures for solving optimisation problems, modelled upon the controlled cooling of physical materials.

The rule representation scheme, fitness function and genotype/phenotype distinction described previously for the GA based package was also used within the simulated annealing toolkit SAmson (Mann 1995). The same simplification process as described for the GA was performed on the rules produced.

A neighbourhood of a solution was generated by selecting a bit at random and inverting it. An initial temperature of 10 was used within a Lundy and Mees (Lundy & Mees 1986) cooling schedule, with a Beta value of 0.9 and 20 proposed moves spent at each temperature step. Non-monotonicity was introduced within the cooling schedule by means of a threshold parameter. This works by returning the temperature to half its value at the point of the last temperature rise when the threshold percentage of this value is reached. The temperature value at the point of the last temperature rise is considered to be the initial temperature if no rises have yet been performed.

C4.5

+ knowledge seeker (statistically approach)

The C4.5 package generates decision trees, which provide a classification for every object within a database. The package allows the decision tree to be simplified, using a pruning technique which reduces the size of the tree according to a user-defined confidence level.

C4.5 was used to produce decision trees for both databases. As expected, the trees produced for both problems were immense. If they had been used as a set of mutually exclusive rules, most rules would have an unsatisforily low level of applicability.

A 5% confidence level value was used for pruning, giving significantly smaller trees. However, even the pruned trees were massive, and not appropriate for assimilation by humans.

A rule with the desired output was extracted from both pruned and unpruned trees, for each database. The best rule from the two extracted was selected for comparison with other approaches. Two rule extraction methods were used; these are described below.

C4.5 allows the automated extraction of production rules from the decision trees which it produces. These have the advantage of being generally much simpler to understand and significantly more compact than the decision tree. However, for the first database, the majority class was predicted, regardless of the value of the input fields. For the second database, the rule produced was of inferior quality to that produced using the following extraction mechanism.

As we have described previously, the company was interested only in rules which predicted a predetermined output value, which we will denote β_d. Let $b(node_x)$ denote the branch of the test at the node $node_x$ which classifies a subset within which there is the largest proportion of records with output value β_d. This branch is used as the α part of a rule $\alpha_x \Rightarrow \beta_d$. We denote the rule produced by this method $\alpha_r \Rightarrow \beta_d$.

> Set current node $node_c$ to be the root of the decision tree;
> $\alpha_r = \alpha_c$;
> Compute the fitness of $\alpha_r \Rightarrow \beta_d$ using the same function and λ values as the GA and SA;
> **repeat**
> > Set the $node_c$ to equal the child of $node_c$ which classifies a subset within which there is the largest proportion of records with output value β_d;
> > **if** fitness$(\alpha_r \wedge \alpha_c \Rightarrow \beta_d) >$ fitness$(\alpha_r \Rightarrow \beta_d)$
> > **then** $\alpha_r = \alpha_r \wedge \alpha_c$
> **until** α_r remains unchanged

The performance of the rules obtained using this method is tabulated in the results section.

KnowledgeSeeker

The software KnowledgeSeeker (KS) was used to construct decision trees. The simplest tree produced using several sets of parameters was chosen to be converted into rules and used in our comparison. Each node of the tree, terminal and non-terminal, was considered as a rule as read from the root of the tree to that node.

CN2

The CN2 (Clark & Niblett 1989) algorithm was applied to the two problem databases, producing an unordered list of rules. Rules with the required output value were then tested using the same λ values as the SA and GA based packages; the best rule was then compared to rules produced using the other approaches.

A Laplacian measure of expected rule accuracy, which favours more general rules, was used to evaluate rules for selection by CN2. This is defined as $(c+1)/(a+k)$, where k is the number of classes in the domain.

Several setting of star size and significance threshold were experimented with for both problems. These parameters allow control over the search process and rule generality respectively.

1R

The 1R (Holte 1993) system, as part of the MLC++ (Kohavi *et al.* 1994) package, was also applied to both databases. This algorithm produces a rule which bases the classification of examples upon the value of a single attribute. The package initially discretises each field within the training data into intervals, each (except the rightmost) containing at most MIN_INST records. We used a MIN_INST value of 6 for our problems, since this was recommended in (Holte 1993) for most datasets. All objects contained within each interval are assigned the majority class for the interval.

Experimental results

The results for all methods are shown in figure 1. Figures in brackets refer to results achieved using the test database; # refers to the number of inequalities used within the rule. Acc. and App. refer to accuracy and applicability respectively.

Conclusions

In this paper we have looked at very simple rules produced by various techniques. These very simple rules represent significant patterns of knowledge extracted from databases, as it can be seen from their applicability/accuracy. We have also shown that these simple rules are in a format that can be used in a commercial environment as they represent understandable knowledge, extracted automatically, using a flexible method that can be easily controlled to look for specific class descriptions.

Data set	Tool	#	Fitness	Acc. (%)	App. (%)
1	SA	2	1195.61 (1133.36)	80.8 (80.4)	52.5 (52.6)
1	GA	6	1098.97 (1016.99)	84 (83.1)	36.6 (37)
1	C4.5	2	1196.06 (1122.66)	80.6 (80.1)	53.8 (53.8)
1	CN2	2	736.81 (756.75)	85.6 (85.9)	21.7 (22.3)
1	KS	2	494.92 (424.55)	76.3 (75.6)	40.3 (40.0)
1	1R	1055	964.92 (233.82)	75.8 (72.1)	86.7 (86.3)
2	SA	8	3675 (3783)	24.2 (24.4)	10.3 (10.3)
2	GA	8	3675 (3783)	24.2 (24.4)	10.3 (10.3)
2	C4.5	6	3210 (2750)	30.3 (26.7)	6.5 (6.5)
2	CN2	4	2682 (2471)	26.9 (25.5)	6.4 (6.3)
2	KS	3	2028 (1880)	23.8 (18.5)	5.8 (7)
2	1R	2	783 (1214)	9.2 (9.6)	41 (41.1)

Figure 1: Experimental results

We have looked at some of the state of the art techniques for data mining and shown that, for standard datasets, the rules obtained using heuristic techniques are of comparable quality to the rules induced using CN2, and to the rules extracted from C4.5 decision trees using our own method. The other techniques produced worse results.

For non-standard databases, such as our second case study, our methods are superior to all the others and do not require the modification of the database ('balancing') so that the exceptions represent a significant proportion.

The conclusion to our paper must be that we find patterns of very high quality because we set out to look for these patterns, rather than produce a model of the data and then search in the model for patterns. With tree induction methods, for example, every rule must contain the partition at the root of the tree, so the search for rules is immediately constrained. Although at the top of the tree, the partition chosen may be the best, there may be stronger patterns that do not contain this partition. The heuristic techniques described can search for rules freely, without committing themselves to including a particular partition. This freedom gives our method a strong advantage: the user can control the search for rules.

The rules produced using heuristics exhibit all but one of the aforementioned desirable features: automa-

tion, explanation, control and flexibility. The only feature missing is adaptability, and we plan to extend and enhance our techniques to include this.

References

Biggs, D.; de Ville, B.; and Suen, E. 1991. A method of choosing multiway partitions for classification and decision trees. *Journal of Applied Statistics* 18(1):49–62.

Breiman, L.; Friedman, J. H.; Olshen, R. A.; and Stone, C. J. 1984. *Classification and Regression Trees*. Monterey, CA.: Wadsworth and Brooks.

Clark, P. C., and Niblett, T. N. 1989. The CN2 induction algorithm. *Machine Learning* 3(4).

Goonatilake, S., and Treleaven, P. C., eds. 1995. *Intelligent Systems for Finance and Business*. Chichester, West Sussex: Wiley.

Holland, J. H. 1975. *Adaptation in Natural and Artificial Systems*. Ann Arbor: University of Michigan Press.

Holsheimer, M., and Siebes, A. 1994. Data mining: The search for knowledge in databases. *Technical report CS-R9406, CWI Amsterdam*.

Holte, R. C. 1993. Very simple classification rules perform well on most commonly used datasets. *Machine Learning* 11.

Kass, G. V. 1975. Significance testing in automatic interaction detection. *Applied Statistics* 24(2):178–189.

Kirkpatrick, S.; Gelatt, C. D.; and Vecchi, M. P. 1983. Optimisation by simulated annealing. *Science* 220.

Kohavi, R.; John, G.; Long, R.; Manley, D.; and Pfleger, K. 1994. MLC++: A machine learning library in C++. In *Tools with Artificial Intelligence*, 740–743. IEEE Computer Society Press.

Limb, P. R., and Meggs, G. J. 1994. Data mining - tools and techniques. *BT Technol J* 12.

Lundy, M., and Mees, A. 1986. Convergence of an annealing algorithm. *Mathematical programming* 34.

Mann, J. W.; Kapsalis, A.; and Smith, G. D. 1995. The GAmeter toolkit. In Rayward-Smith, V. J., ed., *Applications of Modern Heuristic Methods*. Alfred Waller. chapter 12, 195–209.

Mann, J. W. 1995. X-SAmson v1.0 user manual. *University of East Anglia*.

Quinlan, J. R. 1987. Simplifying decision trees. *International Journal of Man-Machine Studies* 27:221–234.

Quinlan, R. 1993. *C4.5: Programs for Machine Learning*. San Mateo, CA: Morgan Kaufmann.

Rayward-Smith, V. J.; Debuse, J. C. W.; and de la Iglesia, B. 1995. Using a genetic algorithm to data mine in the financial services sector. In Macintosh, A., and Cooper, C., eds., *Applications and Innovations in Expert Systems III*. SGES Publications.

KDD for Science Data Analysis: Issues and Examples

Usama Fayyad
Microsoft Research
One Microsoft Way
Redmond, WA 98052, USA
fayyad@microsoft.com

David Haussler
Computer Science Dept.
University of California, Santa Cruz
Santa Cruz, CA 95064, USA
haussler@cse.ucsc.edu

Paul Stolorz
Jet Propulsion Laboratory
California Institute of Technology
Pasadena, CA 91109, USA
pauls@aig.jpl.nasa.gov

Abstract

The analysis of the massive data sets collected by scientific instruments demands automation as a prerequisite to analysis. There is an urgent need to create an intermediate level at which scientists can operate effectively; isolating them from the massive sizes and harnessing human analysis capabilities to focus on tasks in which machines do not even remotely approach humans—namely, creative data analysis, theory and hypothesis formation, and drawing insights into underlying phenomena. We give an overview of the main issues in the exploitation of scientific datasets, present five case studies where KDD tools play important and enabling roles, and conclude with future challenges for data mining and KDD techniques in science data analysis.

1 Introduction

Scientists in a variety of fields are experiencing a data glut problem. Modern scientific instruments can collect data at rates that, less than a decade ago, were considered unimaginable. Scientific instruments, coupled with data acquisition systems, can easily generate terabytes and petabytes of data at rates as high as gigabytes per hour. Be it a satellite collecting data from a remote sensing platform, a telescope scanning the skies, or a microscope probing the minute details of a cell, the scientist at the other end of this data collection machinery is typically faced with the same problem: what do I do with all this data?

There is a rapidly widening gap between data collection capabilities and the ability of scientists to analyze the data. The traditional approach of a lone investigator, or even a team of scientists, staring at data in pursuit of (often hypothesized) phenomena or in search of some underlying structure is quickly becoming infeasible. The root of the problem is fairly simple: the data is increasing dramatically in size and dimensionality. While it is reasonable to assume that a scientist can work effectively with a few thousand observations, each having a small number of measurements, say 5, associated with it, it is not at all acceptable to assume that a scientist can effectively "digest" millions of data points, each with tens or hundreds of measurements.

Note that large data sets with high dimensionality can be effectively exploited when a problem is fully understood and the scientist knows what to look for in the data via well-defined procedures. In fact, the term used in many scientific disciplines is *data reduction*.

By *reducing* data, a scientist is effectively bringing it down in size to a range that is "analyzable". However, where does this leave us if the phenomena are not completely understood? Since in scientific investigation we are often interested in new knowledge, the problem of effective manipulation and exploratory data analysis is looming as one of the biggest hurdles standing in the way of exploiting the data. If left unanswered, a scientist would have little choice but to use only parts of the collected data and simply "ignore" the rest of it. Since data collection is typically expensive, this would be a clear waste of resources, not to mentioned the missed opportunity for new knowledge and understanding.

2 Data Reduction Versus Automated Analysis

We believe that data mining and knowledge discovery in databases (KDD) techniques for automated data analysis have an important role to play as an interface between scientists and large data sets. Machines are still far from approaching human abilities in the areas of synthesis of new knowledge, hypothesis formation, and creative modelling. The processes of drawing insight and conducting investigative analyses are still clearly in the realm of tasks best left to humans. However, automating the data reduction procedure is a significant niche suitable for computers. Data reduction involves cataloging, classification, segmentation, partitioning of data, and so forth. This stage of the analysis process is well-suited for automation for the following reasons:

1. It requires dealing with the raw data and performing passes over large data sets.
2. Typical data reduction operations are fairly tedious and hence scientists are eager to cooperate in automating them.
3. Data reduction is usually decomposable into simpler independent tasks, hence one only needs to consider solving the easier subproblems individually.
4. Humans reason about the underlying phenomena on levels higher than the low-level data. Sections 3.1, 3.2, and 3.3 provide good examples of how KDD can cover this gap.

Once a data set is reduced (say to a catalog or other appropriate form), the scientist can proceed to analyze it using more traditional (manual), statistical, or visualization techniques. For example, in the case of an astronomy sky survey, astronomers want to analyze catalogs (recognized, cataloged, and classified sky objects) rather than images. Reduction is equally important in time-series data (extracting features measured over sequences), for measurements obtained from spatially separated sensors, and for mapping raw sensor readings (e.g. multi-spectral) to a convenient feature space.

Higher-level "creative" analysis capabilities of humans, which machines are currently notably lacking, are put to better use if the lower level work is automated. The "higher" levels of analysis include theory formation, hypothesis of new laws and phenomena, filtering what is useful from background, and searching for hypotheses that require a large amount of highly specialized domain knowledge.

2.1 Data Considerations

Data comes in many forms: from measurements in flat files to mixed (multi-spectral/multi-modal) data that include time-series (e.g. sonar signatures or DNA sequences), images, and structured attributes. Most data mining algorithms in statistics [10] and KDD [12] are designed to work with data in flat files of feature vectors.

Image Data: common in science applications, it offers unique advantages in that it is relatively easy for humans to explore. Since the display format is predetermined, it is also fairly easy to display results (e.g. detections, classes). A user interface involving interactive and incremental analysis is also feasible since humans can "digest" a large number of values when represented as an image. On the other hand, image data poses serious challenges on the data mining side. Feature extraction becomes the dominant problem. Using individual pixels as features is typically problematic since a small subarea of an image easily turns into a high-dimensional vector (e.g. a 30×30 pixel region contains 900 individual values), and thus much more training data would be required to perform recognition or classification (see section 3.2). This is compounded by the fact that often the mapping from pixels to meaningful features is quite complex and noisy.

Time-series and sequence data: while it is easy to visualize for a single variable, time series data of multiple measurements are difficult to deal with, especially if the variables are collected at different rates (time scales). Time-series of continuous values are typically fairly non-smooth with random spiking and dipping. A discrete sequence of a single variable, such as a DNA molecule, can be quite complex and difficult to analyse due to its nonstationary behaviour, and the sometimes subtle signals associated with change of underlying hidden state variables that govern the process. Challenges include extracting stationary characteristics of an entire series, if it is stationary, and if not, segmentation to identify and extract non-stationary behavior and transitions between quantitatively and qualitatively different regimes in the series. Transition probabilities between process state variables must be inferred from the observed data. In many application areas, these problems have been attacked using Hidden Markov Models (HMMs) (see section 3.3).

Numerical measurements vs. categorical values: While a majority of measurements (pixels or sensors) are numeric, some notable examples (e.g. protein sequences, section 3.3) consist of categorical measurements. The advantage of dealing with numerical data is that the notion of "distance" between any two data points (feature vectors) is easier to define. Many classification and clustering algorithms rely fundamentally on the existence of a metric distance and ability to define means and centroids.

Structured and sparse data: In some problems variables may have some structure to them (e.g. hierarchical attributes or conditional variables that have different meanings under different circumstances). In other cases different variables are measured for different observations. Turning these data sets into standard flat file (feature vector) form is unlikely to be useful since it results in high dimensional sparse data sets. Unfortunately, there are few algorithms that are capable of dealing with structured data (e.g. [2, 6]).

Reliability of data (sensor vs. model data): Often, raw sensor-derived data is "assimilated" to provide a smooth homogeneous data product. For example regular gridded data is often required in climate studies, even when data points are collected haphazardly. This raises the question of data reliability - some data points need to be dealt with especially carefully, as they may not correspond to direct sensor-derived information.

3 Brief Case Studies

We shall briefly review five case studies in order to illustrate the contribution and potential of KDD for science data analysis. For each case, the focus will primarily be on impact of application, reasons why KDD systems succeeded, and limitations/future challenges.

3.1 Sky Survey Cataloging

The 2nd Palomar Observatory Sky Survey is a major undertaking that took over six years to complete [21]. The survey consist of 3 terabytes of image data containing an estimated 2 billion sky objects. The 3,000 photographic images are scanned into 16-bit/pixel resolution digital images at $23,040 \times 23,040$ pixels per image. The basic problem is to generate a survey catalog which records the attributes of each object along with its class: star or galaxy. The attributes are defined by the astronomers. Once basic image segmentation is performed, 40 attributes per object are measured. The problem is identifying the class of each object. Once the class is known, astronomers can conduct all sorts of scientific analyses like probing Galactic structure from star/galaxy counts, modelling evolution of galaxies, and studying the formation of large structure in the universe [28]. To achieve these goals we developed the SKICAT system (Sky Image Cataloging and Analysis Tool) [27].

Determining the classes (star vs. galaxy) for faint objects in the survery is a difficult problem. The majority of objects in each image are faint objects whose class cannot be determined by visual inspection or classical computational approaches in astronomy. Our goal was to classify objects that are at least one isophotal magnitude fainter than objects classified in previous comparable surveys. We tackled the problem using decision tree learning algorithms [11] to accurately predict the classes of objects. Accuracy of the procedure was verified by using a very limited set of high-resolution CCD images as ground truth.

By extracting rules via statistical optimization over multiple trees [11] we were able to achieve 94% accuracy on predicting sky object classes. Reliable classification of faint objects increased the the size of data that is classified (usable for analysis) by 300%. Hence astronomers were able to extract much more out of the data in terms of new scientific results [27]. In fact, recently this helped a team of astronomers discover 16 new high red-shift quasars in the universe in at least one order of magnitude less observation time [7]. These objects are extremely difficult to find, and are some of the farthest (hence oldest) objects in the universe. They provide valuable and rare clues about the early history of our universe.

SKICAT was successful for the following reasons:

1. The astronomers solved the feature extraction problem: the proper transformation from pixel space to feature space. This transformation implicitly encodes a significant amount of prior knowledge.
2. Within the 40 dimensional feature space, we believe at least 8 dimensions are needed for accurate classification. Hence it was difficult for humans to discover which 8 of the 40 to use, let alone how to use them in classification. Data mining methods contributed by solving the difficult classification problem.
3. Manual approaches to classification were simply not feasible. Astronomers needed an automated classifier to make the most out of the data.
4. Decision tree methods, although involving blind greedy search, proved to be an effective tool for finding the important dimensions for this problem.

Directions being pursued now involve the unsupervised learning (clustering) version of the problem. Unusual or unexpected clusters in the data might be indicative of new phenomena, perhaps even a new discovery. In a database of hundreds of millions of objects, automated analysis techniques are a necessity since browsing the feature vectors manually would only be possible for a small fraction of the survey. The idea is to pick out subsets of the data that look interesting, and ask the astronomers to focus their attention on those, perhaps perform further observations, and explain why these objects are different. A difficulty here is that new classes are likely to be a rare in the data, so algorithms need to be tuned to looking for small interesting clusters rather than ignoring them (see Section 4).

3.2 Finding Volcanoes on Venus

The Magellan spacecraft orbited the planet Venus for over five years and used synthetic aperture radar (SAR) to map the surface of the planet penetrating the gas and cloud cover that permanently obscures the surface in the optical range. The resulting data set is a unique high-resolution global map of an entire planet. In fact, we have more of the planet Venus mapped at the 75m/pixel resolution than we do of our own planet Earth's surface (since most of Earth's surface is covered by water). This data set is uniquely valuable because of its completeness and because Venus is most similar to Earth in size. Learning about the geological evolution of Venus could offer valuable lessons about Earth and its history.

The sheer size of the data set prevents planetary geologists from effectively exploiting its content. The first pass of Venus using the left-looking radar resulted in over 30,000 1000×1000 pixel images. The data set was released on 100 CD-ROMs and is available to anyone who is interested. Lacking the proper tools to analyze this data, geologists did something very predictable: they simply examined browse images, looked for large features or gross structure, and cataloged/mapped the large-scale features of the planet. This means that the scientist operated at a much lower resolution, ignoring the potentially valuable high resolution data actually collected. Given that it took billions of dollars to design, launch, and operate the sensing instruments, it was a priority for NASA to insure that the data is exploited properly.

To help a group of geologists at Brown University analyze this data set [1], the JPL Adaptive Recognition Tool (JARtool) was developed [4]. The idea behind this system is to automate the search for an important feature on the planet, small volcanoes, by training the system via examples. The geologists would label volcanoes on a few (say 30-40) images, and the system would automatically construct a classifier that would then proceed to scan the rest of the image database and attempt to locate and measure the estimated 1 million small volcanoes. Note the wide gap between the raw collected data (pixels) and the level at which scientists operate (catalogs of objects). In this case, unlike in SKICAT, the mapping from pixels to features would have to be done by the system. Hence little prior knowledge is provided to the data mining system.

Using an approach based on matched filtering for focus of attention (triggering on any candidates that vaguely resemble volcanoes; and with a high false detection rate), followed by feature extraction based on projecting the data onto the dominant eigenvecotrs in the training data, and then classification learning to distinguish true detections from false alarms, JARtool can match scientist performance for certain classes of volcanoes (high probability volcanoes versus ones which scientists are not sure about) [4]. Limitations of the approach include sensitivity to variances in illumination, scale, and rotation.

The use of data mining methods here was well-motivated because:

1. Scientists did not know much about image processing or about the SAR properties. Hence they could easily label images but not design recognizers; making the training-by-example framework natural and justified.
2. Fortunately, as is often the case with cataloging tasks, there was little variation in illumination and orientation of objects of interest. Hence the mapping from pixels to features can be performed automatically.
3. The geologists did not have any other easy means for finding the small volcanoes, hence they were motivated to cooperate by providing training data and other help.
4. The result is to extract valuable data from an expensive data set. Also, the adaptive approach (training by example) is flexible and would in principle allow us to reuse the basic approach on other problems.

With the proliferation of image databases and digital libraries, data mining systems that are capable of searching for content are becoming a necessity. In dealing with images, the train-by-example approach, i.e. querying for "things that look like this" is a natural interface since humans can visually recognize items of interest, but translating those visual intuitions into pixel-level algorithmic contraints is difficult to do. Future work on JARtool is proceeding to extend it to other applications like classification and cataloging of sun spots.

3.3 Biosequence Databases

In simplest computer form the human genome is a string of about three billion letters. The letters are A, C, G, and T, representing the four nucleic acids, the constituents of DNA, which are strung together to make the chromosomes in our cells. When combined into one string, the chromosomes contain our genetic heritage, a blueprint for a human being. A large international effort is currently underway to obtain this string. This project may be complete in as little as five years. However, obtaining the string is not enough. It has to be interpreted.

According to the central dogma of molecular biology, DNA is transcribed into RNA, and RNA is translated into protein by the molecular machinery within the cell. A piece of DNA that serves as a template for a protein in this fashion is called a gene. It is the proteins that do most of the work within the cell, and each of the approximately 100,000 different kinds of protein in a human cell has a unique structure and function. Certain RNA molecules, called structural RNA molecules, also have key roles other than producing proteins, and each of these also has a unique structure and function. Elucidating the structure and function of proteins and structural RNA molecules, for humans and for other organisms, is the central task of molecular biology.

There are several international databases of genetic sequences that coordinate, to a certain extent, the archiving of biosequences. The largest DNA database is GENBANK, maintained by the National Center for Biotechnology Information (NCBI) in Bethesda, with a database of about 400 million letters of DNA from a variety of organisms, and growing very rapidly. Two prominent protein databases are PIR and SWIS-SPROT. After the redundancies are removed from these protein databases, they contain about 200,000 different protein sequences.

The most pressing data mining tasks for biosequence databases are:
1. Find the genes in the DNA sequences of various organisms. It turns out that the genes are interspersed with DNA that has other functions, such as gene regulation, and it is difficult to locate the exact boundaries of the genes themselves, so that they may be extracted from the DNA database. Gene-finding programs such as GRAIL [29], GeneID [16], GeneParser [24], GenLang [3], FGENEH [23], Genie [19] and EcoParse [18] use neural nets and other AI or statistical methods (discussed further below) to locate genes in DNA sequences. Looking for ways to improve the accuracy of these methods is a major thrust of current research in this area.
2. Once a gene has been correctly extracted from the

DNA, it is straightforward to determine the protein that it codes for, using the well known genetic code. Proteins can be represented as sequences over a 20 letter alphabet of amino acids. This is referred to as the primary structure of the protein. Each three consecutive letters of DNA code for one letter of protein according to the genetic code. While it is easy to determine the primary structure of a protein, in the cell the protein sequence folds up on itself in a fashion that is unique to each protein, giving it a higher order structure. Understanding this higher order structure is critical to understanding the protein's function. The situation is similar for structural RNA molecules. The second pressing task for biosequence database mining is to develop methods to search the database for sequences that will have similar higher order structure and/or function to the query sequence, rather than doing a more naive string matching, which only pays attention to matches in the primary structure.

One statistical method that has shown promise in biosequence database mining is the use of Hidden Markov Models (HMMs) [17]. Two popular systems that use this method are HMMer [8] and SAM [15]. A hidden Markov model [20] describes a series of observations by a "hidden" stochastic process—a Markov process. In speech recognition, where HMMs have been used extensively, the observations are sounds forming a word, and a model is one that by its "hidden" random process generates certain sequences of sounds, constituting variant pronunciations of a single word, with high probability. In modeling proteins, a word corresponds to a protein sequence, and a family of proteins with similar structure and/or function, such as the globin proteins, which include the oxygen-carrying protein hemoglobin found in red blood cells, can be viewed as a set of variant pronunciations of a word. Hence, here the observations are the amino acids, and a model of a protein family such as the globin family is one that generates sequences of amino acids forming globins with high probability. In this way, the model describes not just one particular globin sequence, but the general structure of a globin sequence, explicitly modeling the possibility that in some globins, extra amino acids may be inserted in some places in the primary structure and deleted in other places.

It has been conjectured that there are only a few thousand different protein families in biology [5]. Once an HMM has been built for each of these families, or for the different protein domains within the sequences in these families, then it may be possible to assign tentative structure and function to newly discovered protein sequences by evaluating their likelihood under each of the HMMs in this model library, again, in analogy with the way that isolated words are recognized by HMM-based speech recognition systems. One difference is that in biology, the dictionary of fundamentally different protein structures/families is not simply provided to the designer of such a system, but must to a certain extent itself be discovered as part of the modeling process. This leads to a third data mining task, that of clustering protein sequences into families of related sequences to be modeled by a common HMM.

HMMs and variants of HMMs have also been applied to the gene-finding problem [19, 18], and to the problem of modeling structural RNA [9, 22]. The gene-finding methods GeneParser, Genie, and Eco-Parse mentioned above are examples of this. RNA analysis uses an extension of HMMs known as stochastic context-free grammars. This extension permits one to model certain types of interactions between the letters of the sequence that are distant in the primary structure but adjacent in the folded RNA structure, without incurring the huge computational overhead of the general protein threading models. However, there is still some significant overhead, making large database searches quite slow. On the other hand, using these models, one is able to do search based directly on high order structural similarity between molecules, which gives much better discrimination.

Computer-based analysis of biosequences is having an increasing impact on the field of biology. Computational biosequence analysis and database searching tools are now an integrated and essential part of the field, and have lead to numerous important scientific discoveries in the last few years. Most of these have resulted from database searches that revealed unexpected similarities between molecules that were previously not known to be related. However, these methods are increasingly important in the direct determination of structure and function of biomolecules as well. Usually this process relies heavily on the human application of biological knowledge and laboratory experiment, in conjunction with the results from the application of several different fairly simple programs that do statistical analysis of the data and/or apply simple combinatorial methods. HMMs and related models have been more successful in helping scientists with this task because they provide a solid statistical model that is flexible enough to incorporate important biological knowledge, Such knowledge is incorporated the form of hidden state structure and *a priori* parameter estimates. The key challenge for the future is to build computer methods that can interpret biosequences using a still more complete integration of biological knowledge and statistical methods at the outset, allowing the biologist to operate at a higher level in the interpretation process where his or her creativity and insight can be of maximal value.

3.4 Earth Geophysics - Earthquake Photography from Space

Important signals about temporal processes are often buried within noisy image streams, requiring the application of systematic statistical inference techniques. Consider for example the case of two images taken before and after an earthquake, at a pixel resolution of say 10 meters. If the earthquake fault motions are only up to 5 or 6 meters in magnitude, a relatively common scenario, then it is essentially impossible to describe and measure the fault motion by simply comparing the two images manually (or even by naive differencing by computer). However, by repeatedly registering different local regions of the two images, a task that is known to be do-able to subpixel precision, it is possible to infer the direction and magnitude of ground motion due to the earthquake. This fundamental concept is broadly applicable to many data mining situations in the geosciences and other fields, including earthquake detection, continuous monitoring of crustal dynamics and natural hazards, target identification in noisy images and so on.

Data mining algorithms of this kind need to simultaneously address three distinct problems in order to be successful, namely 1)design of a statistical inference engine that can reliably infer the fundamental processes to acceptable precision, 2) development and implementation of scalable algorithms on scalable platforms suitable for massive datasets, and 3) construction of automatic and reasonably seamless systems that can be used by domain scientists on a large number of datasets.

One example of such a geoscientific data mining system is Quakefinder [25], which automatically detects and measures tectonic activity in the Earth's crust by examination of satellite data. Quakefinder has been used to automatically map the direction and magnitude of ground displacements due to the 1992 Landers earthquake in Southern California, over a spatial region of several hundred square kilometers, at a resolution of 10 meters, to a (sub-pixel) precision of 1 meter. It is implemented on a 256-node Cray T3D parallel supercomputer to ensure rapid turn-around of scientific results. The issues of scalable algorithm development and their implementation on scalable platforms are quite general with serious impact to data mining with genuinely massive datasets.

The system addressed a definite scientific need, as there was previously no area-mapped information about 2D tectonic processes available at this level of detail. In addition to automatically measuring known faults, the system also enabled a form of automatic knowledge discovery by indicating novel unexplained tectonic activity away from the primary Landers faults that had never before been observed.

Quakefinder was successful for the following reasons:

1. It was based upon an integrated combination of techniques drawn from statistical inference, massively parallel computing and global optimization.
2. Scientists were able to provide a concise description of the fundamental signal recovery problem.
3. Portions of the task based upon statistical inference were straightforward to automate and parallelize, while still ensuring accuracy.
4. The relatively small portions of the task not so easily automated, such as careful measurement of fault location based on a computer-generated displacement map, are accomplished very quickly and accurately by humans in an interactive environment.

The limitations of the approach include the fact that it relies upon successive images being "similar enough" to each other to allow inference based upon cross-correlation measures. This is not always the case in regions where, for example, vegetation growth is vigorous. The method also requires reasonably cohesive ground motions over a number of pixels. It does not, however, require co-registered images, in contrast to many satellite image applications. Nevertheless, the overall system provides a fast, reliable, high-precision change analyzer able to measure earthquake fault activity to high resolution. The field of remote sensing is likely to become increasingly populated with data mining systems of this type in the future, in which dynamic phenomena are extracted directly from raw data, in addition to successful classification systems that deal with static imagery. One of the primary challenges for remote sensing will be generalization and extension of systems such as Quakefinder to deal with spatio-temporal information in an efficient, accessible and understandable form.

3.5 Atmospheric Science

Analysis of atmospheric data is a another classic area where processing and data collection power has far outstripped our ability to interpret the results. The mismatch between pixel-level data and scientific language that understands spatio-temporal patterns such as cyclones and tornadoes is huge. A collaboration between scientists at JPL and UCLA, has developed CONQUEST (COncurrent QUErying Space and Time) [26], a scientific information system implemented on parallel supercomputers, to bridge this gap.

Parallel testbeds (MPP's) were employed by Conquest to enable rapid extraction of spatio-temporal features for content-based access. In some cases, the features are known beforehand, e.g. detection of cyclone tracks. Other times indexable features are hidden in the enormous mass of data. Hence one of the goals here has been the development of "learning" algorithms on MPPs which look for novel patterns, event clusters or correlations on a number of different spatial and temporal scales. MPPs are also used by CONQUEST to service user queries requiring complex and costly computations on large datasets.

An atmospheric model can generate gigabytes of data covering several years of simulated time on a $4° \times 5°$ resolution grid. We have implemented parallel queries concerning the presence, duration and strength of extratropical cyclones and distinctive "blocking features" in the atmosphere, which can scan through this dataset in minutes. Other features of interest are being added, including the detection and analysis of ocean currents and eddies. Upon extraction, the features are stored in a relational database (Postgres). This content-based indexing dramatically reduces the time required to search the raw datasets of atmospheric variables when further queries are formulated. Also featured are parallel implantations of singular value decomposition and neural network pattern recognition algorithms, in order to identify spatio-temporal features as a whole, in contrast to the separate treatment of spatial and temporal information components that has often been used in the past to study atmospheric data.

The long term goal of projects such as Conquest is the development of flexible, extensible, and seamless environments for scientific data analysis, which can be applied ultimately to a number of entirely different scientific domains. Challenges here include the ability to formulate compound queries spread across several loosely federated databases, and the construction and integration of high-bandwidth I/O channels to deal with the massive sizes of datasets involved. Alghough these ideas and systems are still in their infancy, their potential impact on fields that are currently overwhelmed by the sheer volume of high-resolution spatial and temporal imagery cannot be overestimated.

4 Issues and Challenges

Several issues need to be considered when contemplating a KDD application in science data sets. We summarize some of these below.

Feature extraction: Can the scientist provide transformations from low-level data to features? While some classification problems might be too difficult for humans to perform, it is often possible for the user to provide significant amounts of domain knowledge by stating key attributes to measure. Often, sufficient information is contained in the attributes, but the scientist does not know how to use the high-dimensional feature space to perform classification (e.g. in the SKICAT and the gene-finding problems).

Minority (low probability) classes: in problems of automated discovery where algorithms are being used to sift through large amounts of data, the new class of interest may occur only with very low probablity (e.g. one case per million). Traditional clustering techniques would ignore such cases as "noise". Random sampling would fail by definition. Specialized algorithms or biased sampling schemes are needed.

High degree of confidence: a dimension along which science applications of data mining differ from their commercial or financial counterparts is that high acuracy and precision in prediction and description are required (e.g. in SKICAT, a 90% or better confidence level was required, otherwise results of cataloging cannot be used to test or refute competing theories). Similar high accuracies are required in gene-finding.

Data mining task: The choice of task (see [13] for a list of tasks) is important. For example, supervised classification is generally easier to perform than unsupervised learning (clustering). Rather than simply discriminating between given classes, a clustering algorithm must "guess" what the key (hidden) variable is. Regression (where the class variable is continuous) can be easier to do than classification, hence it may be better to map a classification problem into a regression problem where one is attempting to predict the *probability* of a class or some related smooth quantity.

Understandability of derived models: is an important factor if ultimately the findings need to be interpreted as knowledge or explained. In cases where certain steps are being automated in pre-processing (e.g. JARtool), understandability may not be an issue.

Relevant domain knowledge: unfortunately, other than at the stage of feature definition, most current data mining methods do not make use of domain knowledge. Such knowledge can be critical in reducing the search space an algorithm has to explore. In science applications a large body of knowledge on the topic at hand is typically available.

Scalable machines and algorithms: The sheer scale of modern-day datasets require the highest level of computational resources to enable analysis within reasonable time scales. Apart from the issue of raw CPU power, many data mining applications require fast I/O as the fundamental resource, while others rely on large internal memory. Scalable I/O and scalable computing platforms, together with suitably crafted scalable algorithms, are crucial ingredients.

In conclusion, we point out that KDD applications in science may in general be easier than applications in business, finance, or other areas. This is due mainly to the fact that the science end-users typically know the data in intimate detail. This allows them to intuitively guess the important transformations. Scientists are trained to formalize intuitions into procedures/equations making migration to computers an easier matter. Background knowledge is usually available in well-documented form (papers and books) providing backup resources when the initial data mining attempts fail. This luxury (sometimes a burden) is not usually available in fields outside of science. Finally, the fact that scientists typically use high-tech instruments and equipment in their daily chores biases them (as a community) to look favourably upon new techniques for analysis that in other communities may be shunned as "experimental".

5 Acknowledgements

The authors are grateful to all their collaborators on the projects described within this summary paper. They are too numerous to list here. The work described in this paper was performed in part at Jet Propulsion Laboratory, California Institute of Technology under a contract from the National Aeronautics and Space Administration.

References

[1] J. Aubele, L. Crumpler, U. Fayyad, P. Smyth, M. burl, and P. Perona (1995), In *Proc. 26th Lunar and Planetary Science Conference*, 1458, Houston, TX: LPI/USRA.

[2] Auriol, Manago, Althoff, Wess, and Dittrich (1995) "Integrating Induction and Case-Based Reasoning : Methodological Approach and First Evaluations" in *Advances in Case-Based Reasoning*, Haton J.P., Keane M. & Manago M. (Eds.) pp. 18-32, Springer Verlag, 1995.

[3] S. Dong and D. B. Searls (1994). "Gene Structure Prediction by Linguistic Methods", *Genomics*, 162:705–708.

[4] M.C. Burl, U. Fayyad, P. Perona, P. Smyth, and M.P. Burl (1994). "Automating the Hunt for Volcanoes on Venus", in *proc. of Computer Vision and Pattern Recognition Conference (CVPR-94)*, pp. 302-308, IEEE CS Press.

[5] C. Chothia (1992). "One thousand families for the molecular biologist", *Nature*, 357:543–544.

[6] S. Djoko, D. Cook, and L. Holder (1995). "Analyzing the Benefits of Domain Knowledge in Substructure Discovery", in *Proc. of KDD-95: First International Conference on Knowledge Discovery and Data Mining*, Menlo Park, CA: The AAAI Press.

[7] J.D. Kennefick, R.R. De Carvalho, S.G. Djorgovski, M.M. wilber, E.S. Dickinson, N. Weir, U. Fayad, and J. Roden (1995). *Astronomical Journal*, 110-1:78-86.

[8] S. Eddy (1995). "Multiple alignment using hidden Markov models", *Proc. Conf. on Intelligent Systems in Molecular Biology*, AAAI/MIT Press.

[9] S. Eddy and R. Durbin (1994). "RNA sequence analysis using covariance models", *Nulceic Acids Research*, 22:2079-2088.

[10] J. Elder and D. Pregibon (1996). "Statistical Perspectives on KDD", in *Advances in Knowledge Discovery in Databases*, U. Fayyad et al (Eds.). Cambridge, MA: MIT Press.

[11] U.M. Fayyad, N. Weir, and S. Djorgovski (1993) Skicat: A machine learning system for the automated cataloging of large-scale sky surveys. In *Proc. of 10th International Conference on Machine Learning*, pp 112–119.

[12] U. Fayyad, G. Piatetsky-Shapiro, P. Smyth and R. Uthurusamy (1996). *Advances in Knowledge Discovery in Databases*, Cambridge, MA: MIT Press.

[13] U. Fayyad, G. Piatetsky-Shapiro, P. Smyth (1996). "From Data Mining to Knowledge Discovery: An Overview", in *Advances in Knowledge Discovery in Databases*, U. Fayyad et al (Eds.). Cambridge, MA: MIT Press.

[14] J. W. Head et al. (1992) Venus volcanism: classification of volcanic features and structures, associations, and global distribution from magellan data. *Journal Geophysical Res.*, 97(E8):13153–13197.

[15] R. Hughey and A. Krogh (1995). "SAM: Sequence alignment and modeling software system", *tech. Rep. UCSC-CRL-95-7*, University of California, Santa Cruz.

[16] R. Guigo, S. Knudsen, N. Drake, and T. Smith (1992) Prediction of Gene Structure. *J. Mol. Biol.* 226:141–157",

[17] A. Krogh, M. Brown, I. S. Mian, K. Sjölander, and D. Haussler (1994). "Hidden Markov models in computational biology: Applications to protein modeling", *J. Mol. Biol.*, 235:1501–1531

[18] A. Krogh, I. S. Mian and D. Haussler (1994) "A Hidden Markov Model that finds genes in *E. coli* DNA", *Nucleic Acids Research*, 22:4768-4778.

[19] D. Kulp, D. Haussler, M. Reese, and F. Eeckman (1996). "A generalized hidden Markov model for the recognition of human genes in DNA", *Proc. Conf. on Intelligent Systems in Molecular Biology* AAAI Press.

[20] L. R. Rabiner (1989) "A tutorial on hidden Markov models and selected applications in speech recognition", *Proc. IEEE* vol. 77:257–286.

[21] I. Reid et al D., (1991) "The Second Palomar Sky Survey". *Publications of the Astronomical Society of the Pacific*, vol. 103, no. 665.

[22] Y. Sakakibara, M. Brown, R. Hughey, I. S. Mian, K. Sjölander, R.C. Underwood, and D. Haussler (1994). "Stochastic Context-Free Grammars for tRNA modeling", *Nulceic Acids Research*, 22:5112-5120.

[23] V. Solovyev, A. Salamov, and C. Lawrence (1994). "Predicting internal exons by oligonucleotide composition and discriminant analysis of splicable open reading frames", *Nucl. Acids Res.* 22:5156–5163.

[24] E.E. Snyder and G.D. Stormo (1993). Identification of coding regions in genomic DNA sequences: an application of dynamic programming and neural networks, *Nucl. Acids Res.* 21:607–613.

[25] P. Stolorz, C. Dean, R. Crippen, and R. Blom (1995), "Photographing Earthquakes from Space", in *Concurrent Supercomputing Consortium Ann. Rep.*, ed. T. Pauna, 20-22.

[26] P. Stolorz et al (1995) "Fast Spatio-Temporal Data Mining of Large Geophysical Datasets", in *Proc. 1st International Conf. on Knowledge Discovery and Data Mining*, pp. 300-305, AAAI Press.

[27] N. Weir, U.M. Fayyad, and S.G. Djorgovski (1995) Automated Star/Galaxy Classification for Digitized POSS-II. *The Astronomical Journal*, 109-6:2401-2412.

[28] N. Weir, S.G. Djorgovski, and U.M. Fayyad (1995) Initial Galaxy Counts From Digitized POSS-II. *Astronomical Journal*, 110-1:1-20.

[29] Y. Xu, J.R. Einstein, M. Shah, and E.C. Uberbacher (1994). "An improved system for exon recognition and gene modeling in human DNA sequences.", *Proc. Conf. on Intelligent Systems in Molecular Biology*, Menlo Park, CA: AAAI/MIT Press.

Data Mining and Model Simplicity: A Case Study in Diagnosis

Gregory M. Provan
Rockwell Science Center
1049 Camino dos Rios
Thousand Oaks, CA 91360.
provan@risc.rockwell.com

Moninder Singh
Dept. of Computer and Information Science
University of Pennsylvania
Philadelphia, PA 19104-6389
msingh@gradient.cis.upenn.edu

Abstract

We describe the results of performing data mining on a challenging medical diagnosis domain, acute abdominal pain. This domain is well known to be difficult, yielding little more than 60% predictive accuracy for most human and machine diagnosticians. Moreover, many researchers argue that one of the simplest approaches, the naive Bayesian classifier, is optimal. By comparing the performance of the naive Bayesian classifier to its more general cousin, the Bayesian network classifier, and to selective Bayesian classifiers with just 10% of the total attributes, we show that the simplest models perform at least as well as the more complex models. We argue that simple models like the selective naive Bayesian classifier will perform as well as more complicated models for similarly complex domains with relatively small data sets, thereby calling into question the extra expense necessary to induce more complex models.

Introduction

In any data mining task, one key question that needs to be determined is the type of model that one attempts to learn from the database. One rule of thumb is to try the simplest model first, and see how well the model fits the data, incrementally increasing model complexity to try to obtain better fit of model to data. During this process, attributes that are determined to be irrelevant to the particular task (e.g., classification) may be deleted from the database, other attributes included, etc.

In this paper we present results on applying data mining techniques to a medical diagnosis domain, the diagnosis of acute abdominal pain. The diagnosis of acute abdominal pain is well known to be a difficult task both for physician and machine. Depending on the assumptions used in reporting statistics the accuracy rates vary, but most machine diagnostic systems achieve accuracy of little more than 60% (Todd & Stamper 1994). Moreover, there has been great debate in the literature about whether the naive Bayesian classifier is optimal for this domain (Todd & Stamper

1994). The naive Bayesian model makes the strong assumption that the attributes are conditionally independent given the class variable, yet has been shown to perform remarkably well in this domain, and possibly better than any other approach (Todd & Stamper 1994).

One paradoxical question we attempt to address is that fact that no approach outperformed the naive Bayesian classifier on this domain. In particular, we examine two questions pertaining to model simplicity in this domain: (a) does modeling attribute dependence given the class variable improve performance?; and (b) how many attributes facilitate accurate diagnosis? In addressing hypothesis (a), we compare the performance of the naive Bayesian classifier with that of the Bayes network classifier, an extension of the naive Bayesian classifier that models attribute non-independence given the class variable. The Bayesian network classifier (Singh & Provan 1995) has been shown to outperform the naive Bayesian classifier on several UC-Irvine domains, so it may prove better than the naive Bayesian classifier on this domain. In addressing hypothesis (b), we compare the performance of classifiers using all attributes with those using attributes selected by an attribute-selection algorithm that has produced small models whose accuracy rivals that of much larger models that contain all attributes (Provan & Singh 1996; Singh & Provan 1995). Clearly, since data collection can be a costly process, having the smallest model possible is an advantage if the small model has accuracy comparable to that of the full model.

The following sections of the paper describe in turn the Bayesian network representation and performance measure, the application domain, our experimental studies, and a summary of our contributions.

Bayesian Network Representation

This section summarizes the Bayesian network representation and the performance measure used in this paper.

Representation: A Bayesian network consists of a qualitative network structure $\mathcal{G}$ and a quantitative probability distribution θ over the network structure. The qualitative network structure $\mathcal{G}(N, V)$ consists of a directed acyclic graph (DAG) of nodes N and arcs V, where $V \subseteq N \times N$. Each node i corresponds to a discrete random variable A_i with finite domain Ω_{A_i}.

Arcs in the network represent the dependence relationships among the variables $A = \{A_1, A_2, ..., A_n\}$. An arc into node i from node j may represent probabilistic dependence of A_i on A_j, and is precisely specified using the notion of parents of a node. The parents of A_i, $pa(A_i)$, are the direct predecessors of A_i in $\mathcal{G}$. The absence of an arc from node i to j indicates that variable A_j is conditionally independent of variable A_i given $pa(A_j)$.

The quantitative parameter set θ consists of the conditional probability distributions $P(A_i | pa(A_i))$ necessary to define the joint distribution $P(A_1, A_2, ..., A_n)$. We can write the unique joint distribution specified by $\mathcal{G}$ as

$$P(A_1, A_2, \ldots, A_n) = \prod_{i=1}^{n} P(A_i | pa(A_i)). \quad (1)$$

The naive Bayesian classifier assumes that the attributes are conditionally independent given the class variable C. A naive Bayesian classifier is a Bayesian network whose structure is restricted to having arcs only from the class node to the feature nodes, i.e. the only parent node in Equation 1 is the node for C. The joint distribution is thus given by

$$P(C, A_1, A_2, \ldots, A_n) = P(C) \prod_{i=1}^{n} P(A_i | C). \quad (2)$$

Performance: The performance of Bayesian networks is measured by conducting inference on the networks using belief updating method, such as Lauritzen-Spiegelhalter's (1988) clique-tree inference algorithm. Inference in naive Bayesian networks is linear in the number of attributes, and is done using Bayes' rule and the assumption of feature independence within each class. Inference is more complicated for Bayesian networks: it is NP-hard (Cooper 1990). Pearl (1988), among others, reviews Bayesian network inference; details are beyond the scope of this paper.

Application Domain

This section discusses the domain of acute abdominal pain, focusing on the models used for the diagnosis.

Diagnosis of Acute Abdominal Pain

The diagnosis of acute abdominal pain is considered to be a classic Bayesian problem, as findings are probabilistically (rather than deterministically) related to underlying diseases, and prior information can make a significant difference to a successful diagnosis.

The most serious common cause of acute abdominal pain is appendicitis, and in many cases a clear diagnosis of appendicitis is difficult, since other diseases such as Non-Specific Abdominal Pain (*NSAP*) can present similar signs and symptoms (findings). The tradeoff is between the possibility of an unnecessary appendectomy and a perforated appendix, which increases mortality rates five-fold. The high incidence of acute abdominal pain, coupled with the poor diagnosis accuracy, make any improvements in diagnostic accuracy significant.

The Use of (Naive) Bayesian Classifiers

A full model for this domain typically has three variable types: observable, intermediate (latent) and disease. Observable variables correspond to findings that can be observed directly, such as nausea, vomiting and fever. Disease variables correspond to diseases that are the underlying causes for a case of acute abdominal pain, such as appendicitis or NSAP. Latent variables correspond to physiological states that are neither directly observable nor are underlying diseases, but are clinically relevant (as determined by the domain expert) to determining a diagnosis. Examples include peritonitis and inflammation. Such models typically do not make strong assumptions about conditional independence of latent or observable variables given the disease variable. Models with such a structure are described in (Provan 1994; Todd & Stamper 1994).

A naive model typically ignores the class of latent variables, or if it includes any latent variables it assumes that they are independent of any observable variables given the disease variable. This latter assumption does not correspond to known physiological principles; in addition, including latent variables should improve diagnostic performance, since more information is being used. Hence, it appears that a full model should outperform a naive model.[1]

However, neither the empirical nor the theoretical evidence fully supports this hypothesis. The empirical evidence provides inconclusive evidence about the effect on diagnostic accuracy of capturing dependencies in Bayesian models. Following de Dombal et al.'s publication of a successful naive Bayesian model for the diagnosis of acute abdominal pain (de Dombal *et al.* 1972), many researchers have studied empirically the effect of independence assumptions on diagnostic accuracy. Some studies have demonstrated the influence on diagnostic accuracy of capturing dependencies. For example, Seroussi (1986) reported a 4% increase in diagnostic accuracy (from 63.7% to 67.7%) by accounting for pairwise interactions using a Lancaster model; other researchers (Fryback 1978; Norusis & Jacquez 1975) have shown that capturing conditional dependencies may improve diagnostic accuracy. In contrast, other studies have shown no statistically significant difference between the two approaches (Todd & Stamper 1993), and some have

---

[1]We ignore the cost of data collection in model construction.

even found independence Bayesian classifiers to be optimal (Todd & Stamper 1994; Edwards & Davies 1984; de Dombal 1991). Fryback (1978) has studied the sensitivity of diagnostic accuracy to conditional independence assumptions in a Bayesian model for medical diagnosis. He showed empirically that large models with many inappropriate independence assumptions can be less accurate than smaller models which do not have to make such inappropriate independence assumptions. Fryback suggests that model size should be increased incrementally in cases where conditional independence assumptions are not all known, rather than starting from a large model. The most detailed comparison of several different approaches (Todd & Stamper 1994) has shown the naive classifier to outperform classifiers based on a neural network, decision tree, Bayesian network (hand-crafted network structure with induced parameters), and nearest neighbor model, among others.

In the machine learning community, several researchers have found induced classifiers to be fairly robust to independence assumptions (Langley, Iba, & Thompson 1992; Singh & Provan 1995; Domingos & Pazzani 1996). ¿From a theoretical perspective, there is little research into why this might be the case. For example, Hilden (1984) has outlined a class of probability distributions for which modeling conditional dependencies does not improve diagnostic accuracy. Domingos and Pazzani (1996) have shown that modeling conditional independencies does not improve diagnostic accuracy (i.e., classification tasks), but does improve probability estimation. However, much more work remains to be done.

Experimental Studies

Acute Abdominal Pain Database

The abdominal pain data used for this study consists of 1270 cases, each with 169 attributes. The class variable, final diagnosis, has 19 possible values, and the variables have a number of values ranging from 2 to 32 values. This data was collected and pre-screened by Todd and Stamper, as described in (Todd & Stamper 1993). The resulting database addresses acute abdominal pain of gynaecological origin, based on case-notes for patients of reproductive age admitted to hospital, with no recent history of abdominal or back pain. In compiling the database, the first 202 cases were used in the design of the database itself; thus, they cannot be used for the purpose of testing any model. Moreover, out of the 1270 cases, the diagnosis of only 895 cases was definitely known (definite diagnoses); the remaining 375 cases were assigned the best possible diagnosis, as a presumed diagnosis. Finally, 97 patients occur more than once in the database.

An additional 53 variables representing pathophysiological states and refinements of the final diagnosis were recorded. However, these variables were not used by us since their values are ordinarily no more observable than the final diagnosis. The final diagnosis is used as a measure of diagnostic performance.

Experimental Design

Our experiments address two hypotheses:

1. Does a Bayesian network classifier have better accuracy than a naive Bayesian classifier?

2. Can attribute selection produce networks with comparable accuracy (even through they are a fraction of the size of the full networks)?

Four Bayesian networks were induced from the data, using only the first 169 attributes. The networks were pairs of naive and Bayesian network classifier, with each pair consisting of networks containing all attributes and attributes selected based on an information criterion. For inducing networks with all attributes, we run the algorithm in question. For inducing networks with *selected* attributes, we first select the attributes, and then run the induction algorithm using data for only the selected attributes. We ran a set of preliminary experiments to determine the selection algorithm that produced final networks with the highest predictive accuracy. In comparing three information-based algorithms (as described in (Singh & Provan 1996)) and a belief-network wrapper approach (as described in (Singh & Provan 1995; Provan & Singh 1996)), we decided on using an information-based approach we call CDC to select attributes.

To define the CDC metric, we need to introduce some notation. Let C be the class variable and A represent the attribute under consideration. Let Δ be the subset of attributes already selected. Let k be the number of classes and let m be the number of possible values of A. Moreover, let $\Delta = \{A_1, \ldots, A_q\}$ and let s be the cardinality of the cross product of the sets of values of these variables, i.e., $s = \times_{i=1}^{q} |A_i|$. Given that the set Δ is instantiated to its lth unique instantiation, let $p_{i/l}$ represent the probability that the class variable is instantiated to its ith value and let $p_{j/l}$ be the probability that A is instantiated to its jth value. Similarly, $p_{ij/l}$ is the probability that the class variable takes on its ith value and the attribute A takes on its jth value, given that Δ is instantiated to its lth unique instantiation. The CDC metric is a conditional extension of the complement of Mantaras's (1991) distance metric (d_N), i.e. $1 - d_N$. Following Singh and Provan (1996), we can then define the CDC metric as follows:

$$CDC(A, \Delta) = \frac{\sum_{l=1}^{s} p_l \left(H_{C_l} + H_{A_l} - H_{Cell_l} \right)}{\sum_{l=1}^{s} p_l H_{Cell_l}},$$

where $H_{Cell_l} = -\sum_{i=1}^{k} \sum_{j=1}^{m} p_{ij/l} \log p_{ij/l}$, $H_{A_l} = -\sum_{j=1}^{m} p_{j/l} \log p_{j/l}$, and $H_{C_l} = -\sum_{i=1}^{k} p_{i/l} \log p_{i/l}$.

The feature selection algorithm uses a forward selection search, starting with the assumption that Δ

is empty. It then adds incrementally (to Δ) that attribute A (from the available attributes) that maximizes $CDC(A, \Delta)$. The algorithm stops adding attributes when there is no single attribute whose addition results in a positive value of the information metric.[2] Complete details are given in (Singh & Provan 1996).

To maintain consistency with Todd and Stamper's careful comparison (Todd & Stamper 1994) of several induction approaches, we adopted their experimental method of using a cross-validation strategy to evaluate the different methods. Since the first 202 cases had been used during the construction of the database itself, they were not used for testing purposes. The remaining 1068 cases were divided into 11 subsets (10 consisting of 101 cases each while the 11th had 58 cases) which were successively used for testing models induced from the remaining 10 sets plus the first 202 cases. Moreover, for each run, we removed from each training set all repeat presentations of any patient. The performance measure we used was the classification accuracy of a model on the test data, where the classification accuracy is the percentage of test cases that were diagnosed correctly. Inference on the Bayesian networks was carried out using the the HUGIN (Anderson *et al.* 1989) system.

Results

Our first set of experiments compared the performance of the four different approaches listed above, averaged over 11 trials. We use the following notation: naive-ALL and CB for the naive Bayesian and Bayesian network classifier using all attributes, respectively; and Naive-CDC and CDC for the naive Bayesian and Bayesian network classifier using selected attributes, respectively.

Table 1 summarizes the network structure for these runs. Note that using attribute selection reduces the network to roughly 10% of the nodes and 2.3% of the edges for the regular Bayesian networks, and roughly 10% of the nodes and 9% of the edges for the naive networks. This is a dramatic reduction, especially considering the fact that the selective networks have comparable performance to their non-selective counterparts.

Table 2 shows the results of variable selection on network structure. This table shows the attributes that were selected on average by our variable selection approach. The attributes are numbered from 1 to 169, as denoted in the original database. The important point to note is that the number of nodes selected comes from a small subset of the full set of nodes.

Table 3 summarizes the predictive accuracies for our experiments. The second row of Table 3 shows that the naive classifier (using all attributes) performed the best

---

[2]We take the value of the CDC metric to be zero if the denominator is zero.

Table 1: "Average" network structure on experiment using all cases. Structure is based on 11 runs, and describes the average number of nodes and edges.

APPROACH	Nodes	Edges
Naive-ALL	170	169
CB	170	589.8
CDC	17.36	19.56
Naive-CDC	17.36	16.36

Table 2: Network structure resulting from variable selection. Structure is based on 11 runs, and describes the nodes selected.

VARIABLE FREQUENCY	VARIABLE SET
always	3, 29, 37, 68, 112, 152, 169
mostly	4, 5, 32, 38
sometimes	26, 45, 167

over all cases in the database, although not statistically better than the selective naive classifier.

The third row of Table 3 shows the predictive accuracies when a prior set of nodes was used during network induction. This set of nodes, {3, 29, 37, 68, 112, 152, 169}, is the set that was always selected by CDC. Using a paired-t test showed that using this prior did not make a statistically significant difference to the predictive accuracies of the induced classifiers over not using this prior (the first row of the table).

The fourth row of Table 3 shows the predictive accuracies when only cases with definite diagnoses were used. Here, the differences over using all cases are statistically significant. Comparing the induction approaches for the definite diagnosis data, there is no statistically significant difference between the naive methods and CDC even though Naive-CDC has the greatest accuracy (around 3% more).

To further study the dependencies in the database, we computed a covariance matrix for the database, and looked at the variables with the highest correlation (conditional on the class variable) in the covariance matrix. Based on this matrix (which we do not reproduce due to its size), and on computing a pairwise correlation measure described in (Domingos & Pazzani 1996), we observe that many variables are relatively highly correlated, yet the naive classifier performed better than any other approach. A second observation is that the variables with the highest variance are always included in the selective networks.

Table 3: Predictive accuracy for the four induction approaches, based on the different scenarios. The best predictive accuracy in any row is shown in boldface.

SCENARIO	Naive-ALL	CB	CDC	Naive-CDC
all cases	**60.60±5.59**	57.16±5.65	57.88±4.71	58.89±5.18
"network" prior	**61.95±5.18**	57.16±5.65	57.05±5.80	57.09±5.77
definite diagnosis	67.84±5.34	66.91±8.25	69.54±3.16	**70.53±5.22**

Experiments on Synthetic Data

There are two possible explanations for the unexpectedly high accuracy of the naive Bayesian classfier: the classifiers themselves do not require dependencies for this domain,[3] or the data does not allow the more complex classifiers to estimate parameters accurately enough to be able to classify cases accurately.

To disambiguate the effects of classifier and data, we have run a set of experiments using synthetic Bayes networks with controlled dependencies among the attributes given the class variable. Each network has a five-valued class variable and 13 attributes with between 3 and 5 values. We controlled the attribute dependencies given the class variable by defining three different sets of conditional probability distributions, reflecting (given the class variable): (1) attribute independence ($P(A_k|C, A_{k-1}, ..., A_1) = P(A_k|C)$ for $k = 2, ..., 13$), (2) weak attribute dependence, and (3) strong attribute dependence. We simulated 2000 cases from each network, and learned networks from the simulated data.

Table 4 describes the results of inducing networks from the synthetic data, as averaged over 20 runs. This table shows that this classification task is indeed sensitive to attribute dependencies. For the data with no dependencies, the naive and Bayesian network approaches both learned naive networks with statistically indistinguishable predictive accuracies. However, for the data with dependencies the naive and Bayesian network approaches learned networks with significantly different predictive accuracies, differing by almost 20% for the data with strong dependencies, and slightly less for the data with weak dependencies.

Abdominal Pain Data Revisited

Further analysis of our results show that restrictions of the data lead to the naive classifiers outperforming the Bayesian network classifiers. On closer examination of the data (restricting our attention to cases with a "definite diagnosis"), we found that 2 of the 19 classes accounted for almost 67% of the cases, whereas each of the other classes accounted for 7% or less of the cases. For each of the 2 most common classes, since the

---

[3]Domingos and Pazzani (1996) suggest that the classification task itself is insensitive to the presence or absence of attribute dependencies given the class variable.

probability distribution was induced from many cases, the more complex model (CDC) was significantly better than all other methods, correctly classifying about 89% of the cases. Both selective classifiers significantly outperformed both non-selective classfiers on the cases involving these two classes.

On the other hand, on the cases involving the other 17 classes, naive classifiers performed better than the Bayesian networks, with CDC-naive being the best (though not significantly better). This is because the more complex models could not accurately estimate their more complicated distributions from so few cases, leading to poor predictive accuracy.

These results offer some insights into the observed behavior of the various methods on the abdominal data set. In complex domains with many attributes, such as the abdominal pain domain, feature selection may play a very important part in learning good classifiers for diagnosis; this is especially true when the data set is relatively small. In such cases, it is difficult to accurately learn parameters for the larger networks, more so in the case of Bayesian networks which may pick up spurious dependencies.

Moreover, in domains where there are sufficient cases (as for the two main classes in the abdominal pain data set), Bayesian networks should outperform naive Bayesian classifiers since they can easily model attribute dependencies. However, if the number of cases is small, then the simpler method may perform at least as well as the more complex Bayesian networks.

Discussion

One of the key findings of this work is that for this domain, as well as for a large number of other domains described in (Domingos & Pazzani 1996; Singh & Provan 1995; Provan & Singh 1996), simple models (i.e. naive Bayesian classifiers) perform as well as more complex models. A second key finding is that feature selection further increases model simplicity with no performance penalty. In addition, the more complex the model, the better feature selection increases performance (Singh & Provan 1995). We have shown how only 10% of the attributes provide accuracy comparable to using all the attributes. This can lead to significant savings in data collection and inference.

Our experiments with synthetic networks have shown that attribute dependencies given the class vari-

Table 4: Predictive accuracy for induction algorithms for synthetic networks. Dependencies referred to are between attributes, given the class variable. Accuracies are averaged over 20 runs.

	Cases	CB	CDC	Naive ALL	CDC-naive
"Strong" dependencies	2000	83.65 ± 2.29	82.94 ± 2.10	65.31 ± 2.68	65.7 ± 2.65
"Weak" dependencies	2000	83.06 ± 1.34	82.25 ± 1.78	67.7 ± 1.78	67.7 ± 1.97
No dependencies	2000	87.31 ± 1.00	86.94 ± 1.06	87.31 ± 1.00	86.94 ± 1.06

able do affect classifier performance. Assuming sufficient data with attribute dependencies given the class variable, modeling the dependencies produces a classifier that performs almost 20% better than the naive Bayesian classifier. As a consequence, we argue that the robustness of the naive classifier to attribute correlations is primarily due to the data and the domain under consideration. The robustness of the abdominal pain data to attribute dependencies most likely occurs because the Bayesian network is overfitted to the data.

Our study has shown that data screening can make a big difference to classifier performance. Using the data with just definite diagnoses produces networks with better predictive accuracies than that of the networks induced using all the cases. When all cases are used, the models are both trained and tested on cases whose diagnoses may have been incorrect. This may cause the Bayesian network classifiers to pick up spurious dependencies. In contrast, naive classifiers will not be affected as much: the only thing that changes is the set of probabilities in the network.

Acknowledgements The second author was supported by an IBM Cooperative Fellowship and NSF grant #IRI92-10030. We gratefully acknowledge that HUGIN has been kindly supplied to the second author for his doctoral research.

References

Anderson, S.; Olesen, K.; Jensen, F.; and Jensen, F. 1989. HUGIN - A Shell for building Bayesian Belief Universes for Expert Systems. In *Proceedings IJCAI*, 1080–1085.

Cooper, G. 1990. The computational complexity of probabilistic inference using Belief networks. *Artificial Intelligence* 42:393–405.

de Dombal, F.; Leaper, D.; Staniland, J.; McCann, A.; and Horrocks, J. 1972. Computer-aided diagnosis of acute abdominal pain. *British Medical Journal* 2:9–13.

de Dombal, F. 1991. The diagnosis of acute abdominal pain with computer assistance. *Annals Chir.* 45:273–277.

Domingos, P., and Pazzani, M. 1996. Beyond independence: Conditions for the optimality of the simple Bayesian classifier. In *Proc. Machine Learning Conference*.

Edwards, F., and Davies, R. 1984. Use of a Bayesian algorithm in the computer-assisted diagnosis of appendicitis. *Surg. Gynecol. Obstet.* 158:219–222.

Fryback, D. G. 1978. Bayes' theorem and conditional nonindependence of data in medical diagnosis. *Computers and Biomedical Research* 11:429–435.

Hilden, J. 1984. Statistical diagnosis based on conditional independence does not require it. *Comput. Biol. Med.* 14:429–435.

Langley, P.; Iba, W.; and Thompson, K. 1992. An analysis of Bayesian classifiers. In *Proceedings of the Tenth National Conference on Artificial Intelligence*, 223–228. AAAI Press.

Lauritzen, S.L., and Spiegelhalter, D.J. 1988. Local computations with probabilities on graphical structures and their application to expert systems. *Journal of the Royal Statistical Society (Series B)*, 50:157–224.

Lopez de Mantaras, R. 1991. A distance-based attribute selection measure for decision tree induction. *Machine Learning* 6:81–92.

Norusis, M., and Jacquez, J. 1975. Diagnosis I: Symptom nonindependence in mathematical models for diagnosis. *Comput. Biomed. Res.* 8:156–172.

Pearl, J. 1988. *Probabilistic Reasoning in Intelligent Systems: Networks of Plausible Inference*. San Mateo, CA: Morgan Kaufman.

Provan, G. M., and Singh, M. 1996. Learning Bayesian networks using feature selection. In Fisher, D., and Lenz, H., eds., *Learning from Data: AI and Statistics V, Lecture Notes in Statistics*, **112**. Springer Verlag. 291–300.

Provan, G. 1994. Tradeoffs in knowledge-based construction of probabilistic models. *IEEE Trans. on SMC* 11: 287–294.

Seroussi, B. 1986. Computer-aided diagnosis of acute abdominal pain when taking into account interactions. *Method. Inform. Med.* 25:194–198.

Singh, M., and Provan, G. M. 1995. A comparison of induction algorithms for selective and non-selective Bayesian classifiers. In *Proc. 12th Intl. Conference on Machine Learning*, 497–505.

Singh, M., and Provan, G. M. 1996. Efficient learning of selective Bayesian network classifiers. In *Proc. 13th Intl. Conference on Machine Learning*. To appear.

Todd, B. S., and Stamper, R. 1993. The formal design and evaluation of a variety of medical diagnostic programs. Technical Monograph PRG-109, Oxford University Computing Laboratory.

Todd, B. S., and Stamper, R. 1994. The relative accuracy of a variety of medical diagnostic programs. *Methods Inform. Med.* 33:402–416.

Automated Discovery of Medical Expert System Rules from Clinical Databases based on Rough Sets

Shusaku Tsumoto and Hiroshi Tanaka

Department of Information Medicine, Medical Research Institute,
Tokyo Medical and Dental University,
1-5-45 Yushima, Bunkyo-city Tokyo 113 Japan.
E-mail: tsumoto.com@mri.tmd.ac.jp, tanaka@cim.tmd.ac.jp

Abstract

Automated knowledge acquisition is an important research issue to solve the bottleneck problem in developing expert systems. Although many inductive learning methods have been proposed for this purpose, most of the approaches focus only on inducing classification rules. However, medical experts also learn other information important for diagnosis from clinical cases. In this paper, a rule induction method is introduced, which extracts not only classification rules but also other medical knowledge needed for diagnosis. This system is evaluated on a clinical database of headache, whose experimental results show that our proposed method correctly induces diagnostic rules and estimates the statistical measures of rules.

Introduction

One of the most important problems in developing expert systems is knowledge acquisition from experts(Buchanan and Shortliffe 1984). In order to automate this problem, many inductive learning methods, such as induction of decision trees(Breiman, et al. 1984; Quinlan 1993), rule induction methods(Michalski 1983; Michalski, et al. 1986; Quinlan 1993) and rough set theory(Pawlak 1991; Ziarko 1993), are introduced and applied to extract knowledge from databases, which shows that these methods are appropriate.

However, most of the approaches focus only on inducing classification rules, although medical experts also learn other information important for medical diagnostic procedures. Focusing on their learning procedures, Matsumura et al. propose a diagnostic model, which consists of three reasoning processes, and develop an expert system, called RHINOS(Rule-based Headache and facial pain INformation Organizing System)(Matsumura, et al. 1986).

Since RHINOS diagnostic processes are found to be based on the concepts of set theory, it is expected that a set-theoretic approach can describe this diagnostic model and knowledge acquisition procedures.

In order to characterize these procedures, we introduce the concepts of rough set theory, which clarifies set-theoretic characteristics of the classes over combinatorial patterns of the attributes, precisely discussed by (Pawlak 1991). Based on this theory, we develop a program, called PRIMEROSE-REX (Probabilistic Rule Induction Method based on Rough Sets and Resampling methods for Expert systems), which extracts rules for an expert system from clinical databases, and applies resampling methods to the estimation certainty factors of derived rules.[1]

This system is evaluated on the datasets of RHINOS domain. The results show that the proposed method induces RHINOS diagnostic rules correctly from databases and that resampling methods can estimate the performance of these rules and certainty factors.

The paper is organized as follows: in Section 2, we discuss RHINOS diagnostic model. Section 3 shows rough set theory and representation of RHINOS rules based on this theory. Section 4 presents an algorithm for induction of RHINOS diagnostic rules. Section 5 gives experimental results. Section 6 and Section 7 discusses the problems of our work and related work, respectively. Finally, Section 8 concludes this paper.

RHINOS

RHINOS is an expert system which diagnoses clinical cases on headache or facial pain from manifestations. In this system, a diagnostic model proposed by Matsumura(Matsumura, et al. 1986) consists of the following three kinds of reasoning processes: exclusive reasoning, inclusive reasoning, and reasoning about complications.

First, exclusive reasoning excludes a disease from candidates when a patient does not have a symptom which is necessary to diagnose. Secondly, inclusive reasoning suspects a disease in the output of the exclusive process when a patient has symptoms specific to a disease. Finally, reasoning about complications suspects complications of other diseases when some symptoms which cannot be explained by the diagnostic conclusion are obtained.

---

[1]This system is an extension of PRIMEROSE, which induces classification rules from databases, based on rough sets and resampling methods(Tsumoto and Tanaka 1995).

Each reasoning is rule-based, and all the rules needed for the diagnostic processes are acquired from medical experts in the following way.

(1)Exclusive Rules The premise of an exclusive rule is equivalent to the necessity condition of a diagnostic conclusion. From the discussion with medical experts, we select the following six basic attributes which are minimally indispensable to defining the necessity condition: *1. Age, 2. Pain location, 3. Nature of the pain, 4. Severity of the pain, 5. History since onset, 6. Existence of jolt headache.* For example, the exclusive rule of common migraine is defined as:

```
In order to suspect common migraine,
the following symptoms are required:
pain location: not eyes,
nature :throbbing or persistent or radiating,
history: paroxysmal or sudden and
jolt headache: positive.
```

One of the reason why we select the six attributes is to solve the interface problem of expert systems: if the whole attributes are considered, we also have to input the symptoms which are not needed for diagnosis. To make exclusive reasoning compact, the only minimal requirements are chosen. It is notable that this kind of selection can be viewed as the ordering of given attributes, which can be induced from databases automatically. Therefore we intend to formulate induction of exclusive rules by using the whole given attributes. After the induction, the minimal requirements for describing exclusive rules can be acquired.

(2)Inclusive Rules The premises of inclusive rules are composed of a set of manifestations specific to a disease to be included. If a patient satisfies one set of symptoms, we suspect this disease with some probability. This rule is derived by asking the following items for each disease to the medical experts: *1. a set of manifestations by which we strongly suspect a disease. 2. the probability that a patient has the disease with this set of manifestations:SI(Satisfactory Index) 3. the ratio of the patients who satisfy the set to all the patients of this disease:CI(Covering Index) 4. If the total sum of the derived CI(tCI) is equal to 1.0 then end. Otherwise, goto 5. 5. For the patients of this disease who do not satisfy all the collected set of manifestations, goto 1.* Therefore a positive rule is described by a set of manifestations, its satisfactory index (SI), which corresponds to *accuracy measure*, and its covering index (CI), which corresponds to *total positive rate*. Note that SI and CI are given empirically by medical experts.

For example, one of three positive rules for common migraine is given as follows.

```
If history: paroxysmal, jolt headache: yes,
nature: throbbing or persistent,
prodrome: no, intermittent symptom: no,
```

Table 1: A Small Database

	age	loc	nat	prod	nau	M1	class
1	50-59	occ	per	0	0	1	m.c.h.
2	40-49	who	per	0	0	1	m.c.h.
3	40-49	lat	thr	1	1	0	migra
4	40-40	who	thr	1	1	0	migra
5	40-49	who	rad	0	0	1	m.c.h.
6	50-59	who	per	0	1	1	m.c.h.

DEFINITIONS: loc: location, nat: nature, prod: prodrome, nau: nausea, M1: tenderness of M1, who: whole, occ: occular, lat: lateral, per: persistent, thr: throbbing, rad: radiating, m.c.h.: muscle contraction headache, migra: migraine, 1: Yes, 0: No.

```
persistent time: more than 6 hours,
and location: not eye,
then common migraine is suspected with
accuracy 0.9 (SI=0.9) and this rule covers
60 percent of the total cases (CI=0.6).
```

(3)Disease Image This rule is used to detect complications of multiple diseases, acquired fromm all the possible manifestations of the disease. Using this rule, we search for the manifestations which cannot be explained by the conclusions. Those symptoms suggest complications of other diseases. For example, the disease image of common migraine is:

```
The following symptoms can be explained by
common migraine: pain location: any or
depressing: not or jolt headache: yes or ...
```

Therefore, when a patient who suffers from common migraine is depressing, it is suspected that he or she may also have other disease.

As shown above, three kinds of rules are straightforward, and an inducing algorithm is expected to be implemented on computers easily. Thus, we introduce rough set theory in order to describe these algorithms as shown in the next section.

Formalization of Rules
Probabilistic Rules

In order to describe three kinds of diagnostic rules, we first define probabilistic rules, using the following three notations of rough set theory(Pawlak 1991). To illustrate the main ideas, we use a small database shown in Table 1.

First, a combination of attribute-value pairs, which is corresponding to a complex in AQ (Michalski 1983), is denoted by an equivalence relation R_f, which is defined as follows.

Definition 1 (Equivalence Relation) *Let U be a universe, and V be a set of values. A total function f from U to V is called an assignment function of an* *attribute. Then, we introduce an equivalence relation R_f such that for any $u, v \in U$, $uR_f v$ iff $f(u) = f(v)$.*

For example, $[age = 50 - 59]\&[loc = occular]$ will be one equivalence relation, denoted by $R_f = [age = 50 - 59]\&[loc = occular]$. Secondly, a set of samples which satisfy R_f is denoted by $[x]_{R_f}$, corresponding to a star in AQ terminology. For example, when $\{2, 3, 4, 5\}$ is a set of samples which satisfy $[age = 40 - 49]$, $[x]_{[age=40-49]}$ is equal to $\{2, 3, 4, 5\}$. [2]

Finally, thirdly, U, which stands for "Universe", denotes all training samples.

According to these notations, probabilistic rules are defined as follows:

Definition 2 (Probabilistic Rules) *Let R_f be an equivalence relation specified by some assignment function f, D denote a set whose elements belong to a class d, or positive examples in all training samples (the universe), U. Finally, let $|D|$ denote the cardinality of D. A probabilistic rule of D is defined as a quadruple, $< R_f \overset{\alpha,\kappa}{\to} d, \alpha_{R_f}(D), \kappa_{R_f}(D) >$, where $R_f \overset{\alpha,\kappa}{\to} d$ satisfies the following conditions:* [3]

$$(1) \qquad [x]_{R_f} \cap D \neq \phi,$$

$$(2) \qquad \alpha_{R_f}(D) = \frac{|[x]_{R_f} \cap D)|}{|[x]_{R_f}|},$$

$$(3) \qquad \kappa_{R_f}(D) = \frac{|[x]_{R_f} \cap D)|}{|D|}.$$

In the above definition, α corresponds to the accuracy measure: if α of a rule is equal to 0.9, then the accuracy is also equal to 0.9. On the other hand, κ is a statistical measure of how proportion of D is covered by this rule, that is, a coverage or a true positive rate: when κ is equal to 0.5, half of the members of a class belong to the set whose members satisfy that equivalence relation.

For example, let us consider a case of a proposition $[age = 40 - 49] \to m.c.h.$ Since $[x]_{[age=40-49]}$ is equal to $\{2, 3, 4, 5\}$ and D is equal to $\{1, 2, 5, 6\}$, $\alpha_{[age=40-49]}(D) = |\{2, 5\}|/|\{2, 3, 4, 5\}| = 0.5$ and $\kappa_{[age=40-49]}(D) = |\{2, 5\}|/|\{1, 2, 5, 6\}| = 0.5$. Thus, if a patient, who complains a headache, is 40 to 49 years old, then m.c.h. is suspected, whose accuracy and coverage are equal to 0.5.

RHINOS Diagnostic Rules

By the use of these notations, RHINOS diagnostic rules are described in the following way.

---

[2]In this notation, "n" denotes the nth sample in a dataset (Table 1).

[3]It is notable that this rule is a kind of probabilistic proposition with two statistical measures, which is an extension of Ziarko's variable precision model(VPRS) (Ziarko 1993).

(1) Exclusive rules: $R \overset{\alpha,\kappa}{\to} d \quad s.t. \quad R = \wedge_i R_i = \wedge \vee_j [a_j = v_k]$, and $\kappa_{R_i}(D) = 1.0$. [4] In the above example, the relation R for migraine is described as: $[age = 40 - 49] \wedge ([location = lateral] \vee [location = whole]) \wedge [nature = throbbing] \wedge ([history = paroxysmal] \vee [history = persistent]) \wedge [jolt = yes] \wedge [prod = yes] \wedge [nau = yes] \wedge [M1 = no] \wedge [M2 = no]$.

(2) Inclusive rules: $R \overset{\alpha,\kappa}{\to} d \quad s.t. \quad R = \vee_i R_i = \vee \wedge_j \vee_k [a_j = v_k]$, $\alpha_{R_i}(D) > \delta_\alpha$, and $\kappa_{R_i}(D) > \delta_\kappa$.

In the above example, the simplest relation R for migraine, is described as: $[nature = throbbing] \vee [history = paroxysmal] \vee [jolt = yes] \vee [M1 = yes]$. However, induction of inclusive rules gives us two problems. First, SI and CI are overfitted to the training samples. Secondly, the above rule is only one of many rules which are induced from the above training samples. Therefore some of them should be selected from primary induced rules under some preference criterion. These problems will be discussed in the next section.

(3) Disease Image: $R \overset{\alpha,\kappa}{\to} d \quad s.t. \quad R = \vee R_i \vee [a_i = v_j]$, and $\alpha_{R_i}(D) > 0$ $(\kappa_{R_i}(D) > 0)$.

In the above example, the relation R for migraine is described as:
$[age = 40 - 49] \vee [location = lateral] \vee [location = whole] \vee [nature = throbbing] \vee [severity = strong] \vee [severity = weak] \vee [history = paroxysmal] \vee [nausea = yes] \vee [jolt = yes] \vee [M1 = no] \vee [M2 = no]$.

As shown in the formal definition of these rules, a coverage $\kappa_R(D)$ play an important role in classification of diagnostic rules.

Induction of Rules

An induction algorithm of RHINOS rules consists of two procedures. One is an exhaustive search procedure to induce the exclusive rule and the disease image for each disease through all the attribute-value pairs, corresponding to *selectors* in AQ (Michalski 1983), and the other is a postprocessing procedure to induce inclusive rules through the combinations of all the attribute-value pairs, which corresponds to *complexes* in AQ.

Exhaustive Search

Let D denote training samples of the target class d, or *positive examples*. This search procedure is defined as shown in Figure 1. In the above example in Table 1, let d be migraine and $[age = 40 - 49]$ be selected as $[a_i = v_j]$. Since the intersection $[x]_{[age=40-49]} \cap D(=$

---

[4]Strictly Speaking, this proposition should be written as: $d \to R$. However, for comparison with other two rules, we choose this notation.

```
procedure Exhaustive Search;
  var
    L : List; /* A list of elementary relations */
  begin
    L := P₀; /* P₀: A list of elementary relations */
    while (L ≠ {}) do
      begin
        Select one pair [aᵢ = vⱼ] from L;
        if ([x]₍ₐᵢ₌ᵥⱼ₎ ∩ D ≠ φ) then do
          /* D: a set if positive examples */
          begin
            R_di := R_di ∨ [aᵢ = vⱼ];
              /* Disease Image */
            if (κ₍ₐᵢ₌ᵥⱼ₎(D) > δ_κ)
              then L_ir := L_ir + {[aᵢ = vⱼ]};
              /* Candidates for Inclusive Rules */
            if (κ₍ₐᵢ₌ᵥⱼ₎(D) = 1.0)
              then R_er := R_er ∧ [aᵢ = vⱼ];
              /* Exclusive Rule */
          end
        L := L - [aᵢ = vⱼ];
      end
  end {Exhaustive Search};
```

Figure 1: An Algorithm for Exhaustive Search

```
procedure Postprocessing Procedure;
  var
    i : integer;    M, Lᵢ : List;
  begin
    L₁ := L_ir; /* Candidates for Inclusive Rules */
    i := 1;    M := {};
    for i := 1 to n do
      /* n: Total number of attributes */
      begin
        while ( Lᵢ ≠ {} ) do
          begin
            Select one pair R = ∧[aᵢ = vⱼ] from Lᵢ;
            Lᵢ := Lᵢ - {R};
            if    (α_R(D) > δ_α)
              then  do S_ir := S_ir + {R};
              /* Include R as Inclusive Rule */
            else M := M + {R};
          end
        Lᵢ₊₁ := (A list of the whole combination of
                  the conjunction formulae in M);
      end
  end
end {Postprocessing Procedure };
```

Figure 2: An Algorithm for Postprocessing Procedure

$\{3, 4\}$) is not equal to ϕ, this pair is included in the disease image. However, since $\alpha_{[age=40-49]}(D) = 0.5$, this pair is not included in the inclusive rule. Finally, since $D \subset [x]_{[age=40-49]}(= \{2, 3, 4, 5\})$, this pair is also included in the exclusive rule.

Next, the other attribute-value pair for age, $[age = 50 - 59]$ is selected. However, this pair will be abandoned since the intersection of $[x]_{[age=50-59]}$ and D is empty, or $[x]_{[age=50-59]} \cap D = \phi$.

When all the attribute-value pairs are examined, not only the exclusive rule and disease image shown in the above section, but also the candidates of inclusive rules are also derived. The latter ones are used as inputs of the second procedure.

Postprocessing Procedure

Because the definition of inclusive rules is a little weak, many inclusive rules can be obtained. In the above example, an equivalence relation $[nau = 1]$ satisfies $D \cap [x]_{[nau=1]} \neq \phi$, so it is also one of the inclusive rules of "m.c.h.", although SI of that rule is equal to 1/3. In order to suppress induction of such rules, which have low classificatory power, only equivalence relations whose SI is larger than 0.5 are selected. For example, since the above relation $[age = 40-49]$ is less than this precision, it is eliminated from the candidates of inclusive rules. Furthermore, PRIMEROSE-REX minimizes the number of attributes not to include the attributes which do not gain the classificatory power, called *dependent* variables. This procedure can be described as shown in Figure 2. In the above example in Table 1, the coverage of an attribute-value pair $[prod =$

0] for "m.c.h" takes a maximum value. Furthermore, since the accuracy $\alpha_{[prod=0]}(D)$ is equal to 1.0, it is included in inclusive rules of "m.c.h". The next maximum one is $[M1 = 1]$, whose coverage is equal to 1.0. Since this accuracy is also equal to 1.0, it is also included in inclusive rules. At this point, we have two inclusive rules as follows: $[prod = 0] \overset{\alpha=1.0,\kappa=1.0}{\to}$ "m.c.h." and $[M1 = 1] \overset{\alpha=1.0,\kappa=1.0}{\to}$ "m.c.h." Repeating these procedures, all the inclusive rules are acquired.

Estimation of Statistical Measures

The above definition of statistical measures shows that small training samples causes their overestimation. In the above example, both of the measures are equal to 1.0. This means that this rule correctly diagnoses and covers all the cases of the migrane. However, in general, these meanings hold only in the world of the small training samples. In this sense, accuracy and coverage are biased. Thus, we should correct these biases by introducing other estimating methods, since the biases cannot be detected by the induced method.

Note that this problem is similar to that of error rates of discriminant function in multivariate analysis (Efron 1982), the field in which resampling methods are reported to be useful for the estimation.

Hence the resampling methods are applied to estimation of accuracy and coverage, as shown in the following subsection.

Cross-Validation and the Bootstrap

Cross-validation method for error estimation is performed as following: first, all training samples $\mathcal{L}$ are split into V blocks: $\{\mathcal{L}_1, \mathcal{L}_2, \cdots, \mathcal{L}_V\}$. Secondly, repeat for V times the procedure in which rules are induced from the training samples $\mathcal{L} - \mathcal{L}_i (i = 1, \cdots, V)$ and examine the error rate err_i of the rules using $\mathcal{L}_i$ as test samples. Finally, the whole error rate err is derived by averaging err_i over i, that is, $err = \sum_{i=1}^{V} err_i / V$ (this method is called V-fold cross-validation). Therefore this method for estimation of coverage and accuracy can be used by replacing the calculation of err by that of coverage and accuracy, and by regarding test samples as unobserved cases.

On the other hand, the Bootstrap method is executed as follows: first, empirical probabilistic distribution (F_n) is generated from the original training samples (Efron 1982). Secondly, the Monte-Carlo method is applied and training samples are randomly taken by using F_n. Thirdly, rules are induced by using new training samples. Finally, these results are tested by the original training samples and statistical measures, such as error rate are calculated. These four steps are iterated for finite times. Empirically, it is shown that repeating these steps for 200 times is sufficient for estimation (Efron 1982).

Interestingly, Efron shows that estimators by 2-fold cross-validation are asymptotically equal to predictive estimators for completely new pattern of data, and that Bootstrap estimators are asymptotically equal to maximum likelihood estimators and are a little overfitted to training samples (Efron 1982). Hence, the former estimators can be used as the lower bounds of both measures, and the latter as their upper bounds.

Furthermore, in order to reduce the high variance of estimators by cross validation, we introduce repeated cross validation method, which is firstly introduced by Walker (Walker and Olshen 1992). In this method, cross validation methods are executed repeatedly (safely, 100 times)(Tsumoto and Tanaka 1995), and estimates are averaged over all the trials. In summary, since our strategy is to avoid the overestimation and the high variabilities, combination of repeated 2-fold cross-validation and the Bootstrap method is adopted in this paper.

Experimental Results

We apply PRIMEROSE-REX to the following three medical domains: headache(RHINOS domain), whose training samples consist of 1477 samples, 10 classes, and 20 attributes, cerebulovasular diseases, whose training samples consist of 620 samples, 15 classes, and 25 attributes, and meningitis, whose training samples consists of 213 samples, 3 classes, and 27 attributes. In these experiments, δ_α and δ_κ are set to 0.75 and 0.5, respectively. The experiments are performed by the following four procedures. First, these samples are randomly split into half (new training samples) and half (new test samples). For example, 1477 samples are split into 738 training samples and 739 training samples. Secondly, PRIMEROSE-REX, AQ15 and CART are applied to the new training samples. Thirdly,

Table 2: Experimental Results (Headache)

Method	ER-A	IR-A	DI-A
PR-REX	95.0%	88.3%	93.2%
Experts	98.0%	95.0%	97.4%
CART	–	85.8%	–
AQ15	–	86.2%	–
R-CV	72.9%	78.7%	83.8%
BS	98.4%	91.6%	95.6%

DEFINITIONS: PR-REX: PRIMEROSE-REX,
ER-A: Exclusive Rule Accuracy,
IR-A: Inclusive Rule Accuracy,
DI-A: Disease Image Accuracy

Table 3: Experimental Results (Cerebulovasculuar Diseases)

Method	ER-A	IR-A	DI-A
PR-REX	91.0%	84.3%	94.3%
Experts	97.5%	92.9%	93.6%
CART	–	79.7%	–
AQ15	–	78.9%	–
R-CV	72.9%	78.7%	83.8%
BS	93.4%	92.5%	95.9%

the repeated cross validation method and the bootstrap method are applied to the new training samples in order to estimate the accuracy and coverage of PRIMEROSE-REX. Finally, the induced results are tested by the new test samples. These procedures are repeated for 100 times and all the estimators are averaged over 100 trials.

Experimental results are shown in Table 2 to 4. Exclusive rule accuracy(ER-A) means how many training samples that do not belong to a class are excluded correctly from the candidates. Inclusive rule accuracy(IR-A) is equivalent to the averaged classification accuracy. Finally, disease image accuracy(DI-A) shows how many symptoms, which cannot be explained by diagnostic conclusions, are detected by the disease image. The first row is the results obtained by using PRIMROSE-REX, and the second one is the results derived from medical experts. And, for comparison, we compare the classification accuracy of inclusive rules with that of CART and AQ-15, which is shown in the third and fourth row. Finally, in the fifth and sixth row, we present the results of estimation by repeated cross-validation method (R-CV) and the bootstrap method (BS). These results can be summarized to the following three points. First, the induced rules perform a little worse than those of medical experts. Secondly, our method performs a little better than classical empirical learning methods, CART and AQ15. Finally, thirdly, R-CV estimator and BS estimator can be regarded as the lower boundary and

Table 4: Experimental Results (Meningitis)

Method	ER-A	IR-A	DI-A
PR-REX	88.9%	82.5%	92.6%
Experts	95.4%	93.2%	96.7%
CART	–	81.4%	–
AQ15	–	82.5%	–
R-CV	64.3%	61.3%	73.8%
BS	89.5%	93.2%	98.2%

the upper boundary of each rule accuracy. Hence the interval of these two estimators can be used as the estimators of accuracy and coverage of each rule.

Discussion

Exclusive Rule

As discussed in Section 3, we intend to formulate induction of exclusive rules by using the whole given attributes, although the original exclusive rules are described by the six basic questions. Therefore induced exclusive rules have the maximum number of attributes whose conjunction R also satisfies $\kappa_R(D) = 1.0$. If this maximum combination includes the six basic attributes as a subset, then this selection of basic attributes is one of good choices of attributes, although redundant. Otherwise, the given six attributes may be redundant or the induced results may be insufficient. For the above example shown in Table 1, the maximum combination of attributes is {age, location, nature, history, jolt, prod, nau, M1, M2 }. [5] Since this set does not include an attribute "severity", the six given attributes or the induced results are insufficient in this small database. In this case, however, the sixth attributes are acquired by medical experts through a large number of experienced cases. Thus, the induced attributes should be revised by using additional samples in the future.

On the contrary, in the database on headache, the maximum combination is 13 attributes, derived as follows: Age, Pain location, Nature of the pain, Severity of the pain, History since onset, Existence of jolt headache, Tendency of depression, and Tenderness of M1 to M6, which is a superset of the six basic attributes. Thus, this selection can be a good choice.

In this way, the induction of maximum combination can be also used as a "rough" check of induced results or our diagnosing model on exclusive rules, which can be formulated in the following way. [6]

Let A and E denote a set of the induced attributes for exclusive rules and a set of attributes acquired from

---

[5] Severity cannot be a member, since $[sever = weak] \lor [sever = strong]$ is included in both exclusive rules.

[6] This discussion assumes that the whole attributes are sufficient to classify the present and the future cases into given classes.

domain experts. Thus, the following four relations can be considered. First, if $A \subset E$, then A is insufficient or E is redundant. Second, if $A = E$, then both sets are sufficient to represent a diagnosing model in an applied domain. Third, if $A \supset E$, then A is redundant or E is insufficient. Finally, fourth, if intersection of A and E is not empty ($A \cap E \neq \phi$), then either or both sets are insufficient.

Reader may say that the above relations are weak and indeterminate. However, the above indefinite parts should be constrained by information on domain knowledge. For example, let us consider the case when $A \subset E$. When E is validated by experts, A is insufficient in the first relation. However, in general, E can be viewed as A obtained by large samples, and $A \supset E$ should hold, which shows that a given database is problematic. Moreover, the constraint on exclusive rules, $\kappa_R(D) = 1.0$, suggests that there exist a class which does not appear in the database, because the already given classes cannot support $\kappa_R(D) = 1.0$, that is, $[x]_R \cap D \neq D$ will hold in the future.

On the other hand, when E is not well given by experts and A is induced from sufficiently large samples, E will be redundant, which means that the proposed model for E does not fit to this database or this domain.

This kind of knowledge is important, because we sometimes need to know whether samples are enough to induce knowledge and whether an applied inducing model is useful to analyze databases.

Thus, the above four relations give a simple examination to check the characteristics of samples and the applicability of a given diagnosing model. It is our future work to develop more precise checking methodology for automated knowledge acquisition.

Related Work
Discovery of Association Rules

Mannila et al.(Mannila, et al. 1994) report a new algorithm for discovery of association rules, which is one class of regularities, introduced by Agrawal et al.(Agrawal, et al. 1993). Their method is very similar to our method with respect to the use of set-theoretical operations.

(1) Association Rules: The concept of association rules is similar to our induced rules. Actually, association rules can be described in the rough set framework.

That is, we say that an association rule over r (training samples) satisfies $W \Rightarrow B$ with respect to γ and σ, if

$$|[x]_W \cap [x]_B| \geq \sigma n, \qquad (1)$$

and

$$\frac{|[x]_W \cap [x]_B|}{|[x]_W|} \geq \gamma, \qquad (2)$$

where n, γ, and σ denotes the size of training samples, a confidence threshold, and a support threshold, respectively. Also, W and B denote an equivalence relation and a class, respectively. Furthermore, we also say that W is *covering*, if

$$|[x]_W| \geq \sigma n. \qquad (3)$$

It is notable that the left side of the above formulae (6) and (8) correspond to the formula (3) as to κ, coverage, and the left side of the formula (7) corresponds to (2) as to α, accuracy. The only difference is that we classify rules, corresponding to association rules, into three categories: exclusive rules, inclusive rules, and disease image.

The reason why we classify these rules is that this classification reflects the diagnostic model of medical experts, which makes the computational speed of diagnostic reasoning higher.

(2) Mannila's Algorithm:

Mannila introduces an algorithm to find association rules based on Agrawal's algorithm (Mannila, et al. 1994). The main points of their algorithm are the following two procedures: database pass and candidate generation. Database pass produces a set of attributes L_s as the collection of all covering sets of size s in C_s. Then, the candidate generation calculates C_{s+1}, which denotes the collection of all the sets of attributes of size s, from L_s. Then, again, the database pass procedure is repeated to produce L_{s+1}. The effectiveness of this algorithm is guaranteed by the fact that all subsets of a covering set are covering.

The main difference between Mannila's algorithm and PRIMEROSE-REX is that Mannila uses the check algorithm for covering to obtain association rules, whereas we use both accuracy and coverage to compute and classify rules.

In the discovery of association rules, all the combinations of attribute-value pairs in C_s have the property of covering. On the other hand, our algorithm does not focus on the above property of covering. It selects an attribute-value pair which has both high accuracy and high coverage. That is, PRIMEROSE-REX does not search for regularities which satisfy covering, but search for regularities important for classification.

Thus, interestingly, when many attribute-value pairs have the covering property, or covers many training samples, Mannila's algorithm will be slow, although PRIMEROSE-REX algorithm will be fast in this case. When few pairs cover many training samples, Mannila's algorithm will be fast, and our system will not be slower.

Acknowledgements

This research is supported by Grants-in-Aid for Scientific Research No.08680388 from the Ministry of Education, Science and Culture in Japan.

References

Agrawal, R., Imielinski, T., and Swami, A. (1993). Mining association rules between sets of items in large databases, *Proceedings of the 1993 International Conference on Management of Data (SIGMOD 93)*, pp. 207-216.

Breiman, L., Freidman, J., Olshen, R., and Stone, C. (1984). *Classification And Regression Trees*. Belmont, CA: Wadsworth International Group.

Buchanan, B. G. and Shortliffe, E. H.(eds.) (1984). *Rule-Based Expert Systems*, Addison-Wesley.

Efron, B. (1982). *The Jackknife, the Bootstrap and Other Resampling Plans*. Society for Industrial and Applied Mathematics, Pennsylvania.

Mannila, H., Toivonen, H., Verkamo, A.I. (1994). Efficient Algorithms for Discovering Association Rules, *Proceedings of the AAAI Workshop on Knowledge Discovery in Databases (KDD-94)*, pp.181-192, AAAI press, CA.

Matsumura, Y., et al. (1986). Consultation system for diagnoses of headache and facial pain: RHINOS. *Medical Informatics*, **11**, 145-157.

Michalski, R. S. (1983). A Theory and Methodology of Machine Learning. Michalski, R.S., Carbonell, J.G. and Mitchell, T.M., *Machine Learning - An Artificial Intelligence Approach*. Morgan Kaufmann, Palo Alto.

Michalski, R. S., Mozetic, I., Hong, J., and Lavrac, N. (1986). The Multi-Purpose Incremental Learning System AQ15 and its Testing Application to Three Medical Domains. *Proceedings of the fifth National Conference on Artificial Intelligence*, 1041-1045, AAAI Press, Palo Alto.

Pawlak, Z. (1991). *Rough Sets*. Kluwer Academic Publishers, Dordrecht.

Quinlan, J.R. (1993). *C4.5 - Programs for Machine Learning*, Morgan Kaufmann, CA.

Tsumoto, S. and Tanaka, H.(1994). Induction of Medical Expert System Rules based on Rough Sets and Resampling Methods. *Proceedings of the 18th Symposium on Computer Applications on Medical Care*(Washington, D.C.), pp.1066-1070. Philadelphia: Hanley & Belfus, INC., November.

Tsumoto, S. and Tanaka, H. (1995). PRIMEROSE: Probabilistic Rule Induction Method based on Rough Sets and Resampling Methods. *Computational Intelligence*, **11**, 389-405.

Walker, M. G. and Olshen, R. A. (1992). Probability Estimation for Biomedical Classification Problems. *Proceedings of the sixteenth Symposium on Computer Applications on Medical Care*, McGrawHill, New York.

Ziarko, W. (1993). Variable Precision Rough Set Model. *Journal of Computer and System Sciences*, **46**, 39-59.

Automated Discovery of Active Motifs in Multiple RNA Secondary Structures

Jason T. L. Wang
Computer & Information Sci. Dept.
New Jersey Institute of Technology
Newark, New Jersey 07102, USA
jason@village.njit.edu

Bruce A. Shapiro
Division of Basic Sciences
National Institutes of Health
Frederick, Maryland 21702, USA
bshapiro@ncifcrf.gov

Dennis Shasha
Courant Institute of Math. Sciences
New York University
New York, New York 10012, USA
shasha@cs.nyu.edu

Kaizhong Zhang
Computer Science Dept.
The University of Western Ontario
London, Ontario, Canada N6A 5B7
kzhang@csd.uwo.ca

Chia-Yo Chang
Computer & Information Sci. Dept.
New Jersey Institute of Technology
Newark, New Jersey 07102, USA
changc@homer.njit.edu

Abstract

In this paper we present a method for discovering approximately common motifs (also known as active motifs) in multiple RNA secondary structures. The secondary structures can be represented as ordered trees (i.e., the order among siblings matters). Motifs in these trees are connected subgraphs that can differ in both substitutions and deletions/insertions. The proposed method consists of two steps: (1) find candidate motifs in a small sample of the secondary structures; (2) search all of the secondary structures to determine how frequently these motifs occur (within the allowed approximation) in the secondary structures. To reduce the running time, we develop two optimization heuristics based on sampling and pattern matching techniques. Experimental results obtained by running these algorithms on both generated data and RNA secondary structures show the good performance of the algorithms. To demonstrate the utility of our algorithms, we discuss their applications to conducting the phylogenetic study of RNA sequences obtained from GenBank.

Introduction

Data mining is fun and useful (Agrawal 1994). Most of the research has been concentrating on record-oriented applications (Piatetsky-Shapiro & Frawley 1991; Silberschatz, Stonebraker, & Ullman 1991; Han, Cai, & Cercone 1993). Here we study a different type of data mining, namely, discovering structural patterns in scientific data. We focus on finding approximately common motifs (also known as *active motifs*) in multiple RNA secondary structures. This problem is important in computational biology (Le *et al.* 1989). For example, in predicting secondary structures for a given mRNA, one may first find a set of 'optimal' and 'sub-

optimal' structures using existing algorithms (Zuker 1989). Then to determine which one among these structures is closest to the one occurring naturally, one may search for active motifs in the structures (Le *et al.* 1989). The motifs appearing in many predicted structures are more likely to be present in the real structure. Finding active motifs in secondary structures of different RNA molecules is useful as well. Often, the information obtained from such motifs, in conjunction with results obtained from sequence alignments, helps to conduct the phylogenetic study of the structure for a class of sequences (Shapiro & Zhang 1990).

To find the motifs in RNA secondary structures by a computer, we need a suitable representation for the structures. This paper adopts the tree representation previously proposed in (Shapiro & Zhang 1990). We define both the helical stems and loops to be nodes in a tree. Figure 1 illustrates a RNA secondary structure and its tree representation. The structure is decomposed into five terms: stem, hairpin, bulge, internal loop and multi-branch loop. In the tree, H represents hairpin nodes, I represents internal loops, B represents bulge loops, M represents multi-branch loops, R represents helical stem regions (shown as connecting arcs) and N is a special node used to make sure the tree is connected. The tree is considered to be an ordered one where the ordering is imposed based upon the 5' to 3' nature of the molecule. This representation allows one to encode detailed information of RNA by associating each node with a property list. Common properties may include sizes of loop components, sequence information and energy.

We consider a motif in a tree T to be a connected subgraph of T, viz., a subtree U of T with certain nodes being cut at no cost. (Cutting at a node n in U means removing n and all its descendants, i.e., removing the subtree rooted at n.) The dissimilarity measure used in comparing two trees is the *edit distance*, i.e., the minimum weighted number of insertions, deletions and substitutions (also known as relabelings) of nodes used to transform one tree to the other (Shapiro & Zhang 1990; Wang *et al.* 1994c). Deleting a node n makes the children of n the children of the current parent of n. Inserting n below a node p makes some consecutive subsequence of the children of p become the children of n. For the purpose of this work, we assume that all the edit operations have unit cost.

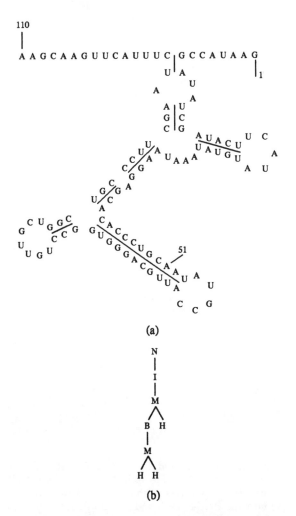

Figure 1: Illustration of a typical RNA secondary structure and its tree representation. (a) Normal polygonal representation of the structure. (b) Tree representation of the structure.

Example: Consider the set S of three trees in Fig. 2(a). Suppose only exactly coinciding connected subgraphs occurring in all the three trees and having size greater than 2 are considered as 'active motifs.' Then S contains two active motifs shown in Fig. 2(b). If connected subgraphs having size greater than 4 and

occurring in all the three trees within distance one are considered as active motifs, i.e., one substitution, insertion or deletion of a node is allowed in matching a motif with a tree, then S contains two active motifs shown in Fig. 2(c).

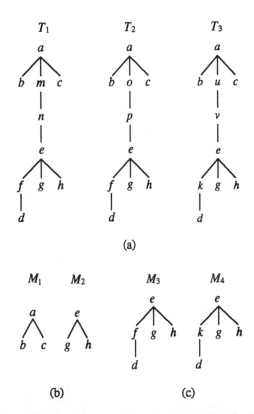

Figure 2: (a) The set S of three trees (these trees are hypothetical ones solely used for illustration purposes). (b) Two motifs exactly occurring in all three trees. (c) Two motifs approximately occurring, within distance 1, in all three trees.

To discover such active motifs in multiple RNA secondary structures (trees), we extend our previous sequence motif discovery technique (Wang *et al.* 1994a, 1994b) to find candidate motifs among a small sample of the secondary structures and then check them against all the structures. Some previously published techniques may solve similar problems when the motifs meet some restrictions, for example, when the motifs are exact matches (Le *et al.* 1989), their topologies are known in advance (Chevalet & Michot 1992), or they are translated into sequences where the tree structure is not considered during searching (Konings & Hogeweg 1989). In contrast, our approach can discover approximately common motifs without prior knowledge of their topologies, positions, or occurrence frequency in the trees. In this aspect our work is similar to the pattern discovery in sequences and graphs reported in (Djoko, Cook, & Holder 1995; Mannila, Toivonen, & Verkamo 1995; Tsumoto & Tanaka 1995). We use RNA molecules as an example in the paper, though our techniques should generalize to any scientific domains where data are naturally represented as trees.

Our Approach

Terminology

We say a tree T contains a motif M within distance d (or M approximately occurs in T within distance d) if there exists a subtree U of T such that the *minimum* distance between M and U is less than or equal to d, allowing zero or more cuttings at nodes from U. Let S be a set of trees. The occurrence number of a motif M is the number of trees in S that contain M within the allowed distance. Formally, the occurrence number of a motif M with respect to distance d and set S, denoted $occurrence\_no_S^d(M)$, is k if there are k trees in S that contain M within distance d. For example, consider Fig. 2 again. Let S contain the three trees in Fig. 2(a). Then $occurrence\_no_S^0(M_1)$ $= occurrence\_no_S^0(M_2) = 3$; $occurrence\_no_S^1(M_3) =$ $occurrence\_no_S^1(M_4) = 3$. Given a set S of trees, our algorithm finds all the motifs M where M is within the allowed distance $Dist$ of at least $Occur$ trees in S and $|M| \geq Size$, where $|M|$ represents the size, i.e., the number of nodes, of the motif M. ($Dist$, $Occur$ and $Size$ are user-specified parameters.)

Discovery Algorithm

Our algorithm consists of two phases: (1) find promising motifs among a randomly chosen sample A of the trees in S; and (2) calculate the occurrence numbers of the promising motifs in all of S to determine which promising motifs satisfy the specified requirements.

Phase (1) consists of two sub-phases. In sub-phase A, we consider all

$$\binom{|A|}{2} = \frac{|A|(|A|-1)}{2}$$

tree pairs in the sample. Then we find candidate motifs from the tree pairs as follows. Suppose the nodes in a tree T are numbered according to some order (e.g., a preorder numbering). Let $t[i]$ represent the node of T whose position in the left-to-right preorder traversal of T is i; $T[i]$ represents the subtree rooted at $t[i]$. We find, for each pair of sample trees T_1 and T_2, the largest approximately common motifs, within distance $Dist$, between $T_1[i]$ and $T_2[j]$ for all $1 \leq i \leq |T_1|$, $1 \leq j \leq |T_2|$. (The asymptotic time complexity of the algorithm is $O(Dist^2 n_1 n_2 (\min\{h_1, l_1\})(\min\{h_2, l_2\}))$, where n_i, $i = 1, 2$, is the number of nodes in tree T_i, h_i is the height of T_i and l_i is the number of leaves in T_i.) Let C contain the found motifs M with $|M| \geq Size$; these constitute candidate motifs. For each candidate motif M, the tree pairs from which M is discovered are recorded.

In sub-phase B, we store the candidate motifs into a prefix tree PRET (similar to Kosaraju's (1989) suffix

tree for trees). Each candidate motif M is decomposed into a collection of paths, called *p-strings*. Each *p*-string contains a sequence of nodes starting at the root of M and ending at a leaf of M. For example, Fig. 3(a) shows four candidate motifs; Fig. 3(b) shows the *p*-strings of one of the motifs.

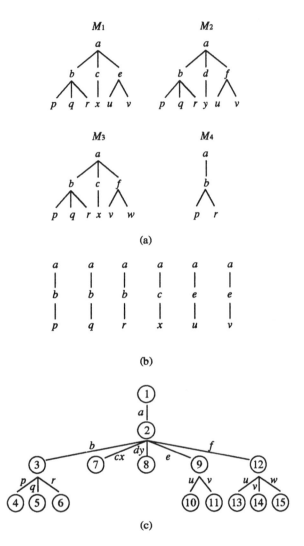

Figure 3: (a) Four candidate motifs M_1, M_2, M_3 and M_4. (b) M_1's *p*-strings. (c) Illustration of the PRET, constructed by inserting the *p*-strings of the motifs in (a) into the PRET; each node in the PRET is labeled by its preorder number.

The edges of the PRET are labeled with characters such that the concatenation of the edge labels on the path from the root to a leaf of the PRET is a *p*-string of some candidate motif. We insert the *p*-strings of candidate motifs into the PRET as into a trie except that if a series of nodes have only one child, we collapse these nodes to a single node whose parent edge is associated with a string instead of a single character. Figure 3(c) shows an example PRET (the nodes with the labels 7 and 8 show the result of a collapsing). For each node v in the PRET, let $string(v)$ be the string on the edge labels from the root to v. We associate v with two fields: $motif(v)$ and $count(v)$. The field $motif(v)$ tells which candidate motifs contain $string(v)$ ($string(v)$ may be a p-string or a prefix of some p-string in the candidate motifs). The field $count(v)$ shows the number of sample trees that contain $string(v)$ within the allowed distance. This field is calculated by traversing the PRET in a bottom-up fashion (e.g., by a postorder traversal) and counting the values in the field $motif(v)$ during the traversal.[1] The PRET can be constructed asymptotically in $O(N)$ time and space where N is the total length of all p-strings contained in the candidate motifs in $\mathcal{C}$ (Kosaraju 1989). After constructing the PRET, we traverse the PRET in a top-down fashion (e.g., by a preorder traversal), pruning unlikely candidate motifs using the optimization heuristics described in the next subsection. The result is a set of "promising" motifs.

In phase (2), we calculate the occurrence numbers of the promising motifs with respect to the entire set $\mathcal{S}$. Determining which are the most likely is a statistical exercise. We use *simple random sampling without replacement* (Cochran 1977) to select sample trees from the set $\mathcal{S}$. Consider a candidate motif M. Let N (n, respectively) denote the number of trees in the set $\mathcal{S}$ (the sample $\mathcal{A}$, respectively) that contain M within the allowed distance. $|\mathcal{S}|$ denotes the set size and $|\mathcal{A}|$ denotes the sample size; $F = N/|\mathcal{S}|$ and $f = n/|\mathcal{A}|$. If it is assumed that f is normally distributed, then we obtain the following.

Fact: *With probability = 99%, F is in the interval $(\hat{F}_L, \hat{F}_U)$ where*

$$\hat{F}_L = f - (t\sqrt{\frac{|\mathcal{S}| - |\mathcal{A}|}{|\mathcal{S}| - 1}}\sqrt{\frac{f(1-f)}{|\mathcal{A}|}} + \frac{1}{2|\mathcal{A}|}),$$

$$\hat{F}_U = f + (t\sqrt{\frac{|\mathcal{S}| - |\mathcal{A}|}{|\mathcal{S}| - 1}}\sqrt{\frac{f(1-f)}{|\mathcal{A}|}} + \frac{1}{2|\mathcal{A}|}).$$

The symbol t is the value of the normal deviate corresponding to the desired confidence probability. When the probability = 99%, $t = 2.58$ (Cochran 1977). The values of $|\mathcal{S}|$, $|\mathcal{A}|$ are given; f, n can be obtained from phase (1) of the discovery algorithm. Thus, if the estimator $(\hat{F}_U \times N) < Occur$ for the candidate motif M, then with probability $\geq 99\%$, M won't satisfy the specified requirements. We therefore eliminate it from consideration.

When checking whether a promising motif M occurs in a tree $T \in \mathcal{S}$ within the allowed distance $Dist$, we add variable length don't cares (VLDCs) to M as the

---

[1]The tree pairs from which a candidate motif is discovered are recorded. For each $string(v)$, we add up the numbers of distinct trees from which the candidate motifs in the field $motif(v)$ are discovered and assign the sum to the field $count(v)$.

new root and leaves to form a VLDC pattern V and then compare V with T using the pattern matching algorithm developed in (Zhang, Shasha, & Wang 1994). (A VLDC can be matched, at no cost, with a path or portion of a path in T. The algorithm calculates the minimum distance between V and T after implicitly computing an optimal substitution for the VLDCs in V, allowing zero or more cuttings at nodes from T.)

Besides statistical filtering, we incorporate a second optimization heuristic to eliminate the redundant calculation of occurrence numbers (an expensive dynamic programming calculation that must be repeated for every tree in $\mathcal{S}$). We say M_1 is a *sub-pattern* of M_2 if for every p-string of M_1, represented as $string(u)$ in the PRET, there exists a p-string of M_2, represented as $string(v)$ in the PRET, such that v is a descendant of u in the PRET. Observe that $occurrence\_no_{\mathcal{S}}^k(M_1) \geq occurrence\_no_{\mathcal{S}}^k(M_2)$ for all $0 \leq k \leq Dist$. Thus if M_2 is in the final output set, then we need not bother matching M_1 against trees in $\mathcal{S}$, since it will be too. If M_1 is not in the final output set, M_2 won't be either, since its occurrence number will be even lower.

By traversing the PRET in a top-down preorder traversal, we implicitly incorporate the preceding optimization heuristics. Let u, v be two nodes in the PRET where v is an descendant of u. Observe that $occurrence\_no_{\mathcal{S}}^k(string(u)) \geq occurrence\_no_{\mathcal{S}}^k(string(v))$ for all $0 \leq k \leq Dist$. Furthermore, for any p-string P of a motif M, $occurrence\_no_{\mathcal{S}}^k(P) \geq occurrence\_no_{\mathcal{S}}^k(M)$ for all $0 \leq k \leq Dist$. Thus in visiting a node u, we check the field $count(u)$ and use our sampling formula described above to estimate $string(u)$'s occurrence number. Suppose it is estimated that the occurrence number of $string(u)$ is below $Occur$, we eliminate all the motifs containing $string(u)$ from further consideration. Furthermore, we prune all motifs containing $string(v)$ where v is a descendant of u in the PRET. After traversing the PRET, we only calculate the occurrence numbers of the unpruned motifs with respect to the entire set $\mathcal{S}$.

Experimental Results

Data and Parameters

We carried out a series of experiments to evaluate the effectiveness and speed (measured by elapsed CPU time) of our approach. The programs were written in C and run on a SUN SPARC workstation under the SUN operating system version 4.1.2. The data was a set of randomly generated 80 trees. To make the experiments manageable, the size of the trees was fixed at 15. Each node label of the generated trees was drawn randomly from the range A to Z. To gain a better understanding of the performance of our algorithms, we also tested the algorithms on real RNA secondary structures. Eighty secondary structures (trees) were selected randomly from the database in the National

Cancer Institute. The sizes of the secondary structures ranged from 10 to 15.

The experimental parameters and their base values were as follows: $SetSize = 80$, $SizeRatio = 80\%$, $Size = 5$ (i.e., the minimum size of an interesting motif is 5), $Dist = 1$ and $Occur = 70$. The sample size was obtained by multiplying $SetSize$ by $SizeRatio$. Twenty samples were chosen randomly; each time one sample was used in running the set and the average was plotted.[2] The metric used to evaluate the effectiveness of our algorithms was $HitRatio = (NumDiscovered/TotalNum) \times 100\%$ where $NumDiscovered$ is the number of interesting motifs discovered by our techniques. $HitRatio$ stands for the percentage of the interesting motifs obtained from the exhaustive search method. By exhaustive search, we mean selecting as candidates all motifs in the set that satisfy the size constraint. One would like this percentage to be as high as possible.

Performance Analysis

Figure 4 compares the effectiveness of our optimized approach (the discovery algorithm with the optimizations) with a non-optimized approach for varying sample sizes. Figure 5 compares their running times with that of the exhaustive search method. It can be seen that very few qualifying motifs were missed by the two proposed optimization heuristics (Fig. 4). Both heuristics sped up the discovery algorithm by a factor of 10. Moreover, our optimized approach was 10,000 times faster than the brute force method (Fig. 5).

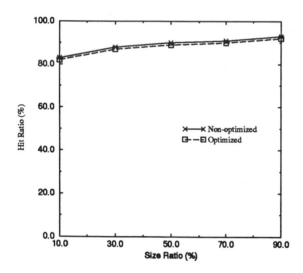

Figure 4: Performance of the pruning techniques for varying sample sizes.

[2]The results obtained from the generated and real data, for both the base values and other parameter values, were rather consistent. Hence, we only present here the results for the RNA molecules with the base values.

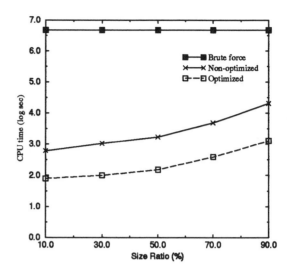

Figure 5: Comparison of the running times between the brute force method, our optimized approach and the approach without optimizations.

Phylogenetic Study

In this experiment, we were interested in seeing whether active motifs help with the phylogenetic study. We selected three families of mRNA sequences from GenBank (Burks *et al.* 1991) pertaining to the poliovirus, human rhinovirus and coxsackievirus. Poliovirus contained two sequences: polio3 sabin strain and pol3mut; human rhinovirus contained two sequences: rhino 2 and rhino 14; and coxsackievirus also contained two sequences: cox5 and cvb305pr. We folded the 5' non-coding region of these mRNA sequences and transformed the resulting suboptimal structures into trees using the algorithm developed in (Shapiro & Zhang 1990). This resulted in 6 files, where each file contained 3,000 trees and the trees had between 70 and 180 nodes.

Using the proposed method, we found 100 most active tree-structured motifs (i.e., those with the largest occurrence numbers) for each sequence. It was observed that rhino 2 had very few active motifs appearing in its family uniquely, whereas the other 5 sequences had many such motifs. To avoid biased results, we took away rhino 2. Then we found the intersections of every two sequences' motifs. Figure 6 summarizes the results. The figure shows that one can get more intersections from sequences of the same family. This result indicates that closeness in motif corresponds to closeness in family. Consequently, one may use the motifs as a way to predict ancestry.

Acknowledgments

We would like to thank the KDD referees whose comments helped to improve the paper. This work was supported by NSF grants IRI-9224601 and IRI-9224602, by ONR grant N00014-92-J-1719 and by the Natural Sciences and Engineering Research Council of

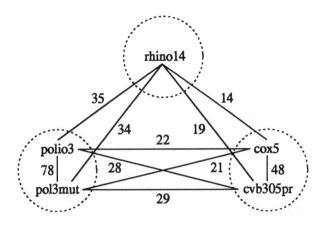

Figure 6: Sequences belonging to the same family are placed in the same circle. Each line connects two sequences and is associated with the number of the intersections of the two sequences' motifs.

Canada under Grant No. OGP0046373.

References

Agrawal, R. 1994. Tutorial: Database Mining. In Proceedings of the Thirteenth ACM SIGACT-SIGMOD-SIGART Symposium on Principles of Database Systems, 75–76.

Burks, C.; Cassidy, M.; Cinkosky, M. J.; Cumella, K. E.; Gilna, P.; Hayden, J. E.-D.; Keen, G. M.; Kelley, T. A.; Kelly, M.; Kristofferson, D.; and Ryals, J. 1991. GenBank. *Nucleic Acids Research* 19:2221–2225.

Chevalet, C., and Michot, B. 1992. An Algorithm for Comparing RNA Secondary Structures and Searching for Similar Substructures. *Comput. Applic. Biosci.* 8:215–225.

Cochran, W. G. 1977. *Sampling Techniques.* New York: Wiley.

Djoko, S.; Cook, D. J.; and Holder, L. B. 1995. Analyzing the Benefits of Domain Knowledge in Substructure Discovery. In Proceedings of the First International Conference on Knowledge Discovery & Data Mining, 75–80.

Han, J.; Cai, Y.; and Cercone, N. 1993. Data-Driven Discovery of Quantitative Rules in Relational Databases. *IEEE Transactions on Knowledge and Data Engineering* 5(1):29–40.

Konings, D. A. M., and Hogeweg, P. 1989. Pattern Analysis of RNA Secondary Structure – Similarity and Consensus of Minimal Energy Folding. *J. Mol. Biol.* 207:597–614.

Kosaraju, S. R. 1989. Efficient Tree Pattern Matching. In Proceedings of the Thirtieth Annual Symposium on Foundations of Computer Science, 178–183.

Le, S.-Y.; Owens, J.; Nussinov, R.; Chen, J.-H.; Shapiro, B. A.; and Maizel, J. V. 1989. RNA Secondary Structures: Comparison and Determination of Frequently Recurring Substructures by Consensus. *Comput. Applic. Biosci.* 5(3):205–210.

Mannila, H.; Toivonen, H.; and Verkamo, A. I. 1995. Discovering Frequent Episodes in Sequences. In Proceedings of the First International Conference on Knowledge Discovery & Data Mining, 210–215.

Piatetsky-Shapiro, G., and Frawley, W. J. eds. 1991. *Knowledge Discovery in Databases.* Menlo Park, CA: AAAI Press/The MIT Press.

Shapiro, B. A., and Zhang, K. 1990. Comparing Multiple RNA Secondary Structures Using Tree Comparisons. *Comput. Applic. Biosci.* 6(4):309–318.

Silberschatz, A.; Stonebraker, M.; and Ullman, J. D. 1991. Database Systems: Achievements and Opportunities. *Communications of the ACM* 34(10):94–109.

Tsumoto, S., and Tanaka, H. 1995. Automated Discovery of Functional Components of Proteins from Amino-Acid Sequences Based on Rough Sets and Change of Representation. In Proceedings of the First International Conference on Knowledge Discovery & Data Mining, 318–324.

Wang, J. T. L.; Chirn, G.-W.; Marr, T. G.; Shapiro, B. A.; Shasha, D.; and Zhang, K. 1994a. Combinatorial Pattern Discovery for Scientific Data: Some Preliminary Results. In Proceedings of the 1994 ACM SIGMOD International Conference on Management of Data, 115–125.

Wang, J. T. L.; Marr, T. G.; Shasha, D.; Shapiro, B. A.; and Chirn, G.-W. 1994b. Discovering Active Motifs in Sets of Related Protein Sequences and Using Them for Classification. *Nucleic Acids Research* 22(14):2769–2775.

Wang, J. T. L.; Zhang, K.; Jeong, K.; and Shasha, D. 1994c. A System for Approximate Tree Matching. *IEEE Transactions on Knowledge and Data Engineering* 6(4):559–571.

Zhang, K.; Shasha, D.; and Wang, J. T. L. 1994. Approximate Tree Matching in the Presence of Variable Length Don't Cares. *Journal of Algorithms* 16(1):33–66.

Zuker, M. 1989. On Finding All Suboptimal Foldings of an RNA Molecule. *Science* 244:48–52.

Detecting Early Indicator Cars in an Automotive Database:

A Multi-Strategy Approach

Ruediger Wirth & Thomas P. Reinartz

Daimler-Benz AG
Research & Technology F3S/E
PO Box 2360
89013 Ulm, Germany
e-mail: {wirth,reinartz}@dbag.ulm.DaimlerBenz.COM

Abstract

No company so far achieved the ultimate goal of zero faults in manufacturing. Even high-quality products occasionally show problems that must be handled as warranty cases. In this paper, we report work done during the development of an early warning system for a large quality information database in the automotive industry. We present a multi-strategy approach to flexible prediction of upcoming quality problems. We used existing techniques and combined them in a novel way to solve a concrete application problem. The basic idea is to identify sub populations that, at an early point in time, behave like the whole population at a later time. Such sub populations act as early indicators for future developments. We present our method in the context of a concrete application and present experimental results. At the end of the paper, we outline how this method can be generalised and transferred to other KDD application problems.

Introduction

No company so far achieved the ultimate goal of zero faults in manufacturing. Even very high-quality products, like Mercedes-Benz vehicles, occasionally show problems that must be handled as warranty cases. At Mercedes-Benz, such cases are recorded in a large database, which contains information on all Mercedes vehicles. For each vehicle, information on its technical configuration and its repair history is stored. This information includes faults and their repairs, the mileage at the repair time, costs associated with the repair, and the area where the repair was performed, for example. Currently, this quality information database contains about 7 million vehicles; the net size of the database is about 25 Giga bytes.

Domain experts access this database for various tasks including

- observation of product quality in the field,
- early detection of important faults and their causes,
- prediction of warranty costs,
- initiation of actions for product improvement.

Most database analyses are currently limited to standardised SQL queries and descriptive statistics. Nevertheless, users expect a lot of useful information hidden in these databases that is not accessible by conventional methods. *Knowledge Discovery in Databases* (KDD) (cf. Piatetsky-Shapiro & Frawley 1991; Frawley, Piatetsky-Shapiro, & Matheus 1992; Fayyad *et al.* 1996) has the potential to disclose this hidden information and also to improve the analysis capabilities by facilitating the tasks of the users.

A successful application of KDD techniques in the quality information domain at Mercedes-Benz will have high impact on the business. Warranty costs belong to the best-kept secrets of a company. Typically, a lot of money and prestige are involved. As an indication of the magnitude of this problem area, consider publicized recall actions of car manufacturers. Such actions can easily cost dozens of millions of dollars, not counting the negative impact on the image of the company.

The presented application domain has been tackled following the task model proposed by Reinartz & Wirth (1995) and Wirth & Reinartz (1995). In a thorough application analysis we first elicited the users' requirements, expectations and prior knowledge. Various application goals were identified in this phase. One of these goals is the development of an early warning system for quality problems. In this paper, we present a particular multi-strategy approach to prediction that is very useful for an early warning system. This approach is very flexible, not tied to particular techniques, and can be generalised to other KDD problems such as focusing.

Scientifically, this application domain serves to evaluate and improve KDD techniques. In particular, we develop and refine a methodology of KDD to guide a user through the process. This methodological approach is task oriented and not driven by techniques. It is based on a systematic refinement of tasks that will be finally mapped to techniques. This task refinement provides us with a framework to set up trials with different techniques until the best combination of techniques is found. Thus, the iterative and interactive nature of the KDD process (Fayyad *et al.*, 1996, Brachman & Anand 1994) is supported. Here, we focus on the application point of view.

As argued in Wirth & Reinartz (1995), the main bottleneck for KDD applications is not the lack of techniques. The challenge is to exploit and combine existing algorithms in the most profitable way in the context of real applications. Most successful KDD applications (e.g., SKICAT (Fayyad, Weir, & Djorgovski 1993), OpportunityExplorer (Anand & Kahn 1993)) did not rely on sophisticated new techniques. The reason for their success was the intelligent combination and adaptation of known techniques w.r.t. the constraints of the application problem. Once developed, these methods (i.e., combinations of techniques) can be transferred to other similar application problems. The application reported in this paper follows the same spirit. We rely on existing (although slightly modified) techniques, which we combined in a novel way to solve a concrete application problem. The resulting method can now be transferred to similar KDD application problems.

The paper is organised as follows. First, we describe the application problem in more detail. Then, we outline our solution approach. We first identified the tasks that need to be solved and refined these tasks until they could be mapped to KDD techniques. We describe our concrete realisation and show experimental results. Finally, we critically assess the results, sketch potential benefits of our approach to KDD in general, and point out future work.

Application Problem

Currently, Mercedes-Benz is developing an early warning system on top of the quality information database mentioned in the previous section. The early warning system should discover upcoming quality problems as soon as possible. The earlier quality problems are detected the earlier product improvement actions can be initiated to save future warranty costs. Furthermore, an early warning system can help to avoid expensive recall actions. If an upcoming quality problem with a line of cars is discovered early enough, there may be time to overcome this problem by preventive maintenance actions at regular maintenance intervals, for example. Expensive follow-up faults can be prevented and the customer does not realise that there could have been a problem in the future.

The current system is based on conventional information technology and simple descriptive statistics. It is rigid, restricted in its capabilities, and consumes a lot of resources because it operates on the whole database. Using a KDD approach, we aim at making the system more flexible, less expensive, faster in terms of computing time, and capable to warn even earlier.

The solution approach described in this paper was inspired by the following observation. The experts look at sub populations of the cars if they want to get a first idea about the rate of certain faults. For instance, people in certain countries seem to be more concerned with the paint of a car. If the experts want to check the quality of the paint they look at the cars in this country first. Any problem with the paint is likely to be observed there first. Taxis are another sub population which is watched closely because they drive many miles in a short period.

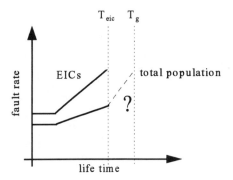

Figure 1: Predicting fault rates using early indicator cars

The question was, could this approach be generalised and automated. Do there exist sub populations of cars which, in certain aspects, behave like the whole population of cars at a later point in time? If yes, how can they be characterized by easily observable attributes? In the following, we call such sub populations early indicator cars (EICs).

Figure 1 illustrates the idea of EICs. Assume we observe a certain aspect of the fault profile, for instance a fault rate, over the life time of cars. The lower line in the diagram shows the accumulated fault rate for a certain fault for cars from the same production period. Assume that we are now at time T_{eic} and we want to predict the fault rate at time T_g. If we had EICs then we could compute the fault rate for the EICs at time T_{eic} and use this value as predicted value for the fault rate of the whole population at time T_g. In this example, the EICs would indicate an increasing fault rate although the total fault rate still looks fine at time T_{eic}.

The discussion above suggests the following high-level procedure. First, select a production period which is used for learning. It needs to be a period in the past such that the values of the relevant attributes at time T_g are already known. In the following, we will call this production period the learning production period. From this learning production period we derive a procedure for the identification of EICs which is independent from a particular production period. This identification procedure will then be applied to subsequent production periods. Each production period then has its own set of EICs which are used for prediction.[1]

---

1 From another point of view, the identification procedure for EICs could be viewed as a particular prediction model.

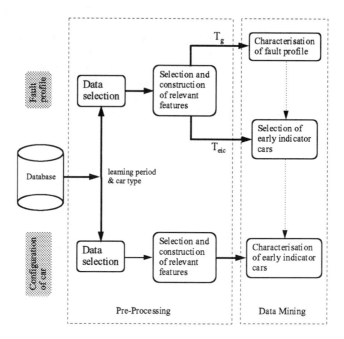

Figure 2: Main steps for detecting EICs

In the context of an early warning system, EICs are an attractive concept because they promise the following benefits:

- Significant changes in the fault profile will be detected earlier. Such changes include upcoming new quality problems, a change in the fault rate or average costs for certain faults.

- Analyses can be performed on smaller sets of vehicles. Thus, resources are saved which can be used for different or more detailed analyses. Some analyses, for instance the application of sophisticated learning algorithms, may not even be possible on the whole population.[2]

- The EICs can be used to predict various aspects of the fault profile, e.g., values, interesting events, and trends. Thus, prediction is much more flexible than with traditional statistical methods like time series analyses.

While EICs alone will not be sufficient for a comprehensive early warning system, they will certainly form a very powerful central part.

Solution Approach

In this section, we describe our approach to detection of EICs. We pursued a task-oriented approach. We first identified the tasks that needed to be solved, refined these

tasks and made them more precise until they could be mapped to KDD techniques. Different techniques could have been applied to solve the tasks. In the next sections, we describe one particular choice of techniques and report experimental results.

Basic idea

Our solution approach consists of three major steps.
1. Characterize the fault profile for the whole population of cars at a certain time T_g.
2. Select EICs.
3. Generate an identification procedure for EICs.

In the first step, the fault profile of the whole population of cars at a certain time T_g is characterized. A fault profile is a vague term which could be characterized in various ways. In any case, it will be described in terms of fault relevant attributes.

In the second step, EICs need to be selected. For this purpose, we compute the values for the fault attributes at an earlier time T_{eic}. Those cars which fit the fault profile of the whole population at T_{eic} are considered to be EICs.

The identification procedure for EICs must take into account that EICs need to be identified at production time or shortly after. Therefore, we cannot use attributes that relate directly to the fault profile. EICs need to be characterized by easily observable attributes, like type and configuration of a car or areas where it was sold. This requires the use of two separate sets of attributes. One set is related to the fault profile and the other set contains attributes that can be observed at production time. Figure 2 shows the procedure.

---

2 Therefore, the EIC approach is closely linked to the focusing problem in KDD.

Realisation

In this section, we describe techniques and set-up of experiments we conducted to assess the applicability of the approach outlined in the previous sections.

The main choice for the realisation concerned the fault profile. We decided to represent the fault profiles as a hierarchy of classes. Classes contain cars which are similar according to a set of attributes which domain experts judged to be relevant for the fault profile.

The characterization of a fault profile can then be mapped to a (conceptual) clustering task (e.g., Gennari, Langley, & Fisher 1989). For several reasons, we selected the hierarchical conceptual clustering algorithm ECOBWEB (Reich 1994) for this clustering task. ECOBWEB can handle both numeric and symbolic attributes and provides some other features, like the hierarchy correction to avoid ordering effects, which proved to be useful. Since we chose a clustering approach for the first step, the second step must be defined accordingly.

The second step is the selection of EICs. We compute values of the fault attributes for a selected earlier time T_{eic} for all cars included in the first step. The resulting instances are then examined how similar they are to classes from the first step. If an instance is similar to an existing class, then we assume that this instance fits the fault profile at time T_g and could thus serve as an early indicator car. If the instance is not similar to any existing class, then it cannot be an early indicator.

This second step can be reduced to a test whether the instances of time T_{eic} can be assigned to existing classes of the hierarchy. For this test, ECOBWEB was slightly modified. ECOBWEB is an incremental hill climbing system. Each instance is presented incrementally and ECOBWEB tries to incorporate this instance. In the simplest case, the instance can be added to an existing class. The description of the class will then be adapted but the structure of the hierarchy remains unchanged. Other operators change the structure of the hierarchy by splitting classes, merging classes, or adding a new class. All of these operators are tentatively applied, their result is evaluated, and the best operator is permanently executed.

We changed ECOBWEB such that the operators are evaluated but not executed. If one of the structure changing operators wins, then the instance does not fit into the existing hierarchy. In other words, it does not fit into the fault profile of time T_g. If the structure preserving operator wins, then the instance fits and is considered to be an early indicator car.

Using this test, we selected a sub population of cars that are considered as early indicator cars. If we were only interested in the present production period we could simply take this set for future prediction tasks. Since we are really interested in identifying early indicator cars for future production periods, we need to characterize the early indicator cars independent of the production period. This characterization could then be used to identify the set of EICs for each subsequent production period.

Therefore, in the third step we try to discriminate EICs and NonEICs using attributes that can be easily observed at production time or shortly after. We selected attributes which described the configuration of the car (e.g., engine type, transmission type, special equipment), the sales area, and the average mileage, which can be easily calculated from the information collected at the first maintenance visit to the garage.

This task can be mapped to a standard classification task with two classes, EIC and NonEIC.[3] Both classes are described using the configuration attributes and the average mileage per day. The latter attribute is computed from the mileage that is observed at the first maintenance in the garage. The resulting instances were then assigned to two classes according to the result of the second step. Finally, we employed two standard rule learning programs, CN2 (Clark & Niblett 1988) and C4.5 (Quinlan 1993), to learn descriptions for these two classes.

These descriptions are independent of the fault profile and a particular production period. The identification procedure for EICs for a production period now is simply to select all cars from this period which fit the description.

Experimental Results

In this section, we present results of our experiments. Numbers in diagrams have been modified because the actual numbers are confidential. The interpretation of the diagrams remains valid.

For our experiments, we chose a learning production period of three months in 1991. The times T_g and T_{eic} were set to 12 and 6 months, respectively. Faults were restricted to faults in the injection system. In cooperation with domain experts we selected 8 attributes which are relevant for the fault profile. Among others, these attributes described average mileage between two faults, average time between two faults, total number of faults in the period, and costs per faults. For each car produced in the learning production period, values for these attributes were computed for life times T_g and T_{eic}. There were 2628 cars considered.

First, ECOBWEB was used to cluster the resulting instances and to construct a class hierarchy based on the attribute values for T_g. Then, attribute values at time T_{eic} were used for selection of EICs as described in the previous section. About one third of the cars (i.e., 862 cars) were classified as EICs.

Then, we selected 28 attributes that can be easily observed early in the life time of the car. We applied both CN2 and C4.5 with different parameter settings until the learning result seemed to be reasonable. It turned out that EICs and NonEICs were not easy to separate. In retrospect, this is not surprising since the vast majority of cars had no quality problems during the first 12 months. For a large portion of these cars their assignment to one of the two classes was almost random.

---

3 Later, we will see that results became better after we introduced a third class.

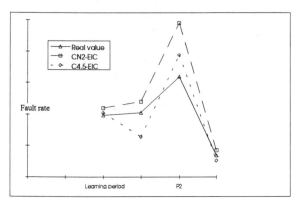 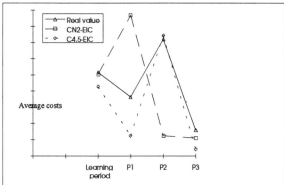

Figure 3: Evaluation results

After this observation, we tried to bias the algorithms towards cars that actually had a quality problem. We introduced a third class containing the EICs which had at least one fault. Now, both CN2 and C4.5 could better discriminate NonEICs from the other two classes. After some iterations with different parameter settings two rule sets were produced.

The resulting rules could be used in two ways to extract EICs. Rules for EICs could be applied directly to identify EICs or rules for NonEICs could be applied to exclude Non-EICs. The latter alternative turned out to be better.

This identification procedure was applied to cars from the learning production period and three subsequent production periods. This resulted in eight sets of EICs. Each set contained about one third of the cars produced during the respective period. The goal of the experiments was to predict different fault rates, average costs per car, and a hot list of faults. The values of the EICs six months after the production date were used to predict the corresponding twelve months values of the whole set.

Figure 3 shows the results for the prediction of the fault rate (total number of faults divided by the number of produced cars) at the left and the average cost per car at the right, respectively. Other tests, for instance predicting fault rates for individual parts produced similar results.

CN2-EICs overestimated fault rates but picked up trends accurately.[4] On costs they performed badly. The predictions of C4.5-EICs were always pretty close to the actual values, both for fault rates and costs. In many cases

In addition to predicting values, we also used EICs to predict hot lists of faults. It turned out that for most cases, ranking and relative frequency of individual faults were predicted accurately. In some cases, however, there were significant deviations from the predicted values. We suspect that these deviations are interesting in their own right. At least some of them may indicate unexpected developments that deserve attention by domain experts.

In summary, the results exceeded our expectations. They show that EICs exist and can be identified

automatically. The feasibility of this approach has been proved.

Conclusions

In this paper, we presented a multi-strategy approach to flexible prediction and demonstrated its feasibility. Our experiments showed that the EIC approach can be used to predict future developments. It will now be further refined and incorporated in an early warning system for quality problems.

The experiments are an example for a typical KDD process. After the identification of the prediction learning task we went through several steps of pre-processing, applied various data mining techniques to the pre-processed data, and evaluated and revised the results in a post-processing stage of the KDD process. Methodological considerations helped us to structure this process and to generalise the results.

Applicability of the EIC approach

Based on our experience with transferring the EIC approach[5], we expect that its applicability and its benefits depend on the domain. Probably, EICs neither exist in all application domains nor can they address all aspects of an application problem. Nevertheless, if EICs exist, as in our quality information domain, they can be use for different purposes.

EICs provide a flexible way of prediction. They are not fixed to prediction of values of just one attribute. They can predict different attributes or events, depending on the application domain. They can also predict different trends, which is very important for any decision support system.

Furthermore, EICs are an intelligent, innovative approach to sampling. Analyses can be performed on EICs instead of the whole population. If the method is applied as described in this paper, then the time aspect has

---

4 In this application domain, trend prediction is sufficient. Specific quantitative values are not necessary.

5 If we generalise the approach described in this paper, it would be more appropriate to talk about early indicator instances instead of early indicator cars. Nevertheless, we use the acronym EIC throughout this paper.

to be considered. EICs are a sample for the whole population at a later point in time. However, the approach can easily be generalised such that the EICs are selected according to different criteria. For instance, in the quality information domain it is also interesting to consider regional effects. Identify a set of regions such that the cars sold in these regions behave like the whole population of cars.

Finally, EICs can also be used for detecting deviations. If EICs are believed to be good predictors then any deviation in the prediction deserves attention of domain experts.

Future work

Although the experimental results with the chosen techniques were very good, there is much room for refinement of the EIC approach. For the experiments reported here some more or less arbitrary choices were made which need to be investigated more systematically. The task refinement process made these choices and parameters explicit and provides a framework for further experiments. Further experiments will address both domain specific and methodological refinements of the EIC approach.

The domain specific refinements concern selection of attributes and data. For instance, the length of the production period was taken to be three months. Other values, perhaps taking seasonalities into account, may lead to better results. Also, times T_g and T_{eic} were arbitrarily set to twelve and six months, respectively. Again, other values may lead to better results. These choices might even depend on the type of fault. Furthermore, attributes describing the fault profile were highly aggregated. In subsequent experiments we will also investigate more fine-grained attributes.

Methodological refinements address the usage of different techniques for the various tasks of the EIC approach and the extension to other application domains. For instance, in the quality information domain we are performing similar experiments with Kohonen networks (Kohonen, 1988) for the clustering sub task. Additionally, we are exploring completely different methods for the representation of a fault profile. At the end, we will have a variety of combinations of techniques which realise the EIC approach. We will then apply the EIC approach to other domains. We expect that the choice of the best realisation of the EIC approach depends on both the domain and the data. Our methodological framework allows us to explore the alternatives systematically and to select the most appropriate one.

Acknowledgments: We thank our domain experts at Mercedes-Benz for their support and access to the quality information database. Lothar K. Becker partly implemented and evaluated our approach.

References

Anand, T., & Kahn, G. (1993). Opportunity explorer: Navigating large databases using knowledge discovery templates. *Proceedings of 1993 AAAI Workshop on Knowledge Discovery in Databases*, pp. 45-51.

Brachman, R.J., & Anand, T. (1994). The process of knowledge discovery in databases: A first sketch. *Proceedings 1994 AAAI Workshop on Knowledge Discovery in Databases*, pp. 1-12.

Clark, P., & Niblett, T. (1989). The CN2 induction algorithm. *Machine Learning 3*, pp. 261-283.

Fayyad, U.M., Piatetsky-Shapiro, G., Smyth, P., & Uthurasamy, R. (1996). *Advances in Knowledge Discovery and Data Mining*. Cambridge, MA: MIT Press.

Fayyad, U.M., Weir, N., & Djorgovski, S. (1993). Automated cataloging and analysis of sky survey image databases: The SKICAT system. *Proc. CIKM*, pp. 527-536.

Frawley, W.J., Piatetsky-Shapiro, G., & Matheus, C.J. (1992). Knowledge discovery in databases: An overview. *AI Magazine*, Fall, pp. 57-70.

Gennari, J.H., Langley, P., & Fisher, D. (1989). Models of incremental concept formation. *Artificial Intelligence*, 40, pp. 11-61.

Kohonen, T. (1988). *Self-organisation and associative memory*. Berlin: Springer.

Quinlan, J.R. (1993). *C4.5: Programs for Machine Learning*. San Mateo, CA: Morgan Kaufmann.

Piatetsky-Shapiro, G., & Frawley, W.J. (eds.) (1991). *Knowledge discovery in databases*. Menlo Park, CA: AAAI Press / MIT Press.

Reich, Y. (1994). Macro and micro perspectives of multi-strategy learning. in: Michalski, R.S., & Tecuci, G. (eds.) *Machine Learning: A Multi-strategy Approach*, Vol. IV, San Francisco, CA: Morgan Kaufmann, pp. 379-401.

Reinartz, T.P., & Wirth, R. (1995). The need for a task model for knowledge discovery in databases. in: Kodratoff, Y., Nakhaiezadeh, G., & Taylor, C. (eds.) Workshop notes *Statistics, Machine Learning, and Knowledge Discovery in Databases*. MLNet Familiarisation Workshop, Heraklion, Crete, pp. 19-24.

Wirth, R., & Reinartz, T.P. (1995). *Towards a task model for Knowledge Discovery in Databases*. Internal Report, Daimler-Benz Research & Technology, Ulm, Germany.

making sense out of data

Knowledge Discovery and Data Mining: Towards a Unifying Framework

Usama Fayyad
Microsoft Research
One Microsoft Way
Redmond, WA 98052, USA
fayyad@microsoft.com

Gregory Piatetsky-Shapiro
GTE Laboratories, MS 44
Waltham, MA 02154, USA
gps@gte.com

Padhraic Smyth
Information and Computer Science
University of California, Irvine
CA 92717-3425, USA
smyth@.ics.uci.edu

Abstract

This paper presents a first step towards a unifying framework for Knowledge Discovery in Databases. We describe links between data mining, knowledge discovery, and other related fields. We then define the KDD process and basic data mining algorithms, discuss application issues and conclude with an analysis of challenges facing practitioners in the field.

1 Introduction

Across a wide variety of fields, data are being collected and accumulated at a dramatic pace. There is an urgent need for a new generation of computational techniques and tools to assist humans in extracting useful information (knowledge) from the rapidly growing volumes of data, These techniques and tools are the subject of the emerging field of knowledge discovery in databases (KDD). This paper is an initial step towards a common framework that we hope will allow us to understand the variety of activities in this multidisciplinary field and how they fit together. We view the knowledge discovery process as a *set* of various activities for making sense of data. At the core of this process is the application of *data mining* methods for pattern[1] discovery. We examine how data mining is used and outline some of its methods. Finally, we look at practical application issues of KDD and enumerate challenges for future research and development.

2 KDD, Data Mining, and Relation to other Fields

Historically the notion of finding useful patterns in data has been given a variety of names including data mining, knowledge extraction, information discovery, information harvesting, data archaeology, and data pattern processing. The term *data mining* has been mostly used by statisticians, data analysts, and the management information systems (MIS) communities. It has also gained popularity in the database field. The term KDD was coined at the first KDD workshop in 1989 (Piatetsky-Shapiro 1991) to emphasize that "knowledge" is the end product of a data-driven discovery. It has been popularized in artificial intelligence and machine learning.

In our view KDD refers to the overall *process* of discovering useful knowledge from data while *data mining* refers to a particular *step* in this process. Data mining is the application of specific algorithms for extracting patterns from data. The distinction between the KDD process and the data mining step (within the process) is a central point of this paper. The additional steps in the KDD process, such as data preparation, data selection, data cleaning, incorporating appropriate prior knowledge, and proper interpretation of the results of mining, are essential to ensure that useful knowledge is derived from the data. Blind application of data mining methods (rightly criticised as "data dredging" in the statistical literature) can be a dangerous activity easily leading to discovery of meaningless patterns.

KDD has evolved, and continues to evolve, from the intersection of research fields such as machine learning, pattern recognition, databases, statistics, artificial intelligence, knowledge acquisition for expert systems, data visualization, and high performance computing. The unifying goal is extracting high-level knowledge from low-level data in the context of large data sets.

KDD overlaps with machine learning and pattern recognition in the study of particular data mining theories and algorithms: means for modeling data and extracting patterns. KDD focuses on aspects of finding *understandable* patterns that can be interpreted as *useful or interesting knowledge*, and puts a strong emphasis on working with large sets of real-world data. Thus, scaling properties of algorithms to large data sets are of fundamental interest.

KDD also has much in common with statistics, particularly exploratory data analysis methods. The sta-

[1]Throughout this paper we use the term "pattern" to designate *pattern* or *model* extracted from the data.

tistical approach offers precise methods for quantifying the inherent uncertainty which results when one tries to infer general patterns from a particular sample of an overall population. KDD software systems often embed particular statistical procedures for sampling and modeling data, evaluating hypotheses, and handling noise within an overall knowledge discovery framework. In contrast to traditional approaches in statistics, KDD approaches typically employ more search in model extraction and operate in the context of larger data sets with richer data structures.

In addition to its strong relation to the database field (the 2nd 'D' in KDD), another related area is *data warehousing*, which refers to the popular business trend for collecting and cleaning transactional data to make them available for on-line analysis and decision support. A popular approach for analysis of data warehouses has been called OLAP (*on-line analytical processing*), after a set of principles proposed by Codd (1993). OLAP tools focus on providing multi-dimensional data analysis, which is superior to SQL in computing summaries and breakdowns along many dimensions. OLAP tools are targeted towards simplifying and supporting interactive data analysis, while the KDD tool's goal is to automate as much of the process as possible.

3 Basic Definitions

We define KDD (Fayyad, Piatetsky-Shapiro, & Smyth 1996) as

Knowledge Discovery in Databases is the *nontrivial process of identifying valid, novel, potentially useful, and ultimately understandable patterns in data.*

Here *data* is a set of facts (e.g., cases in a database) and *pattern* is an expression in some language describing a subset of the data or a model applicable to that subset. Hence, in our usage here, extracting a *pattern* also designates fitting a model to data, finding structure from data, or in general any high-level description of a set of data. The term *process* implies that KDD is comprised of many steps, which involve data preparation, search for patterns, knowledge evaluation, and refinement, all repeated in multiple iterations. By *non-trivial* we mean that some search or inference is involved, i.e. it is not a straightforward computation of predefined quantities like computing the average value of a set of numbers. The discovered patterns should be *valid* on new data with some degree of certainty. We also want patterns to be *novel* (at least to the system, and preferably to the user) and *potentially useful*, i.e., lead to some benefit to the user/task. Finally, the

patterns should be *understandable*, if not immediately then after some post-processing.

The above implies that we can define quantitative measures for evaluating extracted patterns. In many cases, it is possible to define measures of certainty (e.g., estimated prediction accuracy on new data) or utility (e.g. gain, perhaps in dollars saved due to better predictions or speed-up in response time of a system). Notions such as novelty and understandability are much more subjective. In certain contexts understandability can be estimated by simplicity (e.g., the number of bits to describe a pattern). An important notion, called **interestingness** (e.g. see Piatetsky-Shapiro & Matheus 1994, Silberschatz & Tuzhilin 1995), is usually taken as an overall measure of pattern value, combining validity, novelty, usefulness, and simplicity. Interestingness functions can be explicitly defined or can be manifested implicitly via an ordering placed by the KDD system on the discovered patterns or models.

Data Mining is a step in the KDD process consisting of applying data analysis and discovery algorithms that, under acceptable computational efficiency limitations, produce a particular enumeration of patterns over the data (see Section 5 for more details).

Note that the space of patterns is often infinite, and the enumeration of patterns involves some form of search in this space. Practical computational constraints place severe limits on the subspace that can be explored by a data mining algorithm.

KDD Process is the *process* of using the database along with any required selection, preprocessing, subsampling, and transformations of it; to apply data mining methods (algorithms) to enumerate patterns from it; and to evaluate the products of data mnining to identify the subset of the enumerated patterns deemed "knowledge".

The data mining component of the KDD process is concerned with the algorithmic means by which patterns are extracted and enumerated from data. The overall KDD process (Figure 1) includes the *evaluation* and possible *interpretation* of the "mined" patterns to determine which patterns may be considered new "knowledge." The KDD process also includes all of the additional steps described in Section 4. The notion of an overall user-driven process is not unique to KDD: analogous proposals have been put forward in statistics (Hand 1994) and in machine learning (Brodley and Smyth 1996).

4 The KDD Process

The KDD process is interactive and iterative, involving numerous steps with many decisions being made by

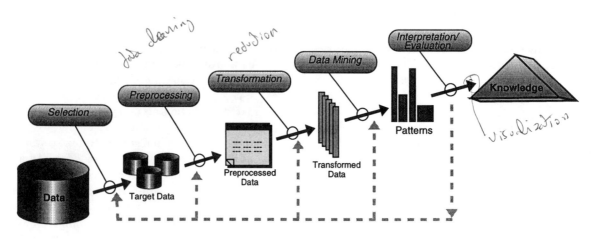

Figure 1: An overview of the steps comprising the KDD process.

the user. Brachman & Anand (1996) give a practical view of the KDD process emphasizing the interactive nature of the process. Here we broadly outline some of its basic steps:

1. Developing an understanding of the application domain and the relevant prior knowledge, and identifying the *goal* of the KDD process from the customer's viewpoint.

2. Creating a target data set: selecting a data set, or focusing on a subset of variables or data samples, on which discovery is to be performed.

3. Data cleaning and preprocessing: basic operations such as the removal of noise if appropriate, collecting the necessary information to model or account for noise, deciding on strategies for handling missing data fields, accounting for time sequence information and known changes.

4. Data reduction and projection: finding useful features to represent the data depending on the goal of the task. Using dimensionality reduction or transformation methods to reduce the effective number of variables under consideration or to find invariant representations for the data.

5. Matching the goals of the KDD process (step 1) to a particular data mining *method*: e.g., summarization, classification, regression, clustering, etc. Methods are described in Section 5.1, and in more detail in (Fayyad, Piatetsky-Shapiro, & Smyth 1996).

6. Choosing the data mining algorithm(s): selecting method(s) to be used for searching for patterns in the data. This includes deciding which models and parameters may be appropriate (e.g. models for categorical data are different than models on vectors over the reals) and matching a particular data mining method with the overall criteria of the KDD process (e.g., the end-user may be more interested in

understanding the model than its predictive capabilities — see Section 5.2).

7. Data mining: searching for patterns of interest in a particular representational form or a set of such representations: classification rules or trees, regression, clustering, and so forth. The user can significantly aid the data mining method by correctly performing the preceding steps.

8. Interpreting mined patterns, possibly return to any of steps 1–7 for further iteration. This step can also involve visualization of the extracted patterns/models, or visualization of the data given the extracted models.

9. Consolidating discovered knowledge: incorporating this knowledge into another system for further action, or simply documenting it and reporting it to interested parties. This also includes checking for and resolving potential conflicts with previously believed (or extracted) knowledge.

The KDD process can involve significant iteration and may contain loops between any two steps. The basic flow of steps (although not the potential multitude of iterations and loops) is illustrated in Figure 1. Most previous work on KDD has focused on step 7 – the data mining. However, the other steps are as important for the successful application of KDD in practice.

Having defined the basic notions and introduced the KDD process, we now focus on the data mining component, which has by far received the most attention in the literature.

5 The Data Mining Step of the KDD Process

The data mining component of the KDD process often involves repeated iterative application of particular data mining methods. The objective of this section is to present a very brief overview of the primary goals of data mining, a description of the methods used to address these goals, and a very brief overview of data mining algorithms which incorporate these methods.

The knowledge discovery *goals* are defined by the intended use of the system. We can distinguish two types of goals: **Verification**, where the system is limited to verifying the user's hypothesis, and **Discovery**, where the system autonomously finds new patterns. We further subdivide the Discovery goal into **Prediction**, where the system finds patterns for the purpose of predicting the future behaviour of some entities; and **Description**, where the system finds patterns for the purpose of presenting them to a user in a human-understandable form. In this paper we are primarily concerned with discovery-oriented data mining.

Most data mining methods are based on tried and tested techniques from machine learning, pattern recognition, and statistics: classification, clustering, regression, and so forth. The array of different algorithms under each of these headings can often be quite bewildering to both the novice and experienced data analyst. It should be emphasized that of the very many data mining methods advertised in the literature, there are really only a few fundamental techniques. The actual underlying model representation being used by a particular method (i.e., the functional form of f in the mapping $x \rightarrow f(x)$) usually comes from a composition of a small number of well-known options: polynomials, splines, kernel and basis functions, threshold/Boolean functions, etc. Thus, algorithms tend to differ primarily in goodness-of-fit criterion used to evaluate model fit, or in the search method used to find a good fit.

5.1 Data Mining Methods

Although the boundaries between prediction and description are not sharp (some of the predictive models can be descriptive, to the degree that they are understandable, and vice versa), the distinction is useful for understanding the overall discovery goal. The relative importance of prediction and description for particular data mining applications can vary considerably. However, in the context of KDD, description tends to be more important than prediction. This is in contrast to many machine learning and pattern recognition applications where prediction is often the primary goal. The goals of prediction and description are achieved via the following primary data mining methods.

Classification: learning a function that maps (classifies) a data item into one of several predefined classes.

Regression: learning a function which maps a data item to a real-valued prediction variable and the dis-covery of functional relationships between variables.

Clustering: identifying a finite set of categories or clusters to describe the data. Closely related to clustering is the method of *probability density estimation* which consists of techniques for estimating from data the joint multi-variate probability density function of all of the variables/fields in the database.

Summarization: finding a compact description for a subset of data, e.g., the derivation of summary or association rules and the use of multivariate visualization techniques.

Dependency Modeling: finding a model which describes significant *dependencies* between variables (e.g., learning of belief networks).

Change and Deviation Detection: discovering the most significant changes in the data from previously measured or normative values

5.2 The Components of Data Mining Algorithms

Having outlined the *general methods* of data mining, the next step is to construct *specific algorithms* to implement these methods. One can identify three primary components in any data mining algorithm: *model representation*, *model evaluation*, and *search*. This reductionist view is not necessarily complete or fully encompassing: rather, it is a convenient way to express the key concepts of data mining algorithms in a relatively unified and compact manner—(Cheeseman 1990) outlines a similar structure.

Model Representation: the language used to describe discoverable patterns. If the representation is too limited, then no amount of training time or examples will produce an accurate model for the data. It is important that a data analyst fully comprehend the representational assumptions which may be inherent in a particular method. It is equally important that an algorithm designer clearly state which representational assumptions are being made by a particular algorithm. Note that more powerful representational power for models increases the danger of overfitting the training data resulting in reduced prediction accuracy on unseen data.

Model Evaluation Criteria: quantitative statements (or "fit functions") of how well a particular pattern (a model and its parameters) meet the goals of the KDD process. For example, predictive models are often judged by the empirical prediction accuracy on some test set. Descriptive models can be evaluated along the dimensions of predictive accuracy, novelty, utility, and understandability of the fitted model.

Search Method: consists of two components: *parameter search* and *model search*. Once the model representation (or family of representations) and the model evaluation criteria are fixed, then the data mining problem has been reduced to purely an optimization task: find the parameters/models from the selected family which optimize the evaluation criteria. In *parameter search* the algorithm must search for the parameters which optimize the model evaluation criteria given observed data and a fixed model representation. *Model search* occurs as a loop over the parameter search method: the model representation is changed so that a family of models are considered.

5.3 Data Mining Algorithms

There exist a wide variety of data mining algorithms. For a brief review of the most popular of these see (Fayyad, Piatetsky-Shapiro, & Smyth 1996) and the references therein. Popular model representations include decision trees and rules, nonlinear regression and classification, example-based methods (including nearest-neighbour and case-based reasoning methods), probabilistic graphical dependency models (including Bayesian networks), and relational learning models (including inductive logic programming).

An important point is that each technique typically suits some problems better than others. For example, decision tree classifiers can be very useful for finding structure in high-dimensional spaces and are also useful in problems with mixed continuous and categorical data (since tree methods do not require distance metrics). However, classification trees may not be suitable for problems where the true decision boundaries between classes are described by a 2nd-order polynomial (for example). Thus, there is no 'universal' data mining method and choosing a particular algorithm for a particular application is something of an art. In practice, a large portion of the applications effort can go into properly formulating the problem (asking the right question) rather than in optimizing the algorithmic details of a particular data mining method (Hand 1994; Langley and Simon 1995).

6   Application Issues

For a survey of applications of KDD as well as detailed examples, see (Piatetsky-Shapiro et al 1996) for industrial applications and (Fayyad, Haussler, & Stolorz 1996) for applications in science data analysis. Here, we examine criteria for selecting potential applications, which can be divided into practical and technical categories. The practical criteria for KDD projects are similar to those for other applications of advanced technology, and include the potential impact of an application,

absence of simpler alternative solutions, and strong organizational support for using technology. For applications dealing with personal data one should also consider the privacy/legal issues (Piatetsky-Shapiro 1995).

The technical criteria include considerations such as the *availability of sufficient data (cases)*. In general, the more fields there are and the more complex the patterns being sought, the more data are needed. However, strong prior knowledge (see below) can reduce the number of needed cases significantly. Another consideration is the *relevance of attributes*. It is important to have data attributes relevant to the discovery task: no amount of data will allow prediction based on attributes that do not capture the required information. Furthermore, *low noise levels (few data errors)* is another consideration. High amounts of noise make it hard to identify patterns unless a large number of cases can mitigate random noise and help clarify the aggregate patterns. *Changing and time-oriented data*, while making the application development more difficult, makes it potentially much more useful, since it is easier to retrain a system than to retrain a human. Finally, and perhaps one of the most important considerations is *prior knowledge*. It is very useful to know something about the domain — what are the important fields, what are the likely relationships, what is the user utility function, what patterns are already known, and so forth.

6.1   Research and Application Challenges

We outline some of the current primary research and application challenges for KDD. This list is by no means exhaustive and is intended to give the reader a feel for the types of problems that KDD practitioners wrestle with.

Larger databases: Databases with hundreds of fields and tables, millions of records, and multi-gigabyte size are quite commonplace, and terabyte (10^{12} bytes) databases are beginning to appear. Methods for dealing with large data volumes include more efficient algorithms (Agrawal et al. 1996), sampling, approximation methods, and massively parallel processing (Holsheimer et al. 1996).

High dimensionality: Not only is there often a very large number of records in the database, but there can also be a very large number of fields (attributes, variables) so that the dimensionality of the problem is high. A high dimensional data set creates problems in terms of increasing the size of the search space for model induction in a combinatorially explosive manner. In addition, it increases the chances that a data mining algorithm will find spurious patterns that are not valid in general. Approaches to this problem include methods to reduce the effective dimensionality of the problem and the use of prior knowledge to identify irrelevant variables.

Overfitting: When the algorithm searches for the best parameters for one particular model using a limited set of data, it may model not only the general patterns in the data but also any noise specific to that data set, resulting in poor performance of the model on test data. Possible solutions include cross-validation, regularization, and other sophisticated statistical strategies.

Assessing statistical significance: A problem (related to overfitting) occurs when the system is searching over many possible models. For example, if a system tests N models at the 0.001 significance level, then on average, with purely random data, $N/1000$ of these models will be accepted as significant. This point is frequently missed by many initial attempts at KDD. One way to deal with this problem is to use methods which adjust the test statistic as a function of the search, e.g., Bonferroni adjustments for independent tests, or randomization testing.

Changing data and knowledge: Rapidly changing (non-stationary) data may make previously discovered patterns invalid. In addition, the variables measured in a given application database may be modified, deleted, or augmented with new measurements over time. Possible solutions include incremental methods for updating the patterns and treating change as an opportunity for discovery by using it to cue the search for patterns of change only (Matheus, Piatetsky-Shapiro, and McNeill 1996). See also (Mannila, Toivonen, & Verkamo 1995; Agrawal & Psaila 1995).

Missing and noisy data: This problem is especially acute in business databases. U.S. census data reportedly has error rates of up to 20%. Important attributes may be missing if the database was not designed with discovery in mind. Possible solutions include more sophisticated statistical strategies to identify hidden variables and dependencies (Heckerman 1996; Smyth et al. 1996).

Complex relationships between fields: Hierarchically structured attributes or values, relations between attributes, and more sophisticated means for representing knowledge about the contents of a database will require algorithms that can effectively utilize such information. Historically, data mining algorithms have been developed for simple attribute-value records, although new techniques for deriving relations between variables are being developed (Djoko, Cook, & Holder 1995; Dzeroski 1996).

Understandability of patterns: In many applications it is important to make the discoveries more understandable by humans. Possible solutions include graphical representations (Buntine 1996; Heckerman 1996), rule structuring, natural language generation, and techniques for visualization of data and knowledge. Rule refinement strategies (e.g. Major & Mangano 1995) can be used to address a related problem: the discovered knowledge may be implicitly or explicitly redundant.

User interaction and prior knowledge: Many current KDD methods and tools are not truly *interactive* and cannot easily incorporate prior knowledge about a problem except in simple ways. The use of domain knowledge is important in all of the steps of the KDD process as outlined in Section 4. Bayesian approaches (e.g. Cheeseman 1990) use prior probabilities over data and distributions as one form of encoding prior knowledge. Others employ deductive database capabilities to discover knowledge that is then used to guide the data mining search (e.g. Simoudis et al. 1995).

Integration with other systems: A stand-alone discovery system may not be very useful. Typical integration issues include integration with a DBMS (e.g. via a query interface), integration with spreadsheets and visualization tools, and accommodating real-time sensor readings. Examples of integrated KDD systems are described by Simoudis, Livezey, and Kerber (1995), and Stolorz et al (1995).

7   Concluding Remarks

We have presented some definitions of basic notions in the KDD field. A primary aim is to clarify the relation between knowledge discovery and data mining. We provided an overview of the KDD process and basic data mining methods. Given the broad spectrum of data mining methods and algorithms, our brief overview is inevitably limited in scope: there are many data mining techniques, particularly specialized methods for particular types of data and domains. Although various algorithms and applications may appear quite different on the surface, it is not uncommon to find that they share many common components. Understanding data mining and model induction at this component level clarifies the task of any data mining algorithm and makes it easier for the user to understand its overall contribution and applicability to the KDD process.

This paper represents a step towards a common framework that we hope will ultimately provide a unifying vision of the common overall goals and methods used in KDD. We hope this will eventually lead to a better understanding of the variety of approaches in this multi-disciplinary field and how they fit together.

Acknowledgments

We thank Sam Uthurusamy, Ron Brachman, and KDD-96 referees for their valuable suggestions and ideas.

Bibliography

Agrawal, R. and Psaila, G. 1995. Active Data Mining, In *Proceedings of KDD-95: First International Conference on Knowledge Discovery and Data Mining*, pp. 3-8, Menlo Park, CA: AAAI Press.

Agrawal, R., Mannila, H., Srikant, R., Toivonen, H., and Verkamo, I. 1996. Fast Discovery of Association Rules, in *AKDDM*, AAAI/MIT Press, 307–328.

Brachman, R. and Anand, T. 1996. The Process of Knowledge Discovery in Databases: A Human Centered Approach, in *AKDDM*, AAAI/MIT Press, 37–58.

Brodley, C. E., and Smyth, P. 1996 Applying classification algorithms in practice. *Statistics and Computing*, to appear.

Buntine, W. 1996. Graphical Models for Discovering Knowledge, in *AKDDM*, AAAI/MIT Press, 59–82.

Cheeseman, P. 1990. On Finding the Most Probable Model. In *Computational Models of Scientific Discovery and Theory Formation*, Shrager, J. and Langley P. (eds). Los Gatos, CA: Morgan Kaufmann, 73–95.

Codd, E.F. 1993. Providing OLAP (On-line Analytical Processing) to User-Analysts: An IT Mandate. E.F. Codd and Associates.

Djoko, S., Cook, D., and Holder, L. 1995. Analyzing the Benefits of Domain Knowledge in Substructure Discovery, in *Proceedings of KDD-95: First International Conference on Knowledge Discovery and Data Mining*, Menlo Park, CA: The AAAI Press.

Dzeroski, S. 1996. Inductive Logic Programming for Knowledge Discovery in Databases, in *AKDDM*, AAAI/MIT Press.

Fayyad, U. M., G. Piatetsky-Shapiro, P. Smyth, and R. Uthurusamy, 1996. *Advances in Knowledge Discovery and Data Mining*, (AKDDM), AAAI/MIT Press.

Fayyad, U.M., Haussler, D. and Stolorz, Z. 1996. KDD for Science Data Analysis; Issues and Examples. *Proc. 2nd Int. Conf. on Knowledge Discovery and Data Mining (KDD-96)*, Menlo Park, CA: AAAI Press.

Fayyad, U.M., Piatetsky-Shapiro, G., and Smyth, P. 1996. From Data Mining to Knowledge Discovery: An Overview, in *AKDDM*, AAAI/MIT Press, pp. 1–30.

Hand, D. J. 1994. Deconstructing statistical questions. *J. Royal. Stat. Soc. A*, 317–356.

Heckerman, D. 1996. Bayesian Networks for Knowledge Discovery, in *AKDDM*, AAAI/MIT Press, 273–306.

Holsheimer, M., Kersten, M.L., Mannila, H., and Toivonen, H. 1996. Data Surveyor: Searching the Nuggets in Parallel, in *AKDDM*, AAAI/MIT Press.

Langley, P. and Simon, H. A. 1995. Applications of machine learning and rule induction. *Communications of the ACM*, 38, 55–64.

Major, J. and Mangano, J. 1995. Selecting among Rules Induced from a Hurricane Database. *Journal of Intelligent Information Systems* 4(1):39–52.

Mannila, H., Toivonen, H. and Verkamo, A.I. 1995. Discovering Frequent Episodes in Sequences, In *Proceedings of KDD-95: First International Conference on Knowledge Discovery and Data Mining*, pp. 210-215, Menlo Park, CA: AAAI Press.

Matheus, C., Piatetsky-Shapiro, G., and McNeill, D. 1996. Selecting and Reporting What is Interesting: The KEFIR Application to Healthcare Data, in *AKDDM*, Cambridge, MA: AAAI/MIT Press, 495-516.

Piatetsky-Shapiro, G. 1991. Knowledge Discovery in Real Databases, *AI Magazine*, Winter 1991.

Piatetsky-Shapiro, G., Matheus, C. 1994. The Interestingness of Deviations. In *Proceedings of KDD-94*. Fayyad, U. M. and Uthurusamy, R., (eds.), AAAI Press report WS-03, Menlo Park, CA: AAAI Press.

Piatetsky-Shapiro, G. 1995. Knowledge Discovery in Personal Data vs. Privacy – a Mini-symposium. *IEEE Expert*, April.

Piatetsky-Shapiro, G., Brachman, R., Khabaza, T., Kloesgen, W., and Simoudis, E., 1996. An Overview of Issues in Developing Industrial Data Mining and Knowledge Discovery Applications, In Proceedings of KDD-96, Menlo Park, CA: AAAI Press.

Silberschatz, A. and Tuzhilin, A. 1995. On Subjective Measures of Interestingness in Knowledge Discovery. In *Proceedings of KDD-95: First International Conference on Knowledge Discovery and Data Mining*, pp. 275-281, Menlo Park, CA: AAAI Press.

Simoudis, E., Livezey, B., and Kerber, R. 1995. Using Recon for Data Cleaning, In *Proceedings of KDD-95: First International Conference on Knowledge Discovery and Data Mining*, pp. 275-281, Menlo Park, CA: AAAI Press.

Smyth, P., Burl, M., Fayyad, U. and Perona, P. 1996. Modeling Subjective Uncertainty in Image Annotation, in *AKDDM*, AAAI/MIT Press, 517–540.

Stolorz, P. et al. 1995. Fast Spatio-Temporal Data Mining of Large Geophysical Datasets, In *Proceedings of KDD-95: First International Conference on Knowledge Discovery and Data Mining*, pp. 300–305, AAAI Press.

An Overview of Issues in Developing Industrial Data Mining and Knowledge Discovery Applications

Gregory Piatetsky-Shapiro
GTE Laboratories
40 Sylvan Road
Waltham, MA 02154
gps@gte.com

Ron Brachman
AT&T Research
600 Mountain Avenue
Murray Hill, NJ 07974
rjb@research.att.com

Tom Khabaza
ISL
Berk House, Basing View
Basingstoke RG21 4RG
UK, tomk@isl.co.uk

Willi Kloesgen
GMD, D-53757
Sankt Augustin, Germany
kloesgen@gmd.de

Evangelos Simoudis
IBM Almaden Research Center
650 Harry Road, San Jose, CA 95120
simoudis@almaden.ibm.com

Abstract

This paper surveys the growing number of industrial applications of data mining and knowledge discovery. We look at the existing tools, describe some representative applications, and discuss the major issues and problems for building and deploying successful applications and their adoption by business users. Finally, we examine how to assess the potential of a knowledge discovery application.

1 Introduction

A significant need exists for a new generation of techniques and tools with the ability to *intelligently* and *automatically* assist humans in analyzing the mountains of data for nuggets of useful knowledge. These techniques and tools are the subject of the emerging field of data mining and knowledge discovery in databases (Fayyad et al. 1996). This paper examines a growing number of industrial applications in this field (see Fayyad, Haussler, and Stolorz 1996 for a survey of scientific applications). We survey the existing data mining tools, describe some representative applications, and discuss the major issues and problems for building and deploying successful applications.

Knowledge Discovery in Databases (KDD) is an umbrella term used to describe a large variety of activities for making sense of data. We will use the term *knowledge discovery* to describe the overall process of finding useful patterns in data, which includes not only the data mining step of running the discovery algorithms, but also pre- and post-processing, and various other activities (see Section 3).

The knowledge discovery *goals* are defined by the intended use of the system. We can distinguish two types of goals: **verification**, where the system is limited to verifying the user's hypothesis (the most prevalent type of data analysis to date), and **discovery**, where the system autonomously finds new patterns. We further subdivide the Discovery goal into **prediction**, where the system finds patterns for the purpose of predicting the future behaviour of some entities; and **description**, where the system finds patterns for the purpose of presenting them to a user in a human-understandable form. Although the boundaries between prediction and description are not sharp – some of the predictive models can be descriptive (to the degree that they are understandable), and some of the descriptive models could be used for prediction – this distinction is useful for understanding the discovery goal.

The framework for knowledge discovery and the data mining tasks of classification, regression, clustering, summarization, dependency modeling, and deviation detection are discussed in more detail in (Fayyad, Piatetsky-Shapiro, & Smyth 1996).

2 Data Mining Tools

Data mining in the industry today is still primarily verification-oriented and performed mainly by analysts whose primary training and professional duties are in statistics or data analysis. By and large, the tools used are not expressly "data mining tools", but rather statistical analysis tools like S and SAS, graph and chart-drawing software and spreadsheets, and database query engines. Direct programming in languages like C and awk is typically used for complex analyses, usually on data selected from a database, but dumped into a flat file for further manipulation.

Among the tools that support data mining[1] – see `<http://info.gte.com/~kdd/siftware.html>` for a catalog, the first group is **generic, single-task tools**. There are many dozens of such tools available, especially for classification, using primarily decision trees, neural networks, example-based, and rule-discovery approaches. Such tools mainly

---

[1]sometimes called *siftware* because this is software for *sifting* through the data

support only the data mining step in the knowledge discovery process and require significant pre- and post-processing. The target user of such tools is typically a consultant or a developer who would integrate them with other modules as part of a complete application.

The next group is **generic, multi-task tools.** These tools perform a variety of discovery tasks, typically combining classification (perhaps using more than one approach), visualization, query/retrieval, clustering, and more. They include Clementine, Darwin, IBM Intelligent Miner, IMACS, MLC++, MOBAL, and SGI MineSet.

These tools support more of the KDD Process and simplify embedding of discovered knowledge in the application. Usually, the target user of such tools is a "power" analyst who understands data manipulation. Generally such tools require appropriate training and some tool customization before being used by domain experts, but there are some exceptions.

Clementine, in particular, is reported to have been widely used without customization by a variety of end-users ranging from business analysts to biochemists. This is made possible by Clementine's highly graphical user interface to data mining functions.

Another example is the IMACS system (Brachman et al. 1993), which used a knowledge representation system to represent domain and task objects and integrate various aspects of the discovery process. IMACS allowed the user to create new, object-centered views over data that was stored in arbitrary ways (relational database, flat files). Data could be segmented in a simple way using these views, and new segments could be defined easily from old ones. This was one big step towards allowing a business user to interact with data in terms s/he was familiar with, since the views (or "concepts") were expressed entirely in the user's terms rather than being slaved to database schemas created for other purposes.

Finally, the last group is **domain-specific tools.** These tools support discovery only in a specific domain and already talk the language of the end user, who needs to know very little about the analysis process. Examples of such tools include Opportunity Explorer (Anand 1995) which generates reports on changes in retail sales, IBM Advanced Scout <http://www.research.ibm.com/xw-scout> which analyzes basketball game statistics and finds patterns of play that coaches can use, and HNC Falcon <http://www.hnc.com/>, a neural network-based system for credit-card fraud detection.

These systems and others represent a growing trend in moving data mining technology into the business world. The key elements that help make the core statistical, machine learning, and other data mining technologies accessible to a mainstream user include

- putting the problem in the business user's terms, including viewing the data from a business model perspective (both concepts and rules);

- support for specific key business analyses like segmentation;

- presentation of results in a form geared to the business problem being solved; and

- support for an iterative exploratory process protracted in time, as examined in the next section.

3 Knowledge Discovery Process

The core of the knowledge discovery process is the set of data mining tasks, used to extract and verify patterns in data. However, we should emphasize that this core takes only a small part (estimated as 15 to 25% of the overall effort) of the entire process of knowledge discovery. No complete methodology for this process yet exists, but knowledge discovery takes place in a number of stages (more about this in Brachman & Anand, 1996):

- Data and task discovery - the process of becoming familiar with both the data that will be analyzed and the task that the business user needs to accomplish. This is more significant than it may sound, especially when the data is to be pulled from multiple sources, and when the analysis will not be done by the business user;

- Acquisition - bringing the data into the appropriate environment for analysis;

- Integration and checking - confirming the expected form and broad contents of the data, and integrating into tools as required;

- Data cleaning - removing records with errors or outliers (if considered insignificant), etc.; looking for obvious flaws in the data and removing them;

- Model and hypothesis development - simple exploration of the data by passive techniques, and elaboration by deriving new data attributes where necessary; selection of an appropriate model in which to do analysis; development of initial hypotheses to test;

- Data mining step - application of the core discovery procedures to discover patterns and new knowledge, or to verify hypotheses developed prior to this step;

- Testing and verification - assessing the discovered knowledge: testing predictive models on test sets, analyzing segmentation etc.;

- Interpretation and use - integration with existing domain knowledge, which may confirm, deny or challenge the newly discovered patterns; if predictive, subsequent use on novel data sets.

Throughout the process, we also have presentation or visualization of results as an integral activity. A key thing to note about this process is that it is not simple and linear, but thoroughly iterative and interactive, the results of analysis being fed back into the modeling and hypothesis derivation process to produce improved results on subsequent iterations. This activity takes time, and if it is applied to data generated on a regular basis (e.g., quarterly or yearly results) can have a very long lifespan.

4 Representative Applications

Numerous knowledge discovery applications and prototypes have been developed for a wide variety of domains including marketing, finance, manufacturing, banking, and telecommunications. A majority of the applications have used predictive modeling approach, but there were also a few notable applications using other methods. Here we describe some of the representative examples.

4.1 Marketing

Leading market research companies such as A.C. Nielsen and Information Resources in USA, GfK and Infratest Burke in Europe apply KDD tools to the rapidly growing sales and marketing databases. Because of a strong competitive pressure, the often saturated market potential and maturity of products, there is a shift from a quality to an information competition where detailed and comprehensive knowledge on the behavior of customers and competitors is crucial.

Market research companies collect data on special markets, analyze this data and sell data and analyses to their clients. The clients add their own data for further analyses. Medium sized datasets are captured when market research companies perform surveys (e.g. 2000 persons interviewed each month) or organize test samples of households. BehaviorScan approaches provide test households with special alternative TV commercials. Much larger data sets are available in the form of point of sale data, when e.g. purchases in supermarkets are captured by scanners.

Marketing, which has been a long time user of statistical and other quantitative methods, has been in the forefront of adopting new knowledge discovery techniques. Most marketing applications fall into the broad area called "Database Marketing" (or "mailshot response" in Europe). This is an approach which relies on analysis of customer databases, using a number of techniques including interactive querying, market segmentation to identify different customer groups, and predictive modeling to forecast their behaviour. Business Week (Berry 1994) has estimated that over half of all retailers are using or planning to use database marketing, and those who do use it have good results

such as 10-15% increase in credit card use reported by American Express.

An interesting application to predict television audiences using neural networks and rule induction was developed by Integral Solutions for the BBC. Rule induction was used to examine which factors play the most important role in relating the size of a program's audience to its scheduling slot. The final models were equivalent to the best performance of human experts, but highly robust against change, because the models could be retrained from up-to-date data (Fitzsimons, Khabaza, & Shearer 1993).

Other applications are more descriptive – their focus is to find patterns that will help market analysts make better decisions. Among the first systems developed and deployed in this area were Coverstory (Schmitz, Armstrong, & Little 1990) and Spotlight (Anand & Kahn 1992), which analyzed supermarket sales data and produced reports, using natural language and business graphics, on the most significant changes in a particular product volume and share broken down by region, product type, and other dimensions. In addition, causal factors such as distribution channels and price changes were examined and related to changes in volume and share. These systems were quite successful – Spotlight was reported to be among the best selling products of A.C. Nielsen.

Spotlight was later extended into Opportunity Explorer system (Anand 1995), which supports the sales representative of a consumer packaged good company in examining the business with a single retailer. This is accomplished by presentations that highlight the advantages for the retailer if additional products are stocked or special promotions are performed. A new feature of Opportunity Explorer was generation of interactive reports with hyperlinks (even before the Web!), which allowed easy navigation between different report sections.

The MDT (Management Discovery Tool) system, a product under development at AT&T and NCR, incorporates several other innovative ideas to allow a business person to directly interface with data. MDT incorporates a set of business rules (encoded as metadata) that make it easy to set up monitors that detect significant deviations in key business indicators. To accommodate the mainstream business user, MDT provides a limited set of analysis types, including summarization, trend analysis, and measure and segment comparison.

Another marketing area is Market basket analysis, which looks at associations between different products bought by the customer. These methods are generally based on the association discovery algorithms (Agrawal et al. 1996). A number of companies, including IBM and SGI offers tools for Market basket analysis.

4.2 Investment

Many financial analysis applications employ predictive modeling techniques, such as statistical regression or neural networks, for tasks like portfolio creation and optimization and trading model creation. Such applications have been in use for several years. To maintain a competitive advantage, the users and developers of such applications rarely publicize their exact details and effectiveness.

We can, however, mention a few examples. Fidelity Stock Selector fund is using neural network models to select investments and has performed quite well until recently. However the output of those models is evaluated by the fund manager Brad Lewis before the action is taken, so it is not clear how to divide the credit between man and machine.

Morgan Stanley and Co. has developed AI (Automated Investor) system which identifies good trading opportunities by using clustering, visualization, and prediction. The system has been deployed and is being evaluated.

Daiwa Securities used MATLAB toolkit to build a portfolio management tool which analyzes a large number of stocks and selects an optimal portfolio based on the stock risk and expected rate of return (Pittaras 96).

LBS Capital Management uses expert systems, neural nets and genetic algorithms to manage portfolios totalling $600 million and since its start in 1993, their system has outperformed the broad stock market (Hall, Mani, & Barr 1996).

Carlberg & Associates have developed a neural network model for predicting S&P 500 Index, <http://carlassoc.com/> using interest rates, earnings, dividends, the dollar index, and oil prices. The model was surprisingly successful and explained 96% of the variation in the S&P 500 index from 1986 to 1995.

In these applications, predictive accuracy is paramount compared to the ability to use the extracted knowledge to explain a recommended action. Thus, the main focus is ensuring that modeling methods do not overfit the data.

4.3 Fraud Detection

Not all the systems developed for this have been publicized, for obvious reasons, but several are worth mentioning.

The HNC Falcon credit risk assessment system, developed using a neural network shell, is used by a large percentage of retail banks to detect suspicious credit card transactions. Falcon deployment was facilitated by the fact that credit card transaction data is captured by just a few companies. Even though each such company uses its own data format, every bank issuing credit cards uses one of these few formats. Therefore, an application that can work with even one format effectively can easily be adopted by a large number of banks.

The FAIS system (Senator et al. 1995) from US Treasury's Financial Crimes Enforcement Network, is used to identify financial transactions that may be indicative of money laundering activity. FAIS uses data from common government forms and consists of a combination of off-the-shelf and custom built components. Its use is expected to expand to a variety of government agencies that are concerned with the detection of suspicious financial transactions indicative of money laundering operations. FAIS has the hardest data quality problem because much of its data comes from poorly handwritten notes.

AT&T has developed a system for detecting the international calling fraud by displaying the calling activity in a way that lets the user quickly see the unusual patterns (Eick & Fyock 1996).

The Clonedetector system, developed by GTE (Davis & Goyal 1993), is using customer profiles to detect the cellular cloning fraud. If a particular customer suddenly starts calling in a very different way, fraud alert automatically kicks in.

Another cellular fraud detection system is under development at NYNEX. The developers first mine the data to discover indicators of fraudulent usage. Subsequently, they automatically generate detection systems by feeding these indicators into a detector constructor program, which uses the indicators to instantiate detector templates. Finally, the system learns how to combine the detectors for optimal performance.

5 Manufacturing and Production

Controlling and scheduling technical production processes is a an application of KDD with a high potential profit. The goal is to discover process conditions that lead to good quality products. At present, large volumes of data generated during a production process are often only poorly exploited. Also, the relations between the control, process, and quality variables are not completely understood by the engineers. In addition, time and space constraints, which play an especially important role in manufacturing, are not well handled by most data mining tools.

A typical example is a project which is run in a large chemical company in Europe to analyze a production process in a plant for polymeric plastics. Data includes control variables (e.g. quantities of raw material, the heating parameters), the process variables (temperatures, pressures, and chemical reaction times), and quality variables measured in a laboratory. Quality variables are determined several times a day, process and control variables nearly continuously. Even simple approach of introducing separate variables for distinct time points (process variables measured every hour), and applying rule-inducing discovery methods to the resulting data can lead to valuable insights into the manufacturing process.

Another example is the CASSIOPEE troubleshooting system, developed by a joint venture of General Electric and SNECMA using the KATE discovery tool. The system is applied by three major European airlines to diagnose and predict problems for BOEING 737. To derive families of faults, clustering methods are used. CASSIOPEE received the European first prize for innovative applications (Manago and Auriol 96).

5.1 Telecommunication

Another application area involving a strong time component is the management of telecommunication networks. These large and complex networks produce large amounts of alarms daily. The sequence of alarms contains valuable knowledge about the behavior of the network. Regularities in the alarms can be used in fault management systems for filtering redundant alarms, locating problems in the network, and predicting severe faults.

At the University of Helsinki, the Telecommunication Alarm Sequence Analyzer (TASA) was built in cooperation with a manufacturer of telecommunication equipment and three telephone networks (Mannila, Toivonen, & Verkamo 1995). The system uses a novel framework for locating frequently occurring alarm episodes from the alarm stream and presenting them as rules. Large sets of discovered rules can be explored with flexible information retrieval tools supporting interactivity and iteration. In this way, TASA offers pruning, grouping, and ordering tools to refine the results of a basic brute force search for rules. The system has discovered rules that have been integrated into the alarm handling software of the telephone networks.

5.2 Other Areas

Health care is an information-rich and high payoff area, ripe for data mining. One of the first applications in this area is KEFIR (Matheus, Piatetsky-Shapiro, & McNeill 1996). The system performs an automatic drill-down through data along multiple dimensions to determine the most interesting deviations of specific quantitative measures relative to their previous and expected values. It explains "key" deviations through their relationship to other deviations in the data, and, where appropriate, generates recommendations for actions in response to these deviations. KEFIR uses a Web browser to present its findings in a hypertext report, using natural language and business graphics.

Improving data quality is another important application area. One aspect of data quality is the automatic detection of errors. A number of applications were developed for checking data (in particular financial trading data), detecting errors currently impossible to detect by conventional means. Another aspect of data quality is the identification of related and duplicate entities – an especially acute problem for database marketers and catalog senders. Identification of duplicate claims was performed by Merge/Purge system (Hernandez & Stolfo 1995), successfully used on data from Welfare Department of the State of Washington.

Basketball statistics are also plentiful, and IBM Advanced Scout helps NBA coaches and league officials organize and interpret the data amassed at every game. A sample finding from a Jan 6, 1995 game between Knicks and Cavaliers is that when Mark Price played the 1Guard position, John Williams attempted four jump shots and made each one. Advanced Scout not only finds this pattern, but explains that it is interesting because it differs considerably from the average shooting percentage of 49.30% for the Cavaliers during that game. This is the kind of pattern that coaches might not ordinarily detect, yet it conveys valuable information about possible improvements in their strategy. Scout has been used by several NBA teams (US News 95).

5.3 Discovery Agents

Finally, a novel and very important type of discovery system has appeared recently – Discovery Agents. Although the idea of active triggers has long been analyzed in the database field, really successful applications of this idea appeared only with the advent of the Internet. These systems ask the user to specify a profile of interest and search for related information among a wide variety of public domain and proprietary sources.

To mention a few examples, the Firefly is personal music recommendation agent – asks user their opinion of several music pieces and then suggests other music that the user may like <http://www.ffly.com/>.

Crayon <http://crayon.net/> allows users to create their own free newspaper (supported by ads). Farcast <http://www.farcast.com/> and NewsHound <http://www.sjmercury.com/hound/> from San Jose Mercury automatically search information from a wide variety of sources, including newspapers and wire services, and email relevant documents directly to the user.

6 Application Development Issues

While the data mining and knowledge discovery technology is quite well developed, its practical application in industry is hampered by a number of difficulties, reviewed below.

Insufficient training: graduates of business schools will be familiar with verification-driven analysis techniques, occasionally with predictive modeling, and very seldom with other discovery techniques. Extending the training of business analysts to acknowledge the full range of techniques available can alleviate this problem; it can also be addressed by making the discovery techniques easily available to business users (see sec. 2).

Inadequate tool support: most available data mining tools support at most one of the core discovery techniques, typically only prediction. Other methods, such as clustering, deviation detection, visualization, summarization are also needed, as well as methods for dealing with exceptions (rare cases) which may be significant in some applications. The tools must also support the complete knowledge discovery process (section 3) and provide a user interface suitable for business users rather than technologists. Some integrated toolkits are now emerging which satisfy these requirements.

Data inaccessibility: for a given business problem, the required data is often distributed across the organization in a variety of different formats, and is often poorly organized or maintained. For this reason, data acquisition and pre-processing usually play a very significant part in any knowledge discovery project. Data warehousing is now becoming widespread, and can potentially alleviate such problems. Both warehousing and data mining often serve to highlight the problems of data quality in an organization, but can also help to solve them.

Overabundance of patterns: when search for patterns has a wide scope, a very large number of patterns can be discovered. Proper statistical controls are needed to avoid discoveries due to chance, while domain knowledge can help to focus on the interesting findings. Rule refinement (Major & Mangano 1995) and other generalization methods could be used to further compress findings.

Changing and time-oriented data: many applications deal with behaviour that changes significantly over time (e.g. stock market or fashions). Such applications are on one hand more challenging because common algorithms suitable for flat tables do not work well with sequential and other time-oriented patterns. On the other hand, such applications can become especially successful, since it is easier to retrain a system than to retrain a human. The improvement in decision-making due to regular updating of decision-making tools is referred to as "volatility benefit". A few recent data mining methods are designed for handling deviation detection and time-oriented data (Agrawal & Psaila 1995, Berndt & Clifford 1996, Mannila, Toivonen, & Verkamo 1995).

Space oriented data: other applications, especially in manufacturing, biology, and geographically-oriented systems, are dealing with spatial data. Here again there are special types of patterns which require special algorithms (Stolorz et al. 1995). Geographical information systems have been very successful in helping to find some types of spatial patterns visually.

Complex data: Other types of information, including text, images, audio, video, and anything related to the Web present an even grander challenge with potentially great rewards.

Scalability: Although many papers (including this one) talk about needing to mine vast amounts of data, none of the tools can do that today. Data warehouses that start at 200GB are not infrequent today, yet current tools can at best deal with 1GB at a time. Progress, however, is being made towards using massively parallel and high performance computing which will help to deal with large databases.

Privacy: When dealing with databases of personal information, governments and businesses have to be careful to adequately address the legal and ethical issues of invasion of privacy (see Piatetsky-Shapiro 1995).

7   Assessing Benefits Of KDD Applications

The domains suitable for data mining are those that are information rich, have a changing environment, do not already have existing models, require knowledge-based decisions, and provide high payoff for the right decisions. Given a suitable domain, we examine costs and benefits of a potential application by looking at the following factors.

- Alternatives: there should be no simpler alternative solutions.

- Relevance: relevant factors should be included.

- Volume: there should be a sufficient number of cases (several thousands at least). Extremely large databases may be a problem when the results are needed quickly.

- Complexity: the more variables (fields) there are the more complex is the application. Complexity is also increased for time-series data.

- Quality: Error rate should be relatively low.

- Accessibility: data should be easily accessible – accessing data or merging data from different sources increases the cost of an application.

- Change: although dealing with change is more difficult, it can also be more rewarding (the volatility benefit) since the application can be automatically and regularly "re-trained" on up-to-date data.

- Expertise: The more expertise available, the easier is the project. It should be emphasized that expertise on the form and meaning of the data is just as important as knowledge of problem-solving in the domain.

Although the challenges are many and the difficulties are substantial, the future of data mining applications looks bright. There is a widespread realization of the potential value of data mining and a growing number of researchers and developers are working on the topic. However, data mining by itself is only a part of the overall application and all other components, as described in Section 3 need to be addressed for a successful application.

Acknowledgments: We thank Usama Fayyad and Sam Uthurusamy for encouraging us to put together this survey, a version of which will also appear in Communications of ACM. Robert Golan helped with information on financial data mining. Colin Shearer (ISL) has contributed much useful material to this article.

8   References

Anand, T. and Kahn, G. 1992. SPOTLIGHT: A Data Explanation System. In *Proceedings Eighth IEEE Conference on Applied AI*, 2–8. Washington, D.C.: IEEE Press.

Anand, T. 1995. Opportunity Explorer: Navigating Large Databases Using Knowledge Discovery Templates. *Journal of Intelligent Information Systems* 4(1):27–38.

Agrawal, R., Mannila, H., Srikant, R., Toivonen, H., Verkamo, A. 1996. Fast Discovery of Association Rules. In *AKDDM*, Cambridge, MA: AAAI/MIT Press.

Agrawal, R., and Psaila, G. 1995. Active Data Mining. In *Proceedings of KDD-95*, 3–8, Menlo Park, CA: AAAI Press.

Brachman, R., et al. 1993. Integrated Support for Data Archaeology. In *Proceedings of KDD-93 Workshop*, Menlo Park, CA: AAAI Press.

Brachman, R. and Anand, T. 1996. The Process of Knowledge Discovery in Databases: A Human Centered Approach. In *AKDDM*, Cambridge, MA: AAAI/MIT Press.

Berndt, D. and Clifford, J. 1996. Finding Patterns in Time Series: A Dynamic Programming Approach. In *AKDDM*, Cambridge, MA: AAAI/MIT Press.

Berry, J. 1994. Database Marketing. *Business Week*, 56–62, Sep 5.

Codd, E.F. 1993. Providing OLAP (On-line Analytical Processing) to User-Analysts: An IT Mandate. E.F. Codd and Associates.

Davis, A. and Goyal, S. 1993. Management of Cellular Fraud: Knowledge- Based Detection, Classification and Prevention. In *Proceedings of 13th Int. Conf. on AI, Expert Systems and Natural Language*, Avignon, France, Vol. 2, pp. 155-164.

Eick, S. and Fyock, D. 1996. Visualizing Corporate Data, *AT&T Technical Journal*, January/February, pp. 74–86.

Fayyad, U., Piatetsky-Shapiro, G., Smyth, P., and Uthurusamy, R. eds. 1996. *Advances in Knowledge Discovery and Data Mining* (AKDDM). Cambridge, MA: AAAI/MIT Press.

Fayyad, U., Piatetsky-Shapiro, G., and Smyth, P. 1996. Knowledge Discovery and Data Mining: Towards a Unifying Framework. In *Proceedings of KDD-96*, Menlo Park, CA: AAAI Press.

Fayyad, U., Haussler, D., and Stolorz, P. 1996. KDD for Science Data Analysis: Issues and Examples. In *Proceedings of KDD-96*, Menlo Park, CA: AAAI Press.

Fitzsimons, M., Khabaza, T., and Shearer, C. 1993. The Application of Rule Induction and Neural Networks for Television Audience Prediction. In *Proc. of ESOMAR/EMAC/AFM Symposium on Information Based Decision Making in Marketing*, Paris, November, pp 69-82.

Hall, J., Mani, G., and Barr, D. 1996. Applying Computational Intelligence to the Investment Process. In *Proc. of CIFER-96: Computational Intelligence in Financial Engineering*. Piscataway, NJ: IEEE Press.

Hernandez, M. and Stolfo, S. 1995. The Merge/Purge Problem for Large Databases. In *Proc. of the 1995 ACM-SIGMOD Conference*, 127–138. NY: ACM Press.

Major, J., and Mangano, J. 1995. Selecting among Rules Induced from a Hurricane Database. *Journal of Intelligent Information Systems* 4(1):39–52.

Manago, M. and Auriol, M. 1996. Mining for OR. *ORMS Today*, February, Special issue on Data Mining, 28–32.

Mannila, H., Toivonen, H., and Verkamo, A. 1995. Discovering Frequent Episodes in Sequences, In *Proceedings of KDD-95*, 210–215. Menlo Park, CA: AAAI Press.

Matheus, C., Piatetsky-Shapiro, G., and McNeill, D. 1996. Selecting and Reporting What is Interesting: The KEFIR Application to Healthcare Data. In *AKDDM*, Cambridge, MA: AAAI/MIT Press, 495–516.

Piatetsky-Shapiro, G. 1995. Knowledge Discovery in Personal Data vs. Privacy – a Minisymposium. *IEEE Expert*, April 1995.

Schmitz, J., Armstrong, G. and Little, J. D. C. 1990. CoverStory – Automated News Finding in Marketing. In *DSS Transactions*, ed. L. Volino, 46–54. Providence, R.I.: Institute of Management Sciences.

Senator, T. et al. 1995. The Financial Crimes Enforcement Network AI System (FAIS), *AI Magazine*, Winter 1995, 21–39.

Stolorz, P. et al. 1995. Fast Spatio-Temporal Data Mining of Large Geophysical Datasets. In *Proceedings of KDD-95*, 300–305, Menlo Park, CA: AAAI Press.

US News & World Report, December 11, 1995. "Basketball's new high-tech guru: IBM software is changing coaches' game plans."

Linear-Time Rule Induction

Pedro Domingos
Department of Information and Computer Science
University of California, Irvine
Irvine, California 92717, U.S.A.
pedrod@ics.uci.edu
http://www.ics.uci.edu/~pedrod

Abstract

The recent emergence of data mining as a major application of machine learning has led to increased interest in fast rule induction algorithms. These are able to efficiently process large numbers of examples, under the constraint of still achieving good accuracy. If e is the number of examples, many rule learners have $O(e^4)$ asymptotic time complexity in noisy domains, and C4.5RULES has been empirically observed to sometimes require $O(e^3)$. Recent advances have brought this bound down to $O(e \log^2 e)$, while maintaining accuracy at the level of C4.5RULES's. In this paper we present CWS, a new algorithm with guaranteed $O(e)$ complexity, and verify that it outperforms C4.5RULES and CN2 in time, accuracy and output size on two large datasets. For example, on NASA's space shuttle database, running time is reduced from over a month (for C4.5RULES) to a few hours, with a slight gain in accuracy. CWS is based on interleaving the induction of all the rules and evaluating performance globally instead of locally (i.e., it uses a "conquering without separating" strategy as opposed to a "separate and conquer" one). Its bias is appropriate to domains where the underlying concept is simple and the data is plentiful but noisy.

Introduction and Previous Work

Very large datasets pose special problems for machine learning algorithms. A recent large-scale study found that most algorithms cannot handle such datasets in a reasonable time with a reasonable accuracy (Michie, Spiegelhalter, & Taylor 1994). However, in many areas—including astronomy, molecular biology, finance, retail, health care, etc.—large databases are now the norm, and discovering patterns in them is a potentially very productive enterprise, in which interest is rapidly growing (Fayyad & Uthurusamy 1995). Designing learning algorithms appropriate for such problems has thus become an important research problem.

In these "data mining" applications, the main consideration is typically not to maximize accuracy, but to extract useful knowledge from a database. The learner's output should still represent the database's contents with reasonable fidelity, but it is also important that it be comprehensible to users without machine learning expertise. "If ... then ..." rules are perhaps the most easily understood of all representations currently in use, and they are the focus of this paper.

A major problem in data mining is that the data is often very noisy. Besides making the extraction of accurate rules more difficult, this can have a disastrous effect on the running time of rule learners. In C4.5RULES (Quinlan 1993), a system that induces rules via decision trees, noise can cause running time to become cubic in e, the number of examples (Cohen 1995). When there are no numeric attributes, C4.5, the component that induces decision trees, has complexity $O(ea^2)$, where a is the number of attributes (Utgoff 1989), but its running time in noisy domains is dwarfed by that of the conversion-to-rules phase (Cohen 1995). Outputting trees directly has the disadvantage that they are typically much larger and less comprehensible than the corresponding rule sets. Noise also has a large negative impact on windowing, a technique often used to speed up C4.5/C4.5RULES for large datasets (Catlett 1991).

In algorithms that use reduced error pruning as the simplification technique (Brunk & Pazzani 1991), the presence of noise causes running time to become $O(e^4 \log e)$ (Cohen 1993). Fürnkranz and Widmer (1994) have proposed *incremental reduced error pruning (IREP)*, an algorithm that prunes each rule immediately after it is grown, instead of waiting until the whole rule set has been induced. Assuming the final rule set is of constant size, IREP reduces running time to $O(e \log^2 e)$, but its accuracy is often lower than C4.5RULES's (Cohen 1995). Cohen introduced a number of modifications to IREP, and verified empirically that RIPPERk, the resulting algorithm, is competitive with C4.5RULES in accuracy, while retaining an average running time similar to IREP's (Cohen 1995).

Catlett (Catlett 1991) has done much work in making decision tree learners scale to large datasets. A preliminary empirical study of his peepholing technique shows that it greatly reduces C4.5's running time without significantly affecting its accuracy.[1] To the best of our knowledge, peepholing has not been evaluated on any large real-world datasets, and has not been applied to rule learners.

A number of algorithms achieve running time linear in e by forgoing the greedy search method used by the learners above, in favor of exhaustive or pruned near-exhaustive search (e.g., (Weiss, Galen, & Tadepalli 1987; Smyth, Goodman, & Higgins 1990; Segal & Etzioni 1994)). However, this causes running time to become exponential in a, leading to a very high cost per example, and making application of those algorithms to large databases difficult. Holte's 1R algorithm (Holte 1993) outputs a single tree node, and is linear in a and $O(e \log e)$, but its accuracy is often much lower than C4.5's.

Ideally, we would like to have an algorithm capable of inducing accurate rules in time linear in e, without becoming too expensive in other factors. This paper describes such an algorithm and its empirical evaluation. The algorithm is presented in the next section, which also derives its worst-case time complexity. A comprehensive empirical evaluation of the algorithm is then reported and discussed.

The CWS Algorithm

Most rule induction algorithms employ a "separate and conquer" method, inducing each rule to its full length before going on to the next one. They also evaluate each rule by itself, without regard to the effect of other rules. This is a potentially inefficient approach: rules may be grown further than they need to be, only to be pruned back afterwards, when the whole rule set has already been induced. An alternative is to interleave the construction of all rules, evaluating each rule in the context of the current rule set. This can be termed a "conquering without separating" approach, by contrast with the earlier method, and has been implemented in the CWS algorithm.

In CWS, each example is a *vector* of *attribute-value pairs*, together with a specification of the *class* to which it belongs; attributes can be either *nominal* (symbolic) or *numeric*. Each rule consists of a conjunction of *antecedents* (the *body*) and a *predicted class* (the *head*). Each antecedent is a condition on a single attribute. Conditions on nominal attributes are equality tests of the form $a_i = v_{ij}$, where a_i is the attribute and v_{ij} is one of its legal values. Conditions on numeric attributes are inequalities of the form $a_i > v_{ij}$ or $a_i < v_{ij}$. Each rule in CWS is also associated with a vector of class probabilities computed from the examples it cov-

[1]Due to the small number of data points (3) reported for the single real-world domain used, it is difficult to determine the exact form of the resulting time growth (linear, log-linear, etc.).

Table 1: The CWS algorithm.

Procedure CWS

Let $RS = \emptyset$.
Repeat
    Add one active rule with empty body to RS.
    For each active rule R in RS,
        For each possible antecedent AV,
            Let $R' = R$ with AV conjoined to its body.
            Compute class probs. and pred. class for R'.
            Let $RS' = RS$ with R replaced by R'.
            If $Acc(RS') > Acc(RS)$ then let $RS = RS'$.
        If RS is unchanged then deactivate R.
Until all rules are inactive.
Return RS.

---

ers; the predicted class is the one with the highest probability. For class C_i, $P_r(C_i)$ is estimated by n_{ri}/n_r, where n_r is the total number of examples covered by rule r, and n_{ri} is the number of examples of the ith class among them. When a test example is covered by more than one rule, the class probability vectors of all the rules covering it are summed, and the class with the highest sum is chosen as the winner. This is similar to the approach followed in CN2 (Clark & Boswell 1991), with the difference that probabilities are used instead of frequencies. In a system like CN2, this could give undue weight to rules covering very few examples (the "small disjuncts" (Holte, Acker, & Porter 1989)), but we have verified empirically that in CWS this problem is largely avoided. Examples not covered by any rules are assigned to the class with the most examples in the training set.

CWS is outlined in pseudo-code in Table 1. Initially the rule set is empty, and all examples are assigned to the majority class. In each cycle a new rule with empty body is tentatively added to the set, and each of the rules already there is specialized by one additional antecedent. Thus induction of the second rule starts immediately after the first one is begun, etc., and induction of all rules proceeds in step. At the end of each cycle, if a rule has not been specialized, it is deactivated, meaning that no further specialization of it will be attempted. If the rule with empty body is deactivated, it is also deleted from the rule set. A rule with empty body predicts the default class, but this is irrelevant, because a rule only starts to take part in the classification of examples once it has at least one antecedent, and it will then predict the class that most training examples satisfying that antecedent belong to. A rule's predicted class may change as more antecedents are added to it. $Acc(RS)$ is the accuracy of the rule set RS on the training set (i.e., the fraction of examples that RS classifies correctly). Most rule induction algorithms evaluate only the accuracy (or entropy, etc.) of the changed rule on the examples that it still covers. This ignores the effect of any other rules that cover those examples, and also the effect of uncovering some examples by specializing the rule, and leads to a tendency for overspecialization that has to be countered by pruning. CWS avoids this through its global evaluation procedure and interleaved rule induction.

Let e be the number of examples, a the number of attributes, v the average number of values per attribute, c the number of classes, and r the number of rules produced. The basic step of the algorithm involves adding an antecedent to a rule and recomputing $Acc(RS')$. This requires matching all rules with all training examples, and for each example summing the class probabilities of the rules covering it, implying a time cost of $O[re(a + c)]$. Since there are $O(av)$ possible antecedents, the cost of the inner loop ("For each AV", see Table 1) is $O[avre(a + c)]$. However, this cost can be much reduced by avoiding the extensive redundancy present in the repeated computation of $Acc(RS')$. The key to this optimization is to avoid rematching all the rules that remain unchanged when attempting to specialize a given rule, and to match the unchanged antecedents of this rule with each example only once. Recomputing $Acc(RS')$ when a new antecedent AV is attempted now involves only checking whether each example already covered by the rule also satisfies that antecedent, at a cost of $O(e)$, and updating its class probabilities if it does, at a cost of $O(ec)$. The latter term dominates, and the cost of recomputing the accuracy is thus reduced to $O(ec)$, leading to a cost of $O(eavc)$ for the "For each AV" loop.

In more detail, the optimized procedure is as follows. Let $Cprobs(R)$ denote the vector of class probabilities for rule R, and $Cscores(E)$ denote the sum of the class probability vectors for all rules covering example E. $Cscores(E)$ is maintained for each example throughout. Let R be the rule whose specialization is going to be attempted. Before the "For each AV" loop begins, R is matched to all examples and those which satisfy it are selected, and, for each such example E, $Cprobs(R)$ is subtracted from $Cscores(E)$. $Cscores(E)$ now reflects the net effect of all other rules on the example. Each possible antecedent AV is now conjoined to the rule in turn, leading to a changed rule R' (or $R'(AV)$, to highlight that it is a function of AV). New class probabilities for R' are computed by finding which examples E' among the previously-selected ones satisfy AV. These probabilities are now added to $Cscores(E')$ for the still-covered examples E'. Examples that were uncovered by the specialization already have the correct values of $Cscores(E)$, since the original rule's $Cprobs(R)$ were subtracted from them beforehand. All that remains is to find the new winning class for each example E. If the example was previously misclassified and is now correctly classified, there is a change of $+1/e$ in the accuracy of the rule

Procedure CWS

Let $RS = \emptyset$.
Let $Cscores(E) = 0$ for all E, C.
Repeat
    Add one active rule R_n with empty body to RS.
    Let $Cprobs(R_n) = 0$ for all C.
    For each active rule R in RS,
        For each example E covered by R,
            Subtract $Cprobs(R)$ from $Cscores(E)$.
        For each possible antecedent AV,
            Let $\Delta Acc(AV) = 0$.
            Let $R' = R$ with AV conjoined to it.
            Compute $Cprobs(R')$ and its pred. class.
            For each example E' covered by R'
                Add $Cprobs(R')$ to $Cscores(E')$.
            For each example E covered by R
                Assign E to class with max. $Cscore(E)$.
                Compute $\Delta Acc_E(AV)$ (-1/e, 0 or +1/e).
                Add $\Delta Acc_E(AV)$ to $\Delta Acc(AV)$.
        Pick AV with max. $\Delta Acc(AV)$.
        If $\Delta Acc(AV) > 0$ then $R = R'(AV)$,
            else deactivate R.
        For each ex. E covered by R ($R = R'$ or not)
            Add $Cprobs(R)$ to $Cscores(E)$.
Until all rules are inactive.
Return RS.

set. If it was previously correctly classified, the change is $-1/e$. Otherwise there is no change. Summing this for all the examples yields the global change in accuracy. As successive antecedents are attempted, the best antecedent and maximum global change in accuracy are remembered. At the end of the loop the best antecedent is permanently added to the rule, if the corresponding change in accuracy is positive. This simply involves repeating the procedure above, this time with permanent effects. If no antecedent produces a positive change in accuracy, the rule's original class probabilities $Cprobs(R)$ are simply re-added to the $Cscores(E)$ of all the examples that it covers, leaving everything as before. This procedure is shown in pseudo-code in Table 2. Note that the optimized version produces exactly the same output as the non-optimized one; conceptually, the much simpler Table 1 is an exact description of the CWS algorithm.

The total asymptotic time complexity of the algorithm is obtained by multiplying $O(eavc)$ by the maximum number of times that the double outer loop ("Repeat ...For each R in RS ...") can run. Let s be the output size, measured as the total number of antecedents effectively added to the rule set. Then the double outer loop runs at most $O(s)$, since each computation within it (the "For each AV" loop) adds at most one antecedent. Thus the total asymptotic time complexity of CWS is $O(eavcs)$.

The factor s is also present in the complexity of other rule induction algorithms (CN2, IREP, RIPPERk, etc.), where it can typically grow to $O(ea)$. It can become a significant problem if the dataset is noisy. However, in CWS it cannot grow beyond $O(e)$, because each computation within the double outer loop ("Repeat ... For ...") either produces an improvement in accuracy or is the last one for that rule, and in a dataset with e examples at most e improvements in accuracy are possible. Ideally, s should be independent of e, and this is the assumption made in (Fürnkranz & Widmer 1994) and (Cohen 1995), and verified below for CWS.

CWS incorporates three methods for handling numeric values, selectable by the user. The default method discretizes each attribute into equal-sized intervals, and has no effect on the asymptotic time complexity of the algorithm. Discretization can also be performed using a method similar to Catlett's (Catlett 1991), repeatedly choosing the partition that minimizes entropy until one of several termination conditions is met. This causes learning time to become $O(e \log e)$, but may improve accuracy in some situations. Finally, numeric attributes can be handled directly by testing a condition of each type ($a_i > v_{ij}$ and $a_i < v_{ij}$) at each value v_{ij}. This does not change the asymptotic time complexity, but may cause v to become very large. Each of the last two methods may improve accuracy in some situations, at the cost of additional running time. However, uniform discretization is surprisingly robust (see (Dougherty, Kohavi, & Sahami 1995)), and can result in higher accuracy by helping to avoid overfitting.

Missing values are treated by letting them match any condition on the respective attribute, during both learning and classification.

Empirical Evaluation

This section describes an empirical study comparing CWS with C4.5RULES and CN2 along three variables: running time, accuracy, and comprehensibility of the output. All running times were obtained on a Sun 670 computer. Output size was taken as a rough measure of comprehensibility, counting one unit for each antecedent and consequent in each rule (including the default rule, with 0 antecedents and 1 consequent). This measure is imperfect for two reasons. First, for each system the meaning of a rule is not necessarily transparent: in CWS and CN2 overlapping rules are probabilistically combined to yield a class prediction, and in C4.5RULES each rule's antecedent side is implicitly conjoined with the negation of the antecedents of all preceding rules of different classes. Second, output simplicity is not the only factor in comprehensibility, which is ultimately subjective. However, it is an acceptable and frequently used approximation, especially when the systems being compared have similar output,

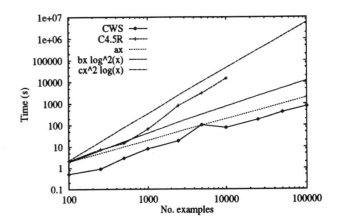

Figure 1: Learning times for the concept $abc \lor def$.

as here (see (Catlett 1991) for further discussion).

A preliminary study was conducted using the Boolean concept $abc \lor def$ as the learning target, with each disjunct having a probability of appearing in the data of 0.25, with 13 irrelevant attributes, and with 20% class noise (i.e., each class label has a probability of 0.2 of being flipped). Figure 1 shows the evolution of learning time with the number of examples for CWS and C4.5RULES, on a log-log scale. Recall that on this type of scale the slope of a straight line corresponds to the exponent of the function being plotted. Canonical functions approximating each curve are also shown, as well as $e \log^2 e$, the running time observed by Cohen (Cohen 1995) for RIPPERk and IREP.[2] CWS's running time grows linearly with the number of examples, as expected, while C4.5RULES's is $O(e^2 \log e)$. CWS is also much faster than IREP and RIPPERk (note that, even though the log-log plot shown does not make this evident, the difference between e and $e \log^2 e$ is much larger than e).

CWS is also more accurate than C4.5RULES for each number of examples, converging to within 0.6% of the Bayes optimum (80%) for only 500 examples, and reaching it with 2500, while C4.5RULES never rises above 75%. CWS's output size stabilizes at 9, while C4.5RULES's increases from 17 for 100 examples to over 2300 for 10000. Without noise, both systems learn the concept easily. Thus these results indicate that CWS is more robust with respect to noise, at least in this simple domain. CN2's behavior is similar to C4.5RULES's in time and accuracy, but it produces larger rule sets.

The relationship between the theoretical bound of $O(eavcs)$ and CWS's actual average running time was investigated by running the system on 28 datasets from the UCI repository[3] (Murphy & Aha 1995). Figure 2

[2] The constants a, b and c were chosen so as to make the respective curves fit conveniently in the graph.

[3] Audiology, annealing, breast cancer (Ljubljana), credit

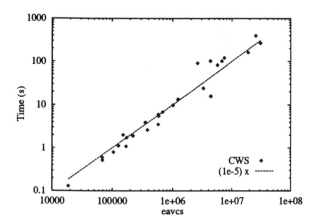

Figure 2: Relationship of empirical and theoretical learning times.

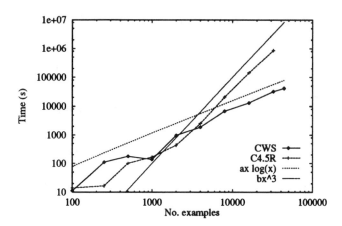

Figure 3: Learning times for the shuttle database.

plots CPU time against the product *eavcs*. Linear regression yields the line $time = 1.1 \times 10^5\ eavcs + 5.1$, with a correlation of 0.93 ($R^2 = 0.87$). Thus *eavcs* explains almost all the observed variation in CPU time, confirming the prediction of a linear bound.[4]

Experiments were also conducted on NASA's space shuttle database. This database contains 43500 training examples from one shuttle flight, and 14500 testing examples from a different flight. Each example is described by nine numeric attributes obtained from sensor readings, and there are seven possible classes, corresponding to states of the shuttle's radiators (Catlett 1991). The goal is to predict these states with very high accuracy (99–99.9%), using rules that can be taught to a human operator. The data is known to be relatively noise-free; since our interest is in induction algorithms for large noisy databases, 20% class noise was added to the training data following a procedure similar to Catlett's (each class has a 20% probability of being changed to a random class, including itself).

The evolution of learning time with the number of training examples for CWS and C4.5RULES is shown in Figure 3 on a log-log scale, with approximate asymptotes also shown, as before. CWS's curve is approximately log-linear, with the logarithmic factor attributable to the direct treatment of numeric values that was employed. (Uniform discretization resulted in linear time, but did not yield the requisite very high accuracies.) C4.5RULES's curve is roughly cubic. Ex-

trapolating from it, C4.5RULES's learning time for the full database would be well over a month, while CWS takes 11 hours.

Learning curves are shown in Figure 4. CWS's accuracy is higher than C4.5RULES's for most points, and generally increases with the number of examples, showing that there is gain in using the larger samples, up to the full dataset. Figure 5 shows the evolution of output size. CWS's is low and almost constant, while C4.5RULES's grows to more than 500 by $e = 32000$. Up to 8000 examples, CN2's running time is similar to C4.5RULES's, but its output size grows to over 1700, and its accuracy never rises above 94%.[5] In summary, in this domain CWS outperforms C4.5RULES and CN2 in running time, accuracy and output size.

Compared to the noise-free case, the degradation in CWS's accuracy is less than 0.2% after $e = 100$, the rule set size is similar, and learning time is only degraded by a constant factor (of a few percent, on average). Thus CWS is again verified to be quite robust with respect to noise.

Conclusions and Future Work

This paper introduced CWS, a rule induction algorithm that employs a "conquering without separating" strategy instead of the more common "separate-and-conquer" one. CWS interleaves the induction of all rules and evaluates proposed induction steps globally. Its asymptotic time complexity is linear in the number of examples. Empirical study shows that it can be used to advantage when the underlying concept is simple and the data is plentiful but noisy.

Directions for future work include exploring ways of boosting CWS's accuracy (or, conversely, broadening the set of concepts it can learn effectively) without affecting its asymptotic time complexity, and applying it to larger databases and problems in different areas.

---

screening (Australian), chess endgames (kr-vs-kp), Pima diabetes, echocardiogram, glass, heart disease (Cleveland), hepatitis, horse colic, hypothyroid, iris, labor negotiations, lung cancer, liver disease, lymphography, mushroom, postoperative, promoters, primary tumor, solar flare, sonar, soybean (small), splice junctions, voting records, wine, and zoology.

[4]Also, there is no correlation between the number of examples e and the output size s ($R^2 = 0.0004$).

[5]For $e > 8000$ the program crashed due to lack of memory. This may be due to other jobs running concurrently.

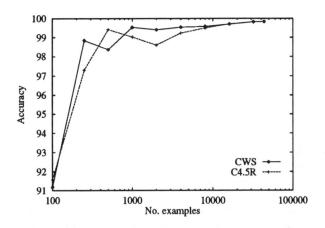

Figure 4: Learning curves for the shuttle database.

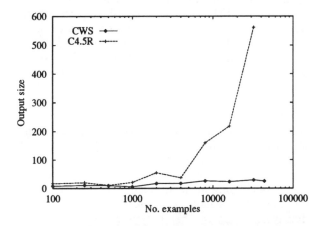

Figure 5: Output size growth for the shuttle database.

Acknowledgments

This work was partly supported by a JNICT/PRAXIS XXI scholarship. The author is grateful to Dennis Kibler for many helpful comments and suggestions, and to all those who provided the datasets used in the empirical study.

References

Brunk, C., and Pazzani, M. J. 1991. An investigation of noise-tolerant relational concept learning algorithms. In *Proceedings of the Eighth International Workshop on Machine Learning*, 389–393. Evanston, IL: Morgan Kaufmann.

Catlett, J. 1991. *Megainduction: Machine Learning on Very Large Databases*. Ph.D. Dissertation, Basser Department of Computer Science, University of Sydney, Sydney, Australia.

Clark, P., and Boswell, R. 1991. Rule induction with CN2: Some recent improvements. In *Proceedings of the Sixth European Working Session on Learning*, 151–163. Porto, Portugal: Springer-Verlag.

Cohen, W. W. 1993. Efficient pruning methods for separate-and-conquer rule learning systems. In *Proceedings of the Thirteenth International Joint Conference on Artificial Intelligence*, 988–994. Chambery, France: Morgan Kaufmann.

Cohen, W. W. 1995. Fast effective rule induction. In *Proceedings of the Twelfth International Conference on Machine Learning*, 115–123. Tahoe City, CA: Morgan Kaufmann.

Dougherty, J.; Kohavi, R.; and Sahami, M. 1995. Supervised and unsupervised discretization of continuous features. In *Proceedings of the Twelfth International Conference on Machine Learning*, 194–202. Tahoe City, CA: Morgan Kaufmann.

Fayyad, U. M., and Uthurusamy, R., eds. 1995. *Proceedings of the First International Conference on Knowledge Discovery and Data Mining*. Montréal, Canada: AAAI Press.

Fürnkranz, J., and Widmer, G. 1994. Incremental reduced error pruning. In *Proceedings of the Eleventh International Conference on Machine Learning*, 70–77. New Brunswick, NJ: Morgan Kaufmann.

Holte, R. C.; Acker, L. E.; and Porter, B. W. 1989. Concept learning and the problem of small disjuncts. In *Proceedings of the Eleventh International Joint Conference on Artificial Intelligence*, 813–818. Detroit, MI: Morgan Kaufmann.

Holte, R. C. 1993. Very simple classification rules perform well on most commonly used datasets. *Machine Learning* 11:63–91.

Michie, D.; Spiegelhalter, D. J.; and Taylor, C. C., eds. 1994. *Machine Learning, Neural and Statistical Classification*. New York: Ellis Horwood.

Murphy, P. M., and Aha, D. W. 1995. UCI repository of machine learning databases. Machine-readable data repository, Department of Information and Computer Science, University of California at Irvine, Irvine, CA.

Quinlan, J. R. 1993. *C4.5: Programs for Machine Learning*. San Mateo, CA: Morgan Kaufmann.

Segal, R., and Etzioni, O. 1994. Learning decision lists using homogeneous rules. In *Proceedings of the Twelfth National Conference on Artificial Intelligence*, 619–625. Seattle, WA: AAAI Press.

Smyth, P.; Goodman, R. M.; and Higgins, C. 1990. A hybrid rule-based/Bayesian classifier. In *Proceedings of the Ninth European Conference on Artificial Intelligence*, 610–615. Stockholm, Sweden: Pitman.

Utgoff, P. E. 1989. Incremental induction of decision trees. *Machine Learning* 4:161–186.

Weiss, S. M.; Galen, R. M.; and Tadepalli, P. V. 1987. Optimizing the predictive value of diagnostic decision rules. In *Proceedings of the Sixth National Conference on Artificial Intelligence*, 521–526. Seattle, WA: AAAI Press.

Learning from biased data using mixture models

A.J. Feelders
Data Distilleries Ltd.
Kruislaan 419
1098 VA Amsterdam
The Netherlands
email: ad@ddi.nl

Abstract

Data bases sometimes contain a non-random sample from the population of interest. This complicates the use of extracted knowledge for predictive purposes. We consider a specific type of biased data that is of considerable practical interest, namely non-random partially classified data. This type of data typically results when some screening mechanism determines whether the correct class of a particular case is known. In credit scoring the problem of learning from such a biased sample is called "reject inference", since the class label (e.g. good or bad loan) of rejected loan applications is unknown. We show that maximum likelihood estimation of so called mixture models is appropriate for this type of data, and discuss an experiment performed on simulated data using mixtures of normal components. The benefits of this approach are shown by making a comparison with the results of sample-based discriminant analysis. Some directions are given how to extend the analysis to allow for non-normal components and missing attribute values in order to make it suitable for "real-life" biased data.

Introduction

It frequently occurs that company data bases used for data mining contain a non-random sample from the population of interest. This situation complicates generalization of the patterns found in the data base, especially when the knowledge extracted is intended for predictive purposes.

We discuss a special case of such a "biased" data base, that is of considerable practical interest. We consider data bases of *partially* classified data, where the "mechanism" that determines whether the class label of a particular case is known, is non-random. Furthermore, we assume that the objective of the data mining excercise is to learn a classification rule that is able to predict the class label of an unseen case that is taken at random from the population of interest.

The situation described above typically occurs when some kind of "screening mechanism" determines whether the correct class of a particular case is known. For example, a bank decides on the basis of a combination of attributes, whether a loan application is accepted or rejected. Only when the loan is accepted will the bank eventually be able to label the loan as "good" or "bad", depending on the payment behaviour of the client. For the loan applications that are rejected, the correct class label cannot be determined with certainty. When the bank wants to use the data base to learn to tell the difference between good and bad applications, a problem arises. If only the classified cases are used, bias is introduced, since the classified cases are a non-random sample from the population of interest. A rule thus learned will only generalize reliably to the group of applicants that pass the screening mechanism (Feelders, le Loux, & Zand 1995). Furthermore, one is not able to determine in this way whether one has been incorrectly rejecting a particular group of applicants. In the credit-scoring literature, this problem is known as the *reject inference* problem. For convenience we continue to use this term, although the problem is obviously more general than credit-scoring alone. Similar cases of screening may for example occur in application areas such as marketing, insurance, and medicine.

In the next section, we formulate and classify the reject inference problem as a problem of learning with missing data. It turns out that likelihood-based approaches are appropriate for this class of missing-data problems. After that we derive the appropriate likelihood based on a mixture model formulation of the problem. We present a case study, using simulated data, to show the potential benefits of the approach. Finally, we draw a number of conclusions and indicate how mixture modeling may be applied to reject inference in more realistic situations.

Reject inference as a missing data problem

Reject inference may be formulated as a missing data problem, where the attributes X are completely observed, and the class label Y is missing for some of the observations. Following the classification used in (Little & Rubin 1987), we distinguish between the following situations, according to whether the probability of Y being missing

1. is independent of X and Y,
2. depends on X but not on Y,
3. depends on Y, and possibly X as well.

If case 1 applies, both sampling-based and likelihood-based inference may be used without the results being biased. For sampling-based, one could just perform the analysis on the classified observations, and ignore the unclassified ones. In the credit-scoring example, case 1 would apply when loan applications are accepted at random, e.g. by simply accepting all applications up to a certain number. This way of "buying experience" has been used to a certain extent by credit institutions, although there are obvious economic factors that constrain the use of this method (Hsia 1978). One may of course also consider using the standard selection mechanism, but accepting rejects with a predetermined probability. This bias could then be corrected easily by weighting the observations according to their probability of ending up in the sample.

Case 2 applies, when the observed values of Y are a random sample of the sampled values within subclasses defined by the values of X (Little & Rubin 1987). This is the case for the reject inference problem, since applications with particular predefined combinations of attributes are accepted and the other applications are rejected. Under these conditions, the missing-data mechanism is ignorable for likelihood-based inference, but not for sampling-based inference.

Finally, if case three applies the missing-data mechanism is nonignorable.

From the foregoing we conclude that likelihood-based inference is a viable approach to the reject inference problem, and start the analysis by formulating the appropriate likelihood, using mixture models.

Mixture distributions

Mixture distributions (Everitt & Hand 1981; Titterington, Smith, & Makov 1985; McLachlan & Basford 1988) are distributions which can be expressed as superpositions of a number of component distributions. Henceforth we assume that the number of components equals the relevant number of classes, so each component models a class-conditional distribution.

As an example, one might express the income density function in the form

$$f(income) = f_1(income; b)\pi_b + f_2(income; g)\pi_g$$

where π_b and π_g are, respectively, the probabilities that a loan application is bad or good (called the mixing proportions), and f_1 and f_2 are the income density functions for bad and good applications. Thus the density function of income has been expressed as a superposition of two conditional density functions. This idea is easily generalized to the multivariate case, e.g. when the joint density of income and age is expressed as a mixture of the joint densities of these features for

bad and good loans respectively. In general, a finite mixture can be written as

$$f(\mathbf{x}) = \sum_{i=1}^{c} \pi_i f_i(\mathbf{x}; \boldsymbol{\theta}_i)$$

where c is the number of components, π_i the mixing proportions and $\boldsymbol{\theta}_i$ the component parameter vectors. Usually, one assumes that it is unknown from which component observations are drawn, and one wants to estimate the *mixing proportions* and the parameters θ_i of the component distributions.

Suppose there are available attribute vectors $\mathbf{x}_j$ observed on m entities of unknown class, and sampled from a mixture C of $C_1, \ldots, C_c$ in unknown proportions $\pi_1, \ldots, \pi_c$. Then the relevant parameters can be estimated using maximum likelihood, taking the following likelihood function

$$L_1(\Psi) = \prod_{j=1}^{m} \left\{ \sum_{i=1}^{c} \pi_i f_i(\mathbf{x}_j; \boldsymbol{\theta}_i) \right\}$$

where $\Psi = (\boldsymbol{\pi}', \boldsymbol{\theta}')'$ denotes the vector of all unknown parameters.

Likelihood L_1 is appropriate when all observations are of unknown class. When we also include n classified observations, the likelihood has to be adjusted accordingly. With respect to the classified entities one distinguishes between two sampling schemes, separate sampling and mixture sampling. In case of separate sampling, random samples of size n_i are drawn from each class separately. Consequently, the relative frequencies n_i/n of the classes do not give any information about the mixing proportions. In case of mixture sampling, the classified entities are obtained by sampling from mixture C, and the resulting relative frequencies of the different classes do provide information on the mixing proportions. For reasons that become clear shortly, we proceed with formulating the likelihood under the assumption that the classified entities have been obtained by mixture sampling.

$$L_2(\Psi) = L_1(\Psi) \prod_{j=m+1}^{m+n} \left\{ \sum_{i=1}^{c} z_{ij} \pi_i f_i(\mathbf{x}_j; \boldsymbol{\theta}_i) \right\}$$

where z_{ij} equals 1 if observation j has class-label i, and zero otherwise.

For computational convenience one often considers the loglikelihood $L_3 = \log L_2$

$$L_3(\Psi) = \sum_{j=1}^{m} \log \left\{ \sum_{i=1}^{c} \pi_i f_i(\mathbf{x}_j; \boldsymbol{\theta}_i) \right\} + \sum_{j=m+1}^{m+n} \sum_{i=1}^{c} z_{ij} \log(\pi_i f_i(\mathbf{x}_j; \boldsymbol{\theta}_i))$$

Let us recall that likelihood L_2 was formulated under the assumption that both the classified and unclassified cases are random samples from the relevant mixture C.

This does unfortunately not apply to the situation considered here, since the selection of classified and unclassified observations has been performed in a systematic way; an observation is not classified if it is located in some subregion of the attribute space. If one assumes however that the total sample of size $m+n$ is a random sample from mixture C, then it can be shown (see (McLachlan 1992), section 2.8) that the relevant likelihood, apart from a combinatorial additive term, reduces to L_2. This means that one can estimate the parameters of the class-conditional (component) distributions using likelihood L_2, even when the separation between classified and unclassified observations is non-random.

A maximum likelihood estimate of Ψ can be obtained using the EM algorithm. The general strategy is based on optimizing the complete-data loglikelihood

$$L_C = \sum_{j=1}^{m+n} \sum_{i=1}^{c} z_{ij} \log(\pi_i f_i(\mathbf{x}_j; \boldsymbol{\theta}_i))$$

In the first E-step, one uses some initial estimate $\Psi^{(0)}$, to calculate the expectation of the complete-data loglikelihood. This is done by calculating the posterior probabilities

$$(1) \qquad \tau_{ij} = \frac{\pi_i f_i(\mathbf{x}_j)}{\sum_{i=1}^{c} \pi_i f_i(\mathbf{x}_j)}$$

of group membership for the unclassified cases, and entering these as values of z_{ij} in the complete-data loglikelihood. In the M-step, the algorithm chooses $\Psi^{(k)}$ that maximizes the complete-data loglikelihood that was formed in the last E-step. The E and M steps are alternated repeatedly until convergence. It has been shown that, under very weak conditions, this algorithm will yield a local maximum of likelihood L_2 of the incomplete-data specification. For a more detailed and rigorous account of the application of EM to this problem, the reader is referred to (McLachlan 1992), pages 39–43.

Example of reject inference using mixture models

In this section we give an example of the possibility of performing reject inference using mixture models. To this end we generate a synthetic data set of loan applications, and a decision rule to determine whether a loan application is accepted or rejected. For the sake of simplicity we assume that only two normally distributed attributes are recorded for each loan application. The 1000 bad loans are drawn from the following distribution

$$\mu_b = \begin{pmatrix} 96.8 \\ 15.6 \end{pmatrix} \qquad \Sigma_b = \begin{pmatrix} 584.6 & -39.7 \\ -39.7 & 3.6 \end{pmatrix}$$

The 1000 good loans are drawn from

$$\mu_g = \begin{pmatrix} 137.8 \\ 9.2 \end{pmatrix} \qquad \Sigma_g = \begin{pmatrix} 720.8 & 44.5 \\ 44.5 & 9.2 \end{pmatrix}$$

	Predicted		
True	Bad	Good	Total
Bad	959	41	1000
Good	49	951	1000
Total	1008	992	2000

Table 1: True vs. Predicted class of loans: quadratic discriminant

	Reject	Accept	Total
Bad	966	34	1000
Good	240	760	1000
Total	1206	794	2000

Table 2: True class vs. Accept/Reject

The parameter estimates resulting from the particular sample drawn are $\hat{\pi}_b = \hat{\pi}_g = 0.5$,

$$\hat{\mu}_b = \begin{pmatrix} 98.0 \\ 15.5 \end{pmatrix} \qquad \hat{\mu}_g = \begin{pmatrix} 135.8 \\ 9.1 \end{pmatrix}$$

and for the covariance matrices

$$\hat{\Sigma}_b = \begin{pmatrix} 553.0 & -38.1 \\ -38.1 & 3.6 \end{pmatrix} \qquad \hat{\Sigma}_g = \begin{pmatrix} 734.0 & 45.0 \\ 45.0 & 9.3 \end{pmatrix}$$

Since within each class, the attributes are normally distributed, with unequal covariance matrices, a quadratic discriminant function is optimal. Quadratic discriminant analysis was performed on the complete sample. The in-sample prediction performance of the resulting function is summarized in table 1. Overall, 95.5% of the observations is classified correctly. This classification result can be obtained if the correct class of all loan applications is known, which is not the case since part of the loan applications is rejected.

For each application the following score is calculated

$$S = 0.16x_1 - x_2$$

If $S > 10$, the loan is accepted, otherwise it is rejected. This score function represents the acceptance policy of the bank, which may have been determined by loan officers or by analysis of historical data. On the particular sample drawn, this yields the results as shown in table 2. The fraction of accepted loans that turns out to be bad is quite low, $34/794 \approx 4.3\%$. On the other hand, quite a number of the rejected loans are in fact good loans, $240/1206 \approx 20\%$. The predictive accuracy of the quadratic discriminant function (estimated on the complete sample) on the rejected loans is summarized in table 3. The overall accuracy of the quadratic discriminant function on the rejected loans is approximately 95.4%.

Next, we removed the class label of the rejected loans for the analysis that follows. This corresponds to the

	Predicted		
True	Bad	Good	Total
Bad	957	9	966
Good	46	194	240
Total	1003	203	1206

Table 3: True vs. Predicted class of rejected loans: quadratic discriminant

situation that the bank faces in practice. It is interesting to obtain an estimate of how many loans are incorrectly rejected, and perhaps more importantly, which of the rejected loans are in fact very likely to be good risks. We try to answer these questions in the subsequent analysis.

Application of EM algorithm

In order to estimate the class-conditional densities of good and bad loans, using the partially classified data, we use a program for fitting a mixture of normal distributions with arbitrary covariance matrices. The number of classified cases from each group must be larger than the number of attributes p, in order to avoid the occurrence of singularities in the likelihood.

The program used has been taken from (McLachlan & Basford 1988), pages 218–224. The program uses EM to find maximum likelihood estimates for the component parameters and the mixing proportions. Under the normality assumption, the likelihood estimates of π_i, μ_i, and Σ_i satisfy

$$\hat{\pi}_i = \frac{\sum_{j=1}^{m} \hat{\tau}_{ij} + \sum_{j=m+1}^{m+n} z_{ij}}{m+n}$$

and

$$\hat{\mu}_i = \frac{\sum_{j=1}^{m} \hat{\tau}_{ij}\mathbf{x}_j + \sum_{j=m+1}^{m+n} z_{ij}\mathbf{x}_j}{\sum_{j=1}^{m} \hat{\tau}_{ij} + \sum_{j=m+1}^{m+n} z_{ij}}$$

and finally

$$\hat{\Sigma}_i = \frac{\sum_{j=1}^{m} \hat{\tau}_{ij}(\mathbf{x}_j - \hat{\mu}_i)(\mathbf{x}_j - \hat{\mu}_i)'}{\sum_{j=1}^{m} \hat{\tau}_{ij} + \sum_{j=m+1}^{m+n} z_{ij}} + \frac{\sum_{j=m+1}^{m+n} z_{ij}(\mathbf{x}_j - \hat{\mu}_i)(\mathbf{x}_j - \hat{\mu}_i)'}{\sum_{j=1}^{m} \hat{\tau}_{ij} + \sum_{j=m+1}^{m+n} z_{ij}}$$

Where, because of the normality assumption the posterior probability τ_{ij} that $\mathbf{x}_j$ belongs to C_i is obtained by substituting

$$(2\pi)^{-p/2}|\Sigma_i|^{-1/2} \exp\{-1/2(\mathbf{x}_j - \mu_i)'\Sigma_i^{-1}(\mathbf{x}_j - \mu_i)\}$$

for $f_i(\mathbf{x}_j)$ into equation 1. These equations are solved by substituting the initial estimates into the right-hand sides of the equations to obtain new estimates, which are substituted into the right-hand sides, and so on, until convergence.

In case of random classification, the classified observations can be used to choose reasonable initial estimates for the mixing proportions, mean vectors and covariance matrices. This procedure is not the most sensible here since the classified observations are not a random sample from mixture C. Therefore, the intial estimates were determined as follows. The size of the total sample of loan applications equals $m + n$. There are n accepted applications and m rejected applications. The class label of the rejected applications is missing.

Furthermore, the accepted loans can be subdivided in bad (b) and good (g) loans ($n = b + g$). Then the initial estimates for the mixing proportions are chosen as follows

$$\hat{\pi}_b^{(0)} = (b+m)/(n+m), \qquad \hat{\pi}_g^{(0)} = g/(n+m)$$

The initial estimates of $\hat{\mu}_b$, $\hat{\mu}_g$, $\hat{\Sigma}_b$ and $\hat{\Sigma}_g$ are also calculated from $b + m$ and g respectively. The rationale is that one simply assumes that all rejects are in fact bad loans (which is the reason they were rejected in the first place).

Thus we get the following initial estimates for the mixing proportions

$$\hat{\pi}_b^{(0)} = \frac{1206 + 34}{2000} = 0.62, \qquad \hat{\pi}_g^{(0)} = \frac{760}{2000} = 0.38$$

For the covariance matrices we have

$$\hat{\Sigma}_b^{(0)} = \begin{pmatrix} 562.9 & -30.1 \\ -30.1 & 9.7 \end{pmatrix} \qquad \hat{\Sigma}_g^{(0)} = \begin{pmatrix} 552.7 & 48.4 \\ 48.4 & 8.7 \end{pmatrix}$$

Finally, for the group means we get

$$\hat{\mu}_b^{(0)} = \begin{pmatrix} 100.4 \\ 14.4 \end{pmatrix} \qquad \hat{\mu}_g^{(0)} = \begin{pmatrix} 143.8 \\ 8.9 \end{pmatrix}$$

After 15 iterations the algorithm converged, yielding the following parameter estimates. For the mixing proportions

$$\hat{\pi}_b^* = 0.507, \qquad \hat{\pi}_g^* = 0.493$$

For the covariance matrices

$$\hat{\Sigma}_b^* = \begin{pmatrix} 552.8 & -38.7 \\ -38.7 & 3.7 \end{pmatrix} \qquad \hat{\Sigma}_g^* = \begin{pmatrix} 739.7 & 46.2 \\ 46.2 & 9.3 \end{pmatrix}$$

The estimates for the group means are

$$\hat{\mu}_b^* = \begin{pmatrix} 98.3 \\ 15.4 \end{pmatrix} \qquad \hat{\mu}_g^* = \begin{pmatrix} 136.0 \\ 9.1 \end{pmatrix}$$

To test the sensitivity of the solution to the initial estimates, we performed the same analysis with initial estimates determined on the classified observations only. In that case, the initial estimates for the mixing proportions are way of,

$$\hat{\pi}_b^{(0)} = 34/794 = 0.043, \qquad \hat{\pi}_g^{(0)} = 760/794 = 0.957$$

The initial estimates for the means and covariance of good loans are near the true value, but for the bad

	Predicted		
True	Bad	Good	Total
Bad	959	7	966
Good	51	189	240
Total	1010	196	1206

Table 4: True vs. Predicted class of rejected loans: mixture model

	Predicted		
True	Bad	Good	Total
Bad	966	0	966
Good	169	71	240
Total	1135	71	1206

Table 5: True vs. Predicted class of rejected loans: linear case

loans they are strongly biased because of the selection effect. For the covariance matrices we have

$$\hat{\Sigma}_b^{(0)} = \begin{pmatrix} 135.5 & -2.6 \\ -2.6 & 0.9 \end{pmatrix} \qquad \hat{\Sigma}_g^{(0)} = \begin{pmatrix} 552.7 & 48.4 \\ 48.4 & 8.7 \end{pmatrix}$$

Finally, for the group means we get

$$\hat{\mu}_b^{(0)} = \begin{pmatrix} 149.0 \\ 11.6 \end{pmatrix} \qquad \hat{\mu}_g^{(0)} = \begin{pmatrix} 143.8 \\ 8.9 \end{pmatrix}$$

After 21 iterations the algorithm converged to the same solution as obtained in the previous analysis.

Most relevant is how well the resulting discriminant rule classifies the rejects. This is summarized in table 4. The proportion of correct classifications of rejects is about 95.2%, which is only slightly worse than the performance of the quadratic discriminant function trained on the complete sample. Perhaps more importantly, 189 of the 196 cases predicted to be good loans are in fact good loans, which is approximately 96.4%.

Comparison to sample-based approaches

To illustrate the severe bias that sample based approaches may suffer from, we have performed linear and quadratic discriminant analysis on the accepted loans, as if it were a random sample from the population of loan applicants. The results for the linear case are summarized in table 5, for the quadratic case in table 6. In both cases, the class priors (mixing proportions) were taken to be the same as the initial estimates in the EM algorithm.

For the linear case, the overall percentage of correct classifications is about 86%. Of the 240 good loans, only 71 are predicted to be good. For the quadratic case, the overall result is about 69.8% correct classifications. Out of 966 bad rejects, 285 (± 30%) are predicted to be good loans.

	Predicted		
True	Bad	Good	Total
Bad	681	285	966
Good	79	161	240
Total	760	446	1206

Table 6: True vs. Predicted class of rejected loans: quadratic case

Discussion

The example discussed has admittedly been constructed to show the possible benefits of the mixture modeling approach to biased data, or more specifically non-random partially classified data. More realistic case studies should be performed to test the practical usefulness of this approach.

One may for example consider situations where the attributes are not real valued, but categorical. In that case mixtures of bernouilli or multinomial components may be used. Problems with mixed real, binary and categorical attributes can be analysed using joint densities with mixed components of the three types (Ghahramani & Jordan 1994; Lawrence & Krzanowski 1996).

One may also consider situations where the class-conditional densities are themselves mixtures. Preliminary data analysis may reveal that a class-conditional density should be modeled as a mixture of component densities rather than a single density. This is for example done in (McLachlan & Gordon 1989) for an application in medicine. A semi-parametric approach is taken in (Hastie & Tibshirani 1996), where a method and algorithm for discriminant analysis by normal mixtures is described. The algorithm can be adjusted quite easily to allow for missing class labels.

Finally, one may also consider situations where missing values occur in the attributes, and not just in the class label. This situation is analysed in (Little & Rubin 1987) and (Ghahramani & Jordan 1994).

Although each of these extensions will obviously complicate the analysis to a certain extent, they can all be handled within the mixture modeling framework using EM to obtain maximum likelihood estimates of the relevant parameters.

Conclusion

The mixture modeling approach is well suited to analyse non-random partially classified data, and avoids the bias that sample-based approaches have. This approach may be applied to any partially classified data set, where some kind of "screening" mechanism determines which observation is classified and which not. Furthermore the mixture modeling framework using EM is flexible enough to allow for non-normal data, class-conditional densities that are mixtures, and missing attribute values. This flexibility indicates that it is also applicable to real-world messy data sets. Performance of realistic case studies, and development of suitable software to perform these studies, must substantiate this claim in the future.

References

Everitt, B., and Hand, D. 1981. *Finite mixture distributions*. London: Chapman and Hall.

Feelders, A.; le Loux, A.; and Zand, J. v. t. 1995. Data mining for loan evaluation at ABN AMRO: a case study. In Fayyad, U., and Uthurusamy, R., eds., *Proceedings of KDD-95*, 106–111. AAAI Press.

Ghahramani, Z., and Jordan, M. I. 1994. Supervised learning from incomplete data via an EM approach. In Cowan, J.; Tesauro, G.; and Alspector, J., eds., *Advances in Neural Information Processing Systems 6*. San Fransisco, CA: Morgan Kaufmann.

Hastie, T., and Tibshirani, R. 1996. Discriminant analysis by gaussian mixtures. *Journal of the Royal Statistical Society B* 58(1):155–176.

Hsia, D. 1978. Credit scoring and the equal credit opportunity act. *The Hastings law journal* 30:371–448.

Lawrence, C., and Krzanowski, W. 1996. Mixture separation for mixed-mode data. *Statistics and Computing* 6:85–92.

Little, R. J., and Rubin, D. B. 1987. *Statistical analysis with missing data*. New York: John Wiley & Sons.

McLachlan, G. J., and Basford, K. E. 1988. *Mixture models, inference and applications to clustering*. New York: Marcel Dekker.

McLachlan, G., and Gordon, R. 1989. Mixture models for partially unclassified data: a case study of renal venous renin in hypertension. *Statistics in Medicine* 8:1291–1300.

McLachlan, G. J. 1992. *Discriminant analysis and statistical pattern recognition*. New York: Wiley.

Titterington, D.; Smith, A.; and Makov, U. 1985. *Statistical analysis of finite mixture distributions*. Chichester: John Wiley & Sons.

Discovery of Relevant New Features
by Generating Non-Linear Decision Trees

Andreas Ittner
Dept. of Computer Science
Chemnitz University of Technology
D-09107 Chemnitz, GERMANY
andreas.ittner@informatik.tu-chemnitz.de

Michael Schlosser
Dept. of Electrical Engineering
Fachhochschule Koblenz
D-56075 Koblenz, GERMANY
schlosser@koblenz.fh-rpl.de

Abstract

Most decision tree algorithms using selective induction focus on univariate, i.e. axis-parallel tests at each internal node of a tree. Oblique decision trees use multivariate linear tests at each non-leaf node. One well-known limitation of selective induction algorithms, however, is its inadequate description of hypotheses by task-supplied original features. To overcome this limitation this paper reports a novel approach to constructive induction, called non-linear decision trees. The crux of this method consists of the generation of new features and the augmentation of the original primitive features with these new ones. This method can be considered as a powerful tool in KDD, because the constructed new features remain understandable and permit an interpretation by experts. The resulted non-linear decision trees are more accurate than their axis-parallel or oblique counterparts. Experiments on several artificial and real-world data sets demonstrate this property.

Introduction

One well-known limitation of selective induction algorithms is its inadequate description of hypotheses by task-supplied primitive features. To overcome this limitation, constructive induction algorithms transform the original feature space into a more adequate space by creating new features and augmenting the primitive features with the new ones. This method can be considered as a powerful tool in Knowledge Discovery and Data Mining (KDD), if the new features "... may be interpreted as useful or interesting knowledge" (Fayyad et al. 1996).

This paper introduces an approach for discovery relevant new features by generating non-linear decision trees (NDT) (Ittner 1995). This kind of decision trees is based on the augmentation of the feature space. Section 2 (The Problem) is dedicated to the problem of feature construction and state of the art solutions. Section 3 (Manufacturing New Features) elaborates the field of manufacturing new features. This is the key idea underpinning the discovery of relevant new features by a non-linear decision tree method. The fourth section (NDT) deals with a comparison of different kinds of decision trees. Moreover, we introduce our novel method for non-linear decision tree generation with respect to feature construction. Results of using this method to classify several real-world and one artificial data sets are presented in section 5 (Experiments). Section 6 (Conclusions) summarizes the lessons learned from these experiments.

The Problem

Good representations are crucial for solving difficult problems in the fields of Artificial Intelligence (AI) as well as in KDD. Feature construction and the extraction of constructed new features are essential steps to achieve this goal. But what does feature construction mean? The following definition of it was stated in (Matheus & Rendell 1989):

Feature Construction: the application of a set of constructive operators $\{o_1, o_2, ..., o_n\}$ to a set of existing features $\{f_1, f_2, ..., f_m\}$ resulting in the construction of one or more new features $\{f'_1, f'_2, ..., f'_N\}$ intended for use in describing the target concept.

The construction of a new feature may be regarded as a combination of existing features, depending on kind of existing features.

The investigation of all combinations of features is a means used to construct a subset of the H most important features from the h possible ones. The number of these combinations is $\binom{h}{H}$. It is obvious that this method is not applicable to practical problems if the feature space is of high dimension. For that reason combinations of features are limited to pairwise or only few combinations and to simple arithmetical operations, like addition, subtraction, multiplication and division up to now.

There are representative examples of systems that perform and employ a variety of feature construction techniques. For instance the system BACON (Langley et al.1984) focuses on the discovery of empirical laws that summarize numerical data. In order to achieve this goal, BACON requires some information about the form that plausible laws may take. The technique used in ABACUS (Falkenhainer & Michalski 1990) depicts quantitative discovery as a search through the space of equations that could possibly describe the behavior of the observed data. This search process mathematically combines variables representing terms to form new terms. For example x and y might be combined to form $x + y$. But also in the field of modeling, producing new features plays an important role. If we consider the problem of classifying the chessboard positions, for example, formed by randomly placing the three pieces White king, White rook and Black king as 'illegal' or 'legal' (Michie et al. 1994). One important step here is to augment the six features (rank and raw of each piece) with fifteen new ones, generated by forming all possible pairwise differences among the original six. In this way it is possible to express in a decision-tree language certain key sub-description, such as crucial same-file and same-rank relations between White rook and Black king.

Manufacturing New Features

In the field of classification there exist many examples of feature construction. Especially in an exploratory study, practitioners often combine features in an attempt to increase the descriptive power of the resulting decision tree/rules (Michie et al. 1994). Data set providers often think that particular combinations, like the sum of two features $x + y$ or ratios like $\frac{x}{x+y}$ are potentially more useful and important than each feature separately.

Background knowledge of a domain is often helpful in determining what combination of the primitive features to use. In the well-known Iris data set (see section Experiments), for example, the product of the features $F3=Petal\ Length$ and $F4=Petal\ Width$ gives a single feature which has the dimension area, and might be labeled as *Petal Area* (Michie et al. 1994). In this case, the single feature *Petal Area* is a basis for a decision rule that produces only four errors in the whole data set. The notion "area", as a the product of length and width, is well-understood in geometry and can be viewed as a new quality in describing the underlying concept of data. Because "... feature construction is a difficult and poorly understood problem" (Matheus & Rendell 1989) one solution is to have a system to construct new features automatically. One approach,

for example, consists of the pairwise generation of the new features from the primitive ones. After the feature construction we can use a selective induction method, for example a decision tree algorithm to evaluate these new features. In the case of Iris data the decision tree, based on the originally existing features, is shown in Figure 1.

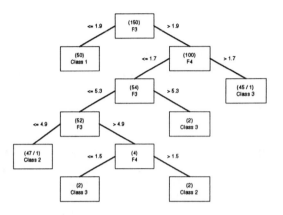

Figure 1: Decision tree of the Iris data set (based on the originally existing primitive features)

After the construction of the pairwise products of the given primitive features and the augmentation to the primitive ones we obtain the following tree [Figure 2].

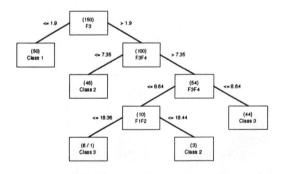

Figure 2: Decision tree of the Iris data set (based on the primitive and new features)

This one is a decision tree with linear or non-linear tests at each internal node. Figure 3 shows the linear and non-linear separations of examples from the three different classes (+,-,x) in the feature space (*F3-F4-space*).

In this case, the simple combination of the original features is the source of power for the resulting decision tree (confer the size of the trees and the expressive power of its internal tests in Figure 1 and 2). Except that, we obtain new ultimately understandable

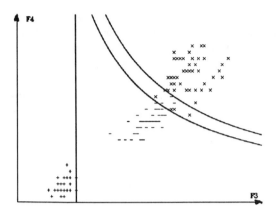

Figure 3: Iris data (linear and non-linear separation)

features ($F3F4$ and $F1F2$) that permit an interpretation by the data set provider. In the spirit of KDD this means "... to make patterns understandable to humans in order to facilitate a better understanding of the underlying data" (Fayyad et al. 1996).

The approach of constructive induction algorithms is not limited to continuous-valued features. There are also many methods for the domain of binary and nominal features. The algorithms FRINGE and GREEDY3 (Pagallo & Haussler 1989) create new Boolean features only by using logical operators to construct new features that are more adequate to describe hypotheses. ID2-of-3 (Murphy & Pazzani 1991) creates M-of-N representations as new Boolean features. X-of-N (Zheng 1995) can be considered as an extension of M-of-N, that constructs new nominal features. The common main advantage of all constructive induction algorithms lies in the stronger expressive power of a concept found by these algorithms. In the following section we describe a method to discover relevant new features as combinations of the continuous primitive ones.

Non-Linear Decision Trees

A decision tree algorithm is an approach of selective induction. This section deals with different decision tree paradigms.

Decision trees have been used for classification since the 1980's. Breiman's work on CART (Breiman et al. 1984) and Quinlan's work (Quinlan 1983), (Quinlan 1986) on ID3 and C4.5 provided the foundations for what has become a large field of research on one of the central techniques of machine learning. Originally decision trees were proposed for classification in domains with symbolic-valued features (Quinlan 1986). Later Quinlan extended them to numeric domains (Quinlan 1993), where the tests have the form $x_i > t$, where x_i is one feature and t is a constant, namely the cut-

point of this feature. Consequently, this binarization can be viewed as a special case of feature construction and an essential requirement for the following feature selection.

This kind of decision trees may be called *univariate* or *axis-parallel*, because the tests on each non-leaf node of the tree are equivalent to axis-parallel hyperplanes in the feature space [Figure 6]. Another class of decision trees tests a linear combination of the features at each internal node (Breiman et al. 1984), (Utgoff & Brodley 1991), (Murthy et al. 1993). This kind is called *multivariate linear* or *oblique* decision tree, because these tests are equivalent to hyperplanes at an oblique orientation to the axes of the feature space [Figure 7]. Note that axis-parallel decision trees produce partitionings of the feature space in form of hyper-rectangles that are parallel to the feature axes, while oblique decision trees produce polygonal partitionings of the feature space. In contrast to these both techniques, our approach, called *non-linear multivariate* decision tree, produces partitionings in form of a curved hypersurface, namely a hypersurface of the second degree [Figure 8].

The novel method introduced now is based on the combination of primitive features and the augmentation of the feature space before tree generation. For example, as a result of combination of the primitive features $f_1 = x_1$ and $f_2 = x_2$ we see a new feature $f_1' = o_1(f_1, f_2) = x_1 o x_2$ as a new dimension in the feature space [Figure 4].

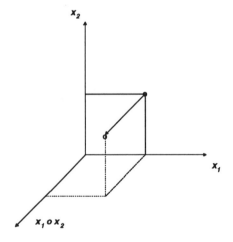

Figure 4: Augmentation of the Feature Space

Because the space of possible new features is exponential, we constrain ourselves to a special kind of feature combination. The key idea is the construction of all possible pairwise products and squares of n numerical primitive features. That means that we use only multiplication as a constructive operator. As a result we obtain $\frac{n^2+3n}{2}$ features. That is the sum of n primitive ones, n squared ones and $\frac{n(n-1)}{2}$ pairwise products of primitive features.

The second applied constructive operator (addition) in this case is a result of linear combinations of these terms. This operator application to the linear terms, products and squares is not explicitly determined by the user. In contrast, the linear combinations result automatically by a decision tree algorithm (see below).

The linear combination of the constructed terms form an equation of a hypersurface of the second degree. For example, in the two-dimensional case, the form of an equation of a curve of the second degree is:

$$ax_1^2 + 2bx_1x_2 + cx_2^2 + 2dx_1 + 2ex_2 + f = 0.$$

An ellipse, a circle, a hyperbola, a parabola, and a pair of two lines are described by this equation. In the m-dimensional case ($m > 2$) we see elliptoids, hyperboloids, paraboloids and so on.

Now we use a decision tree algorithm, in our case OC1 (Murthy et al. 1993), to construct an oblique decision tree in the new created higher-dimensional feature space. This algorithm generates hyperplanes at an oblique orientation as a test of a linear combination of primitive and new created features at each internal node. In general these hyperplanes correspond to non-linear hypersurfaces in the original feature space of primitive features.

If we consider a two-dimensional feature space with the original features x_1 and x_2, for example, the number of dimensions of the new feature space is five. We obtain two renamed features $y_1 = x_1$, $y_2 = x_2$ and three constructed ones, $y_3 = x_1x_2$, $y_4 = x_1^2$ and $y_5 = x_2^2$. Now it is possible to generate an oblique decision tree in this y-feature space. As a result we obtain an oblique decision tree that is equivalent to a non-linear decision tree in the original x-space after a re-transformation of the features.

In the next section, we present empirical studies, using artificial and real-world data sets, that analyze the ability of our approach to construct non-linear decision trees that are more accurate than their axis-parallel or oblique counterparts.

Experiments

We present results of experiments we performed creating NDT on four real-world and one artificial data sets. The results are summarized in Tables 1-3. We compare the accuracies, the number of leaves and the depths of the trees with axis-parallel (C4.5-like) and oblique (OC1) decision trees. The best results are highlighted in the following tables.

Table 1: Accuracy of the Trees (%)

	iris	diab	heart	vehic	spiral
C4.5-like	93.33	72.92	75.93	71.87	56.25
OC1-two	96.00	71.88	75.19	69.03	53.12
OC1-gain	94.67	72.27	77.78	71.04	46.35
OC1-gini	**96.67**	73.18	76.67	68.32	43.75
NDT-two	96.00	**75.00**	**78.15**	72.70	79.69
NDT-gain	**96.67**	73.96	77.41	72.34	**81.25**
NDT-gini	**96.67**	73.18	77.41	**73.76**	76.56

Table 2: Number of Leaves of the Trees

	iris	diab	heart	vehic	spiral
C4.5-like	3.1	12.8	**4.0**	52.4	28.7
OC1-two	3.2	10.6	4.9	51.1	13.0
OC1-gain	**3.0**	11.2	4.8	54.6	17.2
OC1-gini	3.2	8.8	5.6	35.5	12.1
NDT-two	3.2	9.9	6.5	38.2	**8.0**
NDT-gain	**3.0**	13.9	5.3	40.7	9.7
NDT-gini	**3.0**	**5.9**	9.9	**31.7**	9.5

We used the OC1 algorithm with different impurity and goodness measures to construct an axis-parallel tree (C4.5-like) in the original feature space and oblique decision trees in the original and in the new created higher-dimensional feature space, respectively. The measures are the Twoing Rule (two), the Gini-Index (gini), and the Gain Criterion (gain). They are exhaustively described in (Murthy et al. 1994). All our experiments used 10-fold cross-validation trials. Table 4 summarizes the time of computation for the tree generation. The increasing time of computation can be considered as one weakness of our approach.

Data Sets

We used several well-known data sets for our experiments. The data sets are Iris data (iris), Diabetes

Table 3: Depth of the Trees

	iris	diab	heart	vehic	spiral
C4.5-like	2.1	5.9	2.4	13.8	15.7
OC1-two	2.2	4.9	2.6	10.7	6.8
OC1-gain	**2.0**	5.9	**2.1**	14.5	13.1
OC1-gini	2.2	4.2	2.6	**9.6**	8.1
NDT-two	2.2	4.9	2.8	13.3	**6.0**
NDT-gain	**2.0**	5.7	2.4	16.7	8.1
NDT-gini	**2.0**	**3.6**	3.9	12.5	7.5

Table 4: Time of Computation (sec.)

	iris	diab	heart	vehic	spiral
OC1	110	2526	620	5891	382
NDT	192	6766	939	10742	373

Diagnosis (diab), Heart Disease (heart), and Vehicle Silhouettes (vehic). The artificial data set is the Spiral Data Set (spiral).

Spiral Data Set (spiral). This is an artificial data set, which offers the opportunity to demonstrate the ability of non-linear partitioning of feature space exemplarily. Each of the 192 examples is described by two features. Each one belongs to one of two categories. All examples of a class form a spiral in the 2D feature space [Figure 5]. As Figure 5 shows, the examples of the two categories of the artificial spiral data set are quite hard to separate from each other. An axis-parallel, i.e. univariate partitioning of the feature space, is shown in Figure 6.

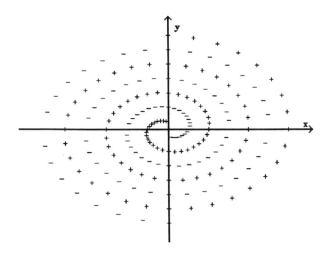

Figure 5: Spiral Data Set

Figure 7 gives an illustration of a multivariate linear partitioning of the feature space with the remarkably number of 38 'hyperplanes'. The oblique decision tree was generated by the OC1 algorithm. Figure 8 shows the non-linear partitioning of the feature space with only 11 curves of the second order. As a special kind of these curves we see two axis-parallel partitioning of the feature space. The corresponding decision tree is a non-linear decision tree that tests a non-linear combination of the original primitive features at each internal node. These tests correspond to tests of a linear combination of the new created features, which can

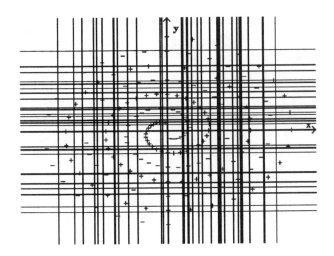

Figure 6: Axis-Parallel Partitioning

be considered as the axes of a higher-dimensional new feature space.

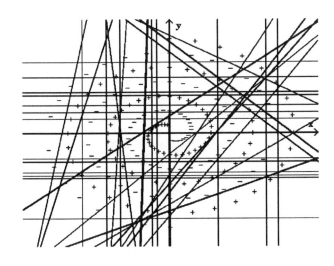

Figure 7: Oblique Partitioning

Conclusions and Further Work

This paper has described a new approach for constructing non-linear decision trees. The ability to produce non-linear splits at each internal node broadens the capabilities of decision tree algorithms and contributes to the society of KDD methods. Our experiments presented here are a convincing demonstration of the usefulness of non-linear separations with respect to the accuracy and the descriptive power of the underlying concept of data. The simple combination of primitive features to new ones gives the opportunity of an oblique partitioning in the higher-dimensional feature space. This oblique partitioning corresponds to a non-

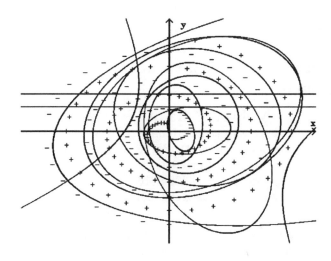

Figure 8: Non-Linear Partitioning of the Space

linear partitioning of the primitive feature space. Our approach fulfills a main goal of KDD to construct new features (patterns), which are easy to understand and to interpret by experts.

The empirical studies have demonstrated that non-linear decision tree algorithms produce more accurate trees than their axis-parallel or oblique counterparts. We plan to extend our experiments with non-linear decision trees to an inductive generation of new features by gradually increasing of the complexity of these ones.

Acknowledgments. The authors thank Werner Dilger, Rainer Staudte and Sarah Malloy for providing comments. Thanks also to two anonymous reviewers for helpful suggestions.

References

Breiman, L., Friedman, J. H., Olshen, R. A. & Stone, C. J. (1984). *Classification and Regression Trees*, Wadsworth International Group.

Brodley, C. E., Utgoff, P. E. (1995). Multivariate Decision Trees, In *Machine Learning*, 19, 45-77.

Falkenhainer, B. C., Michalski, R. S. (1990). Integrating Quantitative and Qualitative Discovery in the ABACUS System. In Y. Kodratoff, R. S. Michalski (eds.), *Machine Learning - An Artificial Intelligence Approach*, Vol. 3, Morgan Kaufmann.

Fayyad, U. M., Piatetsky-Shapiro, G., Smyth, P. (1996). From Data Mining to Knowledge Discovery: An Overview., In Fayyad, U. M., Piatetsky-Shapiro, G., Smyth, P. & Uthurusamy R. (eds.), *Advances in Knowledge Discovery and Data Mining.*, AAAI/MIT Press.

Ittner, A. (1995). *Ermittlung von funktionalen Attributabhängigkeiten und deren Einfluß auf maschinelle Lernverfahren*, Diplomarbeit, TU Chemnitz-Zwickau.

Langley, P., Bradshaw, G. L., Simon, H. A. (1984). Rediscovering Chemistry with the BACON System, In R. S. Michalski, J. G. Carbonell & T. M. Mitchell (eds.), *Machine Learning: An Artificial Intelligence Approach*, Morgan Kaufmann, San Mateo, CA.

Matheus, C. J., Rendell, L. A. (1989). Constructive Induction on Decision Trees. In *Proceedings of the 11th International Joint Conference on Artificial Intelligence (IJCAI-89).*, Morgan Kaufmann.

Michie, D., Spiegelhalter, D. J., Taylor, C. C. (eds.) (1994). *Machine Learning, Neural and Statistical Classification*, Ellis Horwood.

Murphy, P. M., Pazzani, M. J. (1991). ID2-of-3: Constructive induction of M-of-N concepts for discriminators in decision trees, In *Proceedings of the 8th International Machine Learning Workshop*, Morgan Kaufmann.

Murthy, S., Kasif, S., Salzberg, S., Beigel, R. (1993). OC1: Randomized induction of oblique decision trees, In *Proceedings of the 11th National Conference on Artificial Intelligence (AAAI-93)*, MIT-Press.

Murthy, S., Kasif, S., Salzberg, S. (1994). A System for Induction of Oblique Decision Trees, In *Journal of Artificial Intelligence Research*, Vol 2, Morgan Kaufmann.

Pagallo, G., Haussler, D. (1989). Two algorithms that learn DNF by discovering relevant features, In *Proceedings of the 6th International Machine Learning Workshop*, Ithaca N.Y., Morgan Kaufmann.

Quinlan, J. R. (1983). Learning efficient classification procedures and their application to chess end games, In R. S. Michalski, J. G. Carbonell & T. M. Mitchell (eds.), *Machine Learning: An Artificial Intelligence Approach*, Morgan Kaufmann, San Mateo, CA.

Quinlan, J. R. (1986). Induction of decision trees, In *Machine Learning* 1(1):81-106.

Quinlan, J. R. (1993). *C4.5: Programs for Machine Learning*, Morgan Kaufmann, San Mateo, CA.

Utgoff, P. E., Brodley, C. E. (1991). *Linear Machine Decision Trees*, COINS Technical Report 91-10, Dept. of Computer Science, University of Massachusetts.

Zheng, Z. (1995). Constructing Nominal X-of-N Attributes, In *Proceedings of the 14th International Joint Conference on Artificial Intelligence*, Morgan Kaufmann.

Error-Based and Entropy-Based Discretization of Continuous Features

Ron Kohavi
Data Mining and Visualization
Silicon Graphics, Inc.
2011 N. Shoreline Blvd
Mountain View, CA 94043-1389
`ronnyk@sgi.com`

Mehran Sahami
Gates Building 1A, Room 126
Computer Science Department
Stanford University
Stanford, CA 94305-9010
`sahami@cs.stanford.edu`

Abstract

We present a comparison of error-based and entropy-based methods for discretization of continuous features. Our study includes both an extensive empirical comparison as well as an analysis of scenarios where error minimization may be an inappropriate discretization criterion. We present a discretization method based on the C4.5 decision tree algorithm and compare it to an existing entropy-based discretization algorithm, which employs the Minimum Description Length Principle, and a recently proposed error-based technique. We evaluate these discretization methods with respect to C4.5 and Naive-Bayesian classifiers on datasets from the UCI repository and analyze the computational complexity of each method. Our results indicate that the entropy-based MDL heuristic outperforms error minimization on average. We then analyze the shortcomings of error-based approaches in comparison to entropy-based methods.

Introduction

Although real-world classification and data mining tasks often involve continuous features, there exist many algorithms which focus on learning only in nominal feature spaces (Apte & Hong 1996; Cost & Salzberg 1993).

In order to handle continuous features, such algorithms regularly employ simple discretization methods, such as uniform binning of the data, to produce nominal features. Such naive discretization of the data can be potentially disastrous for data mining as critical information may be lost due to the formation of inappropriate bin boundaries. Furthermore, discretization itself may be viewed as a form of knowledge discovery in that critical values in a continuous domain may be revealed. It has also been noted by Catlett (1991) that for very large data sets (as is common in data mining applications), discretizing continuous features can often vastly reduce the time necessary to induce a classifier. As a result, better discretization methods have been developed, but these methods are often not directly compared to each each other, or analyzed for when they may be appropriate to employ.

Dougherty, Kohavi, & Sahami (1995) provided an initial comparison of uniform binning, the discretization method proposed by Holte (1993), and an entropy based method proposed by Fayyad & Irani (1993) using two induction algorithms: C4.5 (Quinlan 1993) and a Naive-Bayesian classifier (Good 1965). Since that study reported that the entropy-based discretization method was the most promising method, we compare that method to two other methods: C4.5-based discretization and error-based discretization.

The C4.5-based discretization is a new entropy-based method that applies C4.5 to each continuous feature separately to determine the number of thresholds and their values. Hence, we still use an entropy-based metric (gain-ratio), but use a different criterion for the number of intervals, *i.e.*, determined by pruning as opposed to Fayyad and Irani's stopping criteria.

The error-based discretization we compare has been proposed by Maass (1994) and used in the T2 algorithm (Auer, Holte, & Maass 1995). Given a number of intervals, k, the method constructs the optimal discretization of a continuous feature with respect to classification error in polynomial time.

We employ the discretization methods listed above in conjunction with C4.5 and Naive-Bayesian classifiers as induction algorithms that are run on the discretized data and show the effectiveness of each discretization method. We also present the computational complexity of each discretization technique. In light of our empirical findings, we analyze situations in which error-based discretization may be inappropriate.

Methods

We briefly describe the induction algorithms and discretization methods we compare.

Induction Algorithms

In our experimental study, we test different discretization methods as applied to C4.5 and Naive-Bayesian classifiers. C4.5 (Quinlan 1993) is a state-of-the-art top-down decision tree induction algorithm. When we discretize features, we declare them nominal, thus C4.5 does a multi-way split on all possible thresholds.

The Naive-Bayesian induction algorithm computes the posterior probability of the classes given the data, assuming independence between the features for each class. The probabilities for nominal features are estimated using counts and a Gaussian distribution is assumed for continuous features (in the undiscretized cases). The Naive-Bayesian classifier used in our experiments is the one implemented in $\mathcal{MLC}$++ (Kohavi et al. 1994).

Discretization Algorithms

We focus on two discretization methods using entropy and a recently developed error-based discretization method. These methods are described below. A comprehensive review of the existing discretization literature is found in Dougherty, Kohavi, & Sahami (1995).

Fayyad and Irani's Method First, we consider discretization based on an entropy minimization heuristic proposed by Fayyad & Irani (1993). The method is similar to that of Catlett (1991) but offers a more motivated heuristic for deciding on the number of intervals. This algorithm uses the class information entropy of candidate partitions to select threshold boundaries for discretization. It finds a single threshold that minimizes the entropy function over all possible thresholds; it is then recursively applied to both of the partitions induced. The *Minimal Description Length Principle* (MDLP) is employed to determine a stopping criteria for the recursive discretization strategy. We refer to this algorithm as **Ent-MDL**.

In our implementation, each split considered in the entropy method takes $O(m \log m)$ time, where m is the number of instances and when we assume a fixed number of classes. If the method chooses k thresholds, then at most $2k + 1$ threshold computations are done. Hence, an upper bound on the time complexity is $O(km \log m)$. This bound could be improved using a smarter implementation that would sort only once. If we assume that the thresholds form a balanced tree, then the time to sort the instances at a given level is $O(m \log m)$ and the time bound can be reduced to $O(\log k \cdot m \log m)$. In practice, we expect the behavior to be somewhere between these two bounds. The space complexity of this method is $O(m)$ because only the feature value and label of each instance is stored.

C4.5 Discretization The C4.5 decision tree induction algorithm can also be used as a discretization method. In this sense, C4.5 is first applied to each continuous feature *separately* to build a tree which contains binary splits that only test the single continuous feature. The C4.5 algorithm uses gain-ratio, an entropy-based metric, to determine the partitions for discrete intervals. We refer to this new method as **C4.5-Disc**.

This method is significantly different from that of Fayyad & Irani (1993) in that the latter employs a top-down stopping criterion based on MDLP, whereas applying C4.5 to a single feature builds a complete tree for that feature and then applies pruning to find an appropriate number of nodes in the tree (*i.e.*, the number of discretization intervals) in a bottom-up approach. After the tree for a single feature is built and pruned using C4.5, we can simply use the threshold values at each node of the induced tree to be the threshold values for a discretization of that continuous feature. We found that C4.5's default pruning confidence (the c parameter) was not pruning enough and forced it to pruned more heavily in order to prevent forming many intervals. To this end, we set the confidence factor to 1 (down from 25). Minor variations of the c value did not have much effect on our experiments. To prevent "overfitting" this value, we did not try to optimize it for our experiments.

The time complexity to discretize features using C4.5 requires that a full single-feature tree be built and then pruned back. The build time dominates the pruning time, but even if only k intervals are finally returned, many more must be constructed. If we assume that at least some constant portion p of the instances (say 10%) are split off each time, then the time bound is $O(\log_{1/(1-p)} m \cdot m \log m)$ because there can be at most $\log_{1/(1-p)} m$ levels in the tree, each taking $O(m \log m)$ time. The space complexity of the C4.5 discretization is $O(m)$ because only the feature value and label of each instance must be stored.

Error-based Discretization Significant work in error-based discretization has only recently been carried out. Maass (1994) developed an algorithm to optimally discretize a continuous feature with respect to error on the training set. This algorithm discretizes a continuous feature by producing an optimal set of k or fewer intervals that results in the minimum error on the training set if the instances were to be classified using only that single feature after discretization. We refer to this algorithm as **ErrorMin**. The maximum number of intervals k is a user-set parameter.

This method has been implemented as part of the T2 induction algorithm (Auer, Holte, & Maass 1995) which induces one or two level decision trees. T2 circumvented the difficulty of providing a good justification for the value of k by simply setting k to be the number of classes plus one. The algorithm employs a dynamic programming approach to efficiently compute the optimal error discretization thresholds. Under the T2 heuristic the time complexity of the algorithm is $O(m(\log m + k^2))$ and the space complexity is $O(m + k^3)$, where m is the number of training instances.

We used the implementation of this algorithm from the T2 induction system, but tried two different approaches to setting the value for k. The first approach is the one proposed for T2 described above, which we call *ErrorMin-T2*. The second approach is to set k to be the same number of intervals proposed by running the *Ent-MDL* method, which allows us to compare them for the same k values; we call this method ***ErrorMin-MDL***.

Results

We begin by presenting the experimental results and then analyze them.

Empirical Findings

Table 1 shows the datasets we chose for our comparison. We chose 17 datasets from the UCI repository (Murphy & Aha 1996) such that each had at least one continuous feature. We used 10-fold cross-validation to determine error rates for the application of each discretization and induction method pair to each dataset. It is important to note that in performing cross-validation we *separately* discretized the training set for each fold. Discretizing all the data once before creating the folds for cross-validation allows the discretization method to have access to the testing data, which is known to result in optimistic error rates.

Figure 1 shows the results for C4.5. We report the error rate for each discretization method used in conjunction with C4.5, normalized by the error rate of the original C4.5 run on the data without any prior discretization. Thus, the relative error bars below 1.0 show an improvement over C4.5 without discretization, whereas values above 1.0 show a degradation in classification performance. More generally, lower values are better. Figure 2 shows the analogous table for Naive-Bayes, normalized by the error rate for Naive-Bayes using the normal distribution (Gaussian) for continuous features.

The results for C4.5 show that *Ent-MDL* does better on average than C4.5 run without discretization, lowering error rate in several instances and never significantly increasing it. C4.5 run using *Ent-MDL* some-

times significantly outperforms C4.5 alone because discretization provides a regularization effect (all the data is used to determine the interval boundaries before training, as opposed to during training where the data is fragmented). The absolute average errors were 16.01% and 17.50% respectively, with the following p-values for the significant differences computed using a t-test: Ionosphere improved with p-value = 0.02, Glass2 improved with p-value = 0.03, and Cleve improved with p-value = 0.05. *Ent-MDL* was, on average, also the best performing discretization method of the four methods we tried. This is a noteworthy result given that this method is entropy-based and does not attempt to directly minimize error, our overall objective function. Looking at all the discretization algorithms, error rates increased significantly only in a few cases and in many cases they slightly decreased.

For the *ErrorMin* method, Hypothyroid and Sick-euthyroid degraded significantly. For hypothyroid, the relative difference is significant with p-value < 0.0002. We examined the discretization methods carefully and noted that with only two features: TSH and FTI, the error of C4.5 is almost as good as with all the features. The *ErrorMin* algorithm discretizes the TSH feature into only two intervals (for all ten folds) even though both heuristics (T2 and MDL) recommended three intervals. The reason for this problem is that *ErrorMin* will never create two adjacent intervals with the same majority class. We explore the impact of this phenomenon in an artificial example.

As reported in previous work (Dougherty, Kohavi, & Sahami 1995), any form of discretization produced large improvements over the Naive-Bayesian algorithm with the normality assumption for continuous variables. Discretization allows for the algorithm to better approximate the true distribution for a continuous variable when that distribution is not normal and thus computes a more accurate posterior probability for an instance to be of a particular class. In the rare cases where the continuous features of a domain are in fact normally distributed (as is the case with Iris and six out of eight features in Diabetes), we find that discretization causes a small increase in error rate, but these are much more the exception than the norm. We find that when discretization is applied, error rates are lower for nine domains, relatively unchanged in six domains, and only worse in two domains. All the discretization methods performed approximately the same, but *Ent-MDL* was a slight winner on average. Also, worth noting is that Naive Bayes run using *Ent-MDL* sometimes significantly outperformed C4.5. For example, performance on Anneal, Cleve, and Glass was better with p-values less than 0.01, and performance

	Dataset	Features		Dataset	Majority		Dataset	Features		Dataset	Majority
		cont	nom	Size	Error			cont	nom	Size	Error
1	anneal	6	32	898	23.83	2	australian	6	8	690	44.49
3	breast cancer	10	0	699	34.48	4	cleve	6	7	303	45.62
5	crx	6	9	690	44.49	6	diabetes	8	0	768	34.89
7	german	24	0	1000	30.00	8	glass	9	0	214	64.46
9	glass2	9	0	163	46.73	10	heart	13	0	270	44.44
11	hepatitis	6	13	155	20.83	12	horse-colic	7	15	368	36.91
13	hypothyroid	7	18	3163	4.77	14	ionosphere	34	0	351	35.87
15	iris	4	0	150	76.67	16	sick-euthyroid	7	18	3163	9.26
17	vehicle	18	0	846	77.41						

Table 1: Datasets, the number of continuous features, nominal features, dataset size, and baseline error (majority inducer on the 10 folds).

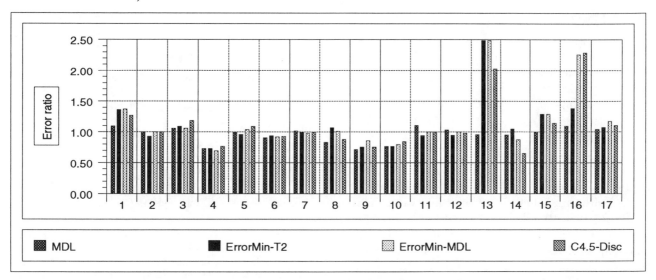

Figure 1: C4.5 with different discretization methods. Error ratios for the different discretization algorithms relative to the original C4.5. Lower values are better.

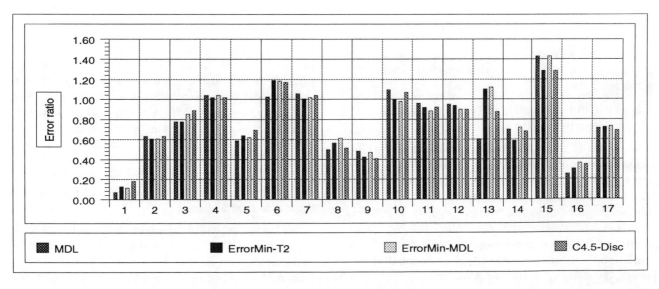

Figure 2: Naive-Bayes with different discretization methods. Error ratios for the different discretization algorithms relative to Naive-Bayes assuming normal distribution. Lower values are better.

on Breast, Diabetes, Glass, and Heart was better with p-values less than 0.05.

The running times for many of these experiments were negligible. The most time intensive datasets to discretize using *Ent-MDL* were Sick-euthyroid and Hypothyroid, which each took about 31 seconds per fold on an SGI Challenge. The longest running time for *ErrorMin* was encountered with the Glass dataset which took 153 seconds per fold to discretize, although this was much longer than any other of the datasets examined. The *ErrorMin* method could not be run on the Letter domain with 300MB of main memory.

Error vs. Entropy

To better understand why the entropy-based methods outperformed *ErrorMin* on some datasets, and why *ErrorMin* would not discretize to the suggested number of intervals, we present a simple example to show the shortcomings of error-based discretization.

Consider a Boolean target function f of two continuous variables, X_1 and X_2 in the range $[0, 1]$, defined as:
$$f(X_1, X_2) = ((X_1 < 0.4) \wedge (X_2 < 0.75)) \vee (X_2 < 0.25).$$

The function and its projection on X_2 are shown in Figure 3. Note that f has only two intervals of interest for X_1 (with threshold 0.4), but three intervals of interest for X_2 (with thresholds 0.25 and 0.75). *ErrorMin* is unable to form the three intervals for X_2. For this function, all instances which have $X_2 < 0.25$ will be positive whereas all instances which have $X_2 \geq 0.75$ will be negative. This leaves a large middle interval ($0.25 \leq X_2 < 0.75$) where instances will either be labeled positive or negative depending on their value for feature X_1. Assuming a uniform distribution of instances, the middle interval will generally have more negative instances. As a result, we will have a majority of negative instances in two adjacent partitions, which is problematic for *ErrorMin* as the following observation shows.

Observation: *ErrorMin* will never generate two adjacent intervals with the same label.

The reason is that these two intervals can always be collapsed into one interval with no degradation in the error. We can thus see an inherent limitation of *ErrorMin*. The implication is that out of eight possible labelings for three intervals in a two-class problem, only two are possible with *ErrorMin*. Entropy-based discretization methods have no such limitation and can partition the space as long as the class distribution between the different partitions is different.

We generated 5,000 instances (uniformly randomly distributed) from this target concept and ran 10-fold cross-validation using *ErrorMin-T2* and *Ent-MDL*.

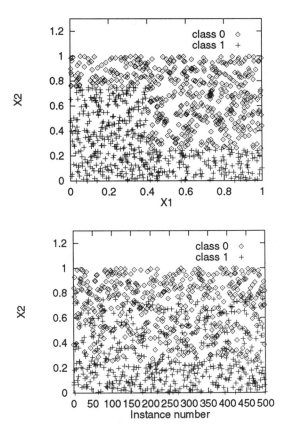

Figure 3: 500 instances from the artificial target concept f (top) and its projection on the second feature (bottom). Note that in the projection all instances below 0.25 are one class, all instances above 0.75 are of the other, and in the range 0.25-0.75, they are mixed.

The *ErrorMin-T2* heuristic recommends three intervals for each feature because this is a two-class problem. For X_1, *ErrorMin-T2* returns three intervals (although there are really only two) in nine out of the ten folds. The second threshold was always very close to the edge at 1.0. As mentioned above, *ErrorMin-T2* returns only two intervals for X_2 in all ten folds, although there are three. The Bayes-error rate for the partitions returned by *ErrorMin-T2* was 10.24%. *Ent-MDL*, on the other hand, found the correct number of partitions and with thresholds very close to the true values. The Bayes-error rate for the partitions returned by *Ent-MDL* was 0.02%.

We conclude that although error-minimization techniques always find the optimal partition to reduce the training-set error for each feature, entropy-based methods might fare better in practice because of feature interaction: as long as the distribution is different enough, a threshold will be formed, allowing other features to make the final discrimination.

Conclusions

Dougherty, Kohavi, & Sahami (1995) describe three axes along which discretization methods can be measured: *supervised* vs. *unsupervised*, *global* vs. *local*, and *static* vs. *dynamic*. The methods examined here are supervised, as they make use of the instance label information while performing discretization, whereas unsupervised methods, such as equal width binning, do not. We did not compare unsupervised methods as the previous work noted that supervised methods have a tendency to work better in practice.

The distinction between global and local methods stems from when discretization is performed. Global discretization involves discretizing all continuous features *prior* to induction. Local methods, on the other hand, carry out discretization *during* the induction process, where particular local regions of the instance space may be discretized differently (such as when C4.5 splits the same continuous feature differently down different branches of a decision tree). All the methods compared here are applied globally. In future work we aim to measure the effectiveness of these methods when applied locally.

Discretization methods often require a parameter, k, indicating the maximum number of intervals to produce in discretizing a feature. Static methods, such as those examined in this work, perform one discretization pass of the data for each feature and determine the value of k for each feature independent of the other features. Dynamic methods conduct a search through the space of possible k values for all features simultaneously, thereby capturing interdependencies in feature discretization. During the course of this study, we looked at dynamic versions of several discretization methods, using the wrapper approach (John, Kohavi, & Pfleger 1994) as a means of searching through the space of the number of discretization intervals for all variables simultaneously. We found no significant improvement in employing dynamic discretization over its static counterpart.

Our results show that *Ent-MDL* is slightly superior to the other methods for the datasets used. We have also described why *ErrorMin* methods are inappropriate in cases where features interact, and analyzed the time and space complexity of the different algorithms.

Acknowledgments We thank Lise Getoor for comments on an earlier version of this paper and Peter Auer for providing us with the code for T2. The second author is supported by an ARPA/NASA/NSF grant to the Stanford Digital Libraries Project. All the experiments reported here were done using $\mathcal{MLC}$++.

References

Apte, C., and Hong, S. 1996. Predicting equity returns from security data. In *Advances in Knowledge Discovery and Data Mining*. AAAI Press and the MIT Press. chapter 22, 541–569.

Auer, P.; Holte, R.; and Maass, W. 1995. Theory and applications of agnostic pac-learning with small decision trees. In *Machine Learning: Proceedings of the Twelfth Int. Conference*. Morgan Kaufmann.

Catlett, J. 1991. On changing continuous attributes into ordered discrete attributes. In Kodratoff, Y., ed., *Proceedings of the European Working Session on Learning*, 164–178. Berlin: Springer-Verlag.

Cost, S., and Salzberg, S. 1993. A weighted nearest neighbor algorithm for learning with symbolic features. *Machine Learning* 10(1):57–78.

Dougherty, J.; Kohavi, R.; and Sahami, M. 1995. Supervised and unsupervised discretization of continuous features. In *Machine Learning: Proceedings of the Twelfth Int. Conference*, 194–202. Morgan Kaufmann.

Fayyad, U. M., and Irani, K. B. 1993. Multi-interval discretization of continuous-valued attributes for classification learning. In *Proceedings of the 13th Int. Joint Conference on Artificial Intelligence*, 1022–1027. Morgan Kaufmann.

Good, I. J. 1965. *The Estimation of Probabilities: An Essay on Modern Bayesian Methods*. M.I.T. Press.

Holte, R. C. 1993. Very simple classification rules perform well on most commonly used datasets. *Machine Learning* 11:63–90.

John, G.; Kohavi, R.; and Pfleger, K. 1994. Irrelevant features and the subset selection problem. In *Machine Learning: Proceedings of the Eleventh Int. Conference*, 121–129. Morgan Kaufmann.

Kohavi, R.; John, G.; Long, R.; Manley, D.; and Pfleger, K. 1994. MLC++: A machine learning library in C++. In *Tools with Artificial Intelligence*, 740–743. IEEE Computer Society Press. http://www.sgi.com/Technology/mlc.

Maass, W. 1994. Efficient agnostic PAC-learning with simple hypotheses. In *Proceedings of the Seventh Annual ACM Conference on Computational Learning Theory*, 67–75.

Murphy, P. M., and Aha, D. W. 1996. UCI repository of machine learning databases. http://www.ics.uci.edu/~mlearn.

Quinlan, J. R. 1993. *C4.5: Programs for Machine Learning*. Los Altos, California: Morgan Kaufmann.

Rethinking the Learning of Belief Network Probabilities

Ron Musick*

Advanced Information Technology Program
Lawrence Livermore National Laboratory
P.O. Box 808, L-419, Livermore, CA 94551
rmusick@llnl.gov

Abstract

Belief networks are a powerful tool for knowledge discovery that provide concise, understandable probabilistic models of data. There are methods grounded in probability theory to incrementally update the relationships described by the belief network when new information is seen, to perform complex inferences over any set of variables in the data, to incorporate domain expertise and prior knowledge into the model, and to automatically learn the model from data. This paper concentrates on part of the belief network induction problem, that of learning the quantitative structure (the conditional probabilities), given the qualitative structure. In particular, the current practice of rote learning the probabilities in belief networks can be significantly improved upon. We advance the idea of applying any learning algorithm to the task of conditional probability learning in belief networks, discuss potential benefits, and show results of applying neural networks and other algorithms to a medium sized car insurance belief network. The results demonstrate from 10 to 100% improvements in model error rates over the current approaches.

Introduction

Belief networks have been accepted as a tool for knowledge discovery in databases for several years now, and have been a growing focus of machine learning research for the past decade. Several uses have been demonstrated in the literature in domains as distinct as document retrieval, medical diagnosis, and telecommunications (D'Ambrosio 1994; Ezawa & Norton 1995; Park, Han, & Choi 1995). A common need across all of these application domains is for robust, flexible and powerful methods for the automatic induction of belief networks. Along with the obvious savings in time and effort, well-constructed automated techniques often lead to improved models, and can help data analysts develop deeper insight into the processes hidden in the data by making it easier to experiment with new ideas.

The main goal of this paper is to influence the current pattern of thought on the effective induction of belief network probabilities. This paper advocates the application of standard machine learning techniques to this problem together with, or in place of, the rote learning techniques that are most common today. We do not address the task of learning the structure of the network.

The conditional probability table (CPT) of a node (variable) in a belief network stores the probabilistic relation between that variable and its parents as a table of conditional probabilities. There is one CPT per node in the network. Inducing the CPTs is a learning problem. Each is a *potentially unique* function from the parent variables to the child, and thus should be open to a wide range of learning techniques. The current approach in most all cases is to learn the conditional probability tables with a simple statistical counting method ("bookkeeping") that can be likened to the rote learning done by chess and checkers programs back in the 60's (Samuel 1963). The bookkeeping approach is seductive because it is the easiest method to implement, is very understandable, and leads to Dirichlet distributions. Dirichlets have nice theoretical properties that can lead to effective measurements of accuracy during inference (Musick 1993). However, the power and flexibility of being able to apply any machine learning technique to CPT learning has advantages that can not be ignored. The following is a brief argument for *incorporating* machine learning techniques into the statistically oriented techniques that are currently in force. The rest of the paper backs these arguments up with results of an implementation of these concepts.

- **Unsupervised Generalization**: Generalization is the heart of the ability to learn and discover new knowledge. It can be argued that most machine learning algorithms generalize by assuming the existence of certain dependencies in the data and generalizing based on those. On the other hand, most statistical techniques (certainly bookkeeping) tend to assume independence in the data (unless specifi-

---

*This research was supported in part by the National Science Foundation under grant Nos. CDA-8722788, and IRI-9058427 while at the University of California, Berkeley.

cally stated with a distribution or a correlation matrix), and so do not generalize unless instructed to. The successes in both fields make it clear that each approach has its place in modeling data.

- **Sparse Data**: Sparse training data is an unavoidable condition in CPT learning. The size of a CPT is the number of unique parent instantiations (columns) times the number of child values (rows.. see Table 1), and in a practical application can be immense. The situation is aggravated by the fact that the training data will not be evenly distributed throughout a table. What often happens is that a small fraction of the columns in a table will together have a very high probability, and thus take in the bulk of the data. The set of low probability columns rarely see relevant data. The implication is that to "cover" a table with training data, the number of samples already likely to be needed must be multiplied by the inverse of the probability of the lowest probability parent instantiation. Bookkeeping further compounds the problem by requiring a significant amount of data supplied to each column in a CPT in order to produce viable estimates. Machine learning algorithms generalize across the data and often produce excellent results under sparse data conditions.

- **Flexibility**: Each CPT is a different learning problem, with unique characteristics. We can take advantage of the uniqueness by applying the algorithm that best fits the learning task. For tables where a linear relationship is expected between child and parent variables, apply linear regression. When the CPT is moderate sized and well covered by data, apply bookkeeping. When the data is sparse or the relation between child and parents is unknown, apply neural nets or decision trees. This ability to tailor the choice of algorithm to match problem characteristics can make a substantial difference in overall performance.

- **Problem Reduction**: In terms of the complexity of the learning task, the bookkeeping algorithm has a much more difficult job than other approaches. For example, if all variables have 5 values, and node X_i has four parents, then the CPT for X_i has 3125 cells or 625 columns for bookkeeping to learn. A effective neural network applied to the same problem (with a construction similar to what we use in Sections 2.2 and 3) need only learn 76 parameters.

The paper continues in Section 2 with a description of the algorithms that have been implemented and applied to the CPT learning problem. Section 3 explains the experimental methodology, and discusses the results of the implementation including comparisons between bookkeeping and other learning alternatives. Section 4 wraps up with a brief conclusion.

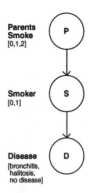

Figure 1: A Smoker Belief Net
This is a belief net showing a simplistic relation between smoking, bronchitis and having parents that smoke.

Methods Used for Learning CPTs

This section describes the bookkeeping (BOOK), neural network (NN), and combination (COMB) algorithms that we have applied to the CPT learning phase of inducing a belief network from training data. We assume that the structure of the belief network is given. Formal details are kept to a minimum in this section; the interested reader can find in-depth descriptions of how these methods and others can be constructed and applied to CPT learning in (Musick 1994).

Bookkeeping

Bookkeeping is a simple matter of counting the training samples that are relevant to each cell in the CPT. Assuming uninformative priors and sampling without replacement, the application of standard statistical inference methodology (maximum likelyhood estimation) leads to the fact that the counts of relevant samples are actually the parameters that describe a beta distribution for each cell[1] of the CPT. A beta distribution $\beta(a, b)$ is similar in shape to a normal that is a bit skewed, and has a mean of $\frac{a}{a+b}$.

Table 1 contains the CPTs for the belief network in Figure 1, and depicts what happens on a bookkeeping update. The CPTs on the left are the original tables with a uniform prior, the CPTs on the right show what happens after updating for one example of Parents smoke = 0, Smoker = 1 and Disease = bronchitis. Each bullet shows where the sample "hits" in each particular table. When the sample hits a cell in the table, the a parameter is incremented, and the rest of the cells in that column have their b parameter incremented. Consider the $Pr(D/S)$ table, in particular the probability that a patient has bronchitis given that he smokes (this cell was "hit" by the sample). This probability starts at a prior of 1/3, and after the sample increases to 1/2, while the probability of Disease

---

[1]Or more generally, a Dirichlet for each column of the table.

		Pr(P)						Pr(P)	
	0	β(1,2)•				0	β(2,2)•	
P	1	β(1,2)			P	1	β(1,3)	
	2	β(1,2)				2	β(1,3)	

		Pr(S|P)						Pr(S|P)		
			P						P	
		0	1	2				0	1	2
S	0	β(1,1)	β(1,1)	β(1,1)	S	0	β(1,2)	β(1,1)	β(1,1)
	1	β(1,1)•	β(1,1)	β(1,1)		1	β(2,1)•	β(1,1)	β(1,1)

		Pr(D|S)					Pr(D|S)	
		S					S	
		0	1				0	1
	b	β(1,2)	β(1,2)•		b	β(1,2)	β(2,2)•
D	h	β(1,2)	β(1,2)	D	h	β(1,2)	β(1,3)
	n	β(1,2)	β(1,2)		n	β(1,2)	β(1,3)

Table 1: **Updating the CPTs**
This shows the update process from the original CPTs on the left to the new CPTs on the right, after a sample of P = 0, S = 1, D = b.

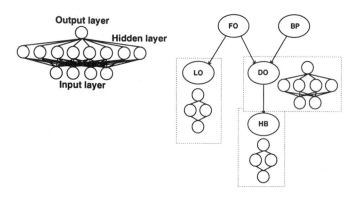

Figure 2: **Applying Neural Nets to Dog Out**
The belief network on the right is for the Dog Out problem, with variables FO = Family Out, BP = dog has Bowel Problems, LO = outside Lights Out, DO = the Dog is Outside, and HB = you can Hear the dog Barking. The neural network on the left shows the structure of the networks in the belief network CPTs, and also happens to be the size of a network applied to the same problem. The goal is to predict whether or not the dog is outside, based on whether the outside lights are on, if the dog is barking, and so on.

= halitosis starts at 1/3 and drops to 1/4. Thus for bookkeeping each complete sample is relevant to an entire column in every CPT. Note also that bookkeeping makes a strong independence assumption; a sample relevant to one column in a CPT is independent of any other column in that CPT.

Neural Networks

The job of the neural network is to produce a density function for each column of the CPT, without any predetermined requirements on the family of functions that could be discovered. Figure 2 is a graphical example of applying neural networks to learn three of the tables in the Dog Out problem (Charniak 1991). Let

T_i be the CPT for node X_i, and π_{ij} be a unique parent instantiation for the node. The general process for learning a CPT with NN is for each T_i:

1. Retrieve from the database the instances that are relevant to T_i.

2. Construct a neural network NN_{T_i} and initialize it.

3. Train NN_{T_i} on the samples, where the value of the variable X_i serves as the classification of each datum.

4. Apply input combination π_{i1} to the neural network and read off the distribution for the CPT column $Pr(X_i|\Pi_1)$ from the output units.

5. Normalize the output and write the values into the CPT for the belief network.

6. Repeat steps 4 and 5 for all input combinations π_{i2} through π_{im}.

The network used for the results described below is a 3-layer feed forward network constructed to learn density functions, and incorporates ideas of momentum and adaptive parameters. A network can be built for any combination of input/output variables, including nodes with binary, discrete, continuous, and nominal values. Details of the construction and mapping into CPT learning can be found in (Musick 1994). Note that while bookkeeping provides a distribution for each cell in the CPT, neural networks in general will only provide a point probability.

It should be made clear that this paper is *not* trying to promote this *particular* neural network construction as the best for the problem of CPT learning. In fact, we do not make that claim for any of the algorithms proposed here. Our claim is that effective CPT learning requires the ability to apply a wide range of learning techniques; this construction is used to demonstrate that point.

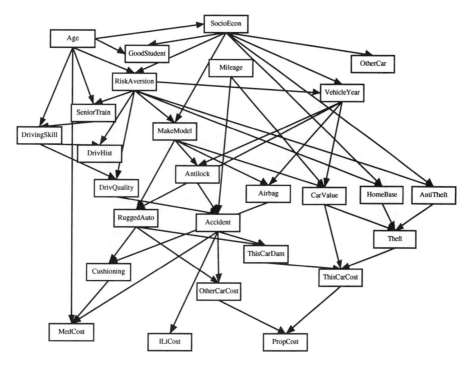

Figure 3: **Car Insurance Database**
This is the model of an insurance database, it includes binary, nominal, discrete and continuous variables.

COMB

COMB is probably the most interesting approach tested. COMB combines both BOOK and NN learning approaches *within one CPT*. The combination is done by choosing to learn data-rich columns with BOOK and the data-poor columns with NN. Specifically, columns with 20 samples or less are learned with NN, columns with more are learned with BOOK. Results are combined on a column by column basis instead of cell by cell since any one sample is relevant to exactly one column. The improvement in the overall model error rate with COMB is impressive.

Results and Comparisons

This section describes the results of an implementation of the above ideas.

Experimental Methodology

The belief network used in this paper is a realistic, moderately sized car insurance network (Russell *et al.* 1995) with 27 binary, discrete, nominal, and continuous nodes, 52 arcs and over 1400 conditional probabilities. The goal is to help predict how much financial risk is incurred from various policy holders given data about age, socio-economic class, and so on. Keep in mind that in high volume industries like insurance or finance, a 1% improvement in risk assessment could be quite valuable.

We need an objective measure of model error rates as a basis from which to compare the different approaches.

To enable this, the training data has been *generated* in a very particular way. Figure 3 is taken to be "The" belief network B_S that represents the actual process occurring in the real world. This network is then used to generate a large database (typically on the order of one hundred thousand samples) which is used as the data seen by BOOK, NN, and COMB. The induced belief network B_D has the same structure as B_S, but the CPTs are constructed using a random sample from the large database. The learned belief net B_D is then compared to "The" belief net B_S for model evaluation.

Two methods are used to score the models, the *mean error*, and the *weighted error*. The mean error is the square root of the mean squared error between the predicted probability and the correct probability from all cells in all of the CPTs. The weighted error is the same thing, but with each error weighted by the probability of that related event occurring. Note that one implication of the mean error scoring system is that a data-rich column counts the same as a data-poor column. The mean error metric makes sense in domains where the data-poor columns of the CPT are valuable but scarce data points (for example, drug testing in the medical domain, where the cost of each sample might be a human life). The weighted error metric is more useful when the cost of an error is the same for high and low probability columns.

Finally, all of the results that follow stem from running this process 10 times: generate a random sample of the given size, pass the sample to three separate pro-

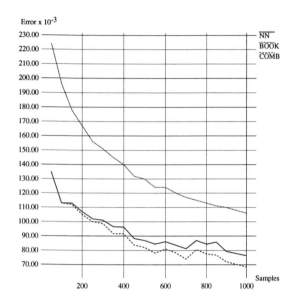

Figure 4: **Car Insurance Database, Mean Error Metric**
The results of applying NN, BOOK and COMB to the car insurance database as the sample size is increased to 1000 samples. This graph uses the mean error metric. BOOK is the topmost curve, COMB the bottommost.

cesses BOOK, NN and COMB, learn the CPTs, then generate the error measurements.

Experiments

Figures 4 and 5 show the learning performance as the total number of samples is varied from 50 to 1000. The learning curves in Figure 4 were built using the mean error metric, the curves in Figure 5 using the weighted error metric.

The most obvious basic trend is that no matter which error metric is used, for low numbers of samples NN significantly outperforms BOOK. In fact, based on other tests we have run (more than five different belief nets, and different learning algorithms including decision trees) it is fair to say that when the data is sparse relative to the size of the overall learning task, the more traditional machine learning algorithms like neural nets and decision trees significantly outperform BOOK.

The second noticeable aspect of these figures is that there seems to be very different stories being told by the two error metrics. The mean error metric shows NN doubling the performance of BOOK all the way out to 1000 samples and more, while the weighted error metric shows BOOK beginning to outperform NN at about 350 samples. The explanation of this is that the low-probability columns (data-poor columns) in all the CPTs far outnumber the medium and high probability columns. BOOK is expected to perform very well for CPT cells and columns for which there is alot of data, and it is exactly these columns that the weighted error

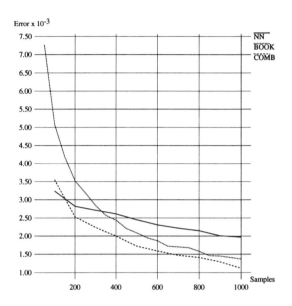

Figure 5: **Car Insurance Database, Weighted Probability Metric**
The results of applying NN, BOOK and COMB to the car insurance database as the sample size is increased to 1000 samples. This graph uses the weighted error metric. The BOOK curve starts high and ends in the middle.

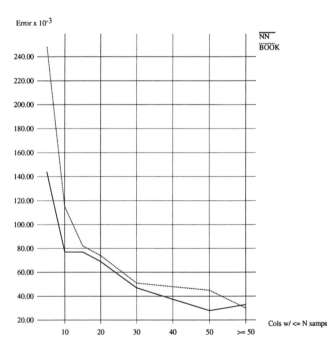

Figure 6: **Error As A Function Of Samples Per Column**
The results of applying NN and BOOK to the car insurance database on 100 samples.

metric is weighting more heavily.

The most interesting feature is that the new algorithm, COMB, consistently outperforms both NN and BOOK. COMB uses NN to learn low-probability columns, and BOOK to learn high probability columns. Even with the weighted error metric on the largest sample (1000 instances), the contribution from NN on the data-poor columns in COMB leads to more than a 10% improvement over the BOOK error rate.

In order to get a better feeling for where and how the improvements are taking place, we clustered columns in the CPTs according to the relative sparseness of the training data. Based on this, Figure 6 should be interpreted as follows: The X axis represents the columns in the CPTs that have seen ≤ 10 samples, 10 to 20 samples, and so on, up to the last point on the axis which represents all of the rest of the columns, all of which are data-rich. The Y axis is the mean error over those clusters. The general expectation is for high error on the data-poor columns to the left, and low error on the data-rich columns to the right. The error metric used for this graph is mean error.

What we see from this graph is that for the CPT columns with relatively little data (less than 50 samples per column), NN outperforms BOOK at all points along the curve.

Conclusion

We tested have several other belief networks and learning algorithms in addition to what is described here, and the results can all be boiled down to the same general conclusions. The nature of the CPT learning problem is that even in the face of massive data sets, data will be sparse for large CPTs. Bookkeeping requires large amounts of data in order to be effective. Machine learning oriented algorithms tend to be more accurate under sparse data conditions. Finally, the ability to freely tailor any learning algorithm to match the unique characteristics of each CPT has the potential to dramatically improve the predictive performance of any belief network model.

References

Charniak, E. 1991. Bayesian networks without tears. *AI Magazine* 12(4):50–63.

D'Ambrosio, B. 1994. Symbolic probabilistic inference in large bn2o networks. In *Proceedings of the Tenth Conference on Uncertainty in Artificial Intelligence*, 128–135.

Ezawa, K., and Norton, S. 1995. Knowledge discovery in telecommunication services data using bayesian networks. In *Proceedings of the First International Conference on Knowledge Discovery and Data Mining*, 100–105.

Musick, R. 1993. Maintaining inference distributions in belief nets. In *Proceedings of the Ninth Conference on Uncertainty in Artificial Intelligence*.

Musick, R. 1994. *Belief Network Induction*. Ph.D. Dissertation, UCB Tech Report CSD-95-863. University of California, Berkeley, Berkeley, CA.

Park, Y.; Han, Y.; and Choi, K. 1995. Automatic thesaurus construction using bayesian networks. In *Proceedings of the Fourth International Conference on Information and Knowledge Management*, 212–217. ACM Press.

Russell, S. J.; Binder, J.; Koller, D.; and Kanazawa, K. 1995. Local learning in probabilistic networks with hidden variables. In *Proceedings of the Fourteenth International Joint Conference on Artificial Intelligence*. Montreal, Canada: Morgan Kaufmann Publishers.

Samuel, A. 1963. Some studies in machine learning using the game of checkers. In Feigenbaum, E. A., and Feldman, J., eds., *Computers and Thought*. New York: McGraw-Hill.

Clustering using Monte Carlo Cross-Validation

Padhraic Smyth*
Department of Information and Computer Science
University of California, Irvine
CA 92717-3425
smyth@ics.uci.edu

Abstract

Finding the "right" number of clusters, k, for a data set is a difficult, and often ill-posed, problem. In a probabilistic clustering context, likelihood-ratios, penalized likelihoods, and Bayesian techniques are among the more popular techniques. In this paper a new cross-validated likelihood criterion is investigated for determining cluster structure. A practical clustering algorithm based on *Monte Carlo cross-validation* (MCCV) is introduced. The algorithm permits the data analyst to judge if there is strong evidence for a particular k, or perhaps weaker evidence over a sub-range of k values. Experimental results with Gaussian mixtures on real and simulated data suggest that MCCV provides genuine insight into cluster structure. v-fold cross-validation appears inferior to the penalized likelihood method (BIC), a Bayesian algorithm (AutoClass v2.0), and the new MCCV algorithm. Overall, MCCV and AutoClass appear the most reliable of the methods. MCCV provides the data-miner with a useful data-driven clustering tool which complements the fully Bayesian approach.

Introduction

Cluster analysis is the process of automatically searching for natural groupings in a data set and extracting characteristic descriptions of these groups. It is a fundamental knowledge discovery process. *Clustering algorithms* (of which there are many) typically consist of a specification of both (1) a *criterion* for judging the quality of a given grouping and (2) a *search method* for optimizing this criterion given data (see Jain and Dubes (1988) for an overview).

A particularly vexing question, which is often glossed over in published descriptions of clustering algorithms, is "how many clusters are there in the data ?". Formal methods for finding the "optimal" number of clusters are few. Furthermore, "optimality" can be difficult to pin down in this context without some assumptions being made. One viewpoint is that the problem of finding the best number of clusters is fundamentally ill-defined

---

*Also with the Jet Propulsion Laboratory 525-3660, California Institute of Technology, Pasadena, CA 91109.

and best avoided (cf. Gelman et al , page 424, in a mixture modelling context). While we sympathize with this view we adopt a more pragmatic approach in this paper, namely, let the data tell us as much as possible about cluster structure, including the number of clusters in the data. If either the data are too few, or the measurement dimensions too noisy, then the data may not reveal much. However, when the data contain interesting structure one seeks an algorithmic technique which can reveal this structure. A fundamental point is that the process of structure discovery in data needs to be interactive, i.e., the data analyst must interpret the results as they see fit.

In this paper we limit our attention to Gaussian mixture models: however, any probabilistic clustering model for which a likelihood function can be defined is amenable to the proposed approach. The method could conceivably be extended to clustering algorithms which do not possess clear probabilistic semantics (such as the k-means family of algorithms), but this is not pursued here.

Probabilistic Clustering Using Mixture Models

Finite Mixture Models

The probabilistic mixture modelling approach to clustering is well-known: one assumes that the data are generated by a linear combination of component density functions resulting in a mixture probability density function of the form:

$$f_k(\underline{x}|\Phi_k) = \sum_{j=1}^{k} \alpha_j g_j(\underline{x}|\underline{\theta}_j) \qquad (1)$$

where $\underline{x}$ is a particular value of a d-dimensional feature vector $\mathbf{X}$, k is the number of components in the model, $\underline{\theta}_j$ are the parameters associated with density component g_j, the α_j are the "weights" for each component j, and $\Phi_k = \{\alpha_1, \ldots, \alpha_k, \underline{\theta}_1, \ldots, \underline{\theta}_k\}$ denotes the set of parameters for the overall model. We will adopt the notation that $\hat{\Phi}_k$ denotes parameters which have been *estimated* from data. It is assumed that $\sum_j \alpha_j = 1$ and $\alpha_j > 0, 1 \leq j \leq k$.

The component density functions are often assumed to be multivariate Gaussian with parameters $\underline{\theta}_j = \{\underline{\mu}_j, \Sigma_j\}$ where $\underline{\mu}_j$ and Σ_j are the mean and covariance matrix, respectively. Thus the mean $\underline{\mu}_j$ specifies the *location* of the jth component density in feature space and the covariance matrix Σ_j prescribes how the data belonging to component j are typically dispersed or scattered around $\underline{\mu}_j$. The flexibility of this model has led to its widespread application, particularly in applied statistics (McLachlan and Basford 1988), and more recently in machine learning and knowledge discovery (Cheeseman and Stutz 1996).

Estimating the Clusters from Data

Clustering (in this mixture model context) is as follows:

1. Assume that the data are generated by a mixture model, where each component is interpreted as a cluster or class ω_j and it assumed that each data point must have been generated by one and only one of the classes ω_j.

2. Given a data set where it is not known which data points came from which components, infer the characteristics (the parameters) of the underlying density functions (the clusters).

In particular, given an "unlabelled" data set $D = \{\underline{x}_1, \ldots, \underline{x}_N\}$, and assuming that the number of clusters k and the functional forms of the component densities g_j in Equation 1 are fixed, estimate the model parameters $\hat{\Phi}_k$. Given $\hat{\Phi}_k$, one can then calculate the probability that data point $\underline{x}$ belongs to class ω_j (by Bayes' rule):

$$\hat{p}(\omega_j | \underline{x}) = \frac{g_j(\underline{x}|\hat{\underline{\theta}}_j)\hat{\alpha}_j}{\sum_{l=1}^{k} g_l(\underline{x}|\hat{\underline{\theta}}_l)\hat{\alpha}_l} \quad 1 \leq j \leq k, \quad (2)$$

where $\hat{\theta}$ denotes an estimate of the true parameter θ. Here, $\hat{\alpha}_j = \hat{p}(\omega_j)$, i.e., an estimate of the marginal or prior for each cluster. Since the mixture likelihood (or posterior) surface (as a function of the parameters) can have many local maxima, and no closed form solution for the global maximum exists, parameter estimation for mixtures is non-trivial. Much of the popularity of mixture models in recent years is due to the existence of efficient iterative estimation techniques (in particular, the expectation-maximization (EM) algorithm).

Choosing the Number of Clusters k

Above we have assumed that k, the number of clusters, is known *a priori*. While there may be situations where k is known, one would often like to determine k from the data if possible. Prior work on automatically finding k can roughly be divided into three categories.

The classical approach is based on hypothesis testing, where hypothesis k states that the underlying density is a mixture of k components. As discussed in Titterington, Smith and Makov (1985, Section 5.4), these techniques are largely unsatisfactory due to the "failure of standard regularity conditions" on the mixture likelihood function.

A second approach is the full Bayesian solution where the posterior probability of each value of k is calculated given the data, priors on the mixture parameters, and priors on k itself. A potential difficulty with this approach is the computational complexity of integrating over the parameter space to get the posterior probabilities on k. The AutoClass algorithm (Cheeseman and Stutz 1996) uses various approximations to get around the computational issues. Sampling techniques have also been applied to this problem with some success (cf. Diebolt and Robert 1994).

A third method (related to the Bayesian approach, see Chickering and Heckerman, 1996) is that of penalized likelihood (such as the Bayesian Information Criterion (BIC) and various coding-based (e.g., MDL/MML) criteria). A penalty term is added to the log-likelihood to penalize the number of parameters (e.g., Sclove 1983). A significant problem here is that the general assumptions underlying the asymptotic optimality of the penalized criteria do not hold in the mixture modelling context (Titterington, Smith and Makov, Section 5.4).

In theory, the full Bayesian approach is fully optimal and probably the most useful of the three methods listed above. However, in practice it is cumbersome to implement, it is not necessarily straightforward to extend to non-Gaussian problems with dependent samples, and the results will be dependent in a non-transparent manner on the quality of the underlying approximations or simulations. Thus, there is certainly room for exploring alternative methods.

Cross-Validated Likelihood for Choosing k

Let $f(\underline{x})$ be the "true" probability density function for $\underline{x}$. Let $D = \{\underline{x}_1, \ldots, \underline{x}_N\}$ be a random sample from f. Consider that we fit a set of finite mixture models with k components to D, where k ranges from 1 to $k_{\max}$. Thus, we have an indexed set of estimated models, $f_k(\underline{x}|\hat{\Phi}_k), 1 \leq k \leq k_{\max}$, where each $f_k(\underline{x}|\hat{\Phi}_k)$ has been fitted to data set D.

The data log-likelihood for the kth model is defined as

$$L_k(D) = \log\left(\prod_{i=1}^{N} f_k(\underline{x}_i|\hat{\Phi}_k)\right) = \sum_{i=1}^{N} \log f_k(\underline{x}_i|\hat{\Phi}_k). \quad (3)$$

Assume that the parameters for the kth mixture model were estimated by maximizing this likelihood as a function of Φ_k, keeping the data D fixed (standard maximum likelihood estimation). We then get that $L_k(D)$ is a non-decreasing function of k since the increased flexibility of more mixture components allows better fit to the data (increased likelihood). Thus, $L_k(D)$ can not directly provide any clue as to the *true* mixture structure in the data, if such structure exists[1].

Imagine that we had a large test data set D^{test} which is not used in fitting any of the models. Let $L_k(D^{\text{test}})$ be the log-likelihood as defined in Equation 3, where the models are fit to the training data D but the likelihood is evaluated on D^{test}. We can view this likelihood as a function of the "parameter" k, keeping all other parameters and D fixed. Intuitively, this "test likelihood" should be a more useful estimator (than the training data likelihood) for comparing mixture models with different numbers of components.

However, in practice, we can not afford, or do not have available, a large independent test set such as D^{test}. Let $\hat{L}_k^{cv}$ be a cross-validation estimate of $L_k(D^{\text{test}})$—we discuss in the next section the particulars of how $\hat{L}_k^{cv}$ is calculated. What can $\hat{L}_k^{cv}$ tell us about how close the model $f_k(\underline{x}|\hat{\Phi}_k)$ is to the true data-generating density f? Following Silverman (1986, p.53) and Chow, Geman, and Wu (1983), it can be shown under appropriate assumptions that

$$E\left[\hat{L}_k^{cv}\right] \approx -E\left[\int f(\underline{x}) \log \frac{f(\underline{x})}{f_k(\underline{x}|\hat{\Phi}_k)} d\underline{x}\right] + C \quad (4)$$

where C is a constant independent of k and $f_k(\underline{x}|\hat{\Phi}_k)$, and the expectation E is taken with respect to all random samples of size N_t generated from the true density $f(\underline{x})$. N_t is the amount of data used to train the model, which in a cross-validation setup will be less than N.

The term in square brackets is the Kullback-Leibler (K-L) information distance between $f(\underline{x})$ and $f_k(\underline{x}|\hat{\Phi}_k)$, namely $I(f, f_k(\hat{\Phi}_k))$. $I(f, f_k(\hat{\Phi}_k))$ is strictly positive unless $f = f_k(\hat{\Phi}_k)$. Thus, the k which minimizes $I(f, f_k(\hat{\Phi}_k))$ tells us which of the mixture models is closest to the true density f. From Equation 4, $\hat{L}_k^{cv}$ is an approximately unbiased estimator (within a constant) of the expected value of the K-L distance $-I(f, f_k(\hat{\Phi}_k))$. Given that f (and $I(f, f_k(\hat{\Phi}_k))$) is unknown, maximizing $\hat{L}_k^{cv}$ over k is a reasonable estimation strategy and is the approach adopted in this paper.

A Monte Carlo Cross-Validated Clustering Algorithm

Choosing a Particular Cross-Validation Method

There are several possible cross-validation methods one could use to generate $\hat{L}_k^{cv}$. v-fold cross validation (vCV) consists of partitioning the data into v disjoint subsets. $v = 1$ yields the well-known "leave-one-out" cross validated estimator, but this is well-known to suffer from high variance. $v = 10$ has been a popular choice in practice (e.g., the CART algorithm for

---

[1]Traditionally this is the departure point for penalized likelihood and likelihood ratio testing methods.

decision tree classification). In *Monte Carlo cross validation* (MCCV) the data are partitioned M times into disjoint train and test subsets where the test subset is a fraction β of the overall data (Burman 1989, Shao 1993). The key distinction between MCCV and vCV is that in MCCV the different test subsets are chosen randomly and need not be disjoint. Typically β can be quite large, e.g., 0.5 or larger, and hundreds or thousands of runs (M) can be averaged. In the regression context it was shown by Shao (1993) that keeping β relatively large reduces estimation variability in the test data (compared to vCV methods). Intuitively, the MCCV estimates should be unbiased (being an average of M individually unbiased estimates) and have desirable variance properties: however, there are few theoretical results available on MCCV in general and none on MCCV in a likelihood estimation context.

Specification of the MCCV Algorithm

The algorithm operates as follows. The outer loop consists of M cross-validation runs over M randomly-chosen train/test partitions. For each partition, k is varied from 1 to $k_{\max}$ and the EM algorithm is used to fit the k components to the training data.

The EM algorithm is initialized using a variant of the k-means algorithm, which is itself initialized randomly. To avoid local minima, the k-means algorithm is run t times (default value is $t = 10$) from different starting points and the highest likelihood solution used to begin the EM estimation. The EM estimation is constrained away from singular solutions in parameter space by limiting the diagonal elements of the component covariance matrices Σ_j to be greater than ϵ (default value is $\epsilon = 0.001\sigma$ where σ is the standard deviation of the unclustered data in the relevant dimension). The EM algorithm iterates until the change in likelihood is less than δ (default value is $\delta = 10^{-6}$), or up to a prespecified maximum number of iterations (default is 30), whichever occurs first. Keeping the maximum number of EM iterations small allows for quicker execution of the algorithm: the intuition is that since we are averaging multiple cross-validation runs, it is sufficient that the EM estimates be somewhere near a peak in the likelihood surface—this assumption warrants further investigation.

Each of the fitted models with k components are then applied to the unseen data in the test partition, and the test-data log-likelihood (Equation 3) is calculated for each. As indicated earlier, this is repeated M times, and the M cross-validated estimates are averaged for each k to arrive at $\hat{L}_k^{cv}, 1 \leq k \leq k_{\max}$. Similarly the standard deviation over the M runs can be calculated for each k, indicating the variability of the likelihood estimates.

The data analyst can plot the $\hat{L}_k^{cv}$ as a function of k along with the standard deviations to see what the data says about the number of clusters. Another approach is to roughly calculate the posterior probabilities for each k, where one effectively assumes equal priors on the values of k:

$$p(k|D) \approx \frac{\exp(\hat{L}_k^{cv})}{\sum_{l=1}^{k_{max}} \exp(\hat{L}_l^{cv})}, \quad 1 \leq k \leq k_{max}.$$

The distribution of $p(k|D)$ is essential to interpreting the results in the following sense. If one of the $p(k|D)$'s is near 1, then there is strong evidence for that particular number of clusters. If the $p(k|D)$'s are more spread out, then the data are not able to resolve the cluster structure, although "bunching" about a particular k value may allow one to focus on a sub-range of k. It is not recommended that the procedure be implemented as a "black-box" where simply the maximum k value is reported.

The complexity of the EM algorithm for fixed k is $O(kd^2NE)$ where d is the dimensionality of the data, and E denotes the average number of iterations of the EM algorithm. Thus, the overall computational complexity of the MCCV clustering algorithm is $O(Mk_{max}^2 d^2 NE)$, i.e., *linear* in the number of samples N if one assumes that E does not depend on N.

Experimental Results
Overall Experimental Methodology

The MCCV algorithm was evaluated on both simulated and real data sets. Unless stated otherwise, the algorithm was run with $M = 20$ (the number of runs) and $\beta = 0.5$ (the fraction of data left out in each run). The value of $M = 20$ was chosen for pragmatic reasons to reduce simulation time (the MCCV procedure is currently coded in MATLAB which is not particularly efficient). The value of $\beta = 0.5$ was based on some initial experimentation which suggested that keeping the cross-validation train and test partitions roughly the same size gave better results than the more "traditional" 90/10 type partitions. Other details of these experiments are omitted here due to lack of space.

Three other methods were compared to MCCV: AutoClass v2.0 (from the authors at NASA Ames), vCV (with $v = 10$), and BIC (using the standard $(q_k/2)\log N$ penalty term where q_k is the number of parameters in the mixture model with k components). The v-CV and BIC methods used the same version of the EM algorithm as MCCV. The maximum number of classes for each of the algorithms (k_{max}) was set to 8 or 15, depending on the true number of classes in the data.

It is important to note that all of the algorithms have random components. The initialization of the EM algorithm (used by each of the clustering algorithms) for fixed k is based on randomly choosing k initial cluster means. The cross-validation algorithms contain further randomness in their choice of particular partitions of the data. Finally, the simulated data sets can be regenerated randomly according to the probability model. An ideal set of experiments would average over

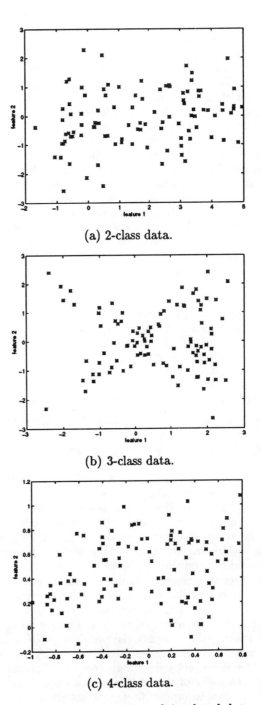

(a) 2-class data.

(b) 3-class data.

(c) 4-class data.

Figure 1: 2-d scatterplots of simulated data.

all of these sources of randomness. Thus, although the experiments in principle could be more extensive (for example, by averaging results over multiple simulated realizations of the simulated problems for a given N) they nonetheless provide clear insight into the general behavior of the algorithms.

Experiments were run on relatively small-sample, low-dimensional data sets (Figures 1 and 2). From a data mining viewpoint this may seem uninteresting. In fact, the opposite is true. *Small sample sizes* are the most challenging problems for methods which seek to extract structure from data (since the MCCV algorithm scales roughly linearly with sample size, scaling up to massive data sets does not pose any particular problems). The focus on *low-dimensional* problems was driven by a desire to evaluate the method on problems where the structure can easily be visualized, the availability of well-known data sets, and the use (in this paper) of full-covariance Gaussian models (which scale poorly with dimensionality from an estimation viewpoint). For all data sets the classes are roughly equiprobable.

Finally due to space limitations we only summarize the experimental results obtained, namely, provide the value of k which maximizes the relevant criterion for each algorithm. Note that, as discussed in the previous section, this is *not* the recommended way to use the MCCV algorithm: rather the full posterior probabilities and variances for each k should be reported and interpreted by the user.

Details of Experiments on Simulated Data

Table 1 contains a brief summary of the experimental results on simulated data.

Experiment 1 consisted of a "control" experiment: data from a single 2-dimensional Gaussian (with $\Sigma = I$ (the identity matrix)). BIC, AutoClass, and MCCV correctly determined the presence of only a single class. vCV on the other hand exhibited considerable variability and incorrectly detected multiple clusters. In general, across different experiments, the vCV method (with $v=10$) was found to be an unreliable estimator compared to the other methods.

The second simulation problem consists of 2 Gaussian clusters in 2 dimensions, both with covariance matrices $\Sigma_1 = \Sigma_2 = I$ and means $\mu_1 = (0,0), \mu_2 = (0,3)$. There is considerable overlap of the clusters (Figure 1(a)) making this a non-trivial problem. MCCV finds evidence of only one cluster with $N = 100$, but for $N = 600, 1200$ it correctly finds both clusters. This conservative tendency of the MCCV algorithm (whereby it finds evidence to support fewer clusters given less data) is pleasing and was noted to occur across different data sets. BIC and AutoClass detected the same number of clusters as MCCV: vCV was consistently incorrect on this problem.

The 3-Class problem (Figure 1(b)) follows the simulated Gaussian structure (in two dimensions) used in

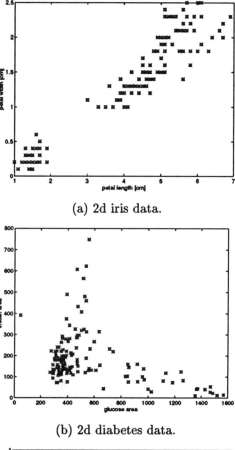

(a) 2d iris data.

(b) 2d diabetes data.

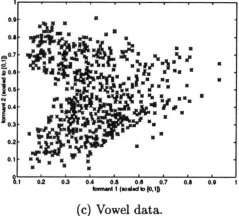

(c) Vowel data.

Figure 2: 2-d scatterplots of real data.

Table 1: Experimental results on simulated data.

Problem	Sample Size	BIC	AC	vCV	MCCV	Truth
1-Class	50	1	1	2	1	1
	200	1	1	1	1	1
	800	1	1	5	1	1
2-Class	100	1	1	4	1	2
	600	2	2	3	2	2
	1200	2	2	3	2	2
3-Class	100	3	3	4	3	3
	600	3	3	3	3	3
	1200	3	3	4	3	3
4-Class	100	2	3	5	3	4
	500	3	4	5	4	4
	1000	4	4	6	4	4

Banfield and Raftery (1993). Two of the clusters are centred at $(0,0)$ but are oriented in "orthogonal" directions. The third cluster overlaps the "tails" of the other two and is centred to the right. MCCV, BIC and AutoClass each correctly detected 3 clusters: once again, vCV was not reliable.

The final simulation problem (Figure 1(c)) contains 4 classes and is taken from Ripley (1994) where it was used in a supervised learning context (here, the original class labels were removed). vCV is again unreliable. Each of BIC, MCCV and AutoClass "zero-in" on the correct structure given enough data, with BIC appearing to require more data to find the correct structure.

Real Data Sets

Below we discuss the application of MCCV (and the comparison methods) to several real data sets. Table 2 contains a brief summary of the results. Each of these data sets has a known classification: the clustering algorithms were run on the data with the class label information removed. Note that unlike the simulated examples, the number of classes in the original classified data set is not necessarily the "correct" answer for the clustering procedure, e.g., it is possible that the a particular class in the original data is best described by two or more "sub-clusters," or that the clusters are in fact non-Gaussian.

Iris Data The classic "iris" data set contains 150 4-dimensional measurements of plants classified into 3 species. It is well known that 2 of the species are overlapped in the feature-space and the other is well-separated from these 2 (Figure 2(a)). MCCV indicates 2 clusters with some evidence of 3. AutoClass found 4 clusters and BIC found 2 (the fact that vCV found 3 clusters is probably a fluke). It is quite possible that the clusters are in fact non-Gaussian and, thus, do not match the clustering model (e.g., the measurements have limited precision, somewhat invalidating the Gaussian assumption). Given these caveats, and

the relatively small sample size, each of the methods are both providing useful insight into the data.

Diabetes Data Reaven and Miller (1979) analyzed 3-dimensional plasma measurement data for 145 subjects who were clinically diagnosed into three groups: normal, chemically diabetic, or overtly diabetic. This data set has since been analyzed in the statistical clustering literature by Symons (1981) and Banfield and Raftery (1993). When viewed in any of the 2-dimensional projections along the measurement axes, the data are not separated into obvious groupings: however, some structure is discernible (Figure 2(b)). The MCCV algorithm detected 3 clusters in the data (as did vCV and AutoClass). BIC incorrectly detected 4 classes. It is encouraging that the MCCV algorithm found the same number of classes as that of the original clinical classification. We note that the "approximate weight of evidence" clustering criterion of Banfield and Raftery (1993) (based on a Bayesian approximation) was maximized at $k = 4$ clusters and indicated evidence of between 3 to 6 clusters.

Speech Vowel Data Peterson and Barney (1952) measured the location of the first and second prominent peaks (formants) in 671 estimated spectra from subjects speaking various vowel sounds. They classified the spectra into 10 different vowel sounds based on acoustic considerations. This data set has since been used in the neural network literature with the best cross-validated classification accuracies being around 80%. As can be seen in Figure 2(c) the classes are heavily overlapped. Thus, this is a relatively difficult problem for methods which automatically try to find the correct number of clusters. AutoClass detected 5 clusters, while MCCV detected 7, with some evidence between 6 and 9 clusters. BIC completely underestimated the number of clusters at 2. Given the relatively small sample size (one is fitting each cluster using only roughly 30 sample points), the MCCV algorithm is do-

Table 2: Experimental results on non-simulated data.

Problem	Sample Size	BIC	AC	vCV	MCCV	"Truth"
Iris	150	2	4	3	2	3
Diabetes	145	4	3	3	3	3
Vowels	671	2	5	8	7	10

ing well to indicate the possibility of a large number of clusters.

Discussion

The MCCV method performed roughly as well as AutoClass on the particular data sets used in this paper. The BIC method performed quite well, but overall was not as reliable as MCCV or AutoClass. vCV (with v=10) was found to be largely unreliable. Further experimentation on more complex problems may reveal some systematic differences between the Bayesian (AutoClass) and cross-validation (MCCV) approaches, but both produced clear insights into the structure of the data sets used in the experiments in this paper.

We note in passing that Chickering and Heckerman (1996) have investigated a problem which is equivalent to that addressed in this paper, except that the feature vector x is now discrete-valued and and the individual features are assumed independent given the (hidden) class variable. Chickering and Heckerman empirically evaluated the performance of AutoClass, BIC, and other approximations to the full Bayesian solution on a wide range of simulated problems. Their results include conclusions which are qualitatively similar to those reported here: namely that the AutoClass approximation to the full Bayesian solution outperforms BIC in general and that BIC tends to be overly conservative in terms of the number of components it prefers.

The theoretical basis of the MCCV algorithm warrants further investigation. For example, MCCV is somewhat similar to the bootstrap method. A useful result would be a characterization (under appropriate assumptions) of the basic bias-variance properties of the MCCV likelihood estimate (in the mixture context) as a function of the leave-out fraction β, the number of cross-validation runs M, the sample size N, and some measure of the problem complexity. Prescriptive results for choosing β automatically (as developed in Shao (1993) in a particular regression context) would be useful. For example, it would be useful to justify in theory the apparent practical utility of $\beta = 0.5$.

On the practical front, clearly there is room for improvement over the basic algorithm described in this paper. The probabilistic cluster models can easily be extended beyond the full-covariance model to incorporate, for example, the geometric shape and Poisson "outlier" models of Banfield and Raftery (1993) and Celeux and Govaert (1995), and the discrete variable models in AutoClass. Diagnostic tests for detecting non-Gaussianity could also easily be included (cf.

McLachlan and Basford (1988), Section 2.5) and would be a useful practical safeguard.

Some obvious improvements could also be made to the search strategy. Instead of "blindly" searching over each possible value of k from 1 to $k_{\max}$ a more intelligent search could be carried out which "zeros-in" on the range of k which has appreciable posterior probability mass (the current implementation of the AutoClass algorithm includes such a search algorithm).

Data-driven methods for automatically selecting the leave-out fraction method β are also a possibility, or possibly averaging results over multiple values of β. When the data are few relative to the number of clusters present, it is possible for the cross-validation partitioning to produce partitions where no data from a particular cluster is present in the training partition. This will bias the estimate towards lower k values (since the more fractured the data becomes, the more likely this "pathology" is to occur). A possible solution is some form of data-driven *stratified* cross-validation (Kohavi (1995) contains a supervised learning implementation of this idea).

Both the EM and MCCV techniques are amenable to very efficient parallel implementations. For large sample sizes N, it is straightforward to assign $1/p$ of the data to p processors working in parallel which communicate via a central processor. For large numbers of cross-validation runs M, each of p processors can independently run M/p runs.

Finally we note that our attention was initially drawn to this problem in a time-series clustering context using hidden Markov models. In this context, the general MCCV methodology still applies but because of sample dependence the cross-validation partitioning strategy must be modified—this is currently under development. The MCCV approach to mixtures described here can also be applied to supervised learning with mixtures: the MCCV procedure provides an automatic method for determining how many components to use to model each class. Other extensions to learning of graphical models (Bayesian networks) and image segmentation are also possible.

Conclusions

MCCV clustering appears to be a useful idea for determining cluster structure in a probabilistic clustering context. Experimental results indicate that the method has significant practical potential. The method complements Bayesian solutions by being simpler to implement and conceptually easier to extend to more complex clustering models than Gaussian mixtures.

Acknowledgments

The author would like to thank Alex Gray for assistance in using the AutoClass software. The research described in this paper was carried out by the Jet Propulsion Laboratory, California Institute of Technology, under a contract with the National Aeronautics and Space Administration.

References

Banfield, J. D., and Raftery, A. E. 1993. 'Model-based Gaussian and non-Gaussian clustering,' *Biometrics*, 49, 803–821.

Burman, P. 1989 'A comparative study of ordinary cross-validation, *v*-fold cross-validation, and the repeated learning-testing methods,' *Biometrika*, 76(3), 503–514.

Celeux, G., and Govaert, G. 1995. 'Gaussian parsimonious clustering models,' *Pattern Recognition*, 28(5), 781–793.

Cheeseman, P. and Stutz. J. 1996. 'Bayesian classification (AutoClass): theory and results,' in *Advances in Knowledge Discovery and Data Mining*, U. M. Fayyad, G. Piatetsky-Shapiro, P. Smyth, R. Uthurusamy (eds.), Cambridge, MA: AAAI/MIT Press, pp. 153–180.

Chickering, D. M., and Heckerman, D. 1996. 'Efficient approximations for the marginal likelihood of incomplete data given a Bayesian network,' MSR-TR-96-08 Technical Report, Microsoft Research, Redmond, WA.

Chow, Y. S., Geman, S. and Wu, L. D. 1983. 'Consistent cross-validated density estimation,' *The Annals of Statistics*, 11(1), 25–38.

Diebolt, J. and Robert, C. P. 1994. 'Bayesian estimation of finite mixture distributions,' *J. R. Stat. Soc. B*, 56, 363–375.

Gelman, A., J. B. Carlin, H. S. Stern, D. B. Rubin. 1995. *Bayesian Data Analysis*, London, UK: Chapman and Hall.

Jain, A. K., and R. C. Dubes. 1988. *Algorithms for Clustering Data*, Englewood Cliffs, NJ: Prentice Hall.

Kohavi, R. 1995. 'A study of cross-validation and bootstrap for accuracy estimation and model selection,' *Proc. Int. Joint. Conf. AI*, Montreal.

McLachlan, G. J. and K. E. Basford. 1988. *Mixture Models: Inference and Applications to Clustering*, New York: Marcel Dekker.

Peterson, G. and Barney, H. 1952. 'Control methods used in the study of vowels,' . *J. Acoust. Soc. Am.*, 24, 175–184.

Reaven, G. M., and Miller, R. G. 1979. 'An attempt to define the nature of chemical diabetes using a multi-dimensional analysis,' *Diabetologia*, 16, 17–24.

Ripley, B. D. 1994. 'Neural networks and related methods for classification (with discussion),' *J. Roy. Stat. Soc. B*, 56, 409–456.

Sclove, S. C. 1983. 'Application of the conditional population mixture model to image segmentation,' *IEEE Trans. Patt. Anal. Mach. Intell.*, PAMI-5, 428–433.

Shao, J. 1993. 'Linear model selection by cross-validation,' *J. Am. Stat. Assoc.*, 88(422), 486–494.

Silverman, B. W. 1986. *Density Estimation for Statistics and Data Analysis*, Chapman and Hall.

Symons, M. 1981. 'Clustering criteria and multivariate normal mixtures,' *Biometrics*, 37, 35–43.

Titterington, D. M., A. F. M. Smith, U. E. Makov. 1985. *Statistical Analysis of Finite Mixture Distributions*, Chichester, UK: John Wiley and Sons.

Harnessing Graphical Structure in Markov Chain Monte Carlo Learning

Paul E. Stolorz
Jet Propulsion Laboratory
California Institute of Technology
Pasadena, CA 91109
pauls@aig.jpl.nasa.gov

Philip C. Chew *
University of Pennsylvania
Philadelphia PA
chew@upenn5.hep.upenn.edu

Abstract

The Monte Carlo method is recognized as a useful tool in learning and probabilistic inference methods common to many datamining problems. Generalized Hidden Markov Models and Bayes nets are especially popular applications. However, the presence of multiple modes in many relevant integrands and summands often renders the method slow and cumbersome. Recent mean field alternatives designed to speed things up have been inspired by experience gleaned from physics. The current work adopts an approach very similar to this in spirit, but focusses instead upon dynamic programming notions as a basis for producing systematic Monte Carlo improvements. The idea is to approximate a given model by a dynamic programming-style decomposition, which then forms a scaffold upon which to build successively more accurate Monte Carlo approximations. Dynamic programming ideas alone fail to account for non-local structure, while standard Monte Carlo methods essentially ignore all structure. However, suitably-crafted hybrids can successfully exploit the strengths of each method, resulting in algorithms that combine speed with accuracy. The approach relies on the presence of significant "local" information in the problem at hand. This turns out to be a plausible assumption for many important applications. Example calculations are presented, and the overall strengths and weaknesses of the approach are discussed.

Introduction

The Monte Carlo method has been used for a number of years to estimate complex multidimensional integrals for systems containing many degrees of freedom [5]. It has been particularly successful when applied to systems in which each variable interacts with other variables with a constant interaction strengh that remains the same, or similar, throughout the system. However, when significant inhomogeneities appear in the interaction strengths over different parts of the system, Monte Carlo methods become much less efficient. The problem is basically a manifestation of the multiple modes that appear in the integrand in this regime,

---

*Current address:EECS Department, Massachusetts Institute of Technology

which makes it difficult for the Monte Carlo procedure to jump between the various modes.

One well-known example of this distinction is supplied by the notorious Ising model [9]. Although the Ising model was originally developed as an abstraction to model physical systems, it turns out to be essentially equivalent to Hidden Markov Models and several other architectures useful in machine learning [2, 3, 8, 19]. It is therefore an excellent testing ground for describing and testing new Monte Carlo sampling ideas. A standard Ising model consists of a collection of binary elements with constant energetic interactions between all its elements. It can be simulated with reasonable efficiency by a Monte Carlo sampling procedure. However, as soon as the interaction strengths become heterogeneous (a common situation in the machine learning context), corresponding to a physical system known as an Ising spin glass, Monte Carlo simulations exhibit huge equilibration problems. In fact, understanding the extreme case of zero temperature for an Ising spin glass, which amounts to finding the minimum energy states, has been proven to be an NP-Complete problem.

The situation becomes even worse when various recently developed improvements, such as clustering methods, are considered [6]. These methods, based upon the simultaneous re-arrangement of blocks of variables, are often thought of as the introduction of auxiliary variables to the problem [2, 3]. They have been outstandingly successful at improving equilibration times for regular Ising models, but they break down completely in the spin glass case. Modifications that attempt to address the disorder present in spin glasses have been developed, but the results are somewhat disappointing [17].

A complementary approach to Monte Carlo methods that has existed in the physics literature for many years is the use of "transfer matrices" [9]. Transfer matrices can be used when the system under investigation consists only of local interactions in a small number dimensions. In this case the integrands or summands of interest can be calculated exactly by recursively building up the model under consideration a few units at a time. Recursive approaches such as this are extremely powerful when only local interactions are involved, because they are immune to equilibration problems, regardless of whether disorder is present. Of course, NP-Completeness does not vanish as a difficulty. It manifests itself in the need for an exponentially growing memory requirement in at least one dimension. However, for many problems such as the investigation of graphical models in data mining, this is not always a severe drawback, as the problems are often organized roughly as causal chains. Hidden Markov Models, for example, are arranged as linear chains. The difficulty is that for many interesting and useful models there may be a small number of "non-local" interactions between units quite distant in the chain. In this case a transfer matrix approach obviously cannot be used.

The Monte Carlo method described in this paper is designed to combine the best features of Monte Carlo and transfer matrix methods, and to apply them to problems where neither approach is successful on its own. The method is a variant of the Hastings generalization [4] of the classic Metropolis method [5]. It applies to models with discrete variables, in which a substantial number of interactions are local, but with a smaller number of non-local interactions present.

Review of Metropolis Monte Carlo

In this section standard Monte Carlo methods such as the Metropolis method will be reviewed, with an emphasis on the crucial points at which computational overhead due to heterogeneity enters the picture. Some of the ideas will be presented in a slightly non-standard way, which will help to motivate the modifications and alternatives that follow in the next section.

Suppose we have a system described by a cost function $E(C)$ (or energy function, or Hamiltonian function), associated with each of an enormous number of configurations C. These functions can be related by the Hammersly-Clifford theorem to an enormous class of probability distributions useful in the learning context, so they good starting point for a general Monte Carlo discussion. For concreteness, consider the calculation of the "average energy" over the entire set of configurations, defined by

$$< E >= \sum_C E_C e^{-\beta E_C} / Z \qquad (1)$$

where β is a positive fixed parameter, and

$$Z = \sum_C e^{-\beta E_C} \qquad (2)$$

is a normalization constant. The average energy occurs frequently in the study of statistical mechanics, where β is interpreted as the inverse temperature. It is also extensively used in image processing applications, where β denotes the amount of noise in an image.

The question we want to answer is: how can $< E >$ be estimated without considering each and every configuration C? One simple way to do this is to evenly sample the space of configurations N times, and to estimate $< E >$ by

$$< E >\approx \sum_{i=1}^{N} E_i e^{-\beta E_i} / \sum_{i=1}^{N} e^{-\beta E_i} \qquad (3)$$

The main problem with this approach can be seen by rewriting $< E >$ in the following form:

$$< E >= \sum_E E N(E) e^{-\beta E} / Z \qquad (4)$$

where $N(E)$ is the number of states of energy E. The trade-off between the functions $N(E)$ and $e^{-\beta E}$ lies at the heart of statistical mechanics. Consider for example their product Π, which represents the probability of obtaining energy E,

$$\Pi(E) = N(E) e^{-\beta E} / Z \qquad (5)$$

Since the product is extremely peaked, all the important contributions to $< E >$ will come from a small band of the energy spectrum. Unfortunately, the even sampling of configuration space will select a great number of states with high energy (since there are a large number of these!), which will subsequently make very little contribution because of their small exponential weighting factor.

The essence of the importance sampling idea is to *generate* states in proportion to the probability distribution $e^{-\beta E_c}/Z$, hereafter referred to as the Boltzmann distribution. The average energy is then estimated from

$$< E >= 1/N \sum_i^N E_i \qquad (6)$$

In this way most of the generated states can be made to fall within the range of important energies, and they will all make meaningful contributions to the sum.

Let's see in a little more detail how this works in the Metropolis method, a widely used method for generating the Boltzmann distribution. We generate a chain of states, beginning with state C_1, by randomly making some change to C_1 to create a new configuration C_2, This new configuration is accepted or rejected according to the transition probability distribution

$$W(C_1 -> C_2) = T(C_1 -> C_2) A(C_1 -> C_2) \qquad (7)$$

where $T(C_1 -> C_2)$ is the probability of selecting state C_2 given C_1, and

$$A(C_1 -> C_2) = min(1, P(C_2)/P(C_1)) \qquad (8)$$

is the probability of accepting the choice C_2 in the Markov chain. $T(C_1 -> C_2)$ can be almost any distribution, provided only that it is symmetric with respect to the choice of C_1 and C_2.

Under mild conditions, it can be proved that the states of this Markov chain will be asymptotically distributed with Boltzmann weight. Satisfied now that the chain of states $C_1, C_2, C_3....$ is producing states in proportion to the Boltzmann distribution, we ask ourselves the following question: "What is the probability P_E, given energy E_1, of going to a new energy level E_2 by a Metropolis move?" Suppose that the Metropolis move only allows one variable in the whole state to be changed. Well, we have

$$P_E(E_1 -> E_2) = T_E(E_1 -> E_2)A(C_1 -> C_2) \quad (9)$$

where $T_E(E_1 -> E_2)$ is the probability of selecting a state of energy E_2 given a state of energy E_1, and where

$$T_E(E_1 -> E_2) \propto N(E) \quad (10)$$

since by randomly choosing a new state in the configuration space, there will be slightly more chance of obtaining a higher energy state than a lower energy state (there are more of them available). Hence the procedure samples energy E near the peak of the product distribution $\Pi(E)$: there is more chance of choosing a higher energy than lower energy by random selection, which is compensated for by smaller Boltzmann weight. The process of randomly selecting a new state "near" an old one in state space is really a *de facto* way of sampling the density of states $N(E)$ around the energy E. By choosing a nearby state, we make sure that the allowed range of E that is explored remains small for trial new states, so that we remain near the peak of $\Pi(E)$ when the Boltzmann weight is factored in, and so that the whole procedure is reasonably efficient.

Why is the above interpretation of the Metropolis procedure illuminating? Because it tells us precisely what motivates the first step in a Metropolis algorithm of generating new configurations by making relatively small changes to old configurations: namely, in the absence of any other information, *it is the only way we know of to sample the configuration space in proportion to the density of states $N(E)$ in a controlled (usually small) energy interval around the old energy E*. This observation is crucial to understanding how Monte Carlo methods break down when applied to disordered systems. For a homogeneous system, for example, the configuration space can be searched ergodically by making small changes to a series of configurations. One will eventually wander over a large region of the configuration space. However, when disorder is introduced, this is no longer the case: by considering only small changes to successive configurations, we can easily end up being stuck in areas of configuration space separated by entropic barriers (i.e. large configuration changes) from other areas.

The interpretion also suggests what must be done in order to to generate a more efficient Monte Carlo procedure: find other ways of searching configuration space while retaining condition in italics above.

New method - Theory

Consider to begin with the concrete example of a simple 1-dimensional Ising model of discrete units S_i connected by nearest-neighbor interactions, together with a dilute concentration of long-range interactions. Denote this cost function by

$$H = H_0 + H_{nl} \quad (11)$$
$$= -\sum_{<ij>} J_{ij}S_iS_j - \sum_{>ij<} J_{ij}S_iS_j \quad (12)$$

where H_0 decribes the nearest-neighbor interactions (the summation $<ij>$), and H_{nl} the long-range interactions (the summation $>ij<$. When the interaction strengths J_{ij} in this model vary along the 1D chain, the energy surface defined by H_0 is in general a highly complex one, displaying many local minima, and gives rise to severe ergodicity problems when a Monte Carlo procedure is applied. For small system sizes, the difficulty can be circumcumvented by using a computer to generate the exact partition function Z recursively, although this approach can no longer be used when long-range interactions are introduced. However, when the number of long-range interactions introduced is quite dilute, it can be expected that their main effect will be to alter the H_0 energy landscape in a limited way. It follows that a Monte Carlo procedure which makes maximum explicit use of the information contained in H_0 (as the transfer matrix does) will be extremely useful, particularly if it is able to sample H_0 efficiently across a large portion of the state space. It is just such an algorithm that is described here.

The first step towards this goal is to construct the exact density of states for the local cost function H_0. This can be achieved by adding one discrete variable at a time to build up a large system recursively. Given a model containing $L - 1$ variables, the appropriate recursion is

$$N_0[L][E][s] = N_0[L - 1][E - \Delta(s)][s] + N_0[L - 1][E - \Delta'(s')][s'] \quad (13)$$

where s and s' denote the possible values of the last variable in the system (assumed to have two values in this case), and E labels the various possible energy levels. The procedure is illustrated in Figure 1.

The idea of building up the density of states recursively by computer is due to Bhanot and Creutz [14]. Related recursions have been used by many authors. However, the uniquely attractive feature of the Bhanot and Creutz formalism is the fact that it can be generalized to perform the following task. By retaining in memory every step $N_0[L][E][s]$ of the build-up process, states of any given energy E can be straightforwardly reconstructed by simply back-tracking through the array $N_0[L][E][s]$, starting at the desired energy level E. This observation has been applied to the analysis of short-range spin glasses [12] and protein models [13]. It is a broadly useful extension for the deceptively simple reason that it allows states of identical energy H_0, but radically different structure, to be generated easily in a way that is directly controlled by the exact density of states. A small set of possible reconstructions is displayed in Figure 2. Note the similarity of the method to the classic technique of dynamic programming [11].

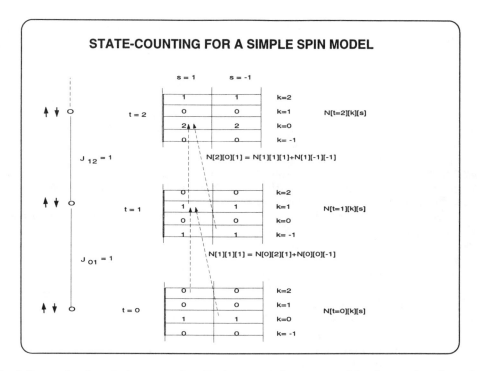

STATE-COUNTING FOR A SIMPLE SPIN MODEL

Figure 1: On the left are the first 3 elements of a 1D chain with binary variables (up or down), with the associated density of states on the right, showing the basic recursion for the first 3 steps.

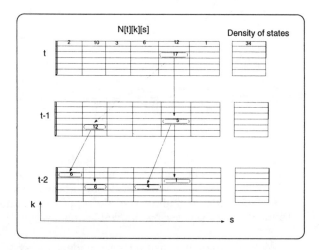

Figure 2: Recursive reconstruction of states with well-controlled energies from density of states array

The array $N_0[L][E][s]$, and its associated back-tracking procedure, can now be used to embed the following unusual form of Monte Carlo method for the full Hamiltonian H. Given a state C_i, choose a new state C_j according to the transition matrix

$$T_{ij}^0 = \frac{N_0(E_j)}{\sum_{k=i,i\pm1} N_0(E_k)} \quad if\,k = i, i \pm 1 \quad (14)$$

$$= 0; \quad otherwise \quad (15)$$

This sampling is straightforward to implement by com-puter using the information contained in N_0. Now apply a generalized Metropolis-like acceptance criterion, with acceptance probability

$$A_{ij} = min(1, \frac{T_{ji}^0 p_j}{T_{ij}^0 p_i}) \quad (16)$$

$$p_j = e^{-\beta(H_0 + H_{nl})} \quad (17)$$

This type of generalized Metropolis procedure was first introduced by Hastings [4], and has also been used in physics computations based on renormalization ideas [10]. The key idea in our implementation is that of choosing the local density of states as the Hastings transition function. Because this function is built up recursively, while retaining a large amount of structural information about the configuration space of the system at each stage, this in turn allows large configurational rearrangements to be attempted with a high chance of success.

In order to guarantee asymptotic convergence to the Boltzmann distribution, it is advisable that the algorithm possess the property of detailed balance. It is easy to see that detailed balance is satisfied by this procedure: the overall transition probability W_{ij} satisfies

$$\frac{W_{ij}}{W_{ji}} = \frac{T_{ij}^0 A_{ij}}{T_{ji}^0 A_{ji}} = \frac{p_j}{p_i} \quad (18)$$

Any choice of selection probability of course satisfies detailed balance under this generalised Metropolis procedure. The original Metropolis method is recovered by using a symmetric selection matrix. What is the advantage of using the asymmetric selection matrix T_{ij}^0 instead of the symmetric Metropolis form? It is the fact that a single step of the sampling procedure is now capable of generating a new state which is completely different than the current state, and yet has identical local energy H_0. The algorithm is therefore totally impervious to the "landscape complexity" of the local Hamiltonian H_0, and is able to traverse the state space of H_0 across many local minima with high efficiency. It is only the modications that are introduced by the non-local portion of the Hamiltonian H_{nl} that can lead to trouble in the form of inefficient sampling of the state space. The method thus provides a mechanism for generating highly efficient non-local moves in the state space. An obvious caveat is of course that the local portion of the Hamiltonian must reflect some reasonable fraction of the structure of the overall full Hamiltonian.

The method has been introduced here in a manner familiar from statistical physics, in which the density of states is separated from an exponential Boltzmann factor. However, the general idea is by no means restricted to the situation of an integrand or summand separable in this way. A perfectly feasible alternative would be to generate the entire product $N_0(E)exp(-\beta E)$ recursively, and to use this function as the Hastings transition function. The overriding point is simply the ability to distinguish between a local portion of the Monte Carlo summand that can be built up recursively, and a separate non-local portion that can be dealt with as a Monte Carlo correction.

New Method - Simulations

We have investigated the properties of this new algorithm by introducing modifications to the simplest type of Markov model, namely a 1D Ising model. Local 1D Ising models containing 1000 spins were prepared, with random nearest-neighbor interactions. Non-local interactions were then inserted randomly between any two spins in the system, creating models in which on average 20% of the interactions were non-local. Note that 2D and 3D Ising models correspond to very particular choices for non-local interactions, so the formalism is actually quite general in scope. The model is a prototype of the most natural kind of generalized Hidden Markov Model. For example, it can be applied to model and predict 3-dimensional protein folding [13], in which non-local interactions are known to play an important role. Hidden Markov Models have been applied in the past to perform protein sequence alignment using local information only.

Monte Carlo simulations were run using the Metropolis algorithm, and various window sizes for the hybrid procedure discussed here. The window size represents the size of 1D subsystem to which the density of states procedure was applied. In order to measure the convergence properties of the various algorithms,

the autocorrelation function of the energy and magnetization was then measured. The results are shown in Figure 3. This is a standard method of characterising equilibration times. Notice the dramatic improvement in equilibration times displayed in this figure as the "window size" W is increased from 1 (the regular Metropolis method) up to the limit of the system size. The procedure is clearly able to capture the structure of the local 1D energy function easily, and is only slowed down by the relatively small number of non-local interactions. Overall, an improvement of at least 2 orders of magnitude is supplied by the method.

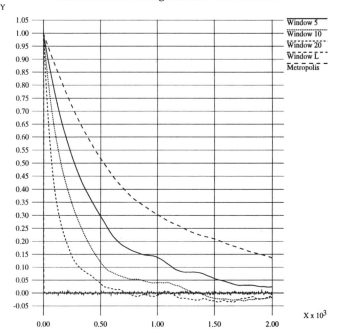

Figure 3: Results for 1D spin model with 20% non-local interactions. Shown are the magnetization autocorrelation functions for simulations using different window sizes (see text), including the Metropolis case and a window of size L covering the whole spin system.

We have also experimented with model Ising systems containing 10% non-local interactions, with similar results. In addition, equilibration times are known to depend strongly on the temperature at which the system is simulated. At high enough tempatures, all simulations are straightforward - it is only at low temperature that these issues become problematic. We find similar behaviour in the autocorrelation function over a range of temperatures, confirming the value of the approach as a general method.

Conclusions

What are the limitations and drawbacks of this approach to Monte Carlo simulation? To begin with, it requires the use of discrete variables. Secondly, the problem tackled must have a reasonable amount of linear structure in its graphical representation. However, this condition is already substantially looser than the restriction to purely local interactions required by many approaches to learning in graphical models. In fact, the basic recursive computational apparatus used as the underpinning of the hybrid Monte Carlo presented here is analogous to exact recursive EM procedures used in HMM learning, and to exact inference methods used by Bayesian nets [1, 13]. The unique feature of the current work is their use as a scaffold on which to build a general Monte Carlo procedure for more complex models as well.

One particular advantage of the method is that it enables extensive use of the Hastings Monte Carlo approach without being restricted to a choice of new configurations from univariate distributions. Historically this has been the main limitation hampering the liberal use of the Hastings approach. This aspect is in fact the key to the development of genuinely efficient Monte Carlo methods for complex interacting systems. It is not enough in general to generate new configurations by making substantial changes to just one variable, no matter how clever the change. Rather, large configurational changes in several variables simultaneously are required, while at the same time avoiding large alterations to the energy of the states involved. The method outlined here is a step towards the realization of this goal for certain classes of graphical models.

Acknowledgements

The research described in this paper was performed at the Jet Propulsion Laboratory, California Institute of Technology, under a contract with the National Aeronautics and Space Administration. Support for PCC was provided by the University Scholars Program at the University of Pennsylvania.

References

[1] D. Heckerman, M. Jordan and P. Smyth (1995), "Conditional Independence graphs for Hidden Markov Probability Models", *Tech. Report submitted for publication.*

[2] A.F. Smith and G.O. Roberts (1993). "Bayesian computation via the Gibbs sampler and related Markov chain Monte Carlo methods (with discussion)", *J. Roy. Stat. Soc.* B55, 3-23.

[3] J.E. Besag and P.J. Green (1993). "Spatial Statistics and Bayesian computation (with Discussion)", *J. Roy. Stat. Soc.* B55, 25-37.

[4] W.K. Hastings (1970). "Monte Carlo sampling methods using Markov chains and their applications", *Biometrika*, 57, 97-109.

[5] N. Metropolis, A.W. Rosenbluth, M.N. Rosenbluth, A.H. Teller and E. Teller (1953). "Equations of state calculations by fast computing machines", *J. Chem. Phys.* 21, 1087-1091.

[6] R.H. Swendsen and J.S. Wang (1987). "Nonuniversal critical dynamics in Monte Carlo simulations", *Phys. Rev. Lett.* 58, 86-88.

[7] R.M. Neal 1994. "Sampling from Multimodal Distributions Using Tempered Transitions", *Univ. of Toronto Tech. Report 9421.*

[8] J. York and D. Madigan (1992). "Markov Chain Monte Carlo Methods for Hierarchical Bayesian Expert Systems", *Proc. 4th Int. Workshop on AI and Statistics*, 433-439.

[9] R.P. Feynman (1972). *Statistical Mechanics: A Set of Lectures.*

[10] K.E. Schmidt (1983). *Phys. Rev. Lett.* 51, 2175-2178.

[11] R. Bellman (1957). *Dynamic Programming.*

[12] P. Stolorz (1993). "Recursive Approaches to Short-range Disordered Systems in the Low-temperature Regime", *Phys. Rev.* B48, 3085-3091.

[13] P. Stolorz (1994). "Recursive Approaches to the Statistical Physics of Lattice Proteins", *Proc. 27th Hawaii International Conf. on System Sciences*, Vol V, 316-325.

[14] G. Bhanot, M. Creutz and J. Lacki (1992), "*Phys. Rev. Lett.* 69, 1841-1843.

[15] L. Saul and M. Jordan (1995). "Exploiting Tractable Substructure in Intractable Networks", *Adv. in Neur. Inf. Proc.Syst.* to appear.

[16] E. Marinari and G. Parisi (1992). "Simulated tempering: a new Monte Carlo scheme", *Europhys. Lett.* 19, 451-458.

[17] D. Kandel, E. Domany and A. Brandt (1989). "Simulations withoug critical slowing down: ising and three-state Potts models:, *Phys. Rev.* B40, 330-344.

[18] B.A. Berg and T. Celik (1992). "New approach to spin-glass simulations", *Phys. Rev. Lett.* 69, 2292-2295.

[19] R.M. Neal (1994). "Probabilistic inference using Markov Chain Monte Carlo methods", *Univ. of Toronto Tech. Report CRG-TR-93-1.*

Imputation of missing data using machine learning techniques

Kamakshi Lakshminarayan, Steven A. Harp, Robert Goldman and **Tariq Samad**

3660 Technology Drive
Honeywell Technology Center
Minneapolis, MN55418, USA
klakshmi@src.honeywell.com

Abstract

A serious problem in mining industrial data bases is that they are often incomplete, and a significant amount of data is missing, or erroneously entered. This paper explores the use of machine-learning based alternatives to standard statistical data completion (data imputation) methods, for dealing with missing data. We have approached the data completion problem using two well-known machine learning techniques. The first is an unsupervised clustering strategy which uses a Bayesian approach to cluster the data into classes. The classes so obtained are then used to predict multiple choices for the attribute of interest. The second technique involves modeling missing variables by supervised induction of a decision tree-based classifier. This predicts the most likely value for the attribute of interest. Empirical tests using extracts from industrial databases maintained by Honeywell customers have been done in order to compare the two techniques. These tests show both approaches are useful and have advantages and disadvantages. We argue that the choice between unsupervised and supervised classification techniques should be influenced by the motivation for solving the missing data problem, and discuss potential applications for the procedures we are developing.

Introduction

We have experimented with using various machine learning techniques for completing industrial maintenance databases. These databases are usually (in our experience, always) incomplete and contaminated with erroneous data. Tools for completing partial data based on past experience would be useful both as preprocessing for further analysis and to provide assistance to people performing data entry. We have experimented with Autoclass, a Bayesian unsupervised learning method and C4.5, a decision-tree based supervised learning method. We describe our experiments, describe the results and draw conclusions. Both offer viable imputation and may be used in combination.

Structure of this paper

The organization of this paper is as follows. The first section describes the magnitude of the missing data problem in the type of industrial data bases maintained by Honeywell and its divisions. The next section introduces the two machine learning techniques which we have explored as potential data completion approaches, and describes how they could be used for data completion. The first of these two techniques, Autoclass, is an unsupervised clustering strategy due to Cheeseman et al. (1988) which uses a Bayesian approach to cluster the data into classes. The classes so obtained are then used to predict multiple choices for the attribute of interest. The second technique involves modelling missing variables by supervised induction of a decision tree-based classifier, C4.5, due to Quinlan (1993). This predicts the most likely value for the attribute of interest. The next section then presents empirical results from applying these two machine learning techniques for predicting missing data. The last two sections discusse potential applications of the procedures we are developing, related work in statistics respectively.

The Missing data problem

Like many businesses involved in the manufacture and service of complex equipment, Honeywell and its customers compile vast amounts of maintenance data. For a number of reasons, this data is plagued with errors and lacunae. We discuss the type of data with which we are working in this section.

Honeywell and its customers routinely compile maintenance information for plant and building equipment installed in various locations. Entry in these data bases is carried out by field personnel, and for various reasons is plagued by a high proportion of missing data fields. In addition, the entered data is sometimes erroneous, or is in a non-standard format and frequently has spelling errors.

The magnitude of the problem for a typical industrial process maintainence data base studied by one of Honeywell's business units, Honeywell Loveland Controls, is shown in Figure 1. This data base contains maintainence information from process control devices. Values for 82 variables or features are recorded in this data base. Some of these variables are symbolic and others are numeric. The variables measure properties

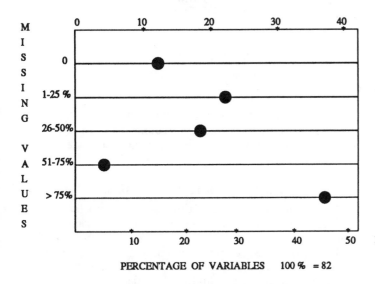

NUMBER OF VARIABLES

MISSING VALUES

PERCENTAGE OF VARIABLES   100 % = 82

Figure 1: Distribution of variables by missing values. Total number of variables = 82. Total number of records = 4383. Number of complete records = 0.

of the devices such as the manufacturer and model of the device, as well as states of the devices at various times such as calibration error, and pass/fail results of testing. Of the 4383 records in this data base, none of the records were complete and only 41 variables out of 82 have more than 50% of the records complete. This level of incompleteness of the data base seriously limits its usefulness to both analysts and field personnel.

Machine learning techniques for missing data imputation

We experimented with two machine learning (ML) systems: Autoclass and C4.5. These are sophisticated systems for unsupervised and supervised machine learning, respectively. In this section we briefly discuss these two tools.

Autoclass

The first algorithm we explored as a possible data completion tool was Autoclass, a program developed by Cheeseman et al.(1988) to automatically discover clusters in data. It is based on Bayesian classification theory (Hanson, Stutz & Cheeseman 1990) and belongs to the general family of unsupervised learning or clustering algorithms. The choice of Autoclass as a data completion tool was motivated by the fact it could be used to predict different attributes after a single learning session. This makes its use economical in terms of time, and is in direct contrast to supervised learning methods which need to be trained separately for each attribute to be predicted. One interesting feature of Autoclass is that it automatically searches for classes,

and, has limits preventing data overfitting, since it trades predictive accuracy versus complexity of classes. Readers interested in more details about this algorithm are referred to Cheeseman & Stutz (1996).

The input to Autoclass is separate files containing the training and test data and a file containing a description of the various fields/features in the data set. This description specifies the distribution of each feature: whether it is continuous or discrete valued and which fields contain missing values. Autoclass models each continuously distributed variable as being normally distributed, and each discrete variable as having an underlying multinomial distribution. The task of Autoclass is to divide the data set into number of classes, and determine probability distributions for each feature given each class. In order to avoid "overfitting" (in the extreme, assigning each case to its own class), a penalty is assessed for the complexity of the classification. The trade-off between prediction and complexity is accomplished by the fact that each parameter in the model brings its own multiplicative Bayesian prior to the model, thereby lowering the marginal likelihood of the model.

The output of Autoclass consists of the following:

- *The optimal classification for the training data.* Autoclass can automatically choose the number of classes or it can use a number suggested by the experimenter.

- *A conditional probability distribution of features given classes.* For discrete attributes, the description will specify the conditional probability of each feature value, given each class. I.e., for each class c and feature f, $P(f(x)|\text{class}(x) = c)$. For continuous attributes, the conditional probability distribution will be specified by giving the mean and variance of a Gaussian random variable. Autoclass models missing values for attributes as another discrete value, 'failure to observe'. In the case of discrete valued attributes, this would mean that there is yet another possible value which could be observed, namely failure to observe'. In the case of independent continuous valued attributes, the value observed could be 'failure to observe' with a probability p, (determined from the data), and a real number with probability $(1 - p)$.

- *A ranking of the variables according to importance in generating the classification.* This gives a rough heuristic measure of the "influence" of each attribute used in the classification.

- A probabilistic assignment of each case in the training and test data set to its class. I.e., for each case, x, and class, c, $P(\text{class}(x) = c)$.

Autoclass does not directly predict values of variables or features for the data in a test set. Rather, for each case x, Autoclass provides a probability distribution over the set of classes $\mathcal{C}$: $P(\text{class}(x) = C)$. We may use the conditional probability of features given classes to infer the most likely value or values of missing values of attributes of a case, given its class membership. To illustrate, let us assume that Autoclass after learning on the training set, classifies a test case x, as belonging to C_1 with probability 0.8, and C_2 with a probability of 0.2, based on the non-missing attribute values of x. If the value of a discrete attribute a is missing for this case, we could pick the most probable value of a in C_1 for the training cases, as the predicted value of attribute a for x. Another possibility is to pick the n most frequent values of attribute a in C_1 for the training cases, as potential candidates for prediction. Since class membership is probabilistic we chose the most likely class of each test case to predict its missing values. An alternative approach would be to predict a distribution over the value space for missing attributes, where the distribution is determined by the case's probablistic membership in various classes. In the case of a continuous attribute, we could use the mean of the distribution for the class as our prediction. The application involved in this paper involves prediction of missing values for discrete attributes only.

C4.5

The second machine learning approach to data completion we explored was C4.5, a supervised learning algorithm for decision tree induction developed by Quinlan (1993). C4.5 uses an information-based measure, usually gain ratio, as a splitting criterion in inducing its decision trees. A splitting criterion is a test, usually about the an input attribute's value, which partitions the cases into dis-joint sets. More details about C4.5's methodology for constructing decision trees can be found in Quinlan (1993). C4.5 takes as input a files containing training (pre-classified) and test cases, and a description of various attributes. Unlike Autoclass, C4.5 can be directly used to predict missing attribute values. This is done by using the values of the target attribute (for discrete-valued attributes) which is to be predicted for test cases, as the classes used for training. The training data should therefore have the target attribute value specified. C4.5 does not naturally handle continuous variables as target classes. One way to get around this would be to use intervals on the real line as classes, for continuous variables. One disadvantage with C4.5 compared to Autoclass, is that each candidate attribute for prediction needs a separate training session.

C4.5 uses a probablistic approach to handle missing values in the training and test data. Any case from the training set is assigned a weight w_i of having outcome O_i for the value of a particular attribute. If the outcome is known and has value O_i, then $w_i = 1$, and, all other outcomes are assigned a weight 0 for this case. If the outcome is missing, then the weight of any outcome O_j for that attribute, is the relative frequency of that outcome, among all training cases whose out-

Subset	Records	ML technique used
A	2117	Autoclass
B	257	-
C	235	Autoclass, C4.5

Table 1: Various subsets of data used in experiments

comes for this attribute are known. The approach used for the test data is similar. Of course, the target variable/attribute cannot be missing in the case of training data.

Experiments and results

We conducted several experiments with Autoclass and C4.5 to determine how well they predicted missing values in our experimental data set. For the purpose of the experiments described in this paper, we assumed that data was missing at random, and ignored the mechanism of missing data. We also assumed that there was no particular pattern missing, i.e. there was no correlations between the occurrence of missing values for different variables.

Data Used. A subset consisting of 2117 records culled from the data base described in Figure 1, was chosen for experimentation. Fourteen attribute fields identified by the domain expert as the most interesting were chosen for the initial analysis. We will refer to this chosen subset as data set A. The target feature chosen for prediction was the manufacturer of the device. There were a total of 52 manufacturers represented in the data base, of which 30 were represented more than once. Of the 2117 records, only 257 (subset B) had the value for the manufacturer specified, the remaining records had this value missing. Of the 257 records with the manufacturer specified, in 22 cases, the manufacturer was a singleton: there was only one record with that manufacturer in the entire data set. Accordingly, we culled those records to get a data set (subset C) of 235 records. Table 1 summarizes the details of the data chosen for the experiments.

Experiment 1. C4.5 was used to learn and predict values for the target variable, manufacturer, on the subset C. Since C4.5 is a supervised classifier it could not be trained on cases where the manufacturer value was missing. A ten-way cross-validation was done to evaluate the accuracy of prediction. In other words, the set C was partitioned randomly into ten subsets of similar size. Nine of these were used as the training set, and the induced tree was used for predicting on the tenth subset (test set). This process was repeated until all ten subsets were used as test sets. The average error over all the test sets was 22.6%.

Experiment 2. A 10-way cross-validation similar to that with C4.5 in Experiment 1 was done for Autoclass with subset C. The manufacturer was predicted for cases in the test set using the approach described in the previous section. The average error on all the test cases was 48.7%.

Experiment 3. This is similar to experiment 2 above in all details, except that the data set $(A - C)$ is added to each training set. Prediction is made on the same subsets as in experiment 2. The average error on test cases was again 48.7%. Considering the results of experiment 2 above, it appears that giving Autoclass the additional set of training cases was not helpful.

Experiment 4. Autoclass was used to cluster the 2117 records in data set A. *The manufacturer variable was not used as part of the input feature space.* The best (Autoclass uses the log posterior probability value for a classification to rank alternate models) classification produced by Autoclass had ten classes. When the classification was compared to distribution of manufacturers for the data points in C, it was found that each manufacturer tended to cluster in a few classes. This is illustrated in Figure 3. In order to evaluate this clustering the leave one out cross-validation task was done. As a benchmark for performance on this task, a prediction based only on the relative frequency of the manufacturer in the data was made. The top three choices for the manufacturer of each case in C were picked using Autoclass results and directly by relative frequency from the data itself. If the manufactuer for a given data point in C, was one of the top three choices, a hit was scored for that method of prediction. Autoclass scored a hit 82% (error rate 18%) of the time, while prediction from relative frequency in the data scored a hit 50% of the time.

The current version of C4.5 does not lend itself to multiple imputation since, it predicts the only best possible value for the target variable. We are working on extending the algorithm to allow C4.5 to do multiple imputation so that a comparison with Autoclass on the multiple prediction task is possible.

Experiment 5. One way to combine unsupervised and supervised learning methods is to use the former for feature extraction, and use the extracted features as input to the supervised classifier. Autoclass as mentioned earlier assigns to each case a probablistic classification. We used Autoclass to classify all the 2117 data points (subset A) after leaving out the manufacturer variable in the data base. The classes of each data point in C was given as input to C4.5, along with the usual information as in experiment 1 above. The results (error rate = 20.1% Table 2), indicate no statistically significant difference, (the t-test was used to compare the means of the 10-way cross validation results in experiment 1 and 5), between using the Autoclass class as an input feature, versus not using it as an input feature.

Autoclass ranks the input variables according to their contribution to the classification. When the two most highly ranked variables were removed from the input feature space of C4.5, and the same 10-way cross-validation was done the average error rate (21.3%) was again found to be not significantly different from experiment 1. This suggests that Autoclass may be used for feature extraction prior to using a decision tree based algorithm to decrease the input feature space for the latter. One interesting effect is that when the Autoclass class of each data point is given as input to C4.5, all the 'best' trees grown have the autoclass class as the root node.

Other results with Autoclass. In addition to a classification, there are interesting results which fall out of the Autoclass classification. One such result is depicted in Figure 2. It is seen here that records classified as belonging to class 7, have a higher linearity error, (deviation from linearity is an input feature, and high deviations from linearity are undesirable for the sensor devices in this data base), as compared to records in other classes. Since manufacturers (see Figure 3) are not distributed uniformly across the classes, in this case we can infer that devices from certain manufacturers are prone to a higher linearity error than others.

Conclusions

Applications of missing data imputation

There are several applications for the procedures we are developing. One application would be to directly assist the field personnel gathering data by offering likely options at data entry time. For example, a user entering information about a particular device could be offered a list of manufacturers to choose from. The choices would be ordered by the likelihood of manufacturers given the already entered information. Unsupervised approaches such as Autoclass, approaches are particularly useful for this since:

1. It can be used to predict multiple choices for an attribute;

2. It can be used to predict multiple target variables, unlike decision tree-based algorithms which have to be re-learned for each target variable.

Autoclass performs poorly when predicting a single value for a target variable, although results from experiment 4 indicate that it has a high accuracy when predicting multiple choices for the same target variable.

A second application of missing value completion is to render existing data bases more useful to analysts. This would allow the generation of more comprehensive summaries and charts (under the completion assumptions) using their regular tools. A decision tree algorithm such as C4.5 or a combination of C4.5 and Autoclass (as in experiment 5) would be useful for such data completion due to its high accuracy when predicting single values for missing data.

A third application would be in the detection of erroneous data. Filled-in-fields of records can be compared to the best guesses of the completion procedure. Outliers can then be examined by analysts or other procedures.

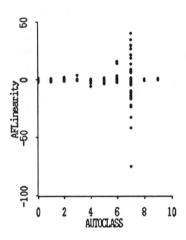

Figure 2: Distribution of linearity error against classes.

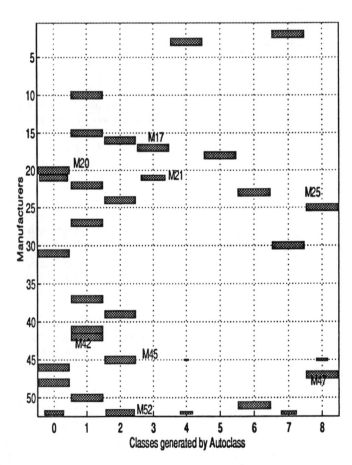

Figure 3: Each manufacturer is clustered in a few classes. The length of the boxes indicate relative proportion of each manufacturer in various classes.

Expt	Data	Method	Test error %	Comments
1	C	C4.5	22.6	
2	C	AC	48.7	
3	A	AC	48.7	Error not different from expt 2.
4	A	AC	18	Predict top 3 manufs.
4	A	Rel. freq in data	50	Predict top 3 manufs.
5	C	AC + C4.5	20.1	AC used as additional input feature.

Table 2: Comparison of results across experiments.

Related work

While the issue of missing data has been addressed in statistical research, most of this work has been directed toward statistical analysis of data with missing values. Some examples of this work are maximum-likelihood techniques, such as the EM algorithm, (Dempster, Laird & Rubin, (1977)). These techniques are helpful in parameter estimation in the presence of missing data, rather than imputation or the filling of missing values, (a.k.a. record completion). Statistical imputation, a less extensively researched field compared to statistical analysis with missing data, encompasses techniques such as mean imputation, regression imputation, hot-deck imputation etc. The former two have the disadvantage that they can be used only in cases where the data is continuous valued, and so cannot be used in cases where the missing data fields pertain to discrete valued attributes. Hot-deck imputation on the other hand can be used for numeric or symbolic valued features. In this method, an imputed value is selected from an estimated distribution for each missing value. This approach carries the same disadvantage as C4.5 in that each attribute needs to be handled individually unlike Autoclass. Currently, we are investigating this approach in order to compare its predictive accuracy with the ML-techniques described in this paper. See Little & Rubin(1987) for an overview of statistical analysis and imputation in databases with missing data.

Summary

We have demonstrated that ML-techniques could be used for missing data imputation in data bases. We have compared the performance of two such techniques, one a supervised classification algorithm, and the other an unsupervised clustering strategy. We also demonstrate how an unsupervised classifier could be used in combination with a supervised classifier. We discussed potential applications of such data imputation techniques and have argued that the choice of an unsupervised versus a supervised technique depends upon the motivation for solving the missing data problem.

References

Cheeseman, P., and Stutz, J. 1996. Bayesian Classification (Autoclass): Theory And Results In: *Advances in Knowledge Discovery and Data Mining*, Eds. Fayyad, U.M., Piatetsky-Shapiro, G., Smyth, P. and Uthurusamy, R. Pub. Menlo Park, California: AAAI Press.

Cheeseman, P., Kelly, J., Self, M., Stutz, J., Taylor, W., and Freeman, D. 1988. Bayesian Classification. In Proceedings of American Association of Artificial Intelligence(AAAI), 607-611, San Mateo, California:Morgan Kaufmann Publishers Inc.

Dempster, A.P., Laird, N.M. and Rubin, D.B. 1977. Maximum Likelihood from incomplete data via the EM algorithm (with discussion), *Journal of Royal Statistical Society* B39:1-38.

Hanson, R., Stutz, J. and Cheeseman, P. 1990. Bayesian Classification Theory, Technical Report, FIA-90-12-7-01, NASA, Ames.

Little, R.J., & Rubin, D.B. 1987. *Statistical Analysis with Missing Data*, New York: John Wiley & Sons.

Quinlan, J.R., 1993. *C4.5 Programs For Machine Learning*, San Mateo, California: Morgan Kaufmann Publishers Inc.

Discovering generalized episodes using minimal occurrences

Heikki Mannila and Hannu Toivonen
University of Helsinki
Department of Computer Science
P.O. Box 26, FIN-00014 Helsinki, Finland
Heikki.Mannila@cs.Helsinki.FI, Hannu.Toivonen@cs.Helsinki.FI

Abstract

Sequences of events are an important special form of data that arises in several contexts, including telecommunications, user interface studies, and epidemiology. We present a general and flexible framework of specifying classes of *generalized episodes*. These are recurrent combinations of events satisfying certain conditions. The framework can be instantiated to a wide variety of applications by selecting suitable primitive conditions. We present algorithms for discovering frequently occurring episodes and episode rules. The algorithms are based on the use of minimal occurrences of episodes; this makes it possible to evaluate confidences of a wide variety of rules using only a single analysis pass. We present empirical results on the behavior of the algorithms on events stemming from a WWW log.

Introduction

Sequences of events are a common form of data that can contain important knowledge to be discovered. Examples of such data are telecommunications network alarms, user interface actions, crimes committed by a person, occurrences of recurrent illnesses, etc. Recently, interest in knowledge discovery from sequences of events has increased: see, e.g., (Dousson, Gaborit, & Ghallab 1993; Laird 1993; Wang *et al.* 1994; Morris, Khatib, & Ligozat 1995; Bettini, Wang, & Jajodia 1996).

In a previous paper (Mannila, Toivonen, & Verkamo 1995) we showed how sequences of events can be analyzed by locating frequently occurring *episodes* from them. An episode is a combination of events with a partially specified order; it occurs in a sequence, if there are occurrences of the events in an order consistent with the given order, within a given time bound.

In a telecommunication application, the rules found using the methods of (Mannila, Toivonen, & Verkamo 1995) have proven to be useful and they have been integrated in alarm handling software (Hätönen *et al.*

1996). However, application studies both in the telecommunications domain and elsewhere have shown that there is a need for extensions to the methods.

In this paper we study what types of episodes can be efficiently discovered from long sequences of events. We present a simple and powerful framework for building episodes out of predefined predicates, and describe how such episodes can be discovered efficiently. The framework allows one to express arbitrary unary conditions on the individual events, and to pose binary conditions on the pairs of events, giving one the possibility to exactly target the types of event combinations that are interesting in the applications.

The algorithms described in the paper are based on *minimal occurrences* of episodes. In addition to being simple and efficient, this formulation has the advantage that the confidences and frequencies of rules with different time bounds can be obtained quickly, i.e., there is no need to rerun the analysis if one only wants to modify the time bounds. In case of complicated episodes, the time needed for recognizing the occurrence of an episode can be significant; the use of stored minimal occurrences of episodes eliminates unnecessary repetition of the recognition effort.

Episodes: patterns in event sequences

We use a fairly standard way of modeling events in time. Given the set $R = \{A_1, \ldots, A_m\}$ of *event attributes* with domains $D_{A_1}, \ldots, D_{A_m}$, an *event* e over R is a $(m+1)$-tuple $(a_1, \ldots, a_m, t)$, where $a_i \in D_{A_i}$ and t is a real number, the *time* of e. We refer to the time of e by $e.T$, and to an attribute $A \in R$ of e by $e.A$. An *event sequence* $\mathcal{S}$ is a collection of events over R, i.e., a relation over $R \cup \{T\}$, where the domain of attribute T is the set of real numbers.

An *episode* P on variables $\{x_1, \ldots, x_k\}$, denoted $P(x_1, \ldots, x_k)$, is a conjunction

$$\bigwedge_{i=1}^{k} \varphi_i(y_i, z_i),$$

where $y_i, z_i \in \{x_1, \ldots, x_k\}$ are event variables, and each conjunct $\varphi_i(x, y)$ has one of the forms $\alpha(x.A)$, $\beta(x.A, y.B)$, or $x.T \leq y.T$. Here A and B are event attributes, α is a predefined unary predicate on D_A, and β is a predefined binary predicate on $D_A \times D_B$. We assume that the available unary predicates include testing for equality with a constant, and that the binary predicates include equality. The *size* $|P|$ of an episode P is the number of conjuncts not involving time in P.

Example 1 In the telecommunications domain, event attributes are, e.g., *type*, *module*, and *severity*, indicating the type of alarm, the module that sent the alarm, and the severity of the alarm, respectively. An episode might look as follows:

$$x.type = 2356 \ \wedge \ y.type = 7401,$$

or

$$x.type = 2356 \ \wedge \ y.type = 7401 \ \wedge$$
$$x.T \leq y.T \ \wedge \ x.module = y.module.$$

The first episode indicates that two alarms of type 2356 and 7401 have to occur, whereas the second says that alarm 2356 has to precede 7401 and that the alarms have to come from the same module. Specification of, e.g., this condition was not possible in the framework of (Mannila, Toivonen, & Verkamo 1995).

The episode

$$x.type = 2356 \ \wedge \ y.type = 7401 \ \wedge$$
$$neighbor(x.module, y.module)$$

captures the situation when alarms of type 2356 and 7401 are sent from adjacent modules. □

Example 2 In analyzing a WWW log, the events have attributes *page* (the accessed page), *host* (the accessing host), and time. An example episode is

$$x.page = p_1 \ \wedge \ y.page = p_2 \ \wedge \ x.host = y.host,$$

indicating accesses to p_1 and p_2 from the same host. □

An episode $P(x_1, \ldots, x_k)$ *occurs* in a sequence of events $\mathcal{S} = (e_1, \ldots, e_n)$, *at interval* $[t, t']$, if there are disjoint events $e_{j_1}, \ldots, e_{j_k}$ such that $P(e_{j_1}, \ldots, e_{j_k})$ is true,[1] and $t \leq min_i\{e_{j_i}.T\}$ and $t' \geq max_i\{e_{j_i}.T\}$.

Note that one could write an SQL query that tests whether an episode of the above form occurs in a sequence, when the sequence is represented as a relation over $R \cup \{T\}$. The evaluation of such a query would, however, be quite inefficient, as the sequence form of the data could not easily be used. The recent work on sequence data in databases (see (Seshadri, Livny, & Ramakrishnan 1996)) provides interesting openings towards the use of database techniques in the processing of queries on sequences.

An occurrence of an episode P at $[t, t']$ is *minimal* if P does not occur at any proper subinterval $[u, u'] \subset [t, t']$. The *set of (intervals of) minimal occurrences* of an episode P is denoted by $mo(P)$:

$$mo(P) = \{[t, t'] \mid [t, t'] \text{ is a minimal occurrence of } P\}.$$

An *episode rule* is an expression $P[V] \Rightarrow Q[W]$, where P and Q are episodes, and V and W are real numbers. The informal interpretation of the rule is that if episode P has a minimal occurrence at interval $[t, t']$ with $t' - t \leq V$, then episode Q occurs at interval $[t, t'']$ for some t'' such that $t'' - t \leq W$.[2]

Example 3 An example rule in the WWW log is

$$x.page = p_1 \ \wedge \ y.page = p_2 \ \wedge$$
$$x.host = y.host \ [60]$$
$$\Rightarrow \quad x.page = p_1 \ \wedge \ y.page = p_2 \ \wedge$$
$$z.page = p_3 \ \wedge \ x.host = y.host \ \wedge$$
$$y.host = z.host \ [120]$$

expressing that if some host accesses pages p_1 and p_2 within a minute, page p_3 is likely to be accessed from the same host within two minutes. □

An episode $P(x_1, \ldots, x_k)$ is *serial*, if P includes conjuncts enforcing a total order between the x_i's. The episode is *parallel*, if there are no conditions on the relative order of the events.

The *frequency freq(P)* of an episode P in a given event sequence $\mathcal{S}$ is defined as the number of minimal occurrences of P in the sequence $\mathcal{S}$, $freq(P) = |mo(P)|$. Given a *frequency threshold min_fr*, an episode P is *frequent* if $freq(P) \geq min\_fr$.

The *episode rule discovery task* can now be stated as follows. Given an event sequence $\mathcal{S}$, a class $\mathcal{E}$ of episodes, and time bounds V and W, find all frequent episode rules of the form $P[V] \Rightarrow Q[W]$, where $P, Q \in \mathcal{E}$.

To make episode rule discovery feasible, the class of episodes has to be restricted somehow. We consider the restricted but interesting task of discovering episodes from the following classes $\mathcal{E}_S(\Gamma, \Delta)$ and $\mathcal{E}_P(\Gamma, \Delta)$. The class $\mathcal{E}_S(\Gamma, \Delta)$ consists of serial episodes with unary predicates from Γ and binary predicates from Δ. The class $\mathcal{E}_P(\Gamma, \Delta)$ is defined to consist of parallel episodes, with predicates from Γ and Δ.

---

[1] For reasons of brevity we omit the standard formal definition of satisfaction of a formula, and just use the notation $P(e_{j_1}, \ldots, e_{j_k})$ to indicate this.

[2] There is a number of variations for the relationship between the intervals; e.g., rules that point backwards in time can be defined in a similar way.

Differences to the previous model The episodes described in (Mannila, Toivonen, & Verkamo 1995) were based on conditions on the event types. That is, of our examples only the first episode of Example 1 would be representable within that framework. In the applications it is necessary to be able to state both more relaxed and more restricted episode specifications by having conditions related to, e.g., the network topology. That is, binary predicates are necessary. Also, there was only one fixed time bound associated with a rule. In the applications it is preferable to have two bounds, one for the left-hand side and one for the whole rule, such as "if A and B occur within 15 seconds, then C follows within 30 seconds".

One notable difference in the algorithms is that here we are able to give methods that can be used to compute the confidences of rules of the above form for various values of the time bounds; the previous methods had to make one pass through the data for each time bound. There are also some smaller technical differences, e.g., the exact definition of the confidence of a rule is somewhat changed (and is now more natural, it seems to us).

The work most closely related to ours is perhaps (Srikant & Agrawal 1996). They search in multiple sequences for patterns that are similar to the serial episodes of (Mannila, Toivonen, & Verkamo 1995) with some extra restrictions and an event taxonomy. Our methods can be extended with a taxonomy by a direct application of the similar extensions to association rules. Also, our methods can be applied on analyzing several sequences; there is actually a variety of choices for the definition of frequency of an episode in a set of sequences.

There are also some interesting similarities between the discovery of frequent episodes and the work done on inductive logic programming (see, e.g., (Muggleton 1992)); a noticeable difference is caused by the sequentiality of the underlying data model, and the emphasis on time-limited occurrences. Similarly, the problem of looking for one occurrence of an episode can be viewed as a constraint satisfaction problem.

Finding minimal occurrences of frequent episodes

In this section we describe the algorithms used to locate the minimum occurrences of frequent episodes from the classes $\mathcal{E}_P$ and $\mathcal{E}_S$. The algorithms are based on the idea of first locating minimal occurrences of small episodes, and using this information to generate candidates for possibly frequent larger episodes.

An episode P is *simple*, if it includes no binary predicates. Recognition of simple episodes turns out to

be considerably easier than for arbitrary episodes, as is shown by the following two theorems.

Theorem 4 Finding whether a simple serial or parallel episode P has an occurrence in an event sequence $\mathcal{S}$ can be done in time $|P||\mathcal{S}|$. $\square$

Theorem 5 Finding whether a serial or parallel episode P has an occurrence in an event sequence $\mathcal{S}$ is an NP-complete problem. $\square$

One should not be discouraged by the NP-completeness result, however; the situations used in the reduction are highly contrived. It seems that in practice episodes similar to the ones in our examples can be recognized and discovered fast.

We move to the discovery algorithm for simple episodes. Given an episode $P = \bigwedge_{i=1}^{k} \varphi_i(y_i, z_i)$, a *subepisode* P_I of P determined by a set $I \subseteq \{1, \ldots, k\}$ is simply $P_I = \bigwedge_{i \in I} \varphi_i(y_i, z_i)$. The basic properties of simple episodes are given in the following lemmas.

Lemma 6 (i) If an episode P is frequent in an event sequence $\mathcal{S}$, then all subepisodes P_I are frequent. (ii) If $[t, t'] \in mo(P)$, then P_I occurs in $[t, t']$ and hence there is an interval $[t_I, t'_I] \in mo(P_I)$ such that $t \leq t_I \leq t'_I \leq t'$. $\square$

Lemma 7 Let P be a simple serial episode of size k, and let $[t, t'] \in mo(P)$. Then there are subepisodes P_1 and P_2 of P of size $k-1$ such that for some $t_1 \in [t, t'[$ and $t_2 \in]t, t']$ we have $[t, t_1] \in mo(P_1)$ and $[t_2, t'] \in mo(P_2)$. $\square$

Note that Lemma 7 does not hold for general episodes: a minimal occurrence of a general episode does not necessarily start with a minimal occurrence of a subepisode.

Lemma 8 Let P be a simple parallel episode of size k, and let $[t, t'] \in mo(P)$. Then there are subepisodes P_1 and P_2 of P of size $k-1$ such that for some $t_1, t_2, t'_1, t'_2 \in [t, t']$ we have $[t_1, t'_1] \in mo(P_1)$ and $[t_2, t'_2] \in mo(P_2)$, and furthermore $t = \min\{t_1, t_2\}$ and $t' = \max\{t'_1, t'_2\}$. $\square$

We use the same algorithm skeleton as in the discovery of association rules (Agrawal & Srikant 1994; Mannila, Toivonen, & Verkamo 1994). Namely, having found the set L_k of frequent simple episodes of size k, we form the set C_{k+1} of *candidate episodes* of size $k+1$, i.e., episodes whose all subepisodes are frequent, and then find out which candidate episodes $P \in C_{k+1}$ are really frequent by forming the set $mo(P)$.

Algorithm 9, below, discovers all frequent simple serial episodes. The discovery of simple parallel episodes is similar; the details of steps 9 and 10 are a bit different.

Algorithm 9 Discovery of frequent simple serial episodes.

Input: An event sequence $\mathcal{S}$, unary predicates Γ and binary predicates Δ, and a frequency threshold min_fr.
Output: All frequent simple episodes from $\mathcal{E}_S(\Gamma, \Delta)$ (and their minimal occurrences).
Method:

1. $C_1 :=$ the set of episodes of size 1 in $\mathcal{E}_S(\Gamma, \Delta)$;
2.   **for all** $P \in C_1$ compute $mo(P)$;
3. $L_1 := \{P \in C_1 \mid P \text{ is frequent}\}$;
4. $i := 1$;
5.   **while** $L_i \neq \emptyset$ **do**
6. $C_{i+1} := \{P \mid P \in \mathcal{E}_S(\Gamma, \Delta)$, all sub-episodes of P are in $L_i\}$;
7. $i := i + 1$;
8.   **for all** $P \in C_i$ **do**
9.   select subepisodes P_1 and P_2;
10.   compute $mo(P)$ from $mo(P_1)$ and $mo(P_2)$;
11.   **od**;
12. $L_i := \{P \in C_i \mid P \text{ is frequent}\}$;
13.   **od**;
14.   **for all** i and all $P \in L_i$, output P and $mo(P)$.

Finding the minimal occurrences For simple serial episodes, the two subepisodes are selected on line 9 so that P_1 contains all events except the last one and P_2 in turn contains all except the first one. P_1 and P_2 also contain all the predicates that apply on the events in the episode. The minimal occurrences of P are then computed on line 10 by

$$mo(P) = \{[t, u'] \mid \text{there are } [t, t'] \in mo(P_1) \text{ and } [u, u'] \in mo(P_2) \text{ such that } t < u, t' < u', \text{ and } [t, u'] \text{ is minimal}\}.$$

Note the correspondence to Lemma 7.

For simple parallel episodes, the subepisodes P_1 and P_2 contain all events except one; the omitted events must be different. Again, P_1 and P_2 contain all the applicable predicates. See Lemma 8 for the idea of how to compute the minimal occurrences of P. To optimize the efficiency, $|mo(P_1)| + |mo(P_2)|$ should be minimized.

The minimal occurrences of a candidate episode P can be found in a linear pass over the minimal occurrences of the selected subepisodes P_1 and P_2. The time required for one candidate is thus $O(|mo(P_1)| + |mo(P_2)| + |mo(P)|)$, which is $O(n)$, where n is the length of the event sequence.

While minimal occurrences of episodes can be located quite efficiently from minimal occurrences, the size of the data structures may be even larger than the original database, especially in the first couple of itera-

tions. A solution is to use in the beginning other pattern recognition methods.

Finding general episodes The recognition problem for general episodes is considerably harder than that for simple episodes. The difficulty is caused by the failure of Lemma 7. Consider as an example the event sequence

$$(page_1, host_1, 1), (page_1, host_2, 2), (page_2, host_2, 3),$$
$$(page_2, host_1, 4), (page_3, host_1, 5),$$

and the episode P

$$x.host = y.host \wedge y.host = z.host.$$

The minimal occurrences of the two (actually equivalent) subepisodes $x.host = y.host$ and $y.host = z.host$ of P are at $[2, 3]$, whereas $mo(P) = \{[1, 5]\}$.

While the minimal occurrences of a general episode cannot be built as easily from the minimal occurrences of subepisodes as for simple episodes, the occurrence of subepisodes is still a necessary condition for the occurrence of the whole episode (Lemma 6). We use this property to implement a simple exhaustive search method for finding minimal occurrences of general episodes; the use of minimal occurrences of subepisodes guarantees that the exhaustive search has to be applied only to small slices of the long event sequence.

Finding minimal occurrences of general episodes In line 9 of Algorithm 9 choose incomparable subepisodes P_1 and P_2 of P such that $|mo(P_1)| + |mo(P_2)|$ is as small as possible. Then, for each pair of intervals $[t_1, t_1'] \in mo(P_1)$ and $[t_2, t_2'] \in mo(P_2)$ such that $\max(t_1', t_2') - \min(t_1, t_2) \leq W$ search for a minimal occurrence of P in the time interval $[\max(t_1', t_2') - W, \min(t_1, t_2) + W]$. Here W is the upper bound on the length of minimal occurrences. The search can be done using basically exhaustive search, as the sizes of episodes and the number of events in such small intervals are small. We omit the details.

A problem similar to the computation of frequencies occurs in the area of active databases. There triggers can be specified as composite events, somewhat similar to episodes. In (Gehani, Jagadish, & Shmueli 1992) it is shown how finite automata can be constructed from composite events to recognize when a trigger should be fired. This method is not practical for episodes since the deterministic automata could be very large.

Finding confidences of rules

In this section we show how the information about minimal occurrences of frequent episodes can be used to

min_fr	Number of frequent episodes and informative rules							
	Time bounds U (s)							
	15, 30		30, 60		60, 120		15, 30, 60, 120	
50	1131	617	2278	1982	5899	7659	5899	14205
100	418	217	739	642	1676	2191	1676	3969
250	111	57	160	134	289	375	289	611
500	46	21	59	49	80	87	80	138

Table 1: Experimental results: number of episodes and rules

obtain confidences for various types of episode rules without looking at the data again.

Recall that an episode rule is an expression $P[V] \Rightarrow Q[W]$, where P and Q are episodes, and V and W are real numbers. To find such rules, first note that for the rule to be interesting, also the episode $P \wedge Q$ has to be frequent. So rules of the above form can be enumerated by looking at all frequent episodes $M = \wedge_{i \in I} \alpha_i$, and then looking at all partitions of I as $I = J \cup K$, and forming the left and right-hand sides as subepisodes: $P = M_J$ and $Q = M_K$. The evaluation of the confidence of the rule $P[V] \Rightarrow Q[W]$ can be done in one pass through the structures $mo(P)$ and $mo(Q)$, as follows.

For each $[t, t'] \in mo(P)$ with $t' - t \leq V$, locate the minimal occurrence $[s, s']$ of Q such that $t \leq s$ and $[s, s']$ is the first interval in $mo(Q)$ with this property. Then check whether $s' - t \leq W$.

The time complexity of the confidence computation is $O(|mo(P)| + |mo(Q)|)$. If one wants to find the confidences of rules of the form $P[V] \Rightarrow Q[W]$ for all $V, W \in U$ for some set of times U, then by using a table of size $|U|^2$ one can in fact evaluate all these in time $O(|mo(P)| + |mo(Q)| + |U|^2)$. For reasons of brevity we omit the details.

Experimental results

We have experimented with the methods using as test data a part of the WWW server log from the Department of Computer Science at the University of Helsinki. The log contains requests to see WWW pages at the department's server; such requests can be made by WWW browsers at any host in the Internet.

An event in the log can be seen as consisting of the attributes *page, host,* and *time*. The number of events in our data set is 116308, and it covers three weeks in February and March, 1996. In total, 7634 different pages are referred to from 11635 hosts. Requests for images have been excluded from consideration. For simplicity, we only considered the *page* and *time* attributes; we used relatively short time bounds to reduce the probability of unrelated requests contributing

min_fr	Execution times (s)			
	Time bounds U (s)			
	15, 30	30, 60	60, 120	15, 30, 60, 120
50	158	210	274	268
100	80	87	103	104
250	56	56	59	58
500	50	51	51	52

Table 2: Experimental results: execution times

to the frequencies.

We experimented with frequency thresholds *min_fr* between 50 and 500, and with time bounds between 15 s and 2 min. (In three cases we used two time bounds, i.e., $U = \{V, W\}$, and in one case we searched simultaneously for all combinations of four time bounds in U.) Episode rules discovered with these parameters should reveal the paths through which people navigate when they know where they want to go.

Table 1 shows the number of frequent episodes and the number of informative rules with confidence at least 0.2. (A rule with time bounds V, W is considered informative if its confidence is higher than with time bounds V', W' where $V' < V$ and $W' > W$.)

The number of frequent episodes is in the range from 40 to 6000, and it seems to grow rather fast when the frequency threshold becomes lower. Our data is relatively dense, and therefore the effect of the time bounds on the number of frequent episodes is roughly linear. The largest frequent episodes consist of 7 events. Note that the method is robust in the sense that a change in one parameter extends or shrinks the collection of frequent episodes but does not replace any.

Table 2 shows the execution times for the experiments on a PC (90 MHz Pentium, 32 MB memory, Linux operating system). The data resided in a 3.0 MB flat text file.

The experiments show that the method is efficient. The execution times are between 50 s and 5 min. Note, in particular, that searching for episodes with several different time bounds (the right-most columns in the tables) is as fast as searching for episodes with only the largest time bound. Minimal occurrences are thus a very suitable representation for queries with different time bounds.

Following are some examples of the episode rules found (we use the titles of the pages here, or their English translations, which should be self-explanatory).

- "Department Home Page", "Spring term 96" [15 s] ⇒ "Classes in spring 96" [30 s] (confidence 0.83). In other words, in 83 % of the cases where the departmental home page and the spring term page had been accessed within 15 seconds, the classes page was requested within 30 seconds (that is, within 30 seconds from the request for the departmental home page).

- "Research at the department" ⇒ "Staff of the department" [2 min] (confidence 0.29). (There is no time bound for the left-hand side since there is only one event.)

- "Department Home Page", "Department Home Page in Finnish", "Classes in spring 96", "Basic courses" [15 s] ⇒ "Introduction to Document Preparation (IDP)", "IDP Course Description", "IDP Exercises" [2 min] (confidence 0.42).

Experiments with the data set of (Mannila, Toivonen, & Verkamo 1995) show that — with comparable parameters — the present method is as fast or faster than the one presented in (Mannila, Toivonen, & Verkamo 1995). The new method has, however, two important advantages: the rule formalism is more useful, and rules with several different time bounds can be found with the same effort.

Concluding remarks

We have presented a framework for generalized episodes, and algorithms for discovering episode rules from sequences of events. The present framework supplies sufficient power for representing desired connections between events.

The work presented here is in many ways preliminary. Perhaps the most important extensions are facilities for rule querying and compilation, i.e., methods by which the user could specify the episode class in high-level language and the definition would automatically be compiled into a specialization of the algorithm that would take advantage of the restrictions on the episode class. Other open problems include a theoretical analysis of what subclasses of episodes are recognizable from episodes in polynomial time, and the combination of episode techniques with intensity models.

References

Agrawal, R., and Srikant, R. 1994. Fast algorithms for mining association rules in large databases. In *Proceedings of the Twentieth International Conference on Very Large Data Bases (VLDB'94)*, 487 – 499.

Bettini, C.; Wang, X. S.; and Jajodia, S. 1996. Testing complex temporal relationships involving multiple granularities and its application to data mining. In *Proceedings of the Fifteenth ACM SIGACT-SIGMOD-SIGART Symposium on Principles of Database Systems (PODS'96)*. To appear.

Dousson, C.; Gaborit, P.; and Ghallab, M. 1993. Situation recognition: Representation and algorithms. In *Proceedings of the Thirteenth International Joint Conference on Artificial Intelligence (IJCAI-93)*, 166 – 172.

Gehani, N.; Jagadish, H.; and Shmueli, O. 1992. Composite event specification in active databases. In *Proceedings of the Eighteenth International Conference on Very Large Data Bases (VLDB'92)*, 327 – 338.

Hätönen, K.; Klemettinen, M.; Mannila, H.; Ronkainen, P.; and Toivonen, H. 1996. Knowledge discovery from telecommunication network alarm databases. In *12th International Conference on Data Engineering (ICDE'96)*, 115 – 122.

Laird, P. 1993. Identifying and using patterns in sequential data. In Jantke, K.; Kobayashi, S.; Tomita, E.; and Yokomori, T., eds., *Algorithmic Learning Theory, 4th International Workshop*, 1 – 18. Berlin: Springer-Verlag.

Mannila, H.; Toivonen, H.; and Verkamo, A. I. 1994. Efficient algorithms for discovering association rules. In Fayyad, U. M., and Uthurusamy, R., eds., *Knowledge Discovery in Databases, Papers from the 1994 AAAI Workshop (KDD'94)*, 181 – 192.

Mannila, H.; Toivonen, H.; and Verkamo, A. I. 1995. Discovering frequent episodes in sequences. In *Proceedings of the First International Conference on Knowledge Discovery and Data Mining (KDD'95)*, 210 – 215.

Morris, R. A.; Khatib, L.; and Ligozat, G. 1995. Generating scenarios from specifications of repeating events. In *Second International Workshop on Temporal Representation and Reasoning (TIME-95)*.

Muggleton, S. 1992. *Inductive Logic Programming*. London: Academic Press.

Seshadri, P.; Livny, M.; and Ramakrishnan, R. 1996. SEQ: Design & implementation of sequence database system. In *Proceedings of the 22nd International Conference on Very Large Data Bases (VLDB'96)*. To appear.

Srikant, R., and Agrawal, R. 1996. Mining sequential patterns: Generalizations and performance improvements. In *International Conference on Extending Database Technology (EDBT'1996)*.

Wang, J. T.-L.; Chirn, G.-W.; Marr, T. G.; Shapiro, B.; Shasha, D.; and Zhang, K. 1994. Combinatorial pattern discovery for scientific data: Some preliminary results. In *Proceedings of ACM SIGMOD Conference on Management of Data (SIGMOD'94)*, 115 – 125.

Metapattern Generation for Integrated Data Mining

Wei-Min Shen
Information Sciences Institute and
Computer Science Department
University of Southern California
4676 Admiralty Way
Marina del Rey, CA 90292
shen@isi.edu

Bing Leng
Inference Corporation
4th Fl, 8410 W Bryn Mawr Ave
Chicago, IL 60631
leng@inference.com

Abstract

Metapatterns (also known as metaqueries) have been proposed as a new approach to integrated data mining, and applied to several real-world applications successfully. However, designing the right metapatterns for a given application still remains a difficulty task. In this paper, we present a metapattern generator that can automatically generate metapatterns from new databases. By integrating this generator with the existing metapattern-based discovery loop, our system has now become both interactive and automatic. It can suggest new metapatterns for humans to choose and test, or pursue these metapatterns on its own. This ability not only makes the process of data mining more efficient and productive, but also provide a new method for unsupervised learning of relational patterns. We have applied this method to several simple databases and obtained some encouraging results.

Introduction

Metapatterns (also known as metaqueries) (Shen *et al.* 1995; Kero *et al.* 1995; Fu & Han 1995; Shen & Leng 1996) have been proposed as a new data mining approach to integrate induction, deduction, and human guidance. They are second-order expressions, such as

$$P(X, Y) \wedge Q(Y, Z) \Rightarrow R(X, Z),$$

where P, Q, and R are variables for predicates and X, Y, and Z are variables for objects. Metapatterns are used to control the discovery loop shown in Figure 1. For the deductive part of the loop, metapatterns outline data-collecting strategies and serve as the basis for the generation of specific queries. Queries are generated by instantiating the variables in the left-hand side of metapatterns with relevant table names and column names in the database of interest and then run against the database to collect relevant data. For example, one possible query instantiated from the above metapattern is:

$$parent(X, Y) \wedge brother(Y, Z) \Rightarrow uncle(X, Z).$$

The final results of discovered patterns are associated with probability factors to reflect how much support received from the underlying databases and provide handlers to deal with noise. For the inductive part of the loop, metapatterns serve as generic descriptions of classes of pattern to be discovered: A metapattern determines which inductive action to apply, and what format the final results should be in. Furthermore, since metapatterns are declarative expressions, they serve as a search control interface between humans and systems. By examing, selecting, and executing different metapatterns, human users can expand or contract the search space and change the search direction at will. For more detailed description of metapatterns, readers are encouraged to read (Shen *et al.* 1995) and (Shen & Leng 1996).

Although metapatterns are powerful tools for data mining and have been applied successfully to several real-world applications (Shen 1992; Shen *et al.* 1995; Fu & Han 1995), designing the right metapatterns for a given application is not an easy task. If a metapattern is too specific, then it may miss the interesting patterns. If a metapattern is too general, then it may exhaust the computing resources that are available. To generate the right metapatterns, one must not only understand the nature of the underlying data, but also analyze the patterns discovered from the previous metapatterns.

To illustrate how productive metapatterns are generated manually, consider our experience in the chemical research domain as an example. Following a suggestion by a chemist, we initially used a metapattern to find the relationship between a set of compounds that have different percentages of the ingredients 'A322' and 'B721' and their chemical properties. However, the patterns returned based on this metapattern did not show any trends. When we showed the results to the chemist, he discovered that these compounds also contained auxiliary chemicals that may affect the properties in a different way. Given this knowledge, we constrained the metapattern so that the compounds that had such auxiliary ingredients were not considered. Sure enough, the resulting patterns showed many clear trends. We can see from this example that if domain experts can directly interact with the system (i.e., metapatterns can be automatically generated and offered to them to choose and test), then the entire discovery process can be much more efficient and pro-

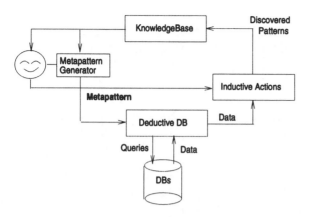

Figure 1: The Metapattern-Based Discovery Loop

ductive. The system should provide suggestions and feedback of metapatterns so the experts can discover new knowledge and try better metapatterns.

For this purpose, we have developed a metapattern generator for the metapattern-based discovery loop. Given a completely new database, the generator first identifies, by examining the types and ranges of the data columns, a set of *significant connections* among tables. Using these connections, a connection graph is then built and all the loops in this graph are found. These loops are then used to generate an initial set of *transitivity metapatterns*. These initial metapatterns are then run against the database; based on the results, new metapatterns are generated dynamically by adding more constraints to the more plausible metapatterns. Since transitivity metapatterns are among the most general types of metapatterns, this top-down approach can generate many interesting metapatterns (and patterns) automatically. In fact, we have applied this approach to some of the well-known examples in the literature of supervised learning of relation patterns, and demonstrated that our system can learn these concepts without "supervision," that is, without requiring humans to pre-label the data as positive or negative examples of some pre-specified target concepts.

The Metapattern Generator

As shown in Figure 1, the metapattern generator will be placed in parallel with the human user and will generate metapatterns based on either the meta-knowledge of the database (e.g., schema), or the patterns that are discovered with other metapatterns. Human users can interact with the generator by examining, selecting, and executing the metapatterns, and they can also create metapatterns by themselves as before. The motivation for having this generator is to give human users suggestions for new metapatterns so that the more expert users can get inspirations, and the less expert users can learn how to perform data mining in a particular domain by observation.

The Space of Metapatterns

In order to generate metapatterns, we must first understand the nature of the set of all possible metapatterns. In this paper, we consider Horn clause metapatterns and assume that the underlying databases are relational. Thus, a predicate variable in a metapattern can be bound to relational table names or built-in predicates (such as *equal* or *greaterThan*), and an object variable can be bound to column names or constant values (such as the integer "20" or the language "English").

For a fixed length, metapatterns can be ordered from the most general to the most specific, depending on how many variables, either for predicates or for objects, are present. For example, among all metapatterns that have three binary (second-order) predicates, the most general ones include:

$$P(X,Y) \wedge Q(Y,Z) \Rightarrow R(X,Z) \qquad \text{(MP-1)}$$
$$P(X,Y) \wedge Q(X,Z) \Rightarrow R(X,W) \qquad \text{(MP-2)}$$
$$P(X,Y) \wedge Q(Y,Z) \Rightarrow R(X,W) \qquad \text{(MP-3)}$$

These metapatterns are the most general because they contain only variables. On the other hand, the most specific metapatterns corresponding to the general ones listed above (MP-1, MP-2, and MP-3) include:

$$\text{authorOf('Orwell','AnimalFarm')} \wedge$$
$$\text{writtenIn('AnimalFarm','English')} \rightarrow \text{canWrite('Orwell','English')}$$

$$\text{likes('John',}tools\text{)} \wedge \text{hasHobby('John','Carpenter')} \rightarrow$$
$$\text{ownsOne('John',}hammer\text{)}$$

$$\text{livesIn('Mary','House1')} \wedge \text{costs('House1',900893)} \rightarrow$$
$$\text{Income('Mary','High')}$$

All the variables in these metapatterns are bound to specific table names (e.g., likes), column names (e.g., *tools*), or constant values (e.g. 'John'). We define a *family* of metapatterns to be the set of all metapatterns of length n. The metapatterns in a family are partially ordered by the number of variables they contain. One can traverse a family of metapatterns from the general to the specific by incrementally instantiating the predicate variables with table names and built-in predicates and the object variables with column names and in turn constant values.

Notice that *not* all metapatterns in a family are interesting. In order to have some prediction value, a metapattern must be *connected*. That is, the predicate on the right-hand side must share at least one variable with some predicate on the left-hand side. For example, the metapattern $P(X,Y) \wedge Q(Y,Z) \Rightarrow R(U,V)$ is not interesting because its right-hand side is not connected to the left-hand side. Furthermore, predicates like $P(X,X)$ or $p(X,X)$ are not considered interesting because they do not link to others.

With the families of metapatterns so defined, one natural question to ask is whether the length of metapatterns can be arbitrarily long. Fortunately, for any given set of databases, the length of the longest metapatterns is bounded because metapatterns must be connected and there is only a fixed number of tables, columns, built-in predicates, and values that are presented in the databases. (Even if a column is typed "real", the number of distinct values in the column is finite because of the implementation.) Therefore, it is meaningful to define the *space* of all possible metapatterns for an application to be the union of all possible families of metapatterns.

Generating Metapatterns Based on Data Schema and Ranges

The space of metapatterns is very large and it is infeasible to enumerate them all. Our approach is to start with the set of most general metapatterns, and incrementally generate interesting ones as the process of discovery continues. Our goal is not to cover all the metapatterns but to guide the discovery process in fruitful directions.

Among all the general metapatterns, the transitivity metapattern (see MP-1 for example) is the most interesting. In essence, it subsumes many other types of metapatterns, such as implication, inheritance, transfers-through, and function dependency (Shen 1992). In this section, we describe how transitivity meatpatterns are generated. How other types of metapatterns are generated based on transitivities will be described in the section after the next.

The set of all possible transitivity metapatterns can be generated based on the data schema and ranges of the databases. The idea is to first identify the sets of columns that are significantly connected, and then use these sets to build metapatterns.

Two columns, from different database tables, are significantly connected, if they have the same type and have ranges that overlap each other above a user specified threshold o, where $0 < o < 1$. The degree of overlapping is computed as follows. Let C_x and C_y be two columns, and V_x and V_y be their value sets, respectively, then the overlapping of C_x and C_y is the maximum number of the shared values relative to either V_x or V_y, as follows:

$$Overlap(C_x, C_y) = \max\left(\frac{|V_x \cap V_y|}{|V_x|}, \frac{|V_x \cap V_y|}{|V_y|}\right)$$

where $|\cdot|$ denotes the cardinality of a set. Here domain knowledge may be used to eliminate unnecessary connections (e.g., height vs. temperature) or suggest and establish syntactically different connections (e.g., color vs. light frequency). Each pair of columns that are connected are then given a reference name, and these connections will be represented in a significant connection table (SCT), where each row is a connection, each column is a table, and each non-empty entry is the name of a connected data field (or column).

To illustrate the idea, consider for example an abstract database shown in Figure 2. In this database, there are four tables, t_1 to t_4, each has some columns c_{ij}. For simplicity, the value ranges of each column are also listed along with the schema. (In reality, value ranges can be obtained by simple SQL queries.)

Schema and Data Ranges			
Table	Columns Type[ValueRange]		
t_1	c_{11}, char(2)	c_{12}, int[2–7]	c_{13}, real[0.4–0.8]
t_2	c_{21}, int[12–17]	c_{22}, real[0.1–0.7]	c_{23}, char(3)
t_3	c_{31}, int[13–16]	c_{32}, char(2)	
t_4	c_{41}, char(3)	c_{42}, real[0.0–0.1]	c_{43}, int[4–7]

Table t_1		
c_{11}	c_{12}	c_{13}
jj	5	0.5
nn	5	0.8
ll	7	0.5
qq	5	0.5
kk	5	0.6
pp	4	0.6
mm	2	0.5
nn	4	0.6
kk	4	0.4
nn	5	0.4

Table t_2		
c_{21}	c_{22}	c_{23}
14	0.5	mmm
14	0.6	iii
14	0.3	jjj
12	0.7	nnn
12	0.1	lll
15	0.6	ppp
15	0.4	mmm
13	0.6	ooo
16	0.6	ooo
17	0.4	mmm
14	0.4	lll
14	0.6	kkk
15	0.3	mmm
12	0.5	mmm
15	0.4	nnn
15	0.6	ooo
16	0.5	ppp
16	0.7	ppp

Table t_3	
c_{31}	c_{32}
14	oo
15	kk
16	mm
15	kk
16	ll
15	ll
15	mm
13	oo
16	oo
14	mm
13	mm
14	mm

Table t_4		
c_{41}	c_{42}	c_{43}
nnn	0.0	5
mmm	0.0	6
rrr	0.1	4
mmm	0.0	4
ooo	0.1	7
jjj	0.0	4
kkk	0.0	5
mmm	0.0	5
jjj	0.1	4
mmm	0.0	5
jjj	0.0	5
jjj	0.0	5
lll	0.0	7
nnn	0.1	4

Figure 2: An Example Database

Given these information, pairs of columns that are connected can be easily determined according to our definition. For example, suppose the threshold o for overlapping is set to 0.6, then column c_{13} in table t_1 and column c_{22} in table t_2 are connected because they have the same data type and their overlapping is 0.9. A reference name, X_1, is then created for this pair of connected columns. After considering every pair of columns, a significant connection table, shown in the upright part of Figure 3, is constructed. As we can see, every connected pair of columns is represented as a row in this SCT. For instance, columns c_{13} and c_{22} are in the first row, where c_{13} is under t_1 while c_{22} is under t_2.

For reasons that will become clear later, we also represent the information in SCT as a graph G, where each node in G is an non-empty entry in the SCT, and each edge connects two non-empty entries that are on the same row or column in the SCT. For example, the graph built from the SCT in Figure 3 is shown in the lower-left part of Figure 3, where node (t_1, X_1) and node (t_2, X_1) represent two non-empty entries, c_{13} and c_{22}, in the SCT. Since they are in the same row, there is an horizontal edge between them. Similarly, node (t_1, X_1) and node (t_1, X_2) represent two non-empty entries, c_{13} and c_{11}, in the same column of the SCT, so there is a vertical edge between them.

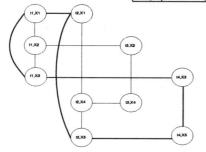

SCT

	t_1	t_2	t_3	t_4
X_1	c_{13}	c_{22}		
X_2	c_{11}		c_{32}	
X_3	c_{12}			c_{43}
X_4		c_{21}	c_{31}	
X_5		c_{23}		c_{41}

Figure 3: A Significant Connection Table (SCT) and its graph G

The graph G generated above provides a basis for generating all possible transitivity patterns in a given database. The idea is to find all the cycles in the graph with alternated vertical and horizontal edges, and convert each of these cycles into a "cycle" of predicates before generating a set of transitivity patterns.

Finding cycles in a graph can be accomplished by using a standard transitive closure algorithm with some simple augmentation to enforce the alternating edge constraint. A graph G cannot have more than $|G|!$ cycles because the length of a cycle, without duplicated nodes, cannot be greater than the number of the nodes in the graph. To convert a cycle of graph nodes into a cycle of predicates is also a straightforward task; one can simply rewrite each vertical edge in the cycle by the table name. For example, the cycle indicated by thick lines in Figure 3 is "$(t_2, X_1)(t_2, X_5)(t_4, X_5)(t_4, X_3)(t_1, X_3)(t_1, X_1)(t_2, X_1)$" and it can be rewritten as a cycle of predicates as "$t_2(X_1, X_5), t_4(X_5, X_3), t_1(X_3, X_1),$" where $t_2(X_1, X_5)$ is a rewrite of the vertical edge $(t_2, X_1)(t_2, X_5)$, and $t_4(X_5, X_3)$ is a rewrite of $(t_4, X_5)(t_4, X_3)$, and so on. Using this method, we can generate all cycles of predicates from the graph G, as listed in Figure 4.

$$t_2(X_1 X_5)t_4(X_5 X_3)t_1(X_3 X_1)$$
$$t_2(X_1 X_4)t_3(X_4 X_2)t_1(X_2 X_1)$$
$$t_2(X_5 X_1)t_1(X_1 X_2)t_3(X_2 X_4)t_2(X_4 X_5)$$
$$t_2(X_4 X_5)t_4(X_5 X_3)t_1(X_3 X_1)t_2(X_1 X_4)$$
$$t_1(X_3 X_1)t_2(X_1 X_4)t_3(X_4 X_2)t_1(X_2 X_3)$$
$$t_3(X_2 X_4)t_2(X_4 X_5)t_4(X_5 X_3)t_1(X_3 X_2)$$
$$t_1(X_2 X_3)t_4(X_3 X_5)t_2(X_5 X_1)t_1(X_1 X_2)$$
$$t_2(X_1 X_4)t_3(X_4 X_2)t_1(X_2 X_3)t_4(X_3 X_5)t_2(X_5 X_1)$$
$$t_1(X_1 X_2)t_3(X_2 X_4)t_2(X_4 X_5)t_4(X_5 X_3)t_1(X_3 X_1)$$

Figure 4: All predicate cycles found in the example DB

From the list of all possible cycles of predicates, we can now generate a complete set of transitivity metapatterns by generalizing table names and refer-

ence names and introducing an implication in each cycle. In our current example database, the result is the following set of metapatterns:

$$P_1(Y_1, Y_2) \wedge Q_1(Y_2, Y_3) \Rightarrow R_1(Y_1, Y_3) \quad \text{(MP-4)}$$
$$P_2(Y_1, Y_2) \wedge Q_2(Y_2, Y_3) \wedge W_2(Y_3, Y_4) \Rightarrow R_2(Y_1, Y_4) \quad \text{(MP-5)}$$
$$P_3(Y_1, Y_2) \wedge Q_3(Y_2, Y_3) \wedge W_3(Y_3, Y_4) \wedge V_3(Y_4, Y_5)$$
$$\Rightarrow R_3(Y_1, Y_5) \quad \text{(MP-6)}$$

For example, MP-4 is a generalization of the first two predicate cycles in Figure 4; MP-5 is a generalization of cycles 3 through 7; and MP-6 is a generalization of the last two cycles. This set is complete because it includes all possible transitivity metapatterns in our example database.

Discovering and Evaluating New Patterns

Generating all transitivity metapatterns is not the end of our story. Depending on the strength or interestness of the patterns that are found with these metapatterns, the discovery system should generate more metapatterns that are deemed to be plausible. To do so, let us first examine how discovered patterns are evaluated.

When a metapattern is selected for execution, the system first instantiates it into a set of specific patterns that are possible in the current databases, and then evaluates them to check if they have sufficient support from the actual data. Given the information produced in the process of generating metapatterns, instantiating a metapattern is a straightforward procedure. It simply replaces the variables in the metapattern with specific table names and column names. For example, the predicate variables $P_1, Q_1,$ and R_1 in MP-4 can be bound to table names $t_1, t_2, t_3,$ and t_4 (these are the table names involve in the first two cycles of predicates in Figure 4), and the object variables $Y_1, Y_2,$ and $Y_3,$ can be bound to the reference variables $X_1, X_2, X_3, X_4,$ and $X_5,$ which in turn can be bound to corresponding columns according to the SCT in Figure 3, as follows:

$$t_2(X_1 X_5)t_4(X_5 X_3) \rightarrow t_1(X_3 X_1)$$
$$t_1(X_3 X_1)t_2(X_1 X_5) \rightarrow t_4(X_5 X_3)$$
$$t_4(X_5 X_3)t_1(X_3 X_1) \rightarrow t_2(X_1 X_5)$$
$$t_2(X_1 X_4)t_3(X_4 X_2) \rightarrow t_1(X_2 X_1)$$
$$t_1(X_2 X_1)t_2(X_1 X_4) \rightarrow t_3(X_4 X_2)$$
$$t_3(X_4 X_2)t_1(X_2 X_1) \rightarrow t_2(X_1 X_4)$$
$$\vdots$$

Notice that not all instantiated patterns are supported by the data in the database. We say a pattern is "interesting" only if its significance is above some user specified thresholds. In our approach, each pattern p is evaluated by two values that are computed against the databases: the *base* value p_b which reflects how much the left-hand side of p is supported by the actual data in the database, and the *strength* value p_s which reflects how much the right-hand side is supported by the data satisfying the left-hand side.

The base value is computed as $p_b = \frac{|LHS|}{|DOM(LHS)|}$, where LHS is the set of tuples in the database for which the left-hand side of p is true, and $DOM(LHS)$

is the *domain* of the tables in the left-hand side. A domain of two or more tables is defined as the union of the values of the fields (columns) through which these tables are joined. For example, if two tables S and T are joined by fields $S.a$ and $T.b$, and the field $S.a$ has values $\{v_1, v_2, v_3\}$, and the field $T.b$ has values $\{v_1, v_2, v_4\}$, then the domain of S and T, $DOM(S.a, T.b)$, in this join is the set of $\{v_1, v_2, v_3, v_4\}$, and the cardinality of this domain is $|DOM(S.a, T.b)| = 4$.

The strength value is computed as $p_s = \frac{|RHS|}{|LHS|}$, where LHS is defined the same as above, and RHS is the set of tuples in the LHS that satisfy the right-hand side of p.

A pattern's base and strength values, p_b and p_s, are compared with two user specified thresholds b and s. When both base and strength values are above their thresholds, the pattern is accepted. If the base value is the only one above its threshold, then the pattern is considered plausible. Such a pattern still has enough tuples (for it has a high enough base value) to be constrained to increase the strength value, and is recorded for further search (considered in the next section). A pattern is discarded when both base and strength are below the thresholds. As an example, suppose that the user specified thresholds are $b = 0.1$ and $s = 0.7$, and the following three sample patterns, with their base and strength values, can be found in the example database in Figure 2:

$$t_1(X_2 X_1) t_3(X_4 X_2) \to t_2(X_4 X_1) \quad [0.17, 0.7]$$
$$t_3(X_4 X_2) t_1(X_2 X_3) t_4(X_5 X_3) \to t_2(X_4 X_5) \quad [0.02, 0.5]$$
$$t_2(X_4 X_1) t_1(X_3 X_1) t_4(X_5 X_3) \to t_2(X_4 X_5) \quad [0.15, 0.4]$$

Among these patterns, the first one will be accepted because it has high enough base and strength values. The second one will be discarded because both its base and strength are lower than the thresholds. The third one will be kept as a plausible pattern because it has high enough base although its strength is low. Notice that for any given database, users may need several trial-and-errors to find suitable thresholds. (We are investigating methods to determine these parameters in a more principled way.)

Generating Metapatterns Based on Plausible Patterns

We have seen that with the initial set of metapatterns, a large set of actual patterns may be generated from the database. Some of these patterns are accepted, some discarded and some are still plausible. Interestingly, the plausible patterns provide the basis for dynamically generating more metapatterns. In particular, if a metapattern is associated with many plausible patterns, it will be used to generate more metapatterns by adding additional (meta)constraints to its left-hand side. If we consider these patterns as cycle of predicates, then with some added constraints the resultant patterns are cycles with extra or alternative branches. These types of patterns are beyond the simple transitivities.

Adding constraints to generate new metapatterns is accomplished as follows. Given a candidate metapattern, the system will add to its left-hand side a new (meta)constraint of the form $S(X, W)$, where S is a predicate variable and W is an object variable, while X must be a variable that already exists in the metapattern in order to link the constraint in. For example, one can add $S_1(Y_2, O)$, where O is an object variable, to MP-4 to get:

$$P_1(Y_1, Y_2) \wedge Q_1(Y_2, Y_3) \wedge S_1(Y_2, O) \Rightarrow R_1(Y_1, Y_3) \quad \text{(MP – 7)}$$

or add $S_3(Y_2, Y_3)$ to MP-6 to get:

$$P_3(Y_1, Y_2) \wedge Q_3(Y_2, Y_3) \wedge W_3(Y_3, Y_4) \wedge V_3(Y_4, Y_5) \wedge S_3(Y_2, Y_3)$$
$$\Rightarrow R_3(Y_1, Y_5)$$
$$\text{(MP-8)}$$

The motivation for this generation is to have the system search for an actual constraint, instantiated from S, that can yield patterns that have higher strengths.

The added meta-constraint can be instantiated to either a table that connects (i.e., share a reference name in SCT) to at least one predicate in the pattern or any of the build-in predicates (e.g., *equal*) with some variables that are already in the pattern. It is interesting to notice that the extended metapatterns enable the system to discover patterns that are beyond transitivities. For example, instantiating the metapattern MP-7, if P_1 and R_1 are bound to "ancestor", Q_1 to "parent", S_1 to "gender", and O to "male", then the following "male-ancestor" pattern may be discovered

$$ancestor(Y_1, Y_2), parent(Y_2, Y_3), gender(Y_2, male)$$
$$\to ancestor(Y_1, Y_3)$$

In general, adding a new constraint to the left-hand side of a pattern will reduce the size of LHS, thus the number of plausible patterns will decrease as the length of their left-hand side increases. Furthermore, we only consider to add a constraint to a pattern when it reduces the number of tuples that satisfy the left-hand side of the pattern, so this process of adding constraints will eventually terminate.

Experimental Results

The described system has been applied to two simply databases to show that it can learn relational patterns directly from databases without requiring humans to pre-label the data as positive or negative examples of some pre-specified target concepts. The first database contains a small network used by the FOIL system (Quinlan 1990). From this database, our system learned, without pre-labeling the examples, the same recursive concepts as FOIL and more:

$$linkedTo(X_1 X_3) \to canReach(X_1 X_3) \quad [1.0, 1.0]$$

$$canReach(X_1 X_2) \wedge linkedTo(X_2 X_3)$$
$$\to canReach(X_1 X_3) \quad [0.14, 1.0]$$

$$canReach(X_1 X_3) \to linkedTo(X_1 X_3) \quad [1.0, 0.5]$$

$$canReach(X_1 X_3) \wedge linkedTo(X_2 X_3)$$
$$\to canReach(X_1 X_2) \quad [0.63, 0.4]$$

Although the last two patterns are not true in general, but they are interesting enough patterns in this database and have sufficient support from the data.

The second database contains a set of families used by Hinton's neural network (Hinton 1986). From this database, our system discovered many interesting relations among people, such as

$$husband(X_2, X_1) \rightarrow wife(X_1, X_2) \; [1.0, 1.0]$$

$$niece(X_{65}, X_{78}), brother(X_{78}, X_{66}) \\ \rightarrow nephew(X_{65}, X_{66}) \; [0.22, 1.0]$$

$$daughter(X_{56}, X_{57}) brother(X_{57}, X_{60}) \\ \rightarrow son(X_{56}, X_{60}) \; [0.33, 1.0]$$

$$brother(X_{63}, X_{64}) \rightarrow sister(X_{64}, X_{63}) \; [1.0, 1.0]$$

Again, the last one is not true in general, but a valid pattern in this particular database (i.e., all the families in the database have siblings of opposite gender).

Related Work

The most relevant work to this research includes supervised learning of relation patterns (e.g., (Quinlan 1990; Muggleton & Feng 1990)) and applications of ILP to KDD (e.g., (Dzeroski 1995)). However, most of these approaches learn rules that are rigid logical statements with no allowance for uncertainty, and often assume databases are correct and noise-free. While the patterns discovered by our method have associated probabilities that allows uncertainties and noise. One notable exception in ILP is the CLAUDIEN system (Raedt & Bruynooghe 1993; Laer, Dehaspe, & Raedt 1994), which uses the notion of *clausemodels* that share the same sprit of metapattern and can learn from positive examples only. However, CLAUDIEN requires clausemodels to be given while our system can generate metapatterns automatically. It would be interesting to see if the method described here can also be used to generate clausemodels for CLAUDIEN.

Conclusions and Future Work

In this paper, we have described a method for automatically generating metapatterns from meta-information of databases. With such a method, a metapattern-based, integrated data mining system can become both autonomous and interactive. There are clearly much room for more research in this area. One natural direction is to investigate methods for generating metapatterns that have other types of inductive actions on the right-hand side. The other one is to scale up this approach to large real-world databases. The current application under development is a set of six logistics databases, which have 104 tables, more than 2,000 columns, and over one million tuples. Following a valuable suggestion made by an anonymous reviewer, we will also include function dependency as another important criterion for testing significant connections.

Acknowledgments

We would like to thank Weixiong Zhang for his comments and suggestions on this paper. Special thanks to Eastman Chemical Company, Motorola Inc., and USC/Information Sciences Institution for providing tasks and resources. This work is also supported in part by the National Science Foundation under Grant No. IRI-9529615. Any opinions, findings, and conclusions or recommendations expressed in this material are those of the author(s) and do not necessarilty reflect the views of the National Science Foundation.

References

Dzeroski, S. 1995. Inductive logic programming and knowledge discovery in databases. In *Advances in Knowledge Discovery and Data Mining*. MIT Press. chapter 5.

Fu, Y., and Han, J. 1995. Meta-rule-guided mining of association rules in relational databases. In *DOOD95 Workshop on the Integration of Knowlege Discovery with Deductive and Object Oriented Databases*.

Hinton, G. 1986. Learning distributed representations of concepts. In *Proceedings of the 8th Annual Conference of the Cognitive Science Society*.

Kero, B.; Russell, L.; Tsur, S.; and Shen, W. 1995. An overview of data mining technologies. In *DOOD95 Workshop on the Integration of Knowlege Discovery with Deductive and Object Oriented Databases*.

Laer, W. V.; Dehaspe, L.; and Raedt, L. D. 1994. Applications of a logical discovery engine. In *Proceedings of AAAI Workshop on Knowledge Discovery in Databases*. AAAI Press.

Muggleton, S., and Feng, C. 1990. Efficient induction of logic programs. In *Proceedings of the 1st Conference on Algorithmic Learning Theory*. Tokyo, Japan: Ohmsha.

Quinlan, R. J. 1990. Learning logical definitions from relations. *Machine Learning* 5(3):239–266.

Raedt, L. D., and Bruynooghe, M. 1993. A theory of clausal discovery. In *The Proceedings of the 13th IJCAI*.

Shen, W. M., and Leng, B. 1996. A metapattern-based automated discovery loop for integrated data mining. *IEEE Transactions on Data and Knowledge Engineering*. To appear in the special issue on data mining and knowledge discovery from databases.

Shen, W.; Ong, K.; Mitbander, B.; and Zaniolo, C. 1995. Metaqueries for data mining. In *Advances in Knowledge Discovery and Data Mining*. MIT Press. chapter 15.

Shen, W. 1992. Discovering regularities from knowledge bases. *International Journal of Intelligent Systems* 7(7):623–636.

Automated pattern mining with a scale dimension

Jan M. Żytkow† & Robert Zembowicz

Computer Science Department, Wichita State University, Wichita, KS 67260–0083
† also Institute of Computer Science, Polish Academy of Sciences, Warsaw
{zytkow, robert}@cs.twsu.edu

Abstract

An important but neglected aspect of automated data mining is discovering patterns at different scale in the same data. Scale plays the role analogous to error. It can be used to focus the search for patterns on differences that exceed the given scale and to disregard those smaller. We introduce a discovery mechanism that applies to bi-variate data. It combines search for maxima and minima with search for regularities in the form of equations. Groups of detected patterns are recursively searched for patterns on their parameters. If the mechanism cannot find a regularity for all data, it uses patterns discovered from data to divide data into subsets, and explores recursively each subset. Detected patterns are subtracted from data and the search continues in the residua. Our mechanism seeks patterns at each scale. Applied at many scales and to many data sets, it seems explosive, but it terminates surprisingly fast because of data reduction and the requirements of pattern stability. We walk through an application on a half million datapoints, showing how our method leads to the discovery of many extrema, equations on their parameters, and equations that hold in subsets of data or in residua. Then we analyze the clues provide by the discovered regularities about phenomena in the environment in which the data have been gathered.

Automated data mining: the role of error and scale

Regularities at different scale (also called tolerance) are common in data, when large amounts of datapoints are available. For instance, consider a time series in which the overall linear growth may be altered with a short cycle periodic pattern. Both patterns may be caused by different phenomena. It is possible that those phenomena can be recognized from the discovered patterns. Real data contain information about many phenomena as a rule, not as an exception.

Statistical data analysis offers many methods for data exploration that assist human data miners (Tukey 1977; Hoaglin, Mosteller & Tukey 1983), yet the majority of methods make a small step and require user choice of the next step (Kendall & Ord, 1990). Today's statistical packages, such as Lisp-Stat (Tierney, 1990) offer the user access to medium level operators, but only recently, in the domain of Knowledge Discovery, the research focused on large-scale search for knowledge that can be invoked with a simple command and keeps the user out of the loop (Piatetsky-Matheus, 1991; Kloesgen 1996; 49er: Zytkow Zembowicz, 1993). Such systems become necessary when thousands of exploratory steps are needed.

The need for mining massive data at many scale levels leads to a challenging vision for automated knowledge discovery: develop a mechanism that discovers as many independent patterns as possible, not overlooking patterns at any scale but not accepting spurious regularities which can occur by chance when data are confronted with very large hypotheses spaces. That mechanism should be able to detect patterns of different types, such as equations, maxima and minima, and search for patterns in data subsets if the search fails to detect patterns satisfied by all data.

In this paper we present an automated data mining mechanism that works efficiently for large amounts of data and makes progress on each of these requirements. We report an application of our methods on a large set of bi-variate data, computationally efficient and leading to a number of surprising conclusions. We concentrate on the algorithmic aspect of our system. Because of the paper size limit we do not present the representation of the nascent knowledge and the way in which the unknown elements of knowledge drive the search. This mechanism is a modification of FAHRENHEIT's knowledge representation (Żytkow, 1996).

The roles of error in pattern discovery

Error is a parameter that defines the difference between values of a variable which are empirically non-distinguishable. Scale plays the role analogous to error. It specifies the difference between the values of a variable which we, tentatively, consider unimportant. Because of this analogy, in order to search for patterns at different scale we can simply replace the error with scale in our discovery algorithms.

Let us briefly summarize the roles of error (noise) in the process of automated discovery. Those roles are well-known in statistical data analysis. Consider the data in the form $D = \{(x_i, y_i, e_i) : i = 1, ..., N\}$. Consider the search for equations of the form $y = f(x)$ that fit data (x_i, y_i) within the accuracy of error e_i. For the same $\{(x_i, y_i) : i = 1, ..., N\}$, the smaller are the error values $e_i, i = 1, ..., N$, the closer fit is required between data and equations. Even a constant pattern $y = C$ can fit any data, if error is very large, but the smaller is the error, the more complex equations may be needed to fit the data.

The same conclusions about error apply to other patterns, too. Let us consider maxima and minima. For the same data (x_i, y_i), when the error is large, many differences between the values of y are treated as random fluctuations within error. In consequence, few maxima and minima are detected. When the error is small, however, the same differences may become significant. The smaller is the error, the larger number of maxima and minima shall be detected.

Knowledge of error has been used in many ways during the search conducted by Equation Finder (**EF**: Zembowicz & Żytkow, 1992):

1. The error is used in the evaluation of each equation $y = f(x)$. For each datum, $0.5e_i = \sigma_i$ can be interpreted as the standard deviation of the normal distribution $N(y(x_i), \sigma_i)$ of y's for each x_i, where $y(x_i)$ is the mean value and σ_i is standard deviation. Knowledge of that distribution permits to compute the probability that the data have been generated as a sum of the value $y(x_i)$ and the value drawn randomly from the normal distribution $N(0, \sigma_i)$, for all $i = 1, ..., N$.

2. When the error e_i varies for different data, the weighted χ^2 value $[(y_i - f(x_i))/0.5e_i]^2$ is used to compute the best fit parameters for any model. This enforces better fit to the more precise data.

3. Error is propagated to the parameter values of $f(x)$. For instance, EF computes the error e_a for the slope a in $y = ax$. When patterns are sought for those parameters (e.g., in BACON-like recursive search for multidimensional regularities), the parameter error is used as data error.

4. If the parameter error is larger than the value of that parameter, EF assumes that the parameter value is zero. When $y = ax + b$ and $|a| < e_a$, then the equation is reduced to a constant.

5. EF generates new variables by transforming the initial variables x and y into terms such as $\log(x)$. Error values are propagated to the transformed data and used in search for equations that apply those terms.

Phenomena at different scale

When we collect data about a physical, social or economical process, it is common that the data capture phenomena at different scale. They describe the process, but the values may be influenced by data collection, instruments behavior, and the environment. Different phenomena can be characterized by their scales in both variables. Periodic phenomena, for instance, can have different amplitudes of change in y and differ-

ent cycle length in x. In a time series (x is time) one phenomenon may occur in a daily cycle, the cycle for another can be few hours, while still another may follow a monotonous dependence between x and y. Each phenomenon may produce influence of different scale on the value of y.

Each datum combines the effects of all phenomena. When they are additive, the measured value of y for each x is the total of values contributed by each phenomenon. Given the resultant data, we want to separate the phenomena by detecting patterns that describe each of them individually. The basic question of this paper is how can it be done by an automated system.

Suppose that a particular search method has captured a pattern P in data D. Subtracting P from D produces residua which hold the remaining patterns. Repeated application of pattern detection and subtraction can gradually recover patterns that account for several phenomena. In this process, one has to be cautious of artifacts generated by spurious patterns and propagated to their residua.

It is a good idea to start the search for patterns from large scale phenomena, by using a large value of scale in pattern finding. The phenomena captured at the large values of error follow simple patterns. Many smaller scale patterns can be discovered later, in the residua obtained by subtracting the larger scale patterns.

The roles for maxima and minima

In this paper we concentrate on two types of patterns: maxima/minima, jointly called extrema, and equations. We explore the ways in which the results in one category can feedback the search for patterns of the other type.

A simple algorithm can detect maxima and minima at a given scale δ:

Algorithm: Find Extrema (X_{max}, Y_{max}) and (X_{min}, Y_{min})

```
given ordered sequence of points (xᵢ, yᵢ), i = 1 ... N, and scale δ
    task ← unknown, X_max ← x₁, X_min ← x₁, Y_max ← y₁, Y_min ← y₁
    for i from 2 to N do
        if task ≠ max and yᵢ > Y_min + δ then
            store minimum (X_min, Y_min)
            task ← max, X_max ← xᵢ, Y_max ← yᵢ
        else if task ≠ min and yᵢ < Y_max − δ then
            store maximum (X_max, Y_max)
            task ← min, X_min ← xᵢ, Y_min ← yᵢ
        else if yᵢ > Y_max then X_max ← xᵢ, Y_max ← yᵢ
        else if yᵢ < Y_min then X_min ← xᵢ, Y_min ← yᵢ
    if Y_max − Y_min > δ then ; handle the last extremum, if any
        if task = min then store minimum (X_min, Y_min)
        else if task = max then store maximum (X_max, Y_max)
```

Our discovery mechanism uses maxima and minima detected by this algorithm in several ways. First, if the number of extrema is M, then the minimum polynomial degree tried by Equation Finder is $M + 1$. A degree higher than M may be ultimately needed, because the inflection points also increase the degree of the polynomial. As the high degree polynomials are difficult to interpret and generalize, if $M > 3$, only the periodic functions are tried.

Another application is search for regularities on different properties of maxima and minima, such as the location, and height. Those regularities can be instrumental in understanding the nature of a periodic phenomenon. A regularity on the locations of the subsequent maxima and minima estimates the cycle length. A regularity on the extrema heights estimates the amplitude of a periodic pattern. Jointly, they can guide the search for sophisticated periodic equations.

Still another application is data partitioning at the extrema locations. Data between the adjacent extrema, detected at scale δ, are monotonous at δ, so that the equation finding search similar to BACON1 (Langley et al., 1987) applies in each partition. We use EF, limiting the search to linear equations and term transformations to monotonous (e.g., $x' = \log x, x' = \exp x$). Since all the data in each partition fit a constant at the tolerance level $1/2 \times \delta$, EF is applied with the error set at $1/3 \times \delta$.

Data reduction

The search for extrema at all scales starts at the minimum positive distance in y between adjacent datapoints, or the error of y, if it is known. The search uses the minimum difference between the adjacent extrema as the next scale value. The search terminates at the first scale at which no extrema have been found. Since an extremum at a larger scale must be also an extremum at each lower scale, when the search proceeds from the low end of scale, the extrema detected at a given scale become the input data for the search at the next higher scale. This way the number of data is reduced very fast and the search at all levels can be very efficient. The whole search for extrema at each scale typically takes less than double the time spent at the initial scale.

Algorithm: Detect extrema at all tolerance levels
Given an ordered sequence of points (x_i, y_i), $i = 1 \ldots N$,
$\delta_{min} \leftarrow \left| \min(y_i - y_{i+1}) \right|$, for all $y_i \neq y_{i+1}$, $i = 1 \ldots N$
$\delta \leftarrow \delta_{min}$, data $\leftarrow (x_i, y_i)$, $i = 1 \ldots N$
while data includes more than two points **do**
    Find Extrema $(X_{min/max}, Y_{min/max})$ **in data at scale** δ
    Store δ, store list-of-extrema $(X_{min/max}, Y_{min/max})$
    $\delta \leftarrow \delta + \delta_{min}$, data $\leftarrow$ list-of-extrema $(X_{min/max}, Y_{min/max})$

The search for equations may benefit from another type of data reduction. A number of adjacent data, at a small distance between their x values, can be binned together and represented by their mean value and standard deviation. The size of the bin depends on the tolerance level in the x dimension. The results of binning are visualized in Figures 1 and 2. Each pixel in the x dimension summarizes about 500 data, so that about 0.5 mln data have been reduced to about 1000.

Pattern stability

No scale is a priori more important than another, as patterns can occur at any scale. When the search for patterns is successful at scale δ, the same pattern can often be detected at scales close to δ. Patterns that hold at many levels are called stable (Witkin, 1983). Consider the stability of extrema. Each extremum that occurs at a given level must also occur at all lower

levels. Stability applies to pairs of adjacent extrema and is measured by the range of scale levels over which a given min/max pair is detected as adjacent. Expanding the definition to the set of all extrema at a given scale, we measure stability as the range of scale levels over which the set of extrema does not change.

Stability is important for several reasons. (1) As discussed earlier, when a number of extrema are detected at a given scale, regularities can be sought on their location, height, and width. It is wasteful to detect the same regularities many times at different scales and then realize that they are identical. A better idea is to recognize that the set of extrema is stable over an interval of scale levels, and search for regularities only once. (2) A stable pattern is a likely manifestation of a real phenomenon, while an unstable set of extrema S may be an artifact. Some extrema may be included in S by chance. A slight variation in the tolerance level removes them from S. The search for regularities in such a set S may fail or lead to spurious regularities. It would be a further waste of time to seek their interpretation and generalization.

Since regularities for extrema may lead to important conclusions about the underlying phenomena, our system pays attention to sets of extrema which are stable across many tolerance levels. It searches the sets of extrema and picks the first stable set at the high end of scale.

Algorithm: Detect stable set of extrema at high end of scale
Given a sequence of extrema sets EXTREMA$_i$, ordered by δ_i,
$\delta_{min} \leq \delta_i \leq \delta_{max}$:
    for δ **from** δ_{min} **to** δ_{max} **do**
        Compute the number E_i of extrema in EXTREMA$_i$
    for each different E_i **do**
        Compute the number N_i of occurrences of E_i ;; The higher
        ;; is N_i, the more stable the corresponding set EXTREMA$_i$
    Let N_a, N_b two highest numbers among N_i
    return EXTREMA$_i$ for the minimum(E_a, E_b)
    ;; That among two most stable sets which is of higher scale
    and return δ_{stable} = average(δ) for EXTREMA$_i$

Residual data

Our mechanism treats patterns as additive. It subtracts the detected patterns from data and seek further patterns in the residua. We will now present the details of subtraction and discuss termination of the search.

Both equations and extrema are functional relationships between x and y: $y = f(x)$. Some extrema can be described by equations that cover also many data that extend far beyond a given extremum. For instance, a second degree polynomial that fits one extremum, may at the same time capture a range of data. Equations may not be found, however, for many extrema. Those we represent point by point. In the first case, when $y = f(x)$ is the best and acceptable equation, the residua are computed as $r_i = y_i - f(x_i)$, and they oscillate around $y = 0$. In the second case we remove from the data all datapoints that represent the extremum.

In the first case the data are decomposed into pattern $y = f(x)$ and residua $\{(x_i, r_i), i = 1, \ldots, N\}$, so that $y_i = f(x_i) + r_i$. In the second case, the data are partitioned into the extremum $\{(x_i, y_i) : s(x_i)\}$, where $s(x)$ describes the scope of the extremum, and the residua $\{(x_i, y_i) : \neg s(x_i)\}$.

If the residua (x_i, r_i) deviate from the normal distribution, the search for patterns applies recursively. Eventually no more patterns can be found in residua. This may happen because regularities in the residua are not within the scope of search or because the residua represent Gaussian noise. In the latter case, the final data model is $y = f(x) + N(0, \varepsilon(x))$, where $\varepsilon(x)$ is Gaussian, while $f(x)$ represents all the detected patterns. Since the variability of residua is much smaller than that of the original data, the subtraction of patterns typically takes only a few iterations.

Algorithm: Detect Patterns
  $D \leftarrow$ the initial data
  until data D are random
    seek stable pattern(s) P in D at the highest tolerance levels
    $D \leftarrow$ subtract pattern(s) P from D

Data

As an example we will consider a large number of data collected in a simple experiment. In order to find the theory of measurement error for an electronic balance, we automatically collected the mass readings of an empty beaker placed on the balance. The measurements have been continued for several days, approximately one datapoint per second. Altogether we got 482,450 readings (7.2 megabytes). Fig. 1 illustrates the data. The beaker weighted about 249.130mg. Since the nominal accuracy of the balance is 0.001g=1mg, we expected a constant reading that would occasionally diverge by a few milligrams from the average value. But the results were very surprising. All datapoints have been plotted, but many adjacent data have been plotted at the same value of x.

We can see a periodic pattern consisting of several large maxima with a slower ascent and a more rapid descent. The heights of the maxima seem constant or slightly growing, and they seem to follow a constant cycle. Superimposed on this constant pattern are smaller extrema of different height. Several levels of even smaller extrema are not visible in Figure 1, because the time dimension has been compresses, but they are clear in the original data.

Upon closer examination, one can notice seven data points at the values about 249.430g, that is 0.3g above the average result, a huge distance in comparison to the accuracy of the balance. They can be seen as small plus signs in the upper part of Figure 1. There is one point about 0.3g below the average data. Those data must have been caused by the same phenomenon because they are very special and very similar: they are momentary peaks of one-second duration, at the similar distance from the bulk of the data.

Apparently, several phenomena must have contributed to those data. Can all these patterns be detected in automated way by a general purpose mechanism, or are our eyes smarter than our computer pro-

grams? Can our mechanism find enough clues about those patterns to discover the underlying phenomena?

Results of search for patterns at many scales

We will now illustrate the application of our multi-scale search mechanism on the dataset described in the previous section.

Detect extrema at all tolerance levels: The search for extrema at all levels of tolerance started from 482,450 data and iterated through some 300 scale levels. Since the number of extrema decreased rapidly between the low scale levels, the majority of time has been spent on the first pass through the data. The number of extrema at the initial scale of $1mg$ has been 29,000, so the data have been reduced to 6%. The number of extrema has been under 50 for $\delta > 9mg$.

Find the first stable set of extrema: The algorithm that finds the first stable set has been applied to all 300 sets of extrema. It detected a set stable at the tolerance levels between 30 and 300. The number of extrema has been 17, including 8 maxima and 9 minima. Eight of those are the outliers discussed in Section 2, while the complementary extrema lie within the main body of data. The stable extrema became the focus of the next step. We will focus on the maxima, where the search has been successful.

Use the stable extrema set: A simple mechanism for identification of similar patterns (Żytkow, 1996) excluded one maximum, which differed very significantly from all others in both the height and width (to limit the size of this paper, we do not discuss the extrema widths). That maximum is an artifact accompanying the minimum located $300mg$ under the bulk of the data. When applied to the remaining maxima, the equation finder discovered two strong regularities: (1) maxima heights are constant, (2) the maxima widths are constant (equal one second). No equation has been found for their location. Even if these 1-second deviations from the far more stable readings of mass occurred only seven times in nearly half million data, the pattern they follow may help us sometime to identify their cause.

Subtract patterns from data: Since the seven maxima have the width of 1 datapoint each, according to section 1.6 they have been removed from the original data. 482,442 data remained for further analysis (one single-point minimum has been removed, too).

Detect patterns in the residua: The search for patterns continued recursively in the residual data. Now the extrema have been found at the much more limited range of tolerance levels, between 1 and 43. The numbers of maxima at each scale have been depicted in Table 1 in the rows labeled M_{max}. The stability analysis determined a set of five maxima and the corresponding minima, which have been stable at the scale between 23 and 30. No regularity has been found for extrema locations and amplitudes, but interesting reg-

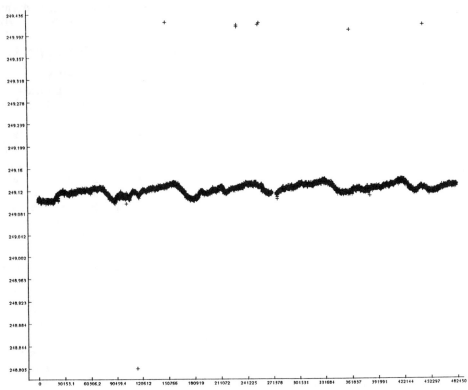

Figure 1: The raw results of mass measurements on an electronic balance over the period of five days (482450 readings).

ularities have been found for heights and locations of the maxima, from the data listed in Table 2.

Max. number	1	2	3	4	5
Height	249.137	249.144	249.143	249.148	249.148
Location	69944	155970	239367	328073	418167

Table 2: The first stable group of maxima, at the scale 23–30 in Table 1.

For those five maxima, stable equations have been found for location and height as functions of the maxima number, M: $location = 86855M - 18261$ and $height = 0.0026M + 249.144$.

The successful regularities have been also found for minima locations and heights. But no equation has been found for all data at the tolerance level $1/6 \times 30mg = 5mg$.

Partition the data: Since no trigonometric equation has been found (cf. section 1.3), the data have been partitioned at the extrema, and search for monotonous equations has been tried and succeeded in each partition, with different equations. For instance, in two segments of data: down-1 (in Figure 2, data for X from about 70,000 to about 90,000) and down-2 (X from 160,000 to 180,000), the equations are linear:

(segment down-1) $y = -1.61 \times 10^{-6} \times x + 249.249$
(segment down-2) $y = -1.46 \times 10^{-6} \times x + 249.371$

By subtracting these regularities from the data, two sets of residua have been generated, labeled down-1 and down-2. Further search, applied to residua in each partition, revealed extrema at lower tolerance levels. The patterns for the stable maxima locations as a function of maxima number M, for instance, have been:

(segment down-1) $location = 1220 \times M + 70,425$
(segment down-2) $location = 1297 \times M + 154,716$

The slope in both equations indicates the average cycle measured in seconds between the adjacent maxima. That cycle is about 21 minutes (1260 seconds).

Physical interpretation of the results

How can we interpret the discovered patterns? Recall that the readings should be constant or fluctuate minimally, as the beaker has not changed its mass.

We do not know what caused the one-second extrema at the highest scale. Perhaps an error in analog-to-digital conversion. But we can interpret many patterns at the lower levels. Consider the linear relation found for maxima locations, $location = 86855M - 18261$. It indicates a constant cycle of 86,855 seconds. When compared to 24 hours (86,400 seconds), it leads to an interesting interpretation: the cycle is just slightly longer than 24 hours. The measurements have been made in May, when each day is few minutes longer then the previous one. These facts make us see a close match

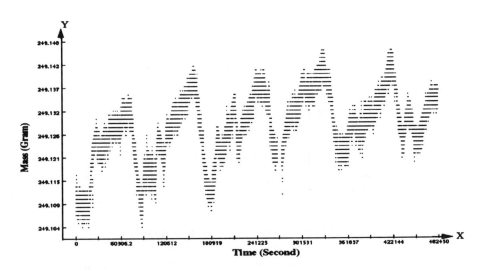

Figure 2: Mass measurements on electronic balance after the outlier extrema have been subtracted.

Scale	1	2	3	4	5	6	7	8	9	10	11	12	13	14	15	16	17	18	19	20	21	22
M_{max}	14337	3114	2308	808	617	267	204	78	46	26	22	16	15	12	12	11	7	7	7	7	6	6
Scale	23	24	25	26	27	28	29	30	31	32	33	34	35	36	37	38	39	40	41	42	43	
M_{max}	5	5	5	5	5	5	5	5	4	3	2	2	2	1	1	1	1	1	1	1	1	

Table 1: The number of maxima (M_{max}) found for different scale values.

between the cycle of day and night and the maxima and minima in the data. The mass is the highest at the end of day. It goes sharply down through the night, which is much shorter than the day in May. Then the mass goes slowly up during the day, until the next sunset.

Why would the balance reflect the time of the day with such a precision? Among many possible explanations we can consider temperature, which changes in a daily cycle. The actual changes in temperature at the balance did not exceed one centigrade and have been hardly noticeable, but if this hypothesis is right, it should apply to other patterns discovered in the same data. The balance has been located in a room with the windows facing east and the morning sun raising temperature from early morning. What about the short term cycles of about 20 minutes? The air conditioning seems the culprit. It turns on and off about every 15–25 minutes, in shorter intervals during the day, in longer intervals at night. The regularities in maxima locations in different data partitions reveal that pattern. The room has been under the influence of both the air-conditioning and from the outside, which explains both the daily cycle and the short term cycle. We could not confirm these conclusions by direct measurements. Few weeks later our discovery lab has been moved to another building.

Acknowledgment: special thanks to Jieming Zhu for his many contributions to the research reported in this paper.

References

Hoaglin, D.C., Mosteller, F., & Tukey, J.W. 1983. *Understanding Robust and Exploratory Data Analysis*, John Wiley & Sons, New York

Kendall, M. & Ord, K. 1990. *Time Series*, Edward Arnold Publ.

Klösgen, W. 1996. Explora: A Multipattern and Multistrategy Discovery Assistant, in U.Fayyad, G.Piatetsky-Shapiro, P.Smyth & R.Uthurusamy eds. *Advances in Knowledge Discovery and Data Mining*, AAAI Press, 249-271.

Langley, P., Simon, H., Bradshaw, G. & Zytkow, J. 1987. *Scientific Discovery: Computational Explorations of the Creative Processes*. MIT Press: Cambridge, Mass.

Piatetsky-Shapiro, G. and C. Matheus, 1991. Knowledge Discovery Workbench, in G. Piatetsky-Shapiro ed. *Proc. of AAAI-91 Workshop on Knowledge Discovery in Databases*, 11–24.

Tierney, L. 1990. *Lisp-Stat: An Object-Oriented Environment for Statistical Computing and Dynamic Graphics*, Wiley, New York, NY.

Tukey, J.W. 1977. *Exploratory Data Analysis*, Addison-Wesley, Reading, MA.

Witkin, A.P., 1983. Scale-Space Filtering, in *Proc. of Intl. Joint Conf. on Artificial Intelligence*, AAAI Press.

Zembowicz, R., & Żytkow, J.M. 1992. Discovery of Equations: Experimental Evaluation of Convergence, in *Proc. of 10th National Conference on Artificial Intelligence*, AAAI Press, 70–75.

Żytkow, J.M. 1996. Automated Discovery of Empirical Laws, to appear in *Fundamenta Informatica*.

A Linear Method for Deviation Detection in Large Databases

Andreas Arning

IBM German Software Development Laboratory
Boeblingen, Germany

Rakesh Agrawal and Prabhakar Raghavan

IBM Almaden Research Center
San Jose, California 95120, U.S.A.

Abstract

We describe the problem of finding deviations in large data bases. Normally, explicit information outside the data, like integrity constraints or predefined patterns, is used for deviation detection. In contrast, we approach the problem from the inside of the data, using the implicit redundancy of the data.

We give a formal description of the problem and present a linear algorithm for detecting deviations. Our solution simulates a mechanism familiar to human beings: after seeing a series of similar data, an element disturbing the series is considered an exception. We also present experimental results from the application of this algorithm on real-life datasets showing its effectiveness.

Index Terms: Data Mining, Knowledge Discovery, Deviation, Exception, Error

Introduction

The importance of detecting *deviations* (or *exceptions*) in data has been recognized in the fields of Databases and Machine Learning for a long time. Deviations have been often viewed as outliers, or errors, or noise in data. There has been work in Statistics on identifying outliers (e.g. (Hoaglin, Mosteller, & Tukey 1983) (Johnson 1992)). There has been work in extending learning algorithms to cope with a small amount of noise (e.g. (Aha, Kibler, & Albert 1991)). Additionally, some work has been done to determine the impact of erroneous examples on the learning results: there is experimental work as in (Quinlan 1986) and quantitative theoretical work as in (Angluin & Laird 1988), extending the valuable work of (Valiant 1984).

Rather than being considered outliers that need to be tolerated during the main-line processing, deviations play the leading part in this paper: the one and only purpose of our proposed method is to discover them. Usually, explicit information sources residing outside the data like integrity constraints (Chamberlin 1996) or predefined error/non-error patterns (Val

1995) are used for deviation detection. We approach the problem from the inside of the data, using the implicit redundancy in the data to detect deviations.

The problem of detecting deviations can be considered to be a special case of clustering of data into two clusters: deviations and non-deviations. However, the usual clustering methods (see (Shavlik & Dietterich 1990)) are biased toward discarding deviations as noise; we, in contrast, try to isolate small minorities. Moreover, these methods generally require the existence of a metrical distance function between data elements. Such is the case with even refined clustering algorithms as (Fisher 1987) (Hanson & Bauer 1989) (Rumelhart & Zipser 1985). Michalski (Michalski & Stepp 1983) replaces the usual Euclidian distance measure between data elements by enriching the measure with conceptual similarity, but still requires a symmetrical distance measure and imposes restrictive constraints on permissible representations. We, on the other hand, only require a function that can yield the degree to which a data element causes the "dissimilarity" of the data set to increase. This function does not have to fulfill the conditions to be metrical.

The literature on Kolmogorov complexity (Li & Vitanyi 1991) is relevant to the problem of deviation detection. We are looking for the subset of data that leads to the greatest reduction in Kolmogorov complexity for the amount of data discarded. Our problem is also related to the Minimum Description Length (MDL) principle (Rissanen 1989). The MDL principle states that the best model for encoding data is the one that minimizes the sum of the cost of describing the data in terms of the model and the cost of describing the model.

Below we give a new measure for deviation detection and an algorithm for detecting deviation. The proposed algorithm has linear complexity. This is a desirable property for a data mining algorithm, as we know from (Agrawal, Imielinski, & Swami 1993) that presents a method for discovering frequent co-occurrences of attribute values in large data sets. But the goal of that algorithm is quite different, and the performance of this system ((Agrawal & Srikant 1994)) is a consequence of ignoring early the seldom occurring values – thus the possible exceptions.

Problem Description

We begin by giving a formal definition of the deviation detection problem.

Exact Exception Problem

Given:

- a set of items I (and thus its power set $\mathcal{P}(I)$);

- a *dissimilarity* function $\mathcal{D}\colon \mathcal{P}(I) \to \mathbb{R}_0^+$;

- a *cardinality* function $\mathcal{C}\colon \mathcal{P}(I) \to \mathbb{R}_0^+$, with $I_1 \subset I_2 \Rightarrow \mathcal{C}(I_1) < \mathcal{C}(I_2)$ for all $I_1, I_2 \subseteq I$.

Define for each $I_j \subset I$, the *smoothing factor*:

$$SF(I_j) := \mathcal{C}(I - I_j) * (\mathcal{D}(I) - \mathcal{D}(I - I_j)).$$

We say that $I_x \subset I, I_x \neq I$ is an *exception set* of I with respect to $\mathcal{D}$ and $\mathcal{C}$ if

$$SF(I_x) \geq SF(I_j) \text{ for all } I_j \subset I.$$

Notes

- Intuitively, an *exception set* is the subset of items that contributes most to the dissimilarity of the itemset I with the least number of items.

- The *smoothing factor* indicates how much the dissimilarity can be reduced by removing a subset I_j of elements from the set I. Observe that SF may be negative for some subset I_j if the dissimilarity of $I - I_j$ is higher than that of the original set I.

- While $\mathcal{D}(I - I_x)$ — the dissimilarity of the reduced set — is important in finding the exception set I_x, the dissimilarity $\mathcal{D}(I_x)$ of the exception set itself is not considered. Nevertheless, it may be valuable to take into account $\mathcal{D}(I_x)$ in further evaluation of the exception set.

- For $\mathcal{D}$, any function can be used that returns a low value if the elements of I are similar to each other, and a higher value if the elements are dissimilar. This function does not require a metrical distance between the items.

- In the most simple case, the function $\mathcal{C}(I - I_j)$ may return $|I - I_j|$, the number of items in the set $I - I_j$. However, to favor small exception sets, this function may be defined by a formula such as $\mathcal{C}(I - I_j) = \frac{1}{|I_j| + 1}$.

- The exception set need not be unique. It can also be empty, e.g. if all items in I are identical. The smoothing factor is 0 in that case.

Example Let

- the set I be the set of integer values $\{1,4,4,4\}$;

- the dissimilarity function $\mathcal{D}\colon \mathcal{P}(I) \to \mathbb{R}_0^+$ be the variance of the numbers in the set, i.e. $\frac{1}{N} \times \sum_{i=1}^{N} (x_i - \overline{x})^2$;

- the cardinality function $\mathcal{C}\colon \mathcal{P}(I) \to \mathbb{R}_0^+$ be the count of elements in the set.

By computing for each candidate exception set I_j the smoothing factor $SF(I_j)$, we get:

I_j	$I - I_j$	$\mathcal{C}(I - I_j)$	$\mathcal{D}(I - I_j)$	$SF(I_j)$
$\{\}$	$\{1,4,4,4\}$	4	1.69	0.00
$\{4\}$	$\{1,4,4\}$	3	2.00	−0.94
$\{4,4\}$	$\{1,4\}$	2	2.25	−1.13
$\{4,4,4\}$	$\{1\}$	1	0.00	1.69
$\{1\}$	$\{4,4,4\}$	3	0.00	5.06
$\{1,4\}$	$\{4,4\}$	2	0.00	3.38
$\{1,4,4\}$	$\{4\}$	1	0.00	1.69

Thus, the candidate set $I_j = \{1\}$ and only this one qualifies as *exception set* I_x with respect to the specified $\mathcal{C}$ and $\mathcal{D}$ functions.

Sequential Exception Problem

There are choices of the functions $\mathcal{C}$ and $\mathcal{D}$ for which the exact exception problem is trivial to solve. There are others for which it is non-trivial but still polynomial-time. For example, given a set of numbers, consider finding the subset whose removal results in the greatest reduction in the variance of the residual set, per element removed (or any similar cardinality function). A priori it is not clear how to do this, but the following schema works: sort the numbers in decreasing order of the distance from their mean. Discard the numbers one by one in this order and at each point compute the smoothing factor. After we have examined all the numbers in this fashion, we would have seen the optimal subset at some point. This example is interesting because it is a case where the optimal order for considering subsets can be computed efficiently.

However, one cannot hope to always find an efficient ordering for examining the elements that yields the optimal solution for every $\mathcal{C}$ and $\mathcal{D}$. Indeed, there exist $\mathcal{C}$ and $\mathcal{D}$ for which the problem is NP-hard by a reduction from Maximum Independent Set in a graph (Garey & Johnson 1979). This motivates the definition of the sequential exception problem.

Sequential Exception

Given:

- a set of items I (and thus its power set $\mathcal{P}(I)$);

- a sequence S of n subsets $I_1, I_2, ..., I_n$ with $2 \leq n \leq |I|$, $I_j \subseteq I$, and $I_{j-1} \subset I_j$;

- a *dissimilarity* function $\mathcal{D}_S$: $\mathcal{P}(I) \rightarrow \mathbb{R}_0^+$ with respect to S;

- a *cardinality* function $\mathcal{C}$: $\mathcal{P}(I) \rightarrow \mathbb{R}_0^+$ with $I_1 \subset I_2 \Rightarrow \mathcal{C}(I_1) < \mathcal{C}(I_2)$ for all $I_1, I_2 \subseteq I$.

Define for each I_j in S, the *smoothing factor*:

$$SF'(I_j) := \mathcal{C}(I_j - I_{j-1}) * (\mathcal{D}_S(I_j) - \mathcal{D}_S(I_{j-1})).$$

We say that $I_x \subset I, I_x = (I_j - I_{j-1}), j > 1$ is a *sequential exception set* of I with respect to $\mathcal{D}_S$, $\mathcal{C}$, and the sequence S if

$$SF'(I_x) \geq SF'(I_j) \text{ for all } I_j \text{ occurring in } S.$$

Observe that the smoothing factor SF for each subset I_j considers the dissimilarity difference with the preceding subset in S instead of considering the dissimilarity of the complementary set $(I - I_j)$ and I.

The sequential exception simulates a mechanism familiar to human beings: after seeing a series of similar data, an element disturbing the series is considered an exception, even without being told explicitly the rules of well-formedness.

Algorithm

The algorithm we propose uses for S the sequence that selects elements of I in the order they appear in input (or a randomization of it). That is, I_{j+1} is derived from I_j by including the next item in the input. In this case, $n = |I|$. We also require that the dissimilarity function be such that $\mathcal{D}(I_j)$ is incrementally computable from the result produced by $\mathcal{D}(I_{j-1})$ and the jth item using constant space. The algorithm is as follows:

[1] Perform steps [2] and [3] m times on randomized input (m is an algorithm parameter).

[2] Performs steps [2.1] through [2.3]:

[2.1] Get the first element i_1 of the item set I making up the one-element subset $I_1 \subseteq I$, and compute $\mathcal{D}_S(I_1)$.

[2.2] For each following element $i_j \in (I - I_{j-1})$ in S, create the subset I_j taking $I_j = I_{j-1} \cup \{i_j\}$; compute the difference in dissimilarity values

$$d_j = \mathcal{D}_S(I_j) - \mathcal{D}_S(I_{j-1}).$$

[2.3] Consider that element i_j with the maximal value of $d_j > 0$ to be the answer for this iteration; if $d_j \leq 0$ for all I_j in S, there is no exception.

[3] If an exception i_j is found in step [2.3], do step [3.1]:

[3.1] For each element $i_k, k > j$ compute $d_{k_0} = \mathcal{D}_S(I_{j-1} \cup \{i_k\}) - \mathcal{D}_S(I_{j-1})$ and $d_{k_1} = \mathcal{D}_S(I_j \cup \{i_k\}) - \mathcal{D}_S(I_j)$. Add to I_x those i_k for which $d_{k_0} - d_{k_1} \geq d_j$.

[4] We now potentially have m competing exception sets I_x, corresponding to each iteration. Select the one with largest value of difference in dissimilarity d_j, scaled with the cardinality function $\mathcal{C}$.

Notes

- Steps [2.1] through [2.3] are performed m times on after randomizing the order of items in input to alleviate the sensitivity of results to the order of input.

- For a motivation for Step [3.1], consider a degenerate scenario. Suppose i_j is such that $\mathcal{D}_S(I_j) - \mathcal{D}_S(I_{j-1})$ is large so that i_j is a candidate exception. Now let i_{j+1} be identical to i_j. In that case, $\mathcal{D}_S(I_{j+1}) - \mathcal{D}_S(I_j)$ will be 0 and i_{j+1} will not be considered an exception. In general, there may be items i_k following i_j that would have caused increase in the dissimilarity, but for the presence of i_j. Step [3.1] adds all such items to the exception set.

Complexity

If the number m of runs with randomized order is kept small, and if the user provided function $\mathcal{D}$ is able to compute $\mathcal{D}(I_j)$ incrementally from $\mathcal{D}(I_{j-1})$ and i_j using constant time and space, then all steps but the randomizing step are constant in space and $O(N)$ in time consumption. Here N is the number of items in the input.

With random access to the data, the randomizing step can be done in $O(N)$ time. If we can rely on an already randomized sequence, we could do instead a random choice of the start record and process the data in wrap-around manner. In that case, this pseudo-randomizing step would also work in linear time.

Experimental Evaluation

We present next the results of applying the proposed algorithm on real-life datasets in order to examine if the algorithm indeed succeeds in isolating deviations.

The datasets are taken from the "UCI Repository of Machine Learning Databases and Domain Theories" (obtainable from `ics.uci.edu` via anonymous ftp in the directory `/usr2/spool/ftp/pub/machine-learning-databases`). We also consider the "fortune cookies" of IBM AIX version 2.2 and a table of IBM stock prices.

Each line in these datasets is considered an item, and the goal is to identify lines that violate frequently occurring character patterns. The same dissimilarity function was used in all the tests.

Dissimilarity Function

The dissimilarity function handles the comparison of character strings. It maintains a pattern in the form of a regular expression that matches all the character strings seen so far. Starting with a pattern that is the same as the first string seen, the pattern may have to be weakened by introducing wildcard characters as more strings are seen to cover them. The dissimilarity function captures this weakening in the covering pattern; the dissimilarity increases when the pattern covering the $j-1$ strings in I_{j-1} does not cover the jth string $\in (I_j - I_{j-1})$.

The dissimilarity function is defined as:

$$\mathcal{D}_S(I_1) := 0;$$

$$\mathcal{D}_S(I_j) := \mathcal{D}_S(I_{j-1}) + j \times \frac{\mathcal{M}_S(I_j) - \mathcal{M}_S(I_{j-1})}{\mathcal{M}_S(I_j)}$$

where $\mathcal{M}_S(I_j)$ is computed from the string pattern that covers all elements:

$$\mathcal{M}_S(I_j) := \frac{1}{3 \times c - w + 2}$$

with c being the total number of characters and w being the number of needed wildcards. For details, see (Arning 1995).

The auxiliary function $\mathcal{M}_S(I_j)$ computes a user customizable maximum value for the elements of I_j in order to find those elements that particularly increase this maximum. In the definition above, it grows with an increasing number of wildcards and a decreasing number of constant characters in a pattern.

Note that a weighting is done in the computation of the distance function by the position j of the string in input; this weighting captures that a weakening of the pattern is quite likely for elements with low index and improbable for elements with high index.

Results

The results reported below show different types of exceptions found on very different datasets. Note that the same dissimilarity function (outlined above) was used in all the tests. To give an idea of the data layout, before giving the exceptions discovered, we list a few initial items of the dataset.

shuttle-landing-control.data

```
2,*,*,*,*,*,2
1,2,*,*,*,*,1
1,1,2,*,*,*,1
1,1,1,*,*,*,1
1,1,3,2,2,*,1
1,*,*,*,*,4,1
2,1,4,*,*,1,1
2,1,4,*,*,2,1
2,1,4,*,*,3,1
2,1,3,1,1,1,1
2,1,3,1,1,2,1
2,1,3,1,2,1,1
2,1,3,1,2,2,1
1,1,3,1,1,3,1
2,1,3,1,2,3,1
```

shuttle-landing-control.data – found exceptions

```
2,*,*,*,*,*,2
```

echocardiogram.data

```
11,0,71,0,0.260,9,4.600,14,1,1,name,1,0
19,0,72,0,0.380,6,4.100,14,1.700,0.588,name,1,0
16,0,55,0,0.260,4,3.420,14,1,1,name,1,0
57,0,60,0,0.253,12.062,4.603,16,1.450,0.788,name,1
19,1,57,0,0.160,22,5.750,18,2.250,0.571,name,1,0
26,0,68,0,0.260,5,4.310,12,1,0.857,name,1,0
13,0,62,0,0.230,31,5.430,22.5,1.875,0.857,name,1,0
50,0,60,0,0.330,8,5.250,14,1,1,name,1,0
19,0,46,0,0.340,0,5.090,16,1.140,1.003,name,1,0
25,0,54,0,0.140,13,4.490,15.5,1.190,0.930,name,1,0
10,1,77,0,0.130,16,4.230,18,1.800,0.714,name,1,1
52,0,62,1,0.450,9,3.600,16,1.140,1.003,name,1,0
52,0,73,0,0.330,6,4,14,1,1,name,1,0
44,0,60,0,0.150,10,3.730,14,1,1,name,1,0
0.5,1,62,0,0.120,23,5.800,11.67,2.330,0.358,name,1
24,0,55,1,0.250,12.063,4.290,14,1,1,name,1,0
0.5,1,69,1,0.260,11,4.650,18,1.640,0.784,name,1,1
0.5,1,62.529,1,0.070,20,5.200,24,2,0.857,name,1,1
22,1,66,0,0.090,17,5.819,8,1.333,0.429,name,1,0
1,1,66,1,0.220,15,5.400,27,2.250,0.857,name,1,1
...
```

echocardiogram.data – found exceptions

```
,?,?,77,?,?,?,?,?,2,?,name,2,?
```

Fortune Cookies

```
* UNIX is a trademark of AT&T Bell Laboratories.
1 bulls, 3 cows.
10.0 times 0.1 is hardly ever 1.0.
A Puritan is someone who is deathly afraid that so
A bad compromise is better than a good battle.  --
A bird in hand is worth two in the bush.  -- Cerva
A bird in the bush can't relieve itself in your ha
A clash of doctrine is not a disaster -- it is an
A conservative is one who is too cowardly to fight
A fanatic is one who can't change his mind and won
A foolish consistency is the hobgoblin of little m
...
```

Fortune Cookies – found exceptions

```
Password:
Quack!
login:
```

Observe that the exception set in this case consist of three items. The algorithm could identify them as exceptions because they are the only ones with no blanks and caused a pattern of the form "* * * *" to be weakened to "*"

IBM stock prices

58/07/01	368.50	313.23	.022561
58/07/02	369.50	314.08	.022561
58/07/03	369.25	313.87	.022561
58/07/04	Market closed		
58/07/07	370.00	314.50	.022561
58/07/08	369.00	313.65	.022561
58/07/09	368.00	312.80	.022561
58/07/10	368.25	313.02	.022561
58/07/11	368.50	313.23	.022561
58/07/14	360.00	306.00	.022561
58/07/15	356.00	302.60	.022561
58/07/16	359.50	305.58	.022561
58/07/17	359.50	305.58	.022561
58/07/18	357.50	303.88	.022561
58/07/21	361.00	306.85	.022561
58/07/22	363.00	308.55	.022561
58/07/23	366.50	311.53	.022561
58/07/24	368.00	312.80	.022561
58/07/25	370.00	314.50	.022561
58/07/28	370.25	314.72	.022561

...

IBM stock prices – found exceptions

58/07/04	Market closed	(317 instances)
59/01/06	2.5% Stock Dividend	(2 instances)
59/05/05	50% Stock Split	(7 instances)
73/10/09	IBM not traded	(1 instance)
88/09/26	Data suspect	(30 instances)

Out of the 9415 records, an exception set of 357 elements was created. We have shown only one exemplar of each exception type. Note that the different instances of an exception type are not duplicates, but differ in the date part.

A Failure and its Analysis

Applying the same dissimilarity function to the following data set, the algorithm did not identify any exception:

house-votes-84.data

```
republican,n,y,n,y,y,y,n,n,n,y,?,y,y,y,n,y
republican,n,y,n,y,y,y,n,n,n,n,n,y,y,y,n,?
democrat,?,y,y,?,y,y,n,n,n,y,n,y,y,n,n
democrat,n,y,y,n,?,y,n,n,n,n,y,n,y,n,n,y
democrat,y,y,y,n,y,y,n,n,n,y,?,y,y,y,y
democrat,n,y,y,n,y,y,n,n,n,n,n,y,y,y,y
democrat,n,y,n,y,y,y,n,n,n,n,n,?,y,y,y
republican,n,y,n,y,y,y,n,n,n,n,n,n,y,y,?,y
republican,n,y,n,y,y,y,n,n,n,n,n,y,y,y,n,y
democrat,y,y,y,n,n,n,y,y,y,n,n,n,n,n,?,?
republican,n,y,n,y,y,y,n,n,n,n,?,?,y,y,n,n
republican,n,y,n,y,y,y,n,n,n,n,y,?,y,y,?,?
democrat,n,y,y,n,n,n,y,y,y,n,n,n,y,n,?,?
democrat,y,y,y,n,n,y,y,y,?,y,y,?,n,n,y,?
republican,n,y,n,y,y,y,n,n,n,n,n,y,?,?,n,?
republican,n,y,n,y,y,y,n,n,n,y,n,y,y,?,n,?
democrat,y,n,y,n,n,y,n,y,?,y,y,y,?,n,n,y
democrat,y,?,y,n,n,n,y,y,y,n,n,n,y,n,y
republican,n,y,n,y,y,y,n,n,n,n,?,y,y,n,n
democrat,y,y,y,n,n,n,y,y,y,n,y,n,n,n,y,y
...
```

However, manual inspection reveals some exceptional items containing the occasionally occurring '?' symbol for the vote; the most outstanding element with many of these seldom values is:

house-votes-84.data – *not* found exception

```
republican,?,?,?,?,?,?,?,?,?,?,?,?,?,?,?,?
```

The reason for this exception not being found is the nature of the dissimilarity function used. For almost any order of the input data, after processing a few data elements the pattern to cover them is changed to "*e*c*a*,,,,,,,,,,,,,,,*"; once two different values "...,n,..." and "...,y,..." are seen in a column, the pattern takes the form "...,*,...". From then on, there is no change in pattern when a "?" appears in the same column as the pattern covers it.

Can we capture these types of exceptions with a more powerful dissimilarity function? We can use a function that maintains for each column some maximum number of values (to enable the membership test with constant space and time consumption), beyond which we use a wildcard symbol for the column. Each column has a partial dissimilarity value, which when summed over all columns gives the total dissimilarity value. Indeed, when using such a dissimilarity function for tabular data, the algorithm could discover the cited exception.

Conclusions and Future Work

This paper is an attempt to give a formal framework to the problem of deviation detection in order to stimulate further work and discussion in the KDD community on this important data mining operation. We also presented a linear algorithm for the sequential exception problem. Our solution simulates a mechanism familiar to human beings: after seeing a series of similar data, an element disturbing the series is considered an exception. A dissimilarity function captures how dissimilar is a new data item from the data items seen so far. This algorithm is suitable for large data bases found in data mining.

Experimental evaluation shows that the effectiveness of our algorithm in isolating deviations depends on the dissimilarity function used. Obviously, if we know the nature of exception we are looking for, we can design a very effective dissimilarity function. But in that case, we do not need a general algorithm and the most effective solution would be to write a special program to do the task. On the other hand, based on experiments with several dissimilarity functions on several datasets, our feeling is that it will be difficult to have a universal dissimilarity function that works well for all datasets.

Nevertheless, it seems possible and helpful to have some predefined dissimilarity functions that can handle typical classes of exceptions found in real-life datasets. The deviation detection algorithm then should work in conjunction with automatic selection of the appropriate function that promises the best results. This could be done by triggering the selection based on the properties of the input data, as well as by conditional selection depending on results of previous runs. Working out the specifics and building such a system is a fruitful direction for future research.

References

Agrawal, R., and Srikant, R. 1994. Fast algorithms for mining association rules. In *Proceedings of the VLDB Conference*.

Agrawal, R.; Imielinski, T.; and Swami, A. 1993. Database mining: A performance perspective. *IEEE Transactions on Knowledge and Data Engineering* 5(6):914–925.

Aha, D. W.; Kibler, D.; and Albert, M. K. 1991. Instance-based learning algorithms. *Machine Learning* 6(1):37–66.

Angluin, D., and Laird, P. 1988. Learning from noisy examples. *Machine Learning* 2(4):343–370.

Arning, A. 1995. *Fehlersuche in großen Datenmengen unter Verwendung der in den Daten vorhandenen Redundanz*. PhD dissertation, Universität Osnabrück, Fachbereich Sprach– und Literaturwissenschaft.

Chamberlin, D. 1996. *Using the New DB2: IBM's Object-Relational Database System*. Morgan Kaufmann.

Fisher, D. H. 1987. Knowledge acquisition via incremental conceptual clustering. *Machine Learning* 2(2):139–172.

Garey, M., and Johnson, D. 1979. *Computers and Intractability: a guide to the theory of NP-completeness*. W. H. Freeman.

Hanson, S. J., and Bauer, M. 1989. Conceptual clustering, categorization, and polymorphy. *Machine Learning* 3(4):343–372.

Hoaglin, D.; Mosteller, F.; and Tukey, J. 1983. *Understanding Robust and Exploratory Data Analysis*. New York: John Wiley.

Johnson, R. 1992. *Applied Multivariate Statistical Analysis*. Prentice Hall.

Li, M., and Vitanyi, P. 1991. *Kolmogorov Complexity*. Springer Verlag.

Michalski, R. S., and Stepp, R. E. 1983. Learning from observation: conceptual clustering. In Michalski et al. (1983). 331–363.

Michalski, R. S.; Carbonell, J. G.; and Mitchell, T. M., eds. 1983. *Machine Learning: An Artificial Intelligence Approach*, volume I. Los Altos, California: Morgan Kaufmann.

Quinlan, J. R. 1986. Induction of decision trees. *Machine Learning* 1(1):81–106.

Rissanen, J. 1989. *Stochastic Complexity in Statistical Inquiry*. World Scientific Publ. Co.

Rumelhart, D. E., and Zipser, D. 1985. Feature discovery by competitive learning. *Cognitive Science* 9:75–112.

Shavlik, J. W., and Dietterich, T. G., eds. 1990. *Readings in Machine Learning*, Series in Machine Learning. Morgan Kaufmann.

Vality Technology Inc. 1995. *Integrity product Overview*.

Valiant, L. G. 1984. A theory of the learnable. *Communications of the ACM* 27(11):1134–1142.

Planning tasks for Knowledge Discovery in Databases;
Performing Task-Oriented User-Guidance.

Robert Engels*
University of Karlsruhe, Institute AIFB,
D-76128, Karlsruhe, Germany
Email: engels@aifb.uni-karlsruhe.de

Abstract

Performing the complex task of Knowledge Discovery in Databases (KDD) requires a break-down of the task-complexity to enable the possibility of performing the KDD-task. Since even more techniques will appear in the future that can solve a variety of KDD-problems, a domain expert that wants to analyse his domain should have the means to work with tools that integrate several of these techniques as well as the techniques themselves. In this paper a framework is proposed for a strategy component that is to be used for a KDD-system that can guide users in breaking down the complexity of a typical KDD-task and supports him in selecting and using several ML-techniques. The goals of such a guidance component are *reuse* of (predefined) taskcomponents in order to decrease development time and to simplify the process of decomposing a KDD-task, task-oriented *planning* in order to break down complexity of a typical KDD-task and *supporting post-processing* (evaluation) of KDD-processes.

Keywords : *User-support, Knowledge Discovery in Databases, Task-decomposition, Reusable Process Components*

Providing User-Guidance for KDD-processes

The question whether there is a need for user-guidance or not is already answered by several studies mentioned in the literature (see i.e. (Consortium 1993), (Mladenic 1995), (Ram & Hunter 1992), (Hunter 1995)). The answer to the "how" question is not so easily answered. There are several approaches that provide a kind of user-support, but a real guidance of a user that helps planning KDD-processes by building up task-decompositions according to the users intentions and helping him to refine and alter his problem statement if necessary is not common.

The framework we propose partly stems from ideas of the field of knowledge acquisition where task-

---
*This work has been partially funded by the Daimler Benz AG, Research & Technology, project no. 096 4 965047 1 E B.

decomposition and reusable task-descriptions are used to describe and specify complex tasks. The user that we see as a typical user of our system is a domain expert that does not have extensive knowledge about KDD and wants an additional tool for the analysis of his database. The expert also has some understanding of the KDD-task in the sense that he knows a little about the several different core tasks that underlie a KDD-process (i.e. visualisation, classification, dependencies, prediction).

User-guidance in a KDD-session is started (as mentioned) with a description of the problem by the expert. This description is to be refined until a clear goal state is defined. This is to be done iteratively and interactively (we do not expect the process to be totally automatical) with a knowledge engineer because it will seldom be the case that the initial problem description is clearly enough specified to form a beginning of the planning process. Once the goal state is described it can be mapped upon a high-level task, where we assume a set of predefined high-level tasks that are defined by the system. Such a high-level task should then be decomposed in a task-structure that breaks down the complexity of the initial task in a sequence of subtasks that together concretise the task and provide a solution for the initial (planning) problem. The task decomposition process consists of a process that has two dimensions, namely the identification of a sequence of subtasks that can perform a certain task, and the identification of several alternative sequences for these subtasks. Pre- and postconditions are defined over tasksequences, as well as a control-flow that is defined over them. The solution (as we will call it, see also section) then consists of a set of algorithms that can be executed in order to get the required "valid, novel, potentially useful, and ultimately understandable patterns in data" as defined in the definition of KDD (Fayyad *et al.* 1996).

Terminology

In this section we will clarify the terminology that is used in our approach to KDD-process guidance. We see this step as necessary because of the diversity in terminology that can be found when analyzing the literature and in order to clear the context we want to use.

The terminology we want to clarify is the terminology that relates to the so-called KDD- guidance module. In the following we clarify the concept of a problem, problem description, tasks, task decomposition, techniques, solution, input data, discovered knowledge and mapping.

Problem: A problem is defined in general as an artifact that contains three elements, an initial state, a goal state and a discrepancy between those.

A well known and usefull distinction at this point can be made between ill-defined problems and well-defined problems, where a problem is called ill-defined when[1]: the goal state is not clearly described, the initial state is not clear (some characteristics relevant to the initial state might be unknown) or the information needed to solve the problem is not available, i.e. a problem is also ill-defined if the characteristics of the initial state are not relatable to the characteristics of the goal state, because then there is no possibility to compare the two. A well-defined problem is a problem were the initial and the goal state are known, and where there is only one pair containing a unique initial state and a goal state, and a discrepancy between the two for which no existing solution exists.

A problem can be stated in a natural language form. It forms the basis upon which a problem description is defined.

Problem Description: A problem description is a pair that consists of a single goal state for the system, and a description of the initial state in which the system is.

The description of the initial state can contain more knowledge than is required to define the discrepancy between the initial and the goal state.

A problem description results from the process of transforming a situation in which only an ill-defined problem exists into a situation in which a well-defined problem exists. The domain expert iteratively refines his/her initial problem statement with regard to indistinctnesses that a knowledge engineer recovers.

Tasks: A task consists of a certain set of inferences that, when executed, transforms a certain state into another state. A task consists of an action that, when performed, bridges the gap between an initial and a goal state.

A task has certain pre- and postconditions, where the preconditions define the possible deployment domain of a task (task resources), and the postconditions the characteristics of the knowledge that results when the task is performed (task effects).

---

[1]See also (Simon 1985) for a theorie on well- and ill-defined problems in an information-processing theory.

Task Decomposition: A task decomposition is a refinement of a task into a task/subtask hierarchy.

The top-level task is identical to the task to be composed, and the leaves of the tree form a set of subtasks to be performed that together can perform the task at the top-node level. A (sub-) task that can not be further decomposed is called a generic or primitive task ((Chandrasekaran, Johnson, & Smith 1992)).

Problem Solving Methods: A Problem Solving Method[2] typically describes how to solve a task by decomposing and defines an order on the subtasks in the decomposition through a controlflow.

One speaks of a task-subtask decomposition if one can reach the functionality of a task by performing a (partial) order of subtasks. This kind of refinement of a task with a subtask structure is a *conjunctive* refinement. The functionality of a certain task is defined in terms of pre- and postconditions of the task and also depends on the (partial) ordering posed upon the subtasks by the controlflow. Typically, the task decomposition can cause a refinement of the tasks' functionality since a subtask might introduce additional or refined pre- and postconditions. The reason for this is that the subtasks of a task would be more specific than their higher-level parents.

Techniques: Techniques refer to algorithms that,when executed, can reach the defined functionality of a (generic) task. Such an algorithm does not necessarily need to be a data mining tool in our context, but can also be a (set of) manual steps that should be performed.

Techniques in our framework thus refer to the (ultimately) implemented algorithms that are available in the KDD-tool. Every technique describes an algorithm and therefore exists of an abstract artifact as well as a description of the parameters that are connected to it. Techniques typically come with parameters that are used for tuning the techniques for several different situations. The abstract artifact is the part that will be used for the mapping on the task-decomposition, where the parameter descriptions can be seen as a definition of the range of application of the artifact.

Solution: With a solution is meant the result of an iterative and interactive (planning-)process, where a domain expert, eventually in cooperation with a knowledge engineer, transforms an "ill- defined" problem into a "well-defined" problem, and where this "well-defined" problem description (together with eventual additionally known domain characteristics) forms the starting point for a planning process in a (semi-) closed world. The result of this planning

---

[2]For more about PSM's and their justification see (Schreiber, Wielinga, & Breuker 1993), (Breuker & van de Velde 1994), for an analysis of a typical PSM see (Fensel 1995).

process is called a *solution* and consists of a task decomposition of a KDD-process that, when followed, provides a way to bridge the gap between initial and goal state in a problem description.

The pair of states that form the problem description forms the basis for a search-process is performed in a "semi-closed" world of possible task decompositions that will ultimately match a specific task-decomposition upon this pair of states. The search space is in principle closed, since one can expect to find a solution when one has a well-defined problem-description that fits on a certain top-level task, although this can not be garantueed in every case due to the uncertainty that is caused by the refinement operator that may introduce (unsatisfiable) new preconditions at every refinement step.

A solution then refers to a (controlflow-determined) sequence of techniques that, when executed, should reach the functionality of the top-node task that is mapped upon the problem-description.

Input Data: Input data refers to the data that is input to the KDD-process, i.e. the data that finally is to be analysed.

Input data can exist of the intensional and extensional descriptions of domain specific knowledge, and forms the data that is subject of analysis.

Discovered Knowledge: With discovered knowledge we refer to the results of the execution of the planned solution for the KDD-problem that is described in the problem description.

We explicitly make a distinction between a *solution* and *discovered knowledge*, where a solution refers to the *result of the planning* that is the main task of the guidance module (i.e. the order of algorithms and their parameter initialisations), and discovered knowledge, that is the result of the *execution* of our solution. The domain expert who provided the problem will be mainly interested in this "discovered knowledge".

Mapping: The mapping process means to map the task decomposition and the resulting controlflow that is defined over it, onto an ordered sequence of techniques that together can bridge the gap between the initial and goal state in the problem description.

This step connects the resulting task-decomposition to techniques. The process of decomposing and mapping is an iterative process that should also provide support for the parameter initialization of the several techniques.

The main terminology as we want to use has been described in this section. The next section will shortly describe the dimensions of which the guidance module consists of.

Dimensions of User-Guidance

User-guidance and support is the main task for our guidance module and is built up around two different dimensions. The first dimension deals with the planning process and supports a user with defining the "what" and "how" of his problem. With the "what" is meant the clarification of his problem (i.e. transforming an ill-defined in a well-defined problem), the "how" refers to the match of the resulting pair of states onto a high-level task that can dissolve the discrepance between initial and goalstate, and decomposing it into an order of subtasks.

The second dimension deals with the execution of the results of the planned task.

Planning the KDD-process

As mentioned, the first step when dealing with a planning task for KDD is to define what the problem really is. Experience with performing KDD-tasks learned us that most initial user-requests for data-analysis are ill-defined, that is, a request is most often vaguely described, lacks clarity, and it is impossible to decide whether there is a solution to the problem or not. If one does not carefully analyse the request it can happen that one analyses another problem as originally stated by the expert. At this point a lot of human interaction is needed of a knowledge engineer with the domain expert that provided the problem.

When a problem description is found, according to the definition in section , then a process of planning is started. The pair of states, that form the well-defined problem, as well as additional knowledge that might be known about the domain (data), form the starting point of a search for a task-decomposition that can bridge the gap between initial and goalstate. This task-decomposition can be seen as a kind of "augmented" hierarchy, since it is not only a hierarchy that provides subtasks for a task, but also poses an order upon those subtasks (as defined in controlflow of PSM-components).

So, summarized, we see the highlevel KDD-process definition in a schema-based way, where a task model for a typical KDD-task is taken to be the schema that should be filled out with building blocks (PSM's) that are partly pre-defined (but can be user-defined as well) according to the goals that are described in the problem-description.

The task-decomposition describes an order of tasks that should be performed in order to solve the problem. A mapping should then take place in order to select appropriate techniques that can perform this order of tasks. Once such an order is found one can go to the executional phase, where the tasks should be actually performed.

Execution of a KDD-solution

A logical step after the planning of the process is, of course, the execution of the set of techniques in the appropriate order and with the appropriate parameter settings.

That this is not a straightforward problem can be seen in the field of planning, where making plans was always treated as the main problem, but lately a growing interest is reported in the execution of such plans, that seem to cause additional problems when executed. One of these additional problems we have to tackle in our KDD-framework are the parameter settings of the several techniques. When executing, the functionality of the implemented techniques can be changed (sometimes a lot) by just changing a single parameter. Supporting the initialisation of those parameters is a prerequisite for a succesful execution of the solution found in the planning process. It might be that parameter settings are initialisable according to the functionality description that is provided by the task-decomposition. In our framework the parameter setting initialisation should also be supported by the mapping process that precedes the execution of the technique sequence. In case of failure there is a possibility to fall back on a set of defaults.

A KDD-process example

In this section we will provide an example of a KDD-process that is performed using a multi-strategy approach as defined in this paper. The example is performed in the field of prediction of warranty costs for cars, and uses data from a rather extensive database that contains all the registrations of new cars with their construction-characteristics and warranty costs.

From the field of KA, several problem solving methods can be taken that form a profound basis for reusable task-components.

In the following we will integrate the assessment PSM (Valente & Löckenhoff 1994) in the task decomposition that we define for our example problem. We propose a division of the KDD-solution for our problem in three subtasks that map on our initial taskmodel for KDD-processes as proposed in (Reinartz & Wirth 1995):

1. A "recognition"-task that has the goal to recognise and extract the relevant early warning cars from the dataset. In terms of our taskmodel this can be seen as a pre-processing stage where focussing on relevant data takes place, and a first learning step, where (given this relevant data) a grouping for data at a specific time t in several classes is performed.

2. A "classification"-task that produces classification rules for the distinguished classes.

3. A "deployment"-task that matches new data-tuples to the set of rules and thus assesses the class-membership of new tuples and that matches the set of EW-tuples (Early-Warning cars) that the "prediction"-task provides in order to match them to a certain (user-defined) treshold.

Actually, a fourth step should be integrated before the other three, namely a focussing step. It is not the case that the data as present in the database can realistically be used, since there are simply to many data-tuples, and too many of them are irrelevant as well. An example is the occurence of trucks and cars in the database, where the problem description already provide a focus on the subset of the tuples in the database that are concerned with cars.

Every task in the KDD-solution of figure 1 has its assumptions about the (meta-) knowledge it needs and about the output it can deliver. Being too specific does not help us much w.r.t. reuse, and being too general neither (a well- known trade-off in Software Engineering (Krüger 1992)).

The overall task of our example approach is decomposed in three steps at the first level of decomposition.

First we will shortly repeat what the problem in our example was[3]:

Give a warning signal at time t if quarantuee costs at time t+x for a (certain type of) car will raise abnormally.

In the next sections we will describe the three subtasks with their decompositions: recognition, classification and deployment.

The "recognition"-task is itself further decomposable in three sub-tasks: a cluster subtask, that clusters a set of database tuples, an "incrementally add" subtask, and an assessment task that estimates the class allocation of the datatuples from the set of datatuples with time t-x. The next subtask on the first level of decomposition is concerned with the production of a set of classification rules for the classes that are found in the "assess class-allocation" subtask. This subtask is concerned with the deployment of these results. In the first subtask an assessment is made of the class-allocation of new datatuples at time t+x. The results of this assessment are gathered and form the input for the second subtask that provides the actual warning signal. Altogether the subdivision in subtasks made it possible to perform the rather complex task that was decomposed in three subtasks (each of which is further decomposed). These tasks where coupled to eachother through a set of pre- and postconditions that reassured the compatibility of the tasks among eachother. Doing so we have a way of defining the compatibility of the subtasks, as well as a way for guiding the planning of technique selection as well as an order in which to execute the selected techniques. Reuse of process components is shown by the multiple usage of a specific PSM, although the example (due to space-restrictions) had to be kept abstract.

---

[3]Where the timeline covers a range from $t - x$ (x days/months/years in the past) over t (present) to $t + x$ (x days/months/years in the future).

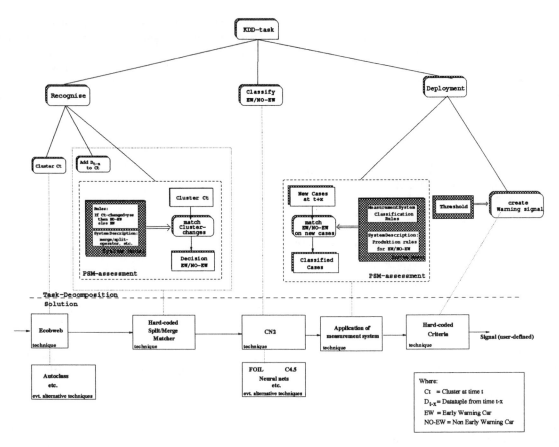

Figure 1: Taskdecomposition of our KDD-solution for the application problem showing integration of the PSM assessment in a (KDD) task decomposition.

Conclusions and related work

For our purposes we see an opportunity to integrate ideas of the several involved disciplines to support breaking down task-complexity of KDD-processes by using task-decompositions. The framework we show here provides a means of flexible planning of a KDD-process according to goals that are made explicit. The user gets support in the sense of pre-defined task-decomposition components and is provided with a means to define those themselve as well. The need for a kind of task-related support is already noticed in (Consortium 1993) and (Thomas, Ganascia, & Laublet 1993).

Therefore we adapted ideas of the KA-community (for example, we did have a look at the ideas on knowledge level modeling as mentioned in KADS (Wielinga, Schreiber, & Breuker 1992), MIKE (Angele, Fensel, & Studer 1996), Components of Expertise (Steels 1990), General Directive Models (van Heijst 1995) and Generic Tasks, (Chandrasekaran, Johnson, & Smith 1992)) and extended the definition of KDD as proposed in (Fayyad *et al.* 1996) in order to introduce the idea of goal-driven KDD. We feel the definition as provided by (Fayyad *et al.* 1996) needed to be extended

by agents, because the 'ultimately understandable patterns', mentioned in the definition, require the notion of an agent in order to be able to define the term 'understandable'. On the other hand we see the need for an extension of this definition with goals since there is a problem defining potentially usefull results when no goals are defined that relate results to needs.

From the field of KDD, the need for breaking down task-complexity in order to solve problems is recognized (see i.e. (Reinartz & Wirth 1995)). Certainly as even more tools will become available to perform data mining, tools that help users selecting and using the right tools for their problems should become available. However, during the KDD-95 conference ((Fayyad & Uthurusamy 1995)) there were not many approaches to be found that dealt with this task-decomposition and user-support problem. Earlier work on the ESPRIT project MLT ((Consortium 1993)), shows a project part that is concerned with the issue of user-guidance and support CONSULTANT (Craw *et al.* 1992), which is later further developed in MUSKRAT (Graner & Sleeman 1993), but no publications are found that do elaborate upon this idea of user-guidance according to tasks and task-decompositions.

An approach that is concerned with the reuse of software components rather than the reuse software processes is the OCAPI system (van den Elst, van Harmelen, & Thonnat 1995). In this approach the idea of modelling processes according to tasks is presented, but, as mentioned, the authors stress the reuse of components rather than of processes. Reuse of components as in OCAPI is also a topic in our framework, where these components exist of data mining techniques rather than image processing programs as in OCAPI. Both approaches share the modelling of pre- and postconditions as well as the modelling of component parameters (that influence the components functionality) at an abstract level.

Furthermore we see a chance for reusing already defined KDD-processes in certain cases were a problem description defines a very similar problem to a previously solved problem (think for example of our specific task description that should be repeatedly performed in order to adjust predictions to new data that is gathered, or that instead of two classes more classes are to be analysed). Here we can see a straightforward need for some kind of reuse of whole KDD-processes, since there is no doubt that developing whole applications again for just a slightly changed problem is not necessary.

The example also showed, although at a rather abstract level, how one can integrate reusable components (like the assessment PSM as described in (Valente & Löckenhoff 1994)) in a task-decomposition. We see a possibility of augmenting a KDD-tool with these structures in order to have a kind of predefined structures that support the definition of certain subtasks, and to be able to define these in a flexible way.

User-guidance performed in this way delivers a solution in the sense that the user interactively defines a sequence of techniques that can solve his problem, and also gets feedback on whether he can expect an answer on his problem definition using the tool or that he should alter his problem definition (i.e. relaxing or specifying the requirements he states in his problem description).

Future work

For the future we plan the further evaluation and implementation of this framework and test it on some more applications. Problems we want to deal with are problems concerning the selection and retrieval of the reusable building blocks according to their functional descriptions, the support of the user by selection of appropriate parameter settings according to the task characteristics and the value of this for task iterations. Integration of more techniques into the framework is also planned.

Acknowledgements

Thanks to Rüdiger Wirth, Thomas Reinartz, the Daimler project group and Rudi Studer for fruitfull discussions on the topics presented in this paper.

References

Angele, J.; Fensel, D.; and Studer, R. 1996. Domain and task modelling in mike. In *Proceedings of the IFIP WG8.1/13.2 Joint Working Conference on Domain Knowledge for Interactive System Design.*

Breuker, J., and van de Velde, W. 1994. *CommonKADS Library for Expertise Modelling.* IOS Press.

Chandrasekaran, B.; Johnson, T. R.; and Smith, J. W. 1992. Task-structure analysis for knowledge modeling. *Communications of the ACM* 35(9):124–137.

Consortium, M. 1993. Final public report. Technical report. Esprit II Project 2154.

Craw, S.; Sleeman, D.; Granger, N.; Rissakis, M.; and Sharma, S. 1992. Consultant: Providing advice for the machine learning toolbox. In Bramer, M., and Milne, R., eds., *Research and Development in Expert Systems*, 5–23.

Fayyad, U., and Uthurusamy, R. 1995. *Proceedings of the first International Conference on Knowledge Discovery & Data Mining.* Menlo Park, California: AAAI Press.

Fayyad, U. M.; Piatetsky-Shapiro, G.; Smyth, P.; and Uthurasamy, R. 1996. *Advances in Knowledge Discovery and Data Mining.* Cambridge, London: MIT press.

Fensel, D. 1995. Assumptions and limitations of a problem-solving method: a case-study. *Proceedings of the 9th Banff Knowledge Acquisition for Knowledge-Based Systems Workhop.*

Graner, N., and Sleeman, D. 1993. Muskrat: a multi-strategy knowledge refinement and acquisition toolbox. In Michalski, R., and Tecuci, G., eds., *Proceedings of the Second International Workshop on Multistrategy Learning*, 107–119.

Hunter, L. 1995. Planning to learn. In Ram, A., and Leake, D., eds., *Goal-Driven Learning.* London, England: MIT press.

Krüger, C. W. 1992. Software reuse. *ACM Computing Surveys* 24(2):131–183.

Mladeniĉ, D. 1995. Automated model selection. In *Proceedings of the Knowledge Level Modelling and Machine Learning Workshop, Crete.*

Ram, A., and Hunter, L. 1992. The use of explicit goals for knowledge to guide inference and learning. *Applied Intelligence* 2(1):46–73.

Reinartz, T., and Wirth, R. 1995. Towards a task model for kdd-processes. In Kodratoff, Y.; Nakhaiezadeh, G.; and Taylor, C., eds., *Workshop notes* Statistics, Machine Learning, and Knowledge Discovery in Databases. *MLNet Familiarisation Workshop*, 19–24.

Schreiber, T.; Wielinga, B.; and Breuker, J. 1993. *KADS: A Principled Approach to Knowledge-Based System Development.* London: Academic Press.

Simon, H. 1985. Information-processing theory of human problem-solving. In Aitkenhead, A., and Slack, J., eds., *Issues in Cognitive Modeling.*, 253–278. Lawrence Erlbaum Ass., London.

Steels, L. 1990. Components of expertise. *AI Magazine.*

Thomas, J.; Ganascia, J.-G.; and Laublet, P. 1993. Model-driven knowledge acquisition and knowledge-biased machine learning: an example of a principled association. In *Workshop proceedings of the 13th Int. Joint Conference on Artificial Intelligence*, volume W16, 220–235.

Valente, A., and Löckenhoff, C. 1994. Assessment. In *(Breuker & van de Velde 1994)*, 155 – 174. IOS-Press.

van den Elst, J.; van Harmelen, F.; and Thonnat, M. 1995. Modelling software components for reuse. In *Seventh International Conference on Software Engineering and Knowledge Engineering*, 350–357. Knowledge Systems Institute.

van Heijst, G. 1995. *The Role of Ontologies in Knowledge Engineering.* Ph.D. Dissertation, University of Amsterdam.

Wielinga, B.; Schreiber, A.; and Breuker, J. 1992. Kads: A modelling approach to knowledge engineering. special issue "the kads approach to knowledge engineering". *Knowledge Acquisition* 4(1):5–53.

Predictive Data Mining with Finite Mixtures

Petri Kontkanen   **Petri Myllymäki**   **Henry Tirri**

Complex Systems Computation Group (CoSCo)
P.O.Box 26, Department of Computer Science
FIN-00014 University of Helsinki, Finland
URL: http://www.cs.Helsinki.FI/research/cosco/
Email: Firstname.Lastname@cs.Helsinki.FI

Abstract

In data mining the goal is to develop methods for discovering previously unknown regularities from databases. The resulting models are interpreted and evaluated by domain experts, but some model evaluation criterion is needed also for the model construction process. The optimal choice would be to use the same criterion as the human experts, but this is usually impossible as the experts are not capable of expressing their evaluation criteria formally. On the other hand, it seems reasonable to assume that any model possessing the capability of making good predictions also captures some structure of the reality. For this reason, in predictive data mining the search for good models is guided by the expected predictive error of the models. In this paper we describe the Bayesian approach to predictive data mining in the finite mixture modeling framework. The finite mixture model family is a natural choice for domains where the data exhibits a clustering structure. In many real world domains this seems to be the case, as is demonstrated by our experimental results on a set of public domain databases.

Introduction

Data mining aims at extracting useful information from databases by discovering previously unknown regularities from data (Fayyad *et al.* 1996). In the most general context, finding such interesting regularities is a process (often called knowledge discovery in databases) which includes the interpretation of the extracted patterns based on the domain knowledge available. Typically the pattern extraction phase is performed by a structure searching program, and the interpretation phase by a human expert. The various proposed approaches differ in the representation language for the structure to be discovered (association rules (Agrawal *et al.* 1996), Bayesian networks (Spirtes, Glymour, & Scheines 1993), functional dependencies (Mannila & Räihä 1991), prototypes (Hu & Cercone 1995) etc.), and in the search methodology used for discovering such structures. A large body of the data mining research is exploratory in nature, i.e., search for any kind of structure in the database in order to understand the domain better.

Akin to the practice of multivariate exploratory analysis in social sciences (Basilevsky 1994), much of the work in the data mining area relies on a task-specific expert assessment of the model goodness. We depart from this tradition, and assume that the discovery process is performed with the expected prediction capability in mind. Consequently, we are trying to answer the question "Which of the models best explains a given database?" by addressing the (in many practical cases more pertinent) question "Which of the models yields the best predictions for future observations from the same process which generated the given database?" In our work the evaluation criteria in the model construction process is based directly on the expected predictive capability of the models, not on more implicit criteria embedded in the search algorithm. The use of predictiveness as a model selection criteria can be justified by the observation that a model with a good predictive capability must have captured some regularities that also reflect properties of the data generating process. We call this approach *predictive data mining*. Predictive data mining is relevant in a wide variety of application areas from credit card fraud detection and sales support systems to industrial process control. Our current work is motivated by large scale configuration problems (e.g., building large generators) where properties of new configurations can be predicted using the regularities in the existing configuration database.

For estimating the expected predictive performance, there exist theoretical measures (see e.g., (Wallace & Freeman 1987; Rissanen 1989; Raftery 1993)) which offer a solid evaluation criterion for the models, but such measures tend to be hard to compute for high-dimensional spaces. In the case of large databases several approximations to these criteria could be used, but many of them are inaccurate with small databases as pointed out in (Kontkanen, Myllymäki, & Tirri 1996a). Alternatively we can choose some prediction problem, and evaluate prediction error empirically by using the available database. An example of such a prediction task would be to predict an unknown attribute value of a data item, given a set of some other instantiated attributes. It should be observed that we do not assume that the set of predicted attributes are fixed in advance during the discovery process — prediction can be seen as a pattern completion task, where the errors in incomplete pattern completion can be used as a *model measure* for the goodness of the model. In this work we adopt the empirical approach and use the crossvalidation method (Stone 1974; Geisser 1975) for model selection on a set of public domain databases.

In the work presented below we have adopted the basic concepts from the general framework of exploring computational models of scientific discovery (Shrager & Langley 1990). Given a database, we do not attempt to discover arbitrary structures, but restrict the possible patterns (models) to be members of a predefined set, which we call *the model space*. Examples of such model spaces are the set of all possible association rules with a fixed set of attributes, or a set of all *finite mixture distributions* (Everitt & Hand 1981; Titterington, Smith, & Makov 1985). A choice of a model space necessarily introduces prior knowledge to the search process. We would like the model space to be simple enough to allow tractable search, yet powerful enough to include models with good prediction capabilities. Therefore in the current work we have restricted ourselves to a simple, computationally efficient set of probabilistic models from the family of finite mixtures. Intuitively this choice reflects our a priori assumption that the real life data is generated by several distinct processes, which is revealed as a cluster structure in the data.

A finite mixture model for a set of random variables is a weighted sum of a relatively small number of independent mixing distributions. The main advantage of using finite mixture models lies in the fact that the computations for probabilistic reasoning can be implemented as a single pass computation (see the next section). Finite mixtures have also a natural means to model multimodal distributions and are universal in the sense that they can approximate any distribution arbitrarily close as long as a sufficient number of component densities can be used. Finite mixture models can also be seen to offer a Bayesian solution to the case matching and case adaptation problems in instance-based reasoning (see the discussion in (Tirri, Kontkanen, & Myllymäki 1996)), i.e., they can also be viewed as a theoretically sound representation language for a "prototype" model space. This is interesting from the a priori knowledge acquisition point of view, since in many cases the domain experts seem to be able to express their expert knowledge very easily by using prototypical examples or distributions, which can then be coded as mixing distributions in our finite mixture framework.

In order to find probabilistic models for making good predictions, we follow the Bayesian approach (Gelman *et al.* 1995; Cheeseman 1995), as it offers a solid theoretical framework for combining both (suitably coded) a priori domain information and inform-

ation from the sample database in the model construction process. Bayesian approach also makes a clear separation between the search component and the model measure, and allows therefore modular combinations of different search algorithms and model evaluation criteria. Our approach is akin to the AutoClass system (Cheeseman *et al.* 1988), which has been successfully used for data mining problems, such as LandSat data clustering (Cheeseman & Stutz 1996).

In the case of finite mixtures, the model search problem can be seen as searching for the missing values of the unobserved latent clustering variable in the dataset. The model construction process consists of two phases: *model class selection* and *model class parameter selection*. The model class selection can be understood as finding the proper number of mixing distributions, i.e., the number of clusters in the data space, and the model class parameter selection as finding the attribute value probabilities for each mixture component. The model search problem in this framework is only briefly outlined in this paper — a more detailed exposition can be found in (Kontkanen, Myllymäki, & Tirri 1996b; 1996a). One should observe that theoretically the correct Bayesian approach for obtaining maximal predictive accuracy would be to use the sum of outcomes of all the possible different models, weighted by their posterior probability, i.e., in our case a "mixture of all the mixtures". This is clearly not feasible for data mining considerations, since such a model can hardly be given any useful semantic interpretation. We therefore use only a single, maximum a posteriori probability (MAP) model for making predictions. The feasibility of this approach is discussed in (Cheeseman 1995).

Bayesian inference by finite mixture models

In our predictive data mining framework the problem domain is modeled by m discrete random variables $X_1, \ldots, X_m$. A *data instantiation* $\vec{d}$ is a vector in which all the variables X_i have been assigned a value,

$$\vec{d} = (X_1 = x_1, \ldots, X_m = x_m),$$

where $x_i \in \{x_{i1}, \ldots, x_{in_i}\}$. Correspondingly we can view the database D as a *random sample* $(\vec{d}_1, \ldots, \vec{d}_N)$, i.e., a set of N i.i.d. (independent and identically distributed) data instantiations, where each $\vec{d}_j$ is sampled from $\mathcal{P}$, the joint distribution of the variables $(X_1, \ldots, X_m)$.

In our work we assume that the database D is generated by K different mechanisms, which all can have their own distributions, and that each data vector originates from exactly one of these mechanisms. Thus the instantiation space is divided into K *clusters*, each of which consists of the data vectors generated by the corresponding mechanism. From the assumptions above it follows that a natural candidate for a probabilistic model family is the family of *finite mixtures* (Everitt

& Hand 1981; Titterington, Smith, & Makov 1985), where the problem domain probability distribution is approximated as a weighted sum of mixture distributions:

$$(1) \qquad P(\vec{d}) = \sum_{k=1}^{K} \left(P(Y = y_k) P(\vec{d} \mid Y = y_k) \right).$$

Here the values of the discrete *clustering random variable* Y correspond to the separate clusters of the instantiation space, and each mixture distribution $P(\vec{d} \mid Y = y_k)$ models one data generating mechanism. Moreover, we assume that the problem domain data is tightly clustered so that the clusters can actually be regarded as points in the instantiation space, and data vectors belonging to the same cluster represent noisy versions of that (unknown) point. Therefore we can assume that the variables X_i inside each cluster are independent by which (1) becomes

$$P(\vec{d}) = P(X_1 = x_1, \ldots, X_m = x_m)$$
$$= \sum_{k=1}^{K} \left(P(Y = y_k) \prod_{i=1}^{m} P(X_i = x_i | Y = y_k) \right).$$

In our model both the cluster distribution $P(Y)$ and the intra-class conditional distributions $P(X_i|Y = y_k)$ are multinomial. Thus a finite mixture model can be defined by first fixing K, the *model class* (the number of the mixing distributions), and then by determining the values of the model parameters $\Theta = (\alpha, \Phi), \Theta \in \Omega$, where $\alpha = (\alpha_1, \ldots, \alpha_K), \alpha_k = P(Y = y_k)$, and

$$\Phi = (\Phi_{11}, \ldots, \Phi_{1m}, \ldots, \Phi_{K1}, \ldots, \Phi_{Km}),$$
$$\Phi_{ki} = (\phi_{ki1}, \ldots, \phi_{kin_i}),$$

where $\phi_{kil} = P(X_i = x_{il}|Y = y_k)$.

Given a finite mixture model Θ that models the cluster structure of the database, *predictive inference* can be performed in a computationally efficient manner. The Bayesian approach to predictive inference (see e.g., (Bernardo & Smith 1994)) aims at predicting unobserved future quantities by means of already observed quantities. More precisely, let $\mathcal{I} = \{i_1, \ldots, i_t\}$ be the indices of the instantiated variables, and let $\mathcal{X} = \{X_{i_s} = x_{i_s l_s}, s = 1, \ldots, t\}$ denote the corresponding assignments. Now we want to determine the distribution

$$P(X_i = x_{il}|\Theta, \mathcal{X}) = \frac{\sum_{k=1}^{K} \left(\alpha_k \phi_{kil} \prod_{s=1}^{t} \phi_{ki_s l_s} \right)}{\sum_{k=1}^{K} \left(\alpha_k \prod_{s=1}^{t} \phi_{ki_s l_s} \right)}.$$

The conditional predictive distribution of X_i can clearly be calculated in time $\mathcal{O}(Ktn_i)$, where K is the number of clusters, t the number of instantiated variables and n_i the number of values of X_i. Observe that K is usually small compared to the sample size N, and thus the prediction computation can be performed very efficiently (Myllymäki & Tirri 1994).

The predictive distributions can be used for classification and regression tasks. In classification problems, we have a special class variable X_c which is used for classifying data. In more general regression tasks, we have more than one variable for which we want to compute the predictive distribution, given that the values of the other variables are instantiated in advance. As in the configuration problems mentioned earlier, finite mixture models can also be used for finding the most probable value assignment combination for all the uninstantiated variables, given the values of the instantiated variables. These assignment combinations are useful when modeling actual objects such as machines, where probability information is in any case used to select a proper configuration with instantiated values for all the attributes.

Learning finite mixture models from data

In the previous section we described how the prediction of any variable could be made given a finite mixture model. Here we will briefly outline how to learn such models from a given database D. Let $D = (\vec{d}_1, \ldots, \vec{d}_N)$ be a database of size N. By learning we mean here the problem of constructing a single finite mixture model $M_K(\Theta)$ which represents the problem domain distribution $\mathcal{P}$ as accurately as possible in terms of the prediction capability. This learning process can be divided into two separate phases: in the first phase we wish to determine the optimal value for K, the number of mixing distributions (the model class), and in the second phase we wish to find MAP parameter values $\hat{\Theta}$ for the chosen model class.

In the Bayesian framework, the optimal number of mixing distributions (clusters) can be determined by evaluating the posterior probability for each model class $\mathcal{M}_K$ given the data:

$$P(\mathcal{M}_K|D) \propto P(D|\mathcal{M}_K)P(\mathcal{M}_K), K = 1, \ldots, N,$$

where the normalizing constant $P(D)$ can be omitted since we only need to compare different model classes. The number of clusters can safely be assumed to be bounded by N, since otherwise the sample size is clearly too small for the learning problem in question. Assuming equal priors for the model classes, they can be ranked by evaluating the *evidence* $P(D|\mathcal{M}_K)$ (or equivalently the stochastic complexity (Rissanen 1989)) for each model class. This term is defined as a multidimensional integral and it is usually very hard to evaluate, although with certain assumptions, the evidence can in some cases be determined analytically (Heckerman, Geiger, & Chickering 1995; Kontkanen, Myllymäki, & Tirri 1996a). In the experimental results presented in the next section we chose another approach and estimated the prediction error empirically by using the crossvalidation algorithm (Stone 1974; Geisser 1975).

After choosing the appropriate model class, there remains the task of finding the actual model (i.e., the model class parameters). In the Bayesian approach, this is usually done by finding the MAP (maximum a posteriori) estimate of parameters by maximizing the posterior density $P(\Theta|D)$. We assume that the prior distributions of the parameters are from the family of Dirichlet densities, since it is *conjugate* (see e.g., (DeGroot 1970)) to the family of multinomials, i.e., the functional form of parameter distribution remains invariant in the prior-to-posterior transformation. Finding the exact MAP estimate of Θ is, however, computationally infeasible task, thus we are forced to use numerical approximation methods. We used here a variant of the *Expectation-Maximization (EM)* algorithm (Dempster, Laird, & Rubin 1977) for this purpose, since the method is easily applicable in this domain and produces good solutions quite rapidly, as can be seen in (Kontkanen, Myllymäki, & Tirri 1996b).

Empirical results

The finite mixture based approach for predictive data mining described above has been implemented as part of a more general software environment for probabilistic modeling. To validate the advocated approach we wanted to test the approach with real data sets, preferably with ones that have been used for other experiments also. The main advantage of using natural databases instead of generated ones is that they are produced without any knowledge of the particular procedures that they are tested on. In addition, although there is no way of telling how the results for a real database generalizes to other problems, we at least know that there are some domains where the results have practical relevance.

Below we report results from an ongoing extensive experimentation with the Bayesian finite mixture modeling method using publicly available datasets for classification problems. The selection of databases was done on the basis of their reported use, i.e., we have preferred databases that have been used for testing many different methods over databases with only isolated results. Many of the databases used are from the StatLog project (Michie, Spiegelhalter, & Taylor 1994). The experimental setups and the best success rates obtained are shown in Table 1.

All our results are crossvalidated, and when possible (for the StatLog datasets) we have used the same crossvalidation schemes (the same number of folds) as in (Michie, Spiegelhalter, & Taylor 1994). The results on each of these datasets are shown in Figures 1–3. In each case, the maximum, minimum and the average success rate on 30 independent crossvalidation runs are given.

Even from these preliminary empirical results it can clearly be seen that the Bayesian finite mixture approach performs well. The general tendency in our experiments is that the success rate first increases with in-

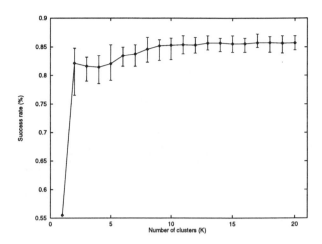

Figure 1: Crossvalidation results with the Australian database.

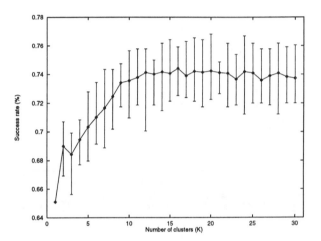

Figure 2: Crossvalidation results with the Diabetes database.

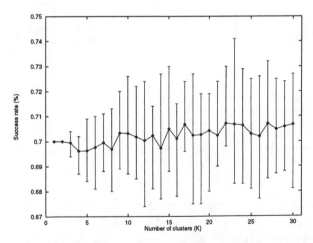

Figure 3: Crossvalidation results with the German Credit database.

dataset	size	#attrs	#CVfolds	#clusters	success rate (%)
Australian	690	15	10	17	87.2
Diabetes	768	9	12	20	76.8
German credit	1000	21	10	23	74.1
Glass	214	10	7	30	87.4
Heart disease	270	14	9	8	84.8
Hepatitis	150	20	5	9	88.0
Iris	150	5	5	4	97.3
Lymphography	148	19	5	19	86.6
Primary tumor	339	18	10	21	50.4

Table 1: Description of the experiments.

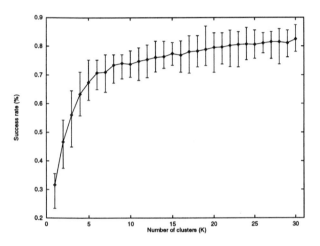

Figure 4: Crossvalidation results with the Glass database.

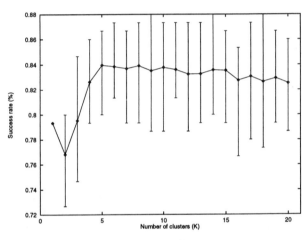

Figure 6: Crossvalidation results with the Hepatitis database.

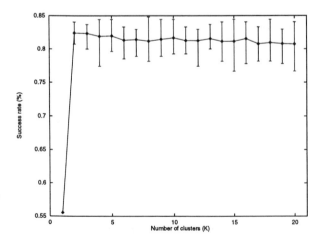

Figure 5: Crossvalidation results with the Heart Disease database.

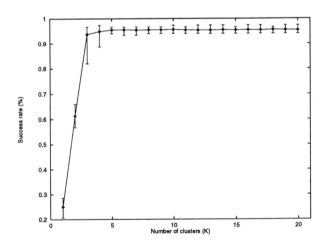

Figure 7: Crossvalidation results with the Iris database.

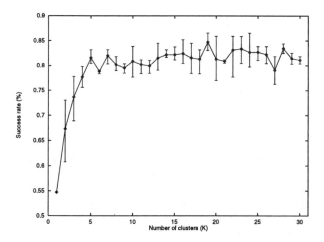

Figure 8: Crossvalidation results with the Lymphography database.

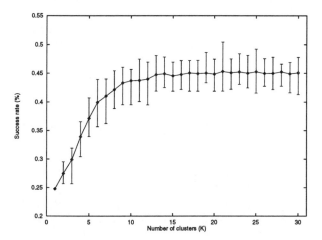

Figure 9: Crossvalidation results with the Primary Tumor database.

creasing number of clusters up to a certain knee point, after which the performance stays relatively constant. Unlike in many other similar studies, the overfitting phenomenon does not seem to have a significant impact here. We believe that this can be explained by the special competitive nature of the EM algorithm in our clustering framework: after the knee point, unnecessary clusters tend to gradually disappear during the EM process, so that the method seems to be able to automatically regulate (to some extent) the number of parameters. This interesting empirical observation deserves further investigation in the future.

In a fielded data mining application, the resulting mixture structure would be given to the expert for evaluation. In our case with the public domain data sets this was not possible (as we did not have the experts available). Instead we investigated the clusters found with the D-SIDE environment, which provides a graphical user interface for displaying predictive dis-

tributions and the mixture structure[1]. For the German credit data, a credit assessment problem, where the attributes were understandable also to a layman, clear interpretations could be given for 6 of the 9 clusters. For example the most influential cluster could be described consisting of working single women (age < 30, 4 − 7 years in the current job), living in an apartment they owned, and requesting a small loan (less than 1800 DM) for furniture or home appliances with very little savings. Needless to say classification suggestion for applicants matching such a description was positive. It should be emphasized that since the mixture model built allows calculation of any predictive distribution, it can also be used explore dependencies between attributes. For example one can investigate what is the effect of being just recently employed to the purpose of the loan.

Although we have reported in Table 1 the model classes (number of clusters) with the best performing single model, sometimes the model class with the highest average success rate could be more useful for data mining purposes. This is due to the fact that because of the small number of repetitions, the variances of the results are quite high, as depicted in the figures. Unfortunately, as these are public domain data, and not industrial applications, we do not have a domain expert available to evaluate our results. However, we are currently also working with several real-world industrial pilot applications.

Conclusion

We discussed the use of finite mixture models for predictive data mining, where the search for unknown structures is guided by expected predictive performance. For the model selection problem, we adopted the Bayesian approach. In this work the predictive performance was measured empirically by using the crossvalidation method. The applicability of the approach was demonstrated empirically by presenting extensive experimental results on a set of public domain databases. In addition to revealing a possible cluster structure in the data, the resulting mixture structure allows also more general inspection of the attribute dependencies by the computationally very efficient predictive Bayesian inference.

Acknowledgments This research has been supported by the Technology Development Center (TEKES). The Primary Tumor, the Breast Cancer and the Lymphography data were obtained from the University Medical Centre, Institute of Oncology, Ljubljana, Yugoslavia. Thanks go to M. Zwitter and M. Soklič for providing the data.

---

[1]A running Java™ prototype of the D-SIDE software is available for experimentation through our WWW homepage at URL "http://www.cs.Helsinki.FI/research/cosco/".

References

Agrawal, R.; Mannila, H.; Srikant, R.; Toivonen, H.; and Verkamo, A. 1996. Fast discovery of association rules. In Fayyad, U.; Piatetsky-Shapiro, G.; Smyth, P.; and Uthurusamy, R., eds., *Advances in Knowledge Discovery and Data Mining*. MIT Press.

Basilevsky, A. 1994. *Statistical Factor Analysis and Related Methods. Theory and Applicatioms*. New York: John Wiley & Sons.

Bernardo, J., and Smith, A. 1994. *Bayesian theory*. John Wiley.

Cheeseman, P., and Stutz, J. 1996. Bayesian classification (AutoClass): Theory and results. In Fayyad, U.; Piatetsky-Shapiro, G.; Smyth, P.; and Uthurusamy, R., eds., *Advances in Knowledge Discovery and Data Mining*. Menlo Park: AAAI Press. chapter 6.

Cheeseman, P.; Kelly, J.; Self, M.; Stutz, J.; Taylor, W.; and Freeman, D. 1988. Autoclass: A Bayesian classification system. In *Proceedings of the Fifth International Conference on Machine Learning*, 54–64.

Cheeseman, P. 1995. On Bayesian model selection. In Wolpert, D., ed., *The Mathematics of Generalization*, volume XX of *SFI Studies in the Sciences of Complexity*. Addison-Wesley. 315–330.

DeGroot, M. 1970. *Optimal statistical decisions*. McGraw-Hill.

Dempster, A.; Laird, N.; and Rubin, D. 1977. Maximum likelihood from incomplete data via the EM algorithm. *Journal of the Royal Statistical Society, Series B* 39(1):1–38.

Everitt, B., and Hand, D. 1981. *Finite Mixture Distributions*. London: Chapman and Hall.

Fayyad, U.; Piatetsky-Shapiro, G.; Smyth, P.; and Uthurusamy, R., eds. 1996. *Advances in Knowledge Discovery and Data Mining*. Cambridge, MA: MIT Press.

Geisser, S. 1975. The predictive sample reuse method with applications. *Journal of the American Statistical Association* 70(350):320–328.

Gelman, A.; Carlin, J.; Stern, H.; and Rubin, D. 1995. *Bayesian Data Analysis*. Chapman & Hall.

Heckerman, D.; Geiger, D.; and Chickering, D. 1995. Learning Bayesian networks: The combination of knowledge and statistical data. *Machine Learning* 20(3):197–243.

Hu, X., and Cercone, N. 1995. Rough sets similarity-based learning from databases. In Fayyad, U., and Uthurusamy, R., eds., *Proceedings of the First International Conference on Knowledge Discovery & Data Mining*, 162–167.

Kontkanen, P.; Myllymäki, P.; and Tirri, H. 1996a. Comparing Bayesian model class selection criteria by discrete finite mixtures. In *Proceedings of the ISIS (Information, Statistics and Induction in Science) Conference*. (To appear.).

Kontkanen, P.; Myllymäki, P.; and Tirri, H. 1996b. Constructing Bayesian finite mixture models by the EM algorithm. Technical Report C-1996-9, University of Helsinki, Department of Computer Science.

Mannila, H., and Räihä, K.-J. 1991. *The design of relational databases*. Addison-Wesley.

Michie, D.; Spiegelhalter, D.; and Taylor, C., eds. 1994. *Machine Learning, Neural and Statistical Classification*. London: Ellis Horwood.

Myllymäki, P., and Tirri, H. 1994. Massively parallel case-based reasoning with probabilistic similarity metrics. In Wess, S.; Althoff, K.-D.; and Richter, M., eds., *Topics in Case-Based Reasoning*, volume 837 of *Lecture Notes in Artificial Intelligence*. Springer-Verlag. 144–154.

Raftery, A. 1993. Approximate Bayes factors and accounting for model uncertainty in generalized linear models. Technical Report 255, Department of Statistics, University of Washington.

Rissanen, J. 1989. *Stochastic Complexity in Statistical Inquiry*. World Scientific Publishing Company.

Shrager, J., and Langley, P., eds. 1990. *Computational Models of Scientific Discovery and Theory Formation*. San Mateo, CA: Morgan Kaufmann Publishers.

Spirtes, P.; Glymour, C.; and Scheines, R., eds. 1993. *Causation, Prediction and Search*. Springer-Verlag.

Stone, M. 1974. Cross-validatory choice and assessment of statistical predictions. *Journal of the Royal Statistical Society (Series B)* 36:111–147.

Tirri, H.; Kontkanen, P.; and Myllymäki, P. 1996. Probabilistic instance-based learning. In Saitta, L., ed., *Machine Learning: Proceedings of the Thirteenth International Conference (to appear)*. Morgan Kaufmann Publishers.

Titterington, D.; Smith, A.; and Makov, U. 1985. *Statistical Analysis of Finite Mixture Distributions*. New York: John Wiley & Sons.

Wallace, C., and Freeman, P. 1987. Estimation and inference by compact coding. *Journal of the Royal Statistical Society* 49(3):240–265.

An Empirical Test of the Weighted Effect Approach to Generalized Prediction Using Recursive Neural Nets[1]

Rense Lange

University of Illinois at Springfield
Springfield, Il 62794-9243
lange@uis.edu

Abstract

The requirement of a strict and fixed distinction between dependent variables and independent variables, together with the presence of missing data, typically imposes considerable problems for most standard statistical prediction procedures. This paper describes a solution of these problems through the "weighted effect" approach in which recursive neural nets are used to learn how to compensate for any main and interaction effects attributable to missing data through the use of an "effect set" in addition to the data of actual cases. Extensive simulations of the approach based on an existing psychological data base showed high predictive validity, and a graceful degradation in performance with an increase in the number of unknown predictor variables. Moreover, the method proved amenable to the use of two-parameter logistic curves to arrive at a three way "low," "high," and "undecided" decision scheme with a-priori known error rates.

Introduction

Most texts on statistical methods (e.g., [1]) present the topic of prediction as the problem of finding an optimal function to predict a set of unknown (dependent) variables from a disjoint set of known (independent) variables. Although this approach is appropriate when testing hypotheses, it may not be applicable in many applied contexts. For instance, when diagnosing a client, physicians and psychologists typically have access to a personal file containing the outcomes on standard tests, together with diverse items of information already gathered by other professionals. Depending on the nature of the case, the distinction between dependent and independent variables is often blurred because: (a) some dependent variables may already be known, whereas some of their indicators (independent variables) are lacking; (b) the same conclusion can often be reached based on different sets of available information; and (c) at any point, practitioners have the option to gather additional information. Since the same variable may occur both as a dependent variable and as an independent variable, the resulting process defies description in terms of a rigid a-priori distinction between these two types of variables.

Situations such as the above would benefit greatly from knowledge discovery systems that allow any set of unknown variables to be predicted from arbitrary collections of already known variables. To achieve this goal in the traditional framework, one might propose to simply re-compute the predictor function each time a new situation arises. Where feasible from a computational and statistical point of view, this approach would require constant access to all appropriate databases. Unfortunately, such databases are often confidential or proprietary, and hence this solution is rarely feasible for large scale applications. Alternatively, one might consider computing a different predictor function for each conceivable pattern of known and unknown variables. However, this approach soon breaks down from a computational point of view. For instance, in a relatively simple application with 30 variables there are a maximum of 2^{30} different patterns of known and unknown variables. Even if only 0.1% of these combinations did actually occur, this would still leave over 1 million cases to be considered.

The present research describes an approach to knowledge discovery that relies on the capability of recursive neural nets to store information such that their performance benefits from knowing which variables can or cannot be used in the prediction process. Because known variables are allowed to differ with respect to their contribution to a particular prediction, the resulting procedure is called a "weighted effect" approach. Following an outline of this approach, later sections describe an empirical evaluation based on an actual data set. Finally, to determine the practical potential of the approach, particular attention is paid to the validity of its predictions.

1. The author wishes to thank James Houran and Joel Adkins for their comments on an earlier version of this paper. I further acknowledge Wayne Penn and Naomi Lynn for their vivid demonstration of the urgent need for more sophisticated thinking tools in order to avoid erroneous conclusions derived by naïve analyses of quantitative data.

A Weighted Effects Approach

To facilitate the presentation, the following terminology is introduced:

(i) The set $\mathbf{V}$ (with elements v) contains all variables that are relevant in a particular context.

(ii) All *known* variables are contained in the subset $\mathbf{IN} \subset \mathbf{V}$.

(iii) All unknown variables are contained in the subset $\mathbf{OUT} \subset \mathbf{V}$.

(iv) For reasons that will become clear later, predictions are the result of the mapping:

$$\mathbf{V'} = \mathbf{F(V,E)},$$

where $\mathbf{E}$ represents the "effect" of knowing [or *not* knowing] the value of each variable v. That is, *all* variables in $\mathbf{V}$ (including the unknown variables in $\mathbf{OUT}$) are input to the function $\mathbf{F}$ to yield an new vector $\mathbf{V'}$ with predicted values (including predictions for already known variables in $\mathbf{IN}$), as moderated by the effects in $\mathbf{E}$.

The author proposes that the effect set $\mathbf{E}$ should contain an entry for every variable in $\mathbf{V}$, such that $e_i = 1$ when the value of the variable is known, and $e_i = -1$ when its value is not known. The rationale behind this assumption is that such weights allow a neural net to learn all linear main and interaction effects [and perhaps some non-linear effects also] associated with the presence or absence of each variable. This claim follows from the observation that the $\mathbf{IN}$ vs. $\mathbf{OUT}$ status of the variables in $\mathbf{V}$ can be thought of as creating a v-factorial $2 \times 2 \times ... \times 2$ analysis of variance (ANOVA) design. It has long been known [2] that any ANOVA design can be translated into an equivalent multiple regression problem through the use of "coded dummy variables." In our particular case where each factor has only two levels, the situation simplifies considerably since all main and interaction effects can be captured by single parameters. Also, in this case the required number of orthogonal dummy variables is equal to number of main and interaction effects.

For instance, assume that we are interested in estimating a dependent variable Y from the two predictor variables A and B in a 2×2 ANOVA design. By defining the three sets of orthogonal dummy weights e_a, e_b, and e_{ab}, least-squares estimates of all main and interaction effects can be obtained by minimizing the expression:

$$\sum_i \sum_j \left(e_a . \alpha + e_b . \beta + e_{ab} . \chi + K - y_{ij} \right)^2,$$

where α represents the main effect of A, β represents the main effect of B, χ represents the $A \times B$ interaction, and K denotes an additive constant. The procedure is illustrated in Figure 1 which shows the predicted y_{ij} as the sum of the dummy variables e_a, e_b, and e_{ab} weighted by their corresponding effects α, β and χ.

e_a	e_b	e_{ab}	
$-1.\alpha$	$-1.\beta$	$-1.\chi$	$= y_{00}$
$-1.\alpha$	$+1.\beta$	$+1.\chi$	$= y_{01}$
$+1.\alpha$	$-1.\beta$	$+1.\chi$	$= y_{10}$
$+1.\alpha$	$+1.\beta$	$-1.\chi$	$= y_{11}$

Figure 1: *Prediction of Y based on the main effects α and β, and their interaction χ in a multiple regression framework using the dummy weights e_a, e_b, and e_{ab}.*

Note that for n predictor variables there are a total of $2^n - (n + 1)$ possible interaction terms, leading to a combinatorial explosion that contradicts our assumption that $\mathbf{E}$ should contain only v items. Notice however that the e_a, e_b, and e_{ab} columns in Figure 1 are related as if:

$$e_{ab} = e_a \text{ XOR } e_b,$$

provided that the weights +1 and -1 are replaced by the truth values T and F, respectively. Thus, the dummy variable e_{ab} need *not* be provided explicitly because it can be learned from e_a and e_b via backpropagation in neural nets with at least one intermediate layer.

In general, the weighted effect approach is predicated on the assumption that interaction effects need not be represented explicitly in $\mathbf{E}$ because they can be learned selectively from training data on an "as needed" basis by neural nets. Thus, the number of interactions that can be accommodated will depend on the size of the layers of the neural net. Also, the order of the interactions is limited by the number of intermediate layers. For example, analogous to XOR problems with three variables, three way interactions require at least two intermediate layers. Thus, the weighted effect approach is best used in situations where higher order interactions are rare. However, such interactions are perhaps best avoided anyway because they typically generalize poorly to new cases.

An Empirical Test

Naturally, the above considerations do not guarantee that adding any main and interaction effects due to (not) knowing predictor variables will improve prediction in actual practice. For this reason, the next sections describe the results of an empirical performance study based on an existing body of psychological data. In particular, all results reported below were derived from a database of 721 cases of hallucinatory episodes experienced by ostensibly normal individuals as described in detail in a psychological study published by Lange et al. [3]. Each case consists of 31 variables, 3 of these are considered continuous, but most (28) are binary categorizations. Since the present research focuses primarily on the predictive quality of the weighted effect approach, the following presentation addresses only the statistical properties of the results. Consequently, variables are simply referred to by their ordinal position in the original database (i.e., 1 through 31), and readers interested in content oriented issues are referred to the aforementioned paper.

Design. In order to test whether addition of the effect set **E** improves prediction, two basic experimental conditions were created:

In the *Effect condition*, the effect set **E** is defined as described in the preceding section, **V** is a copy of a record in the data set, and the function **F** was implemented as a partially recursive neural net. This net has as its outputs the 31 variables in **V'** and as its inputs the 31 + 31 = 62 variables in **V** and **E**. A standard backpropagation algorithm [4] was used with logistic squashing functions over the range -1.0 to +1.0. All variables were scaled over the range -0.9 to +0.9. The 721 cases were randomly divided into a training set and a test set of approximately equal size (i.e., n = 360 or n = 361).

Training Phase. During the training phase, knowledge of predictor variables (or the lack thereof) was simulated by randomly selecting between 0 and 15 variables, using an efficient algorithm described in [5, p. 122]. The thus selected variables were assigned the value 0.0, they were added to **OUT**, and their entry in **E** was set to -0.9. The remaining variables kept their original values, were added to **IN**, and their entry in **E** was set to +0.9. The resulting **V** + **E** were then presented to the backpropagation algorithm. Over 5000 iterations were used to train each of two types of nets: Effect [1], a partially recursive net with one intermediate layer, and Effect [2] a partially recursive net with two intermediate layers.

Test Phase. The weights obtained during the training phase were validated on the test set by randomly selecting between 1 and 15 variables for inclusion in the **OUT** set, and the **E** set was constructed and used exactly as during the forward propagation stage in the training phase. Care was taken to insure that each variable occurred in the **OUT** set about 10,000 times.

The *"Control" condition* was identical to the Effect condition with the exception that no set **E** was used during the training phase. Instead, randomly selected elements of **OUT** were simply assigned the value 0. That is, all results are based on a fully recursive neural net with 2 intermediate layers, 31 outputs (**V'**), but only 31 inputs (**V**). This net is referred to as Control [2].

Main Hypothesis. Figure 2 (solid lines) shows the coefficients of determination (i.e., Pearson r^2) between the actual and the predicted values of the variables in **V** as computed over the cases in the test set. The values shown are the average over all 31 variables. The crucial comparison is between the Effect and Control models with two intermediate layers. It can be seen that our basic hypothesis is supported because the average predictive validity is consistently greater for Effect [2] than for Control [2], for **OUT** sets ranging in size from 1 to 15 unknown variables.

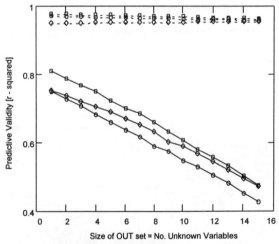

Figure 2: *Average Predictive Validity [Pearson r^2] Over All 31 Variables for Effect Models [1] and [2] and Control Model [1] by size of **OUT** set. (Test data only)*
NOTE: *The definitions of Effect [1], Effect [2], and Control [2] are given in the preceding Design section.*

The performance of Control [1] catches up for larger **OUT** sets. However, it behaves more like the simpler Effect [1] model for smaller **OUT** sets. Nearly identical findings were obtained when using RMS as a performance criterion. Thus, these results clearly show that the effect set **E** improved overall predictive validity.

Although only of tangential importance for the present purposes, Figure 2 also shows that the predictive validity of Control [2] is consistently lower for **IN** variables (diamonds + dotted lines). In other words, the addition of the effect set **E** to the inputs served to minimize distortions in *known* variables in the transformation from **V** to **V'**.

Response Curves

Of particular interest for present validation purposes is the likelihood that a person will be classified correctly as either *"low"* or *"high"* on some dependent variable of interest based on knowledge of his or her predicted score v'. Because most of our variables represent binary categorizations, a person was classified as *"high"* on a variable if this person's *actual* score exceeded 0.0, and the person was classified as *"low"* otherwise. As is customary, the resulting relation between the predicted and the actual score is assumed to follow a logistic "response" curve of the form:

$$P(\text{``high''} \mid v') = \{1 + e^{-(p+q \cdot v')}\}^{-1},$$

where the parameters p and q can be estimated via standard maximum likelihood methods.

For instance, Figure 3 compares the performance of a particular variable (No. 28) under Effect [1] and Effect [2] as derived from about 10,000 data points generated during the training phase (for details see next section). Note that the response curve under Effect [1] (left panel) breaks down over the range $0.2 < v' < 0.5$. Adding an intermediate layer greatly improves this situation as it appears that the Effect [2] net (right panel) smoothes the response curve nicely while providing a "patch" for $0.2 < v' < 0.5$.

Three-Way Decisions. In the following, response curves were used to create a *three-way* decision scheme with arbitrary and adjustable error rates. This can be achieved by selecting two appropriate percentiles in the logistic curve. For instance, the right panel in Figure 3 shows the 40-th and 60-th percentiles (P_{40} and P_{60}) of the logistic curve. By classifying people as *"low"* on Variable 28 if their predicted score falls below P_{40} and as *"high"* if their predicted score exceeds P_{60}, a third category, *"undecided,"* is defined for predicted scores between P_{40} and P_{60}. Naturally, the choice of percentiles used to define these three categories will depend on the nature of the application. In our case, P_{40} and P_{60} were deemed appropriate for all variables and these values were used throughout.

To determine the viability of this approach, the following experiment was performed. *First*, analogous to the procedure described in the design section, the training data set and the connection weights from the training phase were used to generate predictions from randomly constructed **OUT** sets (and corresponding **E** sets) with between 0 and 15 unknown variables. The known classifications and their corresponding predicted values v' were used to generate logistic parameters p and q for all variables, using about 10,000 observations per variable. *Second*, the thus obtained parameters p and q, as well as the already existing connection weights, were then used to generate predictions over the test data set. In particular, randomly constructed **OUT** sets (and corresponding **E** sets) were used with between 1 and 15 unknown variables. Each prediction v' was then classified as "low," "undecided," or "high" depending on the values of P_{40} and P_{60}.

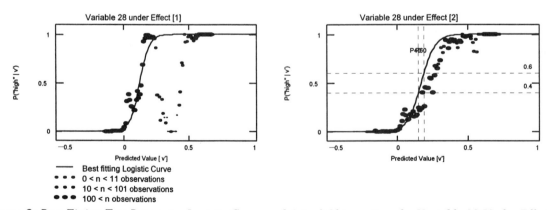

Figure 3: *Best Fitting Two Parameter Logistic Curve and Actual Observations for Variable 28 Under Effect [1] and Effect [2]. (NOTE: Training data only).*

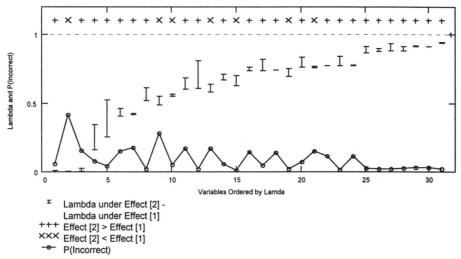

Figure 4: *Proportion of Erroneous Classifications and the Predictive Validity of All 31 Variables Ordered by Their* λ *Coefficients for Effect [1] and Effect [2]. (Test data).*

Because our main interest concerns the correctness of the classification as either "low," "undecided," or "high," predictive validity cannot be determined via Pearson correlation's or RMS values. Instead, the directional and non-parametric λ coefficient was used. The value of this coefficient can be interpreted directly as the proportional increase in classification correctness as the result of knowing the predicted value *v'*. Figure 4 shows the λ values for all 31 variables under Effect [1] and Effect [2] averaged over the 15 **OUT** conditions and ordered by the combined λ magnitudes. It can be seen that the predictability increased by more than 50% for 25 out of the 31 variables, but that the leftmost few variables performed very poorly. It should be pointed out, however, that the low λ values occur mainly for variables showing little variation. Because such variables can be predicted reliably from their modal values, the overall error rate remains relatively low (*M = 0.091*). In fact, the solid line in Figure 4 indicates that only one variable (the second worst) has an overall error rate in excess of 0.3.

Highly similar conclusions were obtained from an analysis of the error rates for the individual categorization as either "low," or "high." Figure 5 shows the average probability of being classified as "high" given that v' > P_{60} (solid curves), or that v' < P_{40} (dotted curves). It can be seen that all but the first three variables perform very satisfactory.

A Comparison of Effect [1] vs. Effect [2]

Throughout the preceding, Effect [2] was slightly superior to Effect [1] in various respects. For instance, Figure 4 (top row) indicates that Effect [2] yielded higher λ values for 24 of the 31 variables (*M = 0.655 vs. M = 0.617*). Also, Effect [2] resulted in slightly more correct overall classifications (*M = 0.913*) than Effect [1] (*M = 0.904*). Although the overall differences are very small, the addition of an intermediate layer had important consequences for some individual variables, as indicated by a detailed analysis of the relation between λ and the size of **OUT** for all 31 variables. Due to space limitations, Figure 6 shows this relation only for the "worst" performing variable (leftmost in Figures 4 and 5), the "best" performing variable (rightmost in Figures 4 and 5), and one "intermediate" performing variable (the fourth in Figures 4 and 5). It can be seen that the "best" variable does not benefit from the additional intermediate layer,

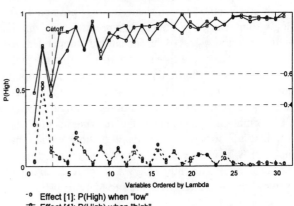

- ⁻º Effect [1]: P(High) when "low"
- ⁻•⁻ Effect [1]: P(High) when "high"
- ⁻º Effect [2]: P(High) when "low"
- ⁻•⁻ Effect [2]: P(High) when "high"

Figure 5: *Proportion "High" Classifications for Actually "High" or "Low" Cases Averaged Over **OUT** Sets of Size 0 to 15. (Test data).*

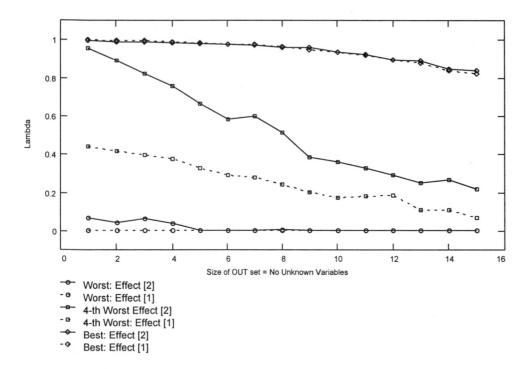

Figure 6: *Predictive Validity* λ *of Three Variables as a Function of the Size of* **OUT** *for Effect [1] and Effect [2] (Test data).*

and that the improvement for the worst variable is limited to small **OUT** sets. However, the "intermediate" variable shows dramatic improvements over the entire range. It is recommended therefore that the decision concerning the desired number of intermediate layers should take the performance of individual variables into account, and that it should not solely be based on overall performance indices.

Discussion

The results presented in this paper strongly support the weighted effects approach since it proved possible to find a single framework to accommodate prediction in situations with varying numbers of dependent and independent variables. In addition, the case study indicated that the method is sufficiently flexible and powerful for practical application, and the current results have already led to new research in psychology and criminology. Further, given that all information is contained in the net's connection weights, it is possible to provide predictions *without* having to provide access to the original data set. For this reason, research is currently underway to provide an expert system type user interface similar to MACIE [4].

Additional study of the weighted effect approach seems desirable. For instance, it is not clear whether the present training approach is optimal or whether more efficient "training schedules" exist. Also, currently the net is used for *all* learning that takes place. It seems desirable, however, to be able to separate the learning associated with the effect set **E** from that associated with **V** in applications containing higher order interaction effects.

Finally, the author feels that further development might benefit from more detailed analyses of the statistical rationale underlying the weighted effect approach as this might lead to increased control over the quality of prediction.

References

[1] Scott, E.M., and Delaney, H.D. (1990). *Designing experiments and analyzing data.* Belmont, CA: Wadsworth.
[2] Cohen, J. (1968). Multiple regression as a general data-analytic system. *Psychological Bulletin*, 70, 426 - 433.
[3] Lange, R., Houran, J., Harte, T., and Havens, R. (1996). Contextual mediation of perceptions of hauntings and poltergeist-like experiences. *Perceptual and Motor Skills*, 755-762.
[4] Gallant, S.I. (1994). *Neural network learning.* Cambridge, Mass.: MIT Press.
[5] Knuth, D.E. (1969). *The art of computer programming.* Vol. II. Reading, Mass.: Addison-Wesley.

Multiple uses of frequent sets and condensed representations
Extended abstract

Heikki Mannila and Hannu Toivonen
University of Helsinki
Department of Computer Science
P.O. Box 26, FIN-00014 University of Helsinki, Finland
Heikki.Mannila@cs.Helsinki.FI, Hannu.Toivonen@cs.Helsinki.FI

Abstract

In interactive data mining it is advantageous to have condensed representations of data that can be used to efficiently answer different queries. In this paper we show how frequent sets can be used as a condensed representation for answering various types of queries.

Given a table r with 0/1 values and a threshold σ, a frequent set of r is a set X of columns of r such that at least a fraction σ of the rows of r have a 1 in all the columns of X. Finding frequent sets is a first step in finding association rules, and there exists several efficient algorithms for finding the frequent sets. We show that frequent sets have wider applications than just finding association rules.

We show that using the inclusion-exclusion principle one can obtain approximate confidences of arbitrary boolean rules. We derive bounds for the errors in the confidences, and show that information collected during the computation of frequent sets can also be used to provide individual error bounds for each clause. Experiments show that this method enables one to obtain different forms of rules from data extremely fast. Furthermore, we define a general notion of condensed representations, and show that frequent sets, samples and the data cube can be viewed as instantations of this concept.

Introduction

Knowledge discovery in databases is an interactive process: one has to be able to look at the data from several different angles. For large data sets, it is not efficient to go back and read the data every time the user wants to see something new from it. A condenced representation of the data for answering most of the needs of the user would be very useful.

One of the most researched areas in data mining is the problem of finding association rules from binary data (Agrawal, Imielinski, & Swami 1993; Houtsma & Swami 1993; Klemettinen *et al.* 1994; Han & Fu 1995; Holsheimer *et al.* 1995; Park, Chen, & Yu 1995; Savasere, Omiecinski, & Navathe 1995; Srikant & Agrawal 1995; Agrawal *et al.* 1996; Srikant & Agrawal 1996; Toivonen 1996). Assuming we have a relation (table) with 0/1-valued attributes R, an association rule is an expression $X \Rightarrow Y$, where $X, Y \subseteq R$. The meaning of such a rule is that whenever a row has a 1 in all the columns of X, it tends to have a 1 also in all the columns of Y.[1]

The algorithms for finding association rules all proceed by first finding frequent sets, i.e., sets X of attributes such that there are sufficiently many rows containing a 1 in each column of X. From the number of such rows it is easy to compute the confidences of association rules.

In this paper we consider additional uses for frequent sets. We show that the collection of frequent sets can actually serve as a condensed representation of the input data for rules with disjunction and negation, a much larger class of rules than simple association rules. These simple observations lead to a considerable widening in the use of frequent sets. Experiments show that this method enables one to obtain generalized rules from data extremely fast.

We analyze formally the use of frequent sets in answering queries concerning complex rules. Our basic tool is the inclusion-exclusion principle. The frequent sets provide some of the terms of this sum. Using the concept of the border of the collection of frequent sets, we are able to derive bounds on the error caused by omitting the rest of the terms.

Finally, we consider the general theory of condensed representations of data. We define what it means for one class of structures to serve as a representation for another with respect to a class of queries. We dis-

---

[1]Note that the input data need not be explicitly in 0/1 form: one can just as well consider association rules based on derived attributes. For example, if the relation contains the attribute Age, one can look for rules containing derived binary attributes such as "Age $\leq$ 40".

cuss how the use of frequent sets, samples and the data cube (Gray *et al.* 1996) can be viewed as instances of this general concept. Our concept can be viewed as a generalization of the notion of ε-approximations from computational geometry (Haussler & Welzl 1987; Mulmuley 1993).

General rules and frequent sets

In this section we describe a simple and basically well-known rule formalism of general boolean rules, show that knowledge of the frequencies of sets is sufficient to determine rule confidences, and give some examples.

Given a set R of 0/1-valued attributes R, a *boolean formula* over R is a formula φ built from the atomic formulae $A = 0$ and $A = 1$, where $A \in R$, using the connectives $\wedge$, $\vee$, and $\neg$, and parenthesis. Given a 0/1 relation r with attributes R, the *frequency* $s(\varphi, r)$ of φ in r is

$$\frac{|\{t \in r \mid \varphi \text{ is true of } t\}|}{|r|},$$

i.e., the fraction of rows where φ holds.

We introduce some shorthand notations for having *all* or *at least one* attribute of a set X equal to 1: For $X = \{A_1, \ldots, A_k\}$ we denote $a(X, r) = s(A_1 = 1 \wedge \cdots \wedge A_k = 1)$ and $o(X, r) = s(A_1 = 1 \vee \cdots \vee A_k = 1)$; we simply use notations $a(X)$ and $o(X)$ if the relation is clear from the context.

A *boolean rule* over R is an expression of the form $\varphi \Rightarrow \psi$, where φ and ψ are boolean formulae. The *confidence* of the rule is $s(\varphi \wedge \psi)/s(\varphi)$.

The following proposition is of course well-known.

Proposition 1 For all boolean formulae φ over R there exists sets $W_1, \ldots, W_m \subseteq R$ and coefficients $e_1, \ldots, e_m \in \{-1, +1\}$ such that for all relations r

$$s(\varphi, r) = \sum_{i=1}^{m} e_i a(W_i, r).$$

□

That is, knowing the special terms $a(X, r)$ is sufficient to determine the number of rows satisfying any boolean formula, and hence also the confidence of any boolean rule.

Example 2 We give some examples of boolean rules and how their confidences can be expressed in terms of the frequencies of conjunctions.

An *association rule* has the form $X \Rightarrow Y$, where $X, Y \subseteq R$, and the confidence is defined to be $a(X \cup Y)/a(X)$.

A rule with *disjunctive right-hand side* has the form $X \Rightarrow Y \vee Z$ and expresses that if a row $t \in r$ has a 1 in

each column of X, then it has a 1 in each column of Y or in each column of Z. The confidence of the rule is

$$\frac{a(X \cup Y) + a(X \cup Z) - a(X \cup Y \cup Z)}{a(X)}.$$

Similarly, we can write a rule with a *disjunctive left-hand side*: $X \vee Y \Rightarrow Z$. The rule states that if a row $t \in r$ has a 1 in each column of X or in each column of Y, then it has a 1 in each column of Z. The confidence of the rule is

$$\frac{a(X \cup Z) + a(Y \cup Z) - a(X \cup Y \cup Z)}{a(X) + a(Y) - a(X \cup Y)}.$$

Rules can also have *negation in the left-hand side*, as in $X \wedge \neg Y \Rightarrow Z$. This means that if a row $t \in r$ has a 1 in each column of X and does not have a 1 in each column of Y, then it has a 1 in each column of Z. The confidence of such a rule is

$$\frac{a(X \cup Z) - a(X \cup Y \cup Z)}{a(X) - a(X \cup Y)}.$$

Negation in the right-hand side is just as easy. The confidence of a rule of the form $X \Rightarrow Y \wedge \neg Z$ is

$$\frac{a(X \cup Y) - a(X \cup Y \cup Z)}{a(X)}.$$

□

Example 3 One of our example data sets r is an enrollment database of courses in computer science. The data set consists of registration information of 4734 students. There is a row per student, containing the courses the student has registered for. On average, a row has 4 courses. The total number of courses is 127. We first discovered all sets X of courses with $a(X, r) \geq 0.05$. The number of frequent sets is 489. We then computed association rules, rules with disjunctions (two disjuncts) on the left or on the right-hand side, and rules with negations, and then used some simple selection tools to locate interesting rules from these sets.

While already association rules produce lots of interesting and sometimes even surprising information about the data set, looking for more complex rules makes it possible to locate more subtle phenomena. For example, we can notice that the confidences of many rules of the form

$$X \Rightarrow C \text{ programming} \vee C \text{ and Unix}$$

have significantly higher confidences than the individual rules

$$X \Rightarrow C \text{ programming}$$
$$X \Rightarrow C \text{ and Unix.}$$

Inspecting the history of the curriculum, this becomes clear: the courses are alternatives to each other. □

Given a relation r with attributes R and a threshold $\sigma \in [0,1]$, the σ-*frequent sets* of r are the subsets X of R such that $a(X,r) \geq \sigma$; this collection is denoted by $Fr(r,\sigma)$ or just $Fr(r)$, if σ is clear from the context. The algorithms for finding association rules compute the collection $Fr(r,\sigma)$, and the quantity $a(X,r)$ for all frequent sets. The time required is roughly proportional to the product of $|Fr(r,\sigma)|$ and $|r|$. These methods are applicable whenever $|Fr(r,\sigma)|$ is not too large.

We show next how the rule confidences can be bounded using frequent sets. The idea is very simple: to get a lower bound on the confidence, just replace every term $a(W)$ such that $W \notin Fr(r)$ in the above formulae either by 0 or σ, depending on whether $a(W)$ occurs positively or negatively within the formula and whether it occurs in numerator or denominator.

For example, to find the confidence of the disjunctive rule $X \Rightarrow Y \vee Z$, we need to know $a(X)$ and $a(X \cup Y) + a(X \cup Z) - a(X \cup Y \cup Z)$. If all these terms are known, we can directly compute the frequency and confidence of the rule. What if some terms are not known? If either $a(X \cup Y)$ or $a(X \cup Z)$ is less than the frequency threshold, then the sum of the unknown terms in the numerator is less than the threshold, and its effect on the confidence can not be very strong. An interesting case is when $a(X \cup Y \cup Z)$ is not known. Then we can simply assume the worst, which is that $a(X \cup Y \cup Z)$ is just below the threshold, and we get a lower bound of $(a(X \cup Y) + a(X \cup Z) - \sigma)/a(X)$ for the confidence of the rule.

Approximate inclusion-exclusion

In the previous section we gave simple examples of how the confidences of general propositional rules can be estimated on the basis of the information about the frequencies of the frequent sets. Such estimations are, however, fairly useless, unless one is able to give bounds on the errors in the estimation. In this section we show how the information collected during the computation of the frequent sets can be used to derive tight bounds on the quality of the approximate confidences; the bounds depend on the boolean formula, and are hence especially accurate.

For simplicity, consider the following approximation problem. Given $W \subseteq R$, we want to know how many rows of r have a 1 in at least one of the columns of W, i.e., we want to compute $o(W)$. This is of course trivial to do by reading the data once, but this can be very costly. What could be done using only the information collected during the computation of the frequent sets?

The inclusion-exclusion formula gives us the expression

$$o(W) = \sum_{\emptyset \neq X \subseteq W} (-1)^{|X|+1} a(X).$$

However, we do not know all terms in the above sum. What we know is the truncated sum

$$\bar{o}(W) = \sum_{\emptyset \neq X \subseteq W, X \in Fr(r)} (-1)^{|X|+1} a(X).$$

The absolute error $e(W)$ caused by using the truncated sum is

$$e(W) = |o(W) - \bar{o}(W)|.$$

We want to bound $e(W)$ somehow.

A similar type of problem has been considered in (Linial & Nisan 1990; Kahn, Linial, & Samorodnitsky 1995), where it is shown that knowing the terms $(-1)^{|X|+1} a(X)$ of the inclusion-exclusion formula for all X with $|X| \leq \sqrt{|W|}$ is sufficient for getting good approximations to the whole sum. Interestingly, the approximation is not formed by simply computing the truncated sum; rather, one uses a linear combination of the terms of the truncated sum. Their results are not, however, applicable to our problem, as the frequent sets do not necessarily provide the required subset of the terms of the inclusion-exclusion formula. See also (Grable 1993; 1994) for related results.

Given r over R, and σ, the *negative border* $Bd^-(r,\sigma)$ of $Fr(r,\sigma)$ consists of sets $W \subseteq R$ not in $Fr(r,\sigma)$ but such that all proper subsets of W are in $Fr(r,\sigma)$. In other words, the negative border consists of the minimal sets that are not frequent. The negative border also defines which sets are frequent and which are not. Given a set X, if X is a superset of some set in the negative border, then X is *not* frequent, otherwise it is frequent.

Example 4 Let $R = \{A,B,C,D\}$. Let r be a relation with attributes R and assume $Fr(r,\sigma) = \{\{A,B\},\{B,C\},\{A,C\},\{A\},\{B\},\{C\},\emptyset\}$. Then $Bd^-(r,\sigma) = \{\{A,B,C\},\{D\}\}$. □

Algorithms that compute the collection of frequent sets also compute the frequencies of sets in the negative border, as the negative border consists of exactly those sets which, on the basis of other information, could be frequent, and whose frequency should therefore be checked. In certain restricted models of computation one can even show that the sets in the border have to be examined (Mannila & Toivonen 1996).

Theorem 5 For all $W \subseteq R$ denote $\mathcal{K} = \{Y \in Bd^-(r) \mid Y \subseteq W\}$. If $\mathcal{K} = \emptyset$, then $e(W) = 0$. Otherwise, let $C = \max\{2^{|\mathcal{K}|-2}/|\mathcal{K}|, 1\}$. Then

$$e(W) \leq C \sum_{Y \subseteq W, Y \in Bd^-(r)} a(Y).$$

Relative error	Number of cases			
$e(W)/\bar{o}(W)$	$\|W\|$			
	2	3	4	5
< 1 %	77	57	20	0
1 − 5 %	16	29	48	10
5 − 10 %	3	6	10	16
10 − 20 %	3	7	13	16
≥ 20 %	1	1	9	58
Total	100	100	100	100
Average error (%)	1.3	2.5	6.2	38.3

Table 1: Distribution of relative error for random disjunctions W of different sizes

Example 6 Continuing Example 4, if we want to approximate the frequency of rows such that at least one attribute has value 1 (i.e., if we want to know $o(\{A, B, C, D\})$, the theorem states that the error is at most $a(\{A, B, C\}) + a(\{D\})$. □

Example 7 We made extensive experiments with a a telecommunications alarm database, where we looked at over 3,300,000 windows of an alarm sequence, and located the frequent sets with threshold 0.0001. There are 128 frequent sets and 713 sets in the negative boundary; only 5 of these, however, have more than 2 elements.

To evaluate the effectiveness of Theorem 5, we generated 100 random disjunctions of size 4 where each disjunct is a frequent alarm, and we used the bound in the theorem to obtain estimates on the size of error. The maximum error bound for the frequency of the disjunction was 0.00041. In 53 cases the absolute error was less than 0.0001, and in 28 cases less than 0.00005.

More interestingly, on average the error bound was only 6.2 % of the estimated size of the disjunction. For 20 cases the error bound was less than 1 % and for another 48 cases less than 5 %; the maximum relative error was 35 %. Table 1 shows the average value and a rough distribution of the relative error for random disjunctions of sizes 2, 3, 4, and 5.

The table shows that the bounds are very accurate for disjunctions of size 2 to 4. In our experiments the bounds were not very useful for disjunctions with 6 or more terms. Experiments with very different alarm databases gave results very similar in nature. Obviously also the frequency threshold has a significant influence on the quality of the bounds: the lower the threshold, the better are the estimates. □

Example 8 In the course enrollment database r we have $|Bd^-(r, 0.05)| = 336$. Theorem 5 gives, e.g., the following results from our database.

- For the set W of courses *Data Structures* and *Database Systems I*, all three terms of the sum are known and $\bar{o}(W) = o(W) = 0.25$ and $e(W) = 0$.
- For a set W of three 'C' or Unix-related courses, 4 out of 7 terms are greater than the threshold and 2 are in the negative border. We have $\bar{o}(W) = 0.24$ and $e(W) \leq 0.017$.
- For a set W of three different intermediate courses, *Theory of Computation*, *Artificial Intelligence*, and *Computer Graphics*, we have 3 out of 7 terms of the sum, and another 3 are in the negative border. The estimated frequency is $\bar{o}(W) = 0.21$ and the error bound $e(W) \leq 0.079$.
- For a W consisting of six programming projects we have $\bar{o}(W) = 0.31$ and $e(W) \leq 0.012$. In this case 7 out of 63 terms exceed the threshold, and another 3 are in the negative border. □

Theorem 5 can also be used to obtain bounds on the error that are independent of the exact frequencies of sets in the border.

Corollary 9 For all $W \subseteq R$ let $K = |Bd^-(r, \sigma) \cap \mathcal{P}(W)|$ and $C = \max\{2^{K-2}, K\}$. Then

$$e(W) \leq C\sigma.$$

Bounds on the error of confidence can be found by assuming opposite errors in the frequencies in the numerator and in the denominator.

Concise representations

In this section we outline a general definition of what it means to represent a class of structures by another, with respect to a set of queries. We discuss how the use of samples, the use of frequent sets, and the data cube (Gray *et al.* 1996) can could be viewed as examples of the same general idea. The concept is based on the notion of ε-approximations widely used in computational geometry and in computational learning theory (Haussler & Welzl 1987; Mulmuley 1993).

We consider a class of structures $\mathcal{S} = \{s_i \mid i \in I\}$, where the index set I can be finite or infinite. Examples of classes of structures are $\mathcal{S}_{R,01}$, the class of all 0/1 relations over the attributes R, $\mathcal{S}_{R,D}$, the class of all relations over the domain D and attributes R, and $\mathcal{S}_E$, the set of all event sequences with event types from the set E.

A query class $\mathcal{Q}$ for $\mathcal{S}$ is a finite set $\{Q_1, \ldots, Q_p\}$ of queries. The value of a query $Q \in \mathcal{Q}$ on a structure $s \in \mathcal{S}$ is denoted by $Q(s)$; the value is assumed to be a real number in the interval $[0, 1]$. Examples of query classes for $\mathcal{S}_{R,01}$ are the *conjunctive* queries $\mathcal{Q}_\wedge = \{Q_W : r \mapsto$

$a(W, r) \mid W \subseteq R\}$ and the *disjunctive* queries $Q_\vee = \{Q'_W : r \mapsto o(W, r) \mid W \subseteq R\}$.

An *ε-adequate representation* for $\mathcal{S}$ with respect to $\mathcal{Q}$ is a class $\mathcal{R} = \{r_i \mid i \in I\}$ of structures and a query evaluation function $m : \mathcal{Q} \times \mathcal{R} \to [0, 1]$ such that for all $Q \in \mathcal{Q}$ and $s_i \in \mathcal{S}$ we have

$$|Q(s_i) - m(Q, r_i)| \leq \varepsilon.$$

That is, the values of queries from $\mathcal{Q}$ on any structure from $\mathcal{S}$ can be evaluated using the corresponding representation from $\mathcal{R}$ and the query evaluation function m.

Example 10 Consider as the class of structures $\mathcal{S}_{R,01}$ the class of all 0/1 relations over the set of attributes R. Consider the query class $\mathcal{Q}_\wedge = \{Q_W \mid W \subseteq R\}$, where for $s \in \mathcal{S}_{R,01}$ we have $Q_W(s) = a(W, s)$, i.e., the fraction of rows of s such that the row has a 1 in each column of W. Then the collection $\{Fr(s, \varepsilon) \mid s \in \mathcal{S}_{R,01}\}$ of the frequent sets of s, for each $s \in \mathcal{S}_{R,01}$, provides an ε-adequate representation of $\mathcal{S}_{R,01}$ with respect to $\mathcal{Q}_\wedge$.

For the telecommunications alarm database we have a 0.0001-adequate representation that consists only of 128 sets. In the case of our course enrollment database r the size of a 0.05-adequate representation is $|Fr(r, 0.05)| = 489$ sets. Note that the number of frequent sets does not depend on the number of rows in the database. □

The notion of an ε-adequate representation is very closely related to the concept of ε-approximations and ε-nets widely used in computational geometry (Haussler & Welzl 1987; Mulmuley 1993). Roughly, given a set N and a collection $\mathcal{S}$ of subsets of N, an ε-approximation is a subset $M \subseteq N$ such that for each $X \in \mathcal{S}$ we have

$$\left| \frac{|X \cap M|}{|M|} - \frac{|X|}{|N|} \right| \leq \varepsilon.$$

Thus an ε-approximation is a subset that gives a good estimate of the sizes of all subsets in $\mathcal{S}$. The ε-adequate representations differ in two respects: the representation does not have to be of the same form as the original data, and we have additionally required that such representations exist for every structure in a class of structures. Still, the results on ε-approximations help in obtaining results about adequate representations.

The existence result for ε-approximations was proved by Vapnik and Chervonenkis, and the sizes of such approximations are naturally connected with the VC-dimension (Vapnik 1982). One can show that samples provide an ε-adequate representation for finite query classes.

The data cube (Gray *et al.* 1996) is a recently introduced summarizing representation for relations with arbitrary values. Using the concepts above, the data cube is 0-adequate representation for the class of queries containing all aggregate functions. An interesting possibility is to diminish the space and time complexity of the data cube by allowing some error. It seems that this can be accomplished by using a similar strategy as in the computation of frequent sets.

The preceding discussion of adequate representations is quite tentative: the usefulness of the notion has yet to be conclusive demonstrated. It seems to us, however, that this concept could serve as a unifying point of view to look at several different types of approximate ways of representing information.

Conclusions

We have shown how the collection of frequent sets can be used as a condensed representation for a relation with 0/1 values. The collection makes it possible to approximate the confidences of arbitrary boolean rules. We have given a strong theorem about the sizes of errors caused by the approximation using the concept of the border of the frequent sets, and have given experimental evidence that the bound is typically extremely good. We have also outlined a possible approach to a general theory of condensed representations and showed how frequent sets, sampling, and also the data cube can be viewed as instances of this concept.

There are several open questions. On the theoretical side, the development of the general notions of condensed representation seems useful. From the practical point of view, a more thorough investigation on the actual sizes of the errors in the approximations could be worthwhile.

References

Agrawal, R.; Mannila, H.; Srikant, R.; Toivonen, H.; and Verkamo, A. I. 1996. Fast discovery of association rules. In Fayyad, U. M.; Piatetsky-Shapiro, G.; Smyth, P.; and Uthurusamy, R., eds., *Advances in Knowledge Discovery and Data Mining*. Menlo Park, CA: AAAI Press. 307 – 328.

Agrawal, R.; Imielinski, T.; and Swami, A. 1993. Mining association rules between sets of items in large databases. In *Proceedings of ACM SIGMOD Conference on Management of Data (SIGMOD'93)*, 207 – 216.

Grable, D. A. 1993. Sharpened bonferroni inequalities. *Journal on Combinatorial Theory, Series B* 57(1):131 – 137.

Grable, D. A. 1994. Hypergraphs and sharpened sieve inequalities. *Discrete Mathematics* 132:75 – 82.

Gray, J.; Bosworth, A.; Layman, A.; and Pirahesh, H. 1996. Data Cube: A relational aggregation operator generalizing group-by, cross-tab, and sub-totals. In *12th International Conference on Data Engineering (ICDE'96)*, 152 – 159.

Han, J., and Fu, Y. 1995. Discovery of multiple-level association rules from large databases. In *Proceedings of the 21st International Conference on Very Large Data Bases (VLDB'95)*, 420 – 431.

Haussler, D., and Welzl, E. 1987. Epsilon-nets and simplex range queries. *Discrete Comput. Geom.* 2:127–151.

Holsheimer, M.; Kersten, M.; Mannila, H.; and Toivonen, H. 1995. A perspective on databases and data mining. In *Proceedings of the First International Conference on Knowledge Discovery and Data Mining (KDD'95)*, 150 – 155.

Houtsma, M., and Swami, A. 1993. Set-oriented mining of association rules. Research Report RJ 9567, IBM Almaden Research Center, San Jose, California.

Kahn, J.; Linial, N.; and Samorodnitsky, A. 1995. Inclusion-exclusion: exact and approximate. Manuscript.

Klemettinen, M.; Mannila, H.; Ronkainen, P.; Toivonen, H.; and Verkamo, A. I. 1994. Finding interesting rules from large sets of discovered association rules. In *Proceedings of the Third International Conference on Information and Knowledge Management (CIKM'94)*, 401 – 407. Gaithersburg, MD: ACM.

Linial, N., and Nisan, N. 1990. Approximate inclusion-exclusion. *Combinatorica* 10(4):349 – 365.

Mannila, H., and Toivonen, H. 1996. On an algorithm for finding all interesting sentences. In *Cybernetics and Systems, Volume II, The Thirteenth European Meeting on Cybernetics and Systems Research*, 973 – 978.

Mulmuley, K. 1993. *Computational Geometry: An Introduction Through Randomized Algorithms*. New York: Prentice Hall.

Park, J. S.; Chen, M.-S.; and Yu, P. S. 1995. An effective hash-based algorithm for mining association rules. In *Proceedings of ACM SIGMOD Conference on Management of Data (SIGMOD'95)*, 175 – 186.

Savasere, A.; Omiecinski, E.; and Navathe, S. 1995. An efficient algorithm for mining association rules in large databases. In *Proceedings of the 21st International Conference on Very Large Data Bases (VLDB'95)*, 432 – 444.

Srikant, R., and Agrawal, R. 1995. Mining generalized association rules. In *Proceedings of the 21st International Conference on Very Large Data Bases (VLDB'95)*, 407 – 419.

Srikant, R., and Agrawal, R. 1996. Mining quantitative association rules in large relational tables. In *Proceedings of ACM SIGMOD Conference on Management of Data (SIGMOD'96)*.

Toivonen, H. 1996. Sampling large databases for finding association rules. In *Proceedings of the 22nd International Conference on Very Large Data Bases (VLDB'96)*. To appear.

Vapnik, V. 1982. *Estimation of Dependencies Based on Empirical Data*. New York: Springer-Verlag.

A Comparison of Approaches For Maximizing Business Payoff of Prediction Models

Brij Masand and Gregory Piatetsky-Shapiro

GTE Laboratories,
40 Sylvan Rd. Waltham MA 02254, USA
email: brij@gte.com, gps@gte.com

Abstract

In many database marketing applications the goal is to predict the customer behavior based on their previous actions. A usual approach is to develop models which maximize accuracy on the training and test sets and then apply these models on the unseen data. We show that in order to maximize business payoffs, accuracy optimization is insufficient by itself, and explore different strategies to take the customer value into account. We propose a framework for comparing payoffs of different models and use it to compare a number of different approaches for selecting the most valuable subset of customers. For the two datasets that we consider, we find that explicit use of value information during the training process and stratified modelling based on value both perform better than post processing strategies.

1 Introduction

The rapidly growing business databases contain much potentially valuable knowledge that could be extracted by Data Mining and Knowledge Discovery Techniques (Piatetsky-Shapiro and Frawley 1991, Fayyad et al. 1996). One of the most widespread applications of data mining is targeted database marketing, which is the use of historical customer records to predict customer behavior.

In our application, historical customer records are used to group the customers into two classes -- those who respond to special offers and those who don't. Using past information collected over several months on usage of telephone services and responses to past offers, our task is to build a model for predicting the customer class in the next month and apply it to several hundred thousand customers. The prediction model is used to rank the customers according to their likelihood of response. Although the response rate for such applications is often low (e.g. 4%), and it is difficult or impossible to predict the class with high accuracy for all customers, a good model can concentrate the likely responders near the top of the list. For example, the top 5% of the list (sorted by the model prediction) may contain 30% of responders (compared to

4% base rate), giving the model a *lift* of 30/4=7.5. For a large customer base, even small improvements in prediction accuracy can yield large improvements in lift.

In this paper we argue that lift measure by itself is not sufficient and that we should take the customer value into account in order to determine the model payoff. Using the predicted behavior and a simple business model we estimate the payoffs from different models and examine different strategies to arrive at an optimal model that maximizes overall business value rather than just accuracy or lift.

In the rest of this paper we explain the business problem and model of business payoffs, present the main experimental hypotheses, results and conclusions.

2 Motivation

When using a predictive model to assign likelihood of response, typically overall accuracy or lift is maximized. To maximize business value however, we need to maximize not only prediction accuracy but identify a group of customers that are not only highly likely to respond but are going to be "high value" customers. How might one arrive at such a model? Is it enough to just select the estimated high value customers from the group of predicted reponders as a post processing step or might it be beneficial to have the predictive model itself take the value into account while building the model? We examine these questions by conducting experiments that contrast different strategies to take value into account.

3 Description of the business problem

Given billing information on customers for a given month, we want to predict the customer behavior for the next month

Table 1:
Example data fields from Customer Billing Record (Aug 95)

record number	unpaid Balance	total Amt Billed	prev Bill Amt	total Peak	cash Payments	monthly Service Charge	service length	optional Feature Charge	ldCarrier	customer service calls	response to offers
1	373.0	519.37	373.0	25.0	0.0	18.0	25.0	4.0	280	2	0
2	0.0	150.25	110.0	37.0	110.0	24.0	12.0	6.0	280	0	1
3	20.0	85.0	60.0	5.0	40.0	10.0	30.0	2.0	280	0	0

and arrive at a ranking of all subscribers for the purpose of extending offers to the top few percent from such a ranked list. The billing data (see Table 1) includes such information as total amount billed, unpaid balances, use of specific (telephone) services, customer service calls plus information on length of service and past marketing behavior e.g. whether they accepted certain offers or not. The sample database we use includes information for 100,000 customers with about two hundred fields per customer per month. A standard approach to this problem is to regard it as a classification problem and use one of the machine learning methods such as neural networks (Rumelhart 1986), decision tree induction (Quinlan 1993) or nearest neighbor classifiers (Dasarathy 1991) and build a predictive model that maximizes some criteria such as overall accuracy, lift in the top 5%.

For the experiments described in this paper, we use a commercial neural network software package from Neuralware. The following steps describe how we prepare the data for modelling.

3.1 Pre-processing and sampling data for analysis

Our first sample database comprises of 25,000 records from a particular market. Based on historical data, typical response rate for this application (responding to offers) are in the vicinity of 7%. For the purpose of building a model we need a more concentrated representation of responders. This is because with a sparse response rate, a learning method can achieve high accuracy by always predicting everyone to be a non-responder.

We create a random sample where we include about 2000 responders and then add enough non-responders to make a dataset of 50-50 concentration of responders. For each one of these individuals we include information from one previous month.

We divide this dataset (about 4000 records) into approximately 2/3 and 1/3 size training and test sets with a 50-50 concentration of responders. A separate random

sample of 6000 records (with no overlap with the train, test sets) is held aside for evaluation purposes.

A second, larger sample is drawn from a different market with 100,000 records and a much lower response rate of about 2%. Following similar steps training and test sets of size about 4000 each are created and a non-overlapping heldaside set of 24,000 records is kept separately for evaluation.

3.2 Reducing the number of data fields for model development

As reported in (Kohavi & Sommerfield 1995) and (Almuallim & Dietterich 1991), reducing or eliminating irrelevant data fields can result in improved classification accuracy. We first excluded fields that have constant values as well l as dependent fields such as tax charges. In order to prune the data fields further, we correlated each field with the target field and arrived at a smaller list of fields per month (about 40). While in general it may not be desirable to exclude fields before the application of a learning procedure, in this case our goal is to compare different learning strategies to maximize business payoff from the models, therefore just including the "best n" fields still serves the purpose of contrasting different modelling strategies.

3.3 Methodology of testing

In order to estimate the accuracy and payoff of different models their ability to predict needs to be tested on a representation of "unseen" data. For our experiments the neural network training was done using the 50-50 train and the test sets, using the test set to prevent overtraining. Once the models were developed, they were applied to the heldaside set to compute the ranked list of subscribers and to estimate model payoffs on unseen data.

3.4 Example predicted performance

Table 2 shows a typical output log which is produced by applying the prediction model to input similar to that in Table 1 (but ignoring the known target value "class" for prediction purposes). The log is sorted by the likelihood of response shown in Column 1 so that subscribers most likely to respond are at the top. Column 3 is the assigned prediction, 1 for response and 0 for no-response. Column 4 "class" is the actual action taken by the customer and finally the last column indicates the typical revenue from the customer from accepting previous offers.The revenue column outputs an estimated revenue, derived from input variables, but is not the variable being predicted.

The "confidence" of prediction is derived from the output of the neural network model. which ranges from 0 to 1. Values above 0.5 are assigned a prediction of 1.0 along with a confidence proportional to the deviation from 0.5. Similarly a prediction of 0 is assigned, with a negative confidence proportional to the absolute deviation from 0.5. The confidence is scaled to range from +100 to -100. It can be seen that the likelihood of response and the typical revenue are not necessarily related.

Table 2: Example output log of predicted output

confidence	Acctno	prediction	class	revenue
89.84	x5195y	1	0	$26.25
87.64	x8102y	1	1	$1007.74
87.45	x1226y	1	1	$679.30
82.45	x2223y	1	1	$942.65
81.45	x3220y	1	0	$297.45
79.45	x4301y	1	0	$359.80
77.45	x2291y	1	1	$281.45
76.45	x1101y	1	1	$940.45
75.45	x2102y	1	0	$564.70
74.45	x3103y	1	1	$522.06
71.45	x1084y	1	0	$393.45
70.25	x7080y	1	1	$207.20
70.05	x6221y	1	1	$18.20

3.5 Business model, estimating overall payoffs, optimal payoff

When we reach a customer that is not likely to respond, we incur the cost of contact. On the other hand, when the customer responds to an offer there is a benefit proportional to their expected usage. For the purpose of estimating the payoff for calling the top few percent of subscribers ranked with the likelihood of response as above, we need a simple cost/benefit model.

If the cost of reaching a customer is c, the expected revenue *is* r, and p is the probability that they will reply positively to an offer, then the overall the expected payoff P of reaching a customer is

$$P = (r * p) - c \qquad (1)$$

For our domain we assume that the cost of reaching a customer by telephone to extend an offer is about $6 per customer, the expected revenue is derived using a value model, and the probability p is about 0.5

If we sum (1) for an output prediction log, similar to that shown in Table 1, we get cumulative payoff results similar to the ones shown in the last two columns of the next table, a lift table.

3.6 Example lift table

Table 3 summarizes the output prediction log, ranked by the most likely responders. The results are for a heldaside sample of 6300 customers, of whom 480 or about 7.5% are known to have responded. The overall accuracy for this log is about 74%.

Column 1 indicates the proportion of the ranked list up to the segment and the remaining columns describe summary statistics. The "hit rate" or response rate in that segment indicates the concentration of responders in that segment while the "cumulative abs hits" indicate the total responders up to that segment. One column of particular interest is the "cum% captured of all hits" which shows the cumulative percentage of *all true* responders present in the list that far. For instance we would expect the 5% segment to have at least 5% of all responders and the 10% to have at least 10% of all responders, so the actual percentage, in this case 30.0 and 43% for 5% and 10% respectively represent a "lift" of 6 and 4.3 approximately. Therefore calling the top 5% subscribers from this list is about 6 times more efficient than calling a random group of subscribers.

If we sum the payoff per customer we get the payoff per segment and the cumulative payoff in the last column. We can see that as the concentration of responders drops, the payoff per segment becomes negative as the cost of reaching non-responders overrides the benefit of potential response. There is an estimated "optimal" number of people to call, in this case about 15% giving an estimated optimal payoff of about $72 k for this group. If this was linearly scaled to 100,000 customers this payoff would represent about $1.1 million. (In practice we have observed a non-linear scaling, giving a higher lift and payoff for larger samples).

Table 3: Example lift table for ranked output log for 6,300 customers

seg-ment	hit rate per seg-ment	cum abs hits	cum% of all hits cap-tured	lift	payoff per seg (x 1000)	cum payoff (x 1000)
5%	45.71	144	30.00	6.00	61.13	61.13
10%	19.68	206	42.92	4.29	8.02	69.15
15%	15.24	254	52.92	3.53	3.14	72.29
20%	7.30	277	57.71	2.89	-0.48	71.81
30%	6.35	322	67.08	2.24	-0.15	71.40
50%	5.71	392	81.67	1.63	-2.08	67.97
70%	3.02	431	89.79	1.28	-4.54	58.99
80%	2.54	447	93.12	1.16	-4.63	54.36
90%	1.75	458	95.42	1.06	-5.05	49.31
100%	3.49	480	100.0	1.0	-3.37	45.94

The figure below (based on slightly different data from the above table) shows an optimal cutoff point from the ranked prediction log for an optimal payoff. Here the optimal point is about 11% for a payoff of $82k.

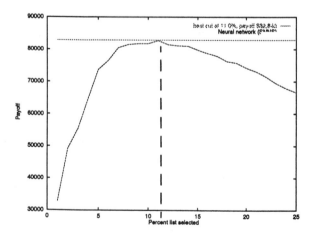

4 Main experimental hypotheses: Value based training vs. post processing

Given the above definition of business payoff in this domain, we now examine different strategies for the task of optimizing the payoff. Essentially we would like to rank the subscriber base in such a way that the people who are most likely to respond are at the top of the ranked list. In addition, we would like to identify a group of customers that are likely to respond to high value offers. For example, it might be better to extend offers to a smaller group of people with a moderate likelihood of response but with the high expected revenue, rather than a group of customers that with a higher likelihood of response but a lower expected revenue.

We ask the question: Is it enough to use a predictive model to arrive at ranked list of subscribers, and then, as a post processing step select the "high value" customers (as estimated from their past behavior) or is it necessary to somehow include the notion of value in the training process itself? Should we stratify customers into high value customers and low value customers and build different models for them? We examine and contrast the following four approaches:

4.1 Baseline payoff calculation

Using a basic predictive model we establish a baseline payoff against which all improvements can be measured. The payoff calculations are done as explained in sections 3.4 and 3.5. It is important to note that what we call "value" (various sources of revenue) are present as some of the inputs, although their use is to predict a likelihood of any response at all (a classification problem) rather than an absolute magnitude of the response (a regression problem).

4.2 Post Processing

We examine a simple strategy to re-rank the basic ranked list using a criteria that takes both likelihood of response and the actual estimated value (which is estimated from the input revenue variables). We use a product of the two factors as a composite rank factor. This simulates "expected value" even though the likelihood as estimated from the neural net prediction is not a strict probability. Thus subscribers with a high likelihood but low estimated value may not be near the top of the list because another subscriber with a moderate likelihood but high value might have a higher composite score.

4.3 Value based training

To develop a model which directly takes value into account, we predict expected payoff (a continuous variable) rather than response/no-response. We modify the target field to be the expected payoff in case of response and the expected cost in case of non-response. For example, instead of a 1 or a 0 as target attributes, the new attributes are a positive number based on their previous revenue or a constant negative value based on the average cost of reaching someone and making the offer. The following table illustrates the augmented target variable.

Table 4: Example Augmented input records

Acctno	class	augmented value target	revenue
x5195y	0	-$6	$26.25
x8102y	1	$1007.74	$1007.74
x1226y	1	$679.3	$679.30
x2223y	1	$942.65	$942.65
x3220y	0	-$6	$297.45
x4301y	0	-$6	$359.80
x2291y	1	$281.4	$281.45

4.4 Modelling stratifed groups based on value

It is reasonable to expect that separate models for stratified groups of customers may have better overall accuracy and payoffs. To explore this we stratify the customer base into two classes: high revenue customers comprising the top 25% as judged by previous revenue, and low revenue customers comprising the remaining 75%. Using these classes we divide both the training and test sets into two groups and build two separate models for high and low revenue customers. The models are than applied to the two similar divisions of the heldaside set and then the two sets of predictions are combined using the using the following two strategies:

4.4.1 Straight Merge of Stratified logs

In this case the entire output logs from the two different stratified groups are merged and then resorted to rank them and the optimal payoff is recomputed.

4.5 Merge of "optimal" subsets from the logs

In this case instead of combining all the records from the two stratified groups, only the optimal number of

subscribers corresponding to the optimal payoff from each stratified model output (as described in section 3.5) are combined and then resorted and the optimal payoff point is again recomputed.

5 Main Results

Tables 5 and 6 compare the optimum payoffs achieved on the heldaside sets from the two datasets by using the strategies described above. Dataset 2 has larger number of

Table 5: Dataset 1, Comparison of Optimum payoffs (x $1000)

	experiment	input 5	input 10	input 15	input 25	input 35	mean (std dev)
1	basic optpayoff	72.0	73.4	72.3	723	71.8	72.35 (0.6)
2	basic resorted opt payoff	72.2	72.0	72.4	72.6	72.3	72.29 (0.2)
3	value training opt payoff	77.8	78.0	77.6	78.3	77.7	77.88 (0.3)
4	strat1 merge opt payoff	73.6	74.1	72.0	71.7	71.1	72.51 (1.3)
5	strat2 opt-merge opt payoff	77.0	78.1	77.6	76.5	77.2	77.27 (0.6)

records with a lower overall response rate (2% vs. 7%)

The first column describes the type of experiment while the other columns show variations on datasets using varying number of inputs for model building, in order to test the effect of strategies on models of different complexities. Input 5, 10 etc. mean that the first 5, the first 10 variables etc. were used as inputs from a possible 40 preselected and pre-ranked variable set as described in section 3.2

The first row describes the optimum payoff using a straight prediction model and computing the payoff as described in section 3.4. The second row describes results for re-sorting the ranked list by using the product of the response likelihood ("confidence" in Table 2) and the previous revenue of the customer. Row 3 describes the results for predicting the expected payoff rather than response/non-response. Row 4 describes the results from merging the entire output logs from the two stratified models while the last row describes the results obtained by merging only optimum subsets from the output of the two stratified models.

Table 6: Dataset 2, Comparison of Optimum payoffs (x $1000)

	experiment	input 5	input 10	input 15	input 25	input 35	mean (std dev)
1	basic opt payoff	55.0	52.7	54.5	57.3	57.1	55.3 (1.9)
2	basic resorted opt payoff	57.6	56.2	56.4	59.0	58.2	57.5 (1.2)
3	value training opt payoff	58.6	59.3	58.8	58.5	58.8	58.8 (0.3)
4	strat1 merge opt payoff	54.7	53.3	54.0	53.1	52.9	53.6 (0.7)
5	strat2 opt-merge opt payoff	58.3	58.1	56.6	57.2	57.1	57.4 (0.7)

5.1 Improvements using post processing

We found that re-ranking based on the product of the likelihood of response and estimated revenue does not results in a significant change for Dataset 1 while for Dataset 2 there is an improvement (95% confidence level for a test comparing the difference between means of two populations)

5.2 Improvements using value based training

As can be seen by comparing the third and the first row of Tables 5 and 6, the results from the value based training are significantly better than the payoffs from the basic model and also consistently better than the post processing strategy

5.3 Improvements using training based on stratified models

We expected the results to improve significantly using the straight merge from the stratified models but the best comparable results to value based training were obtained by merging the optimum subsets from the stratified model outputs.

5.4 Comparison of optimal payoffs with best accuracy and lift

More details related to the experiments for Dataset 1 in Table 5 can be found in Table 7 where the first column indexes the experiments from Table 5 and the remaining

Table 7: Comparison of Optimum payoffs vs. accuracy and lift

	experiment	opt payoff	opt cutoff (%)	overall accuracy	lift at 5%
1	basic input 5	72.05	29.06	72.8	4.97
1	basic input 10	73.42	34.59	75.66	5.36
1	basic input 15	72.27	35.14	74.14	5.23
1	basic input 25	72.26	37.89	74.05	5.23
1	basic input 35	71.77	36.69	73.41	5.4
2	basic resorted 5	72.17	28.7	72.8	4.27
2	basic resorted 10	71.98	19.56	75.66	4.66
2	basic resorted 15	72.38	22.64	74.14	4.97
2	basic resorted 25	72.63	20.26	74.05	4.79
2	basic resorted 35	72.30	18.87	73.41	4.84
3	value training 5	77.79	35.39	65.62	4.47
3	value training 10	77.96	37.69	63.7	4.98
3	value training 15	77.58	28.12	59.25	4.66
3	value training 25	78.35	25.57	58.03	4.84
3	value training 35	77.73	33.7	60.04	4.84
4	basic merge strat1 5	73.65	39.32	73.22	5.14
4	basic mergestrat110	74.15	41.02	74.85	5.36
4	basic merge strat1 15	71.92	53.31	74.03	5.05
4	basic merge strat1 25	71.75	36.52	72.94	4.27
4	basic merge strat1 35	71.08	31.48	73.71	5.01
5	basic optmerge strat2 5	77.0	37.33	34.17	3.83
5	basic optmerge strat2 10	78.13	33.43	33.92	3.63
5	basic optmerge strat2 15	77.56	32.84	39.04	3.76
5	basic optmerge strat2 25	76.48	38.12	34.97	2.81
5	basic optmerge strat2 35	77.22	36.12	34.02	2.33

columns describe parameters such as accuracy and lift. It is generally expected that high accuracy and high lift will be correlated with a high payoff model, however as can be seen from Table 7, the best payoffs are not correlated with the best accuracy or highest lift. This is consistent with the explanation that when we rank subscribers with just the likelihood of response, there is no necessary correlation between high likelihood of response and high magnitude (high value) of response. Thus the strategy which achieves high lift in predicting subscribers may not have the highest payoff value.

Another dimension of comparison can be the optimal percent of subscribers selected for the optimal payoff. For a comparable payoff, a smaller set of selected subscribers would be preferable.

6 Conclusions

We address the problem of identifying an optimal subset of customers with highest estimated payoff for extending offers to them. We find that for our domain, using neural network models on two datasets, different in size and response rates, the value based training strategies and the stratified optimal merge approach outperform the simple post processing strategy based on re-ranking using expected value estimates.

6.1 Discussion and Analysis

One might ask whether the high value stratified group (top 25%) is not sufficient by itself to produce the highest payoffs. We found that there are enough moderate value responders in the remaining 75% such that the payoff from the top 25% alone cannot match the highest payoffs from the value based training.

While new re-ranking factors for post processing can perhaps be discovered by methods such as Genetic Programming or manual heuristics, we show a definite improvement using a value based response variable for training across a range of model complexity as measured by different number of inputs. It's not clear yet if this approach would apply to different domains with a similar sparse response rate and value criteria (e.g. a domain such as credit card attrition).

6.2 Extensions

Methods such C4.5 and KNN classification can also be modified for value based training. We are adding bootstrap error estimates for the optimum payoffs to better assess the statistical significance of the relative ranking of different strategies. We are also experimenting with variations of value based training such as re-ranking the output logs of the value based model and also doing value based training on stratified sets.

7 Acknowledgments

We would like to thank John Vittal for his support of this project.

8 References

Almuallim H. and Dietterich T. 1991. Learning with Many Irrelevant Features. In Proceedings of AAAI-91, 547-552. Menlo Park, CA: AAAI Press.

Dasarathy, B.V. 1991. *Nearest Neighbor Norms: NN Pattern Classification techniques*. Los Alamitos, CA: IEEE Press.

Fayyad, U., Piatetsky-Shapiro, G., P. Smyth, and Uthurusamy, R. 1996. *Advances in Knowledge Discovery and Data Mining*, Cambridge, MA: AAAI/MIT Press.

Kohavi, R. and Sommerfield, D. 1995. Feature Subset Selection Using the Wrapper Method: Overfitting and Dynamic Search Space Topology. In Proceedings of KDD-95: First International Conference on Knowledge Discovery and Data Mining, 192--197. Menlo Park, CA: AAAI Press.

Piatetsky-Shapiro, G. and Frawley, W. 1991. *Knowledge Discovery in Databases*, Cambridge, MA: AAAI/MIT Press.

Rumelhart, D. E., Hinton, G. E. & Williams, R. J. 1986. Learning internal representations by error propagation. In *Parallel Distributed Processing: Explorations in the microstructure of cognition. Volume I: Foundations*. Cambridge, MA: MIT Press/Bradford Books, pp 318 - 362.

Quinlan, J. R. 1993. *C4.5: Programs for Machine Learning*. Los Gatos, CA: Morgan Kauffman.

Scaling Up the Accuracy of Naive-Bayes Classifiers: a Decision-Tree Hybrid

Ron Kohavi

Data Mining and Visualization
Silicon Graphics, Inc.
2011 N. Shoreline Blvd
Mountain View, CA 94043-1389
ronnyk@sgi.com

Abstract

Naive-Bayes induction algorithms were previously shown to be surprisingly accurate on many classification tasks even when the conditional independence assumption on which they are based is violated. However, most studies were done on small databases. We show that in some larger databases, the accuracy of Naive-Bayes does not scale up as well as decision trees. We then propose a new algorithm, NBTree, which induces a hybrid of decision-tree classifiers and Naive-Bayes classifiers: the decision-tree nodes contain univariate splits as regular decision-trees, but the leaves contain Naive-Bayesian classifiers. The approach retains the interpretability of Naive-Bayes and decision trees, while resulting in classifiers that frequently outperform both constituents, especially in the larger databases tested.

Introduction

Seeing the future first requires not only a wide-angle lens, it requires a multiplicity of lenses
—Hamel & Prahalad (1994), p. 95

Many data mining tasks require classification of data into classes. For example, loan applications can be classified into either 'approve' or 'disapprove' classes. A *classifier* provides a function that maps (classifies) a data item (instance) into one of several predefined classes (Fayyad, Piatetsky-Shapiro, & Smyth 1996). The automatic induction of classifiers from data not only provides a classifier that can be used to map new instances into their classes, but may also provide a human-comprehensible characterization of the classes. In many cases, interpretability—the ability to understand the output of the induction algorithm—is a crucial step in the design and analysis cycle. Some classifiers are naturally easier to interpret than others; for example, decision-trees (Quinlan 1993) are easy to visualize, while neural-networks are much harder.

Naive-Bayes classifiers (Langley, Iba, & Thompson 1992) are generally easy to understand and the induction of these classifiers is extremely fast, requiring only a single pass through the data if all attributes are discrete. Naive-Bayes classifiers are also very simple and easy to understand. Kononenko (1993) wrote that physicians found the induced classifiers easy to understand when the log probabilities were presented as evidence that adds up in favor of different classes.

Figure 1 shows a visualization of the Naive-Bayes classifier for Fisher's Iris data set, where the task is to determine the type of iris based on four attributes. Each bar represents evidence for a given class and attribute value. Users can immediately see that all values for petal-width and petal length are excellent determiners, while the middle range (2.95-3.35) for sepal-width adds little evidence in favor of one class or another.

Naive-Bayesian classifiers are very robust to irrelevant attributes, and classification takes into account evidence from many attributes to make the final prediction, a property that is useful in many cases where there is no "main effect." On the downside, Naive-Bayes classifiers require making strong independence assumptions and when these are violated, the achievable accuracy may asymptote early and will not improve much as the database size increases.

Decision-tree classifiers are also fast and comprehensible, but current induction methods based on recursive partitioning suffer from the fragmentation problem: as each split is made, the data is split based on the test and after two dozen levels there is usually very little data on which to base decisions.

In this paper we describe a hybrid approach that attempts to utilize the advantages of both decision-trees (*i.e.*, segmentation) and Naive-Bayes (evidence accumulation from multiple attributes). A decision-tree is built with univariate splits at each node, but with Naive-Bayes classifiers at the leaves. The final classifier resembles Utgoff's Perceptron trees (Utgoff 1988), but the induction process is very different and geared toward larger datasets.

The resulting classifier is as easy to interpret as

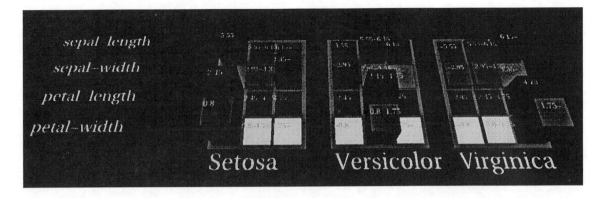

Figure 1: Visualization of a Naive-Bayes classifier for the iris dataset.

decision-trees and Naive-Bayes. The decision-tree segments the data, a task that is consider an essential part of the data mining process in large databases (Brachman & Anand 1996). Each segment of the data, represented by a leaf, is described through a Naive-Bayes classifier. As will be shown later, the induction algorithm segments the data so that the conditional independence assumptions required for Naive-Bayes are likely to be true.

The Induction Algorithms

We briefly review methods for induction of decision-trees and Naive-Bayes.

Decision-tree (Quinlan 1993; Breiman *et al.* 1984) are commonly built by recursive partitioning. A univariate (single attribute) split is chosen for the root of the tree using some criterion (*e.g.*, mutual information, gain-ratio, gini index). The data is then divided according to the test, and the process repeats recursively for each child. After a full tree is built, a pruning step is executed, which reduces the tree size. In the experiments, we compared our results with the C4.5 decision-tree induction algorithm (Quinlan 1993), which is a state-of-the-art algorithm.

Naive-Bayes (Good 1965; Langley, Iba, & Thompson 1992) uses Bayes rule to compute the probability of each class given the instance, assuming the attributes are conditionally independent given the label. The version of Naive-Bayes we use in our experiments was implemented in $\mathcal{MLC}$++ (Kohavi *et al.* 1994). The data is pre-discretized using the an entropy-based algorithm (Fayyad & Irani 1993; Dougherty, Kohavi, & Sahami 1995). The probabilities are estimated directly from data based directly on counts (without any corrections, such as Laplace or *m*-estimates).

Accuracy Scale-Up: the Learning Curves

A Naive-Bayes classifier requires estimation of the conditional probabilities for each attribute value given the label. For discrete data, because only few parameters need to be estimated, the estimates tend to stabilize quickly and more data does not change the underlying model much. With continuous attributes, the discretization is likely to form more intervals as more data is available, thus increasing the representation power. However, even with continuous data, the discretization is global and cannot take into account attribute interactions.

Decision-trees are non-parametric estimators and can approximate any "reasonable" function as the database size grows (Gordon & Olshen 1984). This theoretical result, however, may not be very comforting if the database size required to reach the asymptotic performance is more than the number of atoms in the universe, as is sometimes the case. In practice, some parametric estimators, such as Naive-Bayes, may perform better.

Figure 2 shows learning curves for both algorithms on large datasets from the UC Irvine repository[1] (Murphy & Aha 1996). The learning curves show how the accuracy changes as more instances (training data) are shown to the algorithm. The accuracy is computed based on the data not used for training, so it represents the true generalization accuracy. Each point was computed as an average of 20 runs of the algorithm, and 20 intervals were used. The error bars show 95% confidence intervals on the accuracy, based on the left-out sample.

In most cases it is clear that even with much more

---

[1]The Adult dataset is from the Census bureau and the task is to predict whether a given adult makes more than $50,000 a year based attributes such as education, hours of work per week, *etc.*.

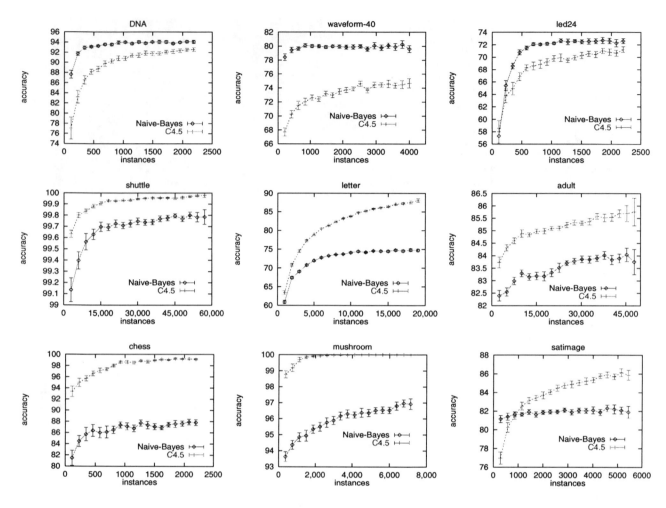

Figure 2: Learning curves for Naive-Bayes and C4.5. The top three graphs show datasets where Naive-Bayes outperformed C4.5, and the lower six graphs show datasets where C4.5 outperformed Naive-Bayes. The error bars are 95% confidence intervals on the accuracy.

data, the learning curves will not cross. While it is well known that no algorithm can outperform all others in all cases (Wolpert 1994), our world does tend to have some smoothness conditions and algorithms can be more successful than others in practice. In the next section we show that a hybrid approach can improve both algorithms in important practical datasets.

NBTree: The Hybrid Algorithm

The NBTree algorithm we propose is shown in Figure 3. The algorithm is similar to the classical recursive partitioning schemes, except that the leaf nodes created are Naive-Bayes categorizers instead of nodes predicting a single class.

A threshold for continuous attributes is chosen using the standard entropy minimization technique, as is done for decision-trees. The utility of a node is computed by discretizing the data and computing the 5-fold cross-validation accuracy estimate of using Naive-Bayes at the node. The utility of a split is the weighted sum of the utility of the nodes, where the weight given to a node is proportional to the number of instances that go down to that node.

Intuitively, we are attempting to approximate whether the generalization accuracy for a Naive-Bayes classifier at each leaf is higher than a single Naive-Bayes classifier at the current node. To avoid splits with little value, we define a split to be *significant* if the relative (not absolute) reduction in error is greater than 5% and there are at least 30 instances in the node.

Direct use of cross-validation to select attributes has not been commonly used because of the large overhead involved in using it in general. However, if the data is discretized, Naive-Bayes can be cross-validated in time that is linear in the number of instances, number of attributes, and number of label values. The reason is

Input: a set T of labelled instances.
Output: a decision-tree with naive-bayes categorizers at the leaves.

1. For each attribute X_i, evaluate the utility, $u(X_i)$, of a split on attribute X_i. For continuous attributes, a threshold is also found at this stage.

2. Let $j = \arg \max_i(u_i)$, *i.e.*, the attribute with the highest utility.

3. If u_j is not significantly better than the utility of the current node, create a Naive-Bayes classifier for the current node and return.

4. Partition T according to the test on X_j. If X_j is continuous, a threshold split is used; if X_j is discrete, a multi-way split is made for all possible values.

5. For each child, call the algorithm recursively on the portion of T that matches the test leading to the child.

Figure 3: The NBTree algorithm. The utility $u(X_i)$ is described in the text.

that we can remove the instances, update the counters, classify them, and repeat for a different set of instances. See Kohavi (1995) for details.

Given m instances, n attributes, and ℓ label values, the complexity of the attribute selection phase for discretized attributes is $O(m \cdot n^2 \cdot \ell)$. If the number of attributes is less than $O(\log m)$, which is usually the case, and the number of labels is small, then the time spent on attribute selection using cross-validation is less than the time spent sorting the instances by each attribute. We can thus expect NBTree to scale up well to large databases.

Experiments

To evaluate the NBTree algorithm we used a large set of files from the UC Irvine repository. Table 1 describes the characteristics of the data. Artificial files (*e.g.*, monk1) were evaluated on the whole space of possible values; files with over 3,000 instances were evaluated on a left out sample which is of size one third of the data, unless a specific test set came with the data (*e.g.*, shuttle, DNA, satimage); other files were evaluated using 10-fold cross-validation. C4.5 has a complex mechanism for dealing with unknown values. To eliminate the effects of unknown values, we have removed all instances with unknown values from the datasets prior to the experiments.

Figure 4 shows the absolute differences between the accuracies for C4.5, Naive-Bayes, and NBTree. Each line represents the accuracy difference for NBTree and one of the two other methods. The average accuracy for C4.5 is 81.91%, for Naive-Bayes it is 81.69%, and

for NBTree it is 84.47%.

Absolute differences do not tell the whole story because the accuracies may be close to 100% in some cases. Increasing the accuracy of medical diagnosis from 98% to 99% may cut costs by half because the number of errors is halved. Figure 5 shows the ratio of errors (where error is 100%-accuracy). The shuttle dataset, which is the largest dataset tested, has only 0.04% absolute difference between NBTree and C4.5, but the error decreases from 0.05% to 0.01%, which is a huge relative improvement.

The number of nodes induced by NBTree was in many cases significantly smaller than that of C4.5. For example, for the letter dataset, C4.5 induced 2109 nodes while NBTree induced only 251; in the adult dataset, C4.5 induced 2213 nodes while NBTree induced only 137; for DNA, C4.5 induced 131 nodes and NBTree induced 3; for led24, C4.5 induced 49 nodes, while NBTree used a single node. While the complexity of each leaf in NBTree is higher, ordinary trees with thousands of nodes could be extremely hard to interpret.

Related Work

Many attempts have been made to extend Naive-Bayes or to restrict the learning of general Bayesian networks. Approaches based on feature subset selection may help, but they cannot increase the representation power as was done here, thus we will not review them.

Kononenko (1991) attempted to join pairs of attributes (make a cross-product attribute) based on statistical tests for independence. Experimentation results were very disappointing. Pazzani (1995) searched for attributes to join based on cross-validation estimates.

Recently, Friedman & Goldszmidt (1996) showed how to learn a Tree Augmented Naive-Bayes (TAN), which is a Bayes network restricted to a tree topology. The results are promising and running times should scale up, but the approach is still restrictive. For example, their accuracy for the Chess dataset, which contains high-order interactions is about 93%, much lower then C4.5 and NBTree, which achieve accuracies above 99%.

Conclusions

We have described a new algorithm, NBTree, which is a hybrid approach suitable in learning scenarios when many attributes are likely to be relevant for a classification task, yet the attributes are not necessarily conditionally independent given the label.

NBTree induces highly accurate classifiers in practice, significantly improving upon both its constituents

Dataset	No attrs	Train size	Test size	Dataset	No attrs	Train size	Test size	Dataset	No attrs	Train size	Test size
adult	14	30,162	15,060	breast (L)	9	277	CV-10	breast (W)	10	683	CV-10
chess	36	2,130	1,066	cleve	13	296	CV-10	crx	15	653	CV-10
DNA	180	2,000	1,186	flare	10	1,066	CV-10	german	20	1,000	CV-10
glass	9	214	CV-10	glass2	9	163	CV-10	heart	13	270	CV-10
ionosphere	34	351	CV-10	iris	4	150	CV-10	led24	24	200	3000
letter	16	15,000	5,000	monk1	6	124	432	mushroom	22	5,644	3,803
pima	8	768	CV-10	primary-tumor	17	132	CV-10	satimage	36	4,435	2,000
segment	19	2,310	CV-10	shuttle	9	43,500	14,500	soybean-large	35	562	CV-10
tic-tac-toe	9	958	CV-10	vehicle	18	846	CV-10	vote	16	435	CV-10
vote1	15	435	CV-10	waveform-40	40	300	4,700				

Table 1: The datasets used, the number of attributes, and the training/test-set sizes (CV-10 denotes 10-fold cross-validation was used).

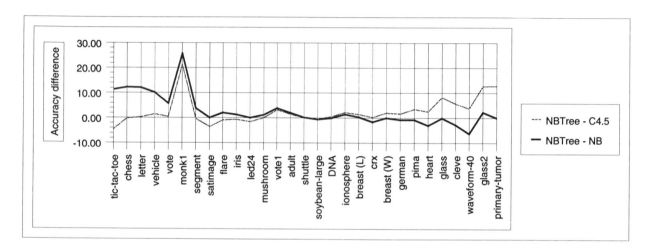

Figure 4: The accuracy differences. One line represents the accuracy difference between NBTree and C4.5 and the other between NBTree and Naive-Bayes. Points above the zero show improvements. The files are sorted by the difference of the two lines so that they cross once.

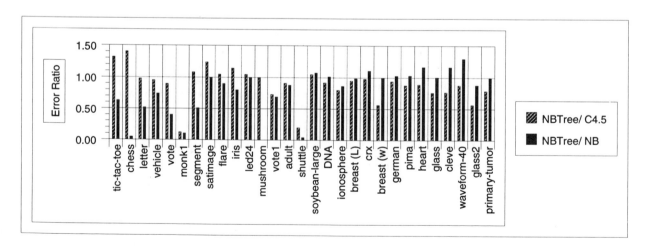

Figure 5: The error ratios of NBTree to C4.5 and Naive-Bayes. Values less than one indicate improvement.

in many cases. Although no classifier can outperform others in all domains, NBTree seems to work well on real-world datasets we tested and it scales up well in terms of its accuracy. In fact, for the three datasets over 10,000 instances (adult, letter, shuttle), it outperformed both C4.5 and Naive-Bayes. Running time is longer than for decision-trees and Naive-Bayes alone, but the dependence on the number of instances for creating a split is the same as for decision-trees, $O(m \log m)$, indicating that the running time can scale up well.

Interpretability is an important issue in data mining applications. NBTree segments the data using a univariate decision-tree, making the segmentation easy to understand. Each leaf is a Naive-Bayes classifiers, which can also be easily understood when displayed graphically, as shown in Figure 1. The number of nodes induced by NBTree was in many cases significantly smaller than that of C4.5.

Acknowledgments We thank Yeo-Girl (Yogo) Yun who implemented the original CatDT categorizer in $\mathcal{MLC}$++. Dan Sommerfield wrote the Naive-Bayes visualization routines in $\mathcal{MLC}$++.

References

Brachman, R. J., and Anand, T. 1996. The process of knowledge discovery in databases. In *Advances in Knowledge Discovery and Data Mining*. AAAI Press and the MIT Press. chapter 2, 37–57.

Breiman, L.; Friedman, J. H.; Olshen, R. A.; and Stone, C. J. 1984. *Classification and Regression Trees*. Wadsworth International Group.

Dougherty, J.; Kohavi, R.; and Sahami, M. 1995. Supervised and unsupervised discretization of continuous features. In Prieditis, A., and Russell, S., eds., *Machine Learning: Proceedings of the Twelfth International Conference*, 194–202. Morgan Kaufmann.

Fayyad, U. M., and Irani, K. B. 1993. Multi-interval discretization of continuous-valued attributes for classification learning. In *Proceedings of the 13th International Joint Conference on Artificial Intelligence*, 1022–1027. Morgan Kaufmann Publishers, Inc.

Fayyad, U. M.; Piatetsky-Shapiro, G.; and Smyth, P. 1996. From data mining to knowledge discovery: An overview. In *Advances in Knowledge Discovery and Data Mining*. AAAI Press and the MIT Press. chapter 1, 1–34.

Friedman, N., and Goldszmidt, M. 1996. Building classifiers using bayesian networks. In *Proceedings of the Thirteenth National Conference on Artificial Intelligence*. To appear.

Good, I. J. 1965. *The Estimation of Probabilities: An Essay on Modern Bayesian Methods*. M.I.T. Press.

Gordon, L., and Olshen, R. A. 1984. Almost sure consistent nonparametric regression from recursive partitioning schemes. *Journal of Multivariate Analysis* 15:147–163.

Hamel, G., and Prahalad, C. K. 1994. *Competing for the Future*. Harvard Business School Press and McGraw Hill.

Kohavi, R.; John, G.; Long, R.; Manley, D.; and Pfleger, K. 1994. MLC++: A machine learning library in C++. In *Tools with Artificial Intelligence*, 740–743. IEEE Computer Society Press. http://www.sgi.com/Technology/mlc.

Kohavi, R. 1995. *Wrappers for Performance Enhancement and Oblivious Decision Graphs*. Ph.D. Dissertation, Stanford University, Computer Science department. ftp://starry.stanford.edu/pub/ronnyk/teza.ps.

Kononenko, I. 1991. Semi-naive bayesian classifiers. In *Proceedings of the sixth European Working Session on Learning*, 206–219.

Kononenko, I. 1993. Inductive and bayesian learning in medical diagnosis. *Applied Artificial Intelligence* 7:317–337.

Langley, P.; Iba, W.; and Thompson, K. 1992. An analysis of bayesian classifiers. In *Proceedings of the tenth national conference on artificial intelligence*, 223–228. AAAI Press and MIT Press.

Murphy, P. M., and Aha, D. W. 1996. UCI repository of machine learning databases. http://www.ics.uci.edu/~mlearn.

Pazzani, M. 1995. Searching for attribute dependencies in bayesian classifiers. In *Fifth International Workshop on Artificial Intelligence and Statistics*, 424–429.

Quinlan, J. R. 1993. *C4.5: Programs for Machine Learning*. Los Altos, California: Morgan Kaufmann Publishers, Inc.

Utgoff, P. E. 1988. Perceptron trees: a case study in hybrid concept representation. In *Proceedings of the Seventh National Conference on Artificial Intelligence*, 601–606. Morgan Kaufmann.

Wolpert, D. H. 1994. The relationship between PAC, the statistical physics framework, the Bayesian framework, and the VC framework. In Wolpert, D. H., ed., *The Mathemtatics of Generalization*. Addison Wesley.

Quakefinder: A Scalable Data Mining System for Detecting Earthquakes from Space

Paul Stolorz and **Christopher Dean**
Jet Propulsion Laboratory
California Institute of Technology
(pauls,ctdean)@aig.jpl.nasa.gov

Abstract

We present an application of novel massively parallel datamining techniques to highly precise inference of important physical processes from remote sensing imagery. Specifically, we have developed and applied a system, Quakefinder, that automatically detects and measures tectonic activity in the earth's crust by examination of satellite data. We have used Quakefinder to automatically map the direction and magnitude of ground displacements due to the 1992 Landers earthquake in Southern California, over a spatial region of several hundred square kilometers, at a resolution of 10 meters, to a (sub-pixel) precision of 1 meter. This is the first calculation that has ever been able to extract area-mapped information about 2D tectonic processes at this level of detail. We outline the architecture of the Quakefinder system, based upon a combination of techniques drawn from the fields of statistical inference, massively parallel computing and global optimization. We confirm the overall correctness of the procedure by comparison of our results with known locations of targeted faults obtained by careful and time-consuming field measurements. The system also performs knowledge discovery by indicating novel unexplained tectonic activity away from the primary faults that has never before been observed. We conclude by discussing the future potential of this data mining system in the broad context of studying subtle spatio-temporal processes within massive image streams.

Introduction

Automatic detection and cataloguing of important temporal processes in massive datasets is a problem of overwhelming scale that has so far eluded automation for the great majority of scientific problems. Careful manual inspection of images by highly-trained scientists is still the standard method of extracting important scientific information from even high-resolution images. This is a time-consuming and extremely expensive process, although there has recently been substantial progress in isolated domains (Fayyad, Weir, & Djorgovski 1993). The goal of this paper is to introduce a data mining system that tackles this problem in the context of analyzing the earth's crustal dynamics, by enabling the automatic detection and measurement of earthquake faults from satellite imagery.

The system, Quakefinder, is applied here to the analysis of data collected by the French SPOT satellite. SPOT is a push-broom detector that collects panchromatic data at 10 meter resolution from a satellite in sun-synchronous orbit around the earth. In our application, images of size 2050 × 2050 pixels are analyzed to detect fault motion to subpixel precision. Although applied initially to the specific problem of earthquake fault analysis, the principals used by Quakefinder are however broadly applicable to a far more general class of calculations involving subtle change-detection in high-resolution image streams. We believe that its success in this domain points the way to a number of such datamining calculations that can directly and automatically measure important temporal processes to high precision from massive datasets. These include problems involving global climate change and natural hazard monitoring, as well as general image understanding problems involving target detection and identification in noisy image streams.

The design and implementation of Quakefinder has been driven by the need to simultaneously address three distinct problems, all of which must be solved in order to enable geophysical analysis of temporal processes from satellite data at the accuracy desired. They are 1) design of a statistical inference engine that can reliably infer the fundamental processes to acceptable precision, 2) development and implementation of scalable algorithms suitable for massive datasets, and 3) construction of an automatic and reasonably seamless system that can be used by domain scientists on a large number of datasets.

The first problem is the design of an inference engine that can infer tectonic ground motion to sub-pixel precision based upon careful comparison of consecutive images. To appreciate the technical challenge involved here, consider briefly the nature of the datasets available in this study, namely SPOT satellite images of the Landers region, taken in June 1991 and June 1992, bracketing the Landers earthquake event. The images consist of panchromatic data taken at 10-meter resolution. Now the ground displacements due to the Landers quake varied in magnitude anywhere up to 7 meters. These ground element motions constitute the fundamental "signal" that we want to mine from the data. Since all the motions are of sub-pixel magnitude, naive pixel-by-pixel change detection methods will fail to extract the events correctly. A careful machine learning technique is required to ensure that reasonable inferences can be drawn about ground displacement to sub-pixel precision.

A distinct, though related, problem stems from the need to map ground motions at or near single pixel resolution. To be perfectly clear, note the distinction here between the term "resolution", denoting the size of ground element associated with a piece of information, and "precision", denoting the accuracy to which this information (e.g. motion) is known. The relatively sophisticated inference methods needed to infer the motion of a single pixel must be repeated over every pixel of an entire image. For even a modest size image containing 2050×2050 pixels, this task represents a huge number of operations. Current workstation technology cannot support these CPU demands, which has led us to implement Quakefinder on massively parallel computing platforms, specifically the 256-node Cray T3D at JPL. The issues of scalable algorithm development and their implementation on scalable platforms that were confronted here are in fact quite general, and are likely to impact the great majority of future datamining efforts geared to the analysis of genuinely massive datasets. They have been investigated previously in the context of data mining and knowledge discovery in (Stolorz et al. 1995).

The third problem is the design and construction of a system architecture that can perform the various computational tasks required automatically. For problems of the scale tackled here, the various components must be linked relatively seamlessly to ensure the rapid delivery of a useful scientific product to geologists. This issue is already important in the context of ground-based analysis, It takes on even greater prominence when considered from the point of view of possible autonomous satellite applications and operations being envisaged by NASA and other agencies and corporations.

The goals of the paper are to describe the basic machine learning techniques used by Quakefinder, to outline the decomposition of these methods onto massively parallel platforms, and to describe their implementation within an overall system usable by domain scientists. We stress the interplay of all three of these components, and argue that all three are essential ingredients for any truly successful datamining system in this domain. We then discuss the results obtained by applying Quakefinder to analysis of the Landers earthquake, outline the overall successes and limitations of the technique, and present future directions that can build upon the work presented here.

Inference Engine

Basic algorithm

The purpose of the basic algorithm is to detect small systematic differences between a pair of images, which we'll call the "before" image I_1 and the "after" image I_2 respectively. This is accomplished at sub-pixel resolution by the following method, dubbed "imageodesy" by its author (Crippen 1992):

1. Match the before and after images by eye as well as possible (i.e. determine the best offsets between the two images in the horizontal and vertical directions).

2. Break the before image up into many non-overlapping templates, each consisting of, let's say, 100 x 100 pixels.

3. For each template, measure the correlation between the before template and the after template at the original position determined in step 1), and at the 24 nearest offset positions.

4. Determine the best template offset Δ_y, Δ_x from the maximum correlation value found in 3).

5. Repeat steps 3) and 4) at successively higher resolution, using bilinear interpolation, or some other interpolation scheme, to generate new templates offset by half a pixel in each direction.

The algorithm relies heavily on the use of sub-pixel image registration for its power. A schematic overview is shown in Figure 1.

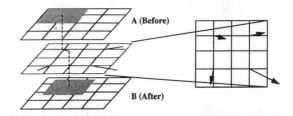

Figure 1: Schematic illustration of the use of subpixel registration to infer displacement maps between image pairs.

This basic idea is a very useful one that has been successfully applied over the years in a number of fields, especially in the context of image enhancement from undersampled image sequences (Crippen 1992; Jacquemod, Odet, & Goutte 1992; Ur & Gross 1992; Wen-Yu-Su & Kim 1994; Kim, Bose, & Valenzuela 1990). Typically, it has been used to automatically account for global effects relating successive images of the same "scene" in an image stream, namely transformations such as translation, rotation and scale changes. We apply the concept here with a highly unusual twist, in that many independent local sub-pixel registrations are performed to uncover the signal of interest, rather than a single global registration.

Probabilistic interpretation

The fundamental imageodesy algorithm can easily be formulated as a maximum likelihood technique. Begin with the notion of a simple 2-point correlation function relating an $N \times N$ template in image 1, centered at pixel location (x, y), to an $N \times N$ template in image 2, centered at pixel location $(x + \Delta_x, y + \Delta_y)$:

$$C(x, y, x + \Delta_x, y + \Delta_y) =$$
$$\frac{1}{N} \sum_i \sum_j I_1(i, j) I_2(i + \Delta_y, j + \Delta_x) - \overline{I_1}\,\overline{I_2} \quad (1)$$

where i and j label the rows and columns of each temp The offset parameters Δ_x, Δ_y between templates in images 1 and 2, referenced to pixel location (x, y) in image 1, can be intepreted as model parameters to be determined. Now define the probability of observing images I_1 and I_2 (the data) as

$$P(I_1, I_2 | x, y, \Delta_x, \Delta_y) =$$
$$e^{C(x,y,x+\Delta_x,y+\Delta_y)} / \sum_{\Delta_x, \Delta_y} e^{C(x,y,x+\Delta_x,y+\Delta_y)} \quad (2)$$

The maximum likelihood estimate for the displacement between images 1 and 2 occurring at pixel location x, y is then given by

$$argmax_{\Delta_x, \Delta_y} P(I_1, I_2 | x, y, \Delta_x, \Delta_y) \quad (3)$$

Imageodesy proceeds by repeating this calculation for a number of disjoint reference templates in image 1, generating a vector field of inferred displacements Δ_x, Δ_y at all template centers x, y.

Generalization to Large-scale Problems

In order to build an area-mapped method applicable to measurement of tectonic activity, we need to improve upon the basic imageodesy method in several different ways:

- Increase the vector field resolution by at least two orders of magnitude, from disjoint templates containing thousands of pixels down to the single pixel level if possible.

- Speed up the basic calculation by at least two orders of magnitude. This is essential if we are to perform vector field computations at or near single pixel resolution in a reasonable time frame.

- Generalize to a more powerful adaptive approach that can improve upon the precision of naive maximum likelihood.

The Quakefinder system achieves these goals by a combination of machine learning and parallel processing methods, providing a fast, reliable, high-precision change analyzer able to measure earthquake fault activity to high resolution. Quakefinder can also be adapted to a range of related problems involving image understanding of temporal processes within remote sensing imagery. The central modification to the inference engine required to accomplish this goal is the insertion of an adaptive learning component to the fault detection software. We outline this modification below.

Adaptive Learning of Earthquake Fault Location and Displacement

The one-shot calculation of fault location and displacement magnitudes provided by the maximum likelihood method is not sufficient to guarantee the accuracy required to reliably measure and predict fault activity. We have solved this problem by embedding the basic maximum likelihood approach within a bootstrapping framework very similar in spirit and approach to the classic EM algorithm for adaptive learning (Dempster, Laird, & Rubin 1977). The EM algorithm has become an extremely popular workhorse in the recent past because of several attractive computational properties, and because it can be interpreted in terms of other fundamental ideas drawn from domains such as statistical physics (Yuille, Stolorz, & Utans 1994).

The approach is motivated by the following line of reasoning. The basic imageodesy method described above is able to roughly locate the position of a fault using maximum likelihood, i.e. with no prior biases for the displacement parameters (within a predefined range), but with a fixed prior template size and shape. The method is a good first approximation when the original templates chosen correspond roughly to the size of "coherent" ground motions in tectonic events. The key to generalizing the approach is to interpret the various template size and shape parameters, denoted by T_{xy}, as unobserved variables that must be iteratively recomputed, with closed form probabilistic expressions for $P(I_1, I_2 | x, y, \Delta_x, \Delta_y)$ available to be maximized with respect to Δ_x, Δ_y once the T_{xy} are specified.

More precisely, given a simple initial guess for template sizes and shapes as uniformly $N \times N$ squares throughout an image, this estimate is easily refined based on the results of the first maximum likelihood iteration, leading to a standard EM-style iterative procedure:

- Locate the estimated fault based on the displacement map inferred in the first ML iteration.

- Redefine in the obvious way the sizes and shapes of all those templates that overlap the estimated fault (E-step).

- Recompute displacement map based on application of ML with updated template parameters (M-step).

Quakefinder Architecture

The architecture of the Quakefinder system is shown in Figure 2. The first step is application of the basic imageodesy method on a Cray T3D to detect the fundamental earthquake signal. This step generates a

The QUAKEFINDER System

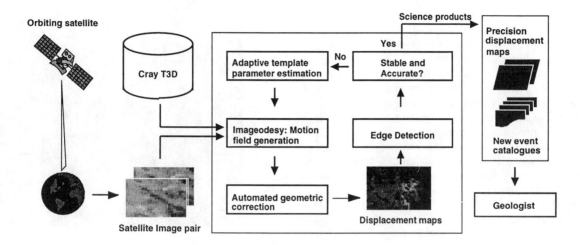

Figure 2: Architecture of the Quakefinder detection and measurement system

vector field of inferred ground motions from a pair of satellite images. The vector field is then passed to a geometric correction module which automatically corrects for spacecraft artifacts. Upon correction, the resulting displacement map is inspected by geologists for evidence of tectonic activity, with faults being mapped and measured. This information is fed in turn into a further adaptive learning component, described above, in order to refine the fault location and magnitude. This iterative procedure is terminated when sufficient accuracy is obtained. The resulting fault outlines are then registered in a catalog as important events.

Geometric corrections

A correction module is necessary because the original computed displacement field does not in general represent directly the ground motion itself. There are typically systematic effects due to slight differences in spacecraft trajectories. They consist primarily of differences in the yaw, pitch and roll of the spacecraft for each trajectory, as well as small differences in orbital height above the target region. These artifacts can be removed straightforwardly, since they appear as well-parametrized global corrections across the entire displacement vector field. A simplex-based optimization package was used to compute the optimal set of parameters characterizing these corrections. This post-processing component has trivial time complexity compared to the displacement field computation itself, and can easily be implemented automatically on workstations instead of a parallel machine.

There are second order corrections which must in principal be accounted for as well. For example, sun angle and view angle differences can introduce spurious

differences between scenes. For the Landers data considered here, these problems are negligible since 1) the images were collected almost exactly one year apart, 2) the SPOT satellite is in sun-synchronous orbit, so time-of-day matches are not a problem, and 3) very similar orbital trajectories were achieved. Radiometric differences are also possible due to vegetation a growth and other events. These are in fact often interesting processes in themselves, although they interfere with the specific task of measuring fault motion. For the desert datasets used here, they are not a major factor in any case. Yaw, pitch and roll can also all vary during a spacecraft overflight of a selected target. Again, this turns out to be a negligible effect for our problem.

Scalable Decomposition on Massively Parallel Processors

The core computation in our approach is that of ground motion inference for a given image pixel. On machines of the workstation class, several hundred such ground motion vectors can be calculated in a matter of days. However, when area-based maps of ground motion are required, workstations are no longer sufficient. For example, for even relatively small images of 2000×2000 pixels, 4 million vectors must now be computed, raising the computational demands by 4 orders of magnitude. The resulting calculation is not accessible to workstations in any reasonable time frame. We have therefore chosen to implement Quakefinder on a 256-node Cray T3D at JPL. The T3D is a massively parallel distributed memory architecture consisting of 256 computing nodes, each based on a DEC Alpha processor running at 150MHz. The nodes are arranged as 3-dimensional tori, allowing each node to communicate directly with up to 6 neighboring nodes of the machine.

MIMD parallel architectures such as the T3D turn out to be ideal architectures on which to implement many image analysis algorithms, including Quakefinder. The best decomposition consists of simply assigning different spatial portions of each image to different nodes of the machine. The vast majority of the calculation can then proceed independently on each node, with very limited communication. This results in a highly efficient parallel algorithm.

A small amount of communication does of course need to be performed periodically. The storage required for some templates will occasionally overlap boundaries between nodes. A standard technique in parallel decomposition handles this problem by tolerating a small amount of memory redundancy. Each node is simply assigned a slightly larger area of the image at the start of the calculation to allow for these overlaps. The overhead required is very small. Thereafter the calculation can proceed entirely in parallel.

Results for the Landers earthquake

We have obtained the following results from applying Quakefinder to SPOT data bracketing the Landers earthquake of June 22, 1992. The images are 2050×2050 pixels in size covering a 400 square kilometer region of the Southern California desert near the town of Landers. The differences between the two images are extremely subtle and are essentially impossible to detect by eye. Ground motion directions calculated for the Landers quake of June 22, 1992 are shown in Figure 3, superimposed on the 1991 panchromatic SPOT image. The major grey-scale discontinuity along the main diagonal of the map. This is the position of the fault break inferred automatically by Quakefinder with no supervised scientific input, based purely on the two raw before and after SPOT images. The black line is ground truth, the known fault location.

The black line represents ground truth superimposed on the computed image to assess its accuracy. It has been determined by extensive field analysis. Note that the major hue discontinuity corresponds very well to the true fault position, including the bends and steps separating the Emerson fault from the Homestead Valley fault. The general motions are right-lateral, as expected. The motion along the SW block appears to have a north to west trend change as the fault trend itself changes from northerly to more westerly. Thus, the motion tends to parallel the fault, as expected. These observations confirm the value of our approach as an efficient method for automatically detecting and measuring the position of known faults.

The area-mapped nature of the products generated by Quakefinder offer an even more interesting capability, namely discovery of entirely new behavior. In the Landers case, it yields suggestive evidence associated with the NE block of the image. This block seems to have two sub-blocks, with relative left-lateral mo-

Figure 3: Preliminary results for displacement map of the 1992 Landers earthquake. A grey-scale wheel shown at lower left encodes the direction of motion of each ground element due to the earthquake, inferred by comparison of two SPOT images. The displacement map is superimposed upon the first (1991) SPOT image to show the main topographic features. Note the correspondence of the direction discontinuities to right-lateral main fault breaks (black lines). Blocks northeast of the main breaks indicate left-lateral warpage above a buried conjugate fault, consistent with the seismic pattern. These results give us high confidence in the accuracy of the method as a general area-based mapping technique for seismic activity. A full color image of this map can be found at http://www-aig.jpl.nasa.gov/mls/quakefinder

tions between them, suggesting a surface or perhaps sub-surface fault conjugate to the main break. Efforts are currently underway to refine this prediction and to confirm it via field studies. Note that alternative technological approaches cannot easily supply this type of knowledge, if at all. Interferometric SAR can measure small ground displacements in one dimension, along a line perpendicular to the spacecraft trajectory, but cannot supply a full 2D map of motions. Movable seismic detectors located by GPS technology can measure full 3D motion quite precisely, but only at a limited number of individual locations. For these reasons, much of the information displayed in Figure 3 has never before been obtained.

Why did Quakefinder work?

A number of ingredients contributed to the success of Quakefinder as a data mining tool. To begin with, it was based upon an integrated combination of techniques drawn from statistical inference, massively parallel computing and global optimization. Secondly, scientists were able to provide a concise description of the fundamental signal recovery problem. Thirdly, resulting tasks based upon statistical inference were straightforward to automate and parallelize on scalable platforms, while still ensuring accuracy. The issues of scalable algorithm development and their implementation on scalable platforms that were addressed here are in fact quite general, and are likely to impact the great majority of future datamining efforts Finally, the relatively small portions of the overall task that were not so easily automated, such as careful measurement of fault location based on a computer-generated displacement map, are accomplished very quickly and accurately by humans in an interactive environment and did not pose an enormous bottleneck for the system.

Conclusions and Future Directions

A number of future data mining investigations are suggested by this work. One obvious one is its extension to the continuous domain, measuring very slowly-varying processes instead of abrupt events. This will require the systematic incorporation of scalable I/O resources to allow the rapid ingestion and processing of continuous image streams. The generality of the basic approach indicates that it will also prove scalable as detector and satellite resolutions improve. For example, plans are now underway for the development and deployment of satellites with 1 meter resolution or better. Extensions of Quakefinder will enable physical processes on the scale of centimeters to be straightforwardly detected and measured automatically, opening new avenues of geophysical analysis from satellite images.

The success of the fundamental technique used here has also created another problem, namely the need to register and catalogue the resulting scientific events systematically, rather than simply scattering them amongst flat files. The point here is that the events inferred by Quakefinder can be used as content-based indices to exploration of related remote-sensing datasets, such as Landsat, Synthetic Aperture Radar, and hyperspectral data. The Conquest/Oasis project begin undertaken as a collaboration between JPL and UCLA is an example of a distributed querying and analysis environment that can potentially exploit spatio-temporal events of the type inferred here (Stolorz et al. 1995).

The Quakefinder system addressed a definite scientific need, as there was previously no area-mapped information about 2D tectonic processes available at this level of detail. In addition to automatically measuring known faults, the system also performed knowledge discovery by indicating novel unexplained tectonic activity away from the primary faults that has never before been observed. It shows dramatically the power of a datamining engine that tackles well-posed scientific problems with a coordinated interdisciplinary approach. There are several other areas that can clearly benefit from the application of datamin-

ing techniques such as this, for example global climate change and natural hazard monitoring, One particularly intriguing prospect is the idea of performing monitoring tasks completely autonomously from largely self-directed spacecraft. This is a serious possibility for studies such as plate tectonics, because it is clear that almost no external information is needed to perform the most important geometric corrections.

Acknowledgements

The research described in this paper was performed on a Cray T3D supercomputer at the Jet Propulsion Laboratory, California Institute of Technology, under a contract with the National Aeronautics and Space Administration. It is a pleasure to acknowledge our colleauges R. Crippen and R. Blom at JPL, who conceived and implemented the original imageodesy algorithm from which Quakefinder is derived, and who provided the SPOT data, geological domain knowledge and numerous insights during the course of this work.

References

Crippen, R. 1992. Measurement of subresolution terrain displacements using SPOT panchromatic imagery. *Episodes* 15:56–61.

Dempster, A.; Laird, N.; and Rubin, D. 1977. Maximum Likelihood from Incomplete data via the EM Algorithm. *J. Roy. Stat. Soc. B* 39:1–38.

Fayyad, U.; Weir, N.; and Djorgovski, S. 1993. Skicat: A machine learning system for the automated cataloging of large-scale sky surveys. In *Proc. of the Tenth International Conference on Machine Learning*, 112–119.

Jacquemod, G.; Odet, C.; and Goutte, R. 1992. Image resolution enhancement using subpixel camera displacement. *Signal Processing* 26:139–146.

Kim, S. P.; Bose, N. K.; and Valenzuela, H. M. 1990. Recursive Reconstruction of High Resolution Image From Noisy Undersampled Multiframes. *IEEE Trans. Acoust. Speech and Sig. Proc.* 38:1013–1027.

Stolorz et al., P. 1995. Fast Spatio-Temporal Data Mining of Large Geophysical Datasets. In *Proceedings of the 1st International Conference on Knowledge Discovery and Data Mining, Montreal, Canada*, 300–305.

Ur, H., and Gross, D. 1992. Improved Resolution from Subpixel Shifted Pictures. *Graphical Models and Image Processing* 54:181–186.

Wen-Yu-Su, and Kim, S. P. 1994. High-Resolution Restoration of Dynamic Image Sequences. *Int. J. Imag. Syst. and Tech.* 5:330–339.

Yuille, A. L.; Stolorz, P. E.; and Utans, J. 1994. Statistical Physics, Mixtures of Distributions and the EM Algorithm. *Neural. Comp.* 6:332–338.

Extensibility in data mining systems

Stefan Wrobel and **Dietrich Wettschereck** and **Edgar Sommer** and **Werner Emde**

GMD, FIT.KI
(Institute of Applied Information Technology, Artificial Intelligence Research Division)
Schloß Birlinghoven, 53754 Sankt Augustin, Germany
E-Mail stefan.wrobel@gmd.de

Abstract

The successful application of data mining techniques ideally requires both system support for the entire knowledge discovery process *and* the right analysis algorithms for the particular task at hand. While there are a number of successful data mining systems that support the entire mining process, they usually are limited to a fixed selection of analysis algorithms. In this paper, we argue in favor of extensibility as a key feature of data mining systems, and discuss the requirements that this entails for system architecture. We identify in which points existing data mining systems fail to meet these requirements, and then describe a new integration architecture for data mining systems that addresses these problems based on the concept of "plug-ins". KEPLER, our data mining system built according to this architecture, is presented and discussed.

Keywords: data mining, system architecture, extensibility, KEPLER

Introduction

Data Mining, or *Knowledge Discovery in Databases* (KDD) aims at finding novel, interesting, and useful information in large real-world datasets (Frawley, Piatetsky-Shapiro, & Matheus 1991; Fayyad, Piatetsky-Shapiro, & Smyth 1996). While building on parent disciplines such as Machine Learning and statistics, the field of data mining differs from these in its stronger orientation to applications on real-world databases. In Machine Learning and statistics, the focus of research tends to be mostly on the *methods* for data analysis, whereas in data mining, the *process* of using such methods to arrive at convincing application results is just as important a topic[1]. For data mining to be successful in practice, good system support for the data mining process can be just as crucial as having the right analysis methods.

Data mining researchers have responded to this challenge by creating data mining systems that combine support for all steps of the data mining process (Fayyad, Piatetsky-Shapiro, & Smyth 1996, p. 10) with a fixed selection of analysis algorithms in one integrated environment. ISL's Clementine (Integral Solutions Ltd. 1996) and Lockheed's Recon (Simoudis, Livezey, & Kerber 1996) are two commercially

---

[1] In fact, some authors reserve the term KDD to denote the entire process, whereas data mining is used to refer to a single analysis step (Fayyad, Piatetsky-Shapiro, & Smyth 1996).

available examples of such systems, the former offering decision trees and neural networks, the latter also including clustering and instance-based algorithms. At the same time, however, with more and more reported applications of data mining, it is becoming increasingly clear that there can never be a fixed arsenal of data mining analysis methods that covers all problems and tasks. New methods are continually becoming available, and in many cases, algorithms are adapted or newly developed specifically for the requirements of a particular application (see e.g. (Apte & Hong 1996; Ezawa & Norton 1995)).

In this paper, we examine *extensibility*, i.e., the capability of integrating new analysis methods with as little effort as possible, as a central requirement for data mining systems to address the above problem. In the following section, we motivate the need for extensiblity with reference to the dynamic nature of the data mining process, and examine the shortcomings of existing data mining architectures in light of extensibility requirements. We then show how an architecture based on the concept of "plug-ins" can overcome these problems, and describe KEPLER, an integrated data mining system developed and implemented as a testbed for our architectural concepts. After an evaluation and discussion of related work, we conclude with pointers to future work.

Motivation and goals of extensibility

Conducting KDD in a given database or set of databases is still an art, perhaps even more so than in KDD's parent disciplines machine learning and statistics. Even in the unlikely situation that there are clear-cut goals at the outset, it is impossible even for a skilled analyst to predict just which analysis method will give the best results. More likely, the goals of data mining will not be clear beforehand, but will evolve as a result of the data mining process. In practice, this means that in many situations, several methods are tried and their results compared or combined to get the desired results. In some situations, algorithms have actually been adapted or developed for a particular application (see e.g. (Apte & Hong 1996; Ezawa & Norton 1995)).

When single-strategy data mining systems are employed, the above means that in many cases, analysts will have to switch from one system to another during the course of working on one data mining problem, incurring all the trivial but extremely time-consuming problems of adapting to different user interfaces and converting data and results back and forth. While existing multi-strategy systems like RECON (Simoudis, Livezey, & Kerber 1996) or CLEMENTINE (Integral Solutions Ltd. 1996) alleviate this problem somewhat by offering multiple analysis algorithms (see related work section below), they still offer a fixed choice of algorithms, leaving the unsolved problem of what to do if the necessary method happens not to be included. Only an *extensible* system architecture can solve this problem in a fundamental way, allowing new methods to be added to the system whenever required.

Of course, in a trivial way, every system is extensible by reprogramming the system to implement a desired method, so we need to be more precise in the meaning of extensibility. An extensible system is a system into which new methods can be integrated without knowledge of system internals and without reprogramming of the system kernel, by people other than the system developers. If a system is extensible in this fashion, different users can extend the system to match the requirements of individual data mining problems. In practice, even though end users will not be able to perform such extensions since some configuration and programming will be required, the concept of extensibility is important for skilled analysts who can integrate new methods without having to switch systems, or for algorithm developers who can make their methods available to end users without having to develop a complete data mining system.

Finally, for extensibility to make sense, it is not sufficient to integrate new methods each with their own user interfaces and different ways of starting tasks and looking at results. Instead, the data mining kernel system must offer mechanisms that allow the user to manage, in a uniform way, the specification of analysis tasks and inspection of results of the different methods. Tasks and results must be first-class objects in the system kernel to allow the user to restart and modify tasks and to compare and combine results. Without integrated and uniform access to the tasks and results of new methods, a lot of the benefits of extensibility for the data mining process are lost: if each new extension has different ways of managing tasks and results, switching methods also means switching to a different user interface, resulting in an unnecessarily high learning overhead for the user.

Architecture

Within multi-strategy tool architectures, a popular distinction is to separate approaches that integrate at the *micro level* and those that integrate at the *macro level* (Emde *et al.* 1993). In macro level integration, each method to be integrated remains a separate module with its own internal representations and storage structures, but is coupled to other modules by receiving inputs and passing results back across a suitable channel. In micro-level integration, all modules directly rely on a common repository of data without transformation, and cooperate during processing, not only when they have finished. Multi-strategy data mining systems have so far mostly been realized by macro-level integration, e.g. in Recon (Simoudis, Livezey, & Kerber

1996) where several modules are linked to a data server. Micro-level integration is only beginning to be attempted, e.g. in the KESO project, where all search modules use a common hypothesis space manager and can share description generation operators (Wrobel *et al.* 1996).

Clearly, it is difficult to make a micro-level integration architecture extensible in the sense defined above, since to integrate a new method, the internals of existing methods and the system kernel must be known. The architecture we have chosen is therefore based on macro-level integration. Each tool that is part of the system is an independent software module and can be realized e.g. in different programming languages. To reach the extensibility goal defined above, we have extended the macro-level integration architecture into the *plug-in* architecture shown in Figure 1.

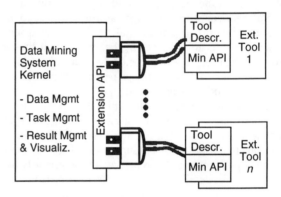

Figure 1: General plug-in architecture

The major components to realize extensibility in this architecture are the following:

- a well-defined and open extension API (application programming interface) through which extensions access data and communicate results back to the system
- declarative extension tool description containing information about the data accepted and needed by an analysis tool and the kinds of results produced
- a task and result manager that offers uniform access to tasks and results (specification, manipulation, visualization), exploiting the declarative specifications in tools
- a minimal tool API which the kernel uses to perform tool-specific functions

The extension API is the basic component towards reaching extensibility. This API must offer hooks for extension tools to access the data in the database and to communicate results back to the system. By making the definition of this API precise and open, it can be ensured that the developer of an extension need only know the API; the internals of the kernel system can be encapsulated. In domains such as image manipulation, this concept of open APIs has led to very simple and extensible systems (this is where we have borrowed the term "plug-in").

As detailed above, however, the situation in data mining is more complex since not only does the "plug-in" need to access data and return results, but the kernel also needs to provide uniform access to the tasks and results being worked on by extensions. Since the tasks of data mining methods vary widely, ranging from classification to clustering to pattern discovery and further, there needs to be a facility with which each extension can declare the required inputs and kind of results. Furthermore, since result types also vary greatly, the extension must be able to declare in which way its results need to be visualized, choosing from the available visualization facilities in the kernel. Alternatively, the API can include visualization operations as well.

Third, the proposed architecture contains a task and result manager that makes use of the declarative information described above to ensure uniform access to tools, whether they be included with the system from the start or added later on. Ideally, based on the declarative specification in the extension, the kernel should be capable of dynamically generating an appropriate graphical user interface to allow the same comfort of usage for all tools. Tasks specifications and results are managed by the analysis task manager, allowing the user to redo and modify each task, check and interrupt tasks that are running (perhaps in parallel), and inspect, test and compare results.

Note that in general, results will not be interpretable to the task manager. This is why in such an architecture, there must be a fourth component, a minimal tool API containing functions that each tool must supply to the kernel. Besides the analysis functionality proper, each tool primarily has to offer hooks for dealing with its results, ranging from simple things like producing printed output to hooks for testing and visualizing results. To simplify this functionality, the kernel's API should include libraries of common testing and visualization functions (e.g. for common results such as decision trees).

The rest of the plug-in architecture contains the standard components that are found in most data mining systems, namely facilities for importing, exporting, selecting, and transforming data.

Kepler

At a general level, the architecture described in the preceding section contains the components that are necessary to make extensibility work: with knowledge of only the API and the tool declaration language, an extension developer can produce a tool that can be plugged in and will be fully supported by the kernel — provided that such APIs (i.e., declarations and facilities) can be designed in such a way and still support more than a narrow class of plug-in tools. We have constructed and fully implemented a data mining system termed KEPLER[2] to prove the feasibility of the proposed architecture. Given the data mining applications we are working on (market study data, 10^4 objects, ecological system analysis, 10^5 objects, protein structure prediction (Dzeroski *et al.* 1996), 10^4 objects), we decided to target KEPLER to medium-range data mining problems (10^4 to 10^6 objects). Our choice was also motivated by the fact that many other published data-mining applications fall into this

class (e.g. (Apte & Hong 1996) 10^4, (Dvzeroski & Grbović 1995) 10^3, (Feelders, le Loux, & van't Zand 1995) 10^5 objects, (Li & Biswas 1995) 10^5, (Sanjeev & Zytkow 1995) 10^3, (Simoudis, Livezey, & Kerber 1995) 10^6), and by the fact that this application size, there exists a number of available ML and KDD algorithms (from our own group and others) that could be used to test the feasibility of the plug-in concept.

KEPLER's general architecture is based on the concept of a *workspace* that stores all data, tasks, and results of a data mining problem domain. Data are represented as relations (with associated key and schema information) and can be organized in different *datasets* (subsets of relations). Tuples are stored in a *data management layer* which is currently mapped to a main memory based storage scheme with disk write-through to compiled files, opening the posibilility of "swapping out" currently unused data. For the target application size, this has turned out to be a good choice. Nonetheless, in future versions of the kernel, the data management layer will map down to a database management system to gain scalability and security.

The extension API of Kepler contains only the elementary calls that are necessary for extensions to access data on a set-oriented or tuple-oriented basis, and to pass back results. When called, each extension receives a *data specification* that it passes back to the kernel whenever it wants to access data; the kernel then maps this to the actual data. This scheme protects extensions from details of data access while still allowing reasonable efficiency since even direct read-through to a database can be realized. A second set of calls is available to pass back results to the kernel as soon as they are generated.

As a tool description language, KEPLER uses parameter and result declarations. Parameter declarations come in two types: inputs and algorithm parameters. Input parameters state what kinds of inputs a tool expects in terms of supplied primitives such as "relation name" or "attribute name" or general parameter types such as "integer", "boolean" or "oneof". These are employed by the task manager in KEPLER to automatically generate the appropriate interface masks to allow the user to specify an analysis task. Similarly, algorithm parameters state the available parameters to influence algorithm behavior, indicating the allowed values in a similar fashion by using predefined parameter types. Here also, KEPLER automatically generates input masks with radio-buttons, sliders, pop-up menus etc. to let the user specify the tool parameters. Hence, KEPLER offers a uniform interface style for all extension tools, minimizing the user's effort to become familiar with a new tool (see Figure 2, next page, for an example of a task window generated from a tool description). Through the task manager, tasks can be created, edited, started and stopped. Cross-validation and other analysis scripts will be possible in the future.

As for analysis results, each tool can declare several result types. However, currently these are only utilized for user information and help. Each extension can pass back to the system kernel as many results of each type as desired; the task manager stores them on disk and allows the user to

---

[2] KEPLER will be demonstrated at the conference.

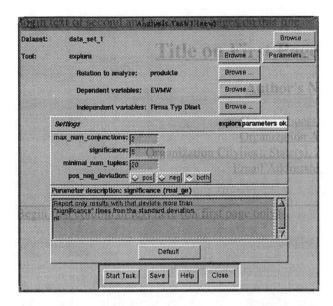

Figure 2: Task window for an EXPLORA task

select and manipulate them. It is also possible for tools to pass back a pointer to a binary results file which is from then on managed by the task manager. As indicated in the previous section, whenever a result needs to be tested on different data or needs to be visualized, the kernel calls the appropriate hooks in the extension tool which in turn can rely again on testing and visualization APIs that the kernel offers as a library.

To test the feasibility of the plug-in concept, we decided to integrate as wide a selection of plug-ins as possible, ranging not only across different methods, but also across different tasks. At first, we chose to include as plug-ins for internal use at our site:

- for classification tasks, the decision tree algorithm C4.5 in the original C version available from Ross Quinlan (Quinlan 1993), a backpropagation neural network realized using SNSS (Zell 1994), as well as our own instance-based method KNN (Wettschereck 1994) and Salzberg's NGE (Salzberg 1991; Wettschereck & Dietterich 1995)).

- for clustering tasks, the AUTOCLASS algorithm (Cheeseman & Stutz 1996) as available from the authors

- for regression tasks, the MARS (multiple adaptive regresssion spline) algorithm of (Friedman 1991), in our own implementation

- the pattern discovery algorithm EXPLORA (Klösgen 1996) developed at GMD (ported from Macintosh to Sun)

All of these are operational in KEPLER at present. To minimize programming overhead, all algorithms were taken as is (except for porting to other platforms as indicated) and used in a compiled form, implementing communication through files which is feasible for the chosen target application size. Summarizing this first experiment with the plug-in concept, we can state that except for reimplementation or porting efforts, the integration of an algorithm of one of the above

types or tasks into KEPLER as a plug-in takes at most one day[3], since all that is involved is the simple parameter declaration and the writing of grammars for file creation and reading.

Given this kind of encouraging evidence, we have extended the plug-in idea to other areas of the system as well. In KEPLER, the user can plug new input formats and new data transformation operators into the system in a very similar fashion. It is therefore no problem to handle applications that require e.g. an unusual aggregation of tuples, a particular re-representation of time series, or some other preprocessing operation for a particular analysis method. For example, a specific transformation (from DINUS (Džeroski, Muggleton, & Russell 1992)) is available for transforming first-order representations (across several relations) into a manageable propositional representation in one relation. These plug-ins complement the standard ASCII input formats and predefined transformation operators like sampling and discretization.

Evaluation

KEPLER has been evaluated on three data mining applications: analysis of retail data, ecological system analysis, and protein structure prediction (Dzeroski *et al.* 1996). In the retail data application (roughly 15.000 tuples), the primary goal was discovery of interesting customer groups (carried out with EXPLORA). In addition, certain customer groups were characterized using C4.5. In the ecosystem domain (roughly 120.000 tuples), the primary goal was to derive ecological conditions for the occurence of certain plants, a secondary goal being clustering of plants into ecological groups. In the protein structure application (ca. 10.000 tuples), the goal was to predict protein structure from spectography data, mostly performed using ILP techniques (Dzeroski *et al.* 1996).

In these applications, all of which required multiple tasks to be solved from the same pool of data, we have found our speed of turning up results to be greatly increased, since all the time usually spent in preprocessing data and changing formats when the method first chosen turns out inappropriate was eliminated. Furthermore, through the automatic generation of graphical interfaces for plug-in tools, even relative newcomers to data analysis (students) produce first results fast. Thus, from an application perspective, KEPLER has reached its goals of offering multiple tools in an integrated, easy-to-use environment.

From the development perspective, in our view, KEPLER has shown that indeed it is possible to realize an extensible data mining system architecture based on the idea of plug-ins. For ourselves as system developers, the concept has resulted in integration times in the order of hours, meaning that new methods (once they are available) can be integrated very fast, resulting in a choice of methods in one system that even with the set of methods described above appears unmatched in any other system.

---

[3]Not including the time it takes to get to know the extension algorithm.

The limits of the present design are in scalability due to the way tools are integrated. To allow this kind of extremely rapid integration, we have used existing code (our own and code made available by others) unchanged, using operating-system level file communication. For the kinds of dataset sizes for which KEPLER is targeted, this has turned out appropriate; it will not, however, scale well much beyond 10^6 objects. To go to these scales would require algorithms to be rewritten to use the kernel's data access facilities directly. When looking at our own and published applications, however, a large number of problems seem to fall in the size range below 10^6 objects.

Related Work

The architectural concepts used here are most closely related to the idea of "external tools" that was realized in the MOBAL knowledge acquisition system (Morik *et al.* 1993; Emde *et al.* 1993). In MOBAL, a number of ILP learning algorithms could be used from within the same graphical environment. However, compared to KEPLER and the general architecture discussed here, MOBAL is lacking in important respects. Analysis tasks and results are not first class objects in MOBAL, making it very difficult for the user to keep track of what was done when and with which tool. Runs cannot be repeated. There is no declarative tool description and no general way of passing inputs and storing results, since it is implicitly assumed that all algorithms are ILP algorithms that always take the entire database as input and always produce first-order Horn clauses as output.

At the general level of multistrategy data mining, there are several tools which can be usefully compared to the work presented here. For commercial tools, there is ISL's CLEMENTINE system (Integral Solutions Ltd. 1996), integrating decision trees and neural networks. This system offers an excellent user interface, but appears limited to classification and clustering tasks. Lockheed's Recon system (Simoudis, Livezey, & Kerber 1996) addresses a wider range of problems, including also instance based methods. Both systems, however, seem to lack the extensibility that characterizes the architecture presented here, and seem to require kernel reprogramming to add new algorithms. Thinking Machine's Darwin system (Thinking Machines Corp. 1996) appears to be more a collection of tools than an integrated system.

Among other multi-strategy systems, there is DBMINER (previously DBLEARN) (Han *et al.* 1992; Han & Fu 1996) which discovers multiple kinds of knowledge, but is based on a single attribute-oriented discovery methods and is not extensible. MLC++ (Kohavi *et al.* 1994) is a collection of C++ programs designed to be configured by a user into a working Machine learning algorithm. Since the source code is available, MLC++ is an extensible system. Extensibility, however, is achieved purely at the programming and algorithm level, as MLC++ is a more a library than a system, not offering the system kernel and user interface support discussed here. The INLEN system (Michalski 1992; Ribeiro, Kaufman, & Kerschberg 1995) is related to the work presented here since it also conceptualizes data man-

agement and analysis as operators, however without a focus on extensibility and closely tied to AQ and related methods. Similarly, GLS (Zhong & Ohsuga 1995), is a multi-strategy system with four fixed analysis methods without extension facilities.

Finally, a useful comparison is with the architectural concepts of the KESO data mining project in which we are also involved (Wrobel *et al.* 1996). In KESO, the very explicit goal at the outset was to create a data mining system capable of handling the very large scale problems ($>>10^6$ objects). Consequently, a macro-level integration as was used in KEPLER was excluded, as it would not have offered the required efficiency. Instead, KESO uses a micro-level integration architecture based on a common hypothesis space manager that maintains a persistent representation of the search space in a database. Different search modules can share subcomponents like the description generator (refinement operator). Since KESO is designed for a particular class of problems (finding interesting subgroups) and extreme efficiency, extensibility across wide task ranges was not of concern. Extending KESO requires reexpressing an algorithm in KESO's framework, but of course (these are the benefits of rewriting and micro-level integration) the newly written search module may use e.g. facilities used in the construction of other methods, like the description generator or a quality computation module.

Conclusion

Based on our own experience and other reported applications, we believe extensibility to be a key feature of any data mining system to keep up with the variability of data mining tasks which does not allow to design a system once and for all that has the right methods for all situations. The key to extensibility is extensibility without system core reprogramming, which allows third parties other than developers to extend a system in their direction without knowing the system's internals. This requires carefully designed extension APIs and declarative tool descriptions so that the kernel may support extensions tools in the same fashion as possible in non-extensible systems. Due to the variety of methods and tasks that could be present in an extensible system, a task manager is a central component of such a system.

With KEPLER, we have realized an extensible system that offers a very wide range of methods and tasks for medium sized data mining problems. The experience of integrating all these different methods shows that the KEPLER's plug-in architecture indeed is a basis for a very rapid extension of the system that does not require kernel reprogramming. Even though we have not proved it in implementation, we nonetheless believe that the plug-in concept can be scaled up to even larger problems with some more effort in designing tool interfaces. Our own future work may move into this direction, but most likely will first concentrate on integrating more extension tools and further refining the system in other applications than the ones it was already tested on. For the distant future, we hope to have the system in a state that allows us to make it available to others and to publish the API specification. This would give developers of new data mining algorithms a simple platform for delivering their methods to uses without having to worry about user interfaces or data access.

References

Apte, C., and Hong, S. 1996. Predicting equity returns from securities data. chapter 22, 542 – 560. In (Fayyad *et al.* 1996).

Cheeseman, P., and Stutz, J. 1996. Bayesian classification (AutoClass): Theory and results. chapter 6, 153 – 180. In (Fayyad *et al.* 1996).

Džeroski, S., and Grbović, J. 1995. Knowledge discovery in a water quality database. 81 – 86. In (Fayyad & Uthurusamy 1995).

Džeroski, S.; Muggleton, S.; and Russell, S. 1992. PAC-learnability of determinate logic programs. In *Proc. 5th ACM Workshop on Comput. Learning Theory*, 128–135.

Dzeroski, S.; Schulze-Kremer, S.; Heidtke, K.; Siems, K.; and Wettschereck, D. 1996. Knowledge discovery for diterpene structure elucidation from 13C NMR spectra. Proc. ECAI-96 workshop on Intelligent Data Analysis for Medicine and Pharmacology.

Emde, W.; Kietz, J.-U.; Sommer, E.; and Wrobel, S. 1993. Cooperation between internal and external learning modules in mobal: different facets of multistrategy learning. MLnet workshop on multistrategy learning, Blanes, Spain.

Ezawa, K., and Norton, S. W. 1995. Knowledge discovery in telecommunications services data using bayesian network models. 100 – 105. In (Fayyad & Uthurusamy 1995).

Fayyad, U., and Uthurusamy, R., eds. 1995. *Proc. First Int. Conf. on Knowledge Discovery and Data Mining*. Menlo Park, CA: AAAI Press.

Fayyad, U.; Piatetsky-Shapiro, G.; Smyth, P.; and Uthurusamy, R., eds. 1996. *Advances in Knowledge Discovery and Data Mining*. Cambridge, USA: AAAI/MIT Press.

Fayyad, U.; Piatetsky-Shapiro, G.; and Smyth, P. 1996. From data mining to knowledge discovery: An overview. chapter 1, 1 – 34. In (Fayyad *et al.* 1996).

Feelders, A.; le Loux, A.; and van't Zand, J. 1995. Data mining for loan evaluation at ABN AMRO: a case study. 106 – 111,. In (Fayyad & Uthurusamy 1995).

Frawley, W.; Piatetsky-Shapiro, G.; and Matheus, C. 1991. Knowledge discovery in databases: An overview. In Piatetsky-Shapiro, G., and Frawley, W., eds., *Knowledge Discovery in Databases*. Cambridge, USA: AAAI/MIT Press. chapter 1, 1 – 27.

Friedman, J. 1991. Multivariate adaptive regression splines (with discussion). *Annals of Statistics* 19(1):1–141.

Han, J., and Fu, Y. 1996. Exploration of the power of attribute-oriented induction in data mining. chapter 16, 399 – 421. In (Fayyad *et al.* 1996).

Han, J.; Cai, Y.; Cercone, N.; and Huang, Y. 1992. DBLEARN: A knowledge discovery system for databases. In *Proc. 1st Int. Conf. Inf. & Knowl. Managmt.*, 473 – 481.

Integral Solutions Ltd. 1996. Clementine data mining system: Decisions from data. WWW http://www.isl.co.uk.

Klösgen, W. 1996. Explora: A multipattern and multi-strategy discovery assistant. chapter 10, 249 – 271. In (Fayyad *et al.* 1996).

Kohavi, R.; John, G.; Long, R.; Manley, D.; and Pfleger, K. 1994. MLC++: A machine learning library in C++. In *Proc. Tools with Artificial Intelligence*, 740 – 743. IEEE Computer Society Press.

Li, C., and Biswas, G. 1995. Knowledge-based scientific discovery in geological databases. 204 – 210. In (Fayyad & Uthurusamy 1995).

Michalski, R. *et. al.*. 1992. Mining for knowledge in databases: The INLEN architecture, initial implementation and first results. *J. Intell. Inf. Sys.* 1(1):85 – 113.

Morik, K.; Wrobel, S.; Kietz, J.-U.; and Emde, W. 1993. *Knowledge Acquisition and Machine Learning: Theory Methods and Applications*. London: Academic Press.

Quinlan, J. R. 1993. *C4.5 — programs for machine learning*. San Mateo, CA: Morgan Kaufman.

Ribeiro, J. S.; Kaufman, K. A.; and Kerschberg, L. 1995. Knowledge discovery from multiple databases. 240 – 245. In (Fayyad & Uthurusamy 1995).

Salzberg, S. 1991. A nearest hyperrectangle learning method. *Machine Learning* 6:277–309.

Sanjeev, A., and Zytkow, J. 1995. Discovering enrollment knowledge in university databases. 246 – 251. In (Fayyad & Uthurusamy 1995).

Simoudis, E.; Livezey, B.; and Kerber, R. 1995. Using Recon for data cleaning. 282 – 287. In (Fayyad & Uthurusamy 1995).

Simoudis, E.; Livezey, B.; and Kerber, R. 1996. Integrating inductive and deductive reasoning for data mining. chapter 14, 353 – 374. In (Fayyad *et al.* 1996).

Thinking Machines Corp. 1996. Darwin: Intelligent data mining. WWW http://www.think.com.

Wettschereck, D., and Dietterich, T. 1995. An experimental comparison of the nearest-neighbor and nearest-hyperrectangle algorithms. *Machine Learning* 19:5–28.

Wettschereck, D. 1994. *A Study of Distance-Based Machine Learning Algorithms*. Ph.D. Dissertation, Oregon State University.

Wrobel, S.; Wettschereck, D.; Verkamo, A. I.; Siebes, A.; Mannila, H.; Kwakkel, F.; and Klösgen, W. 1996. User interactivity in very large scale data mining. Contact keso-develop@cwi.nl.

Zell, A. e. 1994. SNNS user manual, version 3.2. Fakultätsbericht 6/94, IPVR, Universität Stuttgart, Germany.

Zhong, N., and Ohsuga, S. 1995. Toward a multi-strategy and cooperative discovery system. 337 – 342. In (Fayyad & Uthurusamy 1995).

Mining Knowledge in Noisy Audio Data

Andrzej CZYZEWSKI

Technical University of Gdańsk, Faculty of Electronics, Sound Engineering Dept.
Narutowicza 11/12;
80-952 Gdańsk, Poland.
andrzej@next.elka.pg.gda.pl

Abstract

This paper demonstrates a KDD method applied to audio data analysis, particularly, it presents possibilities which result from replacing traditional methods of analysis and acoustic signal processing by KDD algorithms when restoring audio recordings affected by strong noise.

Introduction

Typical applications of computer technologies to audio acoustics only rarely consider the opportunities of data processing with the use of methods which stem from KDD approach. What is essential here is the fact that methods of analysis and signal processing developed on the basis of speech acoustics have not been transferred respectively so far to other related areas, e.g. as an algorithm of intelligent analysis and processing of the musical audio signal. In the meantime the area of audio acoustics has an extensive demand for applications of intelligent signal processing.

The paper demonstrates a KDD method applied to audio data analysis, which was studied at the Sound Engineering Department of the Gdańsk Technical University. Particularly, it presents possibilities which result from replacing traditional methods of analysis and acoustic signal processing by KDD algorithms when restoring audio recordings affected by strong noise.

Previously, the parallel algorithm applied to the removal of clicks has been tested (Czyzewski 1994, 1995a) and the rough set method applied to noise suppression in old audio recordings was tried (Czyzewski 1995b). A new concept of perceptual coding allowing for noise reduction in old musical recordings stemmed from a modification of KDD applications investigated previously by the author (Czyzewski 1995b, 1995c). Perceptual coding provides the way of processing audio signal in such a way that the portions of signal which are perceptible to human hearing sense are to be encoded while the remaining portions of signal or noise are to be rejected. The algorithm processes signal in subbands of the frequency scale corresponding to the critical bands of hearing. The rough set method was employed to building the knowledge base of signal and distortions in such a way that it becomes possible to automatically control the masking threshold in order to maintain the noise affecting audio signals not audible to listeners.

Details of the elaborated and tested algorithms will be presented and results of their application discussed. Some general conclusions concerning knowledge acquisition of audio signal affected by noise and distortions will be added. Potential telecommunications and multimedia applications will be quoted.

Rough set approach to mining signal and noise data

The idea of using KDD approach to the removal of continuous noise from old recordings uses the perceptual coding scheme enhanced by the intelligent decision algorithm based on the rough set method. The rule set used for the determination of thresholds for the selection of eligible components of the signal is obtained by learning from examples. Hence, the data mining process allows one to discern between signal and noise portions of the audio material. Consequently, the masking threshold level can be determined for each data frame allowing one to make the noise inaudible after the execution of the perceptual coding procedure.

Before the details of the elaborated algorithm are presented a brief introduction to the domains of rough sets and of perceptual coding of audio data will be provided.

Basic concepts of the rough set theory

The Boolean traditional logic, which is employed by computers for general use, stems from Cantor's formulation of the definition of a set and operations on sets. However, as numerous examples prove, computers which work on this basis, are not good enough to solve many practical problems which require automatic inference, especially in situations when the data being analyzed carry a certain inaccuracy or irreproducibility and when there is no possibility to create a precise enough model of the decisive process. In such cases, overcoming the axioms of Cantor's definition of sets may turn out to be of purpose and very useful. This situation obviously corresponds to the problems of discerning between signal and noise components in noisy audio patterns. Overcoming the limitations related to Cantor's definition of the set is possible by ignoring the requirement that the set boundaries have to be strictly defined, that is of a set which is precisely defined by its elements. By doing so it is possible to define the set based on its lower and upper approximations. Such a set, since it is not defined fully, may include elements which belong to it many times.

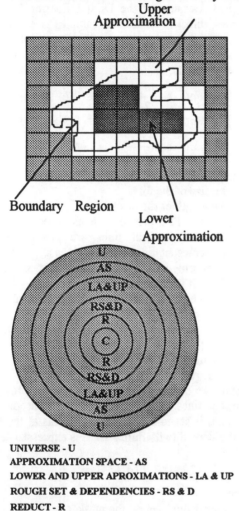

UNIVERSE - U
APPROXIMATION SPACE - AS
LOWER AND UPPER APROXIMATIONS - LA & UP
ROUGH SET & DEPENDENCIES - RS & D
REDUCT - R
CORE - C

Fig. 1. Illustration of elementary notions related to the rough set theory.

Overcoming the traditional axioms applied in the case of rough sets causes the logic based on the rough set theory to acquire completely new features which make it an extremely useful tool for solving many problems which require an intelligent data analysis, searching for hidden relationships between the data and even making the right decisions in situations when incomplete and partially contrary antecedents exist.

The fundamentals of this theory were announced by Pawlak in the early 1980's (Pawlak, 1982). The theory was quickly adopted by the scientific world and is now one of the fast developing methods of artificial intelligence (Pawlak, 1993). The main terms related to defining a rough set are illustrated schematically in Fig. 1. More detailed definitions of these terms can be found in the literature (Slowinski ed., 1992).

The knowledge is represented in a system based on rough sets in a tabular form composed of the following elements:
$$S_R = \langle U, P, D, V_P, V_D, F \rangle$$, where U is a finite set of objects, P - is a finite set of attributes, D - is a special decisive attribute determined by the expert, P is a collection of all conditional attributes in P, V_D - represents the area of decisive attributes, F - is called the knowledge function.

An inductive learning system based on rough set consists of the learning component for the automatic rule derivation from training samples and of the inference system used for decision-making at the recognition stage. Rules are expressions in the following format:

if <condition1>and<condition2>...and<condition n> then <decision>.

Conditions are based on attributes. Attributes should be equal to concrete values or should belong to certain ranges. The decision always use a single rule matching approach.

The knowledge base in rough set method can be conveniently represented in the form of a decision table, in which rows represent objects and columns represent attributes. In the last column decision attributes are collected. The main task for the learning phase (rule generation procedure) is to find the minimum number of maximum composed sets that cover the so called positive region $POS_A(S)$ providing one of the basic notions of the rough set theory (Pawlak, 1982). Consequently, two types of rules are to be derived from the decision table: certain rules and possible rules. An important parameter of possible rules, reflecting quality of them is the rough measure μ_{RS} defined as follows:

$$\mu_{RS} = \frac{|X \cap Y|}{|Y|}$$
(1)

where: X is the concept and Y is the set of all examples described by the rule.

An additional parameter was proposed by the author allowing one to optimize the rule generation process. This parameter was called the rule strength r and is defined as follows:

$$r = c(\mu_{RS} - n_\mu) \qquad (2)$$

where: c - number of cases conforming the rule,

n_μ - the neutral point of the rough measure.

The neutral point of the rough measure n_μ provides one of some parameters of the rule generation system to be set by its operator. This parameter allows one to regulate the influence of possible (uncertain) rules on the process of decision making. More details concerning the rough set concepts are to be found in the rich literature (Slowiński ed., 1992; Wojcik, 1993).

Perceptual coding algorithm

Empirical data reveal that some signals are inaudible in the presence of others both in time and in frequency domain. The level of the barely audible pure tone depends on the difference of frequencies of the signal components and the masking tone, and on the excitation level of the masker. Usually, this dependence is presented as the function of frequency in a linear scale or in a logarithmic scale (Zwicker&Zwicker 1991). It can be observed that the shape varies significantly according to frequency changes. In the literature, some attempts to calculate that shape can be found (Krolikowski, 1996).

Another well-proven phenomenon is the fact that human auditory system analyses spectrum ranges which correspond to subbands, called critical bands. The stimuli frequencies within a critical band are perceived similarly and processed independently from those of other critical bands. Because of the need to use the critical bands scale, the Bark unit for this was defined, which is of the width of one critical band. It can be observed that Bark-to-Hertz dependence can be approximated by the straight line: up to the 8th Bark in the linear frequency scale and from the 8th Bark in the logarithmic one. The above property was taken into account when converting to Bark units in the elaborated algorithm. Moreover, it turns out that masking curves assume almost an uniform shape when calculated versus Bark units. One can notice that the slopes of the curves at the lower frequencies are constant, whereas at the higher ones, the slope depends on the excitation level of the masker.

Basing on the above indications, the elaborated perceptual algorithm for the encoder performs the following operations:

Step 1. On the basis of the sampling frequency, values of frequencies for consecutive spectral lines are computed. Next, they are converted to Bark units.

Step 2. The continuous series of 16-bit samples are grouped into blocks of the length of 512 samples. This size is assumed to be a compromise between high spectral resolution (long blocks) and time resolution requirements (short blocks). Since at the borders of blocks some audible distortions may occur, so called 'block effects', thus overlapping technique with the length of the fold equals to 32 was applied.

Step 3. Because of the Digital Fourier Transform properties, blocks containing samples are windowed before the processing is made. Rectangular-cosine shaped window was used calculated according to the following formula:

$$data(i) = \begin{cases} data \cdot \sin(\frac{\pi}{2} \cdot \frac{i}{L}), & i \in \langle 0, L-1 \rangle \\ data, & i \in \langle L, N-L-1 \rangle \\ data \cdot \cos(\frac{\pi}{2} \cdot \frac{i}{L}), & i \in \langle N-L, N-1 \rangle \end{cases} \qquad (3)$$

where:
L - the size of the fold,
N - the length of the block.

Step 4. The FFT procedure is executed. Amplitudes and phases of spectral lines are calculated using complex representations. Since these values are symmetrical, only half of them is further processed. The remaining part is restored in the decoder.

Step 5. The amplitudes of spectral lines are sorted according to decreasing values of amplitude.

Step 6. Simultaneous masking procedure is executed. Spectral lines with amplitude value remaining below the masking threshold are discarded. Masking curves are represented by uniform curves. For the practical use, shapes of these curves are approximated by straight lines. The slope of the line at the lower frequencies is set to 27 dB/Bark, whereas at the higher ones, the slope S (with minus sign) is expressed as:

$$S = 22 - 0.2 \cdot I \, [\text{dB} / \text{Bark}] \qquad (4)$$

where:
I - denotes the level of the masker.

For each non-masked spectral line, there is a mask level computed, i.e. the excitation value of barely audible tone of the respective frequency.

Step 7. Within every critical band for each spectral line, the minimum mask level is chosen. This approach ensures that after the quantization of non-masked components, the quantization noise is maintained below the audible level.

Step 8. Subjective level of noise is estimated by a human listener. If its value is below the mask level in every critical band - no further actions are performed. If not, new masking thresholds are established to shift the noise below the masking level in each particular subband. This procedure is conceived as a flexible one in order to not to diminish nor to neglect eligible components within the band.

Step 9. After the perceptual processing, every spectral component is quantized or set to 0 (if masked). It would be redundant to encode masked values. Thus, only these components with non-zero magnitudes are processed. However, there is a need to know, for which frequencies spectral lines were neglected if they were. Therefore, an additional piece of information is sent, which defines whether consecutive complex components are transmitted or not. And thus, every package of data is preceded by 256 one-bit flags. If the flag is set to 0 at the kth position, it means that the magnitude and phase for the kth spectral component is not processed (the masking occurred). On the other hand, if the kth value is set to 1, it denotes that the package includes the kth complex component.

The audio samples after quantization can use from 1 to 16 bits. It would be a waste of storage capacity to utilize all 16-bit representation whereas the value can match only a part of it. Thus, it can be assumed that the number of bits used to encode these values is constant in a critical band within the time duration of several frames. In a case, when the word length changes, one needs to send only a new value for appropriate subband. Consequently, the data package is preceded by a number of one-bit flags. When the kth flag is set to 0, it means that the number of bits used to encode spectral components in the kth critical band did not change. When the flag is equal to 1, it denotes that a new number for these bits will be transmitted for the kth band. The number of one-bit flags is equal to the number of critical bands determined by the given sampling frequency.

During the masking procedure, it is evaluated the permissible noise level in each critical band. The level is used for the quantization and should be known to restore sound correctly. Thus, there is a need to store values of the levels for every subband. Fortunately, it turns out that it is essential to precede the audio package by a number of flags informing whether the noise level in consecutive critical bands changed. If so, a new 16-bit value of the level for appropriate band is transmitted. As previously, the number of the one-bit flags refer to the number of utilized critical bands.

Consequently, each 512-sample frame is stored in the format as follows:
256 of one-bit flags of non-masked spectral lines,

up to 25 of one-bit flags. They describe the change of the word length engaged to encode complex components in a critical band,
up to 25 of one-bit flags. They concern the change of permissible noise level in a critical band,
up to 25 of 4-bit values of a new value of word length used to encode spectral components in a critical band,
16-bit values of a new permissible noise level in a critical band,
values of amplitudes and phases of non-masked spectral lines. The value of phases can be encoded using 5 bits, what is recommended in the literature. Consequently, amplitude and phase of the constant complex component is encoded.

The decoder uses the above data for the additive synthesis of sound on the basis of spectral components which have been qualified as non-masked ones.

Knowledge acquisition of signal and of noise

Previously, the rough set approach to the determination of spectral components obtained in the McAulay-Quatieri analysis was tried by the author (Czyzewski 1995b, 1995c). Similar KDD procedure to the one elaborated previously was exploited in the current experiments to derive rules allowing to automatically select the optimal level of the masking threshold in the perceptual coding/filtration procedure.

The masking threshold influencing the selection of spectral components in the encoder should be updated frame by frame basing on the rule set. This rule set is to be acquired on the basis of examples processed during the learning phase. Correspondingly, three classes are to be defined: threshold low (too low), threshold medium or balanced (right) and threshold high (too high). The expressions in brackets correspond to subjective assessment of the effect of filtration. When the threshold is too low, then the noise is clearly audible. When the threshold is too high, many eligible components are removed, so the resulting sound is clean, but poor and distorted. Balanced threshold allows one to remove noise without discarding eligible signal components. As results from above indications, threshold values need to be quantized. The quantization consists in replacing real values of masking threshold by the range representations which are utilized as decision attributes (Slowiński ed., 1992). Practically, the uniform quantization was employed based on 6 dB ranges of magnitude of threshold.

Practically, the learning procedure consists in selecting some short fragments of the recording, automatically setting various threshold levels and assessing the effect subjectively when playing back those fragments after the resynthesis. Correspondingly, each sample fragment is to be represented by a set of threshold values in each critical band and the decision comes from the human expert. That is the way the knowledge base is built with regard to expert subjective assessments of individual examples. Normally, it is sufficient to choose some examples corresponding to the most characteristic fragments of the recording. Typically, up to 5 percent of the whole material should be chosen and assessed on the basis of 2 to 3 seconds portions. This produces a stream of exemplary data to be added to the relevant classes labeled as "low", "right" and too "high". Consequently, the knowledge base is build up to be applicable to the selected fragments (certainly) and to the rest of the whole recording (possibly). The generalization capabilities of KDD algorithms the rough set belongs to proved to work well also with the new patterns representing the material not employed to the training. The rule base represents knowledge acquired during the training of the algorithm. The rule set may contain rules of the following form:

$$\left(s_{k-4}(n-5) \cap s_{k-2}(n-3) \cup s_{k-3}(n-5) \cap s_{k-3}(n-4)\right) \cap \dots$$
$$\cap \left(s_{k-1}(n)=0\right) \cap \left(s_{k-1}(n-1)=0\right) \cap \left(s_{k-2}(n+1)\right)\left(s_{k-1}(n+2)=0\right) \Rightarrow \left(p=p_{\max}\right)$$

(5)

where: $T(b_k) = \{l_1, l_2, \dots, l_{16}\}$ denotes that in the frequency band No. k the threshold value is to be set to the quantized level l_i; $i \in <1,2,\dots,16>$; $k \in <1,2,\dots,24>$

Then, the magnitude of the threshold set in kth critical band is as follows:

$$L_k = 6l_i \quad \text{[dB]} \qquad (6)$$

The exemplary rules presented above are to be determined automatically through the learning from fragments of the recording, packet after packet. As each packet represents the result of FFT transform of 512 samples, thus for each 1s portion of audio sampled with the frequency 22.05 kHz as much as $22.050/512 \cong 43$ rules may be generated.

Thus, initially after typical learning procedure employing 10 or 15 s of exemplary audio material the decision table is constructed containing several hundreds of rules. Usually, such a data collection is superfluous. This feature results from the fact that musical tones duration usually exceeds single packet length. Consequently, many rules and attributes $T(b_k)$ are discarded after the rough set based reduction of the obtained decision table and the resulting knowledge base is automatically compacted. Subsequently, the acquired rule base is used for the automatic setting thresholds for all subbands and all consecutive packets of the whole recording. For the concrete combination of input data many rules are firing, some of them certain (rough measure equal to 1) and some uncertain (rough measure lower than 1) - see eq. 1. According to the rough set method principles, the decision always comes from the single firing rule being the strongest one - see eq. 2. Consequently, the spectrum filtering thresholds are to be updated according to the winning rules. Subsequently, the current packet is processed using threshold values update controlled by the rule conditional attributes. Results of processing noisy recordings with this method are presented in the next paragraph.

Results

Music affected by strong noise was used for the described experiments. The analysis-resynthesis algorithm with the "intelligent" threshold update was applied among others to an exemplary fragment of the song performed by Edith Piaf taken from a very noisy record.

After the perceptual filtration is executed, which is supported by the rough set-based control of masking threshold, the rectified signal was obtained revealing enhanced subjective quality. Results of analyses of music material made before and after the processing are presented in Fig. 2. As is seen from Fig. 2a, spectral analysis of the musical fragment reveals that signal components are accompanied by very strong noise. The noise is broadband (so called hiss) and its components are strong within the whole range of frequency (up to 1/2 sampling freq. which was equal to 22.05 kHz).

Fig. 2b presents spectral analysis of the fragment restored with the perceptual coding algorithm with not properly selected masking thresholds - some eligible signal components are weakened while the higher components of hiss remain still beyond the masking threshold. Fig. 2c presents the result of signal restoration with the perceptual coding algorithm controlled by the rule set derived from eight characteristic portions of the whole recording (time duration of each portion: 2 to 3 s).

Conclusions

KDD algorithms should find their way to more audio applications. The previously conducted experiments related to neural network implementation to the removal of impulse distortions (Czyzewski 1994, 1995a) and the presented exemplary application related to the restoration of noisy audio recordings may support this opinion. There are many potential applications of intelligent algorithms applied to the removal of noise and distortions. Some of them might be used in telecommunications and digital broadcasting, in databases and multimedia-related systems as data reduction and noise suppression techniques.

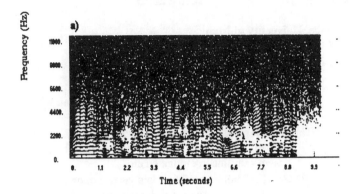

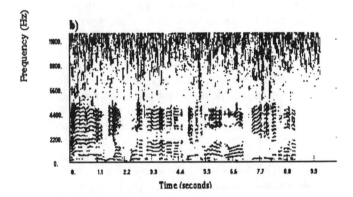

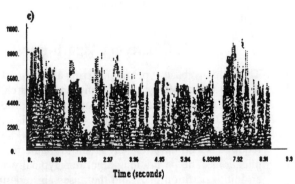

Fig. 2 Results of perceptual filtering of sound with the use of the rule base.

a./ Original fragment of an audio recording affected by strong noise,

b./ The same fragment restored with the use of insufficiently trained algorithm,

c./ Fragment as in Fig. (a) processed employing the final version of the rule set.

Acknowledgment

The presented research project was sponsored by the Committee for Scientific Research, Warsaw, Poland. Grant No. 8 T11D 002 08.

References

1. Czyzewski A. 1994, Artificial Intelligence-Based Processing of Old Audio Recordings. In Preprint of 97th Audio Engineering Society Convention. San Francisco (Preprint No. 3885).

2. Czyzewski A. 1995a. Some Methods For Detection And Interpolation Of Impulsive Distortions In Old Audio Recordings. In Proc. IEEE ASSP Workshop on Applications of Signal Processing to Audio and Acoustics. Mohonk Mountain, N.Y., U.S.A.

3. Czyzewski A. 1995b. Managing Noisy Data in the AI-based Processing of Old Audio Recordings. In Proceedings of International Symposium on Intelligent Data Analysis. Baden-Baden, 17-19 August, 1995.

4. Czyzewski A. 1995c. New Learning Algorithms for the Processing of Old Audio Recordings. In Preprint of 99th Audio Engineering Society Convention. New York (Preprint No. 4078).

5. Pawlak Z. (1982). Rough sets. Journal of Computer and Information Science, vol.11, No.5.

6. Pawlak Z. (1993). Rough Sets - Present State and the Future. Foundations of Computing and Decision Sciences, vol. 18, No.3-4.

7. Slowiński R., ed. 1992. Intelligent Decision Support. Handbook on Applications and Advances of the Rough Sets Theory. Kluwer Academic Publisher, Dordrecht/Boston/London.

8. Wojcik Z.M. 1993. Rough Sets for Intelligent Image Filtering, In Proc. of Rough Sets and Knowledge Discovery Workshop (RSKD), Banff, Canada.

9. Zwicker E., Zwicker U. 1991. Audio Engineering and Psychoacoustics: Matching Signals to the Final Receiver, the Human Auditory System, J. Audio Eng. Soc., vol. 39 (pp. 115-126).

10. Krolikowski R. 1996. Noise reduction in old musical recordings using the perceptual coding of audio. Forthcoming.

A Density-Based Algorithm for Discovering Clusters in Large Spatial Databases with Noise

Martin Ester, Hans-Peter Kriegel, Jörg Sander, Xiaowei Xu

Institute for Computer Science, University of Munich
Oettingenstr. 67, D-80538 München, Germany
{ester | kriegel | sander | xwxu}@informatik.uni-muenchen.de

Abstract

Clustering algorithms are attractive for the task of class identification in spatial databases. However, the application to
large spatial databases rises the following requirements for
clustering algorithms: minimal requirements of domain
knowledge to determine the input parameters, discovery of
clusters with arbitrary shape and good efficiency on large databases. The well-known clustering algorithms offer no solution to the combination of these requirements. In this paper,
we present the new clustering algorithm DBSCAN relying on
a density-based notion of clusters which is designed to discover clusters of arbitrary shape. DBSCAN requires only one
input parameter and supports the user in determining an appropriate value for it. We performed an experimental evaluation of the effectiveness and efficiency of DBSCAN using
synthetic data and real data of the SEQUOIA 2000 benchmark. The results of our experiments demonstrate that (1)
DBSCAN is significantly more effective in discovering clusters of arbitrary shape than the well-known algorithm CLAR-
ANS, and that (2) DBSCAN outperforms CLARANS by a
factor of more than 100 in terms of efficiency.

Keywords: Clustering Algorithms, Arbitrary Shape of Clusters, Efficiency on Large Spatial Databases, Handling Nlj4-
275oise.

1. Introduction

Numerous applications require the management of *spatial*
data, i.e. data related to space. *Spatial Database Systems
(SDBS)* (Gueting 1994) are database systems for the management of spatial data. Increasingly large amounts of data
are obtained from satellite images, X-ray crystallography or
other automatic equipment. Therefore, automated knowledge discovery becomes more and more important in spatial
databases.

Several tasks of *knowledge discovery in databases* (KDD)
have been defined in the literature (Matheus, Chan & Piatetsky-Shapiro 1993). The task considered in this paper is
class identification, i.e. the grouping of the objects of a database into meaningful subclasses. In an earth observation database, e.g., we might want to discover classes of houses
along some river.

Clustering algorithms are attractive for the task of class
identification. However, the application to large spatial databases rises the following requirements for clustering algorithms:

(1) Minimal requirements of domain knowledge to determine the input parameters, because appropriate values

are often not known in advance when dealing with large
databases.

(2) Discovery of clusters with arbitrary shape, because the
shape of clusters in spatial databases may be spherical,
drawn-out, linear, elongated etc.

(3) Good efficiency on large databases, i.e. on databases of
significantly more than just a few thousand objects.

The well-known clustering algorithms offer no solution to
the combination of these requirements. In this paper, we
present the new clustering algorithm DBSCAN. It requires
only one input parameter and supports the user in determining an appropriate value for it. It discovers clusters of arbitrary shape. Finally, DBSCAN is efficient even for large spatial databases. The rest of the paper is organized as follows.
We discuss clustering algorithms in section 2 evaluating
them according to the above requirements. In section 3, we
present our notion of clusters which is based on the concept
of density in the database. Section 4 introduces the algorithm DBSCAN which discovers such clusters in a spatial
database. In section 5, we performed an experimental evaluation of the effectiveness and efficiency of DBSCAN using
synthetic data and data of the SEQUOIA 2000 benchmark.
Section 6 concludes with a summary and some directions for
future research.

2. Clustering Algorithms

There are two basic types of clustering algorithms (Kaufman
& Rousseeuw 1990): partitioning and hierarchical algorithms. *Partitioning algorithms* construct a partition of a database D of n objects into a set of k clusters. k is an input parameter for these algorithms, i.e some domain knowledge is
required which unfortunately is not available for many applications. The partitioning algorithm typically starts with
an initial partition of D and then uses an iterative control
strategy to optimize an objective function. Each cluster is
represented by the gravity center of the cluster (*k-means algorithms*) or by one of the objects of the cluster located near
its center (*k-medoid algorithms*). Consequently, partitioning
algorithms use a two-step procedure. First, determine k representatives minimizing the objective function. Second, assign each object to the cluster with its representative "closest" to the considered object. The second step implies that a
partition is equivalent to a voronoi diagram and each cluster
is contained in one of the voronoi cells. Thus, the shape of all

clusters found by a partitioning algorithm is convex which is very restrictive.

Ng & Han (1994) explore partitioning algorithms for KDD in spatial databases. An algorithm called CLARANS (Clustering Large Applications based on RANdomized Search) is introduced which is an improved k-medoid method. Compared to former k-medoid algorithms, CLARANS is more effective and more efficient. An experimental evaluation indicates that CLARANS runs efficiently on databases of thousands of objects. Ng & Han (1994) also discuss methods to determine the "natural" number k_{nat} of clusters in a database. They propose to run CLARANS once for each k from 2 to n. For each of the discovered clusterings the silhouette coefficient (Kaufman & Rousseeuw 1990) is calculated, and finally, the clustering with the maximum silhouette coefficient is chosen as the "natural" clustering. Unfortunately, the run time of this approach is prohibitive for large n, because it implies O(n) calls of CLARANS.

CLARANS assumes that all objects to be clustered can reside in main memory at the same time which does not hold for large databases. Furthermore, the run time of CLARANS is prohibitive on large databases. Therefore, Ester, Kriegel &Xu (1995) present several focusing techniques which address both of these problems by focusing the clustering process on the relevant parts of the database. First, the focus is small enough to be memory resident and second, the run time of CLARANS on the objects of the focus is significantly less than its run time on the whole database.

Hierarchical algorithms create a hierarchical decomposition of *D*. The hierarchical decomposition is represented by a *dendrogram*, a tree that iteratively splits *D* into smaller subsets until each subset consists of only one object. In such a hierarchy, each node of the tree represents a cluster of *D*. The dendrogram can either be created from the leaves up to the root (*agglomerative approach*) or from the root down to the leaves (*divisive approach*) by merging or dividing clusters at each step. In contrast to partitioning algorithms, hierarchical algorithms do not need *k* as an input. However, a *termination condition* has to be defined indicating when the merge or division process should be terminated. One example of a termination condition in the agglomerative approach is the critical distance D_{min} between all the clusters of *Q*.

So far, the main problem with hierarchical clustering algorithms has been the difficulty of deriving appropriate parameters for the termination condition, e.g. a value of D_{min} which is small enough to separate all "natural" clusters and, at the same time large enough such that no cluster is split into two parts. Recently, in the area of signal processing the hierarchical algorithm Ejcluster has been presented (García, Fdez-Valdivia, Cortijo & Molina 1994) automatically deriving a termination condition. Its key idea is that two points belong to the same cluster if you can walk from the first point to the second one by a "sufficiently small" step. Ejcluster follows the divisive approach. It does not require any input of domain knowledge. Furthermore, experiments show that it is very effective in discovering non-convex clusters. However, the computational cost of Ejcluster is $O(n^2)$ due to the distance calculation for each pair of points. This is acceptable for applications such as character recognition with moderate values for n, but it is prohibitive for applications on large databases.

Jain (1988) explores a density based approach to identify clusters in k-dimensional point sets. The data set is partitioned into a number of nonoverlapping cells and histograms are constructed. Cells with relatively high frequency counts of points are the potential cluster centers and the boundaries between clusters fall in the "valleys" of the histogram. This method has the capability of identifying clusters of any shape. However, the space and run-time requirements for storing and searching multidimensional histograms can be enormous. Even if the space and run-time requirements are optimized, the performance of such an approach crucially depends on the size of the cells.

3. A Density Based Notion of Clusters

When looking at the sample sets of points depicted in figure 1, we can easily and unambiguously detect clusters of points and noise points not belonging to any of those clusters.

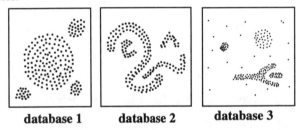

database 1   database 2   database 3

figure 1: Sample databases

The main reason why we recognize the clusters is that within each cluster we have a typical density of points which is considerably higher than outside of the cluster. Furthermore, the density within the areas of noise is lower than the density in any of the clusters.

In the following, we try to formalize this intuitive notion of "clusters" and "noise" in a database *D* of points of some k-dimensional space *S*. Note that both, our notion of clusters and our algorithm DBSCAN, apply as well to 2D or 3D Euclidean space as to some high dimensional feature space. The key idea is that for each point of a cluster the neighborhood of a given radius has to contain at least a minimum number of points, i.e. the density in the neighborhood has to exceed some threshold. The shape of a neighborhood is determined by the choice of a distance function for two points p and q, denoted by *dist(p,q)*. For instance, when using the Manhattan distance in 2D space, the shape of the neighborhood is rectangular. Note, that our approach works with any distance function so that an appropriate function can be chosen for some given application. For the purpose of proper visualization, all examples will be in 2D space using the Euclidean distance.

Definition 1: (Eps-neighborhood of a point) The *Eps-neighborhood* of a point p, denoted by $N_{Eps}(p)$, is defined by $N_{Eps}(p) = \{q \in D \mid dist(p,q) \le Eps\}$.

A naive approach could require for each point in a cluster that there are at least a minimum number (*MinPts*) of points in an Eps-neighborhood of that point. However, this approach fails because there are two kinds of points in a cluster, points inside of the cluster (*core points*) and points on the border of the cluster (*border points*). In general, an Eps-neighborhood of a border point contains significantly less points than an Eps-neighborhood of a core point. Therefore, we would have to set the minimum number of points to a relatively low value in order to include all points belonging to the same cluster. This value, however, will not be characteristic for the respective cluster - particularly in the presence of noise. Therefore, we require that for every point p in a cluster C there is a point q in C so that p is inside of the Eps-neighborhood of q and $N_{Eps}(q)$ contains at least MinPts points. This definition is elaborated in the following.

Definition 2: (directly density-reachable) A point p is *directly density-reachable* from a point q wrt. Eps, MinPts if

1) $p \in N_{Eps}(q)$ and

2) $|N_{Eps}(q)| \geq$ MinPts (core point condition).

Obviously, directly density-reachable is symmetric for pairs of core points. In general, however, it is not symmetric if one core point and one border point are involved. Figure 2 shows the asymmetric case.

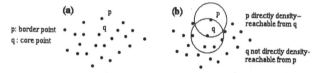

figure 2: core points and border points

Definition 3: (density-reachable) A point p is *density-reachable* from a point q wrt. Eps and MinPts if there is a chain of points $p_1, ..., p_n, p_1 = q, p_n = p$ such that p_{i+1} is directly density-reachable from p_i.

Density-reachability is a canonical extension of direct density-reachability. This relation is transitive, but it is not symmetric. Figure 3 depicts the relations of some sample points and, in particular, the asymmetric case. Although not symmetric in general, it is obvious that density-reachability is symmetric for core points.

Two border points of the same cluster C are possibly not density reachable from each other because the core point condition might not hold for both of them. However, there must be a core point in C from which both border points of C are density-reachable. Therefore, we introduce the notion of density-connectivity which covers this relation of border points.

Definition 4: (density-connected) A point p is *density-connected* to a point q wrt. Eps and MinPts if there is a point o such that both, p and q are density-reachable from o wrt. Eps and MinPts.

Density-connectivity is a symmetric relation. For density reachable points, the relation of density-connectivity is also reflexive (c.f. figure 3).

Now, we are able to define our density-based notion of a cluster. Intuitively, a cluster is defined to be a set of density-connected points which is maximal wrt. density-reachability. Noise will be defined relative to a given set of clusters. Noise is simply the set of points in D not belonging to any of its clusters.

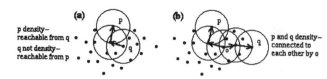

figure 3: density-reachability and density-connectivity

Definition 5: (cluster) Let D be a database of points. A *cluster C* wrt. Eps and MinPts is a non-empty subset of D satisfying the following conditions:

1) ∀ p, q: if $p \in$ C and q is density-reachable from p wrt. Eps and MinPts, then q ∈ C. (Maximality)

2) ∀ p, q ∈ C: p is density-connected to q wrt. EPS and MinPts. (Connectivity)

Definition 6: (noise) Let $C_1, ..., C_k$ be the clusters of the database D wrt. parameters Eps_i and $MinPts_i$, i = 1, ..., k. Then we define the *noise* as the set of points in the database D not belonging to any cluster C_i, i.e. noise = {p ∈ D | ∀ i: p ∉ C_i}.

Note that a cluster C wrt. Eps and MinPts contains at least MinPts points because of the following reasons. Since C contains at least one point p, p must be density-connected to itself via some point o (which may be equal to p). Thus, at least o has to satisfy the core point condition and, consequently, the Eps-Neighborhood of o contains at least MinPts points.

The following lemmata are important for validating the correctness of our clustering algorithm. Intuitively, they state the following. Given the parameters Eps and MinPts, we can discover a cluster in a two-step approach. First, choose an arbitrary point from the database satisfying the core point condition as a seed. Second, retrieve all points that are density-reachable from the seed obtaining the cluster containing the seed.

Lemma 1: Let p be a point in D and $|N_{Eps}(p)| \geq$ MinPts. Then the set O = {o | o ∈ D and o is density-reachable from p wrt. Eps and MinPts} is a cluster wrt. Eps and MinPts.

It is not obvious that a cluster C wrt. Eps and MinPts is uniquely determined by *any* of its core points. However, each point in C is density-reachable from any of the core points of C and, therefore, a cluster C contains exactly the points which are density-reachable from an arbitrary core point of C.

Lemma 2: Let C be a cluster wrt. Eps and MinPts and let p be any point in C with $|N_{Eps}(p)| \geq$ MinPts. Then C equals to the set O = {o | o is density-reachable from p wrt. Eps and MinPts}.

4. DBSCAN: Density Based Spatial Clustering of Applications with Noise

In this section, we present the algorithm DBSCAN (Density Based Spatial Clustering of Applications with Noise) which is designed to discover the clusters and the noise in a spatial database according to definitions 5 and 6. Ideally, we would have to know the appropriate parameters Eps and MinPts of each cluster and at least one point from the respective cluster. Then, we could retrieve all points that are density-reachable from the given point using the correct parameters. But there is no easy way to get this information in advance for all clusters of the database. However, there is a simple and effective heuristic (presented in section section 4.2) to determine the parameters Eps and MinPts of the "thinnest", i.e. least dense, cluster in the database. Therefore, DBSCAN uses global values for Eps and MinPts, i.e. the same values for all clusters. The density parameters of the "thinnest" cluster are good candidates for these global parameter values specifying the lowest density which is not considered to be noise.

4.1 The Algorithm

To find a cluster, DBSCAN starts with an arbitrary point p and retrieves all points density-reachable from p wrt. Eps and MinPts. If p is a core point, this procedure yields a cluster wrt. Eps and MinPts (see Lemma 2). If p is a border point, no points are density-reachable from p and DBSCAN visits the next point of the database.

Since we use global values for Eps and MinPts, DBSCAN may merge two clusters according to definition 5 into one cluster, if two clusters of different density are "close" to each other. Let the *distance between two sets of points* S_1 and S_2 be defined as dist $(S_1, S_2) = \min \{\text{dist}(p,q) \mid p \in S_1, q \in S_2\}$. Then, two sets of points having at least the density of the thinnest cluster will be separated from each other only if the distance between the two sets is larger than Eps. Consequently, a recursive call of DBSCAN may be necessary for the detected clusters with a higher value for MinPts. This is, however, no disadvantage because the recursive application of DBSCAN yields an elegant and very efficient basic algorithm. Furthermore, the recursive clustering of the points of a cluster is only necessary under conditions that can be easily detected.

In the following, we present a basic version of DBSCAN omitting details of data types and generation of additional information about clusters:

```
DBSCAN (SetOfPoints, Eps, MinPts)

// SetOfPoints is UNCLASSIFIED
  ClusterId := nextId(NOISE);
  FOR i FROM 1 TO SetOfPoints.size DO
    Point := SetOfPoints.get(i);
    IF Point.ClId = UNCLASSIFIED THEN
      IF ExpandCluster(SetOfPoints, Point,
            ClusterId, Eps, MinPts) THEN
        ClusterId := nextId(ClusterId)
      END IF
    END IF
  END FOR
END; // DBSCAN
```

SetOfPoints is either the whole database or a discovered cluster from a previous run. Eps and MinPts are the global density parameters determined either manually or according to the heuristics presented in section 4.2. The function SetOfPoints.get(i) returns the i-th element of SetOfPoints. The most important function

used by DBSCAN is ExpandCluster which is presented below:

```
ExpandCluster(SetOfPoints, Point, ClId, Eps,
            MinPts) : Boolean;
  seeds:=SetOfPoints.regionQuery(Point,Eps);
  IF seeds.size<MinPts THEN // no core point
    SetOfPoint.changeClId(Point,NOISE);
    RETURN False;
  ELSE    // all points in seeds are density-
          // reachable from Point
    SetOfPoints.changeClIds(seeds,ClId);
    seeds.delete(Point);
    WHILE seeds <> Empty DO
      currentP := seeds.first();
      result := SetOfPoints.regionQuery(currentP,
                                        Eps);
      IF result.size >= MinPts THEN
        FOR i FROM 1 TO result.size DO
          resultP := result.get(i);
          IF resultP.ClId
              IN {UNCLASSIFIED, NOISE} THEN
            IF resultP.ClId = UNCLASSIFIED THEN
              seeds.append(resultP);
            END IF;
            SetOfPoints.changeClId(resultP,ClId);
          END IF; // UNCLASSIFIED or NOISE
        END FOR;
      END IF; // result.size >= MinPts
      seeds.delete(currentP);
    END WHILE; // seeds <> Empty
    RETURN True;
  END IF
END; // ExpandCluster
```

A call of SetOfPoints.regionQuery(Point,Eps) returns the Eps-Neighborhood of Point in SetOfPoints as a list of points. Region queries can be supported efficiently by spatial access methods such as R*-trees (Beckmann et al. 1990) which are assumed to be available in a SDBS for efficient processing of several types of spatial queries (Brinkhoff et al. 1994). The height of an R*-tree is O(log n) for a database of n points in the worst case and a query with a "small" query region has to traverse only a limited number of paths in the R^*-tree. Since the Eps-Neighborhoods are expected to be small compared to the size of the whole data space, the average run time complexity of a single region query is O(log n). For each of the n points of the database, we have at most one region query. Thus, the average run time complexity of DBSCAN is O(n * log n).

The ClId (clusterId) of points which have been marked to be NOISE may be changed later, if they are density-reachable from some other point of the database. This happens for border points of a cluster. Those points are not added to the seeds-list because we already know that a point with a ClId of NOISE is not a core point. Adding those points to seeds would only result in additional region queries which would yield no new answers.

If two clusters C_1 and C_2 are very close to each other, it might happen that some point p belongs to both, C_1 and C_2. Then p must be a border point in both clusters because otherwise C_1 would be equal to C_2 since we use global parameters. In this case, point p will be assigned to the cluster discovered first. Except from these rare situations, the result of DBSCAN is independent of the order in which the points of the database are visited due to Lemma 2.

4.2 Determining the Parameters Eps and MinPts

In this section, we develop a simple but effective heuristic to determine the parameters Eps and MinPts of the "thinnest" cluster in the database. This heuristic is based on the following observation. Let d be the distance of a point p to its k-th nearest neighbor, then the d-neighborhood of p contains exactly k+1 points for almost all points p. The d-neighborhood of p contains more than k+1 points only if several points have exactly the same distance d from p which is quite unlikely. Furthermore, changing k for a point in a cluster does not result in large changes of d. This only happens if the k-th nearest neighbors of p for k= 1, 2, 3, . . . are located approximately on a straight line which is in general not true for a point in a cluster.

For a given k we define a function *k-dist* from the database D to the real numbers, mapping each point to the distance from its k-th nearest neighbor. When sorting the points of the database in descending order of their k-dist values, the graph of this function gives some hints concerning the density distribution in the database. We call this graph the *sorted k-dist graph*. If we choose an arbitrary point p, set the parameter Eps to k-dist(p) and set the parameter MinPts to k, all points with an equal or smaller k-dist value will be core points. If we could find a *threshold point* with the maximal k-dist value in the "thinnest" cluster of D we would have the desired parameter values. The threshold point is the first point in the first "valley" of the sorted k-dist graph (see figure 4). All points with a higher k-dist value (left of the threshold) are considered to be noise, all other points (right of the threshold) are assigned to some cluster.

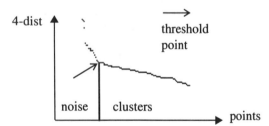

figure 4: sorted 4-dist graph for sample database 3

In general, it is very difficult to detect the first "valley" automatically, but it is relatively simple for a user to see this valley in a graphical representation. Therefore, we propose to follow an interactive approach for determining the threshold point.

DBSCAN needs two parameters, Eps and MinPts. However, our experiments indicate that the k-dist graphs for k > 4 do not significantly differ from the 4-dist graph and, furthermore, they need considerably more computation. Therefore, we eliminate the parameter MinPts by setting it to 4 for all databases (for 2-dimensional data). We propose the following interactive approach for determining the parameter Eps of DBSCAN:

- The system computes and displays the 4-dist graph for the database.
- If the user can estimate the percentage of noise, this percentage is entered and the system derives a proposal for the threshold point from it.
- The user either accepts the proposed threshold or selects another point as the threshold point. The 4-dist value of the threshold point is used as the Eps value for DBSCAN.

5. Performance Evaluation

In this section, we evaluate the performance of DBSCAN. We compare it with the performance of CLARANS because this is the first and only clustering algorithm designed for the purpose of KDD. In our future research, we will perform a comparison with classical density based clustering algorithms. We have implemented DBSCAN in C++ based on an implementation of the R*-tree (Beckmann et al. 1990). All experiments have been run on HP 735 / 100 workstations. We have used both synthetic sample databases and the database of the SEQUOIA 2000 benchmark.

To compare DBSCAN with CLARANS in terms of effectivity (accuracy), we use the three synthetic sample databases which are depicted in figure 1. Since DBSCAN and CLARANS are clustering algorithms of different types, they have no common quantitative measure of the classification accuracy. Therefore, we evaluate the accuracy of both algorithms by visual inspection. In sample database 1, there are four ball-shaped clusters of significantly differing sizes. Sample database 2 contains four clusters of nonconvex shape. In sample database 3, there are four clusters of different shape and size with additional noise. To show the results of both clustering algorithms, we visualize each cluster by a different color (see www availability after section 6). To give CLARANS some advantage, we set the parameter *k* to 4 for these sample databases. The clusterings discovered by CLARANS are depicted in figure 5.

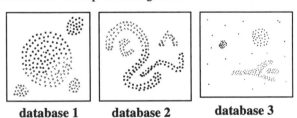

database 1   database 2   database 3

figure 5: Clusterings discovered by CLARANS

For DBSCAN, we set the noise percentage to 0% for sample databases 1 and 2, and to 10% for sample database 3, respectively. The clusterings discovered by DBSCAN are depicted in figure 6.

DBSCAN discovers all clusters (according to definition 5) and detects the noise points (according to definition 6) from all sample databases. CLARANS, however, splits clusters if they are relatively large or if they are close to some other cluster. Furthermore, CLARANS has no explicit notion of noise. Instead, all points are assigned to their closest medoid.

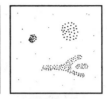

database 1   database 2   database 3

figure 6: Clusterings discovered by DBSCAN

To test the efficiency of DBSCAN and CLARANS, we use the SEQUOIA 2000 benchmark data. The SEQUOIA 2000 benchmark database (Stonebraker et al. 1993) uses real data sets that are representative of Earth Science tasks. There are four types of data in the database: raster data, point data, polygon data and directed graph data. The point data set contains 62,584 Californian names of landmarks, extracted from the US Geological Survey's Geographic Names Information System, together with their location. The point data set occupies about 2.1 M bytes. Since the run time of CLARANS on the whole data set is very high, we have extracted a series of subsets of the SEQUIOA 2000 point data set containing from 2% to 20% representatives of the whole set. The run time comparison of DBSCAN and CLARANS on these databases is shown in table 1.

Table 1: run time in seconds

number of points	1252	2503	3910	5213	6256
DBSCAN	3.1	6.7	11.3	16.0	17.8
CLAR-ANS	758	3026	6845	11745	18029
number of points	7820	8937	10426	12512	
DBSCAN	24.5	28.2	32.7	41.7	
CLAR-ANS	29826	39265	60540	80638	

The results of our experiments show that the run time of DBSCAN is slightly higher than linear in the number of points. The run time of CLARANS, however, is close to quadratic in the number of points. The results show that DBSCAN outperforms CLARANS by a factor of between 250 and 1900 which grows with increasing size of the database.

6. Conclusions

Clustering algorithms are attractive for the task of class identification in spatial databases. However, the well-known algorithms suffer from severe drawbacks when applied to large spatial databases. In this paper, we presented the clustering algorithm DBSCAN which relies on a density-based notion of clusters. It requires only one input parameter and supports the user in determining an appropriate value for it. We performed a performance evaluation on synthetic data

and on real data of the SEQUOIA 2000 benchmark. The results of these experiments demonstrate that DBSCAN is significantly more effective in discovering clusters of arbitrary shape than the well-known algorithm CLARANS. Furthermore, the experiments have shown that DBSCAN outperforms CLARANS by a factor of at least 100 in terms of efficiency.

Future research will have to consider the following issues. First, we have only considered point objects. Spatial databases, however, may also contain extended objects such as polygons. We have to develop a definition of the density in an Eps-neighborhood in polygon databases for generalizing DBSCAN. Second, applications of DBSCAN to high dimensional feature spaces should be investigated. In particular, the shape of the k-dist graph in such applications has to be explored.

WWW Availability

A version of this paper in larger font, with large figures and clusterings in color is available under the following URL: `http://www.dbs.informatik.uni-muenchen.de/ dbs/project/publikationen/veroeffentlichun- gen.html`.

References

Beckmann N., Kriegel H.-P., Schneider R, and Seeger B. 1990. The R*-tree: An Efficient and Robust Access Method for Points and Rectangles, Proc. ACM SIGMOD Int. Conf. on Management of Data, Atlantic City, NJ, 1990, pp. 322-331.

Brinkhoff T., Kriegel H.-P., Schneider R., and Seeger B. 1994 Efficient Multi-Step Processing of Spatial Joins, Proc. ACM SIGMOD Int. Conf. on Management of Data, Minneapolis, MN, 1994, pp. 197-208.

Ester M., Kriegel H.-P., and Xu X. 1995. A Database Interface for Clustering in Large Spatial Databases, Proc. 1st Int. Conf. on Knowledge Discovery and Data Mining, Montreal, Canada, 1995, AAAI Press, 1995.

García J.A., Fdez-Valdivia J., Cortijo F. J., and Molina R. 1994. A Dynamic Approach for Clustering Data. *Signal Processing*, Vol. 44, No. 2, 1994, pp. 181-196.

Gueting R.H. 1994. An Introduction to Spatial Database Systems. *The VLDB Journal* 3(4): 357-399.

Jain Anil K. 1988. *Algorithms for Clustering Data*. Prentice Hall.

Kaufman L., and Rousseeuw P.J. 1990. *Finding Groups in Data: an Introduction to Cluster Analysis*. John Wiley & Sons.

Matheus C.J.; Chan P.K.; and Piatetsky-Shapiro G. 1993. Systems for Knowledge Discovery in Databases, *IEEE Transactions on Knowledge and Data Engineering* 5(6): 903-913.

Ng R.T., and Han J. 1994. Efficient and Effective Clustering Methods for Spatial Data Mining, Proc. 20th Int. Conf. on Very Large Data Bases, 144-155. Santiago, Chile.

Stonebraker M., Frew J., Gardels K., and Meredith J.1993. The SEQUOIA 2000 Storage Benchmark, Proc. ACM SIGMOD Int. Conf. on Management of Data, Washington, DC, 1993, pp. 2-11.

A Method for Reasoning with Structured and Continuous Attributes in the INLEN-2 Multistrategy Knowledge Discovery System

Kenneth A. Kaufman and Ryszard S. Michalski*

Machine Learning and Inference Laboratory,
George Mason University,
Fairfax, Virginia, 22030, USA
{kaufman, michalsk}@aic.gmu.edu

* Also GMU Departments of Computer Science and Systems Engineering
and the Institute of Computer Science, Polish Academy of Sciences

Abstract

Structured attributes have domains (value sets) that are partially ordered sets, typically hierarchies. Such attributes allow knowledge discovery programs to incorporate background knowledge about hierarchical relationships among attribute values. Inductive generalization rules for structured attributes have been developed that take into consideration the type of nodes in the domain hierarchy (anchor or non-anchor) and the type of decision rules to be generated (characteristic, discriminant or minimum complexity). These generalization rules enhance the ability of knowledge discovery system INLEN-2 to exploit the semantic content of the domain knowledge in the process of generating hypotheses. If the dependent attribute (e.g., a decision attribute) is structured, the system generates a system of hierarchically organized rules representing relationships between the values of this attribute and independent attributes. Such a situation often occurs in practice when the decision to be assigned to a situation can be at different levels of abstraction (e.g., this is a liver disease, or this is a liver cancer). Continuous attributes (e.g., physical measurements) are quantized into a hierarchy of values (ranges of values arranged into different levels). These methods are illustrated by an example concerning the discovery of patterns in world economics and demographics.

Introduction

Most symbolic learning systems represent information about objects or events in the form of attribute-value vectors. Attributes used in these systems are typically numerical (i.e., have totally ordered value sets) or nominal (i.e., have unordered value sets). In some applications it is useful to use attributes with value sets that are partially ordered, for example, representing a generalization hierarchy of concepts. Theoretically, almost any attribute can be viewed as having a hierarchical domain. For example, the domain of a numeric variable "age" can be split into a hierarchically organized set of classes—specific numerical values at the lowest level; toddler, child, teen, young adult, middle-age, senior and very senior at the second level; and possibly young, adult and mature at the third level. To represent such concepts, a system needs background knowledge that relates the numerical age with the higher level concepts. In general, the structure of the domain does not have to be fixed; it may be changing with the context of the problem at hand.

Structuring attributes can prove advantageous for a knowledge discovery system. It allows facts, trends and regularities to be revealed both at high and low levels of abstraction, and for background knowledge to be stored and generalizations to be made at the appropriate levels.

The idea of grouping values of attributes into a structure of classes in order to reflect semantic relationships characteristic to the given application domain has led to the introduction of *structured* attributes (Michalski 1980). The domain of a structured attribute is a partially ordered set, typically a hierarchy. Domains of structured variables can be generated by a domain expert (e.g., Karni & Loksh 1996), or by an automatic process using a numerical or conceptual clustering method (e.g., Sokal & Sneath 1973; Michalski & Stepp 1983; Fisher 1987). The structure of the domain can be modified to suit a specific class of problems (e.g., Fisher 1995). Structured attributes can be used as independent (input) variables (Michalski 1980), as well as dependent (output) variables (e.g., Reinke 1984). The roles of structured variables in these two cases differ.

This paper discusses methods for reasoning with structured attributes in the process of data analysis and knowledge discovery. Many of the presented ideas have been adapted for knowledge discovery from the Inferential Theory of Learning, which provides a unifying framework for characterizing learning and discovery processes (Michalski, 1994). Among the novel ideas are the use of "anchor nodes" to guide the inductive generalization process, the use of non-hierarchical attribute domains, and the introduction of different kinds of generalization rules for structured attributes. The use of continuous variables in reasoning is closely related to that of structured attributes in that the way their domains are structured is tailored to the particular discovery problem. The presented ideas and methods have been implemented in the INLEN-2 knowledge discovery system, and are illustrated by an application to a knowledge discovery problem in world demographics.

The Extension-Against Operator and Three Types of Descriptions

An inductive generalization rule (or transmutation) takes input information and background knowledge, and hypothesizes more general knowledge (Michalski 1980; 1994). For example, dropping a condition from a decision rule is a generalization transmutation.

A powerful inductive generalization rule used in the AQ learning program is the *extension-against* operator. If rule **R1:** $[x_i = a]$ **& CTX** characterizes positive concept examples E^+ and rule **R2:** $[x_i = b]$ **& CTX** characterizes negative examples E^- (where the CTX, a context, stands for any additional conditions), then the extension of R1 against R2

$$\text{R1} \longrightarrow \text{R2}$$

produces **R3:** $[x_i \neq b]$, which is the maximal consistent generalization of R1 (Michalski & McCormick 1971; Michalski 1983).

By repeating the extension-against operator until the resulting rule no longer covers any negative examples, a consistent concept description (one that covers no negative examples) can be generated. Such a process can applied to generate a description (cover) that is complete and consistent with regard to all the training examples (i.e., it covers all positive examples and no negative examples).

Another important concept that needs to be explained before introducing the central ideas of this paper is the type of description, as defined in the AQ rule learning methodology (Michalski et al. 1986). By applying the extension-against operator in different ways, one can generate a range of descriptions with different degrees of generality. Here we distinguish three types of descriptions: 1) *discriminant covers* (in which the extension-against is used to create maximal generalizations; such descriptions specify minimal conditions to discriminate between the concept and non-concept examples); 2) *characteristic covers* (in which the extension-against is specialized to create maximally specific generalizations; such generalizations specify the maximal number of conditions that characterize positive examples); and 3) *minimal complexity covers* (in which the extension-against is used to create the simplest possible generalizations).

To illustrate these concepts, consider the diagram shown in Figure 1, which represents a two-dimensional representation space spanned over three-valued attribute *Shape* (Sh) and six-valued attribute *Color* (Co). Positive and negative concept examples are marked by + and -, respectively. The characteristic cover (maximally specific) is represented by the shaded area. It states: *Color is red or yellow or green, and Shape is square or triangle*. A discriminant description (maximum generalization) of the same set of examples states: Color is red, yellow, green or white (or, equivalently, Color is not blue or orange). A minimum complexity description of these examples states: Color is red or yellow or green. The three descriptions are equally consistent with the five input examples.

These three types of descriptions are used in the INLEN-2 system for knowledge discovery in databases. In the following section, we present an extension of these ideas to descriptions with structured attributes (both as independent (input) and dependent (output) variables) and continuous independent attributes.

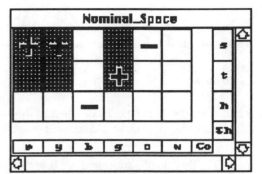

Color is red or yellow or green, and Shape is square or triangle

Figure 1. A characteristic cover of E^+ vs. E^-.

Generalization Rules for Structured Attributes

Structured Input Variables

In order to apply the previously defined extension-against operator to structured attributes, new generalization rules need to be defined. Let us illustrate the problem by an example that uses a structured attribute "Food" shown in Figure 2. Each non-leaf node denotes a concept that is more general than its children nodes. These relationships need to be taken into consideration when developing a generalization of some facts. Suppose the concept to be learned is exemplified by statements: "John eats strip steak" and "John doesn't eat vanilla ice cream." Many consistent generalizations of these facts exist, for example, that John eats strip steak, steak, cattle, meat, meat or vegetables, or anything but vanilla ice cream. The first statement represents a maximally specific description, the last statement represents a maximally general description, and the remaining ones represent intermediate levels of generalization. A problem arises in determining the generalizations of most interest. We approach this problem by drawing insights from human reasoning.

We tend to assign different levels of significance to nodes in a generalization hierarchy. Some cognitive scientists explain this in part with the idea of *basic* level nodes, whose children share many sensorially recognizable commonalities (Roche et al. 1976). Other factors that are important for characterizing nodes are concept typicality (how common are a concept's features among its sibling concepts), and the context in which the concept is being used (Klimesch 1988; Kubat, Bratko, & Michalski 1996).

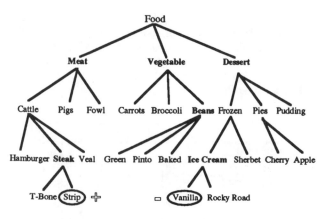

Anchor nodes are shown in bold. Nodes marked by + and - are values occurring in positive and negative examples, respectively.

Figure 2. The domain of a structured attribute "Food."

To capture such preferences simply, we introduce the idea of *anchor nodes* in a hierarchy. Such nodes are the ones that are desirable to use for the given task domain. To illustrate this idea, consider Figure 2 again.

In the presented hierarchy, vanilla and rocky road are kinds of ice cream; ice cream is a frozen dessert, which is a dessert, which is a type of food. In everyday usage, depending on the context, we will typically think of them as ice cream or dessert, but not so typically as frozen dessert or food.

In designing a knowledge discovery system, we should be able to encode the contextual significance of the nodes into the knowledge representation of the system, so that the created rules will represent desirable levels of abstraction. To this end, nodes in the hierarchy that are considered to be at preferable levels of abstraction are marked as *anchor nodes.*

Given the information which nodes are anchors and which are not, different types of descriptions can be created during the generalization phase of knowledge discovery. The meaning of discriminant and characteristic descriptions needs to be properly defined. In building a characteristic description, the following rule is assumed: Generalize positive examples to the next higher anchor node(s) if this maintains consistency conditions. For example, consider the nodes in bold in Figure 2 to be anchors. Then in characteristic mode, the extension of the positive attribute value "Strip" against the negative attribute "Vanilla" would generalize to "Steak." In building a discriminant description from these examples, attribute values are generalized to the most general value that does not cover the nearest anchor node to the value of a negative example. In the example above, the positive value "Strip" would generalize (extend) against the value "Vanilla" to "not Ice Cream." In building the equivalent of minimum complexity descriptions, any of the intermediate anchor nodes could be used if this would simplify the description. For instance, one generalization rule would be to generalize

positive examples to the highest anchor nodes possible, such that consistency is maintained. In this example, the description of "Strip" would generalize to "Meat."

Another feature to increase the power of representing structured variables is that one does not need to limit the domain of structured attributes to strict hierarchies (one parent for every node). Instead, an arbitrary lattice may be used when desired. This feature is useful for representing overlapping or orthogonal classification hierarchies. The nature of the particular problem determines how the nodes are generalized. The system generalizes the nodes in the way that produces the most desirable (for example, the simplest) description.

Generalization in structured domains does not increase the complexity of the extension-against operator, save for the fact that the internal nodes in the hierarchy must now be among the attribute's legal value set, while in an unstructured domain they may or may not be present. Any increase in discovery complexity will come during the postprocessing, when different possible generalizations of the discovered cover will be examined; in the worst case, this will be bounded in number of applications by the number of internal nodes in the tree times the tree's maximum height.

Structured Output Variables

Typically, dependent variables are numeric or nominal. In the latter case, values of an independent variable are independent concepts. Such a representation fails to take advantage of any generalization hierarchies that may exist among values of a dependent variable. For example, when selecting a personal computer to buy, the candidate models may be grouped into IBM-compatible and Macintosh-compatible. Rather than just choosing one system from among the entire set, it may be simpler to organize the knowledge to choose first the general type, and then the specific model of the assumed type. This leads us to the need for using structured attributes as dependent variables and defining an appropriate method for handling them in the process of rule search and generalization.

Given a structured dependent variable (a decision variable), decision rules or descriptions can relate to nodes of the dependent variable at different levels in the hierarchy. The proposed method focuses first on the top-level nodes, creating rules for them. Subsequently, rules are created for the descendant nodes in the context of their ancestors. For example, in the case of the computer selection problem, the generalization operator would first determine how to choose between IBM- and Macintosh-compatible machines, and then generate rules for distinguishing among the machines in each class, and that class alone. The rule for a specific IBM-compatible machine does not attempt to differentiate it from a particular Macintosh; it will be based on the assumption that an IBM-compatible computer is to be selected. Due to this algorithm, the rules at each level of abstraction will tend to be more concise and easier to interpret.

Dynamic Quantization of Continuous Attributes

In some respects, numerical attributes are similar to structured attributes with multiple views. There are different ways to group the values into discrete ranges, and unless definitive background knowledge is available, the optimal organization for a particular discovery problem may not be apparent. Even when numeric values have been quantized into ranges by a domain expert, the expert-generated abstraction schema may not be optimal for the learning task (e.g., Karni & Loksh 1996). Furthermore, a particular set of ranges may be useful for one learning task, but irrelevant to another.

The implemented methodology performs automatic discretization of numeric data using the ChiMerge algorithm (Kerber 1992). With this method, neighboring distinct values of the attribute found in the data are merged into single ranges based on a χ^2 analysis of the classification of the values. When the classification patterns of adjacent ranges are statistically dependent on one another, the ranges are combined into one.

One important consequence of this algorithm is that the grouping of values into intervals will depend on the classification of the input data. Specifically, given a new learning problem from the same data set, the training data will likely be grouped into classes much differently, and thus the set of ranges of a given attribute most likely to generate concise and useful knowledge may be much different. For example, given an auto insurance customer database, there may be little correlation between the set of accident-prone clients and the set of customers who are likely be interested in purchasing a service offered by the company. It is quite possible that the ranges into which the driver's ages are divided that are most useful for the first learning task are not appropriate for the second one. To combat this problem, ChiMerge recomputes the ranges for each numeric variable whenever new sets of data are added or a new discovery problem is specified.

A limitation of the ChiMerge methodology is that it is dependent on the classification of input training examples, and that it therefore can not be used to quantize an output variable (since that would depend on its already having been divided into classes). There are several ways that an output numeric variable can be discretized into a hierarchy of ranges. A domain expert can suggest ranges, ranges can be determined based on some other output variable, conceptual clustering can be used, etc. A discussion and comparison of these methods will be addressed in a forthcoming paper.

Experiments

The above ideas and algorithms have been implemented in the INLEN-2 system for knowledge discovery in data. INLEN-2 belongs to the INLEN family of knowledge discovery programs that use an integrated, multi-operator approach to knowledge discovery (Kaufman, Michalski, & Kerschberg 1991; Michalski et al. 1992). This section illustrates an application of the presented methods to a problem of knowledge discovery in world economics and demographics.

The predominant religion of different countries, as specified in the PEOPLE database of the World Factbook published by the Central Intelligence Agency, is used as an example of a structured attribute. The set of values found in the data contain some natural inclusion relationships. For example, there co-exist labels of "Christian", "Protestant" and "Lutheran" in the database. The organization of some of this attribute's values when structured is shown in Figure 3.

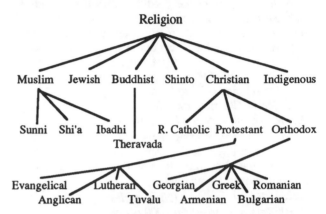

Figure 3. Part of the structure of the PEOPLE database's *Religion* attribute

If the Religion attribute were set up in an unstructured manner, the statement "Religion is Lutheran" would be regarded equally as antithetical to "Religion is Christian" as to the statement "Religion is Buddhist," leading to the possibility that some contradictions (such as "Religion is Lutheran, but not Christian") might be discovered.

Experiments using INLEN-2 have indicated very interesting findings regarding the usage of structured and non-structured attributes. Among the findings regarding their use as independent variables were that structuring attributes led to simpler rules than when the attributes were not structures, and that certain patterns were only found when the domains were structured. These findings are illustrated by the results below:

When INLEN-2 learned rules to distinguish the 55 countries with low (less than 1 per 1000 people) population growth rate (PGR) from other countries, in a version of the PEOPLE database in which the attribute "Religion" was not structured, one of the rules it found was as follows:

PGR < 1 if: *(20 examples)*
   Literacy = 95% to 99%,
   Life Expectancy is 70 to 80 years,
   Religion is Roman Catholic or Orthodox or
      Romanian or Lutheran or
      Evangelical or Anglican or Shinto,
   Net Migration Rate ≤ +20 per 1000 people.

This rule was satisfied by 20 of the 55 countries with low growth rates.

When the same experiment was run with "Religion" structured, a similar rule was discovered:

PGR < 1 if: (14 examples)
  Literacy = 95% to 99%,
  Life Expectancy is 70 to 80 years,
  Religion is Roman Catholic or Orthodox or Shinto,
  Net Migration Rate ≤ +10 per 1000 people.

This rule was satisfied by 14 of the 55 low-growth countries. The removal of some of the Protestant subclasses from the Religion condition and the tightening of the Net Migration Rate condition caused six countries which had been covered by the first rule, not to satisfy this rule. At a slight cost in consistency, simpler, more encompassing rules than either of the above were found:

PGR < 1 if: (21 examples, 1 exception)
  Literacy = 95% to 99%,
  Life Expectancy is 70 to 80 years,
  Religion is Christian or Shinto,
  Net Migration Rate ≤ +10 per 1000 people.

Even when not relaxing the consistency constraint, a concise rule not generated in the unstructured dataset was discovered that described 20 countries including the six omitted in the structured rule:

PGR < 1 if: (20 examples)
  Birth Rate = 10 to 20 per 1000 people,
  Death Rate is 10 to 15 per 1000 people.

Similar differences were obtained using structured output variables. By classifying events at different levels of generality, rules can classify both in general and in specific terms. This tends to reduce the complexity and increase the significance of the rules at all levels of generalization.

In the PEOPLE database it is difficult to learn a set of rules for predicting a country's likely predominant religion given other demographic attributes without using the hierarchies. There are 30 religious categories listed for the 170 countries. The conditions making up the rules will likely have very low support levels (informational significance, defined as number of positive examples satisfying the condition divided by total number of examples satisfying the condition) because a single condition that exists in most of the countries with a certain predominant religion will typically be found, at least occasionally, elsewhere.

When learning rules for distinguishing between the religions in an unstructured format, the highest support level found in the entire rule base was 37% for the awkward condition "Literacy is 70-90% or 95-99%", which described 26 of the 50 Roman Catholic countries, and 43 of the remainder of the world's countries. In contrast, structuring the classification of religions led to several top-level conditions with higher support levels. One condition, with a 63% support level in its ability to distinguish the 88 Christian countries was "Population Growth Rate ≤ 2".

More drastic effects were seen at the lower levels of the hierarchy. In the unstructured dataset, five rules, each with two to five conditions, were required to define the 11 Sunni Muslim countries. The only one to describe more than two of the 11 countries was this set of fragmented conditions:

Religion is Sunni_Muslim if: (4 examples)
  Literacy = 100% or less than 30%,
  Infant Mortality Rate is 25 to 40 or
      greater than 55 per 1000 people,
  Fertility Rate is 1 to 2 or 4 to 5 or 6 to 7,
  Population Growth Rate is 1 to 3 or greater than 4.

The ranges in each of the four conditions are divided into multiple segments, suggesting that this is not at all a strong pattern. In contrast, the structured dataset produced two rules, each with one condition, to distinguish Sunni Muslim countries from other predominantly Islamic nations. The first, "Religion is Sunni_Muslim if Infant Mortality Rate ≥ 40", described all but one of the positive examples (Jordan was the exception), and only one non-Sunni Islamic nation. The second, "Religion is Sunni_Muslim if Birth Rate is 30 to 40" alone discriminated Algeria, Egypt, Jordan and Tajikistan from the rest of the Muslim world.

Experiments also indicate the practical utility of problem-oriented quantization of continuous variables. Advantages include simpler rules that will often have higher accuracy than with a fixed discretization schema. When characterizing different regions of the world based on an economic database, INLEN-2 was able set thresholds that would generate knowledge with high support levels. For example, the allocation of a country's GNP to agriculture of greater than 28% (with that number generated by ChiMerge) was a useful indicator for distinguishing Eastern African countries from other regions of the world.

Conclusion

This paper describes some novel features implemented in the INLEN-2 system for knowledge discovery. Structured and numeric domains share the common trait that many organizational schemas are possible, and the selection of one can have an impact on the success of the discovery process. Structured variables provide a very useful method for providing learning programs with background information about a feature domain, when such is available. A schema for structuring an attribute may be provided either by a domain expert or by a learning system. The implementation of structured attributes can introduce the concepts of generalization, agglomeration, anchor nodes and multiple domain views to a discovery system.

In large databases the structuring of nominal or numeric attributes can assist in the discovery process. In most attribute domains in which there are more than just a few distinct values, structuring of the domain is usually both possible and recommended. There will generally be a way to organize the values according to some classification schema. This allows the import of background knowledge, even to those empirical discovery engines that traditionally rely on a minimum of background knowledge. This domain knowledge, in turn, can result in the discovery of relationships more attuned to the user's existing understanding of the background domain through such techniques as the definition of anchor nodes. Attribute structuring can also be used for output variables. Doing so provides a means for separating the tasks of determining the general class of the decision and determining the specific decision within that class.

By allowing multiple representations of structured and numeric data, adaptive representation selection may be possible, potentially leading to discovering relationships that can alter a user's preconceived notions about the domain. The learning engine can select representations for the attribute domains after, rather than before the learning. These representations may include not only variations on one basis for classification, but also orthogonal classification hierarchies. Similarly, problem-oriented quantization of numeric data may enhance the likelihood of useful results in continuous domains.

Techniques such as anchor nodes and multiple domain views can help create an environment in which a representation space suitable to the problem is selected, while attention is focused on the levels of abstraction of greatest utility to the user. One area for future research is the development of a representation of a node's significance beyond a simple anchor/non-anchor value, and the exploration of thresholds for determining the proper level of generalization in such an environment.

Acknowledgments

This research was conducted in the Machine Learning and Inference Laboratory at George Mason University. The Laboratory's research is supported in part by the Defense Advanced Research Projects Agency under Grant No. N00014-91-J-1854 administered by the Office of Naval Research, in part by the Defense Advanced Research Projects Agency under Grants No. F49620-92-J-0549 and F49620-95-1-0462 administered by the Air Force Office of Scientific Research, in part by the Office of Naval Research under Grant No. N00014-91-J-1351, and in part by the National Science Foundation under Grants No. DMI-9496192 and IRI-9020266.

References

Fisher, D. 1987. Knowledge Acquisition via Incremental Conceptual Clustering. *Machine Learning*, 2:139-172.

Fisher, D. 1995. Optimization and Simplification of Hierarchical Clusterings. *Proceedings of the First International Conference on Knowledge Discovery and Data Mining (KDD-95)*, Montreal, PQ, 118-123.

Karni, R. and Loksh, S. 1996. Generalization Trees as Discovered Knowledge for Manufacturing Management. Forthcoming.

Kaufman, K., Michalski, R.S. and Kerschberg, L. 1991. Mining For Knowledge in Data: Goals and General Description of the INLEN System. In Piatetsky-Shapiro, G. and Frawley, W.J. (Eds.), *Knowledge Discovery in Databases*, Menlo Park, CA: AAAI Press, 449-462.

Kerber, R. 1992. ChiMerge: Discretization of Numeric Attributes. *Proceedings of the Tenth National Conference on Artificial Intelligence (AAAI-92)*, San Jose, CA, 123-127.

Klimesch, W. 1988. *Struktur und Aktivierung des Gedaechtnisses. Das Vernetzungsmodell: Grundlagen und Elemente einer uebergreifenden Theorie.* Bern: Verlag Hans Huber.

Kubat, M., Bratko, I. and Michalski, R.S. 1996. A Review of Machine Learning Techniques. Chapter in *Methods and Applications of Machine Learning and Discovery* (forthcoming).

Michalski, R.S. and McCormick, B.H. 1971. Interval Generalization of Switching Theory. *Proceedings of the 3rd Annual Houston Conference on Computer and System Science*, Houston, TX.

Michalski, R.S. 1980. Inductive Learning as Rule-Guided Generalization and Conceptual Simplification of Symbolic Descriptions: Unifying Principles and a Methodology. *Workshop on Current Developments in Machine Learning*, Carnegie Mellon University, Pittsburgh, PA.

Michalski, R.S. 1983. A Theory and Methodology of Inductive Learning. Chapter in Michalski, R.S., Carbonell, J. and Mitchell, T. (Eds.), *Machine Learning: An Artificial Intelligence Approach*, Palo Alto: Tioga Publishing, Co., 83-134.

Michalski, R.S. (1994). Inferential Theory of Learning: Developing Foundations for Multistrategy Learning. Chapter in *Machine Learning: A Multistrategy Approach*, Michalski, R.S. and Tecuci, G. (Eds.), San Francisco: Morgan Kaufmann, 3-61.

Michalski, R.S., Kerschberg, L., Kaufman, K. and Ribeiro, J. 1992. Mining for Knowledge in Databases: The INLEN Architecture, Initial Implementation and First Results. *Journal of Intelligent Information Systems: Integrating AI and Database Technologies*, 1(1): 85-113.

Michalski, R.S., Mozetic, I., Hong, J. and Lavrac, N. 1986. The AQ15 Inductive Learning System: An Overview and Experiments. Report No. UIUCDCS-R-86-1260, Department of Computer Science, University of Illinois, Urbana, IL.

Michalski, R.S. and Stepp, R.E. 1983. Automated Construction of Classifications: Conceptual Clustering versus Numerical Taxonomy. *IEEE Transactions on Pattern Analysis and Machine Intelligence*, 5(4): 396-410.

Reinke, R.E. 1984. Knowledge Acquisition and Refinement Tools for the Advise Meta-Expert System. Master's Thesis, University of Illinois at Urbana-Champaign.

Rosch, E., Mervis, C., Gray, W., Johnson, D. and Boyes-Braem, P. 1976. Basic Objects in Natural Categories, *Cognitive Psychology*, 8:382-439.

Sokal, R.R. and Sneath, P.H. 1973. *Principles of Numerical Taxonomy*. San Francisco: W.H. Freeman.

Self-Organizing Maps of Document Collections: A New Approach to Interactive Exploration

Krista Lagus, Timo Honkela, Samuel Kaski, and Teuvo Kohonen
Helsinki University of Technology
Neural Networks Research Centre
Rakentajanaukio 2 C, FIN-02150 Espoo, Finland
e-mail: Krista.Lagus@hut.fi

Abstract

Powerful methods for interactive exploration and search from collections of free-form textual documents are needed to manage the ever-increasing flood of digital information. In this article we present a method, WEBSOM, for automatic organization of full-text document collections using the self-organizing map (SOM) algorithm. The document collection is ordered onto a map in an unsupervised manner utilizing statistical information of short word contexts. The resulting ordered map where similar documents lie near each other thus presents a general view of the document space. With the aid of a suitable (WWW-based) interface, documents in interesting areas of the map can be browsed. The browsing can also be interactively extended to related topics, which appear in nearby areas on the map. Along with the method we present a case study of its use.
Keywords: data visualization, document organization, full-text analysis, interactive exploration, self-organizing map.

Introduction

Finding relevant information from the vast material available, e.g., in the Internet is a difficult and time-consuming task. Efficient search tools such as search engines have quickly emerged to aid in this endeavor. However, the basic problem with traditional search methods such as searching by keywords or by indexed contents is the difficulty to devise suitable search expressions, which would neither leave out relevant documents, nor produce long listings of irrelevant hits. Even with a rather clear idea of the desired information it may be difficult to come up with all the suitable key terms and search expressions. Thus, a method of encoding the information based, e.g., on semantically homogeneous *word categories* rather than individual words would be helpful.

An even harder problem, for which search methods are usually not even expected to offer much support, is encountered when interests are vague and hard to describe verbally. Likewise, if the area of interest resides at the outer edges of one's current knowledge, devising search expressions is like finding a path in total darkness, and the results are poor. If there were something like a map of the document collection at hand, a map where documents were ordered meaningfully according to their content, then even partial knowledge of the connections of the desired information to something already familiar would be useful. Maps might help the exploration first by visualizing the information space, and then by guiding one to the desired information as well as to related subjects. A visualized map of the information landscape might even reveal surprising connections between different areas of knowledge.

The self-organizing map (SOM) (Kohonen 1982; 1995; Kohonen *et al.* 1996) is a means for automatically arranging high-dimensional statistical data so that alike inputs are in general mapped close to each other. The resulting map avails itself readily to visualization, and thus the distance relations between different data items can be illustrated in a familiar and intuitive manner.

When suitably encoded textual documents are organized with the SOM algorithm, the map of the document collection provides a general view to the information contained in the document landscape, a view where changes between topics are generally smooth and no strict borders exist. Easy exploration of the document landscape may then be provided, e.g., via the World Wide Web (WWW).

The WEBSOM Method

Before ordering the documents they must be *encoded*; this is a crucial step since the final ordering depends on the chosen encoding scheme. In principle, a document might be encoded as a histogram of its words. Often the computational burden required for treating the histograms would, however, be orders of magnitude too large with the vast vocabularies used for automatic full-text analysis. An additional problem with the word histograms is that the discrete, symbolic words as such retain no information of their relatedness. Synonyms appear to be as distant as any unrelated words, although in a useful full-text analysis method similar words should obviously be encoded similarly.

Since it is not currently feasible to incorporate references to real-life experience of word meanings to a text analysis method, the remaining alternative is to use the statistics of the *contexts* of words to provide information on their relatedness. It has turned out that the size of the word histograms can be reduced to a fraction with the so-called self-organizing semantic maps (Ritter & Kohonen 1989). At the same time, by virtue of the organizing power of the SOM, the semantic similarity of the words can be taken into account in encoding the documents.

Preprocessing Text

Before applying the SOM to a document collection (in this case 8800 articles from a Usenet newsgroup, with a total of 2 000 000 words) we automatically removed some non-textual information from the documents. In the remaining text, numerical expressions and several kinds of common code words were categorized with heuristic rules into a few classes of special symbols. To reduce the computational load the words that occurred only a few times (in this experiment less than 50 times) in the whole data base were neglected and treated as empty slots.

In order to emphasize the subject matters of the articles and to reduce variations caused by the different discussion styles, which were not of interest in this experiment, a group of common words that were not supposed to discriminate any discussion topics were discarded from the vocabulary. In the actual experiment we removed 1000 common words from the vocabulary of 3300 words that remained after discarding the rarest words.

The SOM Algorithm

To provide a general understanding of what the self-organizing map is and why it is suitable for ordering large collections of text documents, the following expedition of thought may be helpful.

Consider an information processing system, such as a brain area, which must learn to carry out different tasks, each of them well. Let us assume that the system may assign different tasks to different sub-units that are able to learn from what they do. Each new task is given to the unit that can best complete the task. Since the units learn, and since they receive tasks that they can do well, they become even more competent in those tasks. This is a model of specialization by competitive

learning. Furthermore, if the units are interconnected in such a way that also the (predefined) *neighbors* of the unit carrying out a task are allowed to learn some of the task, the system also slowly becomes ordered: nearby units have similar abilities, and the abilities change slowly and smoothly over the whole system. This is the general principle of the self-organizing map (SOM). The system is called a *map* and the task is to imitate, i.e., *represent* the input. The representations become ordered according to their similarity relations in an unsupervised learning process. This property makes the SOM useful for organizing large collections of data in general, including document collections.

In the simplest kinds of SOMs the map consists of a regular grid of units, and the task is to represent statistical data, described by vectors $x \in \Re^n$. Each map unit i contains a model vector $m_i \in \Re^n$, and the model vectors are used for representing the data. In the learning process the model vectors change gradually so that finally the map forms an ordered non-linear regression of the model vectors into the data space.

At each step t of the learning process, a data sample $x(t)$ is presented to the units. The node c that best represents the input is then searched for using, e.g., the Euclidean distance to define the quality of the representation: $\|x - m_c\| = min_i\{\|x - m_i\|\}$. Next, the unit c as well as the neighboring units learn to represent the data sample more accurately. The model vector of unit i is updated according to the following learning rule:

$$m_i(t+1) = m_i(t) + h_{ci}(t)[x(t) - m_i(t)]. \quad (1)$$

Here h_{ci} is a "smearing" or neighborhood function expressing how much the unit i is updated when unit c is the winner. The neighborhood function typically is a symmetric, monotonically decreasing function of the distance of units i and c *on the map grid*. During repeated application of (1) with different inputs, model vectors of neighboring map units become gradually similar because of the neighborhood function h_{ci}, eventually leading to global ordering of the model vectors.

The Word Category Map

The word category map that is used for document encoding is organized according to word similarities, measured by the similarity of the contexts of the words. Conceptually related words tend to fall into the same or neighboring map nodes. Nodes may thus be viewed as word categories. The ordering is formed by the SOM algorithm based on the average short contexts of the words (Ritter & Kohonen 1989).

In our experiment, the word contexts were of length three, and consisted of one preceding and one following word in addition to the word that was being encoded. The ith word in the sequence of words is represented by an n-dimensional (here 90) real vector x_i with random number components. The averaged context vector of a word, marked by w, may be expressed as follows:

$$X(w) = \left[\begin{array}{c} E\{x_{i-1}|x_i = w\} \\ \varepsilon w \\ E\{x_{i+1}|x_i = w\} \end{array} \right], \qquad (2)$$

where E denotes the conditional average over the whole text corpus, and ε is a small constant, here 0.2. Now the real-valued vectors $X(w)$, in our experiment of dimension 270, constitute the input vectors given to the word category map. During the training of the map, the averaged context vectors $X(w)$ were used as input.

After the map has self-organized, each map node corresponds to a set of input vectors that are close to each other in the input space. A map node may thus be expected to approximate a set of similar inputs, here averaged word contexts. All the inputs for which a node is the best match are associated with the node. The result is a labeling of the map with words, where each node on the map is associated with all the inputs $X(w)$ for which the node is the closest representative. The word in the middle of the context, that is, the word corresponding to the w part of the context vector, was used as a label of the node. In this method a unit may become labeled by several symbols, often synonymic or describing alternative or opposing positions or characteristics. Examples of map nodes are illustrated in Fig. 1. Interrelated words that have similar contexts tend to appear near each other on the map.

The Document Map

With the aid of the word category map the documents can be encoded as *word category histograms*. Very closely related words (that are in the same category on the map) then contribute identically to the code formed for a document.

It would also be advantageous if words in *similar* categories contributed similarly to the codes of the documents. This is indeed possible to achieve since the word category map is ordered. The relations of the categories are reflected in their distances on the map. Therefore, the contributions of nearby categories can be made similar by *smoothing* the histogram on the word category map, whereby the encoding becomes less influenced by the choices of words made by the authors of the documents. A moderately narrow (e.g., diminishing to the half of the maximum value between two neighboring map units) Gaussian function was found to be a suitable smoothing kernel in our recent experiments.

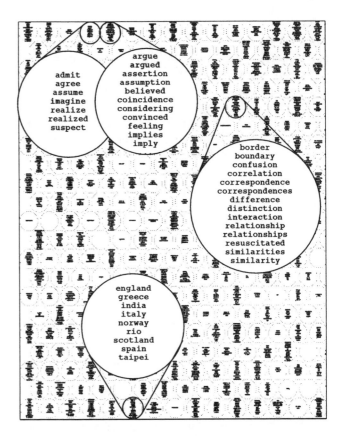

Figure 1: *Sample categories illustrated on a word category map. Similar words tend to occur in the same or nearby map nodes, forming "word categories". The map was computed using a massively parallel neurocomputer CNAPS, and fine-tuned with the SOM_PAK software (Kohonen et al. 1996).*

A representative sample of the encoded documents is presented as input to the SOM, which organizes them by unsupervised learning. After the map is formed, also documents that were *not* used in the learning may be automatically positioned onto the map.

When the learning process is complete the density of the documents in the document space can be visualized as shades of gray on the document map, to illustrate the relations of different map locations (see Fig. 3).

Previous Work on Organizing Documents with the SOM

Several studies have been published on SOMs that map words into grammatical and semantic categories (e.g., by Honkela, Pulkki, & Kohonen 1995; Miikkulainen 1993; Ritter & Kohonen 1989; 1990; and Scholtes 1993). The SOM has also been utilized previously to form a small map based on the titles of scientific documents (Lin, Soergel, & Marchionini 1991). Scholtes has applied the SOM extensively in natural language processing, e.g., developed a neural filter along with a neural interest map for information retrieval (1992a; 1992b). Merkl (1993; Merkl, Tjoa, & Kappel 1994) has used the SOM to cluster textual descriptions of software library components. Quite recently we have also been informed of an approach studied in the University of Arizona AI Lab for organizing WWW-pages.

Exploring Document Maps

We have designed a browsing environment which utilizes the order of the document map. The document collection may be explored with any graphical WWW browser.

Example: Documents from the Usenet Newsgroup sci.lang

To ensure that the WEBSOM method works in realistic applications, we performed a case study with material that is difficult enough from the textual analysis point of view. We organized a map with a collection of 8800 full-text articles that appeared in the Usenet newsgroup "sci.lang" during the latter half of 1995, containing approximately a total of 2 000 000 words. The articles are colloquial, mostly rather carelessly written short documents that contain little topical information to organize them properly. Furthermore, spelling errors are not uncommon. Currently (1 May) over 13 000 articles have been organized by the map.

Viewing the Document Collection

The document maps may be explored via a point-and-click interface: the user may zoom in on any map area by clicking the map image to view the underlying document space in more detail. Fig. 2 presents the four different view levels that one encounters when exploring the material. The view of the whole map (part 1 of Fig. 2) offers a general overview on the whole document collection. The display may be focused to a zoomed map view, deeper to a specific node, and finally to a single document.

In a typical session, the user might start from the overall map view, and proceed to examine further a specific area, perhaps later gradually wandering to close-by areas containing related information. Clickable arrow images are provided for moving around on the map. After finding a particularly interesting node, one may use it as a "trap" or "document bin" which can be checked regularly to see if new interesting articles have arrived. An exploration example of the "sci.lang" map is shown in Fig. 3.

Multiple Applications of the WEBSOM Method

The WEBSOM method is readily applicable to any kind of a collection of textual documents. It is especially suitable for exploration tasks in which the users either do not know the domain very well, or they have only a limited or vague idea of the contents of the full-text database being examined. With the WEBSOM, the documents are ordered meaningfully according to their contents, and thus related documents are located near each other. Maps also help the exploration by giving an overall view of what the document space looks like.

In the World Wide Web, one target of application for the WEBSOM is the organization of home pages instead of newsgroup articles. Also electronic mail messages can be automatically positioned on a suitable map organized according to personal interests. Relevant areas and single nodes on the map could be used as "mailboxes" into which specified information is automatically gathered.

The method can also be used to organize official letters, personal files, library collections, and corporate full-text databases. Especially administrative or legal documents may be difficult to locate by traditional information retrieval methods, because of the specialized terminologies used. The category-based and redundantly encoded approach of the WEBSOM is expected to alleviate the terminology problem.

Conclusions

In this work we have presented a novel method for organizing collections of documents into maps, and a browsing interface for exploring the maps. The method, called the WEBSOM, performs a completely automatic and unsupervised full-text analysis of the document set using self-organizing maps. The result of the analysis, an ordered map of the document space, visualizes the similarity relations of the subject matters of the documents; they are reflected as distance relations on the document map.

The present version of the WEBSOM interface has the basic functionality needed for exploring the document collection: Moving on the document map, zooming in on the map and viewing the contents of the nodes. Many different directions for enhancing the interface are possible. For example, ideal starting points for exploration could be provided by finding the position where a user-specified document would fall on the map. The WEBSOM (Honkela *et al.* 1996) tool is already available for exploring collections of Usenet news articles.

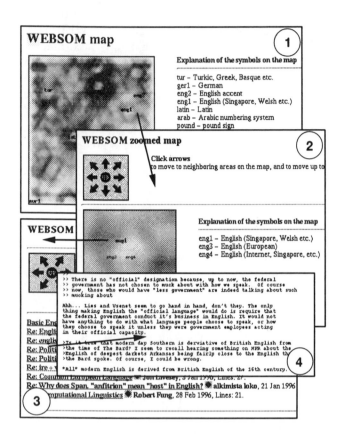

Figure 2: *The different view levels, (1) whole map, (2) zoomed map, (3) map node, and (4) single document, in the order of increasing detail. Moving between the levels or to neighboring areas on the same level is done by mouse clicks on the images or on the document links. Once an interesting area on the map has been found, one may use the arrow images to proceed to explore neighboring areas containing related documents. This can be contrasted with the traditional information retrieval techniques, where the users cannot know whether there are considerable numbers of relevant documents just "outside" the search results.*

Figure 3: *An example of map exploration. The contents of four map nodes in the upper right corner of the sci.lang map are shown. The shades of gray reflect distances between the map locations in the document space, a dark shade corresponding to a long distance. In a distinct area of its own (the upmost arrow), one can find articles on German or written in German. The remaining three neigboring nodes contain articles related to English, for instance, its usage around the world, historical English, and English as a common language for European Union, or for the Internet community. It is to be noted that some of the titles may be quite disassociated from the contents. In long discussions the original title is often used even after the conversation has diverged into several threads.*

References

Honkela, T.; Kaski, S.; Lagus, K.; and Kohonen, T. 1996. Newsgroup exploration with WEBSOM method and browsing interface. Technical Report A32, Helsinki University of Technology, Laboratory of Computer and Information Science, Espoo. WEBSOM home page (1996) available at http://websom.hut.fi/websom/.

Honkela, T.; Pulkki, V.; and Kohonen, T. 1995. Contextual relations of words in Grimm tales analyzed by self-organizing map. In Fogelman-Soulié, F., and Gallinari, P., eds., *Proceedings of the International Conference on Artificial Neural Networks, ICANN-95*, volume 2, 3–7. Paris: EC2 et Cie.

Kohonen, T.; Hynninen, J.; Kangas, J.; and Laaksonen, J. 1996. SOM_PAK: The self-organizing map program package. Technical Report A31, Helsinki University of Technology, Laboratory of Computer and Information Science, Espoo.

Kohonen, T. 1982. Self-organized formation of topologically correct feature maps. *Biological Cybernetics* 43:59–69.

Kohonen, T. 1995. *Self-Organizing Maps*. Berlin: Springer.

Lin, X.; Soergel, D.; and Marchionini, G. 1991. A self-organizing semantic map for information retrieval. In *Proceedings of the 14th Annual International ACM/SIGIR Conference on Research & Development in Information Retrieval.* 262–269.

Merkl, D.; Tjoa, A. M.; and Kappel, G. 1994. A self-organizing map that learns the semantic similarity of reusable software components. In *Proceedings of the 5th Australian Conference on Neural Networks, ACNN'94.* 13–16.

Merkl, D. 1993. Structuring software for reuse - the case of self-organizing maps. In *Proceedings of the International Joint Conference on Neural Networks, IJCNN-93-Nagoya*, volume III, 2468–2471. Piscataway, NJ: IEEE Service Center.

Miikkulainen, R. 1993. *Subsymbolic Natural Language Processing: An Integrated Model of Scripts, Lexicon, and Memory.* Cambridge, MA: MIT Press.

Ritter, H., and Kohonen, T. 1989. Self-organizing semantic maps. *Biological Cybernetics* 61:241–254.

Ritter, H., and Kohonen, T. 1990. Learning 'semantotopic maps' from context. In *Proceedings of the International Joint Conference on Neural Networks, IJCNN-90-Washington-DC*, volume I, 23–26. Hillsdale, NJ: Lawrence Erlbaum.

Scholtes, J. C. 1991a. Kohonen feature maps in full-text data bases: A case study of the 1987 Pravda. In *Proc. Informatiewetenschap 1991, Nijmegen*, 203–220. Nijmegen, Netherlands: STINFON.

Scholtes, J. C. 1991b. Unsupervised learning and the information retrieval problem. In *Proceedings of the International Joint Conference on Neural Networks, IJCNN'91*, 18–21. Piscataway, NJ: IEEE Service Center.

Scholtes, J. C. 1993. *Neural Networks in Natural Language Processing and Information Retrieval.* Ph.D. Dissertation, Universiteit van Amsterdam, Amsterdam, Netherlands.

The Quest Data Mining System

Rakesh Agrawal and **Manish Mehta** and **John Shafer** and **Ramakrishnan Srikant**[*]

IBM Almaden Research Center
San Jose, California 95120, U.S.A.

Andreas Arning and **Toni Bollinger**

IBM German Software Development Laboratory
Boeblingen, Germany

Introduction

The goal of the Quest project at the IBM Almaden Research center is to develop technology to enable a new breed of data-intensive decision-support applications. This paper is a capsule summary of the current functionality and architecture of the Quest data mining System.

Our overall approach has been to identify basic data mining operations that cut across applications and develop fast, scalable algorithms for their execution (Agrawal, Imielinski, & Swami 1993a). We wanted our algorithms to:

- *discover* patterns in very large databases, rather than simply verify that a pattern exists;

- have a *completeness* property that guarantees that all patterns of certain types have been discovered;

- have high performance and near-linear scaling on very large (multiple gigabytes) real-life databases.

We discuss the operations of discovering association rules, sequential patterns, time-series clustering, classification, and incremental mining. Due to space limitation, we only give highlights and point the reader to the relevant information for details. Unfortunately, for the same reason, we have not been able to include a discussion of the related work. Besides proceedings of the KDD, SIGMOD, VLDB, and Data Engineering Conferences, other excellent sources of information about the data mining systems and algorithms include (Piatetsky-Shapiro & Frawley 1991) (Fayyad *et al.* 1995). Further information about Quest can be obtained from http://www.almaden.ibm.com/cs/quest. IBM is making the Quest technology commercially available through the data mining product, IBM Intelligent Miner.

---

[*]Current members of the Quest group.

Association Rules

We introduced the problem of discovering *association rules* in (Agrawal, Imielinski, & Swami 1993b). Given a set of transactions, where each transaction is a set of literals (called items), an association rule is an expression of the form $X \Rightarrow Y$, where X and Y are sets of items. The intuitive meaning of such a rule is that transactions of the database which contain X tend to contain Y. An example of an association rule is: "30% of transactions that contain beer also contain diapers; 2% of all transactions contain both of these items". Here 30% is called the *confidence* of the rule, and 2% the *support* of the rule. The problem is to find all association rules that satisfy user-specified minimum support and minimum confidence constraints. Applications include discovering affinities for market basket analysis and cross-marketing, catalog design, loss-leader analysis, store layout, customer segmentation based on buying patterns, etc. See (Nearhos, Rothman, & Viveros 1996) for a case study of a successful application in health insurance.

Apriori Algorithm

The problem of mining association rules is decomposed into two subproblems (Agrawal, Imielinski, & Swami 1993b):

- Find all combinations of items that have transaction support above minimum support. Call those combinations *frequent* itemsets.

- Use the frequent itemsets to generate the desired rules. The general idea is that if, say, $ABCD$ and AB are frequent itemsets, then we can determine if the rule $AB \Rightarrow CD$ holds by computing the ratio $r = \text{support}(ABCD)/\text{support}(AB)$. The rule holds only if $r \geq$ minimum confidence. Note that the rule will have minimum support because $ABCD$ is frequent.

The Apriori algorithm (Agrawal & Srikant 1994) used in Quest for finding all frequent itemsets is

```
procedure AprioriAlg()
begin
    L₁ := {frequent 1-itemsets};
    for ( k := 2; Lₖ₋₁ ≠ ∅; k++ ) do {
        Cₖ := apriori-gen(Lₖ₋₁);  // New candidates
        forall transactions t in the dataset do {
            forall candidates c ∈ Cₖ contained in t do
                c.count++;
        }
        Lₖ := {c ∈ Cₖ | c.count ≥ min-support}
    }
    Answer := ⋃ₖ Lₖ;
end
```

Figure 1: Apriori Algorithm

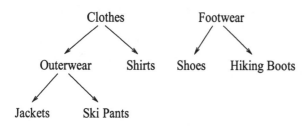

Figure 2: Example of a Taxonomy

given in Figure 1. It makes multiple passes over the database. In the first pass, the algorithm simply counts item occurrences to determine the frequent 1-itemsets (itemsets with 1 item). A subsequent pass, say pass k, consists of two phases. First, the frequent itemsets L_{k-1} (the set of all frequent $(k-1)$-itemsets) found in the $(k-1)$th pass are used to generate the candidate itemsets C_k, using the *apriori-gen()* function. This function first joins L_{k-1} with L_{k-1}, the joining condition being that the lexicographically ordered first $k-2$ items are the same. Next, it deletes all those itemsets from the join result that have some $(k-1)$-subset that is not in L_{k-1}, yielding C_k. For example, let L_3 be {{1 2 3}, {1 2 4}, {1 3 4}, {1 3 5}, {2 3 4}}. After the join step, C_4 will be {{1 2 3 4}, {1 3 4 5} }. The prune step will delete the itemset {1 3 4 5} because the itemset {1 4 5} is not in L_3. We will then be left with only {1 2 3 4} in C_4.

The algorithm now scans the database. For each transaction, it determines which of the candidates in C_k are contained in the transaction using a hash-tree data structure and increments the count of those candidates. At the end of the pass, C_k is examined to determine which of the candidates are frequent, yielding L_k. The algorithm terminates when L_k becomes empty.

Generalizations

Very often, taxonomies (*is-a* hierarchies) over the items are available. An example of a taxonomy is shown in Figure 2: this taxonomy says that Jacket *is-a* Outerwear, Ski Pants *is-a* Outerwear, Outerwear *is-a* Clothes, etc. Users are often interested in generating rules that span different levels of the taxonomy. For example, we may infer a rule that people who buy Outerwear tend to buy Hiking Boots from the fact that people bought Jackets with Hiking Boots and and Ski Pants with Hiking Boots. However, the support for the rule "Outerwear ⇒ Hiking Boots" may not be the sum of the supports for the rules "Jackets ⇒ Hiking Boots" and "Ski Pants ⇒ Hiking Boots" since some people may have bought Jackets, Ski Pants and Hiking Boots in the same transaction. Also, "Outerwear ⇒ Hiking Boots" may be a valid rule, while "Jackets ⇒ Hiking Boots" and "Clothes ⇒ Hiking Boots" may not. The former may not have minimum support, and the latter may not have minimum confidence. This generalization of association rules and the algorithm used in Quest for finding such rules are described in (Srikant & Agrawal 1995).

Another generalization of the problem of mining association rules is to discover rules in data containing both quantitative and categorical attributes. An example of such a "quantitative" association rule might be that "10% of married people between age 50 and 60 have at least 2 cars". We deal with quantitative attributes by fine-partitioning the values of the attribute and then combining adjacent partitions as necessary. We also have measures of partial completeness that quantify the information loss due to partitioning. This generalization and the algorithm for finding such rules used in Quest are presented in (Srikant & Agrawal 1996a).

One potential problem that users experience in applying association rules to real problems is that many uninteresting or redundant rules may be generated along with the interesting rules. In (Srikant & Agrawal 1995) (further generalized in (Srikant & Agrawal 1996a)), a "greater-than-expected-value" interest measure was introduced, which is used in Quest to prune redundant rules.

Sequential Patterns

We introduced the problem of discovering *sequential patterns* in (Agrawal & Srikant 1995). The input data is a set of sequences, called data-sequences. Each data-sequence is a list of transactions, where each transaction is a sets of items (literals). Typically there is a transaction-time associated with each transaction. A *sequential pattern* also consists of a list of sets of items. The problem is to find all sequential patterns with a user-specified minimum *support*, where the support of a sequential pattern is the percentage of data-sequences that contain the pattern.

For example, in the database of a book-club, each data-sequence may correspond to all book selections of a customer, and each transaction to the books selected by the customer in one order. A sequential pattern might be "5% of customers bought 'Foundation', then 'Foundation and Empire', and then 'Second Foundation'". The data-sequence corresponding to a customer who bought some other books in between these books still contains this sequential pattern; the data-sequence may also have other books in the same transaction as one of the books in the pattern. Elements of a sequential pattern can be sets of items, for example, "'Foundation' and 'Ringworld', followed by 'Foundation and Empire' and 'Ringworld Engineers', followed by 'Second Foundation'". However, all the items in an element of a sequential pattern must be present in a single transaction for the data-sequence to support the pattern.

This problem was initially motivated by applications in the retailing industry, including attached mailing, add-on sales, and customer satisfaction. But the results apply to many scientific and business domains. For instance, in the medical domain, a data-sequence may correspond to the symptoms or diseases of a patient, with a transaction corresponding to the symptoms exhibited or diseases diagnosed during a visit to the doctor. The patterns discovered using this data could be used in disease research to help identify symptoms/diseases that precede certain diseases.

Generalizations

The basic definition of sequential patterns was generalized in (Srikant & Agrawal 1996b) to incorporate following features:

- **Introduction of time constraints.** Users often want to specify maximum and/or minimum time gaps between adjacent elements of the sequential pattern. For example, a book club probably does not care if someone bought "Foundation", followed by "Foundation and Empire" three years later; they may want to specify that a customer should support a sequential pattern only if adjacent elements occur within a specified time interval, say three months.

- **Flexible definition of a transaction.** For many applications, it is immaterial if items in an element of a sequential pattern were present in two different transactions, as long as the transaction-times of those transactions are within some small time window. That is, each element of the pattern can be

contained in the union of the items bought in a set of transactions, as long as the difference between the maximum and minimum transaction-times is less than the size of a sliding time window. For example, if the book-club specifies a time window of a week, a customer who ordered the "Foundation" on Monday, "Ringworld" on Saturday, and then "Foundation and Empire" and "Ringworld Engineers" in a single order a few weeks later would still support the pattern "'Foundation' and 'Ringworld', followed by 'Foundation and Empire' and 'Ringworld Engineers'".

In addition, if there were taxonomies (*is-a* hierarchies) over the items in the data, the sequential patterns could now include items across different levels of the taxonomy.

See (Srikant & Agrawal 1996b) for a description of the GSP algorithm used in Quest for finding such generalized sequential patterns.

Time-Series Clustering

Time-series data constitute a large portion of data stored in computers. The capability to find time-series (or portions thereof) that are "similar" to a given time-series or to be able to find groups of similar time-series has several applications. Examples include identifying companies with similar pattern of growth, finding products with similar selling patterns, discovering stocks with similar price movements, determining portions of seismic waves that are not similar to spot geological irregularities, etc.

We introduced a model of time-series similarity in (Agrawal *et al.* 1995a). In this model, two time-series are considered to be similar if they have enough non-overlapping time-ordered pieces (subseries) that are similar. The amplitude of one of the two time-series is allowed to be scaled by any suitable amount and its offset adjusted appropriately before matching the other series. Two subsequences are considered similar if one lies within an envelope of ϵ width around the other, ignoring outliers. The matching subseries need not be aligned along the time axis. Figure 3 captures the intuition underlying our similarity model.

The matching system used in Quest is described in (Agrawal *et al.* 1995a). It consists of three main parts: (i) "atomic" subseries matching, (ii) long subseries matching, and (iii) series matching. The basic idea is to create a fast, indexable data structure using small, atomic subseries that represents all the series up to amplitude scaling and offset, and find atomic matches by doing a self-join on this structure. The initial prototype used the $R+$-tree for this representation. A faster data structure described in (Shim, Srikant, & Agrawal

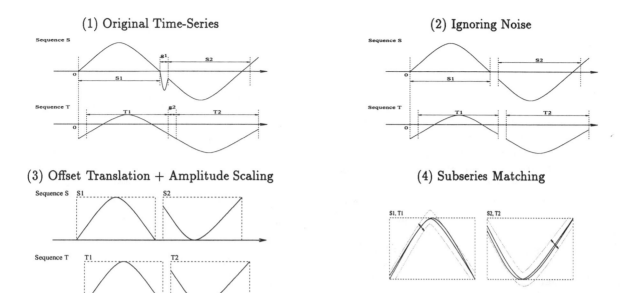

(1) Original Time-Series

(2) Ignoring Noise

(3) Offset Translation + Amplitude Scaling

(4) Subseries Matching

Figure 3: Illustration of Time-series matching

1996) is now used in its place. The second stage employs a fast algorithm for stitching atomic matches to form long subseries matches, allowing non-matching gaps to exist between the atomic matches. The third stage linearly orders the subseries matches found in the second stage to determine if enough similar pieces exist in the two time-series. In every stage, the system allows for the flexibility of user/system-defined matching parameters without sacrificing efficiency.

Classification

Classification is a well recognized data mining operation and it has been studied extensively in statistics and machine learning literature (Weiss & Kulikowski 1991). However, most of the current classification algorithms have the restriction that the training data should fit in memory. In data mining applications, very large training sets with several million examples are common. We therefore wanted to design a classifier that scales well and can handle training data of this magnitude (without resorting to sampling/partitioning). The ability to classify larger training data can also lead to improved classification accuracy.

SLIQ (*S*upervised *L*earning *I*n *Q*uest), described in (Mehta, Agrawal, & Rissanen 1996), is a decision tree classifier, designed to classify large training data. It uses a pre-sorting technique in the tree-growth phase. This sorting procedure is integrated with a breadth-first tree growing strategy to enable classification of disk-resident datasets. In the pruning phase, it uses a pruning strategy based on the Minimum Description Length (MDL) principle. The net result of these techniques is that, given training data that can be handled by another decision tree classifier, SLIQ exhibits the same accuracy characteristics, but executes much faster and produces smaller trees. Moreover, SLIQ can potentially obtain higher accuracies by classifying larger (disk-resident) training datasets which cannot be handled by other classifiers.

While SLIQ was the first classifier to address several issues in building a fast scalable classifier and it gracefully handles disk-resident data that are too large to fit in memory, it still requires some information to stay memory-resident. Furthermore, this information grows in direct proportion to the number of input records, putting a hard-limit on the size of training data. We have recently designed a new decision-tree-based classification algorithm, called SPRINT (*S*calable *Pa*R*allelizable *IN*duction of decision *T*rees) that for the first time removes all of the memory restrictions, and is fast and scalable and easily parallelizable. The algorithm, presented in (Shafer, Agrawal, & Mehta 1996), can classify data sets irrespective of the number of classes, attributes, and examples (records), making it an attractive tool for data mining.

Incremental Mining

As the data mining technology is applied in the production mode, the need for *incremental/active* mining arises (Agrawal & Psaila 1995). Rather than applying a mining algorithm to the whole data, the data is first partitioned according to time periods. The granularity of the time period is application-dependent. The mining algorithm is now applied to each of the partitioned data sets and patterns are obtained for each time period. These patterns are collected into a database. In this database, each statistical parameter of a pattern will have a sequence of values, called the history of the parameter for that pattern. We can now query the database using predicates that select patterns based on the shape of the history of some or all parameters. A shape query language is presented for this purpose in (Agrawal *et al.* 1995b).

The user can specify triggers over the database in which the triggering condition is a query on the shape of the history. As fresh data comes in for the current time period, the mining algorithm is run over this data, and the database is updated with the generated patterns. This update causes the histories of the patterns to be extended. This, in turn, may cause the triggering condition to be satisfied for some patterns and the corresponding actions to be executed.

Such active systems can be used, for instance, to build early warning systems for spotting trends in the retail industry. For example, if we were mining association rules, we would have histories for the support and confidence of each rule. Following the promotion for an item X, the user may specify a notification trigger on the rule $X \Rightarrow Y$; the triggering condition being that the support history remains stable, but the confidence history takes the shape of a downward ramp. Firing of this trigger will signify that if the goal of promoting X was to drag the sale of Y, it was not fulfilled. The loyalists continued to buy X and Y together, but the new buyers cherry-picked X.

Parallelism

Given that mining can involve very large amounts of data, parallel algorithms are needed. Quest algorithms have been parallelized to run on IBM's shared-nothing multiprocessor SP2. The parallel implementation of the mining of association rules is described in (Agrawal & Shafer 1996). This implementation shows linear scale-up for association rules. Mining of sequential patterns is also parallelized using similar techniques. We have also parallelized the SPRINT classification algorithm (Shafer, Agrawal, & Mehta 1996), where all processors work together to build a single classification model. Measurements from these implementations show excellent scaleup, speedup and sizeup characteristics.

System Architecture

Figure 4 shows the system architecture of the Quest system. The mining algorithms run on the server close

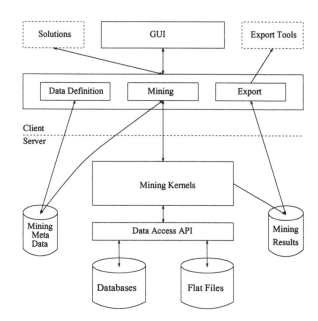

Figure 4: The Quest System Architecture

to the data source. Users interact with the system through a GUI that can run on the same work-station or on a different client machine. There is an open API using which the user can optionally import results of any mining operation into software of choice.

An interesting aspect of the Quest architecture is its I/O architecture. There is a standard stream interface defined for all accesses to input, insulating the algorithm code from data repository details, which are encapsulated in a data access API. Thus, it is easy to add new data repository types to the Quest system.

The Quest system runs both on AIX and MVS platforms, against data in flat files as well as DB2 family of database products. Databases can be accessed in a loosely-coupled mode using dynamic SQL. However, for better performance, it is possible to run the mining algorithm in a tightly-coupled mode described in (Agrawal & Shim 1996).

Future Directions

We plan to continue on the current path of identifying new data mining operations and developing fast algorithms for their execution. Two operations that we are currently focusing on are deviation detection (Arning & Agrawal 1996) and segmentation of high-dimensional data. We are also interested in mining data types other than structured data, such as text, particularly in the context of the world-wide web. Finally, we are also exploring the interaction between discovery-driven and verification-driven data mining, especially in OLAP databases.

Acknowledgment The Quest system is the result of efforts of many who rightfully belong to the author list. They include George Almasi, Ute Baumbach, Dominique Brodbeck, Srinivas Bulusu, Mike Carey, Stefan Dipper, Christos Faloutsos, Takeshi Fukuda, Sakti Ghosh, Ashish Gupta, Howard Ho, Maurice Houtsma, Tomasz Imielinski, Bala Iyer, David Lin, Hansel Miranda, Shinichi Morishita, Leon Pauser, Giuseppe Psaila, Prabhakar Raghavan, Jorma Rissanen, Harpreet Sawhney, Sunita Sarawagi, Ashok Savasere, Kyuseok Shim, Arun Swami, Peter Vigants, Marisa Viveros, Ed Wimmers, and Mohamed Zaït. Bill Bath, Cindy Baune, Tony Clacko, Ron Groves, Barry Mason, and Molly Nicole were some of the early adopters of the Quest system. Finally, the Quest sytem would not have become the reality but for the faith of Chris Arnold, Walter Baur, Ashok Chandra, Bill Cody, Peter Greissl, Laura Haas, Frank Leymann, John McPherson, Dragutin Petkovic, Pat Selinger, Mario Schkolnick, and Irv Traiger.

References

Agrawal, R., and Psaila, G. 1995. Active data mining. In *Proc. of the 1st Int'l Conference on Knowledge Discovery in Databases and Data Mining*.

Agrawal, R., and Shafer, J. 1996. Parallel mining of association rules: Design, implementation and experience. Research Report RJ 10004, IBM Almaden Research Center, San Jose, California. To appear in *IEEE Transactions on Knowledge and Data Engineering*.

Agrawal, R., and Shim, K. 1996. Developing tightly-coupled data mining applications on a relational database system. In *Proc. of the 2nd Int'l Conference on Knowledge Discovery in Databases and Data Mining*.

Agrawal, R., and Srikant, R. 1994. Fast Algorithms for Mining Association Rules. In *Proc. of the 20th Int'l Conference on Very Large Databases*.

Agrawal, R., and Srikant, R. 1995. Mining Sequential Patterns. In *Proc. of the 11th Int'l Conference on Data Engineering*.

Agrawal, R.; Lin, K.-I.; Sawhney, H. S.; and Shim, K. 1995a. Fast similarity search in the presence of noise, scaling, and translation in time-series databases. In *Proc. of the 21st Int'l Conference on Very Large Databases*.

Agrawal, R.; Psaila, G.; Wimmers, E. L.; and Zaït, M. 1995b. Querying shapes of histories. In *Proc. of the 21st Int'l Conference on Very Large Databases*.

Agrawal, R.; Imielinski, T.; and Swami, A. 1993a. Database mining: A performance perspective. *IEEE Transactions on Knowledge and Data Engineering* 5(6):914–925.

Agrawal, R.; Imielinski, T.; and Swami, A. 1993b. Mining association rules between sets of items in large databases. In *Proc. of the ACM SIGMOD Conference on Management of Data*, 207–216.

Arning, A., and Agrawal, R. 1996. A linear method for deviation detection in large databases. In *Proc. of the 2nd Int'l Conference on Knowledge Discovery in Databases and Data Mining*.

Fayyad, U. M.; Piatetsky-Shapiro, G.; Smyth, P.; and Uthurusamy, R., eds. 1995. *Advances in Knowledge Discovery and Data Mining*. AAAI/MIT Press.

Mehta, M.; Agrawal, R.; and Rissanen, J. 1996. SLIQ: A fast scalable classifier for data mining. In *Proc. of the Fifth Int'l Conference on Extending Database Technology (EDBT)*.

Nearhos, J.; Rothman, M.; and Viveros, M. 1996. Applying data mining techniques to a health insurance information system. In *Proc. of the 22nd Int'l Conference on Very Large Databases*.

Piatetsky-Shapiro, G., and Frawley, W. J., eds. 1991. *Knowledge Discovery in Databases*. Menlo Park, CA: AAAI/MIT Press.

Shafer, J.; Agrawal, R.; and Mehta, M. 1996. Fast serial and parallel classification of very large data bases. In *Proc. of the 22nd Int'l Conference on Very Large Databases*.

Shim, K.; Srikant, R.; and Agrawal, R. 1996. The ϵ-k-d-b tree: A fast index structure for high-dimensional similarity joins. Research Report, IBM Almaden Research Center, San Jose, California.

Srikant, R., and Agrawal, R. 1995. Mining Generalized Association Rules. In *Proc. of the 21st Int'l Conference on Very Large Databases*.

Srikant, R., and Agrawal, R. 1996a. Mining Quantitative Association Rules in Large Relational Tables. In *Proc. of the ACM SIGMOD Conference on Management of Data*.

Srikant, R., and Agrawal, R. 1996b. Mining Sequential Patterns: Generalizations and Performance Improvements. In *Proc. of the Fifth Int'l Conference on Extending Database Technology (EDBT)*.

Weiss, S. M., and Kulikowski, C. A. 1991. *Computer Systems that Learn: Classification and Prediction Methods from Statistics, Neural Nets, Machine Learning, and Expert Systems*. Morgan Kaufman.

DBMiner: A System for Mining Knowledge in Large Relational Databases*

Jiawei Han   Yongjian Fu   Wei Wang   Jenny Chiang   Wan Gong   Krzysztof Koperski   Deyi Li
Yijun Lu   Amynmohamed Rajan   Nebojsa Stefanovic   Betty Xia   Osmar R. Zaiane

Data Mining Research Group, Database Systems Research Laboratory
School of Computing Science, Simon Fraser University, British Columbia, Canada V5A 1S6
E-mail: {han, yongjian, weiw, ychiang, wgong, koperski, dli, yijunl, arajan, nstefano, bxia, zaiane}@cs.sfu.ca
URL: http://db.cs.sfu.ca/ (for research group)   http://db.cs.sfu.ca/DBMiner (for system)

Abstract

A data mining system, DBMiner, has been developed for interactive mining of multiple-level knowledge in large relational databases. The system implements a wide spectrum of data mining functions, including generalization, characterization, association, classification, and prediction. By incorporating several interesting data mining techniques, including attribute-oriented induction, statistical analysis, progressive deepening for mining multiple-level knowledge, and meta-rule guided mining, the system provides a user-friendly, interactive data mining environment with good performance.

Introduction

With the upsurge of research and development activities on knowledge discovery in databases (Piatetsky-Shapiro & Frawley 1991; Fayyad *et al.* 1996), a data mining system, DBMiner, has been developed based on our studies of data mining techniques, and our experience in the development of an early system prototype, DBLearn. The system integrates data mining techniques with database technologies, and discovers various kinds of knowledge at multiple concept levels from large relational databases efficiently and effectively.

The system has the following distinct features:

1. It incorporates several interesting data mining techniques, including attribute-oriented induction (Han, Cai, & Cercone 1993; Han & Fu 1996), statistical analysis, progressive deepening for mining multiple-level rules (Han & Fu 1995; 1996), and meta-rule guided knowledge mining (Fu & Han 1995). It also implements a wide spectrum of data mining functions including generalization, characterization, association, classification, and prediction.

2. It performs interactive data mining at multiple concept levels on any user-specified set of data in a database using an SQL-like Data Mining Query Language, DMQL, or a graphical user interface. Users may interactively set and adjust various thresholds, control a data mining process, perform *roll-up* or *drill-down* at multiple concept levels, and generate different forms of outputs, including generalized relations, generalized feature tables, multiple forms of generalized rules, visual presentation of rules, charts, curves, etc.

3. Efficient implementation techniques have been explored using different data structures, including generalized relations and multiple-dimensional data cubes. The implementations have been integrated smoothly with relational database systems.

4. The data mining process may utilize user- or expert-defined set-grouping or schema-level concept hierarchies which can be specified flexibly, adjusted dynamically based on data distribution, and generated automatically for numerical attributes. Concept hierarchies are being taken as an integrated component of the system and are stored as a relation in the database.

5. Both UNIX and PC (Windows/NT) versions of the system adopt a client/server architecture. The latter may communicate with various commercial database systems for data mining using the ODBC technology.

The system has been tested on several large relational databases, including NSERC (Natural Science and Engineering Research Council of Canada) research grant information system, with satisfactory performance. Additional data mining functionalities are being designed and will be added incrementally to the system along with the progress of our research.

Architecture and Functionalities

The general architecture of DBMiner, shown in Figure 1, tightly integrates a relational database system, such as a Sybase SQL server, with a concept hierarchy module, and a set of knowledge discovery modules. The discovery modules of DBMiner, shown in Fig-

---

*Research was supported in part by the grant NSERC-OPG003723 from the Natural Sciences and Engineering Research Council of Canada, the grant NCE:IRIS/Precarn-HMI-5 from the Networks of Centres of Excellence of Canada, and grants from B.C. Advanced Systems Institute, MPR Teltech Ltd., and Hughes Research Laboratories.

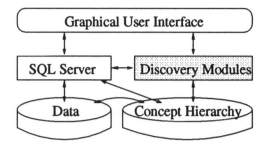

Figure 1: General architecture of DBMiner

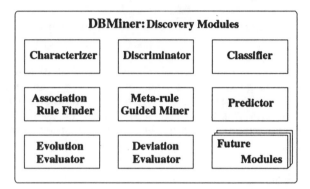

Figure 2: Knowledge discovery modules of DBMiner

ure 2, include characterizer, discriminator, classifier, association rule finder, meta-rule guided miner, predictor, evolution evaluator, deviation evaluator, and some planned future modules.

The functionalities of the knowledge discovery modules are briefly described as follows:

- The **characterizer** generalizes a set of task-relevant data into a *generalized relation* which can then be used for extraction of different kinds of rules or be viewed at multiple concept levels from different angles. In particular, it derives a set of **characteristic rules** which summarizes the general characteristics of a set of user-specified data (called the *target class*). For example, the symptoms of a specific disease can be summarized by a characteristic rule.

- A **discriminator** discovers a set of **discriminant rules** which summarize the features that distinguish the class being examined (the *target class*) from other classes (called *contrasting classes*). For example, to distinguish one disease from others, a discriminant rule summarizes the symptoms that discriminate this disease from others.

- A **classifier** analyzes a set of training data (i.e., a set of objects whose class label is known) and constructs a model for each class based on the features in the data. A set of **classification rules** is generated by such a classification process, which can be used to classify future data and develop a better understanding of

each class in the database. For example, one may classify diseases and provide the symptoms which describe each class or subclass.

- An **association rule finder** discovers a set of association rules (in the form of "$A_1 \wedge \cdots \wedge A_i \rightarrow B_1 \wedge \cdots \wedge B_j$") at multiple concept levels from the relevant set(s) of data in a database. For example, one may discover a set of symptoms often occurring together with certain kinds of diseases and further study the reasons behind them.

- A **meta-rule guided miner** is a data mining mechanism which takes a user-specified meta-rule form, such as "$P(x, y) \wedge Q(y, z) \rightarrow R(x, z)$" as a pattern to confine the search for desired rules. For example, one may specify the discovered rules to be in the form of "$major(s : student, x) \wedge P(s, y) \rightarrow gpa(s, z)$" in order to find the relationships between a student's major and his/her gpa in a university database.

- A **predictor** predicts the possible values of some missing data or the value distribution of certain attributes in a set of objects. This involves finding the set of attributes relevant to the attribute of interest (by some statistical analysis) and predicting the value distribution based on the set of data similar to the selected object(s). For example, an employee's potential salary can be predicted based on the salary distribution of similar employees in the company.

- A **data evolution evaluator** evaluates the data evolution regularities for certain objects whose behavior changes over time. This may include characterization, classification, association, or clustering of time-related data. For example, one may find the general characteristics of the companies whose stock price has gone up over 20% last year or evaluate the trend or particular growth patterns of certain stocks.

- A **deviation evaluator** evaluates the deviation patterns for a set of task-relevant data in the database. For example, one may discover and evaluate a set of stocks whose behavior deviates from the trend of the majority of stocks during a certain period of time.

Another important function module of **DBMiner** is concept hierarchy which provides essential background knowledge for data generalization and multiple-level data mining. Concept hierarchies can be specified based on the relationships among database attributes (called *schema-level hierarchy*) or by set groupings (called *set-grouping hierarchy*) and be stored in the form of relations in the same database. Moreover, they can be adjusted dynamically based on the distribution of the set of data relevant to the data mining task. Also, hierarchies for numerical attributes can be constructed automatically based on data distribution analysis (Han & Fu 1994).

DMQL and Interactive Data Mining

DBMiner offers both an SQL-like data mining query language, DMQL, and a graphical user interface for interactive mining of multiple-level knowledge.

Example 1. To characterize CS grants in the *NSERC96* database related to discipline code and amount category in terms of count% and amount%, the query is expressed in DMQL as follows,

```
use NSERC96
find characteristic rules for "CS_Discipline_Grants"
from award A, grant_type G
related to disc_code, amount, count(*)%, amount(*)%
where A.grant_code = G.grant_code
      and A.disc_code = "Computer Science"
```

The query is processed as follows: The system collects the relevant set of data by processing a transformed relational query, generalizes the data by *attribute-oriented induction*, and then presents the outputs in different forms, including generalized relations, generalized feature tables, multiple (including visual) forms of generalized rules, pie/bar charts, curves, etc.

A user may interactively set and adjust various kinds of thresholds to control the data mining process. For example, one may adjust the generalization threshold for an attribute to allow more or less distinct values in this attribute. A user may also *roll-up* or *drill-down* the generalized data at multiple concept levels.   □

A data mining query language such as DMQL facilitates the standardization of data mining functions, systematic development of data mining systems, and integration with standard relational database systems. Various kinds of graphical user interfaces can be developed based on such a data mining query language. Such interfaces have been implemented in DBMiner on three platforms: Windows/NT, UNIX, and Netscape. A graphical user interface facilitates interactive specification and modification of data mining queries, concept hierarchies, and various kinds of thresholds, selection and change of output forms, roll-up or drill-down, and dynamic control of a data mining process.

Implementation of DBMiner

Data structures: Generalized relation vs. multi-dimensional data cube

Data generalization is a core function of DBMiner. Two data structures, *generalized relation*, and *multi-dimensional data cube*, can be considered in the implementation of data generalization.

A *generalized relation* is a relation which consists of a set of (generalized) attributes (storing generalized values of the corresponding attributes in the original relation) and a set of "aggregate" (*measure*) attributes (storing the values resulted from executing aggregate functions, such as *count*, *sum*, etc.), and in which each

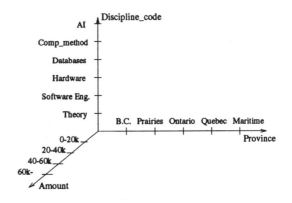

Figure 3: A multi-dimensional data cube

tuple is the result of generalization of a set of tuples in the original data relation. For example, a generalized relation *award* may store a set of tuples, such as "*award(AI, 20_40k, 37, 835900)*", which represents the generalized data for discipline code is "AI", the amount category is "20_40k", and such kind of data takes 37 in count and $835,900 in (total) amount.

A *multi-dimensional data cube* is a multi-dimensional array structure, as shown in Figure 3, in which each dimension represents a generalized attribute and each cell stores the value of some aggregate attribute, such as *count*, *sum*, etc. For example, a multi-dimensional data cube *award* may have two dimensions: "discipline code" and "amount category". The value "AI" in the "discipline code" dimension and "20-40k" in the "amount category" dimension locate the corresponding values in the two aggregate attributes, *count* and *sum*, in the cube. Then the values, *count%* and *amount%*, can be derived easily.

In comparison with the generalized relation structure, a multi-dimensional data cube structure has the following advantages: First, it may often save storage space since only the measurement attribute values need to be stored in the cube and the generalized (dimensional) attribute values will serve only as dimensional indices to the cube; second, it leads to fast access to particular cells (or slices) of the cube using indexing structures; third, it usually costs less to produce a cube than a generalized relation in the process of generalization since the right cell in the cube can be located easily. However, if a multi-dimensional data cube structure is quite sparse, the storage space of a cube is largely wasted, and the generalized relation structure should be adopted to save the overall storage space.

Both data structures have been explored in the DBMiner implementations: the generalized relation structure is adopted in version 1.0, and a multi-dimensional data cube structure in version 2.0. A more flexible implementation is to consider both structures, adopt the multi-dimensional data cube structure when the size of the data cube is reasonable, and switch to the generalized relation structure (by dynamic allocation) otherwise (this can be estimated based on the number of dimensions being considered, and the attribute threshold of each dimension). Such an alternative will be considered in our future implementation.

Besides designing good data structures, efficient implementation of each discovery module has been explored, as discussed below.

Multiple-level characterization

Data characterization summarizes and characterizes a set of task-relevant data, usually based on generalization. For mining multiple-level knowledge, progressive deepening (*drill-down*) and progressive generalization (*roll-up*) techniques can be applied.

Progressive generalization starts with a conservative generalization process which first generalizes the data to slightly higher concept levels than the primitive data in the relation. Further generalizations can be performed on it progressively by selecting appropriate attributes for step-by-step generalization. Strong characteristic rules can be discovered at multiple abstraction levels by filtering (based on the corresponding thresholds at different levels of generalization) generalized tuples with weak support or weak confidence in the rule generation process.

Progressive deepening starts with a relatively high-level generalized relation, selectively and progressively specializes some of the generalized tuples or attributes to lower abstraction levels.

Conceptually, a top-down, progressive deepening process is preferable since it is natural to first find general data characteristics at a high concept level and then follow certain interesting paths to step down to specialized cases. However, from the implementation point of view, it is easier to perform generalization than specialization because generalization replaces low level tuples by high ones through ascension of a concept hierarchy. Since generalized tuples do not register the detailed original information, it is difficult to get such information back when specialization is required later.

Our technique which facilitates specializations on generalized relations is to save a "*minimally generalized relation/cube*" in the early stage of generalization. That is, each attribute in the relevant set of data is generalized to minimally generalized concepts (which can be done in one scan of the data relation) and then identical tuples in such a generalized relation/cube are merged together, which derives the minimally generalized relation. After that, both *progressive deepening* and *interactive up-and-down* can be performed with reasonable efficiency: If the data at the current abstraction level is to be further generalized, generalization can be performed directly on it; on the other hand, if it is to be specialized, the desired result can be derived by generalizing the minimally generalized rela-

tion/cube to appropriate level(s).

Discovery of discriminant rules

The *discriminator* of DBMiner finds a set of discriminant rules which distinguishes the general features of a target class from that of contrasting class(es) specified by a user. It is implemented as follows.

First, the set of relevant data in the database has been collected by query processing and is partitioned respectively into a *target* class and one or a set of *contrasting* class(es). Second, attribute-oriented induction is performed on the target class to extract a *prime target relation/cube*, where a *prime target relation* is a generalized relation in which each attribute contains no more than but close to the threshold value of the corresponding attribute. Then the concepts in the *contrasting* class(es) are generalized to the same level as those in the prime target relation/cube, forming the *prime contrasting relation/cube*. Finally, the information in these two classes is used to generate qualitative or quantitative discriminant rules.

Moreover, interactive drill-down and roll-up can be performed synchronously in both target class and contrasting class(es) in a similar way as that explained in the last subsection (characterization). These functions have been implemented in the discriminator.

Multiple-level association

Based on many studies on efficient mining of association rules (Agrawal & Srikant 1994; Srikant & Agrawal 1995; Han & Fu 1995), a multiple-level association rule finder has been implemented in DBMiner.

Different from mining association rules in transaction databases, a relational association rule miner may find two kinds of associations: *nested association* and *flat association*, as illustrated in the following example.

Example 2. Suppose the "course_taken" relation in a university database has the following schema:

course_taken = (student_id, course, semester, grade).

Nested association is the association between a data object and a set of attributes in a relation by viewing data in this set of attributes as a nested relation. For example, one may find the associations between students and their course performance by viewing "(*course, semester, grade*)" as a nested relation associated with *student_id*.

Flat association is the association among different attributes in a relation without viewing any attribute(s) as a nested relation. For example, one may find the relationships between *course* and *grade* in the *course_taken* relation such as "*the courses in computing science tend to have good grades*", etc.

Two associations require different data mining techniques.

For mining nested associations, a data relation can be transformed into a nested relation in which the tuples which share the same values in the unnested attributes are merged into one. For example, the *course_taken* relation can be folded into a nested relation with the schema,

$$course\_taken = (student\_id, course\_history)$$
$$course\_history = (course, semester, grade).$$

By such transformation, it is easy to derive association rules like *"90% senior CS students tend to take at least three CS courses at 300-level or up in each semester"*. Since the nested tuples (or values) can be viewed as data items in the same transaction, the methods for mining association rules in transaction databases, such as (Han & Fu 1995), can be applied to such transformed relations in relational databases.

Multi-dimensional data cube structure facilitates efficient mining of multi-level flat association rules. A count cell of a cube stores the number of occurrences of the corresponding multi-dimensional data values, whereas a dimension count cell stores the sum of counts in the whole dimension. With this structure, it is straightforward to calculate the measurements such as *support* and *confidence* of association rules. A set of such cubes, ranging from the least generalized cube to rather high level cubes, facilitate mining of association rules at multiple concept levels. □

Meta-rule guided mining

Since there are many ways to derive association rules in relational databases, it is preferable to have users to specify some interesting constraints to guide a data mining process. Such constraints can be specified in a *meta-rule* (or *meta-pattern*) form (Shen *et al.* 1996), which confines the search to specific forms of rules. For example, a meta-rule "$P(x, y) \rightarrow Q(x, y, z)$", where P and Q are predicate variables matching different properties in a database, can be used as a rule-form constraint in the search.

In principle, a meta-rule can be used to guide the mining of many kinds of rules. Since the association rules are in the form similar to logic rules, we have first studied meta-rule guided mining of association rules in relational databases (Fu & Han 1995). Different from the study by (Shen *et al.* 1996) where a meta-predicate may match any relation predicates, deductive predicates, attributes, etc., we confine the search to those predicates corresponding to the attributes in one relation. One such example is illustrated as follows.

Example 3. A meta-rule guided data mining query can be specified in DMQL as follows for mining a specific form of rules related to a set of attributes: *"major, gpa, status, birth_place, address"* in relation *student* for those born in Canada in a *university* database.

find association rules in the form of
$$major(s : student, x) \wedge Q(s, y) \rightarrow R(s, z)$$

related to major, gpa, status, birth_place, address
from student
where birth_place = "Canada"

Multi-level association rules can be discovered in such a database, as illustrated below:

$$major(s, \text{``Science''}) \wedge gpa(s, \text{``Excellent''}) \rightarrow$$
$$status(s, \text{``Graduate''}) \quad (60\%)$$
$$major(s, \text{``Physics''}) \wedge status(s, \text{``M.Sc''}) \rightarrow$$
$$gpa(s, \text{``3.8\_4.0''}) \quad (76\%)$$

The mining of such multi-level rules can be implemented in a similar way as mining multiple-level association rules in a multi-dimensional data cube. □

Classification

Data classification is to develop a description or model for each class in a database, based on the features present in a set of class-labeled training data.

There have been many data classification methods studied, including decision-tree methods, such as ID-3 and C4.5 (Quinlan 1993), statistical methods, neural networks, rough sets, etc. Recently, some database-oriented classification methods have also been investigated (Mehta, Agrawal, & Rissanen 1996).

Our classifier adopts a generalization-based decision-tree induction method which integrates attribute-oriented induction with a decision-tree induction technique, by first performing attribute-oriented induction on the set of training data to generalize attribute values in the training set, and then performing decision tree induction on the generalized data.

Since a generalized tuple comes from the generalization of a number of original tuples, the *count* information is associated with each generalized tuple and plays an important role in classification. To handle noise and exceptional data and facilitate statistical analysis, two thresholds, *classification threshold* and *exception threshold*, are introduced. The former helps justification of the classification at a node when a significant set of the examples belong to the same class; whereas the latter helps ignore a node in classification if it contains only a negligible number of examples.

There are several alternatives for doing generalization before classification: A data set can be generalized to either a minimally generalized concept level, an intermediate concept level, or a rather high concept level. Too low a concept level may result in scattered classes, bushy classification trees, and difficulty at concise semantic interpretation; whereas too high a level may result in the loss of classification accuracy.

Currently, we are testing several alternatives at integration of generalization and classification in databases, such as (1) generalize data to some medium concept levels; (2) generalize data to intermediate concept level(s), and then perform node merge and split for better class representation and classification accuracy; and (3) perform multi-level classification and select a desired level by a comparison of the classification quality at different levels. Since all three classification processes are performed in relatively small, compressed, generalized relations, it is expected to result in efficient classification algorithms in large databases.

Prediction

A predictor predicts data values or value distributions on the attributes of interest based on similar groups of data in the database. For example, one may predict the amount of research grants that an applicant may receive based on the data about the similar groups of researchers.

The power of data prediction should be confined to the ranges of numerical data or the nominal data generalizable to only a small number of categories. It is unlikely to give reasonable prediction on one's name or social insurance number based on other persons' data.

For successful prediction, the factors (or attributes) which strongly influence the values of the attributes of interest should be identified first. This can be done by the analysis of data relevance or correlations by statistical methods, decision-tree classification techniques, or simply be based on expert judgement. To analyze attribute correlation, our predictor constructs a contingency table followed by association coefficient calculation based on χ^2-test by the analysis of minimally generalized data in databases. The attribute correlation associated with each attribute of interest is precomputed and stored in a special relation in the database.

When a prediction query is submitted, the set of data relevant to the requested prediction is collected, where the relevance is based on the attribute correlations derived by the query-independent analysis. The set of data which matches or is close to the query condition can be viewed as similar group(s) of data. If this set is big enough (i.e., sufficient evidence exists), its value distribution on the attribute of interest can be taken as predicted value distribution. Otherwise, the set should be appropriately enlarged by generalization on less relevant attributes to certain high concept level to collect enough evidence for trustable prediction.

Further Development of DBMiner

The DBMiner system is currently being extended in several directions, as illustrated below.

- Further enhancement of the power and efficiency of data mining in relational database systems, including the improvement of system performance and rule discovery quality for the existing functional modules, and the development of techniques for mining new kinds of rules, especially on time-related data.

- Integration, maintenance and application of discovered knowledge, including incremental update of discovered rules, removal of redundant or less interesting rules, merging of discovered rules into a knowledge-base, intelligent query answering using discovered knowledge, and the construction of multiple layered databases.

- Extension of data mining technique towards advanced and/or special purpose database systems, including extended-relational, object-oriented, text, spatial, temporal, and heterogeneous databases. Currently, two such data mining systems, **GeoMiner** and **WebMiner**, for mining knowledge in spatial databases and the Internet information-base respectively, are being under design and construction.

References

Agrawal, R., and Srikant, R. 1994. Fast algorithms for mining association rules. In *Proc. 1994 Int. Conf. Very Large Data Bases*, 487–499.

Fayyad, U. M.; Piatetsky-Shapiro, G.; Smyth, P.; and Uthurusamy, R. 1996. *Advances in Knowledge Discovery and Data Mining.* AAAI/MIT Press.

Fu, Y., and Han, J. 1995. Meta-rule-guided mining of association rules in relational databases. In *Proc. 1st Int'l Workshop on Integration of Knowledge Discovery with Deductive and Object-Oriented Databases*, 39–46.

Han, J., and Fu, Y. 1994. Dynamic generation and refinement of concept hierarchies for knowledge discovery in databases. In *Proc. AAAI'94 Workshop on Knowledge Discovery in Databases (KDD'94)*, 157–168.

Han, J., and Fu, Y. 1995. Discovery of multiple-level association rules from large databases. In *Proc. 1995 Int. Conf. Very Large Data Bases*, 420–431.

Han, J., and Fu, Y. 1996. Exploration of the power of attribute-oriented induction in data mining. In Fayyad, U.; Piatetsky-Shapiro, G.; Smyth, P.; and Uthurusamy, R., eds., *Advances in Knowledge Discovery and Data Mining.* AAAI/MIT Press. 399–421.

Han, J.; Cai, Y.; and Cercone, N. 1993. Data-driven discovery of quantitative rules in relational databases. *IEEE Trans. Knowledge and Data Engineering* 5:29–40.

Mehta, M.; Agrawal, R.; and Rissanen, J. 1996. SLIQ: A fast scalable classifier for data mining. In *Proc. 1996 Int. Conference on Extending Database Technology (EDBT'96)*.

Piatetsky-Shapiro, G., and Frawley, W. J. 1991. *Knowledge Discovery in Databases.* AAAI/MIT Press.

Quinlan, J. R. 1993. *C4.5: Programs for Machine Learning.* Morgan Kaufmann.

Shen, W.; Ong, K.; Mitbander, B.; and Zaniolo, C. 1996. Metaqueries for data mining. In Fayyad, U.; Piatetsky-Shapiro, G.; Smyth, P.; and Uthurusamy, R., eds., *Advances in Knowledge Discovery and Data Mining.* AAAI/MIT Press. 375–398.

Srikant, R., and Agrawal, R. 1995. Mining generalized association rules. In *Proc. 1995 Int. Conf. Very Large Data Bases*, 407–419.

DataMine: Application Programming Interface and Query Language for Database Mining

Tomasz Imielinski and **Aashu Virmani** and **Amin Abdulghani**
{imielins, avirmani,aminabdu}@cs.rutgers.edu
Department of Computer Science
Rutgers University
New Brunswick, NJ 08903
Phone: (908) 445 3551, Fax: (908) 445 0537

Introduction

The main objective of the *DataMine* is to provide application development interface to develop knowledge discovery applications on the top of large databases.

Current database systems have been designed mainly to support business applications. The success of SQL capitalized on a small number of primitives which are sufficient to support a vast majority of applications today. Unfortunately this is not enough to capture the emerging family of new applications dealing with the so called *rule and knowledge discovery*. The goal of the *DataMine* and our work is to make the next step in the development of DBMS and provide much needed support for the rule discovery applications.

A typical knowledge discovery application starts with rule discovery, but rules are not necessarily the end products. For example:

1. Finding the "best" candidates for a marketing promotion package from a large population stored in the database; for example, the best candidates for certain type of insurance may be those who frequent health clubs and are under 40 etc.

2. Finding any strong rules between the age, disease, and residence area, such as "40% of heart disease case in NJ occur in patients older than 50" (rules are statements of the form "if *condition* then *consequent*".)

3. Finding the most distinctive features (as opposed to other states) of NJ heart patients

Finding rules is only the first step in a knowledge discovery application. Typically, a user wants to embed information obtained from the rules in a larger program. For instance, in target marketing applications a company may have a fixed promotion budget and can only offer some limited number of promotions. A promotion mailing application must rank the best candidates for mailing and go "down the list" of most likely candidates until all promotion offerings are taken. To accomplish such a task we need an integrated API for knowledge discovery applications, integrated with the programming language (like C) and with the database query language (such as SQL).

There is no commercial system nor research prototype today which would offer such integrated API for knowledge discovery applications. Today, most systems offer "stand alone" features using tree classifiers, neural nets, and meta-pattern generators. Such systems cannot be embedded into a large application and typically offer just one knowledge discovery feature. The situation today is thus very similar to the situation in DBMS in the early sixties when each application had to build from scratch, without the benefit of dedicated database primitives provided later by SQL and relational database APIs.

The objective of *DataMine* is to fill this gap and bring the database support for knowledge discovery applications *to the same level that exists today for business applications*. What we offer and plan to offer can be summarized as follows:

- Extension of SQL, called M-SQL to generate and selectively retrieve sets of rules from a large database.

- Embedding of M-SQL in the general host language (in a similar way as SQL is embedded in C) to provide API for Knowledge and Data Discovery applications.

Thus, just as SQL does, we are supporting two basic modes: *free form querying* and *embedded querying*. Free form querying allows the user to perform interactive and exploratory data analysis, while embedded querying provides features to run applications which rely on rule discovery, but use rules in some further computations.

Key Features

The key features of the *DataMine* system include:

- Extension of SQL to handle rule mining applications

  The proposed extension uses just one additional primitive - the *MINE* operator.

- Query Optimizer to compile M-SQL queries into efficient execution plans.

- Application Programming Interface (API) with M-SQL embedded into C++ host programming language

Both in the query language as well as in the application programming interface, a *single rule*, and a *set of rules* are the basic objects which are manipulated and queried. Rules are defined as in (Agrawal, Imielinski, & Swami 1993). A rule is an expression of the form:

Body $\Longrightarrow$ Consequent

where Body is a conjunction of descriptors and consequent is a descriptor. A descriptor is a pair (Attribute, Value), and is satisfied by those tuples in the database for which Attribute equals Value. (When the domain of A_i is continuous we also allow ranges of values to also appear as descriptors. Thus, for example, (Age IN $< 30, 40 >$) is a legal descriptor as well). Attributes could either exist in the database originally or could be a user defined method, in which case the evaluation for the method is done at run time.

Additionally, each rule is specified by two parameters: *support* and *confidence*. The **support** of the rule is defined as a number of tuples which satisfy the body of the rule. The **confidence** is defined as the ratio of the number of all tuples which satisfy both the body and the consequent to the number of all tuples which satisfy just the body of the rule.

Eager Evaluation: Since rule queries may possibly take a very long time to execute and in addition, may return very large rule sets, (the rule generation problem is in general of exponential worst case complexity in terms of number of attributes involved) we have implemented a new mode of query evaluation in which the first few rules are generated as soon as possible, and then a certain steady rate of rule production is ensured. This enables the system to keep users interested and let the user cognitively process the returned rules while other rules are generated.

Rule Query Language: The rule query language, M-SQL, (the M stands for Mining) is built as an extension of SQL by including a small set of primitives for data mining. A typical M-SQL query is of the form:

```
Select
    From Mine(C)
```

```
Where
    D-CONDITION
    s1 < Support < s2
    c1 < Confidence < c2
```

C can be a persistent class or a table defined by a "Mine-Free" SQL expression. Mine(C) returns the set of *all* rules as defined above, which are true in C. This set could be very large, but in the presence of constraints and D-Conditions (defined below), an optimized algorithm never actually generates the whole set. Thus, *Mine* is viewed as a logical operator. Let *MUST*, *MAY* and *TARGET* be sets of descriptors. D-CONDITION is defined as a disjunction of atoms of the following form:

$$(MUST \subset Body \subseteq MAY)$$
$$AND \ (Consequent \ IN \ TARGET)$$

This allows specification of conditions imposed on the bodies as well as on consequents of target rules. For example, the query: *"Find all rules in Table T involving the Attributes(methods) Disease, Age and ClaimAmt, which have a confidence of at least 50%"* might be expressed as:

```
select *
from Mine(T) R
where
    R.Body < {(Disease=*),(Age=*),(ClaimAmt=*)}
    and {} < R.Body
    and R.Consequent IN
            {(Disease=*),(Age=*),(ClaimAmt=*)}
    and R.Confidence > 0.5
```

The "from" line in the query allows substitution of Mine(T) for R, for notation simplicity. The above query explicitly disallows rules with empty bodies. However, a rule with an empty body does state a fact about the database, for example, a rule like $\emptyset \Longrightarrow$ **(Sex = 'Male') (30%, 239)** merely states that out of the database of 239 objects, 30 percent are males. Queries are compiled and executed using an efficient algorithm for rule generation (in the case when the data mining mode is used). We describe below the two lines of development we have chosen for the system, i.e. Free Form Querying, and Embedded querying, which complement each other and are each useful in their own ways.

Free Form Querying

Free form querying works in two modes: *data mining mode* and *rule mining mode*. First, the user formulates a rule query. The rule query is specified in M-SQL described above and describes the conditions which the rule should satisfy in order to be included in the answer. The current prototype implements only the graphical "query by example" style version of the language. Then, If a query is processed in the *data mining mode*, it is evaluated on the top of the original database and the requested rules are generated from data in the run time of the query. In the *rule mining mode*, it is assumed that rules have been generated earlier and are stored in a rule base. In this case query behaves like a pattern against which existing rules are matched and retrieved from the rulebase.

Data Mining Mode   This mode forms the core of the mining engine, which is responsible for transforming the query into an optimized algorithm for rule generation depending on the search space requested by the user. If the user has some understanding of the data set, he can exercise greater control over the mining process by specifying a user defined discretization function to be applied to continuous attributes (or one of the several builtin choices), and for instance, restricting the rules from containing redundant information by specifying dependencies that exist among the attributes. On the other hand, for a novice user, who is trying to gain an understanding of the data set, the mining engine can run in a highly interactive mode, where a graphical interface is constantly updated with progress information from the system (see "Exploratory Mining Scenario" later in this paper), and the user can query the rulebase as it is being generated, narrow his preferences about what he wants, and prune the overall rule-space the system must generate. Figure 1 shows a screen snapshot of this mode.

Rule Mining Mode   The rule mining mode helps to browse through the vast numbers of rules which can be generated from a database. In addition to being just a retriever/browser, this mode contains a builtin applications suite or "Macros" (described in more detail later) which run on top of the rulebase, and can help the user query the rulebase in a very effective manner. It also lets the user shuffle back and forth between the rulebase and database asking for tuples that satisfied or violated a given rule and vice-versa. Figure 2 shows one of the screen shots of this mode.

Embedded Querying: API

We demonstrate a number of pilot knowledge discovery applications which were developed using the proposed API, like classification, typicality and "characteristic of" applications. Using these

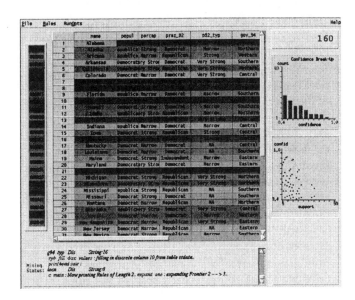

Figure 1: *DataMine system in online-mining mode.*

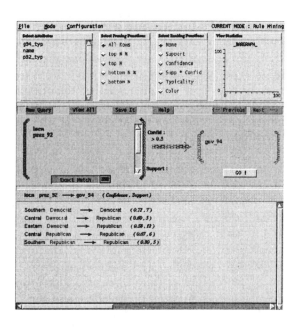

Figure 2: *Rule Manger - query based mining.*

applications one can find the "most typical" heart patients, the most characteristic features of smokers from New Jersey or the best candidates for life insurance in a given population sub-category. One can also "mine around a rule", when a user can look for rules which are similar but stronger than a given one.The key aspect of *DataMine* is that it provides application programming interface to develop new discovery applications.

Our API design mirrors the design of C++ with SQL calls, using standard host language/SQL interface involving cursors. We plan to offer a similar interface between C++ and M-SQL. This requires adding an extra class of *rules* and binding cursor variables which range through rule sets to that rule class. The rule class will be a generic library class with methods directly corresponding to the specific rule attributes. In addition, several visualization primitives are provided which to graphically display the rules, or to display a bar graph based on a certain attribute, or the confidence and support of a set of rules.

Scenarios of Use

In this section we briefly describe what you will see in the Demo of the existing prototype and some of the features which will be added very soon. The first four scenarios are fully supported, the fifth is currently "under construction".

Scenario 1: Mining around a rule

User starts from a specific rule which he wants to check/verify against the data. *DataMine* system additionally offers a possibility of *mining around a rule*, that is not only verifying whether the original rule holds but also *suggesting* other, perhaps stronger rules which are "close" to the original rule which the user wanted to verify.

Scenario 2: Rule Querying

User can query and obtain all rules having certain body, consequent, support, confidence, or a mixture of one of more the above criteria. Once the rules are generated, the user can pick a rule and further mine around it, as in the previous scenario. Alternately, (s)he can obtain all the records in the database which satisfy(violate) the rule, select a subset of these records, look for further rules there etc. This process crosses the border between the rulebase and the database many times and is highly interactive.

Scenario 3: Exploratory Mining

This mode is intended for the user who knows very little about the data, probably not enough to even formulate a query. In this mode, the system looks for all rules between all attributes in the database. This is computationally expensive, but we have

implemented this process in a very incremental way to keep the user interested. Such a user will see the database with tuples (records) changing colors, while mining process is taking place. The colors reflect how many rules, discovered so far, a given record in the database satisfies. The "hottest" (red color) tuples satisfy most of the rules and attract user's interest. The user can then click on such a record and see all the rules which such a record satisfies. In addition, a scatter plot of the confidence vs. support of the rules (see fig. 1) is also constantly updated. The user can zoom a section of this plot and see the rules contained in that confidence and support range. These queries can further lead to mining around a rule if some rule looks particularly interesting to the user.

Scenario 4: Typicality and Atypicality

This is an application which we have built using our API as a proof of concept. From the user specified subset of records it selects the most "typical" and the most "atypical" records. Typical records are the records which satisfy most of the rules, atypical records violate most of the rules. Coloring is used again to make a distinction between typical and atypical records (atypical are blue, typical are red). This application helps in identifying database irregularities and can be useful, for example, in fraud detection.

Scenario 5: Application Development

User constructs a new application on the top of the set of rules generated by a rule query. The graphical API helps the user to write a C program which uses rules as first class objects.

System Platform

The *DataMine* prototype has been built keeping in mind the above features. It currently generates propositional rules matching a specified set of patterns (The patterns could be wildcard, in which case it generates all rules). The mining engine has been implemented in C (about 15,000 lines of code), and the front and back end GUI has been developed using Tcl-Tk (about 20,000 lines of code). It can read data from Ascii files or from a database directly, without any need for preprocessing by the user. The database system used currently is Sybase 10.2, but the design ensures a "loose-coupling" between the database and the engine, so that plugging in modules for other database systems is very straightforward. The systems comes with a smart browser which can let a user query rules by example, perform mining "around" a first guess, and a pilot suite of applications which treat rules as first class objects, and we believe should be part of core M-SQL.

Currently, the system runs on Solaris 2.5 on an UltraSparc 170E, but in the near future, we hope to run a parallelized version of this algorithm on a cluster of 6 UltraSparcs connected via a gigabit switch.

Performance

The DataMine engine can be run in either a "Memory Saver Mode" when it uses more economical data structures (at the cost of time) which conserve memory (less swapping), or a "Performance Mode" where it uses slightly more memory intensive data structures, but performs much better. The idea is that if the data is relatively small (see fig 3 below), then it makes sense to make full use of memory available. The graph below was obtained by mining different fractions of a 1.2 million record database containing seven attributes in both modes, and comparing the performance. The steep rise in the time taken by performance mode (from 50% to 100% of data size) is explained by the fact that extensive swapping began at that point.

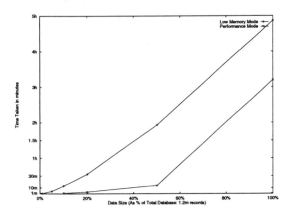

Figure 3: *Performance comparison in two modes of operation.*

Comparison with Relevant Systems

Systems which are compatible in scope include the DBMiner system (Han *et al.* 1996b) which is built on top of DMQL (Han *et al.* 1996a), another query language for rule generation.

However, our system is somewhat different in language design by providing a specific language primitive "Mine" as an extension to SQL. Besides, a query expressed in our language can work in rule generation (data-mining) mode as well as rule retrieval (rule-mining) mode.

In addition, this is, to our knowledge the first prototype of a system which provides an API to facilitate building complex data mining applications.

Conclusions

We believe that a "Query Based" approach is particularly suited for the data mining with human in the loop, where the human actively participates in the data mining process by changing and modifying the data mining requests. It makes an effective tool to provide users with precise specification of their mining interests, and also helps to deal with potentially very large results of data mining. There is a wide variety of applications which are using knowledge discovery techniques today. Typically, each application is handled by a specialized "stand alone" system which is developed from "scratch". The objective of our API design is to provide a platform which will make the knowledge discovery application development faster and easier. SQL and relational APIs increased programmer's productivity for business applications, DataMine will offer similar advantages for knowledge discovery application developers.

References

Agrawal, R., and Srikant, R. 1994. Fast algorithms for mining association rules. In *VLDB-94*.

Agrawal, R.; Ghosh, S.; Imielinski, T.; Iyer, B.; and Swami, A. 1992. An interval classifier for database mining applications. In *VLDB-92*, 560–573.

Agrawal, R.; Imielinski, T.; and Swami, A. 1993. Mining associations rules between sets of items in large databases. In *SIGMOD-93*.

Han, J., and Fu, Y. 1995. Discovery of multiple level association rules from large databases. In *VLDB-95*, 420–431.

Han, J.; Fu, Y.; Koperski, K.; Wang, W.; and Zaiane, O. 1996a. DMQL: A data mining query language for relational databases. In *DMKD-96 (SIGMOD-96 Workshop on KDD)*.

Han, J.; Fu, Y.; Wang, W.; Chiang, J.; Gong, W.; Koperski, K.; and Li, D. 1996b. DBMiner: A system for mining knowledge in large relational databases. to appear in KDD-96.

Imielinski, T., and Hirsh, H. 1993. Query based approach to knowledge discovery. Technical report, Rutgers University, NJ.

Kero, B.; Russell, L.; and Tsur, S. 1995. An overview of database mining techniques. Technical report, Argonne National Laboratory, Argonne, Illinois.

Mannila, H.; Toivonen, H.; and Verkamo, A. I. 1994. Efficient algorithms for discovering association rules. In *KDD-94*.

Piatetsky-Shapiro, G., and Frawley, W. J. 1991. *Knowledge Discovery in Databases.* AAAI/MIT Press.

Quinlan, J. R. 1986. Induction of decision trees. *Machine Learning* 1(1):81–106.

R.Agrawal; Imielinski, T.; and Swami, A. 1993. Database mining: A performance perspective. In *IEEE Transactions on Knowledge and Data Engineering, Special Issue on Learning and Discovery in Knowledge-Based Databases.*

Technology Spotlight

Evaluating the Interestingness of Characteristic Rules

Micheline Kamber
School of Computing Science
Simon Fraser University
Burnaby, BC V5A 1S6, Canada
kamber@cs.sfu.ca

Rajjan Shinghal
Dept. of Computer Science
Concordia University
Montreal, QC H3G 1M8, Canada
shinghal@cs.concordia.ca

Abstract

Knowledge Discovery Systems can be used to generate classification rules describing data from databases. Typically, only a small fraction of the rules generated may actually be of interest. Measures of rule *interestingness* allow us to filter out less interesting rules.

Classification rules may be discriminant ($e \rightarrow h$) or characteristic ($h \rightarrow e$), where e is evidence, and h is an hypothesis. For discriminant rules, e distinguishes h from $\neg h$. For characteristic rules, e summarizes one or more properties common to all instances of h. Both rule types can contribute insight into the data under analysis.

In this paper, we first expand on the rule interestingness measure principles proposed by Piatetsky-Shapiro (1991) and by Major and Mangano (1993) by adding a principle which, unlike the others, considers the difference between discriminant and characteristic rules.

We establish experimentally that the three popular interestingness measures for discriminant rules found in the literature do not fully serve their purpose when applied to characteristic rules. To our knowledge, no interestingness measures for characteristic rules have been published. We propose IC^{++}, an interestingness measure for characteristic rules based on necessity and sufficiency (Duda, Gaschnig, & Hart 1981). IC^{++} obeys each of the rule interestingness principles, unlike the other measures studied. If a given characteristic rule is found to be uninteresting by IC^{++}, three additional measures, which we present, can be used to derive other useful information regarding h and e.

Introduction

Knowledge Discovery Systems (KDSs) can be used to generate patterns describing the data in a given database. Typically, the number of patterns generated is very large, only a small fraction of which may actually be of interest to the KDS user or data analyst. Measures are therefore essential for the ranking of discovered patterns according to their degree of *interestingness*, thereby allowing the filtering out of less useful information.

Such interestingness measures can be objective or subjective. *Objective* measures are based on the structure of the discovered patterns and the statistics underlying them. Such factors include coverage, confidence, statistical significance, strength, simplicity, and redundancy (Agrawal, Imielinski, & Swami 1993; Piatetsky-Shapiro 1991; Major & Mangano 1993; Smyth & Goodman 1992; Hong & Mao 1991; Srikant & Agrawal 1995). *Subjective* measures are based on user beliefs regarding relationships in the data, recognizing that a pattern of interest to one user may not be so to another. Subjective measures evaluate the interestingness of discovered patterns with respect to their unexpectedness or actionability (Silberschatz & Tuzhilin 1995; Piatetsky-Shapiro & Matheus 1994). Here a pattern that contradicts a user expectation, or that a user may act on to his or her advantage, is deemed interesting. Objective and subjective measures are both useful in assessing the interestingness of data patterns. Ideally, given a set of discovered patterns, objective measures can be applied first to filter out those patterns that do not meet structural and statistical requirements. Subjective measures can then be applied to identify the patterns most interesting to the given user.

Different KDSs can generate different types of patterns (e.g., classification rules, association rules, time series patterns, etc.). This paper is concerned with the interestingness of classification rules. Classification rules may be discriminant ($e \rightarrow h$) or characteristic ($h \rightarrow e$), where e is evidence (typically a conjunction of database attribute-value conditions), and h is an hypothesis. For discriminant rules, e distinguishes h from $\neg h$. For characteristic rules, e summarizes one or more properties common to all instances of h. In medicine, for example, discriminant rules may be used to summarize the symptoms sufficient to distinguish one disease from another, whereas characteristic rules may be used to summarize the symptoms necessary for a given disease. Both types of rules can be of interest, contributing insight into the data under analysis.

Principles that all rule interestingness measures should follow have been proposed (Piatetsky-Shapiro 1991; Major & Mangano 1993). In this paper, we first expand on these by proposing an additional principle which, unlike the others, considers the difference between discriminant and characteristic rules.

The measures of Rule Interest, or RI (Piatetsky-Shapiro 1991), J (Smyth & Goodman 1992), and certainty (Hong & Mao 1991) are three popular interestingness measures from the literature for classification rules. Although these measures help assess the interestingness of discriminant rules, we establish experimentally that they do not fully serve their purpose when applied to characteristic rules. To the best of our knowledge, no interestingness measures for characteristic rules have been published. We propose IC^{++}, an objective interestingness measure for characteristic rules, based on technical definitions of necessity and sufficiency (Duda, Gaschnig, & Hart 1981). IC^{++} obeys each of the rule interestingness principles. We also present three other rule interestingness measures. If a given characteristic rule, $h \rightarrow e$, is deemed uninteresting by IC^{++}, these additional measures can be used to derive other useful information regarding h and e.

Rule Interestingness Measure Principles

Given a rule $e \rightarrow h$ or $h \rightarrow e$ we say that the rule is X% *complete* if e satisfies (i.e., is true for, or covers) X% of the tuples satisfying h. A rule is Y% *discriminant* if e satisfies (100-Y)% of the $\neg h$ tuples (i.e., tuples for which h is false). Principles that all rule *interestingness* measures, I, should follow have been proposed by Piatetsky-Shapiro (1991) and by Major and Mangano (1993). The principles consider rule completeness and discriminability. Let $|S|$ denote the size of set S (e.g., $|h \wedge e|$ is the number of tuples satisfying h and e). The principles are:

1. $I = 0$ if h and e are statistically independent of each other (Piatetsky-Shapiro 1991).
2. I increases monotonically with $|h \wedge e|$ when $|h|$, $|\neg h|$, and $|e|$ remain the same (Piatetsky-Shapiro 1991). In other words, the more reliable a rule is, the more interesting it is, provided all other parameters remain fixed. The reliability of a discriminant rule is $|h \wedge e|/|e|$, and is also known as rule confidence or certainty factor. $|e|$ is known as the rule cover.
3. I decreases monotonically with $|h|$ (or $|e|$) when $|h \wedge e|$, $|e|$ (or $|h|$), and $|\neg h|$ remain the same (Piatetsky-Shapiro 1991). That is, the more complete a rule is, the more interesting it is, provided its discriminability remains constant. Similarly, the more discriminant a rule is, the more interesting it is, provided its completeness remains fixed.
4. I increases monotonically with $|e|$ when the rule reliability, $|h|$, and $|\neg h|$ remain the same (Major & Mangano 1993). Essentially, given two rules having the same reliability, but where one rule has a larger cover than the other then the rule with the larger cover is the more interesting of the two.

The above principles hold for both discriminant and characteristic rules. Recall that in discriminant rules, e is intended to discriminate h from $\neg h$, while in characteristic rules, e should be *necessary* for h, i.e., 100% complete for h. However, as noted by philosophers

Rule	e	h	Discrim.	Completeness
A	Fever	Flu	80%	30%
B	Sneezing	Flu	30%	80%

Table 1: Discriminability vs. Completeness.

(e.g., Wittenstein), it frequently happens that not all members of a given class have some property in common. Moreover, this can be the case when dealing with real-world databases, owing to exceptions, noisy, or missing data. Therefore, when mining characteristic rules from real-world databases, the stipulation that e must cover *all* training examples of h should be relaxed (Han, Cai, & Cercone 1993). Hence, our definition of characteristic rules allows for incompleteness.

The interestingness of a rule may be defined as the product of its goodness (reflecting the goodness of fit between the rule and data), and utility (Smyth & Goodman 1992). For characteristic rules, $h \rightarrow e$, utility is $P(h)$; for discriminant rules, $e \rightarrow h$, it is $P(e)$. For characteristic rules, multiplying by utility biases the interestingness function towards the more frequent classes (or the more frequent evidence, for discriminant rules). Depending on the data analyst or application, such a bias may be undesirable. For example, a strong rule found for diagnosing a rare disease may be just as important as an equally strong rule for diagnosing a common disease. (One might argue that recognizing the rare disease is even more important!) Hence, a user may wish to evaluate the interestingness of a rule based on it goodness alone, or on its goodness and utility.

Consider Table 1 and assume for the moment that each class, or piece of evidence, is considered equally important. Suppose that rules A and B are discriminant (i.e., respectively, $Fever \rightarrow Flu$, and $Sneezing \rightarrow Flu$). The object of discriminant rules for the class Flu is to distinguish instances of Flu from $\neg$Flu. Rule A is 80% discriminant, while rule B is 30% discriminant. Therefore, as discriminant rules, rule A is more interesting than rule B. Suppose, instead, that rules A and B are characteristic (i.e., respectively, $Flu \rightarrow Fever$, and $Flu \rightarrow Sneezing$). The object of characteristic rules for Flu is to cover all, or as many as possible, of the Flu tuples. Since rule B is 80% complete and rule A is only 30% complete, as characteristic rules, rule B is the more interesting of the two. Hence, we see a difference in the assessment of interestingness for discriminant and characteristic rules. Thus, we propose a fifth principle for rule interestingness measures.

5. Given two rules where one rule is as complete as the other is discriminant, and vice versa, then for discriminant (characteristic) rules, the more discriminant (complete) rule has greater potential interestingness. If each class or evidence is considered equally important, then the rule with greater potential interestingness is deemed the more interesting. Otherwise, the potential interestingness

(*Pot_I*) may be multiplied by the rule utility in order to bias interestingness towards the more frequent classes (for characteristic rules) or the more frequent evidence (for discriminant rules). Stated formally: Let r_1 and r_2 be rules where r_1 is $X\%$ discriminant and $Y\%$ complete, and r_2 is $Y\%$ discriminant and $X\%$ complete, where $X \neq Y$, $Pot\_I(r_1) \neq 0$, and $Pot\_I(r_2) \neq 0$ where $Pot\_I(r)$ is a measure of the goodness of rule r. If $X > Y$ and r_1 and r_2 are discriminant, then $Pot\_I(r_1) > Pot\_I(r_2)$. If $X < Y$ and r_1 and r_2 are discriminant, then $Pot\_I(r_1) < Pot\_I(r_2)$. If $X > Y$ and r_1 and r_2 are characteristic, then $Pot\_I(r_2) > Pot\_I(r_1)$. If $X < Y$ and r_1 and r_2 are characteristic, then $Pot\_I(r_2) < Pot\_I(r_1)$. If all events are considered equally important, then the interestingness of rule r may be assessed as $I(r) = Pot\_I(r)$. Otherwise, $I(r) = Pot\_I(r) \times Utility(r)$ where $Utility(r)$ is $P(e)$ for discriminant rule, $e \rightarrow h$, or $P(h)$ for characteristic rule, $h \rightarrow e$.

This new principle, unlike the others, considers the difference between discriminant and characteristic rules.

Proposed Interestingness Measures for Characteristic Rules

Let c^{++} be the characteristic rule $h \rightarrow e$, and d^{++} be the discriminant rule $e \rightarrow h$. Our proposed interestingness measures for characteristic rules are based on the measures of necessity and sufficiency defined as $Nec(d^{++}) = P(\neg e|h)/P(\neg e|\neg h)$ and $Suf(d^{++}) = P(e|h)/P(e|\neg h)$ (Duda, Gaschnig, & Hart 1981). The probabilities can be estimated from the given data. Nec can be used to assess the goodness of c^{++}. For example, if $Nec(d^{++}) = 0$, then $\neg e$ invalidates h, meaning $\neg e \rightarrow \neg h$, $e \lor \neg h$, that is $\underline{h \rightarrow e}$. Here, e is *necessary* for h, i.e., e covers all training examples of h, and so the characteristic rule, c^{++}, is certain. If $0 < Nec(d^{++}) < 1$, then $\neg e$ discourages h, meaning that $\neg e$ makes h less plausible. The closer $Nec(d^{++})$ is to 0, the more certain is $h \rightarrow e$. Hence we propose IC^{++} as an interestingness measure for c^{++}, where c^{++} can be any characteristic rule, $h \rightarrow e$ (which may contain negative literals):

$$IC^{++} = \begin{cases} (1 - Nec(d^{++})) \times P(h) & 0 \leq Nec(d^{++}) < 1 \\ 0 & \text{otherwise.} \end{cases}$$

Moreover, if c^{++} is found to be uninteresting by IC^{++}, one may still use Nec and Suf to draw useful conclusions regarding h and e by evaluating the interestingness of other forms of c^{++}, such as $c^{+-} = h \rightarrow \neg e$, $c^{-+} = \neg h \rightarrow e$, or $c^{--} = \neg h \rightarrow \neg e$. If $Nec(d^{++}) \rightarrow \infty$, then $\neg e$ validates h, that is $\neg e \rightarrow h$, $e \lor h$, and $\underline{\neg h \rightarrow e}$ (i.e., c^{-+}). If $1 < Nec(d^{++}) < \infty$, then $\neg e$ encourages h, meaning $\neg e$ makes h more plausible, and the greater $Nec(d^{++})$ is, the more certain is $\neg h \rightarrow e$. Similarly, the smaller $Suf(d^{++})$ is, the more e discourages h, and the more certain $\underline{h \rightarrow \neg e}$ (i.e., c^{+-}) is. The larger $Suf(d^{++})$ is, the more e encourages h, and the more certain $\underline{\neg h \rightarrow \neg e}$ (i.e., c^{--}) is. Thus we propose the

following additional interestingness measures for characteristic rules:

$$IC^{+-} = \begin{cases} (1 - Suf(d^{++})) \times P(h) & 0 \leq Suf(d^{++}) < 1 \\ 0 & \text{otherwise.} \end{cases}$$

$$IC^{-+} = \begin{cases} (1 - 1/Nec(d^{++})) \times P(\neg h) & 1 < Nec(d^{++}) < \infty \\ 0 & \text{otherwise.} \end{cases}$$

$$IC^{--} = \begin{cases} (1 - 1/Suf(d^{++})) \times P(\neg h) & 1 < Suf(d^{++}) < \infty \\ 0 & \text{otherwise.} \end{cases}$$

For example, if $c^{++} = Flu \rightarrow Headache$ is found to be uninteresting by IC^{++}, then IC^{-+} can be used to assess the interestingness of $c^{-+} = \neg Flu \rightarrow Headache$. Since $Nec(d^{++})$ was already computed for the evaluation of IC^{++}, then the evaluation of IC^{-+} is trivial, yet may provide useful information regarding Flu and Headache. Each of the proposed measures lies in the range $[0, 1]$, with 0 and 1 representing the minimum and maximum possible interestingness, respectively. In practice, the maximum interestingness value is equal to the probability of the most frequent hypothesis or class. So as to avoid the problems that can occur when probabilities evaluate to 0 (e.g., the denominator in an equation evaluating to 0), we use Bayesian probability estimates (Shinghal 1992).

By definition, $Nec(d^{++}) = 1$ iff $Suf(d^{++}) = 1$, in which case h and e are independent. One example of such a case is a rule having 0% discriminability and 100% completeness. The Nec and Suf values cause each of the IC measures to return an interestingness value of 0, indicating that any characteristic rule form involving h and e is uninteresting. One may argue, however, that if a characteristic rule is 100% complete, then it should be interesting no matter how well it can discriminate. We, however, adopt the view of Michalski (1983) that the most interesting of characteristic rules for h are also intended to *discriminate* h from $\neg h$. We feel that a characteristic rule is uninteresting if it cannot at all discriminate. This reasoning agrees with rule interestingness principle 1 (Piatetsky-Shapiro 1991). Rather, we feel that what is interesting is the *metafact* that h and e are independent. The four new measures presented here for characteristic rules obey rule interestingness principles 1 to 4 (Piatetsky-Shapiro 1991; Major & Mangano 1993), as well as the proposed principle 5.

Preliminary Results and Analysis

Preliminary results were obtained for characteristic rules mined from a synthetic database of 4000 tuples described by 10 attributes. Rule interestingness was assessed using the proposed IC^{++} measure for characteristic rules, as well as the RI (Piatetsky-Shapiro 1991), J (Smyth & Goodman 1992), and certainty, or 'CE' (Hong & Mao 1991) measures, the last three being popular objective rule interestingness measures from the literature. The measures were also analyzed with respect to principles 1 to 5. The results are summarized below (proofs not shown owing to limited space).

#	$|h \wedge \neg e|$	$|h \wedge e|$	$|\neg h \wedge e|$	$|\neg h \wedge \neg e|$	Nec(d^{++})	Suf(d^{++})	RI(c^{++})	J(c^{++})	CE(c^{++})	IC^{++}	IC^{+-}
1	700	1300	1300	700	1.0000	1.0000	0	0	0.504	0	0
2	0	2000	200	1800	0.0006	9.9552	900.000	0.1289	0.801	0.4997	0
3	200	1800	0	2000	0.1004	1801.0000	900.000	0.0982	0.754	0.4498	0
4	2000	0	1800	200	9.9552	0.0006	-900.000	0.1289	0.000	0	0.4997

Table 2: Characteristic rules evaluated for interestingness.

Only IC^{++} obeys all 5 principles. CE does not obey principle 1, as shown in the scenario representing characteristic rule 1 (Table 2) where h and e are independent. RI does not obey principle 5. For example, from Table 2, rule 2 is as complete (100%) as rule 3 is discriminant, and as discriminant (90%) as rule 3 is complete. Here h and $\neg h$ are equally likely or important. According to principle 5, rule 2 is therefore the more interesting characteristic rule. The IC^{++}, J, and CE measures have ranked the rules accordingly, but RI has not.

The J measure can give misleading results. For example, the J measure finds characteristic rule 4 of Table 2 to be as interesting as rule 2, even though rule 4 fails to identify any of the h tuples, and mistakes 90% of the $\neg h$ tuples for h. Furthermore, the J measure does not obey principle 2, as illustrated by rules 3 and 4 of Table 2.

If IC^{++} finds that a given characteristic rule, c^{++}, is uninteresting, other potentially useful conclusions regarding h and e may be drawn. If h and e are independent (as indicated by a Nec and Suf value of 1), then this knowledge can be reported. Suppose that rule 4 is $Flu \rightarrow \neg Headache$. From the necessity and sufficiency values computed for rule 4 (Table 2), one cannot conclude that Flu and $\neg Headache$ are independent. A user may wish to see if another version of characteristic rule 4 is interesting. The IC^{+-} measure finds that the c^{+-} version of the given rule, i.e., $Flu \rightarrow Headache$ is indeed interesting, with an interestingness value of 0.4997 (Here, IC values close to 0.5 indicate high interestingness). If the necessity and sufficiency values are precomputed, then the application of the remaining IC measures is trivial, yet it can reveal additional useful conclusions regarding the data.

Conclusions

We have proposed IC^{++}, an interestingness measure for characteristic rules. We have also proposed a rule interestingness principle in addition to the four presented by (Piatetsky-Shapiro 1991; Major & Mangano 1993) which, unlike the others, considers the difference between discriminant and characteristic rules. In comparison with the RI, J, and CE measures, IC^{++} is the only one that obeys all five principles. If a given characteristic rule, $h \rightarrow e$, is deemed uninteresting by IC^{++}, three additional measures which we also presented here can be used to derive other useful information regarding h and e. Our future work involves using the measures to guide the discovery of characteristic rules from databases.

Acknowledgements

We thank R.F. Hadley and J. Han for very helpful feedback, as well as the Natural Sciences & Engineering Research Council of Canada for financial support.

References

Agrawal, R.; Imielinski, T.; & Swami, A. 1993. Database mining: A performance perspective. *IEEE Trans. Knowledge & Data Eng.* 5(6):914–925.

Duda, R.O.; Gaschnig, J.; & Hart, P.E. 1981. Model design in the Prospector consultant system for mineral exploration. In B.L. Webber & N.J. Nilsson, eds., *Readings in Artificial Intelligence*, 334–348. Palo Alto, CA: Tioga.

Han, J.; Cai, Y.; & Cercone, N. 1993. Data-Driven Discovery of Quantitative Rules in Relational Databases. *IEEE Trans Knowledge & Data Eng.* 5(1):29–40.

Hong, J. & Mao, C. 1991. Incremental discovery of rules and structure by hierarchical and parallel clustering. In G. Piatetsky-Shapiro & W. J. Frawley, eds., *Knowledge Discovery in Databases*, 177-194. Menlo Park, CA: AAAI/MIT Press.

Major, J.A.; & Mangano, J. 1993. Selecting among rules induced from a hurricane database. In G. Piatetsky-Shapiro, ed., *Proc. AAAI-93 Workshop on Knowledge Discovery in Databases*, 28–44.

Michalski, R.S. 1983. A theory and methodology of inductive learning. *Artificial Intelligence* 20:111–161.

Piatetsky-Shapiro, G. 1991. Discovery, analysis, and presentation of strong rules. In G. Piatetsky-Shapiro & W.J. Frawley, eds., *Knowledge Discovery in Databases*, 229-248. Menlo Park, CA: AAAI/MIT Press.

Piatetsky-Shapiro, G. & Matheus, C.J. 1994. The interestingness of deviations. In *Proc. AAAI-94 Workshop on Knowledge Discovery in Databases*, 25–36.

Shinghal, R. 1992. *Formal Concepts in Artificial Intelligence*. London: Chapman & Hall.

Silberschatz, A. & Tuzhilin, A. 1995. On subjective measures of interestingness in knowledge discovery. In *Proc. 1st International Conf. on Knowledge Discovery in Databases*, 275–281.

Smyth, P. & Goodman, R.M. 1992. An information theoretic approach to rule induction from databases. *IEEE Trans. Knowledge & Data Eng.* 4(4):301–316.

Srikant, R. & Agrawal, R. 1995. Mining generalized association rules. In U. Dayal, P.M.D. Gray, & S. Nishio, eds., *Proc. 21st VLDB Conf.*, 407–419.

The field matching problem: Algorithms and applications

Alvaro E. Monge and **Charles P. Elkan**

Department of Computer Science and Engineering
University of California, San Diego
La Jolla, California 92093–0114

{amonge,elkan}@cs.ucsd.edu

Abstract

To combine information from heterogeneous sources, equivalent data in the multiple sources must be identified. This task is the field matching problem. Specifically, the task is to determine whether or not two syntactic values are alternative designations of the same semantic entity. For example the addresses *Dept. of Comput. Sci. and Eng., University of California, San Diego, 9500 Gilman Dr. Dept. 0114, La Jolla, CA 92093* and *UCSD, Computer Science and Engineering Department, CA 92093-0114* do designate the same department. This paper describes three field matching algorithms, and evaluates their performance on real-world datasets. One proposed method is the well-known Smith-Waterman algorithm for comparing DNA and protein sequences. Several applications of field matching in knowledge discovery are described briefly, including WEBFIND, which is a new software tool that discovers scientific papers published on the worldwide web. WEBFIND uses external information sources to guide its search for authors and papers. Like many other worldwide web tools, WEBFIND needs to solve the field matching problem in order to navigate between information sources.

Introduction

In many knowledge discovery and database mining applications there is a need to combine information from heterogeneous sources. The core issue is to identify equivalent data in the multiple sources. Through this operation, one can navigate from one source to another. This is what is commonly known as a "join" between two tables in relational databases.

In order to perform a join between two relations, one must first determine which columns refer to the same category of entities. This is known as the schema matching problem (Batini *et al.* 1986; Kim *et al.* 1993). Given a solution to the schema matching problem, one still needs to determine whether two specific tuples, i.e. field values, are equivalent. This is the problem studied in this paper. In general the field matching problem is to determine whether or not two field values are syntactic alternatives that designate the same semantic entity.

A solution to the field matching problem can be applied to solve the schema matching problem. The "information learning agent" (ILA) of Etzioni and Perkowitz (1995) learns the schema of other information sources based on the known schema of one source. To learn a new schema, equivalent pieces of information must be detected. The ILA can match (206) 616-1845 and 616.1845 for example, but details of the matching method are not given by Etzioni and Perkowitz (1995). General matching methods are the topic of this paper.

The field matching problem

Many information sources, e.g. relational databases or worldwide web pages, provide information about the same real-world entities, but designate these entities differently. We refer to a designator of an entity as a *field*. Table 1 contains examples of fields designating academic institutions. These examples show that fields can be made up of subfields delimited by separators such as newlines, commas, or spaces. A subfield is itself a field and may be made up of subsubfields, and so on. Two fields are *equivalent* if they are equal semantically, that is if they both designate the same semantic entity. Equivalence may sometimes be a question of degree, so we allow a function solving the field matching problem to return a value between 0.0 and 1.0, where 1.0 means certain equivalence and 0.0 means certain non-equivalence.

There has been little previous research on the field matching problem, although it has been recognized as important in industry for decades. For example tax agencies must do field matching to correlate different pieces of information about the same taxpayer when social security numbers are missing or incorrect. In general, field matching is the central issue in the so-called "merge/purge" task (Hernandez and Stolfo 1995): identifying and combining multiple records, from one database or many, that concern the same entity but are distinct because of data entry errors.

Published previous work deals with special cases of the field matching problem, involving customer addresses (Ace *et al.* 1992), census records (Slaven 1992), or variant entries in a lexicon (Jacquemin and Royaute 1994). The most similar work to ours is due to Hernandez and Stolfo (1995), for the "merge/purge" task. After clustering tuples using indices, Hernandez and Stolfo (1995) use domain-specific equational axioms to identify semantically equivalent tuples inside each cluster. This approach depends on knowledge supplied by a human. We consider domain-independent methods here.

Field matching algorithms

The input to a field matching algorithm is the two fields being tested for semantic equivalence. In the work described here, stop words in the set {*and in for the of on & - /*} are removed before matching, but this is not critical.

A basic field matching algorithm

An atomic string is a sequence of alphanumeric characters delimited by punctuation characters. A simple definition of the degree to which two fields match is the number of their matching atomic strings divided by their average number of atomic strings. Two atomic strings match if they are the same string or if one is a prefix of the other. For example, consider the fields $A =$ *"Comput. Sci. & Eng. Dept., University of California, San Diego"* and $B =$ *"Department of Computer Science, Univ. Calif., San Diego"*. After removing stop words, $k = 6$ strings in the first field match some string in the second field, namely *Comput., Sci., San, Diego, Univ.* and *Calif.* No matches exist for *Eng.* and *Dept.* The overall matching score is $k/((|A| + |B|)/2) = 0.8$.

The algorithm to compute the basic matching score is straightforward. First, the atomic strings of each field are extracted and sorted. Second, each atomic string of one field is searched for in the other field's list of strings. The number of matched atomic strings is recorded. The complexity of the algorithm is dominated by the sort of the atomic strings, which uses time $O(n \log n)$ where n is the maximum number of atomic strings in either field.

The basic field matching algorithm does not take into account abbreviations which are not prefixes. It also does not use information regarding the ordering of the subfields. The algorithms described in the next two subsections attempt to overcome these limitations.

A recursive field matching algorithm

The algorithm here uses the recursive structure of typical textual fields. The base case is that A and B match with degree 1.0 if they are the same atomic string or one abbreviates the other; otherwise their degree of match is 0.0. Each subfield of A is assumed to correspond to the subfield of B with which it has highest score. The score of matching A and B then equals the mean of these maximum scores:

$$match(A, B) = \frac{1}{|A|} \sum_{i=1}^{|A|} \max_{j=1}^{|B|} match(A_i, B_j).$$

Matching of abbreviations uses four patterns:

(i) the abbreviation is a prefix of its expansion, e.g. "Univ." abbreviates "University", or

(ii) the abbreviation combines a prefix and a suffix of its expansion, e.g. "Dept." matches "Department", or

(iii) the abbreviation is an acronym for its expansion, e.g. "UCSD" abbreviates "University of California, San Diego", or

(iv) the abbreviation is a concatenation of prefixes from its expansion, e.g. "Caltech" matches "California Institute of Technology".

Note that case (iii) is a special case of case (iv).

The recursive field matching algorithm has quadratic time complexity. Given A and B, every subfield in A must be compared with every subfield in B. At the lowest level, each atomic string of A is compared with each atomic string of B. An important optimization is to apply memoization to remember the results of recursive calls which have already been made.

The Smith-Waterman algorithm

This method (Smith and Waterman 1981) is a dynamic programming algorithm. It was first developed to find optimal alignments between related DNA or protein sequences.

The Smith-Waterman algorithm has three main adjustable parameters. Given the alphabet Σ, the first parameter is a $|\Sigma| \times |\Sigma|$ matrix of match scores for each pair of symbols in the alphabet. The other parameters are penalties for starting a gap in an alignment, and for continuing a gap.

For matching textual fields we define Σ to be just the lower case and upper case alphabetic characters, the ten digits, and three punctuation symbols space, comma, and period. Our experiments use Smith-Waterman algorithm parameter values chosen in preliminary experiments as being intuitively reasonable and providing good results. The match score matrix is symmetric with all entries -5 except that an exact match scores 5, and approximate matches score 2. An approximate match occurs between two characters if they are both in one of the following subsets: {*d t*} {*g j*} {*l r*} {*m n*} {*b p v*} {*a e i o u*} {*, .*}. The gap start and continue penalties are 5.0 and 1.0 respectively.

Since the Smith-Waterman algorithm allows for gaps of unmatched characters, it should perform well for many abbreviations, and when fields have missing information or minor syntactical differences. On the other hand, subfields out of order will certainly cause problems.

It is important to note that the Smith-Waterman algorithm and the basic algorithm are symmetric, but

internet host	institution
cs.ucsd.edu	computer science department, university of california, san diego
cs.stanford.edu	computer science department, stanford university, palo alto, california
(INSPEC)	Dept. of Comput. Sci., California Univ., San Diego, La Jolla, CA, USA.
(INSPEC)	Dept. of Comput. Sci. Stanford Univ., CA, USA.

Table 1: Example of NETFIND and INSPEC fields.

group size	UCSD	Stanford	mixed
1	31	44	81
2	9	11	25
3	4	7	14
4	1	0	2

Table 2: Equivalent groups in the three datasets

the recursive algorithm is asymmetric when two fields have different numbers of subfields.

An experimental comparison

Each algorithm was tested using three datasets. The first dataset contains 65 fields describing various academic departments at UCSD, and the second dataset contains 87 fields from Stanford, all taken from the INSPEC bibliographic database. The third dataset is the union of the UCSD and Stanford datasets and an additional 29 UCSD and Stanford fields from NETFIND, a service that gives internet host addresses and email addresses (Schwartz and Pu 1994).

For each dataset we identified groups of equivalent fields. For example, the two Stanford fields in Table 1 form a group. Table 2 shows the number of equivalent groups of each size in each dataset. A group of size 1 is a single field for which there was no match in a dataset.

The performance of a field matching algorithm can be evaluated by viewing the problem in information retrieval terms (Salton and McGill 1983). Given a set of possibly equivalent fields, consider each field in turn to be a query, and rank all other fields according to their degree of match as computed by the field matching algorithm. The accuracy of the algorithm then corresponds to retrieval effectiveness as measured by precision and recall. Recall is the proportion of relevant information actually retrieved, while precision is the proportion of retrieved information that is relevant. The amount of retrieved information varies based on what threshold is chosen for match scores. Typically, as recall is increased from 0% to 100%, precision de-

creases from 100% to 0%.

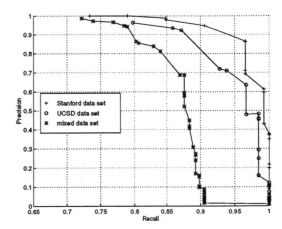

Figure 1: Basic algorithm: recall v. precision.

Figures 1 to 3 show recall versus precision for each algorithm. All algorithms perform worst on the mixed dataset, which is the most diverse. Both the Smith-Waterman algorithm and the recursive algorithm can achieve 100% recall, while the basic algorithm can only achieve 90% recall. The expected tradeoff between recall and precision is visible.

For all levels of recall, the Smith-Waterman algorithm has lower precision than the other two algorithms. The recursive and basic algorithms have similar performance. It appears that these datasets do not require the complexity of the recursive algorithm.

The WEBFIND application

WEBFIND is an application that discovers scientific papers made available by their authors on the worldwide web. The external information sources integrated by WEBFIND are MELVYL and NETFIND. MELVYL is a University of California library service that includes comprehensive databases of bibliographic records, including INSPEC (University of California 1996).

A WEBFIND search starts with the user providing keywords to identify the paper, exactly as he or she would in searching INSPEC directly. A paper can be identified using any combination of the names of its authors, words from its title or abstract, or other bibliographic information. After the user confirms that the right paper has been identified, WEBFIND queries INSPEC to find the institutional affiliation of the principal author of the paper. Then, WEBFIND uses NETFIND to provide the internet address of a host computer with the same institutional affiliation. WEBFIND then uses a search algorithm to discover a worldwide web server on this host, then an author's home page, and finally the location of the wanted paper.

Since institutions are designated very differently in INSPEC and NETFIND, it is non-trivial to decide when an INSPEC institution corresponds to a NETFIND in-

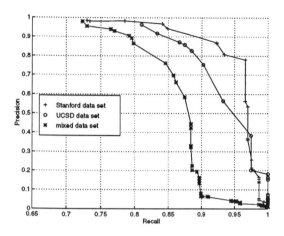

Figure 2: Recursive algorithm: recall v. precision.

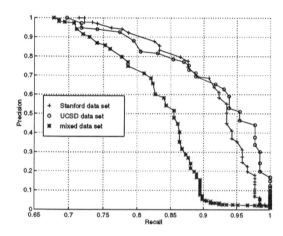

Figure 3: Smith-Waterman algorithm: recall v. precision.

stitution. WEBFIND uses the recursive field matching algorithm to do this.

Monge and Elkan (1996) provide a more lengthy description of WEBFIND, including experiments which show that WEBFIND is successful at finding worldwide web servers and finding web pages designated for authors. WEBFIND is less successful at finding actual papers, most of all because many authors have not yet published their papers on the worldwide web.

Conclusion

This study addresses the problem of reconciling information from heterogeneous sources. Such sources may represent entities differently, so identifying equivalent information is difficult. Future work will use an algorithm that is a hybrid of the Smith-Waterman method and the recursive method described above. This algorithm will take into account field order while allowing for missing fields. Parameter values for the Smith-Waterman component will be learned automatically by tuning on sets of representative data.

Acknowledgments
Alvaro Monge's work is supported by an AT&T Cooperative Research Program Fellowship.

References

J. Ace, B. Marvel, and B. Richer. Matchmaker...matchmaker...find me the address (exact address match processing). *Telephone Engineer and Management*, 96(8):50,52–53, April 1992.

C. Batini, M. Lenzerini, and S. Navathe. A comparative analysis of methodologies for database schema integration. *ACM Computing Surveys*, 18(4):323–364, December 1986.

Oren Etzioni and Mike Perkowitz. Category translation: learning to understand information on the internet. *International Joint Conference on AI*, pages 930–936, 1995.

M. Hernandez and S. Stolfo. The merge/purge problem for large databases. In *Proceedings of the ACM SIGMOD International Conference on Management of Data*, pages 127–138, May 1995.

C. Jacquemin and J. Royaute. Retrieving terms and their variants in a lexicalized unification-based framework. In *Proceedings of the ACM-SIGIR Conference on Research and Development in Information Retrieval*, pages 132–141, July 1994.

W. Kim, I. Choi, S. Gala, and M. Scheevel. On resolving schematic heterogeneity in multidatabase systems. *Distributed and Parallel Databases*, 1(3):251–279, July 1993.

Alvaro E. Monge and Charles P. Elkan. Integrating external information sources to guide worldwide web information retrieval. Technical Report CS96-474, Department of Computer Science and Engineering, University of California, San Diego, January 1996. http://www.cs.ucsd.edu/users/amonge/Papers/WebFind-CS96-474.ps.gz.

Gerard Salton and Michael J. McGill. *Introduction to Modern Information Retrieval*. McGraw Hill, 1983.

Michael Schwartz and Calton Pu. Applying an information gathering architecture to Netfind: a white pages tool for a changing and growing internet. *IEEE/ACM Transactions on Networking*, 2(5):426–439, October 1994.

B.E. Slaven. The set theory matching system: an application to ethnographic research. *Social Science Computer Review*, 10(2):215–229, Summer 1992.

T. F. Smith and M. S. Waterman. Identification of common molecular subsequences. *Journal of Molecular Biology*, 147:195–197, 1981.

Division of Library Automation University of California. Melvyl system welcome page. URL, May 1996. http://www.dla.ucop.edu/.

Discovering Classification Knowledge in Databases Using Rough Sets

Ning Shan, Wojciech Ziarko, Howard J. Hamilton and Nick Cercone

Department of Computer Science, University of Regina
Regina, Saskatchewan, Canada S4S 0A2
E-Mail: {ning,ziarko,hamilton,nick}@cs.uregina.ca

Abstract

The paper presents an approach to data mining involving search for complete, or nearly complete, domain classifications in terms of attribute values. Our objective is to find classifications based on interacting attributes that provide a good characterization of the concept of interest by maximizing predefined quality criteria. The paper introduces the notion of the classification complexity and several other measures to evaluate quality.

Introduction

Knowledge discovery in databases (KDD) or data mining has recently attracted great interest and research activity (Fayyad et al. 1996; Piatetsky-Shapiro & Frawley 1991; Ziarko 1994). One goal is the discovery of relationships between data values. The standard approach to this problem, as discussed by many authors, is to attempt to induce classification rules from data using inductive algorithms (Fayyad et al. 1996; Piatetsky-Shapiro & Frawley 1991; Shan et al. 1995a, 1995b; Ziarko 1994; Ziarko & Shan 1994). A *classification* is a partition of the objects in the domain into equivalence classes based upon the condition attributes. The rules, which have the format "if *conditions* then *decision*," normally properly reflect relationships occurring in the database. Unfortunately, the validity of rules in the domain from which the database was collected is typically questionable.

We observe that (a) databases are often highly incomplete, that is, in the selected attribute-value representation many possible tuples are not present in the database; and (b) in particular, insufficient tuples exist in the database to reliably estimate the probability distributions. As long as we lack sufficient evidence about the completeness of the classification and the reliability of the associated probability estimates, rule extraction from the data and the application of these rules to the original domain is of limited utility. In our approach, rule induction, although important, is only applied after ensuring the completeness of the classification and the reliability of the probability estimates.

We perform three steps prior to rule induction. First, we generalize the condition attributes as necessary to increase the credibility of the classification. Then we identify clusters of interacting attributes, *i.e.*, those with direct or indirect dependencies. Finally, we search for credible classifications of the database tuples based on these clusters. A classification is *credible* if it is complete or almost complete with respect to the domain from which the database was collected. We use evaluation parameters, such as classification complexity, to constrain the search for credible classifications. Classifications which result in the good approximation of the concept of interest, in the rough sets sense (Katzberg & Ziarko 1994; Pawlak 1991), are subsequently selected to obtain the classification rules.

Classifications on Rough Sets

A relational database can be viewed as an information system (Pawlak 1991). Formally, an *information system* S is a quadruple $\langle U, A, V, f \rangle$, where U is a nonempty set of objects called *universe*; A is a finite set of attributes consisting of *condition attributes* C and *decision attributes* D such that $A = C \cup D$ and $C \cap D = \emptyset$; $V = \bigcup_{p \in A} V_p$ is a nonempty finite set of values of attributes A and V_p is the *domain* of the attribute p (the set of values of attribute p); $f : U \times A \rightarrow V$ is an *information function* which assigns particular values from the domain of attributes A to objects such that $f(x_i, p) \in V_p$ for all $x_i \in U$ and $p \in A$.

Any subset of condition attributes defines a classification of the universe of objects U as follows. Let B be a nonempty subset of C, and let x_i, x_j be members of U. The *projection* of the function f onto attributes belonging to the subset B will be denoted as f_B. A binary relation $R(B)$, called an *indiscernibility relation*, is first defined as follows:

$$R(B) \;=\; \{(x_i, x_j) \in U^2 : f_B(x_i) = f_B(x_j)\} \quad (1)$$

We say that x_i and x_j are indiscernible by a set of attributes B in S iff $f(x_i, p) = f(x_j, p)$ for every $p \in B$. $R(B)$ is an equivalence relation on U for every $B \subset C$ which classifies the objects in U into a finite, preferably small, number of *equivalence classes*. The set of equivalence classes is called the *classification* $R^*(B)$. The pair $\langle U, R(B) \rangle$ is called an *approximation space* (Pawlak 1991).

The above model cannot, however, be directly applied to most KDD problems. A database represents only a subset (a sample) U' of the universe U about which we are trying to discover something. Depending on the selection of the information function f, the subset of the attributes B, the size and the distribution of objects in the sample U', we may or may not have all values of the information function f_B in our database. If all values are present then our knowledge about the classification is *complete* (despite not having all domain objects in the database); otherwise our knowledge about the classification is *incomplete*. To properly reason about the relationships occurring in U, the classification must be complete; otherwise, false conclusions may be drawn.

Reduction of Classification Complexity

In KDD-related problems, the universe U is finite and it is highly desirable for it to be small. Only finite classifications are "*learnable*," i.e., we can potentially acquire complete knowledge about such classifications. Unfortunately, most finite classifications are not learnable due to the excessively large number of possible equivalence classes. Only a small fraction of all possible classifications expressible in terms of the indiscernibility relation are learnable.

Classification Complexity

To evaluate the computational tractability of the finite classification learning problem, we introduce the notion of *classification complexity*, defined as the number of equivalence classes in the classification. In practice, this number is usually not known in advance. Instead, a crude upper bound on the classification complexity for a subset of attributes $B \subseteq C$, can be computed "a priori" by (2)

$$TC(B, V) = \prod_{p \in B} card(V_p) \quad (2)$$

The quantity $TC(B, V)$ is called the *theoretical complexity* of the set of attributes B given the set of values

V of the attributes B. If the number of attributes and the size of the domain V_p for each attribute is large, then $TC(B, V)$ grows exponentially large. It is very difficult to find a credible classification based on a large number of attributes unless the attributes are strongly dependent (*e.g.*, functionally dependent) on each other (limiting the number of equivalence classes).

Complexity Reduction

Complexity reduction increases the credibility of the classification by generalizing condition attributes. The information generalization procedure (Shan et al. 1995a, 1995b) applies *attribute-oriented concept tree ascension* (Cai, Cercone & Han 1991) to reduce the complexity of an information system. It generalizes a condition attribute to a certain level based on the attribute's *concept tree*, which is provided by knowledge engineers or domain experts. Trivially, the values for any attribute can be represented as a *one-level* concept tree where the root is the most general value "ANY" and the leafs are the distinct values of the attribute.

The following algorithm, adapted from (Shan et al. 1995a, 1995b), extracts a generalized information system. Two thresholds (the *attribute threshold* and the *theoretical complexity threshold*) constrain the generalization process. Condition attributes are generalized by ascending their concept trees until the number of values for each attribute is less than or equal to the user-specified attribute threshold for that attribute and the theoretical complexity of all generalized attributes is less than or equal to the user-specified theoretical complexity threshold. For each iteration, one attribute is selected for generalization (this selection can be made in many ways (Barber & Hamilton 1996). Lower level concepts of this attribute are replaced by the concepts of the next higher level. The number of possible values at a higher level of an attribute is always smaller than at a lower level, so the theoretical complexity is reduced.

Algorithm EGIS*:
Input: (i) The original information system S with a set of condition attributes C_i ($1 \le i \le n$);
     (ii) a set H of concept trees, where each $H_i \in H$ is a concept hierarchy for the attribute C_i.
     (iii) t_i is a threshold for attribute C_i, and d_i is the number of distinct values of attribute C_i;
     (iv) TC defined by user is a theoretical complexity threshold.
Output: The generalized information system S'
$S' \leftarrow S$
$TC_1 = \prod_{i=1}^{n} d_i$
while $TC_1 > TC$ and $\exists d_i > t_i$ **do**
     Select an attribute $C_i \in C$ such that $\frac{d_i}{t_i}$ is maximal
     Ascend tree H_i one level and make appropriate substitutions in S'
     Remove duplicates from S'

```
        Recalculate $d_i$
        Recalculate $TC_1 = \prod_{i=1}^{n} d_i$
endwhile
```

The side effect of such a transformation is an imprecise concept representation in terms of the rough *lower bound* and *upper bound* (Pawlak 1991).

Quality of Classification

Each combination of values of the decision attribute is a concept. Our main goal is to identify a credible classification for each such concept $F \in R(D)$, based on some interacting attributes B. To evaluate the quality of the classification $R^*(B)$ with respect to the concept F, we use the following criterion (Ziarko & Shan 1995):

$$Q_B(F) = \beta \sum_{E \in R^*(B)} P(E) \times |P(F|E) - P(F)|, \quad (3)$$

and $\beta = \frac{1}{2P(F)(1-P(F))}$.

Criterion (3) represents the average gain in the quality of information, reflected by $P(F|E)$, used to make the classificatory decision F versus $\neg F$. In the absence of the classification $R^*(B)$, the only available information for this kind of the decision is the occurrence probability $P(F)$. The quantity β is a normalization factor to ensure that Q_B is always within the range $[0, 1]$, with 1 corresponding to the exact characterization of the concept (that is, when for every equivalence class E, $P(F|E)$ is either 0 or 1) and 0 corresponding to the situation where the distribution of F within every equivalence class E is the same as in the universe U.

Identifying Interacting Attributes
Local Discovery of Interacting Attributes

The local discovery of interacting attributes has been reported in (Ziarko & Shan 1995). All condition attributes are grouped into disjoint clusters without considering the decision attribute(s). Each *cluster* contains attributes which are directly or indirectly dependent upon each other.

DEP is a generalization of the concept quality measure Q_B (Ziarko & Shan 1995). $DEP(X, Y)$ measures degree of dependency between two groups of attributes X and Y:

$$DEP(X, Y) = \sum_{E \in R^*(Y)} P(E)Q_X(E). \quad (4)$$

The degree of dependency (4) is the average gain in the quality of the characterization of equivalence classes of $R(Y)$ in the approximation space $\langle U, R(Y) \rangle$. Here, we are not concerned about the direction of the dependency. The crucial question is whether $DEP(X, Y)$ or $DEP(Y, X)$ is greater than or equal to a *dependency*

threshold, τ, which is the minimum recognizable dependency level. The generalization procedure for attribute clusters is as follows:

Local ClusterGen Algorithm:
Input : C is a set of condition attributes and
          τ is a dependency threshold.
Output : *AttriCluster* is a set of attribute clusters.
```
AttriCluster ← ∅
while C ≠ ∅ do
    ACluster ← a ∈ C
    C ← C − {a}
    forall attribute x ∈ ACluster do
        forall attribute y ∈ C do
            MaxDep ← Max(DEP({x}, {y}),
                    DEP({y}, {x}))
            if MaxDep ≥ τ then
                ACluster ← ACluster ∪ y
                C ← C − {y}
            endif
        endfor
    endfor
    AttriCluster ← AttriCluster ∪ ACluster
endwhile
```

Global Discovery of Interacting Attributes

The global discovery of interacting attributes is a novel contribution of this paper. A subset of condition attributes is selected based on their relevance to the decision attribute(s).

Global ClusterGen Algorithm:
Input : C is a set of condition attributes
          D is a set of decision attributes, and
          τ is a dependency threshold.
Output : *AttriCluster* is a set of attribute's clusters.
```
AttriCluster ← a ∈ C
C ← C − {a}
Dep ← DEP(AttriCluster, D)
while C ≠ ∅ and Dep < τ do
    forall attribute ā ∈ AttriCluster do
        C' ← AttriCluster ∪ {a}
        Depₐ ← DEP(C', D)
    endfor
    Find the attribute x that has the maximum value of Depₐ
    AttriCluster ← AttriCluster ∪ {x}
    C ← C − {x}
    Dep ← DEP(AttriCluster, D)
endwhile
```

Search for Domain Classifications

Finally, we search for acceptable classifications (*i.e.*, any subset B of a cluster that satisfies the following criteria: (1) the cardinality of B is at most $MaxSize$; (2) the theoretical complexity of B is at most TC; (3) the size of equivalence classes in $R^*(B)$ is at least $MinESize$; and (4) the credibility of the classification is at least $MinCred$.

Algorithm **ClassificationSearch** considers all subsets whose size is at most $MaxSize$. The algorithms starts with an empty subset of attributes and incrementally expands the generated subsets as long as they meet the specified criteria.

ClassificationSearch Algorithm:

Input : *Cluster* is a cluster of attributes generated by the **ClusterGen** algorithm, *MaxSize* is an attribute number threshold, *TC* is a theoretical complexity threshold, *MinESize* is the equivalence class threshold, and *MinCred* is the minimum credibility for the classification.

Output : *ClassificationSet* is a set of attribute subsets of *Cluster*.

$ClassificationSet \leftarrow \emptyset$
$SUB \leftarrow \{\emptyset\}$
while $SUB \neq \emptyset$ **do**
    forall subset $X \in SUB$ **do**
        $MaxSize_X \leftarrow$ the number of attributes in X
        $TC_X \leftarrow$ the theoretical complexity of X
        $MinESize_X \leftarrow Min_{E_i \in R^{\bullet}(X)}(|E_i|)$
        $ECount_X \leftarrow$ the number of equivalence classes in X
        if $(MaxSize_X > MaxSize)$ or $(TC_X > TC)$ or
            $(MinESize_X < MinESize)$ or
            $(ECount_X/TC_X < MinCred)$ **then**
            Remove X from SUB
        endif
    endfor
    if $SUB \neq \emptyset$ **then**
        $ClassificationSet \leftarrow ClassificationSet \cup SUB$
        if $Cluster \notin SUB$ **then**
            $SUB' \leftarrow \emptyset$
            forall subset $X \in SUB$ **do**
                $Cluster_1 \leftarrow$ all attributes in $Cluster$ which have higher numbered than attributes in X
                forall attribute $x \in Cluster_1$ **do**
                    $SUB' \leftarrow SUB' \cup (X \cup \{x\})$
                endfor
            endfor
            $SUB \leftarrow SUB'$
        endif
    endif
endwhile

This algorithm appears exponential in the size of subset B, but it can be reworked to be $2^{MaxSize}$, which is a constant. Large subsets of attributes correspond to prohibitively complex and unlearnable classifications, so the given method is quite feasible for relatively simple classifications which are of the most interest.

Summary and Conclusions

We described an approach to database mining based upon searching for domain classifications. The goal of the search is to find a classification or classifications which jointly provide a good, in the rough sets sense, approximation of the concept of interest. We have introduced measures to evaluate the classifications, such as classification complexity measures, quality of classification and connectivity measures to evaluate the degree of connection between classifications, attributes or the concept of interest. We also presented algorithms for complexity reduction, local and global discovery of interacting attributes, and classification search. After classification search, further steps in the rough sets approach to knowledge discovery involve classification analysis and simplification, rule induction and prediction, if required by an application. These aspects have been omitted here as they are presented in detail in other publications (Shan et al. 1995a, 1995b; Ziarko & Shan 1994).

References

Barber, B. and Hamilton, H.J. 1996. Attribute Selection Strategies for Attribute-Oriented Generalization. In *Proceedings of the Canadian AI Conference (AI'96)*, Montreal, Canada.

Cai, Y., Cercone, N., and Han, J. 1991. Attribute-Oriented Induction in Relational Databases, In *Knowledge Discovery in Database*, pp. 213-228.

Fayyad, U.M., Piatetsky-Shapiro, G., Smyth, P., and Uthurusamy, R. (eds.) 1996. *Advances in Knowledge Discovery and Data Mining*, AAAI Press/The MIT Press.

Katzberg, J. and Ziarko, W. 1994. Variable Precision Rough Sets with Asymmetric Bounds. In *Rough Sets, Fuzzy Sets and Knowledge Discovery*, pp. 167-177.

Pawlak, Z. 1991. *Rough Sets: Theoretical Aspects of Reasoning About Data*, Kluwer.

Piatetsky-Shapiro, G. and Frawley, W. J. (eds.) 1991. *Knowledge Discovery in Databases*, AAAI/MIT Press.

Shan, N., Hamilton, H.J., and Cercone, N. 1995a. GRG: Knowledge Discovery Using Information Generalization, Information Reduction, and Rule Generation. *International Journal of Artificial Intelligence Tools*, in press.

Shan, N., Ziarko, W., Hamilton, H.J., and Cercone, N. 1995b. Using Rough Sets as Tools for Knowledge Discovery. In *Proceedings of the First International Conference on Knowledge Discovery and Data Mining (KDD95)*, Montreal, Canada, pp. 263-268.

Ziarko, W. (ed.) 1994. *Rough Sets, Fuzzy Sets and Knowledge Discovery*, Springer-Verlag.

Ziarko, W. and Shan, N. 1994. KDD-R: A Comprehensive System for Knowledge Discovery in Databases Using Rough Sets. In *Proceedings of the International Workshop on Rough Sets and Soft Computing (RSSC'94)*, pp. 164-173.

Ziarko, W. and Shan, N. 1995. On Discovery of Attribute Interactions and Domain Classifications, In Lin. T.Y (ed.), Special Issue in *Journal of Intelligent Automation and Soft Computing*, in press.

Exceptional Knowledge Discovery in Databases based on Information Theory

Einoshin Suzuki
Division of Electrical and
Computer Engineering, Faculty of Engineering,
Yokohama National University,
156, Tokiwadai, Hodogaya,
Yokohama, 240, Japan.
suzuki@dnj.ynu.ac.jp

Masamichi Shimura
Dept. of Computer Science, Graduate School
of Information Science and Engineering,
Tokyo Institute of Technology,
2-12 Ohokayama, Meguro,
Tokyo, 152, Japan.
shimura@cs.titech.ac.jp

Abstract

This paper presents an algorithm for discovering exceptional knowledge from databases. Exceptional knowledge, which is defined as an exception to a general fact, exhibits unexpectedness and is sometimes extremely useful in spite of its obscurity. Previous discovery approaches for this type of knowledge employ either background knowledge or domain-specific criteria for evaluating the possible usefulness, i.e. the interestingness of the knowledge extracted from a database. It has been pointed out, however, that these approaches are prone to overlook useful knowledge.

In order to circumvent these difficulties, we propose an information-theoretic approach in which we obtain exceptional knowledge associated with general knowledge in the form of a rule pair using a depth-first search method. The product of the ACEs (Average Compressed Entropies) of the rule pair is introduced as the criterion for evaluating the interestingness of exceptional knowledge. The inefficiency of depth-first search is alleviated by a branch-and-bound method, which exploits the upper-bound for the product of the ACEs. MEPRO, which is a knowledge discovery system based on our approach, has been validated using the benchmark databases in the machine learning community.

Introduction

Recently, databases have grown remarkably both in size and in number. Consequently, increasing attention has been paid to the automatic extraction of knowledge from them, i.e. Knowledge Discovery in Databases (KDD) (Frawley et al. 1991). In KDD, the discovered knowledge can be classified into two categories: general knowledge, which holds for numerous examples, and exceptional knowledge, which represents an exception to general knowledge. For instance, "a jumbo jet is a safe means of transportation" is a piece of general knowledge, while "a jumbo jet which does not satisfy condition X is a dangerous means of transportation" is a piece of exceptional knowledge.

Although exceptional knowledge is often overlooked, it represents a different fact from general knowledge and can be extremely useful. Among the approaches for discovering such useful exceptional knowledge, well-known systems include EXPLORA (Hoschka & Klösgen 1991), which employs background knowledge for evaluating the knowledge extracted from a database, and KEFIR (Piatetsky-Shapiro & Matheus 1994) which employs domain-specific criteria.

Since a huge amount of knowledge can be embedded in a database, the discrimination of possibly useful or *interesting* knowledge is one of the most important topics in the KDD community. Especially in the case of discovering exceptional knowledge hidden in databases, the most crucial problem is to define appropriate criteria for evaluating the interestingness of the extracted knowledge (Piatetsky-Shapiro & Matheus 1994). As described above, previous criteria either require background knowledge or are inherently domain-specific. However, the use of such background knowledge can in fact hinder the discovery of interesting knowledge (Frawley et al. 1991). Furthermore, it is difficult to find such criteria in some domains.

In order to circumvent these difficulties, we propose a novel approach which employs neither background knowledge nor domain-specific criteria.

Rule Pair

Let an example e_i be a description about an object stored in a database in the form of a record, then a database contains n examples $e_1, e_2, \cdots, e_n$. An example e_i is represented by a tuple $< a_{i1}, a_{i2}, \cdots, a_{im} >$ where $a_{i1}, a_{i2}, \cdots, a_{im}$ are values for m discrete attributes.

Consider the problem of finding K pieces of knowledge $\{r_1, r_2, \cdots, r_K\}$. We can view a piece of knowledge r_i to be discovered from a database as represented by a **rule pair** $r(\mu, \nu)$:

$$r(\mu, \nu) \equiv \begin{cases} Y_\mu & \to & x \\ Y_\mu \wedge Z_\nu & \to & x' \end{cases} \quad (1)$$

where $Y_\mu = y_1 \wedge y_2 \wedge \cdots \wedge y_\mu$, $Z_\nu = z_1 \wedge z_2 \wedge \cdots \wedge z_\nu$. Here, x, x', y_i, and z_i are **atoms**, each of which is an event representing, in propositional form, a single value assignment to an attribute. Atoms x and x' have the same attribute but different values.

Since an if-then rule in equation (1) represents correlation or causality between its premise and conclusion, every rule pair is assumed to satisfy the following inequalities

$$p(x|Y_\mu) > p(x), \; p(x'|Y_\mu \wedge Z_\nu) > p(x'), \qquad (2)$$

where $Y_\mu = y_1 \wedge y_2 \wedge \cdots \wedge y_\mu$, $Z_\nu = z_1 \wedge z_2 \wedge \cdots \wedge z_\nu$.

A rule pair of equation (1) can be interpreted as "if Y_μ then x, but if Y_μ and Z_ν then x'". Since the event Y_μ occurs more frequently than $Y_\mu \wedge Z_\nu$, the rule $Y_\mu \to x$ represents a piece of general knowledge, and is thus called a **general rule**. On the other hand, the rule $Y_\mu \wedge Z_\nu \to x'$ represents the associated piece of exceptional knowledge, and is thus called an **exceptional rule**.

ACEP: average compressed entropy product

From the point of view of information theory, the rule $Y_\mu \to x$ indicates that each of the $np(x, Y_\mu)$ examples has a code length of $-\log_2 p(x|Y_\mu)$, which is smaller than the original length, $-\log_2 p(x)$, and each of the $np(\overline{x}, Y_\mu)$ examples, a code length of $-\log_2 p(\overline{x}|Y_\mu)$ instead of $-\log_2 p(\overline{x})$. The use of the reduced code length, or the compressed entropy, allows us to measure the information content of an if-then rule quantitatively. The entropy per example compressed by the rule, $\mathrm{ACE}(x, Y_\mu)$, which is called the **Average Compressed Entropy (ACE)**, is given as follows.

$$\mathrm{ACE}(x, Y_\mu) \equiv p(x, Y_\mu) \log_2 \frac{p(x|Y_\mu)}{p(x)}$$
$$+ p(\overline{x}, Y_\mu) \log_2 \frac{p(\overline{x}|Y_\mu)}{p(\overline{x})} \qquad (3)$$

A rule of large information content is useful in the sense that it gives a compact representation for data stored in a database. Since ACE is a measure for the information content of a rule, it can be considered as a function for the usefulness of the rule. Therefore, the interestingness of a rule extracted from a database is evaluated by its ACE. Since ACE increases monotonously as $p(x)$ decreases, as $p(x|Y_\mu)$ increases, or as $p(x, Y_\mu)$ increases, it can be also viewed as a unified criterion for evaluating the unexpectedness, stability, and generality of a rule. Actually, Smyth (Smyth & Goodman 1991) showed various desirable properties of ACE as a criterion for evaluating the interestingness of an if-then rule extracted from a database.

However, an exceptional rule $Y_\mu \wedge Z_\nu \to x'$, whose ACE is high, may not be "interesting" if the ACE of the associated general rule $Y_\mu \to x$ is extremely low. That is, the interestingness of an exceptional rule depends not only on its ACE but also on the ACE of the associated general rule. It is reasonable therefore to represent the interestingness of an exceptional rule in terms of both the above ACEs. Note that interestingness should increase as the ACEs increase, and decrease when they decrease. Among the functions which satisfy these requirements, the add-sum $\mathrm{ACE}(x, Y_\mu) + \mathrm{ACE}(x', Y_\mu \wedge Z_\nu)$ and product $\mathrm{ACE}(x, Y_\mu) \cdot \mathrm{ACE}(x', Y_\mu \wedge Z_\nu)$ are considered as the simplest formulations.

Let us analyze the appropriateness of these functions as evaluation criteria for the interestingness of exceptional knowledge. Consider the case in which the maximums of both ACEs for constant x and x' occur, since we are interested in the rule pairs whose ACEs are close to their respective maximum values. From equation (1) and (2), the following equations (4)~(6) are obtained.

$$\mathrm{ACE}(x, Y_\mu)$$
$$= (a + b) \log_2 \left(\frac{a+b}{a+b+c+d+e+f} \frac{1}{p(x)} \right)$$
$$+ (c + d + e + f)$$
$$\cdot \log_2 \left(\frac{c+d+e+f}{a+b+c+d+e+f} \frac{1}{p(\overline{x})} \right) \qquad (4)$$

$$\mathrm{ACE}(x', Y_\mu \wedge Z_\nu)$$
$$= c \log_2 \left(\frac{c}{a+c+e} \frac{1}{p(x')} \right)$$
$$+ (a + e) \log_2 \left(\frac{a+e}{a+c+e} \frac{1}{p(\overline{x'})} \right) \qquad (5)$$

$$\frac{a+b}{a+b+c+d+e+f} > p(x), \quad \frac{c}{a+c+e} > p(x'), \qquad (6)$$

where $a = p(x, Y_\mu, Z_\nu)$, $b = p(x, Y_\mu, \overline{Z_\nu})$, $c = p(x', Y_\mu, Z_\nu)$, $d = p(x', Y_\mu, \overline{Z_\nu})$, $e = p(\overline{x \vee x'}, Y_\mu, Z_\nu)$, and $f = p(\overline{x \vee x'}, Y_\mu, \overline{Z_\nu})$. Note that the following inequalities hold for these variables.

$$a, b, c, d, e, f \geq 0, \; a + b \leq p(x), \; c + d \leq p(x'),$$
$$e + f \leq p(\overline{x \vee x'}) \qquad (7)$$

A simple calculation shows that both $\mathrm{ACE}(x, Y_\mu)$ and $\mathrm{ACE}(x', Y_\mu \wedge Z_\nu)$ are maximized when $b = p(x)$ and $a = d = e = f = 0$. Let U and V be the maximum value of $\mathrm{ACE}(x, Y_\mu)$ and $\mathrm{ACE}(x', Y_\mu \wedge Z_\nu)$, respectively. From equation (4) and (5), we obtain

$$U = p(x) \log_2 \frac{1}{p(x) + c} + c \log_2 \left(\frac{c}{p(x) + c} \frac{1}{p(\overline{x})} \right),$$
$$V = c \log_2 \frac{1}{p(x')}, \qquad (8)$$

where from equation (6) and (7),

$$0 \leq c \leq p(x'), \; c < p(\overline{x}). \qquad (9)$$

A simple calculation shows that the maximum of the add-sum $U+V$ for constant x and x' occurs when either $\mathrm{ACE}(x, Y_\mu) = 0$ or $\mathrm{ACE}(x', Y_\mu \wedge Z_\nu) \approx 0$. The add-sum function, therefore, is inappropriate as a criterion for interestingness since its maximum value is dominated by one of the ACEs. Actually, using this function to determine interestingness in some databases will yield results which contain useless knowledge.

On the other hand, the product $U \cdot V$ can be proved to possess no such shortcomings, and thus the product of the ACEs, **Average Compressed Entropy Product (ACEP)**, can be considered as one of the simplest functions appropriate for evaluating the interestingness of an exceptional rule. Therefore, the interestingness function is defined by the ACEP, $\text{ACEP}(x, Y_\mu, x', Z_\nu)$.

$$
\begin{aligned}
&\text{ACEP}(x, Y_\mu, x', Z_\nu) \\
&\equiv \quad \text{ACE}(x, Y_\mu) \cdot \text{ACE}(x', Y_\mu \wedge Z_\nu) \quad (10)
\end{aligned}
$$

Discovery Algorithm

Consider a discovery algorithm which generates K rule pairs, where K is a user-specified parameter. The generated rule pairs are the K most interesting ones in the database as defined by ACEP. In the algorithm, a discovery task is viewed as a search problem, in which a node of a search tree represents a rule pair $r(\mu, \nu)$ of equation (1). A depth-first search method with maximum depth D is employed to traverse this tree.

Let $\mu = 0$ and $\nu = 0$ represent the state in which the premises of a rule pair $r(\mu, \nu)$ contain no y_i or no z_i respectively, then we define that $\mu = \nu = 0$ holds in a node of depth 1, and as the depth increases by 1, an atom is added to the premise of the general or exceptional rule. A node of depth 2 is assumed to satisfy $\mu = 1$ and $\nu = 0$; a node of depth 3, $\mu = \nu = 1$; and a node of depth l (≥ 4), $\mu + \nu = l - 1$ ($\mu, \nu \geq 1$). Therefore, a descendant node represents a rule pair $r(\mu', \nu')$ where $\mu' \geq \mu$ and $\nu' \geq \nu$. According to the following theorem, an upper-bound exists for the ACEP of this rule pair.

Theorem 1 *Let* $\text{H}(\alpha) \equiv [\alpha/\{(1 + \alpha)\text{p}(\overline{x})\}]^{2\alpha}/\{(1 + \alpha)\text{p}(x)\}$, α_1 *and* α_2 *satisfy* $\text{H}(\alpha_1) > 1 > \text{H}(\alpha_2)$, *and* $ACEP = \text{ACEP}(x, Y_{\mu'}, x', Z_{\nu'})$. *If* $\text{H}(\text{p}(x', Y_\mu, Z_\nu)/\text{p}(x, Y_\mu)) < 1$ *then,*

$$
\begin{aligned}
ACEP \quad < \quad & \alpha_2 \text{p}(x, Y_\mu)^2 \left\{ \log_2 \left(\frac{1}{1 + \alpha_1} \frac{1}{\text{p}(x)} \right) + \alpha_1 \right. \\
& \left. \cdot \log_2 \left(\frac{\alpha_1}{1 + \alpha_1} \frac{1}{\text{p}(\overline{x})} \right) \right\} \log_2 \frac{1}{\text{p}(x')} , \quad (11)
\end{aligned}
$$

else

$$
\begin{aligned}
ACEP \quad \leq \quad & \left\{ \text{p}(x, Y_\mu) \log_2 \left(\frac{\text{p}(x, Y_\mu)}{\text{p}(x, Y_\mu) + \text{p}(x', Y_\mu, Z_\nu)} \right. \right. \\
& \left. \cdot \frac{1}{\text{p}(x)} \right) + \text{p}(x', Y_\mu, Z_\nu) \\
& \cdot \log_2 \left(\frac{\text{p}(x', Y_\mu, Z_\nu)}{\text{p}(x, Y_\mu) + \text{p}(x', Y_\mu, Z_\nu)} \right. \\
& \left. \left. \cdot \frac{1}{\text{p}(\overline{x})} \right) \right\} \text{p}(x', Y_\mu, Z_\nu) \log_2 \frac{1}{\text{p}(x')} . \quad (12)
\end{aligned}
$$

In other words, if the upper-bound for the current node is lower than $ACEP_K$ (the Kth highest ACEP of the discovered rule pairs), no rule pair exists whose ACEP is higher than $ACEP_K$ in its descendant nodes. This law tells us that there is no need to expand such descendant nodes and that these nodes can be safely cut off. To alleviate the inevitable inefficiency of depth-first search, a Branch-and-Bound Method (BBM) based on $ACEP_K$ is employed in our approach.

Application to Databases

The proposed method was implemented as MEPRO (database Miner based on average compressed Entropy PROduct criterion), and tested with data sets from several domains, including the voting records database (Murphy & Aha 1994).

The voting records database consists of voting records in a 1984 session of Congress, each piece of data corresponding to a particular politician. The class variable is party affiliation (republican or democrat), and the other 16 attributes are yes/no votes on particular motions such as Contra-aid and budget cuts. Table 1 shows the results of asking MEPRO for the 10 best rule pairs, where the maximum search depth D is restricted to 8. A comma and $\mathcal{C}$ in the table represent conjunction and the premise of the general rule respectively, while the columns xY and Y are the respective actual number of occurrences of the event $x \wedge Y$ (conclusion and premise) and Y (premise).

From table 1, we note that interesting exceptional knowledge emerges, confirming that the system is adequate for the task. According to the second rule pair, 91 % of the 253 congressmen who voted "yes" to "adoption" were democrats. However, 17 of these (who voted "yes" to "physician" and "satellite" in addition to "adoption") were republicans. It is found, from this rule pair, that even republicans vote "yes" to "adoption". The premise of this exceptional rule, which can be viewed as giving a partial definition of these republicans, is highly interesting.

The maximum depth should be large enough so that MEPRO investigates rule pairs whose premises have sufficient numbers of atoms. However, in depth-first search, the number of rule pairs grows exponentially as the depth increases. In this section, we show experimental evidence which suggests that BBM is quite effective in alleviating such inefficiency.

Figure 1 shows a plot of the ratio of the number of nodes pruned by BBM to the total number of nodes visited by depth-first search with depth D. The database chosen for this evaluation was the "voting" database. The system was run with six different values of D (3, 4, $\cdots$, 8) and three values of K (10, 50, 100). Note that the ratio decreases as K increases; actually it is 0 if K is equal to or greater than the number of nodes within depth D. The figure shows that BBM is more effective with a larger depth, e.g. it reduces by more than 80 % of the number of nodes searched when $D = 8$. This is especially important since we must go deeper in the tree to obtain useful exceptional knowledge.

Rank	Rule pair	p(x|Y)	p(x)	xY	Y	ACE	ACEP
1	adoption=yes → physician=no	0.87	0.57	219	253	0.175	0.0115
	C, party=rep → physician=yes	1.00	0.41	22	22	0.066	
2	adoption=yes → party=demo	0.91	0.61	231	253	0.195	0.0105
	C, physician=yes, satellite=yes → party=rep	1.00	0.39	17	17	0.054	
3	satellite=yes → physician=no	0.82	0.57	197	239	0.118	0.0104
	C, party=rep → physician=yes	0.95	0.41	37	39	0.088	
4	party=demo → salvador=no	0.75	0.48	200	267	0.135	0.0101
	C, nicaraguan=no, crime=yes → salvador=yes	0.97	0.49	37	38	0.075	
5	crime=yes → party=rep	0.64	0.39	158	248	0.105	0.0101
	C, physician=no → party=demo	0.97	0.61	74	76	0.095	
6	adoption=yes → party=demo	0.91	0.61	231	253	0.195	0.0099
	C, physician=yes, synfuels=no, south-africa=yes → party=rep	1.00	0.39	16	16	0.050	
7	salvador=yes → party=rep	0.74	0.39	157	212	0.182	0.0098
	C, physician=no → party=demo	0.98	0.61	41	42	0.054	
8	crime=yes → salvador=yes	0.78	0.49	194	248	0.151	0.0097
	C, physician=no, satellite=yes, nicaraguan=yes → salvador=no	0.95	0.48	35	37	0.064	
9	nicaraguan=yes → party=demo	0.90	0.61	218	242	0.169	0.0096
	C, physician=yes, synfuels=no → party=rep	1.00	0.39	18	18	0.057	
10	satellite=yes → party=demo	0.84	0.61	200	239	0.094	0.0095
	C, physician=yes, salvador=yes → party=rep	1.00	0.39	32	32	0.100	

Table 1: The 10 best rule pairs from the voting records database.

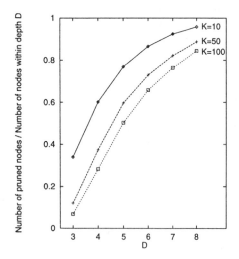

Figure 1: Performance of BBM with varying depth D and number of target rule pairs K.

Conclusion

This paper has described an approach for finding exceptional knowledge using the criterion ACEP (Average Compressed Entropy Product), which requires neither pre-supplied background knowledge nor domain-specific criteria. Consequently, our KDD system MEPRO is immune from the problem of overlooking useful knowledge inherent in the previous approaches which employ either background knowledge or domain-specific criteria. Moreover, we have derived the upper-bound for ACEP and used this in a BBM (Branch-and-Bound Method) to improve search efficiency without altering the discovery results.

Our MEPRO system has been applied to several benchmark databases in the machine learning community. Experimental results show that our system is promising for the efficient discovery of interesting exceptional knowledge. MEPRO is effective in exceptional knowledge discovery in databases where it is difficult to obtain background knowledge a priori. Moreover, it would discover unknown and useful exceptional knowledge in databases where such knowledge is left undiscovered due to the unpredictable misuse of user-supplied background knowledge.

References

Frawley, W. J., Piatetsky-Shapiro, G., and Matheus, C. J. 1991. Knowledge Discovery in Databases: An Overview. In Knowledge Discovery in Databases, 1-27. Piatetsky-Shapiro, G., and Frawley, W. J. (eds). AAAI Press/ The MIT Press.

Hoschka, P., and Klösgen, W. 1991. A Support System For Interpreting Statistical Data. In Knowledge Discovery in Databases, 325-345. Piatetsky-Shapiro, G., and Frawley, W. J. (eds). AAAI Press/ The MIT Press.

Murphy, P. M., and Aha, D. W. 1994. UCI Repository of machine learning databases. http://www.ics.uci.edu/~mlearn/ MLRepository.html. Dept. of Information and Computer Science, University of California.

Piatetsky-Shapiro, G., and Matheus, C. J. 1994. The Interestingness of Deviations. In AAAI-94 Workshop on Knowledge Discovery in Databases, 25-36.

Smyth, P., and Goodman, R. M. 1991. Rule Induction Using Information Theory. In Knowledge Discovery in Databases, 159-176. Piatetsky-Shapiro, G. and Frawley, W. J. (eds). AAAI Press/ The MIT Press.

Interactive Knowledge Discovery from Marketing Questionnaire Using Simulated Breeding and Inductive Learning Methods

Takao TERANO
Graduate School of Systems Management,
The University of Tsukuba, Tokyo
3-29-1 Otsuka, Bunkyo-ku, Tokyo 112, Japan
terano@gssm.otsuka.tsukuba.ac.jp

Yoko ISHINO
Interdiciplinary Course on Advanced
Science and Technology, The University of Tokyo
4-6-1 Komaba, Meguro-ku, Tokyo 153, Japan
ishino@ai.rcast.u-tokyo.ac.jp

Abstract

This paper describes a novel method to acquire efficient decision rules from questionnaire data using both simulated breeding and inductive learning techniques. The basic ideas of the method are that simulated breeding is used to get the effective features from the questionnaire data and that inductive learning is used to acquire simple decision rules from the data. The simulated breeding is one of the Genetic Algorithm (GA) based techniques to subjectively or interactively evaluate the qualities of offspring generated by genetic operations. In this paper, we show a basic interactive version of the method and two variations: the one with semi-automated GA phases and the one with the relatively evaluation phase via the Analytic Hierarchy Process (AHP). The proposed method has been qualitatively and quantitatively validated by a case study on consumer product questionnaire data.

Introduction

Marketing decision making tasks require the acquisition of efficient decision rules from noisy questionnaire data. Unlike popular learning-from-example methods, in such tasks, we must interpret the characteristics of the data without clear features of the data nor pre-determined evaluation criteria. This causes serious KDD problems. Traditionally, statistical methods have been used for these analyses, however, conventional techniques in statistics are too weak because they usually assume the linearity of the models and the form of distributions of the data. During the statistical analysis, emphasis has been placed on understanding trends after identifying target data. Furthermore, marketing requires use of quantitative as well as qualitative analysis. Unfortunately, there are no statistical tools to facilitate to satisfy both requirements simultaneously.

Based on the above background, this paper proposes a novel method to acquire efficient decision rules from questionnaire data. In the following sections, we will describe a method to solve the feature selection problem in inductive learning by the simulated breeding (Dawkins 1986, Sims 1992), genetic algorithms (Goldberg 1989), and the AHP (Saaty 1980) methods. As a result, it will be possible to develop a decision tree with comparatively smaller number of features and which incorporates human subjective evaluations.

Problem Description

First, the techniques used in the method are summarized as follows: (1) Simulated breeding is one of the GA-based techniques to evolve offspring via user interaction based on human preference without explicit evaluation functions; (2) As inductive learning tool, we adopts C4.5 (Quinlan 1993) a noise tolerant successor of ID3, which gives a decision tree or a set of rules from data with attributes-value pairs; and (3) The Analytic Hierarchy Process (AHP)(Saaty 1980) hierarchically decomposes a given problem into its smaller constituent parts and then evaluates the weights of these sub-problems by pair-wise comparison judgements.

Next, in a saturated market domain such as oral care products, marketing decision analysts as domain experts must determine the promotion strategies of new products according to the abstract image of the products to be produced. However, in the task domain, although we can only gather noisy sample data with complicated models, it is critical to get simple but clear rules to explain the characteristics of the products in order to make decisions for promotion.

Third, the difficult points of the research are that 1) the questionnaire data intrinsically involve noises, 2) a distribution of data cannot be previously assumed, 3) selection of appropriate features of the data is inevitable, because of the difficulty in interpreting the results of analysis incorporating all the various features, and 4) we do not know how to define the evaluation criteria in advance for effective explanation.

Forth, the focuses of this research are 1) to classify noisy questionnaire data with multiple features, 2) to select necessary and sufficient features to explain the characteristics of the data, and 3) to generate effective interpretations provided by decision trees or a set of decision rules.

Algorithm for Acquiring Decision Rules

Step 1: Initialization
Select plural number of image words to be explained by decision rules.
Randomly select m sets of individuals with l selected features

Repeat Steps 2-4 until
an appropriate decision tree or a set of decision rules is obtained.

Step 2: Inductive Learning
Apply an inductive learning program to the selected m individuals.
Obtain the corresponding decision trees or sets of decision rules.

step 3: Interactive Evaluation
From among the obtained decision trees or decision rules, two are selected by a user based on the simplicity, correctness & reliability, and the understandability of the decision tree.

step 4: Application of Genetic Operations
Select the best two offspring as parents, apply uniform-crossover operations to them in order to get new sets features, then generate corresponding offspring.

Figure 1: SIBILE-I Algorithm

The procedure of the basic method, SIBILE-I is shown in Figure 1 (Terano, et al. 1995). We call both the algorithm and the system equipped with it SIBILE[1].

In Step 1, we define a set of target concepts to be explained by decision trees. By defining and explaining plural image words simultaneously, we try to solve multi-objective optimization problems. Then, we generate the initial population. The m and l respectively represent the number of individuals and the length of their chromosomes. The number m in simulated breeding is set to very small compared with standard GA-based applications. The chromosomes to represent the features are coded in binary strings, in which a '1' (respectively '0') means that a feature is (not) selected for inclusion in the inductive learning process in Step 2.

In Step 2, the data acquired from the questionnaire is aggregated, each of which has the corresponding fea-

tures in it. Then the m sets of the data are processed by inductive learning programs.

In Step 3, a user or a domain expert must interact with the system. This is a highly knowledge-intensive task. The domain expert judges them based on simplicity, understandability, accuracy, reliability, plausibility, and applicability of the represented knowledge.

The trees selected in Step 3 are set as parents, and in Step 4, new product characteristics are determined by genetic operations. The GA techniques we have adopted are based on the Simple GA found in (Goldberg 1989). The corresponding chromosomes of the selected decision trees become parents for genetic operations. We apply uniform-crossover operations to them in order to get new sets of features to broaden the variety of offspring.

Steps 2 to 4 are repeated until an appropriate decision tree or set of decision rules is obtained. As are illustrated in (Dawkins 1986), the steps required to obtain the appropriate results are very small. In our experiments, it usually takes only less than 10 steps.

Two Variations

Algorithm with Interactive- and Automated-Phases

As stated in the previous section, Step 3 of SIBILE-I requires highly knowledge intensive tasks and times. Furthermore, in the steps in SIBILE-I, the once omitted features of the data will not appear anymore, because the algorithm does not employ mutation operations in GAs. To improve this, we develop a half-automated version: SIBILE-II: first, in the interactive phase, we subjectively evaluate decision trees or sets of decision rules to get the biases of features in the data as is used in the previous section, then in the automated phase, using the biases of the features given in the interaction, genetic operations are applied to develop offspring with *effective* features.

Algorithm with relative evaluation phase via the AHP

This variation: SIBILE-III facilitates the interactive evaluation of offspring represented by decision trees and/or sets of decsion rules. The user feels it convenient to evaluate them pairwisely, instead of comparing them entirely. The evaluation result can be validated by the consistency indices used in the AHP. The variation is easy to implement: we only add the following two sub-steps in Step 3 of SIBILE-I: 1) the interactive pairwise comparison phase and 2) the weight computation phase from the pairwise comparison matrix in the AHP.

---

[1] 'Sibyl' in old French, which stands for Simulated Breeding and Inductive LEarning.

Experimental Results

To validate the effectiveness of the proposed method, we have carried out intensive experiments from a practical case study on consumer product questionnaire data. This section describes the experimental results.

Methods

Questionnaire data to investigate the features of new products in a manufacturing company was used as a case study of the proposed method. The experimental methods are summarized as follows.

- **Questionnaire used:**
  Questionnaire survey conducted with 2,300 respondents by a manufacturing company in 1993 regarding oral care products.

- **Domain Expert:**
  The resulting knowledge was evaluated by a domain expert who is concerned with marketing analysis on the task domain at the manufacturing company. She has been required to interactively and subjectively evaluate the quality of the discovered knowledge from the viewpoints of simplicity, understandability, accuracy, reliability, plausibility, and applicability of the knowledge.

- **Experimental Methods and Implementation:**
  - 16 image words were selected to define product image. Respondents of the questionnaire evaluated how well each of the 16 image words fit the categories (*Fit*, *Moderate*, and *Does not Fit*, which will be respectively denoted as O, M, and X in the following) of the toothpaste brand they mainly use.
  - 16 features words were selected for the evaluation. Respondents of the questionnaire evaluated whether they were *satisfied* or *not satisfied* with their toothpaste brand with regards to each of the 16 features. Therefore, the size of the search space is 2^{16}, which seems small to use Genetic Algorithms, however, it is enough large for using Simulated Breeding. For example, refer to (Bala et al. 1995).

Results

This subsection presents the results of two experimental results (the one for **SIBILE-I** and the other for **SIBILE-II/III**) for the selected images: *innovative* and *effective*. In the experiments, we have tried to discover the knowledge to represent both of the two image words simultaneously. Prior to the experiments, as an initial investigation, we applied C4.5 programs to the data with all 16 features. As a result, we have got a huge *pruned* decision tree with 113 nodes, which was

impossible for even the experienced expert to correctly interpret.

```
CHARACTERISTIC = YES: O (293.0/117.3)
CHARACTERISTIC = NO:
|   LIQUID = YES: O (48.0/21.9)
|   LIQUID = NO:
|   |   COMBINATION = YES: O (120.0/59.3)
|   |   COMBINATION = NO:
|   |   |   FREQUENT-CH = YES: O (198.0/115.3)
|   |   |   FREQUENT-CH = NO:
|   |   |   |   MAKER-VALUE = NO: M (1191.0/595.4)
|   |   |   |   MAKER-VALUE = YES:
|   |   |   |   |   RECOMMENDATION = YES: O (33.0/14.5)
|   |   |   |   |   RECOMMENDATION = NO: M (417.0/236.5)
```

Figure 2: Resulting Decision Tree from Experiment 1

The final results of the decision tree is shown in Figure 2. It took 7 generations or user interaction to obtained the desired results. The decision tree is represented in the form of standard outputs of C4.5 programs.

Results on **SIBILE-II/-III** are also shown in Figure 3 of the set of decision rules.

```
RESULTING DECISION RULES:


Rule 6:                     Rule 7:
    medical-type = YES          medical-type = YES
    liquid = YES                maker-value = YES
    family-use = YES            -> class O [61.5%]
    -> class O [85.7%]
                            Rule 5:
Rule 10:                        characteristics = YES
    characteristics = NO        maker-value = NO
    liquid = YES                family-use = NO
    maker-value = YES           -> class O [58.5%]
    family-use = YES
    -> class O [77.7%]      Rule 9:
                                medical-type = YES
Rule 4:                         family-use = NO
    characteristics = YES       -> class O [57.0%]
    liquid = NO
    family-use = YES       Rule 13:
    -> class O [63.0%]          liquid = YES
                                maker-value = NO
Rule 2:                         family-use = NO
    characteristics = YES       -> class O [53.9%]
    maker-value = YES
    -> class O [62.2%]
```

Figure 3: Resulting Decision Rules from Experiment 2

Discussion

The above experimental results have been evaluated by both quantitative and qualitative ways. Since one of the objectives of this research is to support the creativity of marketing analysts, there is more than one right answer to the questions we are investigating and there are several potential answers left uncovered. With this in mind, the interpretations of the simulation results are described below.

Simplicity of the Decision Rules As depicted in the decision trees obtained, toothpaste with the images of both *innovative* and *effective* were explained by the seven features in the first experiment and the five features in the second experiment. We have got much simpler decision rules than the tree with all 16 features generated by C4.5 programs. It is remarkable that the sizes of the trees do not dramatically change as the generation proceeds. This suggests that in the task domain, the size of the trees does not necessarily become a good measure to evaluate resulting decision rules.

Understandability of the Resulting Rules The decision tree obtained for first experiment explain why the image characteristics both innovative and effective fit the data. For example, from the tree in Figure 2, the user can easily derive the strategy :

Develop a line-up of toothpaste with technical characteristics other brands do not have, a liquid toothpaste, and a combination toothbrush/toothpaste brand.

This strategy is confirmed by the other domain experts to be similar to the company's actual strategy for its brand which was not on the market at the time the questionnaire survey was conducted.

Accuracy Comparison Accuracy does not overcome the other measures in SIBILE, however, it is one of the important measure which can be evaluated among the other methods. Table 1 shows the accuracy comparison results of the tree with all features and the resulting tree generated by the experiment. Furthermore, we have compared the accuracy of resulting decision trees by SIBILE with the other statistical methods: the linear discrimination method (LD)in *SAS* package and the automatic interaction detection (AID) in *S* package. The experimental results are also summarized in Table 1.

The first three columns, the next two columns, and the final two columns respectively indicate the results using all 16 features, the results using selected features in the experiment 1, and the results using selected features in the experiment 2. The data C4.5 with features 1.7.4 and 2.3.4 mean the results which have been selected by the proposed method.

In our task domain, the total accuracy of the resulting rules and the accuracy for Class O are critical to get decision knowledge. Keep this in mind, the figure suggest that the proposed method shows the same level of accuracy among the other method, in spite that the resulting rules are so simple.

Concluding Remarks

The main contributions of the research to KDD are (1) that the combinatorial feature selection problem in inductive learning can be resolved by simulated breeding, which is characterized by subjective and interactive evaluations of offspring generated by genetic operations, (2) that the effectiveness of the proposed method SIBILE has been validated by a case study on practical questionnaire data, and (3) that we have shown the Alife oriented techniques such as simulated breeding can be applied to practical knowledge discovery problems.

The pre-requisites of the proposed method are quite simple and the algorithm is easy to implement. Therefore, we conclude the proposed method is applicable to other task domain problems.

References

Bala, J. W.; Huang, J.; Vafaie, H.; De Jong, K; and Wechsler, H. 1995: Hybrid Learning Using Genetic Algorithms and Decision Trees for Pattern Recognition. in *Proceedings of 14th International Joint Conference on Artificial Intelligence*, 719-724.

Dawkins, R. 1986. *The Blind Watchmaker*. W. W. Norton.

Goldberg, D. E. 1989. *Genetic Algorithms in Search, Optimization and Machine Learning*. Addison-Wesley.

Quinlan, J. R. 1993. *C4.5: Programs for Machine Learning*. Morgan-Kaufmann.

Saaty, T. L. 1980. *The Analytic Hierarchy Process - Planning, Priority Setting, Resource Allocation*. McGraw-Hill.

Sims, K. 1992. Interactive Evolution of Dynamical Systems. in Varela, F. J., Bourgine, P. (eds.) : *Toward a Practice of Autonomous Systems - Proc. 1st European Conf. Artificial Life*, MIT Press: 171-178.

Terano , T.; Ishino, Y.; and Yoshinaga, K. 1995: Integrating Machine Learning and Simulated Breeding Techniques to Analyze the Characteristics of Consumer Goods. in Biethahn, J., Nissen, V. eds.1995. *Evolutionary Algorithms in Management Applications*, Springer-Verlag, 211-224.

Weiss, S. M., and Kulikowski, C. A. 1991. *Computer Systems that Learn*. Morgan-Kaufmann.

Table 1: Accuracy of SIBILE, C4.5, LD, and AID

Methods	C4.5	LD	AID	Sibile	LD	Sibile	LD
Selected Features	All	All	All	Same 1.7.4	Same 1.7.4	Same 2.3.4	Same 2.3.4
Total Accuracy	57.3%	41.4%	56.0%	51.4%	40.6%	52.4%	33.9%
Class O Accuracy	51.8%	48.2%	61.3%	41.3%	37.2%	45.3%	50.4%
Class M Accuracy	81.2%	3?.5%	69.4%	77.5%	43.8%	76.1%	8.2%
Class X Accuracy	0.0%	43.5%	0.9%	0.0%	40.0%	0.0%	66.5%

Representing Discovered Patterns Using Attributed Hypergraph

Yang Wang and Andrew K. C. Wong
Pattern Analysis and Machine Intelligence Group
Department of Systems Design Engineering
University of Waterloo
Waterloo, Ontario N2L 3G1, CANADA
{wang, akcwong}@watnow.uwaterloo.ca

Abstract

One of the fundamental problems in knowledge discovery in databases and other applications of AI is how to represent knowledge and patterns. Existing representation schemes have various shortcomings. In this paper, we propose a new knowledge representation scheme using *attributed hypergraph* (*AHG*), which is simple yet general enough to directly encode different order patterns discovered from large databases. In *AHG*, both the qualitative and quantitative relations are represented as attributed hyperedges. Such representation is lucid and transparent for visualization. Besides, patterns in *AHG* are easy to understand. In the discussion, some basic manipulations of *AHG* for data mining tasks are briefly addressed. The paper ends with examples of pattern representation using *AHG*.

Introduction

For most applications of AI, including machine learning and KDD, the choice of knowledge representation is a difficult task. Woods (Woods 1983) suggests that two measurements, *expressive adequacy* and *notational efficiency*, should be used to evaluate the performance of a knowledge representation.

By knowledge discovery in databases, or Data Mining, we mean automatically process from databases large quantities of data; identify the significant and meaningful patterns; and represent them in a form suitable for achieving the user's goal (Matheus & Piatetsky-Shapiro 1993). Since the goals of such a system are often vaguely defined and change with time, knowledge representation tends to be more important for a KDD system than a conventional classification system. In addition to the requirements proposed by Woods, several other aspects should be considered. First, the representation scheme should offer a mechanism for easy knowledge re-organization or focus on a certain portion of the knowledge to meet the changing goal. Secondly, the represented knowledge should be transparent, easy to be visualized and understood.

Since data in real world databases usually contains noise and uncertainty, patterns extracted by a KDD system are generally probabilistic. It is required that numerical inferences be supported by the representation in addition to logical inference. Finally, since the patterns detected from large databases could be of different orders, and since high order patterns cannot be induced by lower order relations (Wong & Wang 1995), different order patterns should be explicitly represented.

In this paper, after a brief review of popular representation, we propose a new knowledge representation based on *attributed hypergraph* (*AHG*), which is simple yet general enough to encode different order patterns. With such representation, both the qualitative and the quantitative relations are explicitly represented and are easy to understand.

Representation Schemes for KDD

Over the years, numerous knowledge representation schemes have been reported. The most popular ones are decision tree, networks, production rule and logic.

Decision tree is a simple representation popularized by Quinlan's ID3 and successfully applied to inductive learning. Decision tree based systems are found in a wide range of application domains, mostly in the classification-oriented areas. A disadvantage of decision tree is its difficulty for humans to interpret, especially from the viewpoint of expert systems (Smyth & Goodman 1992) and KDD systems (Holsheimer & Siebes 1995). Also, trees are not designed to deal with missing attribute information (Smyth & Goodman 1992). Moreover, since decision trees are mainly designed for classification purposes, they are not suitable for multi-attribute prediction (Fisher 1987).

Trees can be considered as a special case of graphs. Graph representations, such as Bayesian and Markov networks, usually provide more general methods to represent patterns. They directly represent the first order associations between two nodes by links. However, as observed by Pearl (Pearl 1988), graph-based representation, including trees and networks, cannot distinguish between set connectivity and connectivity among their elements. Hence, they are not general enough for representing different order patterns.

Production (if-then) rule is another scheme widely used in expert systems and classification oriented tasks. It explicitly presents the association between a set of observations (left-hand antecedent) and one attribute value (right-hand consequent). Rules are considered easier to understand than trees. However, in KDD applications, with each changing interest, the values of different attributes have to be predicted. Besides, a huge number of rules have to be obtained. This is sometimes impractical in the real world (Wong & Wang 1996). In this case, we need a scheme which can easily re-organize the represented knowledge for different goals of the system.

In addition to attribute (proposition) based representations, relational representations such as Horn clause (see (Kowalski 1979) for an overview) and First Order Logic (see (Muggleton 1992) for an overview) are used in learning systems. They are very powerful and expressive formalisms. Since they are originally designed to formalize mathematical reasoning and later used in logic programming, patterns in them are deterministic rather than probabilistic. To do probabilistic reasoning, special adoptions have to be done. This problem also exists in the structured representations such as semantic networks. Besides, logic based representations are considered less comprehensible and harder to visualize than graph based representations.

The AHG Representation

To overcome the shortcomings of the traditional representations, we here propose an *attributed hypergraph* representation to depict the associations of patterns in a data set. *AHG* is a direct, simple and efficient representation for describing the information at different and/or mixed levels of abstraction. It has been successfully used in 3D scene interpretation and object recognition (Wong & Rioux 1990). In *AHG*, both the qualitative relations (the structure of the hypergraph) and the quantitative relations (the attribute values of vertices and hyperedges) are encoded. Since *AHG* representation is lucid and transparent for visualization, interpretation of different order patterns can be easily achieved. A good number of mature graph algorithms can be adopted to implement various operations for pattern retrieval and re-organization. The computational complexity of this representation will be related to the complexity of the algorithms performing graph operations. Before proposing the *AHG* representation,

we first formalize the definition of a pattern.

Pattern as Event Association in Database

Consider that we have a database D containing M instances. Every instance is described in terms of N fields, $\mathbf{X} = \{X_1, \cdots, X_N\}$. Then each field, X_i, $1 \leq i \leq N$, can be seen as a random variable taking on values from its domain $Dom(X_i)$. In this manner, each instance in D is a realization of $\mathbf{X}$, denoted as $\mathbf{x}_j = \{x_{1j}, \cdots, x_{Nj}\}$, where x_{ij} can assume any value in $Dom(X_i)$.

A *component* of D is either a field or any possible value (range) of a field. Any field X_i, $1 \leq i \leq N$ is a component. *True* can be a component if it is a possible value of a field. An interval $(25, 50)$ can also be a component if it belongs to a domain. An *atomic event*, or *event* for short, is defined as the relationship between two components. Thus, any realizations of the fields, such as $X_1 = True$ and $X_2 \in (25, 50)$ are atomic events. The relationships between two fields such as $X_1 < X_2$, $X_1 \neq X_2$ and $X_1/X_2 = 2.5$ are also events if they are meaningful. A *compound event*, or *composite* for short, is a set of atomic events and/or compound events. The *order* of a composite is its cardinality. Any first order composite is an atomic event. Thus, $[X_1 = True, X_2 \in (25, 50)]$ is a second order composite. A *sub-composite* of a composite is a subset of the composite. Let T be a statistical significance test. If a composite c passes the test, we say that c is a *significant pattern*, or simply a *pattern*, of order $|c|$. The elements of c are said to have a *statistically significant association according to T* or simply they are *associated*.

We argue that most patterns in a database can always be described as event associations. An if-then rule can be seen as an association between its left-hand composite and its right-hand event. Due to the noise in a database, patterns are probabilistic rather than deterministic. In a real world database, the existence of higher order patterns does not guarantee the existence of lower order patterns and *vice versa* (Wong & Wang 1995). Hence, whether or not a composite is a pattern cannot be determined by examining its sub-composites and *vice versa*. This implies that, in general, higher order patterns cannot be synthesized from the lower order ones (Wong & Wang 1995). It requires that different order patterns be represented explicitly.

Representing Patterns in AHG

Let us first give a formal definition of hypergraph.
Def. 1. (Berge 1989) Let $Y = \{y_1, y_2, \cdots, y_n\}$ be a finite set. A *hypergraph* on Y is a family $H = (E_1, E_2, \cdots, E_m)$ of subsets of Y such that

1. $E_i \neq \phi \quad (i = 1, 2, \cdots, m)$, and
2. $\bigcup_{i=1}^{m} E_i = Y$.

The elements $y_1, y_2, \cdots, y_n$ of Y are called *vertices*, and the sets $E_1, E_2, \cdots, E_m$ are the *edges* of the hypergraph, or simply, *hyperedges*.

Def. 2. A *simple hypergraph* is a hypergraph H with hyperedges $(E_1, E_2, \cdots, E_m)$ such that
$$E_i = E_j \Rightarrow i = j.$$
Unless otherwise indicated, we refer to *hypergraph* as *simple hypergraph*.

Def. 3. An *attribute* of a hypergraph is a data structure associated with a hyperedge or a vertex.

Def. 4. An *attributed hypergraph* is a hypergraph such that each of its hyperedges and vertices has an attribute.

In *AHG* representation, each *vertex* represents an atomic event. Each pattern or statistically significant association is represented by a *hyperedge*. The *rank* (*anti-rank*) of a hypergraph is the highest (lowest) order of the patterns detected from the database. For an event e, the *star* $H(e)$ of hypergraph H with center e represents all the patterns related to the event e. Let A be a subset of all atomic events, the *sub-hypergraph* of hypergraph H induced by A represents the event associations in A.

The attributes of both the vertices and the hyperedges depend on the application and the pattern discovery algorithm applied. In (Wong & Wang 1996), we proposed a statistical pattern discovery method based on adjusted residual analysis. In such a case, the attribute of each vertex is the marginal probability of the corresponding atomic event. The attribute of each hyperedge contains the probability of the compound event, the expected probability of the compound event, and the probabilities of sub-compound events one order lower. All of these attributes will be useful for the inference process. Therefore, hyperedges depict the qualitative relations among their elementary vertices, while the attributes associated with the hyperedges and the vertices quantify these relations.

Fig. 1 shows some generalized cases of different order significant associations. The upper part of each case in this figure depicts the event occurrences and their pairwise associations, while the lower part furnishes the hypergraph representation of the associations (attributes not shown). This figure also illustrates that the existence of higher order patterns does not guarantee the existence of lower order patterns and *vice versa*. For instance, Case 3 shows a situation where third order pattern $[A, B, C]$ exists, but there is no second order association between A, B and C. Case 4 depicts a contrary instance such that all of the three second order patterns exist but not the third order pattern.

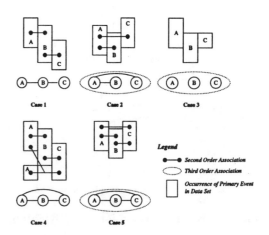

Figure 1: Different Order Significant Associations

Within the *AHG* framework, to manipulate patterns is to operate on the hyperedges, vertices and their attributes. To re-organize knowledge is to select sub-hypergraphs according to the current system goal. If we are classifying a new instance against a field X_1, only the hyperedges containing an event of X_1 are interesting. If the system is later asked to find the patterns related to event $X_2 = True$, only the hyperedges containing this event are focused on. Thanks to a good number of mature algorithms on graphs, these kinds of operations are expected to be computationally efficient. Most database mining problems can be classified into three categories: association, classification, and sequence (Agrawal & Swami 1993). In the *AHG* framework, associations among events are represented as hyperedges. When we consider class labels as a special field, classification can always be treated as using patterns related to this special field to predict the class of a new object. The sequential problem is just a special case of association with a time tag attached.

How to operate on an *AHG* is also application dependent. Basic operators include *Construct()* which constructs an attributed hypergraph from a database, *HighestOrder()* and *LowestOrder()* which find the highest (lowest) order of detected relationships, *Find-Relation()* which extracts all the patterns related to a specified event, and *FindSubEvent()* which extracts all patterns that contain a given composite or its non-empty sub-composites. The last one is to find all the compound events which are considered relevant to the inference process from a set of facts.

Examples of AHG Representation

XOR is a typical high order problem. Case 1 of Fig. 2 shows all the patterns found by applying the algorithm in (Wong & Wang 1995). We note right away that there are only third order patterns. If we are interested in only the patterns related to $C = F$, then a sub-hypergraph shown by Case 2 is extracted. This hypergraph is equivalent to the rule: $(A = T \wedge B = T) \vee (A = F \wedge B = F) \Rightarrow C = F$.

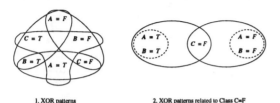

1. XOR patterns   2. XOR patterns related to Class C=F

Figure 2: AHG Representation of XOR Patterns

In the breast cancer database (Wolberg & Mangasarian 1990), each sample is described by 10 attributes and classified into one of the two classes. Fig. 3 shows part of the patterns detected by applying the algorithm proposed in (Wong & Wang 1995) and (Wong & Wang 1996). Here, the values of hypergraph attributes are not shown. To make explicit the class and attribute association, we single out the classes (*benign* and *malignant*). Their associations with other atomic or compound events are shown by the solid lines. Significant compound events associated with a class are enclosed by dotted curves. This *AHG* shows that: 1) any composite c can only be associated with only one of the two classes; and 2) if c is associated with one class, none of the sub-composite of c would appear in hyperedges related to the other class (i.e. the two classes are totally separated). It implies that, theoretically, we can achieve 100% classification accuracy.

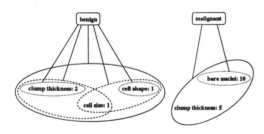

Figure 3: Part of AHG for Breast-Cancer Database

Fig. 4 is the *AHG* of all the second order patterns related to the field *Severity* discovered from a company's injury database. The number on the line indicates the significant level of the pattern. A dash line shows that the pattern is negative, which means that the two connected events are unlikely to happen together. From the figure, for example, we can see that two fields, *Injury_Type* and *Department* have relations with *Severity*. If *Injury_Type* is 1, *Severity* will be higher than 1. The most probable *Severity* level will be 2, since this pattern has the highest sig-

nificant level. On the other hand, only one event of *Department* is related to *Severity*. It depicts that workers in *Department* 1 normally do not have injuries of *Severity* level 2.

Figure 4: Second Order Patterns in an Injury Database

Summary

This paper presents a new pattern representation for KDD. Here, different order patterns are explicitly represented in the form of *AHG* which allows the user to analyze the data at different levels of abstraction. In this *AHG* framework, to re-organize knowledge, relations can be used to induce new hyperedge. Such representation encodes both qualitative and quantitative patterns. Since the framework is transparent to the user, knowledge can be visualized and interpreted by humans without difficulty. Current work concentrates on the inference processes using *AHG* knowledge representation for various data mining tasks.

References

Agrawal, R.; Imielinski, T., and Swami, A. 1993. Database mining: A performance perspective. *IEEE Trans. on KDB* 5(6):914–925.

Berge, C. 1989. *Hypergraph: Combinatorics of Finite Sets*. North Holland.

Fisher, D. H. 1987. Knowledge acquisition via incremental conceptual clustering. *Machine Learning* 2(2):139–172.

Holsheimer, M., and Siebes, A. 1995. Data mining: The research for knowledge in databases. Technical Report CS-R9406, CWI.

Kowalski, R. 1979. *Logic for Problem Solving*. North Holland.

Matheus, C. J.; Chan, P. K., and Piatetsky-Shapiro, G. 1993. Systems for knowledge discovery in databases. *IEEE Trans. on KDB* 5(6):903–913.

Muggleton, S. 1992. *Inductive Logic Programming*. Academic Press.

Pearl, J. 1988. *Probabilistic Reasoning in Intelligent Systems: Networks of Plausible Inference*. Morgan Kaufmann.

Smyth, P., and Goodman, R. M. 1992. Information theoretic approach to rule induction from database. *IEEE Trans. on KDB* 4(4):301–316.

Wolberg, W. H., and Mangasarian, O. L. 1990. Multisurface method of pattern separation for medical diagnosis applied to breast cytology. In *Proc. of the Nat. Aca. of Sci.*, volume 87.

Wong, A. K. C.; Lu, S. W., and Rioux, M. 1990. Recognition and shape synthesis of 3-d object based on attributed hypergraph. *IEEE Trans. on PAMI* 11(3):279–290.

Wong, A. K. C., and Wang, Y. 1995. Discovery of high order patterns. In *Proc. of IEEE Int'l Conf. on SMC*, 1142–1148.

Wong, A. K. C., and Wang, Y. 1996. High order pattern discovery from discrete-valued data. *IEEE Trans. on KDB*. accepted.

Woods, W. A. 1983. What's important about knowledge representation. *Computer* 16(10).

Developing Tightly-Coupled Data Mining Applications on a Relational Database System

Rakesh Agrawal and **Kyuseok Shim**
IBM Almaden Research Center
650 Harry Road, San Jose, CA 95120

Abstract

We present a methodology for tightly coupling data mining applications to database systems to build high-performance applications, without requiring any change to the database software.

Introduction

Most of the current data mining applications have a loose connection with databases. A majority of them treat database simply as a container from which data is extracted to populate main memory data structures before the main execution begins. This approach limits the amount of data the application can handle effectively.

The more database-aware applications use *loosely-coupled* SQL to fetch data records as needed by the mining algorithm. The front-end of the application is implemented in a host programming language, with embedded SQL statements in it. The application uses a SQL `select` statement to retrieve the set of records of interest from the database. A loop in the application program copies records in the result set one-by-one from the database address space to the application address space, where computation is performed on them. This approach has two performance problems: i) copying of records from the database address space to the application address space, and ii) process context switching for each record retrieved, which is costly in a database system built on top of an operating system such as UNIX. The resultant poor performance is often the deterrent in using databases in these applications.

We present a methodology for *tightly-coupled* integration of data mining applications with a relational database system. Instead of bringing the records of database into the application program, we selectively push parts of the application program that perform computation on retrieved records into the database system, thus avoiding the performance degradation cited above. Our approach is based on a novel way of using the user-defined functions in SQL statements. A major attraction of our methodology is that it does not require changes to the database software. We validated our methodology by tightly-coupling the problem of mining association rules (Agrawal, Imielinski, & Swami 1993) on IBM DB2/CS relational database system (Chamberlin 1996). Empirical evaluation using real-life data shows nearly two-fold performance advantage for tight-coupling over loose-coupling. The programming effort in converting the loosely-coupled application to a tightly-coupled one was minimal.

Related Work The idea of realizing performance gains by executing user-specified computations within the database system rather than in the applications has manifested in several systems. Research in database programming languages, object-oriented database systems, and the integration of abstract data types in relational systems has been partially driven by the same motivation. Stored procedures in commercial database products have been designed for the same purpose. For example, Oracle provides a facility to create and store procedures written in PL/SQL as named objects in the database to reduce the amount of information sent over a network. Alternatively, an application can send an unnamed PL/SQL block to the server, which in turn complies the block and executes it. The Illustra DBMS also provides a facility for user-defined aggregations to be performed within the DBMS.

Methodology

Our methodology for developing tightly-coupled applications has the following components:

- Employ two classes of user-defined functions:
  - those that are executed a few times (usually once) independent of the number of records in the table;
  - those that are executed once for each selected record.

The former are used for allocating and deallocating work-area in the address space of the database system and copying results from the database address to the application address space. The latter do computations on the selected records in the database address space, using the work-area allocated earlier.

- To execute a user-defined function once, reference it in the select list of a SQL select statement over a one-record table. In DB2/CS, create this temporary one-record dynamically by using the construct *(value(1))* as *onerecord* in the from clause.

- To execute a user-defined function *udf()* once for each selected record without ping-ponging between the database and application address spaces, have the function return 0. Define the SQL select statement over the table whose records are to be processed, and add a condition of the form *udf() = 1* in the where clause. If there are other conditions in the where clause, those conditions must be evaluated first because the user-defined function must be applied only on the selected records.

- If a computation involves using user-defined functions in multiple SQL select statements, they share data-structures by creating handles in the work-area initially created.

Specifically, our approach consists of the following steps:

- Allocate work-area in the database address space utilizing a user-defined function in a SQL select statement over a one-record table. A handle to this work-area is returned in the application address space using the into clause.

- Setup iteration over the table containing data records and reference the user-defined function encapsulating the desired computation in the where clause of the select statement as discussed above. Pass the handle to the work-area as an input argument to this user-defined function. If the computation requires more than one user-defined function (and hence multiple select statements), have the previous one leave a handle to the desired data structures in the work-area.

- Copy the results from the work-area in the database address space into the application address space using another user-defined function in a SQL select statement over a one-record table.

- Use another user-defined function over a one-record table in a SQL select statement to deallocate the work-area.

We can cast our approach in the object-oriented programming paradigm. We can think of the function to allocate space as a constructor for an object whose data members store the state of the application program in the address space of database system. A collection of member functions generate, save, and query the state of the application program. The function to deallocate space can be thought of as the destructor for the object.

A Case Study

To validate our methodology, we tightly-coupled the data mining application of discovering association rules to IBM DB2/CS. Given a set of transactions, where each transaction is a set of items, an association rule is an expression of the from $X \implies Y$, where X and Y are sets of items. An example of an association rule is: "30% of transactions that contain beer also contain diapers; 2% of all transactions contain both of these items". Here 30% is called the *confidence* of the rule, and 2% the *support* of the rule. The problem is to find all association rules that satisfy user-specified minimum support and minimum confidence constraints.

A transaction is represented as a set of consecutive records in the database. A record consists of a transaction id and an item id; all the items belonging to the same transaction id represent a transaction. The input data comes naturally sorted by transaction id.

Overview of the Apriori Algorithm

Our case study uses the Apriori algorithm for mining association rules (Agrawal & Srikant 1994). The problem of mining association rules is decomposed into two subproblems: i) find all *frequent* itemsets that occur in a specified minimum number of transaction, called *min-support*; ii) use the frequent itemsets to generate the desired rules. We only consider the first subproblem as the database is only accessed during this phase.

The Apriori algorithm for finding all frequent itemsets is given in Figure 1. It makes multiple passes over the database. In the first pass, the algorithm simply counts item occurrences to determine the frequent 1-itemsets (itemsets with 1 item). A subsequent pass, say pass k, consists of two phases. First, the frequent itemsets L_{k-1} (the set of all frequent $(k-1)$-itemsets) found in the $(k-1)$th pass are used to generate the candidate itemsets C_k, using the *apriori-gen()* function. This function first joins L_{k-1} with L_{k-1}, the joining condition being that the lexicographically ordered first $k-2$ items are the same. Next, it deletes all those itemsets from the join result who have some $(k-1)$-subset that is not in L_{k-1}, yielding C_k. For example, let L_3 be {{1 2 3}, {1 2 4}, {1 3 4}, {1 3 5},

```
procedure AprioriAlg()
begin
1.  L_1 := {frequent 1-itemsets};
2.  for ( k := 2; L_{k-1} ≠ ∅; k++ ) do {
3.     C_k := apriori-gen(L_{k-1});  // New candidates
4.     forall transactions t ∈ D do {
5.        forall candidates c ∈ C_k contained in t do
6.           c.count++;
7.     }
8.     L_k := {c ∈ C_k | c.count ≥ min-support}
9.  }
10. Answer := ⋃_k L_k;
end
```

Figure 1: Apriori Algorithm

{2 3 4}}. After the join step, C_4 will be {{1 2 3 4}, {1 3 4 5} }. The prune step will delete the itemset {1 3 4 5} because the itemset {1 4 5} is not in L_3. We will then be left with only {1 2 3 4} in C_4.

The algorithm now scans the database. For each transaction, it determines which of the candidates in C_k are contained in the transaction using a hash-tree data structure and increments their count. At the end of the pass, C_k is examined to determine which of the candidates are frequent, yielding L_k. The algorithm terminates when L_k becomes empty.

Loosely Coupled Integration

Figure 2 shows the sketch of a loosely-coupled implementation of the Apriori algorithm. Lines 4 through 13 determine the frequent 1-itemsets corresponding to line 1 in Figure 1. We open a cursor over the *sales* table, fetch one record at a time from the database to the application program, and increment count for items found in each record. The count array is maintained in the application program. Note that there is one context switch for every record in the *sales* table. At the end of the loop, the count array is scanned to determine the frequent 1-itemsets.

Lines 14 through 33 contain processing for subsequent passes. These lines correspond to lines 2 through 9 in Figure 1. In line 15, we generate candidates in the application program. The database is now scanned to determine the count for each of the candidates. We open a cursor over the *sales* table and fetch one record at a time from the database process to the application process. After all the records corresponding to a transaction have been retrieved, we determine which of the candidates are contained in the transaction and increment their counts. Finally, we determine in the application which of the candidates are frequent.

```
procedure LoosleyCoupledApriori() :
begin
1.  exec sql connect to database;
2.  exec sql declare cur cursor for
           select TID, ITEMID from sales
           for read only;
3.  exec sql open cur;
4.  notDone := true;
5.  while notDone do {
6.     exec sql fetch cur into :tid, :itemid;
7.     if (sqlcode ≠ endOfRec) then
8.        update counts for each itemid;
9.     else
10.       notDone := false
11. }
12. exec sql close cur;
13. L_1 := {frequent 1-itemsets};
14. for ( k := 2; L_{k-1} ≠ ∅; k++ ) do {
15.    C_k := apriori-gen(L_{k-1});  // New candidates
16.    exec sql open cur;
17.    t := ∅; prevTid := -1; notDone := true;
18.    while notDone do {
19.       exec sql fetch cur into :tid, :itemid;
20.       if (sqlcode ≠ endOfRec then) {
21.          if (tid ≠ prevTid and t ≠ ∅) then {
22.             forall candidates c ∈ C_k contained in t do
23.                c.count++;
24.             t := ∅; prevTid := tid;
25.          }
26.          t := t ∪ itemid
27.       }
28.       else
29.          notDone := false;
30.    }
31.    exec sql close cur;
32.    L_k := {c ∈ C_k | c.count ≥ min-support}
33. }
34. Answer := ⋃_k L_k;
end
```

Figure 2: Loosely-coupled Apriori Algorithm

Tightly Coupled Integration

We give a tightly-coupled implementation of the Apriori algorithm in Figure 3 using our methodology. The statement in line 2 creates work-area in the database address space for intermediate results. The handle to this work-area is returned in the host variable *blob*. The statement in line 3 iterates over all the records in the database. However, by making the user-defined function $GenL_1()$ always return 0, we force the function $GenL_1()$ to be executed in the database process for every record, avoiding copying and context switching. Line 3 corresponds to the first pass of the algorithm in which frequency of each item is counted and 1-frequent itemsets are determined. $GenL_1()$ receives the handle for the work-area as an input argument and it saves a handle to the 1-frequent itemsets in the work-area

```
Procedure TightlyCoupledApriori() :
begin
1.  exec sql connect to database;
2.  exec sql select allocSpace() into :blob
        from onerecord;
3.  exec sql select *
        from sales
        where GenL₁(:blob, TID, ITEMID) = 1;
4.  notDone := true;
5.  while notDone do {
6.      exec sql select aprioriGen(:blob) into :blob
            from onerecord;
7.      exec sql select *
            from sales
            where itemCount(:blob, TID, ITEMID) = 1;
8.      exec sql select GenLₖ(:blob) into :notDone
            from onerecord;
9.  }
10. exec sql select getResult(:blob) into :resultBlob
        from onerecord;
11. exec sql select deallocSpace(:blob)
        from onerecord;
12. Compute Answer using resultBlob;
end
```

Figure 3: Tightly-coupled Apriori Algorithm

before it returns.

Lines 4 through 9 correspond to subsequent passes. First the candidates are generated in the address space of the database process by the the user-defined function *aprioriGen()*. We accomplish this by referencing this function in the **select** list of the SQL statement over *onerecord* table (hence ensuring that it is executed once) and providing the handle to the frequent itemsets needed for generating candidates as input argument to the function. The handle to candidates generated is saved in the work-area.

Statement on line 7 iterates over the database. Again, by making the function *itemCount()* return 0, we ensure that this function is applied to each record, but within the database process. Handle to the candidates is available in the work-area provided as input argument to *itemCount()* and this function counts the the support of candidates. This statement corresponds to the statements in line 16-31 in Figure 2.

Next, the function *GenLₖ()* is invoked in the address space of the database process by referencing it in the SQL statement in line 9 over *onerecord* table. In the kth pass, this function generates frequent itemsets with k items and returns a boolean to indicate whether the size of current L_k is empty or not. This value is copied into the host variable *notDone* to determine loop termination in the application program. After the loop exits, the function *getResult()* copies out the result from the database process into the host vari-

able *resultBlob* in the application process. Finally, the function *deallocSpace()* frees up the work-area in the database address space.

Performance

To assess the effectiveness of our approach, we empirically compared the performance of tightly-coupled and loosely-coupled implementations of the Apriori algorithm. Six real-life customer datasets were used in the experiment. These datasets were obtained from department stores, supermarkets, and mail-order companies. We observed that in all cases, tight-coupling gives more than two fold performance advantage over loose-coupling. See (Agrawal & Shim 1995) for details of the performance experiments and results. We would like to mention that work is underway to improve the performance of the implementation of the user-defined functions in DB2/CS. The tightly-coupled implementation would directly benefit from any performance gains from this effort.

Acknowledgments Experiments by Andreas Arning, Toni Bollinger, and Ramakrishnan Srikant brought to our attention the performance penalty of loosely-coupled integration. John McPherson, Pat Selinger, and Don Haderle pointed us to the user-defined functions as a possible way of attacking the performance problem. Don Chamberlin, Guy Lohman, Hamid Pirahesh, Berthold Reinwald, Amit Somani, and Geroge Wilson explained several subtleties of the user-defined functions and stored procedures in DB2/CS. Bob Yost helped us in obtaining the latest versions of DB2/CS. Finally, the generous help and suggestions of Ramakrishnan Srikant were invaluable.

References

Agrawal, R., and Shim, K. 1995. Developing tightly-coupled applications on IBM DB2/CS relational database system: Methodology and experience. Research Report RJ 10005 (89094), IBM Almaden Research Center, San Jose, California. Available from http://www.almaden.ibm.com/cs/quest.

Agrawal, R., and Srikant, R. 1994. Fast Algorithms for Mining Association Rules. In *Proc. of the 20th Int'l Conference on Very Large Databases*.

Agrawal, R.; Imielinski, T.; and Swami, A. 1993. Mining association rules between sets of items in large databases. In *Proc. of the ACM SIGMOD Conference on Management of Data*, 207–216.

Chamberlin, D. 1996. *Using the New DB2: IBM's Object-Relational Database System*. Morgan Kaufmann.

Mining Entity-Identification Rules for Database Integration

M. Ganesh and **Jaideep Srivastava**
Dept. of Computer Science
4-192 EECS Bldg., 200 Union St. SE
University of Minnesota, Minneapolis, MN 55455

Travis Richardson
Apertus Technologies, Inc.
7275 Flying Cloud Dr.
Eden Prairie, MN55344

Abstract

Entity identification (EI) is the identification and integration of all records which represent the same real-world entity, and is an important task in database integration process. When a common identification mechanism for similar records across heterogeneous databases is not readily available, EI is performed by examining the relationships between various attribute values among the records. We propose the use of distances between attribute values as a measure of similarity between the records they represent. Record-matching conditions for EI can then be expressed as constraints on the attribute distances. We show how knowledge discovery techniques can be used to automatically derive these conditions (expressed as decision trees) directly from the data, using a distance-based framework.

Introduction

Many large enterprises are currently faced with the need to integrate several heterogeneous and independently evolved operational data sources (Drew *et al.* 1993). The information infrastructure in such organizations has been developed over several years using a wide range of technologies from file systems to relational and object database management systems[1]. Effective utilization of available resources in such environments is critically dependent on obtaining a consistent and global view of all information in the organization.

Database integration is the process of merging together information represented in more than one component database system, so that a uniform view of the enterprise data is offered to all the users. This activity forms the core of several frequently performed information systems tasks such as database conversion, database synchronization, data/event replication, and data warehousing (Richardson & Srivastava 1995; Inmon 1992). Federated database systems (Sheth & Larson 1990) allow multiple heterogeneous databases to cooperatively provide a uniform integrated schema to the users while still retaining autonomy of local operations. All these paradigms of database integration require the knowledge about how data in different component databases relate to each other.

Database integration process includes two distinct tasks: *Global schema mapping* or *schema integration* resolves all conflicts due to schema mismatches such as homonyms (using same name for different attributes) and synonyms (using different names for the same attributes) (Batini, Lenzerini, & Navathe 1986). Mapping the records in the component databases to a uniform global schema makes it possible to treat all the records uniformly for further processing (Richardson & Srivastava 1995). When the component databases replicate data the mapped global database may contain multiple instances of the same real-world entity. Identification and integration of these instances is the second task in database integration. In this paper we focus on this *Entity Identification (EI)* (Lim *et al.* 1993) problem assuming the schema integration tasks have already been performed. EI problem deserves attention in the current environment where enterprises rely on robust information systems which can provide very accurate information. In many situations there are no common identification mechanisms, such as key attributes, to distinguish records instances which represent the same real-world entity. In this paper, we propose a method to derive the rules for EI directly from examples of similar instances of records, instead of requiring users to specify rules/conditions that identify instances of the same entity. The concept of attribute-value distances is introduced to facilitate this discovery. Since the rules are learned directly from the data, they are expected to be more comprehensive than could be specified by any single user.

---

[1]In this paper we use the term "database" to refer to a wide variety of data sources including relational and non-relational databases, file systems, etc.

Employee

Name	Address	City	Zip	State	Age	ID	TelNum	Salary
Johns Smith	935 Shady Oak	Fridley	55532	MN	28	333444555	421-5533	25000

Student

Name	Street	City	Zipcode	Birthdate	ID	Home Ph	Wagerate
John Smith	729 W. 17th	Fridley	55536	052266	1314156	421-5533	7.95

Mapped global table - Personnel

Name	Address	City	Zip	State	Age	TelNum	Wagerate
Johns Smith	935 Shady Oak	Fridley	55532	MN	28	421-5533	12.02
John Smith	729 W. 17th	Fridley	55536	MN	29	421-5533	7.95

Integrated global table - Personnel

Name	Address	City	Zip	State	Age	TelNum	Wagerate
John Smith	729 W. 17th	Fridley	55536	MN	29	421-5533	19.97

Figure 1: Database integration example

Entity Identification Framework

Figure 1 describes a complete example of the integration steps. Two tables, *Employee* and *Student*, from two different databases are integrated to obtain a single table *Personnel*. The key attributes in the two tables *ID* are homonyms, i.e. their meanings differ even though the names are identical. The *ID* attribute in the *Employee* table refers to social security number whereas the *ID* in the *Student* table corresponds to an university Id. There are no common keys between the two tables. After resolving schema conflicts such as name mismatches between attributes, a mapped global table *Personnel* is created. Entity identification is then performed on the mapped global table to determine entities that possibly occur more than once in this table. This step is required since the component database tables have no common key. The rule used to identify instances of the same entity is given as:

Match any 2 of (*Name, Address, TelNum*)

Two record instances in the mapped global table with names "Johns Smith" and "John Smith" have the same value in the *"TelNum"* field and have *"Name"* values which are very similar. Functions that determine whether each of the attribute value pairs match or do not match are defined for each attribute field. If the match function for the *"Name"* field reports similar names such as the pair above to be a match then the two record instances will be identified as the same enitity. The resulting integrated global table is shown with only one instance for each matching entity sets. Conflicts among attribute values of the integrated instances are resolved (determining the correct value for the attribute fields if different instances have different values for the same field) using user specified rules.

Rules for EI, specify relationships among attribute values of instances of the same entity. These rules are obtained from users who have the knowledge of the data semantics. In many cases the users are not able to specify the exact relationships between attribute values which relate instances of the same records. It is however possible to provide a set of example records which represent the same entity. The record-matching rules are therefore implicitly present in the classification of the records into distinct entities. We describe a framework for learning these rules using the ideas from clustering and classification algorithms (Agrawal, Imielinski, & Swami 1993; Han, Cai, & Cercone 1992; Quinlan 1993). The rules we learn are in the form of decision trees, although any classification system which could explain the learned rules to the users may be used in its place instead.

Figure 2 shows our framework for performing entity identification. A data analyst selects a few records from the mapped global database and labels all instances that represent the same entity with a unique entity Id. This set of records, classified by their entity Id, form a training sample for a learning system. The learning system discovers the attribute value relationships among records which represent the same enitity and also the relationships which classify the records as dissimilar. The relationships thus discovered form the rules which are used on the unclassified records to perform entity identification. It is desirable to have the learning module explain the rules in an understandable form to the data analyst so that s/he can evaluate them. Depending on the results of this evaluation the data analyst can alter the training samples to improve the quality of rules learned. The integrated instances are also monitored by the data analyst for evaluation of the performance of the EI rules.

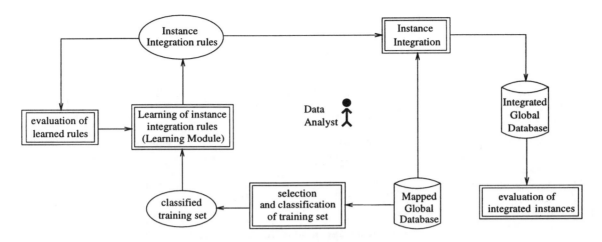

Figure 2: Entity Identification framework

Attribute Distance Functions

EI problem can be viewed as determining the clusters to which the individual records belong, where each cluster represents a real-world entity. We use an initial set of records whose entity identities (EIDs) are known as the training set. The record-matching conditions for any pair of records is an appropriate combination of the relationships between each pair of attribute values in the records. The relationships between similar attribute value pairs is then measured as a distance between their values. A similar pair of attribute values will have a smaller distance between them, compared to a dissimilar pair of values which fall into distant regions of the description space. We measure distances between all such pairs of attribute values to form a vector of distances for a given pair of data records. These distance records are categorized into two classes – "Match" and "No-Match" – depending on whether they measure the distances between two entities with similar EIDs or not. These distance records then form the training set for a learning system which will induce the relationships between attribute distances as the conditions for the source records to match. Entity identification problem is thus reduced to a classification problem and we can use any classification system to learn the rules for EI.

Figure 3 explains the details of the learning module. The training data for the rule induction process is generated from a set of classified records. Using a set of N such records we generate $\frac{N(N-1)}{2}$ distance records, comparing each record against another. Each type of attribute distances is measured using functions which are specific to the attribute type. e.g. distances between two strings may be measured using the edit distance, and distance between two names may be measured using the soundex function (Knuth

1973). These distance records are then assigned the label "Match" if the corresponding classified records have the same EIDs, and the label "No-Match" otherwise. Using these distance records as a training sample, a rule learning system induces the conditions under which a pair of records are similar. These conditions are then applied to any pair of records in the same mapped global database to perform EI.

Experimental Evaluation and Conclusions

We have carried out preliminary experiments to evaluate the effectiveness of our approach to EI in database integration. The experiment used a set of 1100 homogeneized data records from a business customer database. Each of these records in the database represents one of 20 real-world entities. The records were labelled with corresponding EIDs and the number of records corresponding to each of the entities ranged from 6 to a maximum of 524. We measured the effectiveness of the EI rules learned by their performance on unseen test cases and the size of the decision trees. From the data set various sizes of workloads were obtained (50, 100, and 200) and training sets of various sizes are drawn from the corresponding workloads. In our experiments we have varied the training set sizes as 10, 20, 40, 60, 80, and 100% of the test sets. These training sets are used to generate the decision trees for classifying the distance records into one of the two categories, Match or No-Match. The well-known C4.5 algorithm (Quinlan 1993) was used as the rule learning engine. Decision trees learned were then used to classify the corresponding test sets from which the training sets were drawn.

This method was able to achieve very high effectiveness for EI. In most cases the pairwise match errors

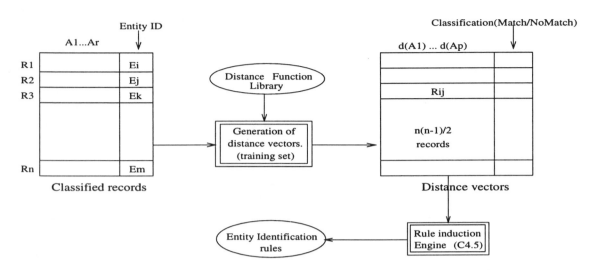

Figure 3: Learning of EI rules

are $\leq$ 0.2%, and the number of records misclassified were $\leq$ 1%. Reasonably small error rates are achieved with about 20% of the data set provided as training set sizes. As we go beyond 40% of the data set as the training set size, the tree sizes increase while bringing only marginal improvement in the classification error rate. At this stage the rules learned have become sensitive to the specific data provided as examples. The size of the decision trees in our experiments varied between 3 and 20 nodes.

We have introduced a framework for the mining of the EI rules directly from examples of integrated instances of entities, to obtain precise rules. Direct application of learning algorithms to this problem is not viable because of the inability to provide examples of all possible entities which may occur in a data set. The concept of attribute-distance functions have been introduced to facilitate this process. Results obtained from our experiments demonstrate that this approach to EI is comparable to the best accuracies of methods where users specify the EI rules without the corresponding human effort. In future work we plan to include attribute-value conflict resolution part of EI. We are currently developing efficient algorithms for performing EI with the distance-based approach and using the distance values computed from the induced rules.

References

Agrawal, R.; Imielinski, T.; and Swami, A. 1993. Database mining: A performance perspective. *IEEE Transactions on Knowledge and Data Engg.* 5(6):914–925.

Batini, C.; Lenzerini, M.; and Navathe, S. B. 1986. A comparitive analysis of methodologies for database schema integration. *ACM Computing Surveys* 18(4):323–364.

Drew, P.; King, R.; McLeod, D.; Rusinkiewicz, M.; and Silberschatz, A. 1993. Report of the workshop on semantic heterogeneity and interoperation in multidatabase systems. *SIGMOD Record* 22(3):47–56.

Han, J.; Cai, Y.; and Cercone, N. 1992. Knowledge discovery in databases: An attribute-oriented approach. In *Proc. of the 18th VLDB Conference*, 547–559.

Inmon, W. H. 1992. *Building the Data Warehouse*. Wiley-QED.

Knuth, D. E. 1973. *The Art of Computer Programming; Vol 3: Sorting and Searching.* Reading, MA: Addison-Wesley.

Lim, E.-P.; Srivastava, J.; Prabhakar, S.; and Richardson, J. 1993. Entity identification in database integration. In *Proc. of the 9th Int'l Conf. on Data Engg.*, 294–301.

Quinlan, J. R. 1993. *C4.5: Programs for Machine Learning.* San Mateo, CA: Morgan Kaufmann.

Richardson, T., and Srivastava, J. 1995. Enterprise/integrator: Using object technology for data integration. In *Proc. of Workshop on Legacy Systems and Object Technology, at OOPSLA 95.*

Sheth, A. P., and Larson, J. A. 1990. Federated database systems for managing distributed, heterogeneous, and autonomous databases. *ACM Computing Surveys* 22(3):183–236.

Undiscovered Public Knowledge: a Ten-Year Update

Don R. Swanson* and Neil R. Smalheiser†

*Division of Humanities, University of Chicago,
1010 E. 59th St.,Chicago, IL 60637; swanson@kiwi.uchicago.edu
†Department of Pediatrics, University of Chicago,
5841 S. Maryland Ave., Chicago, IL 60637; sma2@midway.uchicago.edu

Abstract

Two literatures or sets of articles are complementary if, considered together, they can reveal useful information of scientific interest not apparent in either of the two sets alone. Of particular interest are complementary literatures that are also mutually isolated and noninteractive (they do not cite each other and are not co-cited). In that case, the intriguing possibility arises that the information gained by combining them is novel. During the past decade, we have identified seven examples of complementary noninteractive structures in the biomedical literature. Each structure led to a novel, plausible, and testable hypothesis that, in several cases, was subsequently corroborated by medical researchers through clinical or laboratory investigation. We have also developed, tested, and described a systematic, computer-aided approach to finding and identifying complementary noninteractive literatures.

Specialization, Fragmentation, and a Connection Explosion

By some obscure spontaneous process scientists have responded to the growth of science by organizing their work into specialties, thus permitting each individual to focus on a small part of the total literature. Specialties that grow too large tend to divide into subspecialties that have their own literatures which, by a process of repeated splitting, maintain more or less fixed and manageable size. As the total literature grows, the number of specialties, but not in general the size of each, increases (Kochen, 1963; Swanson, 1990c).

But the unintended consequence of specialization is fragmentation. By dividing up the pie, the potential relationships among its pieces tend to be neglected. Although scientific literature cannot, in the long run, grow disproportionately to the growth of the communities and resources that produce it, combinations of implicitly-related segments of literature can grow much faster than the literature itself and can readily exceed the capacity of the community to identify and assimilate such relatedness (Swanson, 1993). The significance of the "information explosion" thus may lie not in an explosion of quantity per se, but in an incalculably greater combinatorial explosion of unnoticed and unintended logical connections.

The Significance of Complementary Noninteractive Literatures

If two literatures each of substantial size are linked by arguments that they respectively put forward -- that is, are "logically" related, or complementary -- one would expect to gain useful information by combining them. For example, suppose that one (biomedical) literature establishes that some environmental factor A influences certain internal physiological conditions and a second literature establishes that these same physiological changes influence the course of disease C. Presumably, then, anyone who reads both literatures could conclude that factor A might influence disease C. Under such conditions of complementarity one would also expect the two literatures to refer to each other. If, however, the two literatures were developed independently of one another, the logical linkage illustrated may be both unintended and unnoticed. To detect such mutual isolation, we examine the citation pattern. If two literatures are "noninteractive" — that is, if they have never (or seldom) been cited together, and if neither cites the other, — then it is possible that scientists have not previously considered both literatures together, and so it is possible that no one is aware of the implicit A-C connection. The two conditions, complementarity and noninteraction, describe a model structure that shows how useful information can remain undiscovered even though its components consist of public knowledge (Swanson, 1987, 1991).

Public Knowledge / Private Knowledge

There is, of course, no way to know in any particular case whether the possibility of an AC relationship in the above model has or has not occurred to someone, or whether or not anyone has actually considered the two literatures on A and C together, a private matter that necessarily remains conjectural. However, our argument is based only on determining whether there is any printed evidence to the contrary. We are concerned with public rather than private knowledge -- with the state of the record produced rather than the state of mind of the producers (Swanson, 1990d). The point of bringing together the AB and BC literatures, in any event, is not to "prove" an AC linkage, (by considering only transitive relationships) but rather to call attention to an apparently unnoticed association that may be worth investigating. In principle any chain of scientific, including analogic, reasoning in which different links appear in noninteractive literatures may lead to the discovery of new interesting connections.

"What people know" is a common understanding of what is meant by "knowledge". If taken in this subjective sense, the idea of "knowledge discovery" could mean merely that someone discovered something they hadn't known before. Our focus in the present paper is on a second sense of the word "knowledge", a meaning associated with the *products* of human intellectual activity, as encoded in the public record, rather than with the contents of the human mind. This abstract world of human-created "objective" knowledge is open to exploration and discovery, for it can contain territory that is subjectively unknown to anyone (Popper, 1972). Our work is directed toward the discovery of scientifically-useful information implicit in the public record, but not previously made explicit. The problem we address concerns structures within the scientific literature, not within the mind.

The Process of Finding Complementary Noninteractive Literatures

During the past ten years, we have pursued three goals: i) to show in principle how new knowledge might be gained by synthesizing logically- related noninteractive literatures; ii) to demonstrate that such structures do exist, at least within the biomedical literature; and iii) to develop a systematic process for finding them.

In pursuit of goal iii, we have created interactive software and database search strategies that can facilitate the discovery of complementary structures in the published literature of science. The universe or search-space under consideration is limited only by the coverage of the major scientific databases, though we have focused primarily on the biomedical field and the MEDLINE database (8 million records). In 1991, a systematic approach to finding complementary structures was outlined and became a point of departure for software development (Swanson, 1991). The system that has now taken shape is based on a 3-way interaction between computer software, bibliographic databases, and a human operator. The interaction generates information structures that are used heuristically to guide the search for promising complementary literatures.

The user of the system begins by choosing a question

or problem area of scientific interest that can be associated with a literature, C. Elsewhere we describe and evaluate experimental computer software, which we call ARROWSMITH (Swanson & Smalheiser, 1997), that performs two separate functions that can be used independently. The first function produces a list of candidates for a second literature, A, complementary to C, from which the user can select one candidate (at a time) as an input, along with C, to the second function. This first function can be considered as a computer-assisted process of problem-discovery, an issue identified in the AI literature (Langley, et al., 1987; p304-307). Alternatively, the user may wish to identify a second literature, A, as a conjecture or hypothesis generated independently of the computer-produced list of candidates.

Our approach has been based on the use of article titles as a guide to identifying complementary literatures. As indicated above, our point of departure for the second function is a tentative scientific hypothesis associated with two literatures, A and C. A title-word search of MEDLINE is used to create two local computer title-files associated with A and C, respectively. These files are used as input to the ARROWSMITH software, which then produces a list of all words common to the two sets of titles, except for words excluded by an extensive stoplist (presently about 5000 words). The resulting list of words provides the basis for identifying title-word pathways that might provide clues to the presence of complementary arguments within the literatures corresponding to A and C. The output of this procedure is a structured title-display (plus journal citation), that serves as a heuristic aid to identifying word-linked titles and serves also as an organized guide to the literature.

Seven Examples of Literature-Based Knowledge Synthesis

The concept of "undiscovered public knowledge" based on complementary noninteractive literatures was introduced, developed, and exemplified in (Swanson, 1986a, 1986b). Since 1986, we have described six more examples, each representing a synthesis of two complementary literatures in which biomedical relationships not previously noted in print were brought to light. We describe also the hypotheses to which they have led, and the strategies we have followed in finding and identifying these structures (Swanson 1988, 1989a, 1989b, 1990a; Smalheiser & Swanson 1994, 1996). We identify these examples here in terms of A, B, and C, wherein associations between A and B are found in one literature and associations between B and C in another literature, leading us to draw certain inferences about a previously unreported association between A and C. In most cases we analyzed multiple B-terms for a given A and C. In the following description we identify only A and C, and a few of the more important B-connections, along with the main conclusion or hypothesis to which we were led. Other authors have reviewed, extended, or assessed this work (Chen, 1993; Davies, 1989; Garfield, 1994; Gordon & Lindsay, 1996; Lesk, 1991; Spasser, in press).

Example 1, 1986: Dietary Fish Oils (A) and Raynaud's Disease (C)

Dietary fish oils (esp. eicosapentaenoic acid) lead to certain blood and vascular changes (B) that are separately known to be beneficial to patients with Raynaud's disease. One B-linkage, for example, was: dietary eicosapentaenoic acid can decrease *blood viscosity* (B); abnormally high *blood viscosity* has been reported in patients with Raynaud's disease. (Swanson, 1986a, 1986b, 1987). The inference that fish oils may benefit Raynaud patients may be regarded as a successful prediction; two years after publication of the above analysis, the first clinical trial demonstrating such a beneficial effect of fish oil was reported by medical researchers (cited and discussed in Swanson, 1993).

Example 2, 1988: Magnesium Deficiency (A) and Migraine (C).

B consists of eleven indirect connections, which led to a prediction that magnesium deficiency might be implicated in migraine headache. (Two such linkages are, for example: magnesium can inhibit *spreading depression* in the cortex, and *spreading depression* may be implicated in migraine attacks; magnesium-deficient rats have been used as a model of *epilepsy*, and *epilepsy* has been associated with migraine) (Swanson, 1988, 1989b). Since publication of that analysis, more than 12 different groups of medical researchers have reported a systemic or local magnesium deficiency in migraine or a favorable response of migraine patients to dietary supplementation with magnesium (cited and discussed in Swanson, 1993).

Example 3, 1990: Arginine (A) and Somatomedin C (C).

B consists of five physiologic associations leading to the inference that orally administered arginine may increase blood levels of somatomedin C (the latter being known to have a number of beneficial effects). For example, infused arginine stimulates the release of growth hormone, and the latter in turn is known to increase blood levels of somatomedin C (Swanson, 1990a). Our inferences led to a proposal by medical researchers to conduct a clinical trial (discussed further in (Swanson, 1993)).

Example 4, 1994: Dietary Magnesium (A) and Neurologic Disease (C).

Endogenous magnesium ions play a key role in regulating excitotoxicity mediated by the NMDA receptor (B). Excitotoxicity in turn is thought to have an important role in various neurologic diseases. We suggested that the possible effect of manipulating exogenous (e.g. dietary) magnesium on brain function or neurologic disease merits investigation (Smalheiser & Swanson, 1994).

Example 5, 1995: Indomethacin (A) and Alzheimer's Disease (C)

In this example, the A and C literatures are neither disjoint nor noninteractive. Indeed, there is clinical and epidemiologic evidence that indomethacin may have a protective effect against Alzheimer's disease. However, we found certain indirect associations (B) between the two literatures that were not mentioned in the direct (A-C) literature, or elsewhere. One of these B-relationships in particular indicated that indomethacin, because of its anti-cholinergic activity, could adversely affect Alzheimer patients by exacerbating cognitive dysfunction. Because this possibility apparently had not been previously reported, we brought it to the attention of neuroscientists (Smalheiser & Swanson, 1996).

Example 6, 1995: Estrogen (A) and Alzheimer's Disease (C)

As in example 5, the A and C literatures are interactive; estrogen replacement therapy is reported to be associated with a lower incidence of Alzheimer's disease, but the mechanism of such an effect is unknown. We reported several previously-uninvestigated B-relationships, particularly one involving antioxidant activity, that appeared to merit investigation as possible explanations of this intriguing relationship (Smalheiser & Swanson, in press).

Example 7, 1996: Phospholipases (A) and Sleep (C)

The A and C literatures are disjoint and noninteractive, but implicitly related through a set of substances (notably interleukin 1=DF, tumor necrosis factor and endotoxin/lipopolysaccharide) which are well known both to promote sleep and to stimulate one or more phospholipases. This study identified a list of agents whose effects on sleep are especially likely to involve phospholipases; and suggested several straightforward experimental tests of our hypothesis that phospholipases may be involved in endogenous pathways that regulate sleep (Smalheiser & Swanson, in preparation).

Comment

The objects of study in the work summarized here are complementary structures within the scientific literature. The recognition of meaningful associations and ultimately that of complementarity require a high level of subject expertise. The unruly problems of meaning within the natural language of titles and abstracts present serious obstacles to more fully automating this process of knowledge discovery. Our computer aids are therefore designed to enhance and stimulate human ability to see connections and relationships. These aids necessarily derive from the immense databases that provide the routes of intellectual access to the literature. Our goal thus far has been to produce a working practical system that yields immediate results in furthering the aims of biomedical research, and which at the same time generates data and problems that contribute to understanding literature-based scientific discovery.

References

Chen Z. 1993. Let documents talk to each other: A computer model for connection of short documents, *The Journal of Documentation* 49(1):44-54.

Davies, R. 1989. The Creation of New Knowledge by Information Retrieval and Classification. *The Journal of Documentation* 45(4):273-301.

Garfield, E. 1994. Linking literatures: An intriguing use of the Citation Index, *Current Contents* #21, 3-5.

Gordon, M.D. & Lindsay, R. K. 1996. Toward discovery support systems: A replication, re-examination, and extension of Swanson's work on literature based discovery of a connection between Raynaud's and fish oil. *Journal of the American Society for Information Science* 47:116-128.

Kochen, M. 1963. On natural information systems: pragmatic aspects of information retrieval. *Methods of Information in Medicine* 2(4):143-147.

Langley, P., Simon, H. A., Bradshaw, G. L., and Zytkow, J. M. 1987. *Scientific Discovery. Computational Explorations of the Creative Process.* Cambridge, Mass.: MIT Press

Lesk, M. 1991. SIGIR '91: The More Things Change, the More They Stay the Same. In: *SIGIR FORUM.* 25(2):4-7, ACM Press.

Popper, K. R. 1972. *Objective Knowledge* Oxford.

Smalheiser, N.R. and Swanson, D. R. 1994. Assessing a gap in the biomedical literature: magnesium deficiency and neurologic disease. *Neurosci Res Commun* 15(1):1-9.

Smalheiser, N.R. and Swanson, D. R. 1996. Indomethacin and Alzheimer's Disease. *Neurology* 46:583.

Smalheiser, N.R. and Swanson, D. R. (in press) Linking Estrogen to Alzheimer's Disease: An informatics approach. *Neurology*

Spasser, M. (in press) The enacted fate of undiscovered public knowledge. *Journal of the American Society for Information Science.*

Swanson, D. R. 1986a Undiscovered public knowledge. *Library Quarterly* 56(2):103-118.

Swanson, D. R. 1986b. Fish Oil, Raynaud's Syndrome, and Undiscovered Public Knowledge. *Perspectives in Biology and Medicine* 30(1):7-18.

Swanson, D. R. 1987. Two Medical Literatures that are Logically but not Bibliographically Connected. *Journal of the American Society for Information Science* 38(4):228-233.

Swanson, D. R. 1988. Migraine and Magnesium: Eleven Neglected Connections. *Perspectives in Biology and Medicine* 31(4):526-557.

Swanson, D. R. 1989a. Online Search for Logically-Related Noninteractive Medical Literatures: A Systematic Trial-and-Error Strategy. *Journal of the American Society for Information Science* 40:356-358.

Swanson, D. R. 1989b. A Second Example of Mutually-Isolated Medical Literatures Related by Implicit, Unnoticed Connections. *Journal of the American Society for Information Science* 40:432-435.

Swanson, D. R. 1990a. Somatomedin C and Arginine; Implicit Connections Between Mutually-Isolated Literatures. *Perspectives in Biology and Medicine* 33(2):157-186.

Swanson, D. R. 1990b. Medical Literature as a Potential Source of New Knowledge. *Bulletin of the Medical Library Association* 78(1):29-37.

Swanson, D. R. 1990c. Integrative Mechanisms in the Growth of Knowledge: A legacy of Manfred Kochen. *Information Processing & Management* 26(1):9-16.

Swanson, D. R. 1990d. The absence of co-citation as a clue to undiscovered causal connections, in Borgman, C. L., ed. *Scholarly Communication and Bibliometrics.* 129-137. Newbury Park, CA: Sage Publ.

Swanson, D. R. 1991. Complementary Structures in Disjoint Science Literatures. In *SIGIR91 Proceedings of the Fourteenth Annual International ACM/SIGIR Conference on Research and Development in Information Retrieval* Chicago, Oct 13-16, 1991 ed. A. Bookstein, et. al. New York: ACM; p. 280-9.

Swanson, D. R. 1993. Intervening in the Life Cycles of Scientific Knowledge, *Library Trends* 41(4):606-631.

Swanson, D. R. and Smalheiser, N. R. 1997. An interactive system for finding complementary literatures: a stimulus to scientific discovery. Forthcoming.

A Genetic Algorithm-Based Approach to Data Mining

Ian W. Flockhart[a] and Nicholas J. Radcliffe[a,b]
{iwf,njr} @quadstone.co.uk
[a]Quadstone Ltd, 16 Chester Street, Edinburgh EH3 7RA, UK
[b]Department of Mathematics and Statistics, University of Edinburgh,
King's Buildings, EH9 3JZ, UK

Abstract

Most data mining systems to date have used variants of traditional machine-learning algorithms to tackle the task of *directed* knowledge discovery. This paper presents an approach which, as well as being useful for such directed data mining, can also be applied to the further tasks of *undirected* data mining and *hypothesis refinement*. This approach exploits parallel genetic algorithms as the search mechanism and seeks to evolve explicit "rules" for maximum comprehensibility. Example rules found in real commercial datasets are presented.

Introduction

Genetic algorithms (Holland, 1975) have been used successfully in a variety of search and optimisation problems. Work on genetic algorithm-based learning has traditionally been grouped into one of two general approaches. The *Pitt* approach (Smith, 1980) uses a traditional genetic algorithm in which each entity in the population is a set of rules representing a complete solution to the learning problem. The *Michigan* approach (Holland, 1986) has generally used a distinctly different evolutionary mechanism in which the population consists of individual rules, each of which represents a partial solution to the overall learning task.

The system we present here — GA-MINER — is a general pattern search tool supporting several pattern forms and capable of functioning with varying levels of user supervision. Although the system may be used for traditional classification tasks, the emphasis has been placed more on pattern discovery. The authors have sought to divide data mining into three types or levels as follows:

- *Undirected or Pure Data Mining.* Here the concept is that the user asks of the data miner: "Tell me something interesting about my data". The key point is that the user is *not* specifying what kind of rule is desired. The system is left relatively unconstrained and is therefore given the greatest "free-

dom" to discover patterns in the data free of prejudices from the user. It seems likely that in these circumstances there is the greatest scope for finding completely unexpected patterns in the data, which has been one of the "promises" of data mining.

- *Directed data mining.* The user asks something much more specific, such as: "Characterise my high spending customers". Here a much stronger "steer" is being given to the system and the problem usually changes from a general pattern-detection problem to a rather better defined *induction* problem.

- *Hypothesis testing and refinement.* The user conceptually says: "I think that there is a positive correlation between sales of peaches and sales of cream: am I right?". Now the idea is that the system first evaluates the hypothesis but then—if the evidence for it is not strong—seeks to refine it. Depending on what scope for variation the system is allowed, this may make the task even more directed than "directed data mining", or almost as open as "undirected data mining".

GA-MINER is unusual in being applicable to all three kinds of data mining. It is undirected data mining that has been our defining goal, but we have deliberately built a system which allows directed data mining and hypothesis refinement also to be tackled. Directed data mining is achieved by fixing certain parts of the pattern over the course of the run, and hypothesis refinement is achieved by "seeding" the system with the hypothesis but then allowing some or all parts of it to vary.

Related Work on Genetic Algorithm-Based Learning

An early example of a genetic algorithm-based machine learning system is LS-1 (Smith, 1980, 1984), which introduced a structured representation based on the semantics of the problem domain with genetic operators working at each level. GABIL (DeJong *et al.*, 1993) uses the Pitt approach for evolving concept descriptions, which are defined as a collection of possibly overlapping classification rules. COGIN (Greene & Smith, 1993, 1994) addresses multi-class problem domains by introducing competition for coverage of training examples, encouraging the population to work together to solve the concept learning task. Another recent example is REGAL (Neri & Giordana, 1995; Giordana *et al.*, 1994) which also uses a coverage-based approach for multi-concept learning and introduces a new *Universal Suffrage* selection operator to encourage cooperation between population members. Augier *et al.* (1995) present an algorithm, SIAO1, for learning first order logic rules with a genetic algorithm. Domain knowledge may be introduced in the form of domain hierarchies and the algorithm uses a covering technique to ensure that all examples are covered by some rule.

Related Work on Data Mining

GA-MINER has also drawn ideas from a number of non-genetic data mining tools, particularly regarding pattern forms. EXPLORA (Kloesgen, 1994) is an interactive statistical analysis tool for discovery in databases. A number of *statement types* (or patterns) are defined, and users may select the most appropriate for their particular analysis purposes. Forty-Niner (Zytkow & Baker, 1991; Zytkow & Zembowicz, 1993) searches for regularities in databases, that is, a pattern and the range within which it holds. The representation of a range is as a conjunction of attribute/value-sets, while a pattern is either a function (an equation relating the attributes) or a contingency table.

The Reproductive Plan Language

Fast and flexible development of GA-MINER was made possible by its implementation in the *Reproductive Plan Language* RPL2 (Surry & Radcliffe, 1994b, 1994a). RPL2 is an extensible language, interpreter and run-time system for the implementation of stochastic search algorithms, with a special emphasis on evolutionary algorithms such as genetic algorithms. The main features of RPL2 pertinent to GA-MINER are automatic parallelism, support for arbitrary representations (important in the current context as the rule forms are structured and not string-like), and its large library of functions which has allowed almost the entire project to be devoted to an exploration of data mining itself, rather than merely coding up ideas.

Pattern Representation

GA-MINER includes a variety of pattern forms, drawing on ideas from EXPLORA and Forty-Niner, including explicit rule patterns, distribution shift patterns and correlation patterns. The basis for all supported patterns is *subset description*.

Subset descriptions are clauses which are used to select subsets of the database, and form the main heritable units which are manipulated by the genetic algorithm. A subset description consists of a disjunction of conjunctions of attribute-value or attribute-range constraints, shown in *Backus-Naur* form below:

Subset Description	::=	*Clause* [**or** *Clause*]
Clause	::=	*Term* [**and** *Term*]
Term	::=	*Attribute* **in** *Value Set*
	|	*Attribute* **in** *Range*

Patterns are then constructed as higher level interpretations of a number of these subsets. For example, an explicit rule pattern may use two subset descriptions, C and P to represent the *condition* and *prediction* respectively of a rule: "**if** C **then** P". Note that the interpretation of a collection of subset descriptions as a particular form of pattern is defined entirely by the chosen evaluation function. For example, a rule "**when** S, **if** C **then** P" can be constructed from three subset descriptions, S, C and P respectively, combined with an appropriate evaluation function.

In a similar manner, a distribution shift pattern may be formed from two subset descriptions together with a *hypothesis variable*, which is simply a field from the database to which the pattern refers. In this case the subset descriptions C and P and the hypothesis variable A are interpreted as a pattern of the form:

The distribution of A **when** C **and** P
is significantly different from the distribution of A **when** C.

Finally, correlation patterns express a relationship which holds between two hypothesis variables within a particular subset of the database. i.e. patterns of the form:

when C, the variables A and B are correlated.

Since the same underlying representation is used for all pattern forms, the same genetic algorithm may be used to manipulate all these patterns.

Pattern Templates

Pattern templates are used to constrain the system to particular forms of patterns, and allow extensive control over a number of features including the high-level pattern form as described above, the database fields permitted to appear in each of the subset descriptions, the maximum numbers of disjunctions and conjunctions permitted in each subset description and any clauses, terms or fields which must be included as part of a subset description.

The component parts of the pattern template are marked as either *initialised* or *fixed*. Fixed parts of the template are inherited by every pattern in the population and are never modified by crossover or mutation. Initialised parts of the template appear in all newly generated patterns but may be modified during the search.

Undirected data mining may be performed by using a minimal template, and directed data mining by restricting the pattern form more tightly. Hypothesis refinement is achieved by seeding the initial population of the genetic algorithm with patterns based on the template but with additional randomly generated components, and the search is permitted to modify these patterns subject to the constraints specified by the template.

Pattern Evaluation

A number of evaluation functions for estimating pattern interest have been used during the course of this work, mainly based on statistical measures. For example, for rule patterns we have used, among others, information gain (see Frawley, 1991), the J-measure (Smyth & Goodman, 1991) and the form suggested in Piatetsky-Shapiro (1991). Our experience has shown that many of these evaluation mechanisms give qualitatively similar results (Flockhart & Radcliffe, 1995).

While falling short of providing fully satisfactory definitions of interesting patterns, the evaluation functions have been sufficiently successful for the system to discover several useful patterns in the databases provided by our industrial collaborators, GMAP Ltd and Barclays Bank plc. Although the system still produces some non-interesting rules, tautologies are generally discarded early in the search and the pattern templates may be used to steer the system away from obvious domain knowledge.

The Genetic Algorithm

The genetic algorithm in GA-MINER uses a structured population model in which each genome's reproductive partner is selected from within its local neighbourhood (using tournament selection). This helps prolong diversity within the population and encourages local niching, which tends to result in exploration of several areas of the search space and matches well with the goal of finding several patterns in a single run.

The crossover operator is defined at a variety of levels, reflecting the structure of the representation. Disjunct clauses, clauses, terms and attribute values each comprise a single gene at the appropriate level. Within subset descriptions, crossover at the disjunct clause level is based on uniform crossover and enforces positional alignment of component clauses. Both uniform and single-point crossover are used at the clause level, while crossover at the term level is again based on uniform crossover. Mutation is also defined at a variety of levels, with separate probabilities specified for mutating each of the component parts. Clauses, terms and values are added or deleted with specified probabilities and can be regarded as distinct specialisation and generalisation operators.

GA-MINER collects sets of patterns during the run of the algorithm for presentation to the user. A simple heuristic is used for updating the set, based on a strategy of continually replacing either the lowest fitness rule or the most similar rule (if the similarity is over a given threshold) by a higher fitness rule.

Examples of Discovered Patterns

Many patterns of varying strength were discovered within the data provided by our industrial collaborators, however, we restrict ourselves to just two representative examples of the kinds of patterns discovered. Both were found by using the system in "undirected" mode with a minimal pattern template.

Explicit Rule Pattern

if	Proportion of households with 1 child ≥ 0.12 (Approximate percentiles 36% - 100%) (true: 1618 false: 939 unique false: 272)
and	Number of Ford Dealers > 0 (Approximate percentiles 62% - 100%) (true: 936 false: 1621 unique false: 809)
and	Proportion of households with 3+ cars **in** 0.01 .. 0.07 (Approximate percentiles 4% - 86%) (true: 2038 false: 519 unique false: 108)
then	Ford market share segment F (Sierra) **in** 0.06 .. 0.75 (Approximate percentiles 30% - 100%) (true: 1770 false: 787 unique false: 787)

Left hand side matches 19% of the database
Right hand side matches 69% of the database

	Expected	Actual
Accuracy:	69%	93%
Coverage:	20%	27%

The rule above states that there is a 93% probability that Ford market share of segment F (Sierra) is between 0.06 and 0.75 in postal districts where there is at least one Ford dealer, the proportion of households with 1 child is relatively high (in the top 64% of the distribution) and the proportion of households with 3 or more cars is neither very high nor very low. This compares to an expected probability of 69%, under the assumption of no relationship between the left and right hand sides of the rule. The true and false count for each clause show the number of times that clause is true and false respectively, while the unique false count shows the number of times the clause is false when all the others are true. This gives some indication of the relative importance of the terms.

Distribution Shift Pattern

The distribution of "Ford market share of segment D (Escort)"
when   Proportion of households — Council $\geq$ 0.20
            (Approximate percentiles 62% - 10%)
            (true: 929 false: 1628 unique false: 123)
and
            Proportion of households with 2 children $\geq$ 0.11
            (Approximate percentiles 26% - 100%)
            (true: 1854 false: 703 unique false: 233)
and
            Proportion of unemployed in population $\geq$ 0.04
            (Approximate percentiles 52% - 100%)
            (true: 1183 false: 1374 unique false: 48)
and
            Proportion of households with 0 cars $\geq$ 0.31
            (Approximate percentiles 60% - 100%)
            (true: 1015 false: 1542 unique false: 89)

has median 0.28 and is significantly shifted
from the overall distribution which has median value 0.20.

The distribution shift rule above says that Ford market share in segment D is 8% higher in postal districts with a high proportion of council houses, relatively high unemployment, a high proportion of households with no car and relatively few households with 2 children.

Conclusions and Future Work

GA-MINER has demonstrated that genetic algorithms may be used successfully for a variety of pattern discovery tasks in addition to their traditional use in classification and concept learning. Genetic algorithms appear well suited to undirected data mining, given their limited need for user direction and user interaction, however we have also demonstrated that they may be used for more directed forms of data mining through the use of pattern templates. In particular, the authors believe that the system's use for hypothesis refinement holds much promise. The scrutibility of the patterns generated by the system also make results more understandable than those produced by many other unsupervised methods such as neural networks, an essential component for any system which is to be widely used by non-experts.

The system would undoubtedly benefit from increased used of domain knowledge, perhaps in the form of domain hierarchies. Further work to allow some degree of fuzziness in the form of pattern templates would also be useful.

Finally, although GA-MINER has been successfully parallelised and is scalable on main memory databases, it is becoming increasingly apparent that commercial data mining systems will require to access volumes of data far in excess of available main memory. This is likely to mean that effective data mining systems will be dependent more on scalable data warehouse systems than on explicitly parallel algorithms.

Acknowledgements

This work was funded by a research grant from the UK Engineering and Physical Science Research Council's AIKMS programme, and was carried out while the authors were at Edinburgh Parallel Computing Centre.

References

S. Augier, G. Venturini, and Y. Kodratoff, 1995. Learning first order logic rules with a genetic algorithm. In Usama M. Fayyad and Ramasamy Uthurusamy, editors, *Proceedings of the First International Conference on Knowledge Discovery and Data Mining*. AAAI Press.

Kenneth A. DeJong, William M Spears, and Diana F Gordon, 1993. Using genetic algorithms for concept learning. *Machine Learning*, 13:161–188.

Ian W. Flockhart and Nicholas J. Radcliffe, 1995. GA-MINER: Parallel data mining with hierarchical genetic algorithms. Technical Report EPCC-AIKMS-GA-MINER-REPORT, Edinburgh Parallel Computing Centre.

William J. Frawley, 1991. Using functions to encode domain and contextual knowledge in statistical induction. In Gregory Piatetsky-Shapiro and William J. Frawley, editors, *Knowledge Discovery in Databases*, pages 261–275. MIT Press.

Attilio Giordana, Filippo Neri, and Lorenza Saiat, 1994. Search-intensive concept induction. Technical report, Università di Torino, Dipartimento di Informatica, Corso Svizzera 185, 10149 Torino, Italy.

David Perry Green and Stephen F. Smith, 1993. Competition-based induction of decision models from examples. *Machine Learning*, 13:229–257.

David Perry Greene and Stephen F. Smith, 1994. Using coverage as a model building constraint in learning classifier systems. *Evolutionary Computation*, 2(1).

John H. Holland, 1975. *Adaptation in Natural and Artificial Systems*. University of Michigan Press (Ann Arbor).

John H. Holland, 1986. Escaping brittleness: the possibilities of general-purpose learning algorithms applied to parallel rule-based systems. *Machine Learning, an artificial intelligence approach*, 2.

W. Klösgen, 1994. Exploration of simulation experiments by discovery. In *Proceedings of KDD-94 Workshop*. AAAI.

Filippo Neri and Attilio Giordana, 1995. A parallel genetic algorithm for concept learning. In Larry J. Eshelman, editor, *Proceedings of the Sixth International Conference on Genetic Algorithms*. Morgan Kaufman.

Gregory Piatetsky-Shapiro, 1991. Discovery, analysis and presentation of strong rules. In Gregory Piatetsky-Shapiro and William J. Frawley, editors, *Knowledge Discovery in Databases*. MIT Press.

Stephen F. Smith, 1980. *A Learning System Based on Genetic Adaptive Algorithms*. PhD thesis, University of Pittsburgh.

Stephen F. Smith, 1984. Adaptive learning systems. In Richard Forsyth, editor, *Expert Systems, Principles and case studies*. Chapman and Hall Ltd.

Padhraic Smyth and Rodney M. Goodman, 1991. Rule induction using information theory. In Gregory Piatetsky-Shapiro and William J. Frawley, editors, *Knowledge Discovery in Databases*, pages 159–176. MIT Press.

Patrick D. Surry and Nicholas J. Radcliffe, 1994a. *The Reproductive Plan Language RPL2*. Edinburgh Parallel Computing Centre.

Patrick D. Surry and Nicholas J. Radcliffe, 1994b. RPL2: A language and parallel framework for evolutionary computing. In Y. Davidor, H.-P. Schwefel, and R. Männer, editors, *Parallel Problem Solving from Nature III*, pages 628–637. Springer-Verlag, Lecture Notes in Computer Science 866.

Jan M. Zytkow and John Baker, 1991. Interactive mining of regularities in databases. In Gregory Piatetsky-Shapiro and William J. Frawley, editors, *Knowledge Discovery in Databases*, pages 31–53. MIT Press.

Jan M. Zytkow and Robert Zembowicz, 1993. Database exploration in search of regularities. *Journal of Intelligent Information Systems*, 2:39–81.

Deriving Queries from Results using Genetic Programming

Tae-Wan Ryu and Christoph F. Eick

Department of Computer Science
University of Houston
Houston, Texas 77204-3475
{twryu,ceick}@cs.uh.edu

Abstract

This paper centers on the problem of finding commonalities for a set of objects belonging to an object-oriented database. In our approach, commonalities within a set of objects are described by object-oriented queries that compute this set of objects. The paper discusses the architecture of a knowledge discovery system, called MASSON, which employs genetic programming to find such queries. We also report on an experiment that evaluated the knowledge discovery capabilities of the MASSON system.

1. Introduction

A database consists of extensional information and intensional information. Extensional information is physically stored data or database instances. Intensional information is the descriptions and the high-level abstracts of a database such as schema, relationships, and other implicit information. Most traditional database systems have focused on storing, maintaining and accessing the extensional information efficiently in databases. Extracting intensional information with respect to an extensional data collection is relatively difficult using conventional database systems. For example, suppose there is a police suspect database which contains information about persons and their activities, and a police officer has two drug-dealer suspects {Joe, Mary} who may be involved in a particular case. Then the police data analyst may be interested in knowing **"What do Joe and Mary have in common?"**

In order to answer this question, the data analyst has to conduct a time-consuming search process in which he has to find a query or a set of queries that returns the exactly same instances, {Joe, Mary} in this case, as its result. Suppose he found the following SQL form of query,

" *(SELECT ssn name address*
   FROM person purchase
   WHERE (amount-spent > 1000) and (payment-type = 'cash')
      and (store-name = 'flea-market'))"

which returns {Joe, Mary} as its result, which states that they both have spent more than $1,000 cash for shopping in a 'flea-market'. This information might lead the police to investigate suspicious activities in flea-markets. However, in the example we have given in the above, it is not very obvious what kind of queries the user has to write. Accordingly, an automatic tool that facilitates the task for the data analyst is desirable. This paper will describe such a tool for extracting intensional information in an object-oriented database.

2. Deriving Queries From Results

Deriving queries from results is the process of finding a desired query or a set of queries from a set of objects. In this approach, the user's role is not to derive a query but the knowledge discovery in databases (KDD) system (Piatetsky & Frawley 1991) will derive a query or a set of queries by accessing database schema information as well as database instances through the database interface. The user of the KDD-system does not need in-depth knowledge about the database schema. We claim that this approach actually discovers useful or interesting intensional information implicitly stored in a database. We are developing a prototype system called MASSON that employs *deriving queries from results* approach in the context of object-oriented database. Figure 1 depicts the architecture of the system. MASSON takes a database name and object set (or database instances) as its input and accesses the database given from a user for domain knowledge and schema information. The user may also supply domain knowledge to restrict the search space if possible. MASSON uses genetic programming (GP) (Koza 1990) to generate many different queries and to search a query or a set of queries that describe the commonalities of the given object set. The generated queries are sent to an object-oriented database management system (OODBMS) for execution. The system will then evaluate those returned results from OODBMS according to how well they cover the given target object set. Based on the results of the evaluation process the GP search engine will generate new queries based on the principles of evolution by giving fitter query a better chance to reproduce. In order to evaluate an individual query q_i in a population, we use the following fitness function f: $f(q_i) = T - (h_i * h_i)/n_i$, where $n_i > 0$, $T \geq h_i$, and $i = 1, 2, ...$ population size. (T is the cardinality of the set of objects whose commonalities have to be determined, h_i is the number of hits for an individual query q_i, n_i is the cardinality of query q_i's result) This function is our standardized fitness function (Koza 1990), which means the smaller the fitness value,

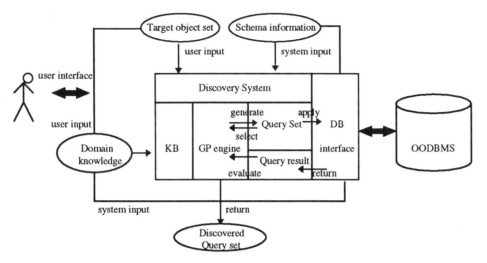

Figure 1: Architecture of MASSON

the fitter the individual is. The above fitness function depends on the number of hits and the cardinality of the query result. If a query does not make any hit ($h_i = 0$), then it has the value T, which is the worst fitness value. If, on the other hand the result of query q_i perfectly matches the set of objects given to the system, then its fitness value $f(q_i)$ is 0 ($h_i = n_i = T$ in this case). We call this case *perfect hit*. However, if a query is too general, it may contain superfluous instances (false positives) even if it made 100% of hits. If, on the other hand, a query is too specific then the number of hits of the query is less than the number of target instances – the difference is the number of false negatives. To cope with false positives and false negatives, we put the number of instances for an individual query, n_i as denominator. Moreover, because we take the square of the number of hits, false positives are punished less severely than false negatives by the fitness function: we are more interested in queries that return the target set or at large portions of the target set, even if they return objects that do not belong to the target set.

Object-oriented queries are used to describe commonalities among objects in our approach. The supported navigational query operators include *SELECT*, *RESTRICTED*, *RELATED*, *GET-RELATED*, and set operators (Ryu & Eick 1996). *SELECT* operator selects all the objects that satisfy the conditional predicate. *RESTRICTED* operator restricts the objects in the given set to those that are related to another class, according to the given predicate. The relationship operator *RELATED* selects all the objects from a class that are related to objects in another class through the relationship links. *GET-RELATED* operator is an inverse operator of RELATED. In addition, the set operators *UNION, INTERSECTION, DIFFERENCE* are supported.

The schema diagram shown in Figure 2 represents our experimental object-oriented database that contains information of persons and their related activities. Each class (or entity set) has slots and their values. A relationship or reverse relationship links a class to another class. The MASSON system was implemented by the PCL (Portable Common Loops) version of the CLOS (Common Lisp Object System) (Paepcke 1993) implementation.

We used GP as a search engine for MASSON (Ryu & Eick 1996). GP searches for a target program in the space of all possible computer programs (queries in our application) randomly composed of functions (query operators) and terminals (basic arguments for each operator) appropriate to the problem domain. Initially, a pre-defined number of queries that are syntactically legal, are generated by randomly selecting operators and their arguments from the function set and the terminal set respectively, forming the initial population. Each individual is evaluated based on the fitness function f. Fitter queries are then selected with higher probability to breed a new population, using three genetic operators: selection, crossover, and mutation. The selection operator is used to choose certain individuals based on their fitness values for generating the next generation. The crossover operation creates two new offsprings by exchanging subtrees between the two parents if we represent a query as a tree. The mutation operation produces a new offspring by replacing one parent subtree with a newly created subtree. The size, shape, and structures of queries can be dynamically changed when crossover or mutation operators are applied to each pair of selected queries (parent queries) during the breeding process. The selection-crossover-mutation cycle is repeated until an user defined termination criteria are satisfied.

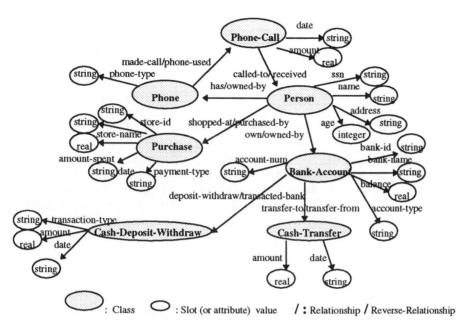

: Class   ◯ : Slot (or attribute) value   **/ :** Relationship **/** Reverse-Relationship

Figure 2: Schema Diagram for Personal Database

3. MASSON at Work

To demonstrate how MASSON works, and to evaluate the knowledge discovery capabilities of MASSON, we manually created 5 benchmark queries, Q1 ~ Q5.

Q1: *"Select persons who have transferred cash to anyone more than 4 times."*
(GET-RELATED (RESTRICTED bank-account (> transfer-to 4))
owned-by
person)

An object set that Q1 computes for a given example database consists of 22 persons. This object set was then used as the target object set when running the MASSON system. The query discovery process starts by generating 100 queries randomly. At generation 33, MASSON found the original query Q1. This was the first query that made a *perfect hit*, which is the case of $f_{33} = 0$ *(since T=h=n=22).* At generation 47, the average fitness value was significantly decreased to 2.83, and the best query that also made a perfect hit and has different semantics was:

"Select persons who have transferred cash to anyone more than 4 times and are age less than 30 or greater than 20."
(GET-RELATED (RESTRICTED BANK-ACCOUNT (> TRANSFER-TO 4))
        OWNED-BY
        (SELECT PERSON (OR (**< AGE 30**) (**> AGE 20**)))))

The predicate in boldface is an additional predicate. Another perfect hit query was also found at generation 81.

Q2: *"Select persons who live in Houston."*
(SELECT person (= address "Houston"))

The first perfect hit query to the object set provided by Q2 was found at generation 122. The query and the semantics were:

"Select persons who have telephone and live in Houston."
(GET-RELATED BANK-ACCOUNT OWNED-BY
  (SELECT (RELATED PERSON HAS PHONE) (= ADDRESS "Houston")))

The query Q2 was found at generation 135. Several other perfect hit queries that was different from Q1 was found.

Q3: *"Select persons who purchased more than $3,000 by cash in one store."*
(RELATED person shopped-at
*(SELECT purchase (AND (> amount-spent **3000**)*
                (= payment-type 1))))

The first perfect hit query was found at generation 70. Even if the exactly same query Q3 was not found during 200 generations, syntactically and semantically almost similar query to Q3 was found at generation 94:

(RELATED PERSON SHOPPED-AT
  (SELECT (SELECT PURCHASE (= PAYMENT-TYPE 1))
      (> AMOUNT-SPENT **3002**)))

The only difference between the discovered query and the query Q3 is the amount 3002 showed in boldface which is different from 3000. Actually, it is not possible to find the exact value 3000 unless the value is stored in the database, since MASSON only generates constants that appear in the database. Therefore we assume it found a query that is approximately the same as the original query Q3. Several other different perfect hit queries were also found.

Q4: *"Select persons that have more than 7 times of suspect activities records or spent more than $5,000 cash in a store."*
(O-UNION
  (RELATED person shopped-at
    (SELECT purchase (AND (> amount-spent 5000) (= payment-type 1))))
  (SELECT person (> nsuspect-act 7)))

Q4 is relatively a complex query. The first query that made perfect hit was found at generation 95:

"Select persons that have more than 7 times of suspect activities records or paid cash when shopping."
(O-UNION
    (SELECT PERSON (> NSUSPECT-ACT 7))
    (RELATED (O-UNION PERSON (SELECT (RESTRICTED (RESTRICTED
        PERSON (>= RECEIVED 3)) (< HAS 0)) (> NSUSPECT-ACT 7)))
    SHOPPED-AT
    (SELECT (GET-RELATED PERSON SHOPPED-AT (GET-RELATED
        PERSON SHOPPED-AT PURCHASE)) (= PAYMENT-TYPE 1))))

Other perfect hit queries was found. However, MASSON could not find the original query Q4 for 200 generations.

Q5: *"Select persons who have transferred more than $2,000 and have called more than 4 times and spent more than $500 cash."*
(O-INTERSECTION
    (GET-RELATED (GET-RELATED
      (SELECT cash-transfer (> amount 2000))
      transfer-from bank-account) owned-by person)
    (GET-RELATED (RESTRICTED (GET-RELATED
      (SELECT phone-call (> amount 500)) phone-used phone)(> made-call 4))
      owned-by person)))

This is another complex query. The first query that made perfect hit to the object set provided by the query Q5 was found at generation 112:

"Select persons who have telephone and have called to two persons not at 11/10/1987 and have made phone calls more than 4 times."
(GET-RELATED PHONE
  OWNED-BY
  (GET-RELATED (RESTRICTED (GET-RELATED PHONE-CALL PHONE-USED
    (GET-RELATED PHONE-CALL PHONE-USED (GET-RELATED (SELECT
    (RELATED (RESTRICTED PHONE-CALL (= CALLED-TO 2)) PHONE-USED
    (RELATED (GET-RELATED PHONE-CALL PHONE-USED PHONE)
      MADE-CALL (RELATED PHONE-CALL CALLED-TO PERSON)))
    (NOT (EQUAL DATE "11 10 87"))) PHONE-USED PHONE)))
    (> MADE-CALL 4)) OWNED-BY
  (GET-RELATED (RESTRICTED (GET-RELATED PHONE-CALL
    PHONE-USED PHONE) (> MADE-CALL 3)) OWNED-BY PERSON)))

MASSON could not find the original query Q5 during 200 generations; however, it found several other queries that made perfect hit. These queries are semantically and syntactically different from Q5. This is an interesting discovery by MASSON since the input object set was obtained by Q5 consisting of a set operator, INTERSECTION. On the other hand, MASSON found those queries that consist of only selection and relationship operators. The semantics of those queries are also different from Q5. Table 1 shows summary for this experiment.

Query	Hit-at	Org	Othr	Nclass	Nvsl	Nop	Nsop	Ncop
Q1	33	Y	2	2	1	2	0	1
Q2	122	Y	6	1	1	1	0	1
Q3	70	Y	4	2	2	2	0	2
Q4	95	N	5	2	3	3	1	3
Q5	112	N	7	5	3	7	1	3

Table 1: Execution results and the complexity for the 5 test queries

The left part of Table 1 shows the benchmark results for the 5 test queries and the right part of the table shows relative complexity of each test query although these are not a precise metrics of complexity measure. In this table, Hit-at is the generation number that made first perfect hit. Org shows whether MASSON found the original query or not. Othr is the number of other queries found that made perfect hit other than the original query. Nclass is the number of classes that each test query traversed. Nvsl, Nop, Nsop, and Ncop are the number of slots, query operators, set operators, and conditional operators respectively. According to the table, the query Q4 and Q5 are relatively more complex than Q1, Q2, and Q3. MASSON could not find the exactly same queries as those queries Q4 and Q5 for 200 generations but found other queries that describe commonalities within the given target set.

4. Summary

In this paper, we proposed a problem on how to extract intensional information or concept descriptions for a set of objects from a database without other knowledge about the given object set. The major contribution of this paper is the presentation of a new approach to discovering commonalities within a given set of objects. We dealt with this problem by introducing *deriving queries from results* approach in which we try to find an object-oriented query that returns a given result or set of results for a given database. These derived queries present intensional information for the given set of objects. MASSON takes a database name and a set of objects belonging to the database as its input and returns a query or a set of queries as the result of the search process. We presented an example that demonstrated how MASSON works, and we reported on an experiment that evaluated MASSON's knowledge discovery capabilities.

References

Ryu, T.W and Eick, C.F. 1996. MASSON: Discovering Commonalities in Collection of Objects using Genetic Programming. *In Proceedings of the Genetic Programming 1996 Conference.*

Koza, John R. 1990. *Genetic Programming: On the Programming of Computers by Means of Natural Selection.* Cambridge, MA: The MIT Press.

Paepcke, Andreas 1993. *Object-Oriented Programming: the CLOS perspective.* Cambridge, MA: The MIT Press.

Piatetsky-Shapiro, G. and Frawley, W.J. 1991. Knowledge Discovery in Databases: An Overview. *Knowledge Discovery in Databases.* AAAI/The MIT press. Pages1-27.

Maintenance of Discovered Knowledge : A Case in Multi-level Association Rules

David W. Cheung[†]   Vincent T. Ng[‡]   Benjamin W. Tam [†]

[†] Department of Computer Science, The University of Hong Kong, Hong Kong. Email: {dcheung|wktam}@cs.hku.hk.

[‡] Department of Computing, Hong Kong Polytechnic University, Hong Kong. Email: cstyng@comp.polyu.edu.hk.

Abstract

An incremental technique and a fast algorithm FUP have been proposed previously for the update of discovered single-level association rules(SLAR). In this study, a more efficient algorithm FUP*, which generates a smaller number of candidate sets when comparing with FUP, has been proposed. In addition, we have demonstrated that the incremental technique in FUP and FUP* can be generalized to some other kdd systems. An efficient algorithm MLUp has been proposed for this purpose for the updating of discovered multi-level association rules(MLAR). Our performance study shows that MLUp has a superior performance over ML-T2 in updating discovered MLAR.

1   Introduction

An association rule(AR) is a strong rule which implies certain association relationships among a set of objects in a database. Since finding interesting AR in databases may disclose some useful patterns for decision support, marketing analysis, financial forecast, system fault prediction, and many other applications, it has attracted a lot of attention in recent data mining research (6). Efficient mining of AR in transaction and/or relational databases has been studied substantially (1; 2; 8; 10; 12; 7; 11; 13).

In our previous study, we have investigated the maintenance problem in SLAR discovery (4). An efficient algorithm FUP (*Fast Update*) has been proposed, which can incrementally update the AR discovered, if updates to a database is restricted to insertions of new transactions. In this paper, we will report two progresses in our study of the maintenance problem in the mining of association rules. (1) A faster version FUP* of FUP has been proposed. The improvement of FUP* over FUP is in the candidate set generation procedure. (2) An algorithm MLUp (stands for M*ulti-Level asso-ciation rules* Up*date*) has been proposed for the update of the discovered MLAR in relation databases (7).

The success of the incremental updating technique used in SLAR and MLAR suggests that, potentially, the technique could be generalized to solve the update problem in some other kdd systems. The remaining of the paper is organized as follows. In Section 2, the faster version FUP* is proposed. In Section 3, the problem of updating MLAR is discussed and the algorithm MLUp for the update of discovered MLAR is discussed. In Section 4, an in-depth performance study of MLUp is presented. Section 5 is the discussion and conclusions.

2   Update of Discovered SLAR

In the following discussion, we use the same notation as used in (4). We summarize the finding of (4) in Lemma 1. For a complete description of FUP, please see (4).

Lemma 1 (4) *A k-itemset X not in the original large k-itemsets L_k can become a* winner, *(i.e., become large) in the updated database $DB \cup db$ only if $X.support_d \geq s \times d$.*   □

A faster update algorithm FUP*

The improvement of FUP* over FUP (4) is in the candidate set generation mechanism. FUP uses the Apriori-gen function defined in (2) to establish a set of candidate sets (4). In fact, it looks for itemsets in Apriori-gen(L'_{k-1}) which does not belong to L_k but appear in some transaction(s) in *db*, whose support count in *db* is larger than or equal to $s \times d$, where the set L'_{k-1} is the set of size-(k-1) large itemset in the update database found in the (k-1)-th iteration of FUP. We find out that the domain in this searching which is the set Apriori-gen(L'_{k-1}) can be further reduced to a smaller set. This finding is supported by the following result. (A result similar to Lemma 2 for partitioned databases has been reported in (5)).

Lemma 2 *A k-itemset X not in the original large k-itemsets L_k can become a* winner *(i.e., become large) in the updated database $DB \cup db$ only if $Y.support_d \geq s \times d$ for all the subsets $Y \subseteq X$.*
Proof. It follows from Lemma 1 that $X.support_d \geq s \times d$. If $Y \subseteq X$, then $Y.support_d \geq X.support_d$. Hence, the condition holds for all the subsets Y of X.   □

From Lemma 2, the candidate sets can be restricted to the sets in Apriori-gen(L^*_{k-1}), where L^*_{k-1} are the itemsets in L'_{k-1}, whose support counts in db are larger than or equal to $s \times d$. In general, L^*_{k-1} is smaller than L'_{k-1}, and hence the number of candidate sets in Apriori-gen(L^*_{k-1}) is smaller than that in Apriori-gen(L'_{k-1}). In the following, we will use Example 1 to illustrate the execution of FUP*. In particular, the example will show that FUP* can reduce significantly the number of candidate sets.

Example 1 A database DB is updated with an increment db such that $D = 1000$, $d = 100$ and $s = 3\%$. $X, Y, Z,$ and W are four items and the size-1 and size-2 large itemsets in DB are $L_1 = \{X, Y, Z\}$ and $L_2 = \{XY, YZ\}$, respectively. Also $XY.support_D = 32$ and $YZ.support_D = 31$. Suppose FUP* has completed the first iteration and found the "new" size-1 itemsets $L'_1 = \{X, Y, W\}$. Moreover, assuming that the support counts of X, Y, and W found in db are 2, 4 and 5, respectively. This example illustrates how FUP* will find out L'_2 in the second iteration, and also its effectiveness in reducing the number of candidate sets.

FUP* first filters out losers from L_2. Note that $Z \in L_1 - L'_1$, i.e., Z has become a loser; therefore, the set $YZ \in L_2$ must also be a loser and is filtered out. For the remaining set $XY \in L_2$, FUP* scans db to update its support count. Assume that $XY.support_{db} = 2$. Since $XY.support_{UB} = (2+32) > 3\% \times 1100$, therefore, XY is large in $DB \cup db$ and is stored in L'_2.

Secondly, FUP* needs to find out the "new" large itemsets from db. For this purpose, FUP* has to find out the set L^*_1 from L'_1, which contains the itemsets in L'_1 that have enough support counts in db. Since $X.support_d = 2 < 3\% \times 100$, $X \notin L^*_1$, i.e., even though X is a winner in the 1st iteration, it will not be used to generate the size-2 candidate sets. On the other hand, both the support counts of Y and W in db are larger than the threshold $3\% \times 100$; therefore they will be used to generate the size-2 candidate sets, i.e., $L^*_1 = \{Y, W\}$. Following that, FUP* applies Apriori-gen on L^*_1 and generates the candidate set $C_2 = \{YW\}$. Note that in FUP, Apriori-gen is applied on $L'_1 = \{X, Y, W\}$ instead of L^*_1, and the set of candidate sets generated will have three itemsets which is three times larger than what is generated in FUP* in this example. This illustrates that FUP* can significantly and effectively reduce the number of candidate sets when comparing with FUP.

Suppose $YW.support_d = 4 > 3\% \times 100$. It follows from Lemma 1 that YW will not be pruned and remain in C_2. Following the pruning of the candidate sets in C_2, FUP* has to update the remaining candidate sets in C_2 against the original database DB. Suppose $YW.support_D = 29$. Since $YW.support_{UD} = 29 + 4 > 3\% \times 1100$, it is a large itemset in the updated database. Therefore YW is added into L'_2. At the end of the second iteration, $L'_2 = \{XY, YW\}$ is returned. □

3 Update of Discovered MLAR

The method used in FUP* (and FUP) could be applied to many other kdd systems to update the knowledge discovered. In particular, it can be used in the systems that are designed to discover various types of associations between generalized items and events. This includes the discovery of MLAR, generalized AR, sequential patterns, episodes, and quantitative AR (7; 12; 3; 9; 13). In the following, we will show that FUP* can be generalized to solve the update problem for MLAR. For this purpose, an algorithm MLUp, which is an adaptation of FUP*, will be proposed.

Mining of MLAR

In the study of mining MLAR, a series of algorithms have been proposed to facilitate a top-down, progressive deepening method based on the algorithms for mining SLAR. The method first finds large data items at the top-most level and then progressively deepens the mining process into their large descendants at lower concept levels. For details on the mining of MLAR, please refer to (7).

Update of discovered MLAR

The problem of updating the discovered MLAR is the same as that in the single-level environment. The only difference is that the rules in all the levels have to be updated instead of updating the rules in only one level. Also, the minimum support thresholds at different levels may not be equal. We use s_m to denote the minimum support threshold at level m for $m \geq 1$.

Since there are several variations of the algorithm in mining MLAR, the update algorithm should be designed according to the strategy used in the initial mining process. The algorithm MLUp we are proposing is associated with the representative mining algorithm ML-T2. The following two results are the bases of MLUp.

Lemma 3 *In a multi-level environment, a level-m 1-itemset X not in the original large 1-itemsets $L[m, 1]$, $(m \geq 1)$, can become a winner (i.e., become large) in the updated database $DB \cup db$ only if all ancestors of X are winners.*
Proof. This follows from the definition of large itemsets in the multi-level environment. □

Following Lemma 3, when MLUp scans the increment db to look for new size-1 winners, it not only has to ensure a candidate itemset has the required support count, but must also check that all its ancestors are large in the updated database. (Because of transitivity, MLUp only needs to check a candidate's immediate ancestor).

Lemma 4 *In a multi-level environment, a level-m k-itemset X not in the original large k-itemsets $L[m, k]$, $(m \geq 1)$, can become a winner (i.e., become large) in the updated database $DB \cup db$ only if $X.support_d \geq s_m \times d$ and $Y.support_d \geq s_m \times d$, for all subset $Y \subseteq X$.*

Proof. This follows directly from Lemmas 1 and 2. □

The implication of the result in Lemma 4 is that the candidate set generation mechanism in FUP* can be applied directly in MLUp for finding new winners in different levels. In the following, we describe the main procedure of the update algorithm MLUp. The input to the algorithm includes the original encoded transaction database $T[1]$, the increment database db, and the old large itemsets $L[m,k]$, $(m \geq 1, k \geq 1)$, and their support counts. Following the conventions in FUP*, the sizes of $T[1]$ and db are denoted by D and d respectively. Moreover, the minimum support threshold for different level is denoted by s_m, $(m \geq 1)$.

MLUp (main steps) :

1. Translate the increment transaction database db into an encoded transaction table $db[1]$ according to the given taxonomy information.

2. At level 1, scan $db[1]$ to update the support counts of the 1-itemsets in $L[1,1]$ to filter out the winners into $L'[1,1]$. In the same scan, find all the 1-itemsets in $db[1]$ which do not belong to $L[1,1]$, whose support count in $db[1]$ is larger than or equal to $s_1 \times d$, and store these 1-itemsets in the candidate set C_1. Subsequently, scan $T[1]$ to find out the new winners in C_1 and store them into $L'[1,1]$. Following that, $T[1]$ is filtered by $L'[1,1]$ to generate the encoded transaction table $T[2]$. Similarly, $db[1]$ is filtered to $db[2]$.

At level m, $(m > 1)$, scan $db[2]$ to update the support counts of the 1-itemsets in $L[m,1]$. An 1-itemset in $L[m,1]$ is a winner only if its immediate ancestor is large in the updated database and its support counts in the updated database is larger than or equal to $s_m \times (D + d)$.

In the same scan, find all level-m 1-itemsets in $db[2]$ which do not belong to $L[m,1]$, whose immediate ancestor belongs to $L'[m-1,1]$ and whose support count in $db[2]$ is larger than or equal to $s_m \times d$. Then store these 1-itemsets in the candidate set C_1. Subsequently, scan $T[2]$ to find out the new winners in C_1 and store them in $L'[m,1]$.

3. The large k-itemsets, $(k > 1)$, for the updated database at level m is derived in three steps:
(1) Remove all the k-itemsets in $L[m,k]$ for which one of its ancestors is not large in the updated database. Then scan $db[2]$ to update the support counts of the remaining itemsets in $L[m,k]$ to find out the winners. (2) Let $L^*[m,k-1]$ be the subsets of itemsets in $L'[m,k-1]$ whose support count in db is larger then or equal to $s_m \times d$. In the same scan on $db[2]$ performed in (1), find all level-m k-itemsets in Apriori-gen($L^*[m,k-1]$) which do not belong to $L[m,k]$, whose support count in $db[2]$ is larger than or equal to $s_m \times d$, and store them in the candidate set C_k. (3) Scan DB to update the support counts of the candidate sets in C_k and find all the level-m size-k winners in C_k, and store them in $L'[m,k]$.

4. At level m, return the union of $L'[m,k]$ for all the k's.

4 Performance Study of MLUp

Extensive experiments have been conducted to assess the performance of MLUp. It was compared with the algorithm ML-T2. The experiments were performed on an AIX system on an RS/6000 workstation with model 410. The result shows that MLUp is much faster than re-running ML-T2 to update the discovered AR. This improvement is not surprising given that FUP also has similar performance in updating SLAR. The databases used in our experiments are synthetic data generated using a technique similar to that in (2).

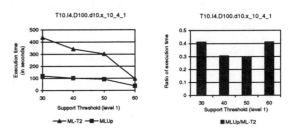

Figure 1: Performance Comparison (level 1)

Our test environments are denoted by T10.I4.D100.d10.s_1_s_2_s_3_s_4, which represents an updated database in which the original database DB has 100 thousands of transactions (D100), the increment db has 10 thousands of transactions (d10). The transactions on average has 10 items (T10), and the average size of the large itemsets is 4 (I4). Moreover, there are four levels in the taxonomy and the minimum supports are denoted by s_i, $(1 \leq i \leq 4)$. The performance comparison between MLUp and ML-T2 in the update of the level-1 AR is plotted in Figure 1 against different minimum support thresholds. Their performance ratios are also presented as bar charts in the same figure. It can be seen that MLUp is 2-3 times faster than ML-T2. MLUp also has similar speed-up over ML-T2 in the updates in the other levels.

As explained before, MLUp reduces substantially the number of candidate sets generated when comparing with ML-T2. In Figure 2, the number of candidate sets generated in MLUp in the same experiment is compared with that in ML-T2. The ratios in the comparison are presented as bar charts in the same figure. The chart shows that the number of candidate sets generated by MLUp is only about 2-3% of that in ML-T2.

A series of updates from 10K to 350K were generated on the databases T10.I4.D100, and the execution times for MLUp and ML-T2 to do the updates on these increments were compared. A gradually level off of the speed-up of MLUp over ML-T2 only appears when the increment size is about 3.5 times the size of the original database. The fact that MLUp still exhibits performance gain when the increment is much larger than the original database shows that it is very efficient.

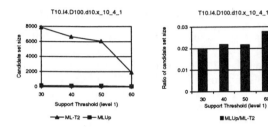

Figure 2: Reduction of Candidate Sets (level 1)

5 Discussion and Conclusions

We have shown that FUP* is an efficient algorithm for updating discovered SLAR. It improves the performance of FUP by significantly reducing its candidate sets.

We have also proposed an efficient algorithm MLUp for updating discovered MLAR. It is an adaptation of the FUP* algorithm in the multi-level environment. The algorithm MLUp is implemented and its performance is studied and compared with the ML-T2 algorithm . The study shows that MLUp has superior performance in the multi-level environment. The success of the incremental updating technique in both the SLAR and MLAR suggests that the technique could be generalized to solve the update problems in some other knowledge discovery systems.

Currently, both FUP* and MLUp are applicable only to a database which allow frequent or occasional updates restricted to insertions of new transactions. We have also investigated the cases of updates including deletions and/or modifications to a transaction database. In FUP* and MLUp, the incremental updating technique has made use of the fact that new winners generated in the updating process must appear and have enough support counts in the increment. However, this does not hold in general in the cases of deletion and modification. For example, in the case of deletion, because the size of the updated database has decreased, some itemsets which are "small" in the orginial database DB, could become large in the updated database, even though it is not contained in any transaction deleted. Consequently, the set of candidate sets cannot be limited to those appear in the increment, and potentially, all itemsets in the updated database have to be considered as candidates. Therefore, the current incremental technique cannot be applied directly to the cases of deletion and modification. However, it is possible to solve the deletion and modification cases if the initial mining process is enhanced to retain more informations to support the update.

The extension of our incremental update technique for the maintenance of other type of knowledge such as generalized AR, episodes, sequential patterns, and quantitative AR is an interesting topic for future research. However, as discussed above, a bigger challenge is to extend this technique to cover the cases of deletion and modification.

References

[1] R. Agrawal, T. Imielinski, and A. Swami. Mining association rules between sets of items in large databases. In *Proc. 1993 ACM-SIGMOD Int. Conf. Management of Data*, pp. 207–216, Washington, D.C., May 1993.

[2] R. Agrawal and R. Srikant. Fast algorithms for mining association rules. In *Proc. 1994 Int. Conf. VLDB*, pp. 487–499, Santiago, Chile, Sept. 1994.

[3] R. Agrawal and R. Srikant. Mining sequential patterns. In *Proc. 1995 Int. Conf. Data Engineering*, pp. 3–14, Taipei, Taiwan, March 1995.

[4] D.W. Cheung, J. Han, V. Ng, and C.Y. Wong. Maintenance of discovered association rules in large databases: An incremental updating technique. In *Proc. 1996 Int'l Conf. on Data Engineering*, New Orleans, Louisiana, Feb. 1996.

[5] D.W. Cheung, J. Han, V. Ng, A. Fu and Y. Fu. A Fast Distributed Algorithm for Mining Association Rules. Technical Report, Dept. of Computer Science, The University of Hong Kong, 1996.

[6] U. M. Fayyad, G. Piatetsky-Shapiro, P. Smyth, and R. Uthurusamy. *Advances in Knowledge Discovery and Data Mining*. AAAI/MIT Press, 1996.

[7] J. Han and Y. Fu. Discovery of multiple-level association rules from large databases. In *Proc. 1995 Int. Conf. VLDB*, pp. 420–431, Zurich, Switzerland, Sept. 1995.

[8] M. Klemettinen, H. Mannila, P. Ronkainen, H. Toivonen, and A. I. Verkamo. Finding interesting rules from large sets of discovered association rules. In *Proc. 3rd Int'l Conf. on Information and Knowledge Management*, pp. 401–408, Gaithersburg, Maryland, Nov. 1994.

[9] H. Mannila, H. Toivonen, and A. I. Verkamo. Discovering Frequent Episodes in Sequences. In *Proc. 1st Int'l Conf. on KDD*, pp. 210–215, Montreal, Quebec, Canada, Aug. 1995.

[10] J.S. Park, M.S. Chen, and P.S. Yu. An effective hash-based algorithm for mining association rules. In *Proc. 1995 ACM-SIGMOD Int. Conf. Management of Data*, pp. 175–186, San Jose, CA, May 1995.

[11] A. Savasere, E. Omiecinski, and S. Navathe. An efficient algorithm for mining association rules in large databases. In *Proc. 1995 Int. Conf. VLDB*, pp. 432–443, Zurich, Switzerland, Sept. 1995.

[12] R. Srikant and R. Agrawal. Mining generalized association rules. In *Proc. 1995 Int. Conf. VLDB*, pp. 407–419, Zurich, Switzerland, Sept. 1995.

[13] R. Srikant and R. Agrawal. Mining quantitative association rules in large relational tables. In *Proc. 1996 ACM-SIGMOD Int. Conf. Management of Data*, Montreal, Canada, June 1996.

Analysing Binary Associations

Arno J. Knobbe, Pieter W. Adriaans

Syllogic

P.O. Box 26, 3990 DA Houten, The Netherlands

Email: {ajknobbe, pieter}@syllogic.nl

Abstract

This paper describes how binary associations in databases of items can be organised and clustered. Two similarity measures are presented that can be used to generate a weighted graph of associations. Each measure focuses on different kinds of regularities in the database. By calculating a Minimum Spanning Tree on the graph of associations, the most significant associations can be discovered and easily visualised, allowing easy understanding of existing relations. By deleting the least interesting associations from the computed tree, the attributes can be clustered.

Introduction

In this paper we investigate new ways of discovering and presenting associations discovered in databases of items. The discovered knowledge will be represented in the form of clusters of items and graphs of relationships between items, and not in the form of rules, which is the traditional form of knowledge representation used for associations (Agrawal et al. 1996, Toivonen et al. 1995). Our particular focus will facilitate easy understanding and interpretation of the discovered associations.

A general problem of discovery algorithms and in particular those that discover association rules, is the great amount of rules that are discovered. By examining rules between sets of items, the emphasis is on completeness rather than on readability. Some solution to this problem have been proposed, such as allowing the user to specify rules of interest, or clustering rules into groups of related structures (Toivonen et al. 1995). Still the user was required to examine lists of rules by hand.

In this paper we focus on associations between single attributes, thus reducing the number of hypothetical associations. We claim that this restricted analysis will discover most of the interesting knowledge contained in the database, while greatly increasing the readability and usefulness of the resulting structure. Experiments show that our focus on simple associations produces acceptable results, and that knowledge expressed in complex rules is, at least to some extent, represented by simple associations, which is a result of the transitivity of simple rules.

An analysis of simple associations produces an association matrix that can easily be visualised in a bar diagram, or in a graph with an association measure with each edge. Still with larger amounts of attributes, such a bar diagram or graph will become too complex and cluttered. We solve this problem by simplifying the association graph by calculating a minimum spanning tree (Cormen & Leiserson 1989, Preparata & Shamos 1985, Prim 1957, Tarjan 1983). The resulting tree can be used to cluster the attributes (Gower & Ross 1969, Preparata & Shamos 1985).

This paper is organised as follows. The following section describes two similarity measures that can be used to generate an association matrix. We compare the properties of each of these similarity measures. The next section describes how minimum spanning trees can be used to reduce the set of associations. This graph can be used to cluster the attributes. Finally we present some experimental results that demonstrate the usefulness of our approach, followed by some conclusions.

Simple association

In this section we focus on finding associations between pairs of attributes. Measures of similarity (amount of association) are calculated by making passes of the database and counting occurrences of 1's for the pair of attributes. Different similarity measures can be thought of, each expressing a particular type of association. We will present two similarity measures, one based on Shannon's information theory (Shannon & Weaver 1949, Li & Vitányi 1993), and one based on conditional probabilities. Other measures can be thought of, but in order to calculate a minimum spanning tree in a later stage, we require all similarity measures to be symmetric in the two associated attributes.

Our similarity measure will be a symmetric function $S(x,y)$ of two attributes x and y, that is calculated from values $p_x(i)$, $p_y(i)$ and $p_{xy}(i,j)$, where i and j may take on the values 0 and 1. $p_x(i)$ is taken to be

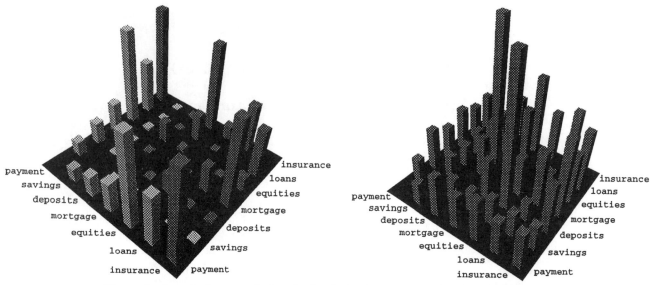

Figure 1: Association matrix for the bank database using $I(x, y)$, and $P(x, y)$.

an estimation of the probability of attribute x being i, and is defined as the number of times x has the value i, divided by the total number of records in the database. Similarly for $p_y(i)$ and $p_{xy}(i, j)$.

The first similarity measure is based on information theory, and is commonly known as *mutual information*. It is defined as

$$I(x, y) = \sum_{i=0}^{1} \sum_{j=0}^{1} p_{xy}(i, j) \lg \frac{p_{xy}(i, j)}{p_x(i) p_y(j)}$$

Clearly $I(x, y)$ is symmetric. For a rationale behind this definition see (Li & Vitányi 1993). The mutual information between two attributes describes the amount of information that one attributes gives about the other. The definition of mutual information describes the amount of information but does not determine the type of relation between two attributes. Two attributes that always have reversed values will be similar according to this measure.

The second measure considered in this paper is based on probability theory. It is defined as

$$P(x, y) = \frac{p_{xy}(1, 1)}{p_x(1) p_y(1)}$$

This measure is closely related to the definition of confidence for association rules (Agrawal et al. 1996). It can be thought of as the ratio between the estimation of the conditional probability $\frac{p_{xy}(1,1)}{p_x(1)}$, and the estimation of the apriori probability $p_y(1)$. The conditional probability coincides with the confidence for an association rule $x \rightarrow y$.

example 1. Fig 1 shows the association matrix for a database of customers of a bank using the two different similarity measures. The database contains 8844

records having seven attributes that describe the seven different classes of products provided by the bank. Fig 1 on the left shows the results of using mutual information as a similarity measure. High bars correspond to pairs of similar attributes. Dark bars are positive relations, light bars are negative. Clearly there is a strong positive relation between payments and insurances, insurances and mortgages, etc., indicated by several dark bars. Apparently there is a negative relation between payments and equities.

Fig 1 on the right shows the results of the similarity measure based on conditional probabilities. The most significant relations are now between equities and deposits, and between insurances and mortgages.

The two measures are biased towards different types of association. $I(x, y)$ will reveal both positive and negative relations, but has a bias towards attributes of which $p_x(1)$ are close to $p_x(0)$. Two attributes that are rarely 1 (or 0) but always at the same time will not be recognised as a significant relation. $P(x, y)$ will reveal relations between attributes that are rarely 1 (see for example equities and deposits) but will only show positive relations. Thus different measures can be used depending on the type of association that is searched for.

Clustering

The association matrix calculated in the previous section can be used to report all association above a certain level. However the end-user would still be required to examine lists of (simple) rules. In this section we consider the graph defined by the association matrix and show how this fully connected graph can be simplified by calculating a *minimum spanning tree* (Cormen & Leiserson 1989, Preparata & Shamos 1985,

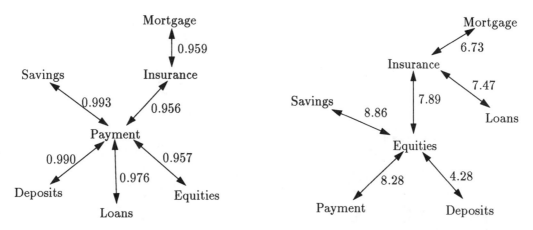

Figure 2: Minimum spanning trees for the bank database using $I(x,y)$, and $P(x,y)$.

Prim 1957, Tarjan 1983). This minimum spanning tree (MST) can then be used to cluster attributes (Cormen & Leiserson 1989).

We define the association graph of a database of items as a fully connect undirected graph $G = (V, E)$, where V is the set of vertices each of which represents an attribute and E the set of edges connecting the attributes. For each edge (x, y) we have a value $d(x, y) = -S(x, y)$ specifying the distance between two attributes, which we define as the negation of the similarity. Note that $d(x, y)$ may be negative.

An acyclic subset $T \subseteq E$ is a MST if it connects all vertices, and minimises the sum

$$\sum_{(x,y) \in T} d(x,y)$$

Two greedy algorithms for computing MSTs, Kruskal's and Prim's algorithm, are described in (Cormen & Leiserson 1989). They both work by growing a tree from a single vertex, adding one edge at a time. They differ in what edge is added to the subset of edges that form the tree at each iteration. Kruskal's algorithm maintains a forest, starting with every vertex being a single tree. At each step two trees are joined by choosing an edge with a minimal weight. Prim's algorithm works by adding edges to a single tree that is a subset of the final MST.

Kruskal's algorithm can be implemented to run in $\mathcal{O}(|E| \lg |V|)$. Prim's algorithm runs in $\mathcal{O}(|E| \lg |V|)$ using ordinary heaps or $\mathcal{O}(|E| + |V| \lg |V|)$ using Fibonacci heaps for finding new edges efficiently. Because $|E| = \mathcal{O}(|V|^2)$ Prim's algorithm will run in $\mathcal{O}(|V|^2 + |V| \lg |V|) = \mathcal{O}(|V|^2)$ which is clearly optimal because an association matrix of complexity $\mathcal{O}(|V|^2)$ needs to be fully examined, if no assumptions on the type of similarity measure are made.

example 2. Fig 2 shows the effect of calculating the MST for the two matrices from example 1. It conveys

the most interesting associations in a readable fashion. Again we see the properties of the two similarity measures in the organisation of the two trees. Payment and equities are connected in the graph on the left because there is a reverse relation between the two attributes. The relation between equities and deposits is only revealed in the right graph because the associated similarity measure does focus on such infrequent associations.

Computation of a MST can be thought of as reducing the complexity of the graph while respecting the connectivity of the graph. We can push the balance between these two goals towards reduction of complexity by repeatedly removing those associations that are least important in the MST. Every removal will cause a subtree to be split into two separate groups. We will thus end up with clusters of attributes that have high internal similarity. Because every association between attributes of two different clusters are less then the single connection that was cut (see (Cormen & Leiserson 1989)), dissimilarity between seperate clusters is guaranteed.

Experiments

We analyse an enrollment database of courses in computer science, using the approach presented in the previous sections. The database consists of 2836 records each describing the courses taken by a single student. On average between six and seven courses were taken by each student, from a total of 127 courses.

An MST containing the 127 courses is computed using the mutual information-based measure $I(x, y)$. Fig 3 show some details of the MST. Clearly the structure of the subtrees seems to coincide with our common knowledge of relations between the subjects that are covered in each course. Fig 3 seems to deal with courses about databases and user interfaces. Apparently the link between these two subjects is made by

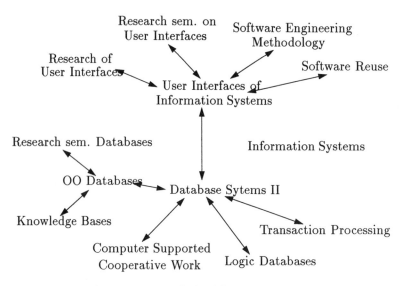

Figure 3: Part of Finnish courses.

'User Interfaces of Information Systems', a course that combines subjects from the two areas.

Clustering on this MST has the effect of putting outlyers in clusters of a single course, such as *'Sem. on Scientific Visualisation'*, *'Computational Geometry'* or *'Principles of Programming Languages (Ada)'*. These courses appear to be taken independently of other available courses. Continuing the clustering process will then split the remaining tree into particular subgroups, such as the area of databases, system programming, etc. A good criterion for continuing the clustering process seems to be hard to define.

Conclusion

This paper describes how information contained in binary associations can be exploited to the fullest. Our approach analyses a subset of the possible associations considered in traditional association rule discovery algorithms, but from the experiments it is clear that it does not suffer from this restriction, and even allows more effective ways of presenting the discovered knowledge.

Two similarity measures for attributes have been presented, each emphasising particular characteristics of associations between attributes. New similarity measures should be examined with the aim of combining useful properties from the presented measures.

By computing the minimum spanning tree of the association graph, we focus on the particular subset of large associations that is sufficient to include all attributes. We intend to examine the effect of reducing or extending this set of associations, especially in the context of clustering.

Acknowledgement
We thank Hannu Toivonen for providing the student enrollment database (in Finnish).

References

Agrawal, R., Mannila, H., Srikant, R., Toivonen, H., Verkamo, A. 1996. *Fast Discovery of Association Rules.* in Advance in Knowledge Discovery and Data Mining.

Cormen, T.H., Leiserson, C.E., Rivest, R.L. 1989. *Introduction to Algorithms.* MIT Press/McGraw-Hill.

Gower, J.C., Ross, G.J.S. 1969. *Minimum spanning trees and single linkage cluster analysis.* Appl. Stat. 18(1), 54-64.

Li, M., Vitányi, P.M.B. 1993. *An Introduction to Kolmogorov Complexity and its Applications.* Springer-Verlag.

Preparata, F.P., Shamos, M.I. 1985. *Computational Geometry: An Introduction.* Springer-Verlag.

Prim, R.C. 1957. *Shortest connection networks and some generalizations.* Bell System Technical Journal, 36:1389-1401.

Shannon, C.E., Weaver, W. 1949. *The Mathematical Theory of Communication.* University of Illinois Press, Urbana, IL.

Tarjan, R.E. 1983. *Data structures and Network Algorithms.* Society for Industrial and Applied Mathematics.

Toivonen, H., Klemettinen, M., Ronkainen, P., Hätönen, K., Mannila, H. 1995. *Pruning and Grouping Discovered Association Rules.* ECML-95 workshop on Statistics, Machine Learning and Knowledge Discovery in Databases.

Growing Simpler Decision Trees to Facilitate Knowledge Discovery

Kevin J. Cherkauer   Jude W. Shavlik

Department of Computer Sciences
University of Wisconsin
1210 West Dayton Street
Madison, WI 53706, USA
cherkauer@cs.wisc.edu, shavlik@cs.wisc.edu

Abstract

When using machine learning techniques for knowledge discovery, output that is comprehensible to a human is as important as predictive accuracy. We introduce a new algorithm, SET-GEN, that improves the comprehensibility of decision trees grown by standard C4.5 without reducing accuracy. It does this by using genetic search to select the set of input features C4.5 is allowed to use to build its tree. We test SET-GEN on a wide variety of real-world datasets and show that SET-GEN trees are significantly smaller and reference significantly fewer features than trees grown by C4.5 without using SET-GEN. Statistical significance tests show that the accuracies of SET-GEN's trees are either not distinguishable from or are more accurate than those of the original C4.5 trees on all ten datasets tested.

Introduction

One approach to knowledge discovery in databases (DBs) is to apply inductive learning algorithms to derive models of interesting aspects of the data. The predictive accuracy of such a model is obviously important. However, human comprehensibility of the learned model is equally vital so that we can add the knowledge it captures to our understanding of the domain or validate the model for critical applications.

To address the issue of human comprehensibility, we introduce SET-GEN, a new algorithmic approach to knowledge discovery that improves the comprehensibility of decision trees grown by a state-of-the-art tree induction algorithm, C4.5 (Quinlan 1993), without reducing tree accuracy. SET-GEN takes a DB of labeled examples (vectors of feature-value pairs) and selects a subset of the available features for training C4.5. Its goal is to choose a set of features that results in

- Predictive accuracy at least as good as that of running C4.5 without SET-GEN

- Significantly smaller decision trees

- Significantly fewer unique input features referenced

Reducing tree size makes it easier to understand the relationships contained in the tree, and referencing fewer features focuses attention on the most important information. We demonstrate SET-GEN on a wide variety of real-world prediction problems and show empirically that it meets our stated goals.

The SET-Gen Algorithm

SET-GEN performs feature-subset selection for decision-tree induction. Table 1 gives pseudocode for the algorithm. SET-GEN applies a genetic algorithm (GA; Goldberg 1989) with a wrapper-style evaluation function (John, Kohavi, & Pfleger 1994) to search many candidate feature subsets. It uses ten-fold cross validation on the training examples to estimate the quality, or *fitness*, of each candidate. That is, the training data is partitioned into ten equal-sized sets, each of which serves as an unseen *validation set* used to estimate the accuracy of a C4.5 decision tree trained on the remaining nine sets using just the candidate features. Fitness is a function of the number of candidate features, the average size of the ten trees, and the average tree accuracy on the validation sets.

SET-GEN maintains a population of the best feature subsets it has found. New subsets are created by applying genetic operators to population members. If a new subset is more fit than the worst member of the population, it replaces that member; otherwise the new subset is discarded. After completing the desired number of subset evaluations, SET-GEN uses the entire training set to grow a single C4.5 tree using only the features in the best subset it has found. It outputs this final tree and the corresponding feature subset.

SET-Gen's Genome

SET-GEN represents a feature subset as a fixed-length vector called a *genome*. Each genome entry may either contain a feature or be empty. The genome in Figure 1 represents a subset comprised of features f_2, f_7, and f_{15}. A feature may occur multiple times and in any position, making SET-GEN's genome somewhat unusual among GAs. An indicator bit vector with one entry per input feature would be more traditional. Our justification for SET-GEN's genome style is twofold. First, the fact that features can appear multiple times potentially slows the loss of diversity that tends to occur during genetic search (Forrest & Mitchell 1993) and allows better features to proliferate. Second, unlike the bit-vector genome, SET-GEN's genome length does not

Table 1: SET-GEN pseudocode.

Algorithm SET-Gen
   Input labeled training examples, program parameters
   Choose pruning level via 10-fold cross validation
     on training data (builds 10 decision trees)
   While perform more evaluations?
     If pop. is not full, *Child* = fill genome randomly
     Else
        Op = choose genetic operator randomly
        Parents = choose parent(s) randomly from
           population proportional to fitness
        Child = Apply(*Op*, *Parents*)
     End If
     Evaluate *Child* fitness via 10-fold cross validation
       on training data (builds 10 decision trees)
     If population is not full, add *Child* to population
     Else
        Worst = population member with worst fitness
        If Fitness(*Child*) > Fitness(*Worst*)
           replace *Worst* with *Child* in population
        Else discard *Child*
     End If
   End While
   FinalFeatures = features present in best pop. member
   FinalTree = grow decision tree from all training data
     using only features in *FinalFeatures*
   Output *FinalTree, FinalFeatures*
End Algorithm SET-Gen

---

		f_7	f_7	f_2		f_7		f_{15}			f_2

Figure 1: An example SET-GEN genome, representing the feature subset $\{f_2, f_7, f_{15}\}$.

depend on the number of input features. By default, SET-GEN's genome size is the same as the number of available features, but if desired one can choose a larger or smaller genome. Smaller genomes bias SET-GEN toward smaller feature subsets and simpler trees. Because trees can be grown faster when there are fewer features to test as splits, this also reduces evaluation time, making the algorithm tractable for larger DBs.

SET-Gen's Genetic Operators

SET-GEN's genetic operators are *Crossover, Mutate,* and *Delete Feature.* Each uses one or two *parent* feature subsets to create a new *child* subset for evaluation.

The *Crossover* operator is a variant of a uniform crossover, and produces a single child from a primary and a secondary parent. First, the genome of one parent is rotated a random distance. Then each entry of the child is filled by copying the corresponding entry of the primary parent with probability $1 - P_c$ and that of the secondary parent with probability P_c (the *crossover rate*). In our experiments, we set P_c to 0.10, so a typical child receives approximately 90% of its genome from the primary parent.

We chose a uniform crossover with a low crossover rate instead of a one-point crossover because we felt that small "tweaks" would more likely improve a current solution than the larger jumps one-point crossover tends to make. This is only an intuition; we have

not yet compared the performance of this crossover to a one-point crossover. SET-GEN's low crossover rate hopefully results in low disruption across generations of high-order schemata involving many features (cf. Goldberg 1989). However, a one-point crossover might take better advantage of lower-level "building blocks" (Goldberg 1989) as individual features could assemble themselves in spatially adjacent fashion to increase their chances of being exchanged as a unit.

SET-GEN's *Mutate* operator uses one parent. Each entry of the child is copied from the parent with probability $1 - P_m$. With probability P_m (the *mutation rate*), it is filled randomly thus: 50% of the time, fill with a feature chosen equiprobably from among all input features; the other 50% of the time, leave the entry empty. P_m is 0.10 for the experiments.

Delete Feature uses one parent to produce a child that is identical except that all occurrences of one (equiprobably chosen) feature in the parent are removed from the child. This operator directly biases SET-GEN toward smaller feature subsets, and thus toward simpler, more comprehensible decision trees.

The initial population members are created by *Mutate* with a temporary mutation rate of 1.00. From then on, each new feature subset is produced by applying one of the genetic operators, chosen equiprobably, to parent(s) picked randomly from the current population proportional to their fitness (Goldberg 1989).

SET-Gen's Fitness Function

The core of SET-GEN is its fitness function, which evaluates feature subsets in terms of the accuracy and simplicity of their resulting trees[1]:

$$Fitness = \tfrac{3}{4}A + \tfrac{1}{4}\left(1 - \tfrac{S+F}{2}\right)$$

where A is the average validation-set accuracy of the trees SET-GEN builds on the training data; S is the average size of these trees, normalized by dividing by the average number of training examples they were built from; and F is the number of features in the subset being evaluated, normalized by the total number of available features. We define F as the number of features present, instead of the average number of features the trees reference, to create a fitness distinction between representations containing the same referenced features but different numbers of extra, unreferenced ones. Without this, there would be no selective pressure to eliminate unused features from the representations. We could instead simply delete all unused features immediately, but this would dramatically reduce the internal diversity of individuals early in the search, before it is apparent whether the unused features would prove valuable under different subset recombinations.

SET-GEN's fitness function is a linear combination of an accuracy term, A, and a simplicity term,

---

[1]The fitness variables are motivated by our previous work on representation Sufficiency, Economy, and Transparency ("SET"; Cherkauer & Shavlik 1996).

Table 2: Summary of datasets used: number of examples, classes, and features (discrete, continuous).

Dataset	Exs	Cls	Fts (Ds, Cn)
Auto Imports[a]	205	6	25 (10, 15)
Credit Approval[a]	690	2	15 (9, 6)
Heart Disease[a]	303	2	13 (8, 5)
Hepatitis[a]	155	2	19 (13, 6)
Lung Cancer[a]	32	3	56 (56, 0)
Lymphography[a]	148	4	18 (15, 3)
Magellan-SAR	611	2	137 (0, 137)
Promoters	468	2	57 (57, 0)
Ribosome Binding	1,877	2	49 (49, 0)
Splice Junctions[a]	3,190	3	60 (60, 0)

[a]Available publicly (Murphy & Aha 1994).

$(1 - \frac{S+F}{2})$. We weight the accuracy term more heavily to encourage SET-GEN to maintain the original accuracy level. All coefficients in the fitness function were chosen prior to running any experiments. Note that A and F (normalized) vary in the range [0, 1]. The normalization used for S attempts to put it on an approximately equivalent [0, 1] scale so that the weights in the fitness function are meaningful to a human. It is simply a heuristic that uses the number of training examples as a rough upper bound for expected tree size. The result is that the simplicity term ranges roughly over [0, 1] to match the range of the accuracy term, and S and F (tree size and number of features) are of about equal importance in the simplicity term.

Empirical Evaluation

We test SET-GEN on ten real-world problems from business, medicine, biology, and vision. These problems vary widely in the number and types of available input features and the number of examples in the DB. The datasets are summarized in Table 2. The Magellan-SAR data consists of features derived from small patches of radar images of the planet Venus, and the task is to determine if a patch contains a volcano (Burl *et al.* 1994). Promoter, Ribosome Binding, and Splice Junction are all problems of detecting different types of biologically significant sites on strands of DNA. Most of the DBs are publicly available through Murphy and Aha (1994). We chose these problems because of their diversity and interest to scientists in their respective fields. We did not preselect these datasets to favor SET-GEN in any way; these are all ten of the datasets we have tested it on to date.

Experimental Methodology

We evaluate SET-GEN and C4.5 by ten-fold cross validation on each problem's entire DB of examples and report average results over the ten folds, or *trials*. Accuracies are measured on the ten unseen test sets of the cross validation. (SET-GEN itself uses cross validation internally on the training examples to evaluate feature subsets, but this occurs inside the SET-GEN

Table 3: SET-GEN parameter settings used (defaults).

Parameter	Value
Population size	100
Feature subsets evaluated	5,000
Genome size	# input feats
Probability a child is produced by *Crossover, Mutate, Del. Feature*	1/3, 1/3, 1/3
Crossover rate, Mutation rate	0.10, 0.10

"black box" and has no bearing on the external cross validation used to assess algorithm performance.)

The amount of tree pruning is a crucial parameter because it greatly affects accuracy, tree size, and number of features referenced. For each trial, both SET-GEN and C4.5 chose the pruning level by doing an initial, internal ten-fold cross-validation of standard C4.5 using only the training examples. The pruning level was chosen from among ten equally spaced confidence levels: 5%, 15%, 25%, ..., 95% (Quinlan 1993), and the one yielding the most accurate trees on the validation sets was then used to train on the entire training set for the remainder of the trial. (Thus, choosing the pruning level is part of SET-GEN and C4.5 training. This process is identical for the two algorithms.)

We fixed all other SET-GEN and C4.5 parameters at their default values. SET-GEN's parameter defaults are summarized in Table 3, and were chosen before running it on any of the datasets used in the experiments. C4.5's parameters are described in Quinlan (1993).

Experimental Results

We compare the average test-set accuracy, tree size, and number of features referenced for the ten pruned trees of C4.5 versus SET-GEN using two-tailed, matched-pair t-tests to check for statistically significant differences at the 0.05 significance level. The unpruned trees give qualitatively similar results, but tend to be larger and thus of less interest from a comprehensibility standpoint, so we do not include those results.

Figure 2 shows the average percent error on the ten unseen test sets of the final pruned trees for each problem. The C4.5 and SET-GEN error rates only differ statistically significantly on the Ribosome Binding problem, where SET-GEN has a lower error rate. SET-GEN thus meets our goal of retaining the accuracy level of standard C4.5.

Figure 3 shows the average number of (internal plus leaf) nodes in the final pruned trees. The size differences between C4.5 and SET-GEN are statistically significant for all datasets except Lung Cancer,[2] and in all ten cases the SET-GEN trees are smaller, frequently by a factor of two or more. Hence, SET-GEN meets our goal of reducing tree size.

Figure 4 shows the average number of unique features referenced by the final pruned trees. The C4.5

---

[2]Lung Cancer has only 32 available examples (Table 2), so variance is quite high.

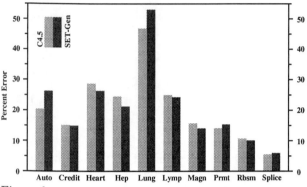

Figure 2: Average test-set error rates of final pruned trees.

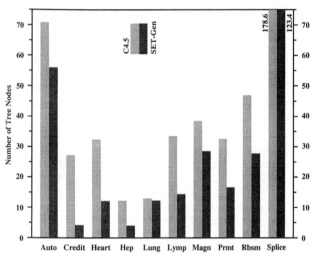

Figure 3: Average number of nodes in final pruned trees.

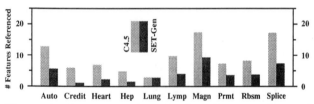

Figure 4: Average number of unique features referenced by final pruned trees.

versus SET-GEN differences are again statistically significant for all datasets except Lung Cancer, and in all ten cases the SET-GEN trees reference fewer features. SET-GEN's advantage over C4.5 here is almost always at least two to one. It thus meets our goal of reducing the number of features referenced.

In summary, these experiments show that SET-GEN simultaneously fulfills all three criteria we set for improving human comprehensibility without accuracy loss on a wide variety of real-world learning problems.

Related Work

The most closely related prior work is by Skalak (1994) and John, Kohavi, and Pfleger (1994). Skalak uses stochastic hill climbing to reduce nearest-neighbor model size, thus lowering computational cost, while re-

taining accuracy. However, his main thrust is selecting prototypical subsets of examples, rather than features. John *et al.* apply greedy feature selection to reduce C4.5 tree size without losing accuracy. In contrast to these systems, SET-GEN's genetic search is not greedy and thus can escape local optima. SET-GEN also focuses more strongly on human comprehensibility than John *et al.* by specifically seeking model simplicity.

Conclusions

Our goal is to induce more comprehensible decision trees to facilitate knowledge discovery, without reducing predictive accuracy. To achieve this, we introduced the SET-GEN feature-selection system and tested it on a wide variety of real-world problems, demonstrating empirically that it meets our goal. SET-GEN dramatically reduced the complexity of induced trees compared to C4.5, both in size and number of features referenced. Moreover, it did so without significantly reducing tree accuracy for any dataset, and in one case it even improved significantly on C4.5's accuracy. We hope SET-GEN will aid experts in better understanding these and other important problems. Our future work will compare SET-GEN to other feature selectors on the comprehensibility dimension and evaluate its current representational assumptions.

Acknowledgements

Thanks to U. Fayyad and P. Smyth for their aid in creating the Magellan-SAR dataset, R. Detrano (Heart Disease data), and M. Zwitter and M. Soklic (Lymphography data). This work was supported in part by a NASA GSRP fellowship held by KJC and ONR grant N00014-93-1-0998.

References

Burl, M.; Fayyad, U.; Perona, P.; Smyth, P.; and Burl, M. 1994. Automating the hunt for volcanoes on Venus. In *IEEE Comp Soc Conf Comp Vision & Pat Rec: Proc.* IEEE Computer Society Press.

Cherkauer, K., and Shavlik, J. 1996. Rapid quality estimation of neural network input representations. In *Advances in Neural Info Proc Sys 8*. MIT Press.

Forrest, S., and Mitchell, M. 1993. What makes a problem hard for a genetic algorithm? some anomalous results and their explanation. *Machine Learning* 13:285–319.

Goldberg, D. 1989. *Genetic Algorithms in Search, Optimization, and Machine Learning.* Reading, MA: Addison-Wesley.

John, G.; Kohavi, R.; and Pfleger, K. 1994. Irrelevant features and the subset selection problem. In *Mach Learn: Proc 11th Intl Conf*, 121–129. Morgan Kaufmann.

Murphy, P., and Aha, D. 1994. Univ. California Irvine repository of machine learning databases. At *http://www.ics.uci.edu/~mlearn/MLRepository.html*.

Quinlan, J. 1993. *C4.5: Programs for Machine Learning.* San Mateo, CA: Morgan Kaufmann.

Skalak, D. 1994. Prototype and feature selection by sampling and random mutation hill climbing algorithms. In *Mach Learn: Proc 11th Intl Conf*, 293–301. Morgan Kaufmann.

Efficient Specific-to-General Rule Induction

Pedro Domingos
Department of Information and Computer Science
University of California, Irvine
Irvine, California 92717, U.S.A.
pedrod@ics.uci.edu
http://www.ics.uci.edu/~pedrod

Abstract

RISE (Domingos 1995; in press) is a rule induction algorithm that proceeds by gradually generalizing rules, starting with one rule per example. This has several advantages compared to the more common strategy of gradually specializing initially null rules, and has been shown to lead to significant accuracy gains over algorithms like C4.5RULES and CN2 in a large number of application domains. However, RISE's running time (like that of other rule induction algorithms) is quadratic in the number of examples, making it unsuitable for processing very large databases. This paper introduces a method for reducing RISE's running time based on partitioning the training set, evaluating rules from one partition on examples from another, and combining the final results at classification time. Partitioning guarantees a learning time that is linear in the number of examples, even in the presence of numeric attributes and high noise. Windowing, a well-known speedup method, is also studied as applied to RISE. In low-noise conditions, both methods are successful in reducing running time whilst maintaining accuracy (partitioning sometimes improves it significantly). In noisy conditions, the performance of windowing deteriorates, while that of partitioning remains stable.

Introduction and Previous Work

Rule induction is one of the major technologies underlying data mining. Given a number of classified examples represented by vectors of symbolic and/or numeric attributes, algorithms like C4.5RULES (Quinlan 1993) and CN2 (Clark & Niblett 1989) produce sets of "if ... then ..." rules that allow us to predict the classes of new examples by performing tests on their attributes. However, the running time of these algorithms is typically quadratic or worse in the number of examples, making it difficult to apply them to the very large databases that are now common in many fields. In C4.5RULES, noise can lead to a cubic running time (Cohen 1995). While some faster variants of rule induction have been proposed (Fürnkranz & Widmer 1994; Cohen 1995), none achieve the ideal

goal of linear time. An alternative approach, and the one that is followed in this paper, is to employ some form of sampling, like windowing (Catlett 1991; Quinlan 1993), peepholing (Catlett 1991), or partitioning (Chan & Stolfo 1995). While often (though not always) reducing running time, sampling techniques can sometimes substantially reduce accuracy, and there may be a trade-off between the two. A reduced-accuracy rule set is preferable to a more-accurate one that is never reached due to lack of time; ideally, however, the loss in accuracy should be as small as possible, given the available time.

RISE (Domingos 1995; in press) is a rule induction algorithm that searches for rules in a specific-to-general direction, instead of the general-to-specific one used by most rule learners. This has several advantages, among them the ability to detect with confidence a higher level of detail in the databases, and a reduction of sensitivity to the fragmentation (Pagallo & Haussler 1990) and small disjuncts problems (Holte, Acker, & Porter 1989). In a study comparing RISE with several induction algorithms (including C4.5RULES and CN2) on 30 databases from the UCI repository (Murphy & Aha 1995), RISE was found to be more accurate than each of the other algorithms in about two-thirds of the databases, in each case with a confidence of 98% or better according to a Wilcoxon signed-ranks test (DeGroot 1986). RISE also had the highest average accuracy and highest rank.

RISE's running time, like that of previous algorithms, is quadratic in the number of examples, and thus the question arises of whether it is possible to reduce this time to linear without compromising accuracy. This paper proposes, describes and evaluates the application of windowing and partitioning to RISE; in both cases, this raises issues and opportunities that are not present in general-to-specific systems.

The next three sections of the paper describe pure RISE, RISE with windowing, and RISE with partitioning. This is followed by an empirical study comparing the three, and discussion of the results.

The RISE Algorithm

RISE searches for "good" rules in a specific-to-general fashion, starting with a rule set that is the training set of examples itself. RISE looks at each rule in turn, finds the nearest example of the same class that it does not already cover, and attempts to minimally generalize the rule to cover it, by dropping conditions (in the case of differing symbolic attributes) and/or expanding intervals (for numeric attributes). If the change's effect on the rule set's leave-one-out accuracy on the training set is positive or null, it is retained; otherwise it is discarded. This procedure is repeated until, for each rule, attempted generalization fails.

At performance time, classification of each test example is performed by finding the nearest rule to it, and assigning the example to the rule's class. The distance measure used is a combination of Euclidean distance for numeric attributes, and a simplified version of Stanfill and Waltz's value difference metric for symbolic attributes (Stanfill & Waltz 1986). When two or more rules are equally close to a test example, the rule that was most accurate on the training set wins. So as to not unduly favor more specific rules, the Laplace-corrected accuracy is used (Niblett 1987).

Windowing

Windowing is applied to RISE in a fashion broadly similar to C4.5's (Quinlan 1993), and proceeds as follows. Initially, only $2\sqrt{e}$ examples randomly extracted from the training set are used for learning. This sample is stratified (i.e., it contains approximately equal proportions of all classes); this makes it possible to still learn classes that have few representatives in the original training set. If the remaining training examples are correctly classified by the resulting rule set, this set is output. Otherwise, the misclassified examples are added to the initial example set, and this process repeats until it produces no improvement in accuracy on two successive expansions, or a maximum number of expansions is reached (5 by default).

Partitioning

In the partitioning approach (Chan & Stolfo 1995), the training data is divided into a number of disjoint subsets, and the learning algorithm is applied to each in turn. The results of each run are combined in some fashion, either at learning or at classification time. In RISE, partitioning is applied by pre-determining a maximum number of examples e_{max} to which the algorithm can be applied at once (100 by default). When this number is exceeded, the training set is randomly divided into $\lceil e/e_{max} \rceil$ approximately equal-sized partitions, where e is the total number of training examples. RISE is then run on each partition separately, but with an important difference relative to a direct application: the rules grown from the examples in partition p are not evaluated on the examples in that partition but on

the examples in partition $p+1$ (modulo the number of partitions). This should help combat overfitting, and the resulting improvement in accuracy may partly offset the degradation potentially caused by using smaller training sets. It is not possible in general-to-specific algorithms, where there is no connection between a specific rule and a specific example.

Because the number of partitions grows linearly with the number of training examples, and RISE's quadratic factor is confined to the examples within each partition and thus cannot exceed a given maximum (e.g., 100^2 if $e_{max} = 100$), the algorithm with partitioning is guaranteed a linear worst-case running time. However, depending on e_{max}, the multiplicative constants can become quite large.

Two methods of combining the results of induction on the individual partitions have been implemented and empirically compared. In the first, all the rule sets produced are simply merged into one, which is output by the learning phase. In the second, the rule sets are kept separate until the performance phase, and each partition classifies the test instance independently. A winning class is then assigned to the example by voting among the partitions, with each partition's weight being the Laplace accuracy of the rule that won within it (see section on RISE). The second method was found to achieve consistently better results, and was therefore adopted. More sophisticated combination methods based on Bayesian theory are currently being studied, but have so far yielded inferior results. Many other combination schemes are possible (e.g., (Chan & Stolfo 1995)).

Empirical Evaluation

The two speedup methods were tested on seven of the UCI repository's largest databases (Murphy & Aha 1995) (in increasing order of size: credit screening (Australian), Pima diabetes, annealing, chess endgames (kr-vs-kp), hypothyroid, splice junctions, and mushroom). Partitioning was tested with $e_{max} = 100$, 200, and 500. Ten runs were carried out for each database, in each run randomly dividing the data into two-thirds for training and one-third for testing. The averaged results are shown in Tables 1 (running times) and 2 (accuracies).

Both speedup methods are effective in reducing RISE's running time, generally without seriously affecting accuracy (chess and annealing with partitioning, and diabetes with windowing, are the exceptions). Windowing often has practically no effect on accuracy. Thus, overall this method appears to be more useful in RISE than in decision tree induction (Catlett 1991). This may be due to several factors, including RISE's lower sensitivity to the global proportions of different classes, and its higher resistance to the fragmentation problem, which enables it to correctly approximate class frontiers using fewer examples.

The effect of partitioning on accuracy is more vari-

Table 1: Experimental results: running times (in minutes and seconds).

Database	RISE	Windowing	Partitioning $e_{max}=100$	$e_{max}=200$	$e_{max}=500$
Credit	4:31	3:21	1:37	1:11	4:38
Pima diabetes	4:15	6:20	1:32	1:13	2:47
Annealing	4:26	2:44	1:43	2:33	2:17
Chess	33:26	10:40	3:10	6:04	12:06
Hypothyroid	105:23	14:46	5:08	10:42	24:06
Splice junctions	110:39	51:28	5:22	12:45	25:48
Mushroom	70:07	10:07	5:55	7:26	14:32

Table 2: Experimental results: accuracies and standard deviations.

Database	RISE	Windowing	Partitioning $e_{max}=100$	$e_{max}=200$	$e_{max}=500$
Credit	82.6±1.5	83.6±1.5	86.4±1.9	86.4±1.5	82.6±1.6
Pima diabetes	71.6±2.5	70.6±2.7	74.4±2.1	73.6±3.3	72.8±2.6
Annealing	97.5±0.9	98.0±1.0	93.6±1.6	96.1±1.6	96.5±1.1
Chess	98.4±0.6	98.4±0.7	94.5±0.5	95.2±0.6	96.6±0.9
Hypothyroid	97.9±0.2	97.5±0.5	97.0±0.3	97.5±0.3	97.9±0.4
Splice junctions	92.5±0.8	92.8±0.7	95.0±0.7	94.6±0.7	94.7±0.6
Mushroom	100.0±0.0	100.0±0.0	98.9±0.1	99.5±0.3	99.8±0.1

able than that of windowing. In some domains a trade-off between partition size and accuracy is observed; however, only in the chess domain does increasing e_{max} from 200 to 500 substantially increase accuracy. More interestingly, in the credit, diabetes and splice junctions domains the opposite trend is observed (i.e., partitioning increases accuracy, and smaller partitions more so than larger ones); this may be attributed to the reduction in overfitting derived from inducing and testing rules on different partitions, to the increase in accuracy that can result from combining multiple models (Wolpert 1992; Breiman in press), and possibly to other factors. In practice, the best partition size should be determined by experimentation on the specific database RISE is being applied to, starting with smaller (and therefore faster) values.

To test the algorithms on a larger problem, and obtain a clearer view of the growth rate of their running times, experiments were conducted on NASA's space shuttle database. This database contains 43500 training examples from one shuttle flight, and 14500 test examples from a different flight. Each example is described by nine numeric attributes obtained from sensor readings, and there are seven possible classes, corresponding to states of the shuttle's radiators (Catlett 1991). The goal is to predict these states with very high accuracy (99–99.9%), using rules that can be taught to a human operator.

The learning time curves obtained for RISE, RISE with windowing and RISE with partitioning (using

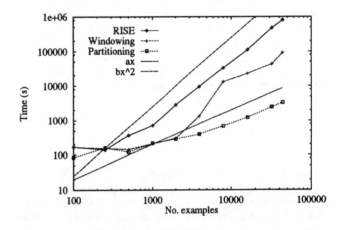

Figure 1: Learning times for the shuttle database.

$e_{max}=100$) are shown in Figure 1 using a log-log scale. Approximate asymptotes are also shown. Windowing reduces running time, but its growth appears to remain roughly quadratic; partitioning reduces it to linear, as expected. The accuracy curves (not shown) are very similar for all systems, converging rapidly to very high values (99% by $e=1000$, etc.), with partitioning lagging slightly behind the other two.

The shuttle data is known to be relatively noise-free. To investigate the effect of noise, the three algorithms (pure RISE, windowing and partitioning) were also applied after corrupting the training data with

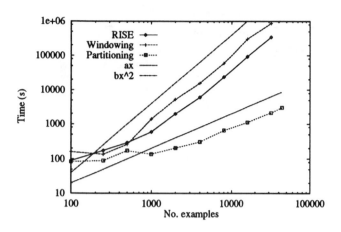

Figure 2: Learning times for the shuttle database with 20% noise.

20% class noise (i.e., each class had a 20% probability of being changed to a random class, including itself). The learning time curves obtained are shown in Figure 2. The time performance of windowing degrades markedly, even with the pre-imposed limit on the number of window expansions, becoming a liability for all $e > 500$. In contrast, partitioning remains almost entirely unaffected. Noise reduces the accuracy of pure RISE and windowing by 3 – 8%, with the smaller differences occurring for larger training set sizes. (Recall that noise was added only to the training set.) The accuracy of partitioning is barely affected, making it consistently more accurate than pure RISE at this noise level. Thus partitioning appears to be the speedup method of choice for noisy databases.

Conclusions and Future Work

This paper studied the application to the RISE rule induction system of two speedup methods, windowing and partitioning. With noise-free data, both were found to effectively reduce running time while maintaining accuracy, but only partitioning reduced the growth rate to linear; in noisy conditions, the use of windowing has a negative effect, while partitioning remains unaffected.

Directions for future research include testing and developing more sophisticated methods of combining the outputs of the individual partitions (e.g., (Chan & Stolfo 1995)), automating the selection of partition size, testing windowing and partitioning on a larger variety of larger databases, and introducing further speedup techniques to RISE.

Acknowledgments

This work was partly supported by a JNICT/PRAXIS XXI scholarship.

References

Breiman, L. Bagging predictors. *Machine Learning*. In press.

Catlett, J. 1991. *Megainduction: Machine Learning on Very Large Databases*. Ph.D. Dissertation, Basser Department of Computer Science, University of Sydney, Sydney, Australia.

Chan, P. K., and Stolfo, S. J. 1995. Learning arbiter and combiner trees from partitioned data for scaling machine learning. In *Proceedings of the First International Conference on Knowledge Discovery and Data Mining*, 39–44. Montréal, Canada: AAAI Press.

Clark, P., and Niblett, T. 1989. The CN2 induction algorithm. *Machine Learning* 3:261–283.

Cohen, W. W. 1995. Fast effective rule induction. In *Proceedings of the Twelfth International Conference on Machine Learning*, 115–123. Tahoe City, CA: Morgan Kaufmann.

DeGroot, M. H. 1986. *Probability and Statistics*. Reading, MA: Addison-Wesley, 2nd edition.

Domingos, P. 1995. Rule induction and instance-based learning: A unified approach. In *Proceedings of the Fourteenth International Joint Conference on Artificial Intelligence*, 1226–1232. Montréal, Canada: Morgan Kaufmann.

Domingos, P. Unifying instance-based and rule-based induction. *Machine Learning*. In press.

Fürnkranz, J., and Widmer, G. 1994. Incremental reduced error pruning. In *Proceedings of the Eleventh International Conference on Machine Learning*, 70–77. New Brunswick, NJ: Morgan Kaufmann.

Holte, R. C.; Acker, L. E.; and Porter, B. W. 1989. Concept learning and the problem of small disjuncts. In *Proceedings of the Eleventh International Joint Conference on Artificial Intelligence*, 813–818. Detroit, MI: Morgan Kaufmann.

Murphy, P. M., and Aha, D. W. 1995. UCI repository of machine learning databases. Machine-readable data repository, Department of Information and Computer Science, University of California at Irvine, Irvine, CA.

Niblett, T. 1987. Constructing decision trees in noisy domains. In *Proceedings of the Second European Working Session on Learning*, 67–78. Bled, Yugoslavia: Sigma.

Pagallo, G., and Haussler, D. 1990. Boolean feature discovery in empirical learning. *Machine Learning* 3:71–99.

Quinlan, J. R. 1993. *C4.5: Programs for Machine Learning*. San Mateo, CA: Morgan Kaufmann.

Stanfill, C., and Waltz, D. 1986. Toward memory-based reasoning. *Communications of the ACM* 29:1213–1228.

Wolpert, D. 1992. Stacked generalization. *Neural Networks* 5:241–259.

Data Mining and Tree-based Optimization

Robert Grossman,* Haim Bodek & Dave Northcutt   Vince Poor

Magnify, Inc.
815 Garfield Street
Oak Park, IL 60304
{rlg, haim, dmn}@magnify.com

Dept. of Electrical Eng.
Princeton University
Princeton, NJ 08540
poor@princeton.edu

Abstract

Consider a large collection of objects, each of which has a large number of attributes of several different sorts. We assume that there are data attributes representing data, attributes which are to be statistically estimated or predicted from these, and attributes which can be controlled or set. A motivating example is to assign a credit score to a credit card prospect indicating the likelihood that the prospect will make credit card payments and then to set a credit limit for each prospect in such a way as to maximize the over-all expected revenue from the entire collection of prospects. In the terminology above, the credit score is called a predictive attribute and the credit limit a control attribute. The methodology we describe in the paper uses data mining to provide more accurate estimates of the predictive attributes and to provide more optimal settings of the control attributes. We briefly describe how to parallelize these computations. We also briefly comment on some of data management issues which arise for these types of problems in practice. We propose using object warehouses to provide low overhead, high performance access to large collections of objects as an underlying foundation for our data mining algorithms.

Introduction

In this paper, we consider a class of data mining problems that are broadly related to optimization. The goal is to maximize an objective function defined on a large collection of objects by setting certain control attributes of each object. In the problems of interest there is additional structure present: the control attributes are dependent upon other attributes, which are statistical in nature. The problem is difficult due to the large amount of data, the large number of attributes, and the complexity of the data. We use data mining techniques to estimate which attributes influ-

---

*Robert Grossman is also a faculty member in the Department of Mathematics, Statistics, and Computer Science at the University of Illinois at Chicago.

ence the control attributes and to estimate these (predictive) attributes from the underlying data attributes of the objects.

A motivating example is to assign a credit score to a credit card prospect indicating the likelihood that the prospect will make credit card payments and then to set a credit limit for each prospect in such a way as to maximize the over-all expected revenue from the entire collection of prospects. Additional details and examples are given in Section 3.

To summarize: we are given a large collection of objects, each of which has a large number of attributes of several sorts. Certain *data* attributes of the objects are given. From these we compute *summary* attributes and estimate *predictive* attributes. The goal is to set the *control* attributes to optimize a given objective function. We use tree-based techniques from data mining to estimate the predictive attributes and to determine which statistical attributes are important for setting the control attributes.

Our over all objective is to derive data mining algorithms that are scalable and data-driven. By scalable we mean algorithms that scale as the number of objects and the number of attributes increases. We are also interested in algorithms which scale as the numerical complexity and data selectivity of a data mining query varies. By data-driven we mean algorithms that do not require sampling, but rather examine all of the data.

To obtain scalable, data driven algorithms, we introduce and exploit three main ideas.

Tree-based Optimization. As the amount of data grows, the number of patterns combinatorially explodes. By focusing on patterns related to the objective function associated with our optimization, we reduce the number of patterns we must examine. We use tree-based techniques as the basis for our optimization algorithms. In particular, one can view the algorithm we use at each leaf of the optimization tree as exploiting a different model for a particular subset of the data: we can think of this as tree-based "micro-modeling".

Parallel Trees. We exploit techniques from parallel and high performance computing to reduce the running time of our algorithms. In particular, we partition the data, separately compute the predictive attributes using tree-based techniques for each partition, and then combine the resulting information. We also compute trees in parallel by passing attribute information at each level of the tree between nodes in a parallel computing environment.

Object Warehouses. Data driven data mining requires that all of the data be examined. In order to manage very large data sets, we use specialized data management techniques which are optimized to provide low overhead, high performance access to complex data, in contrast to traditional transaction-oriented data management systems. More specifically, our data mining algorithms view the data as a distributed collection of objects, which we manage using an object warehouse specially designed for data mining queries.

This is an extended abstract. A full version of this paper will appear elsewhere.

Background and Related Work

There has been increasing interest recently in developing scalable and parallel data mining algorithms. Agrawal et al. (Agrawal et al. 1995) discuss scalable algorithms for discovering associations. Holsheimer et al. (Holsheimer et al. 1996) discuss parallel algorithms for a class of problems which require uncovering relatively few patterns which can cover a database. Fayyad et al. (Fayyad et al. 1996) discuss extracting rules independently from partitioned data using decision trees and then aggregating the results.

Fundamentally, our approach to this class of data mining problems is an outgrowth of the idea of inductive learning (Quinlin 1986) and classification and regression trees (CART) (Breiman 1984). CART is a widely accepted tree-based methodology for performing classification and regression based on adaptation to a training set consisting of attributes vectors paired with correct classifications or function values. There are two basic and significant modifications of CART that are needed in order to apply this notion here. These are: 1) the development of *optimization* trees; and and 2) the parallelization of tree-based techniques, such as CART.

Some Examples

In this section, we describe three motivating problems involving tree-based optimization. These descriptions of the problems are from (Grossman 1996).

Problem A. Account solicitation and management. In this problem, we are a given a large collection of customers or potential customers, ranging from 10^5 to 10^8. Assume that each customer or prospect has several hundred to a thousand attributes describing them.

To be specific, assume that there are one million credit card customers and the goal is to set their credit limit, interest rate and fee structure on the credit card twice a year in order to maximize the life time profit of the customer.

Notice first that there is a natural objective function defined by total life time profit of the collection. Also, notice that there are several types of attributes: 1) data attributes, such as the number, type and amount of purchases over some number of months; 2) summary attributes, which precompute such variables as the average amount of credit used per month, 3) predictive attributes, such as the expected life time revenue of the customer; and 4) control attributes, such as the credit limit, interest rate, and fee of the credit card. The goal is first to use the data attributes to estimate the predictive attributes, and second to use the predictive attributes to set the control attributes in order to optimize the objective function. The role of the precomputed summary attributes is to speed up the computation.

Data mining enters in the following two related manners. Different groups of customers may require different subsets of data attributes in order to best estimate the predictive attributes. The problem is difficult because of the size of the data set and the number of attributes. With three hundred attributes and a million customers it makes sense to break up the collection of customers into sub-collections specified by attribute sequences with the property that predictive attributes of customers belonging to the same sub-collections are estimated from the same collection of attributes. In other words, *attribute discovery* is an important component in estimating predictive attributes.

In addition, different groups of customers may require different models to set the control attributes. A common approach is to work with a parameterized family of models. In other words, *parameter identification and model discovery* is also an important component in setting the control attributes.

Problem B. Anomaly detection. In this problem, we have two collections: 1) a real time stream of transactions producing a transaction collection and 2) a collection of customers. All transactions are associated with a customer, but a small percentage, say 1% are fraudulent in the sense they were generated by a third party different than the customer.

As in the first example, there is an objective function and several types of attributes. In this case, the objective function is usually taken to be a weighted average of the number of false positives and false negatives produced by the algorithm. Data attributes include the merchant, customer, and amount associated with the transaction. Summary attributes include the average dollar amount of a transaction during the past three months. Predictive attributes include the probability that a given customer will purchase a high ticket item from a certain merchant category during the next six months. Control attributes include the score assigned to the transaction indicating the probability of fraud or related actions, such as increased monitoring of the customer or merchant, denying the transaction, or calling the merchant.

Attribute discovery is also important in this problem. The merchant category may be the most important predictor for some customers; for others, the amount of the transaction; for still others, the frequency. Model discovery is also important, low usage and high usage customers may be best served by different models.

Essentially the same problem arises when using attribute-base information to look for anomalous or unusual documents within a large collection of documents.

Problem C. Target Assessment. This is a variant of Problem B. We assume that we have tens to hundreds of thousands of targets and a real time stream of information about the targets. The problem is difficult because the information stream is so large that the information must be classified automatically and the target list so large that only a few of the targets at any time may be examined by a human.

The data attributes include the information itself and metadata such as its source, when it was collected, etc. The information is automatically scored in order to attach it to the relevant target and to measure its significance. Both the relevance and significance score are examples of predictive attributes. Finally control attributes include the action taken, which may range from throwing the information away, to flagging the information and raising the threat posed by the target.

Problem Description

This section gives a general description of the problem. We assume that at the logical level, that there is a large collection of objects and that each object has a variety of attributes. The attributes may be primitive data types (such as integers, floats, or character strings) object valued, or collection valued. As illustrated in the examples above, we assume that the objects have several types of attributes: data attributes, summary attributes, predictive attributes, and control attributes. The data attributes constitute the underlying data of the problem. Summary attributes are precomputed summaries of the data attributes. The predictive attributes are random variables that are estimated from the data attributes, while the control attributes are chosen to optimize the objective function.

In more detail, we are given a very large collection of objects x_1, ..., x_N, where each object x_j has data attributes $x_j[1]$, ..., $x_j[n]$. From the data attributes of an object x_j, we precompute summary attribute(s) $\eta_j = e(x_j)$ and estimate the predictive attribute(s) $\zeta_j = f(x_j, \eta_j)$. Finally, we define control attributes $r_j = g(x_j, \eta_j, \zeta_j)$. Here η_j, ζ_j and r_j may all be vector valued. Our goal is to optimize the objective function

$$h = \sum_j \text{Max}_{r_j} h(x_j, \eta_j, \zeta_j, r_j),$$

by suitably choosing the control attributes r_j.

A Tree-based Optimization Algorithm

In this section, we briefly sketch an algorithm we have developed and implemented to solve problems like the ones described above. There is a precomputation, which in part involves training data:

1. First, we compute the predictive attributes ζ_j using regression trees (Breiman 1984) on training data $\mathcal{L}$. We write $\zeta_j = f(x_j, \eta_j)$ and let T_f denote the corresponding tree. Note that there will be several trees in case ζ_j is vector-valued.

2. Second, we partition the data using a tree. There are several variants: for simplicity we describe only the simplest. We are given an objective function $h(x_j, \eta_j, z_j, r_j)$ and partition the data using a regression tree approximation to h computed on the training data $\mathcal{L}$. Here z_j are the instances of the random variable ζ_j arising in the training data. Denote this tree by T_h. It is important to note that when computing the regression tree, *we do not partition using the control attributes.*

Processing a collection (or stream) of objects using the algorithm requires three steps:

1. In the first step, given an object x_j, we use the tree(s) T_f to compute the predictive attributes ζ_j.

2. In the second step, we apply the tree T_h to the object x_j so that x_j is associated with one of the leaves of T_h.

3. In the third step, we compute the control attributes r_j of x_j using the optimization algorithm appropriate for that leaf. The control attributes r_j are defined to optimize the objective function $h(x_j, \eta_j, \zeta_j, r_j)$. That is

$$h(x_j, \eta_j, \zeta_j, r_j) = \text{Max}_r h(x_j, \eta_j, \zeta_j, r).$$

Loosely speaking, we are using different models and control strategies for each leaf of the tree T_h. Think of this as tree-based micro-modeling. An important advantage is that working with many micro-models that are automatically computed results in a system that is more maintainable that one which uses one or a few models that are derived by a statistician. Traditional approaches typically use a relatively small number of models and thus incur large costs when these models are changed. In contrast, our approach automatically results in a relatively large number of different models, each applying to a relatively small number of cases. This potentially results in more accurate models and decreases the cost when a few models are changed or updated.

Implementation

Numeric and statistically intensive queries and other complex queries are extremely costly when run against data in databases, especially relational databases in which the data is spread over several tables. The high costs associated with these types of queries basically arises from the fact that traditional databases are optimized for relatively simple data, simple queries, and frequent updates. On the other hand, complex queries on complex data perform best using specialized data management systems that are 1) optimized for frequent reads, occasional appends, and infrequent updates and 2) joins and other operations on the data are precomputed. These types of data management systems are sometimes called data warehouses.

We have developed a data warehouse for large collections of objects specifically designed for parallel and distributed data mining. We are currently testing it on 100 gigabyte size data sets. The object warehouse was developed by Magnify, Inc. and is called PATTERN:Store. An earlier version of this system is described in (Grossman et al. 1995).

Using PATTERN:Store, we have experimented with various strategies for growing trees in parallel. This work was undertaken by Magnify, Inc. and is implemented in a system called PATTERN:Predict.

Conclusion

In this paper, we have considered a class of problems with the following structure: We are given data attributes. We precompute summary attributes from these. In the examples of interest to us there are hundreds to a thousand data and summary attributes. From the data and summary attributes we use tree-based techniques to estimate statistical or predictive attributes. Given an objective function, we also use tree-based techniques to discover patterns that are directly relevant to setting the control attributes to maximize a given objective function. This structure arises in a variety of problems ranging from computing scores for credit card prospects to assessing threats in data fusion problems.

By focusing on problems we this type of structure, we can narrow our search to a restricted class of patterns and in this fashion obtain algorithms which can scale. We are interested in algorithms which are data driven in the sense that they examine all of the data. This requires specialized data management techniques. We have developed object warehouses specialized for data mining and used these to develop and test the tree-based optimization algorithms discussed here.

Although this work is preliminary, we feel we have made a contribution by focusing on an important class of problems and by presenting a new algorithm to attack them.

Acknowledgments

This work was supported in part by the Massive Digital Data Systems (MDDS) Program, sponsored by the Advanced Research Development Committee of the Community Management Staff.

References

R. Agrawal, H. Mannila, R. Srikant, H. Toivonen, and A. I. Verkamo, 1996. Fast Discovery of Association Rules. In Advances in Knowledge Discovery and Data Mining, edited U. M Fayyad, G. Piatetsky-Shapiro, P. Smyth, and R. Uthurusamy, 307–328. Menlo Park, California: AAAI Press/MIT Press.

L. Breiman, J. H. Friedman, R. A. Olshen, and C. J. Stone, 1984. *Classification and Regression Trees.* Belmont, California: Wadsworth.

U. M. Fayyad, G. Piatetsky-Shapiro, and P. Smyth, 1996. From Data Mining to Knowledge Discovery: An Overview. In Advances in Knowledge Discovery and Data Mining, edited U. M Fayyad, G. Piatetsky-Shapiro, P. Smyth, and R. Uthurusamy, 1–34. Menlo Park, California: AAAI Press/MIT Press.

U. M. Fayyad, S. G. Djorgovksi and N. Weir, 1996. Automating the Analysis and Cataloging of Sky Surveyes. In Advances in Knowledge Discovery and Data Mining, edited U. M Fayyad, G. Piatetsky-Shapiro, P. Smyth, and R. Uthurusamy, 471–493. Menlo Park, California: AAAI Press/MIT Press.

R. L. Grossman, 1996. Early Experience with a System for Mining, Estimating, and Optimizing Large Collections of Objects Managed Using an Object Warehouse. Proceedings of the Workshop on Research Issues on Data Mining and Knowledge Discovery. Forthcoming.

R. L. Grossman, H. Hulen, X. Qin, T. Tyler, W. Xu, 1995. An Architecture for a Scalable, High Performance Digital Library. In Proceedings of the 14th IEEE Computer Society Mass Storage Systems Symposium, S. Coleman, editor. Los Alamites, California: IEEE Press.

R. L. Grossman and H. V. Poor, 1996. Optimization Driven Data Mining and Credit Scoring. In Proceedings of the IEEE/IAFE 1996 Conference on Computational Intelligence for Financial Engineering (CIFEr). Los Alamites, California: IEEE Press.

M. Holsheimer, M. L. Kersten, and A. P. J. M. Siebes, 1996. Data Surveyor: Searching the Nuggets in Parallel. In Advances in Knowledge Discovery and Data Mining, edited U. M Fayyad, G. Piatetsky-Shapiro, P. Smyth, and R. Uthurusamy, 447–467. Menlo Park, California: AAAI Press/MIT Press.

J. R. Quinlan, 1986. The Induction of Decision Trees. *Machine Learning* 1: 81–106.

Induction of Condensed Determinations

Pat Langley*(LANGLEY@CS.STANFORD.EDU)
Robotics Laboratory, Computer Science Dept.
Stanford University, Stanford, CA 94305

Abstract

In this paper we suggest *determinations* as a representation of knowledge that should be easy to understand. We briefly review determinations, which can be displayed in a tabular format, and their use in prediction, which involves a simple matching process. We describe CONDET, an algorithm that uses feature selection to construct determinations from training data, augmented by a condensation process that collapses rows to produce simpler structures. We report experiments that show condensation reduces complexity with no loss of accuracy, then discuss CONDET's relation to other work and outline directions for future studies.

Introduction

Understandability is a major concern in knowledge discovery and data mining. Although it is important to discover knowledge that is accurate, in many domains it is also essential that users find that knowledge easy to interpret. Most researchers assume that logical rules and decision trees are more understandable than other formalisms, such as neural networks or stored cases. Although the evidence supporting this belief is mainly anecdotal, we will not argue with it here.

Rather, we will assume its validity and focus on a special class of logical rules, known as *determinations*, that we maintain are particularly understandable. This representation differs from other rule frameworks in that all rules in the knowledge base refer to the same attributes. As a result, they can be graphically displayed as a 'truth table', with one column for each attribute (including the class) and one row for each combination of attribute values. We anticipate that users will like this regular structure, especially given its similarity to widely used spreadsheet formats.

In the following sections, we review the representation of determinations and their use in classification, followed by an algorithm for inducing these structures based on recent work in feature selection. Next we present a technique for condensing induced determinations, aimed at further improving their understandabil-

*Also affiliated with the Institute for the Study of Learning and Expertise, 2164 Staunton Court, Palo Alto, CA 94306.

ity. After this, we present experimental studies of these techniques that evaluate the accuracy and complexity of the learned structures. We close with comments on related work and directions for future research.

The Nature of Determinations

Davies and Russell (1987) introduced determinations as a form of background knowledge for use in analogical reasoning, but the idea has more general applications. Briefly, a determination expresses some functional dependency between a set of predictor attributes P and a set of predicted attributes Q, so that, given P, one can infer Q. Of course, such knowledge is useful only if one has information about particular combinations of those attributes' values. Davies and Russell proposed obtaining this information through analogy with stored cases. However, one can also envision a knowledge base containing a separate rule for each combination of predictor values, and we will assume such structures here.

Such determinations are interesting from the perspective of understandability because they can be displayed in a tabular format. Table 1 shows a determination for a simple artificial domain, originally used by Quinlan (1993) to illustrate decision trees, that involves deciding whether to pursue an outdoor activity. This domain includes four predictor attributes – OUTLOOK, HUMIDITY, WINDY, and TEMPERATURE – and one predicted attribute CLASS, which states whether to engage in the activity. This determination includes columns for only three of the predictor variables, because TEMPERATURE does not help to predict CLASS.

One can use a determination for prediction or inference in the same way as any other formalism that involves logical rules. For a given instance, one finds the row (i.e., rule) that specifies a combination of predictor values that match the instance, then infers the value specified for the predicted attribute(s). For now, we will assume that all attributes in a determination are discrete, and that any continuous variables have been transformed into discrete ones either by the knowledge base's developer or through some automatic process.

Although Davies and Russell focused on logical determinations that always held, one can adapt them to

Table 1: A simple determination for outdoor activities.

Outlook	Humidity	Windy	Class
Sunny	High	True	No
Sunny	High	False	No
Sunny	Normal	True	Yes
Sunny	Normal	False	Yes
Overcast	High	True	Yes
Overcast	High	False	Yes
Overcast	Normal	True	Yes
Overcast	Normal	False	Yes
Rain	High	True	No
Rain	High	False	Yes
Rain	Normal	True	No
Rain	Normal	False	Yes

Table 2: A condensed determination based on Table 1.

Outlook	Humidity	Windy	Class
Sunny	High	*	No
Sunny	Normal	*	Yes
Overcast	*	*	Yes
Rain	*	True	No
Rain	*	False	Yes

situations in which each row's outcome is probabilistic. In such domains, the natural strategy is to predict the class most frequently associated with the matched row. Note that learned determinations may lack rows for certain combinations of attribute values if those combinations never occur in the training data. For such situations, Langley and Sage (1994) recommended basing predictions on the nearest matches, while Kohavi (1995) suggested predicting a default value associated with the entire table. We will incorporate the latter technique into the system we describe here.

The ability to display determinations in a tabular format has led Kohavi (1995) to refer to them as *decision tables*. Determinations are also equivalent to what Langley and Sage (1994) have called *oblivious decision trees*, in which each level of the tree involves tests on the same attribute. We will continue to use the term *determinations* here, primarily because it should be familiar to more readers.

Greedy Induction of Determinations

Given a set of predictive attributes, inducing a probabilistic determination from supervised training data is straightforward. For each observed combination of predictive values, one computes a histogram for the class values, then selects the most frequent class for entry in that row of the table. To determine default values, one also computes histograms for the entire training set, then selects the most frequent overall value.

However, the above procedure assumes that the predictive and predicted attributes have been specified. Many data-mining tasks involve supervised learning, so that one knows which attribute must be predicted, but determining the predictive attributes is another matter. Fortunately, some recent work on feature selection has dealt with determinations or closely related representations of knowledge.

For example, Schlimmer (1993) describes a systematic search algorithm that finds all minimal sets of features that predict the training data, though his method

was not well suited for noisy data. Other work has also dealt with this task under different guises. Thus, Langley and Sage (1994) report a greedy algorithm that induces oblivious decision trees, Aha and Bankert (1994) take a similar approach to finding abstract cases for nearest-neighbor classification, and Kohavi (1995) describes a related scheme for creating decision tables.

We have developed a system for learning determinations that operates along similar lines, which we will call ConDet. As Langley and Sage (1994) note, methods for feature selection must take a stance on four basic issues. First, they must specify the state from which search begins; ConDet starts with no features, since we believe that a bias toward simplicity will produce more understandable structures. Second, they require some scheme for organizing search; our system takes a greedy approach, both for purposes of efficiency and to reduce chances of overfitting. Third, they must have some means of evaluating alternative feature sets; ConDet takes a 'wrapper' approach to evaluation (John, Kohavi, & Pfleger, 1994), which invokes the histogram method described above for each candidate feature set considered, combined with an efficient version of leave-one-out to estimate its accuracy. Finally, they must indicate some halting criterion, and our system stops adding features when none of the candidates leads to an increase in the estimated accuracy.

Clearly, our approach to feature selection is far from new, in that ConDet draws heavily on earlier work. We review it here for purposes of completeness rather than novelty. This paper's main goal is to explore the advantages of learning determinations from the viewpoint of finding *understandable* knowledge structures. Again, we posit that determinations, especially when presented in tabular form, should fare better on this dimension than decision trees or arbitrary rule sets. However, this does not mean that their understandability cannot be improved further, as we will find shortly.

Condensing Induced Determinations

As we have seen, ConDet uses a feature-selection method, combined with a simple counting scheme, to induce a determination from data. This formalism has the same representational power as decision trees and arbitrary rule sets, but it may require more rules to encode the same knowledge, and this complexity may

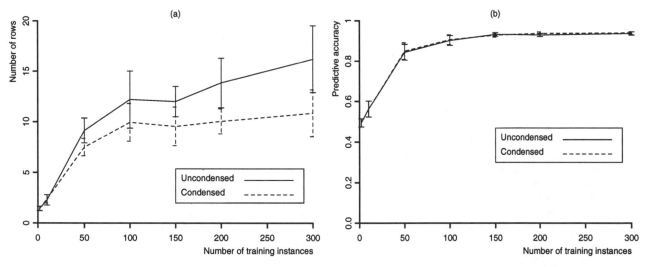

Figure 1: Learning curves for for inducing determinations on chess endgames, with and without its condensation mechanism, measuring (a) complexity of the learned determinations and (b) accuracy on separate test sets.

decrease the inherent comprehensibility. For example, Quinlan's (1986) decision-tree encoding of the twelve-row determination in Table 1 involves only five terminal nodes, which is certainly simpler in some respects.

Fortunately, there exists a compromise that retains the tabular format but allows simpler structures. These *condensed* determinations still display knowledge in terms of rows and columns, but they allow wildcard symbols to indicate that some rows have been collapsed. For example, Table 2 shows a condensed determination that makes the same predictions as the original table. The new structure includes a wildcard '∗' for selected values of HUMIDITY and WINDY, which reduces the total number of rows from twelve to five.

CONDET incorporates a mechanism to condense determinations in this manner. The basic operator involves combining rules (rows) that differ on only one predictive attribute into a rule in which that attribute's values have been replaced with a wildcard. For tractability's sake, we restrict this operation in certain ways. Rather than focusing on pairs of rules, CON-DET combines *all* rules that share a set of attribute values. Also, when the system combines one set of rules that share values, it tries to condense all other sets that have common values on those attributes.

Another constraint aims to maintain the predictive accuracy of the original determination. Here, CONDET combines only sets of rules that predict the same class. When all possible rows of the determination are represented in the training data, this scheme does not alter the deductive closure of the knowledge base. However, the closure can change when some rows are missing, since the situation they describe may now be covered by the condensed rule, which has precedence over the majority class. For this reason, CONDET evaluates each candidate condensation against the training set, retaining it only if it does not hurt the overall accuracy.

In terms of search organization, CONDET takes a greedy approach to condensing its determinations, as it does in constructing them. The system tentatively generates a new table that results from condensing along each attribute, in each case combining all rules that differ on that attribute but have the same class. It selects the condensed table with the highest training set accuracy and continues this process, halting when accuracy decreases. The resulting table may not be condensed in the optimal way, but it provides a reasonable compromise given limited computational resources.

Experiments with Condensation

Our aim in developing CONDET was to improve the comprehensibility of learned determinations without decreasing their accuracy. We posit that determinations with fewer rows will be easier to understand than ones with more rows; we have no hard evidence for this claim, but it seems intuitively plausible and we will assume it here. Thus, to evaluate our system's behavior, we needed two dependent measures – the accuracy of the induced determinations and the complexity (specifically, the number of rows) of this knowledge structure.

We tested CONDET on four domains from the UCI repository, focusing on data sets with only nominal attributes. For each domain, we generated 20 random training sets and 20 associated test sets. We ran CON-DET on all 20 training sets, measuring accuracy on the test sets and complexity of the learned determination, then computed average scores. Because we were interested in the effects of condensation, we collected the same statistics when this process was absent.

Moreover, we hypothesized that differences between the condensed and uncondensed determinations would increase with greater numbers of training cases, because the data would tend to encourage the inclusion of more attributes and thus increase the number of uncompressed rows. For this reason, we collected learning curves, which measure system behavior as one increases the number of training cases. We expected that their accuracies would remain the same throughout the course of learning, while their complexities would diverge for larger numbers of training instances.

Figure 1 shows the comparative learning curves for the domain of chess endgames, which involves two classes and 36 attributes. The results were consistent with our predictions; Figure 1 (a) indicates that, later in the learning curve, condensation consistently leads to simpler determinations, whereas Figure 1 (b) reveals that this process does not reduce accuracy. We observed similar results (which we do not have room to report here) on domains involving mushroom classification and Congressional voting records, with condensation not affecting accuracy but simplifying the determinations. Here the size reduction was smaller, since feature selection left only a few tabular rows to condense. We also tested our algorithm on DNA promoters, a domain that typically gives trouble to induction methods that create axis-parallel splits. Yet the predicted effect occurred even here; condensation led to simpler determinations without reducing accuracy.

Recall that our experiments were not designed to show that CONDET is a particularly effective induction algorithm. Other implementations of the same basic approach may produce simpler determinations and higher accuracies, though the accuracies for CONDET and C4.5 were nearly identical on the domains used in our studies. Rather, our aim was to illustrate that determinations are a viable representation for use in knowledge discovery, that feature selection combined with a simple counting procedure can produce accurate determinations for some natural domains, and that a straightforward condensation process can simplify (and make more understandable) these knowledge structures with no loss in accuracy.

Related and Future Work

The approach to induction described in this paper has clear relations to earlier research. We have noted its strong debt to work on feature selection; nor are we the first to study methods for learning determinations from data, as Schlimmer (1993), Langley and Sage (1994), and Kohavi (1995) have worked on very similar tasks and, in some cases, very similar methods.

At first glance, the condensation process appears more novel, but it holds features in common with compression techniques intended to reduce matching costs and with postpruning methods designed to avoid overfitting. An even stronger connection exists with work in the rough sets community, which often uses tabular representations of knowledge. Shan, Ziarko, Hamilton, and Cercone (1995) report an operation called *value reduction* that reduces the rows in a table by replacing values with wildcards. Their algorithm differs from the one used in CONDET, but the spirit is much the same.

We have made no claims that our particular approaches to the induction and simplification of determinations are the best possible. Rather, this paper's contribution has been to highlight determinations as a promising representation of discovered knowledge, to note that algorithms exist for inducing such descriptions, and to show there are methods that can increase their understandability with no loss in accuracy.

We believe that the most important direction for future work on this topic lies not in developing more refined algorithms, but in testing our predictions about the ease of understanding condensed determinations relative to other formalisms. This will require experiments with human subjects, including measures of their ability to understand knowledge bases, before we can draw firm conclusions about alternative notations.

Acknowledgements

Thanks to S. Sage, R. Kohavi, and G. John for discussions that led to the ideas in this paper. This research was funded by AFOSR Grant No. F49620-94-1-0118.

References

Aha, D. W., & Bankert, R. L. (1994). Feature selection for case-based classification of cloud types. *Working Notes of the AAAI94 Workshop on Case-Based Reasoning* (pp. 106–112). Seattle, WA.

Davies, T. R., & Russell, S. J. (1987). A logical approach to reasoning by analogy. *Proceedings of the Tenth International Joint Conference on Artificial Intelligence* (pp.264–270).Milan: Morgan Kaufmann.

John, G. H., Kohavi, R., & Pfleger, K. (1994). Irrelevant features and the subset selection problem. *Proceedings of the Eleventh International Conference on Machine Learning* (pp. 121–129). New Brunswick, NJ: Morgan Kaufmann.

Kohavi, R. (1994). The power of decision tables. *Proceedings of the 1995 European Conference on Machine Learning* (pp. 174–189). Heraklion, Crete.

Langley, P., & Sage, S. (1994). Oblivious decision trees and abstract cases. *Working Notes of the AAAI94 Workshop on Case-Based Reasoning* (pp. 113–117). Seattle, WA: AAAI Press.

Quinlan, J. R. (1993). *C4.5: Programs for machine learning*. San Francisco: Morgan Kaufmann.

Schlimmer, J. C. (1993). Efficiently inducing determinations: A complete and efficient search algorithm that uses optimal pruning. *Proceedings of the Tenth International Conference on Machine Learning* (pp. 284–290). Amherst, MA: Morgan Kaufmann.

Shan, N., Ziarko, W., Hamilton, H. J., & Cercone, N. (1995). Using rough sets as tools for knowledge discovery. *Proceedings of the First International Conference on Knowledge Discovery and Data Mining* (pp. 263–268). Montreal: Morgan Kaufmann.

SE-trees Outperform Decision Trees in Noisy Domains

Ron Rymon*

Intelligent Systems Program, 901 CL
University of Pittsburgh
Pittsburgh, PA 15260
Rymon@ISP.Pitt.edu

Abstract

As a classifier, a Set Enumeration (SE) tree can be viewed as a generalization of decision trees. At the cost of a higher complexity, a single SE-tree encapsulates many alternative decision tree structures. An SE-tree enjoys several advantages over decision trees: it allows for domain-based user-specified bias; it supports a flexible tradeoff between the resources allocated to learning and the resulting accuracy; and it can combine knowledge induced from examples with other knowledge sources. We show that SE-trees enjoy a particular advantage over simple decision trees in noisy domains. This advantage manifests itself both in terms of accuracy, and in terms of consistency.

SE-tree-based Induction

- SE-trees first proposed as a systematic way to search a space of sets (Rymon, 1992). One way to view learning is as search for kernel (minimal) rules.

- An SE-tree can also be viewed as a generalizing decision tree induction a la Quinlan (1986) and Breiman *et al.* (1984), where nodes can possibly be expanded with *multiple* attributes (Rymon, 1993).

- The Algorithm (simplified version):
  - As in decision trees, recursively partition the training set until a rule qualification condition is met. Except in each node, this is done for all allowed attributes (termed that node's "View").
  - In each node, attributes in the View are scored by the attribute selection measure of choice, e.g., Information Gain, GINI Index, Chi-Square, and then expanded in that order.
  - Systematicity – never go back to higher-scoring attributes – ensures uniqueness of exploration.
  - Only most general rules are retained; if an old rule is subsumed by a new one, it is removed.

- Example (Figure 1):
  - W.l.o.g, suppose attributes are first scored in a lexicographic order, as marked next to the root.

---
*Parts of this work were supported by NASA grant MTPE-94-02; and funding from Modeling Labs.

The root was thus expanded with all attribute-value pairs, in that order.

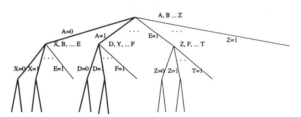

Figure 1: Improving Upon a Given Decision Tree

- In every node, attributes in the View (i.e., those scoring worse at its parent) are re-scored according to same heuristic. For example, in the node {E=1}, attributes F-Z are re-ranked: Z, F, ... T; in the node {Z=1}, the *View* is empty.

- Main features of SE-tree framework:

  - Primary Decision Tree. In Figure 1, note the bold-faced arcs at the left side of the SE-tree. These are exactly same nodes that would have appeared in a decision tree utilizing same heuristic.

  - Union of Many Alternative Decision Trees. Due to its multi-branching, as SE-tree can be viewed as an economical representation of many alternative decision trees: all overlaps are uniquely represented, and only most general rules are retained.

  - User-Specified Exploration Policy. Complete SE-trees are often too large to be entirely searched. They are so searched by a user-specified *exploration policy*. One family of exploration policies begins with the primary decision tree, and then continues to other parts of SE-tree. This is a hill-climbing procedure, where the extent of exploration may depend on resources available. The exploration policy represents user-specified bias.

  - User-Specified Resolution Criterion. As in decision trees, new instances are classified along matching paths, except here there may be *multiple* such paths. User-specified criteria are used to resolve conflicts (note that same conflicts exist

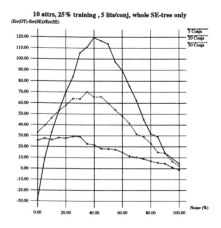
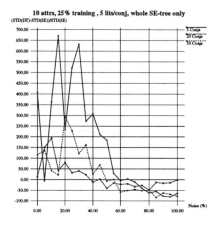
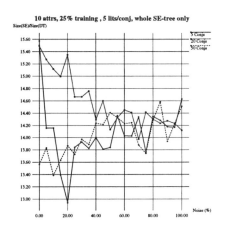

Figure 2: Varying #conj, #lits=5

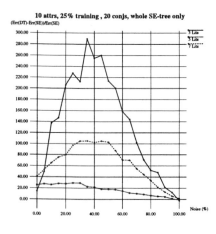
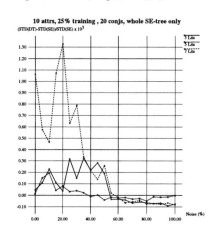
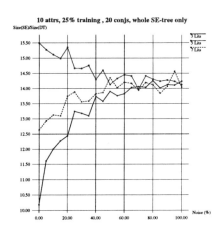

Figure 3: Varying #lits, #conj=20

between alternative decision trees). A resolution criterion can be general (e.g., simple voting), but may also represent domain-based bias.

- Implementation. This family of algorithms for SE-tree-based induction, including a variety of attribute-selection measures, as well as exploration policies and resolution criteria, is implemented in a program called SE-Learn (SE-Learn Home Page).

Hypothesis and Methods

- Hypothesis: SE-trees outperform decision trees in noisy domains.

- Intuitive Explanation: incorporating many alternative decision trees acts to reduce variance error.

- Method of Investigation: empirical, by testing on randomly generated artificial problem sets, with varying noise levels. We compare generalization accuracy of SE-tree and its primary decision tree.

- Using artificial problems, we can control generation and testing parameters. For the main experiment we use the following parameters:

- Problem size: 10 binary attributes + binary class.
- Training set size: 25% of the domain.
- Complexity of target function: using DNF representations, diversity is achieved by varying the number of conjunctions (#conj), and the number of literals per conjunction (#lits).
- Distribution of problems: Uniform over a given choice of #conj and #lits.
- Choice of decision tree program: Information Gain (ID3) is used to select splitting attributes.
- Choice of parametrization for SE-tree framework:
  * Exploration policy and extent: Complete SE-trees only (conservative assumption).
  * Resolution criterion: Simple voting (again a conservative assumption).
- Pruning: Unpruned trees.

- In subsequent experiments, we test sensitivity to important assumptions.

Main Experiment

- Two experiments: varying #conj, and varying #lits.

As aside, it appears as if 20-conj 5-lits functions are more complex than other variations.

- Noise modeled as randomly assigned classes, 0-100%.
- Test complete SE-tree vs. primary decision tree.
- 30 different random problems tested per data point.
- Reporting:
  - Normalized reduction in average error rates:
$$100*(\text{Err}(DT)-\text{Err}(SE))/\text{Err}(SE);$$
  - Normalized reduction in variance:
$$100*(\text{STD}(DT)-\text{STD}(SE))/\text{STD}(SE);$$
  - Cost as complexity ratio: Size(SE)/Size(DT).
- Results (Figures 2, 3):
  - Generally SE-trees have lower error rates (as indicated by positive values).
  - At moderate noise levels, error reduction increases with introduction of additional noise. By definition, it must then drop back; at 100% noise, there is no information in training set.
  - SE-trees are more consistent at moderate noise levels, but less consistent at very high noise levels.
  - Complete SE-trees are more complex. However, they are typically explored partially. Generally, complexity ratios are higher for more complex functions. It appears that noise reduces the ratio for complex functions, and increases it for simpler ones.

Experimental Setting Variations

- Conservative assumption: performed with 20-conjs 5-lits functions, where the relative performance of the SE-tree was poorest: #conj=20 and #lits=5.
1. Alternative attribute selection heuristics (Figure 4). No apparent differences.
2. Training set sizes (Figure 5). Hypothesis still confirmed. However, lower absolute error reduction rates and higher complexity ratios are apparent with fewer training instances.
3. Statistically pruned vs. Unpruned trees (Figure 6). SE-tree still outperforms decision tree. However, in pruned trees, we find smaller error reductions, and larger variations. In pruned trees, complexity ratios are smaller, and drop quickly with noise.

Related Work and Discussion

- Tree averaging. As a joint representation for many alternative decision trees, the SE-tree-based framework bears resemblance to the tree averaging approach taken by Kwok and Carter (1990) and Buntine (1994), as well as Breiman's (1994) bagging.
- Reduction of Variance Error. Dietterich and Kong (1995) distinguish statistical bias from variance error. They indicate that "one important source of variance in C4.5 is the fact that the algorithm must

choose a single split at each node". Noisy domains are characterized by added variance, and SE-trees may relieve some of it.

Dietterich and Kong conclude that "some method is needed for converting a combination of trees (or other complex hypotheses) into a smaller, equivalent hypothesis. These trees are very redundant; how can we remove this redundancy, while still reducing bias and variance?". SE-trees may represent one step in that direction.

- Bootstrap Aggregation. In analyzing where bagging works, Breiman too points to domains exhibiting great variation between alternative classifiers. SE-trees provide an effective way to consider alternative decision trees without the loss of information incurred when subseting the training data.

Conclusion

1. In the presence of noise, a complete SE-tree typically outperforms its own primary decision tree. Results were replicated with different heuristics.
2. At moderate noise levels, the SE-tree advantage generally *increases* with additional noise.
3. At moderate noise levels, the SE-tree is also more consistent.

References

Breiman, L., Friedman, J., Olshen, R., and Stone, C., *Classification and Regression Trees.* Wadsworth, Belmont.

Breiman, L., Bagging Predictors. *Technical Report 421*, Department of Statistics, UC Berkeley.

Buntine, W., Learning Classification Trees. *Artificial Intelligence Frontiers in Statistics*, D. Hand (Ed), Chapman and Hall.

Dietterich, T. G., and Kong, E. B., Machine Learning Bias, Statistical Bias, and Statistical Variance of Decision Tree Algorithms. Technical Report, Department of Computer Science, Oregon State University.

Kwok, S., and Carter, C., Multiple Decision Trees. *Uncertainty in Artificial Intelligence*, 4, pp. 327-335.

Quinlan, J. R., Induction of Decision Trees. *Machine Learning*, 1(1):81-106.

Quinlan, J. R., *C4.5: Programs for Empirical Learning.* Morgan Kaufmann, San Francisco, CA.

Rymon, R., Search through Systematic Set Enumeration. *Third International Conference on Principles of Knowledge Representation and Reasoning*, Cambridge MA, pp. 539-550.

Rymon, R., An SE-tree-based Characterization of the Induction Problem. *Tenth International Conference on Machine Learning*, pp. 268-275, Amherst MA.

Rymon, R., Home page for the SE-Learn software. http://www.isp.pitt.edu/~rymon/SE-Learn.html.

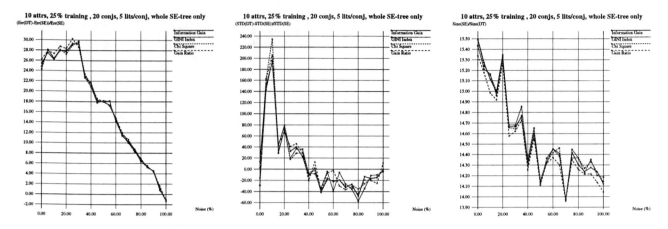

Figure 4: Various Attribute-Selection Heuristics

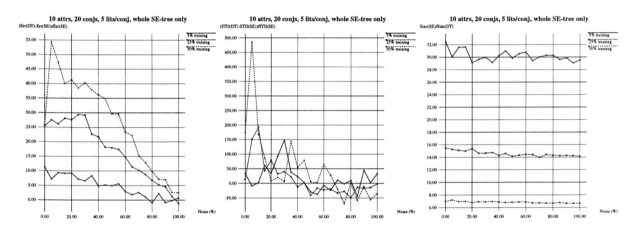

Figure 5: Various Training Set Sizes

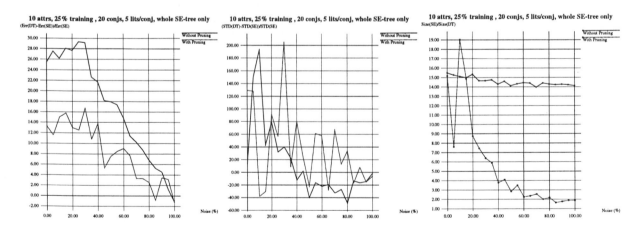

Figure 6: With and Without Pruning

Learning Limited Dependence Bayesian Classifiers

Mehran Sahami

Gates Building 1A, Room 126
Computer Science Department
Stanford University
Stanford, CA 94305-9010
sahami@cs.stanford.edu

Abstract

We present a framework for characterizing Bayesian classification methods. This framework can be thought of as a spectrum of allowable dependence in a given probabilistic model with the Naive Bayes algorithm at the most restrictive end and the learning of full Bayesian networks at the most general extreme. While much work has been carried out along the two ends of this spectrum, there has been surprising little done along the middle. We analyze the assumptions made as one moves along this spectrum and show the tradeoffs between model accuracy and learning speed which become critical to consider in a variety of data mining domains. We then present a general induction algorithm that allows for traversal of this spectrum depending on the available computational power for carrying out induction and show its application in a number of domains with different properties.

Introduction

Recently, work in Bayesian methods for classification has grown enormously (Cooper & Herskovits 1992) (Buntine 1994). Bayesian networks (Pearl 1988) have long been a popular medium for graphically representing the probabilistic dependencies which exist in a domain. It has only been in the past few years, however, that this framework has been employed with the goal of automatically learning the graphical structure of such a network from a store of data (Cooper & Herskovits 1992) (Heckerman, Geiger, & Chickering 1995). In this latter incarnation, such models lend themselves to better understanding of the domain in which they are employed by helping identify dependencies that exist between features in a database as well as being useful for classification tasks. A particularly restrictive model, the Naive Bayesian classifier (Good 1965), has had a longer history as a simple, yet powerful classification technique. The computational efficiency of this classifier has made it the benefactor of a number of research efforts (Kononenko 1991).

Although general Bayesian network learning as well as the Naive Bayesian classifier have both shown success in different domains, each has it shortcomings. Learning in the domain of unrestricted Bayesian networks is often very time consuming and quickly becomes intractable as the number of features in a domain grows. Moreover, inference in such unrestricted models has been shown to be NP-hard (Cooper 1987). Alternatively, the Naive Bayesian classifer, while very efficient for inference, makes very strong independence assumptions that are often violated in practice and can lead to poor predictive generalization. In this work, we seek to identify the limitations of each of these methods, and show how they represent two extremes along a spectrum of data classification algorithms.

Probabilistic Models

To better understand the spectrum we will present shortly for characterizing proabilistic models for classification, it is best to first examine the end points and then naturally generalize.

Bayesian Networks

Bayesian networks are a way to graphically represent the dependencies in a probability distribution by the construction of a directed acyclic graph. These models represent each variable (feature) in a given domain as a node in the graph and dependencies between these variables as arcs connecting the respective nodes. Thus, independencies are represented by the *lack* of an arc connecting particular variables. A node in the network for a variable X_i represents the probability of X_i conditioned on the variables that are immediate parents of X_i, denoted $\Pi(X_i)$. Nodes with no parents simply represent the prior probability for that variable.

In probabilistic classification we would ideally like to determine the probability distribution $P(C|\mathbf{X})$ where C is the class variable and $\mathbf{X}$ is the n-dimensional data vector $(x_1, x_2, ..., x_n)$ that represents an observed instance. If we had this true distribution available to us, we could achieve the theoretically optimal classication

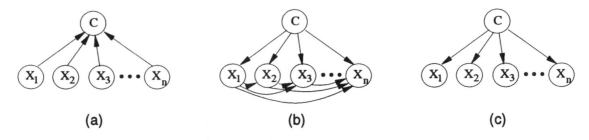

Figure 1: Bayesian networks representing (a) $P(C|\mathbf{X})$, (b) $P(C|\mathbf{X})$ after arc reversal, and (c) Naive Bayes.

by simply classifying each instance $\mathbf{X}$ into the class c_k for which $P(C = c_k|\mathbf{X})$ is maximized. This is known as *Bayes Optimal* classification. This general distribution can be captured in a Bayesian network as shown in Figure 1(a).

It is insightful to apply arc reversal (Shachter 1986) to the network in Figure 1(a) to produce the equivalent dependence structure in Figure 1(b). Here, $\Pi(X_i) = \{C, X_1, ..., X_{i-1}\}$. Now, we can see that the true complexity in such an unrestricted model (i.e. no independencies) comes from the large number of feature dependence arcs which are present in the model.

Since Bayesian networks allow for the modeling of arbitrarily complex dependencies between features, we can think of these models as lying at the most general end of a *feature dependence spectrum*. Thus, Bayesian networks have much representational power at the cost of computationally expensive learning and inference.

Naive Bayes

The Naive Bayesian classifier represents the most restrictive extreme in our spectrum of probabilistic classification techniques. As a Bayesian approach, it predicts the class c_k that maximizes $P(C = c_k|\mathbf{X})$, for a data vector $\mathbf{X}$, under the restrictive assumption that each feature X_i is conditionally independent of every other feature given the class label. In other words: $P(\mathbf{X}|C = c_k) = \prod_i P(X_i|C = c_k)$

The Naive Bayesian model is shown in Figure 1(c). In contrast to Figure 1(b), we see that the Naive Bayesian model allows for no arcs between feature nodes. We can think of the Naive Bayesian algorithm as being at the most restrictive end of the feature dependence spectrum, in that it strictly allows no dependencies between features given the class label.

We now formalize our notion of the spectrum of feature dependence in Bayesian classification by introducing the notion of k-dependence Bayesian classifiers. The proofs of the propositions we give subsequently are straight-forward and are omitted for brevity.

Definition 1 *A k-dependence Bayesian classifier is a Bayesian network which contains the structure of the*

Naive Bayesian classifier and allows each feature X_i to have a maximum of k feature nodes as parents. In other words, $\Pi(X_i) = \{C, \mathbf{X_{d_i}}\}$ where $\mathbf{X_{d_i}}$ is a set of at most k feature nodes, and $\Pi(C) = \emptyset$.

Proposition 1 *The Naive Bayesian classifier is a 0-dependence Bayesian classifier.*

Proposition 2 *The full Bayesian classifier (i.e. no independencies) is a $(N-1)$-dependence Bayesian classifier, where N is the number of domain features.*

Geiger (1992) has defined the related notion of a *conditional dependence tree*. This notion is captured in our general framework as a 1-dependence Bayesian classifier. Friedman & Goldszmidt (1996) have also developed an algorithm, named TAN, which is similar to Geiger's method for inducing conditional trees. These algorithms generate optimal 1-dependence Bayesian classifiers, but provide no method to generalize to higher degrees of feature dependence.

By varying the value of k we can define models that smoothly move along the spectrum of feature dependence. If k is large enough to capture all feature dependencies that exist in a database, then we would expect a classifier to achieve optimal Bayesian accuracy if the "right" dependencies are set in the model[1].

The KDB Algorithm

We presently give an algorithm which allows us to construct classifiers at arbitrary points (values of k) along the feature dependence spectrum, while also capturing much of the computational efficiency of the Naive Bayesian model. Thus we present an alternative to the general trend in Bayesian network learning algorithms which do an expensive search through the space of network structures (Heckerman, Geiger, & Chickering 1995) or feature dependencies (Pazzani 1995).

---

[1]The question becomes one of determining if the model has allowed for enough dependencies to represent the *Markov Blanket* (Pearl 1988) of each feature. We refer the interested reader to Friedman & Goldszmidt (1996) and Koller & Sahami (1996) for more details

Our algorithm, called KDB, is supplied with both a database of pre-classified instances, DB, and the k value for the maximum allowable degree of feature dependence. It outputs a k-dependence Bayesian classifier with conditional probability tables determined from the input data. The algorithm is as follows:

1. For each feature X_i, compute mutual information, $I(X_i; C)$, where C is the class.
2. Compute class conditional mutual information $I(X_i; X_j|C)$, for each pair of features X_i and X_j, where $i \neq j$.
3. Let the used variable list, S, be empty.
4. Let the Bayesian network being constructed, BN, begin with a single class node, C.
5. Repeat until S includes all domain features
   5.1. Select feature X_{max} which is not in S and has the largest value $I(X_{max}; C)$.
   5.2. Add a node to BN representing X_{max}.
   5.3. Add an arc from C to X_{max} in BN.
   5.4. Add $m = \min(|S|, k)$ arcs from m distinct features X_j in S with the highest value for $I(X_{max}; X_j|C)$.
   5.5. Add X_{max} to S.
6. Compute the conditional probabilility tables infered by the structure of BN by using counts from DB, and output BN.

In this description of the algorithm, Step 5.4 requires that we add m parents to each new feature added to the model. To make the algorithm more robust, we also consider a variant where we change Step 5.4 to: Consider m distinct features X_j in S with the highest value for $I(X_{max}; X_j|C)$, and only add arcs from X_j to X_{max} if $I(X_{max}; X_j|C) > \theta$, where θ is a mutual information threshold. This allows more flexibility by not forcing the inclusion of dependencies that do not appear to exist when the value of k is set too high.

Another feature of our algorithm which makes it very suitable for data mining domains is its relatively small computational complexity. Computing the actual network structure, BN, requires $O(n^2 mcv^2)$ time (dominated by Step 2) and calculating the conditional probability tables within the network takes $O(n(m + v^k))$ time, where n is the number of features, m is the number of data instances, c is the number of classes, and v is the maximum number of discrete values that a feature may take. In many domains, v will be small and k is a user-set parameter, so the algorithm will scale linearly with m, the amount of data in DB. Moreover, classifying an instance using the learned model only requires $O(nck)$ time.

We have recently become aware that Ezawa & Schuermann (1995) also have an algorithm similar in flavor to ours, but with some important differences, which attempts to discover feature dependencies directly using mutual information, as opposed to employing a general search for network structure.

Dataset	No. Classes	No. Features	Training Set Size	Testing Set Size
Corral	2	6	128	10-fold CV
LED7	10	7	3200	10-fold CV
Chess	2	36	3196	10-fold CV
DNA	3	180*	3186	10-fold CV
Vote	2	48*	435	10-fold CV
Text	3	3440	1084	454

Table 1: Datasets. *Denotes Boolean encoding.

Dataset	k	Accuracy	
		KDB-orig	KDB-θ
Corral	0	$88.4 \pm 10.5\%$	$88.4 \pm 10.5\%$
	1	$100.0 \pm 0.0\%$	$100.0 \pm 0.0\%$
	2	$96.7 \pm 5.8\%$	$96.7 \pm 5.8\%$
	3	$88.4 \pm 17.2\%$	$100.0 \pm 0.0\%$
LED7	0	$72.9 \pm 2.1\%$	$72.9 \pm 2.1\%$
	1	$73.1 \pm 3.9\%$	$73.0 \pm 2.9\%$
	2	$73.5 \pm 2.3\%$	$72.9 \pm 2.4\%$
	3	$73.2 \pm 2.3\%$	$73.4 \pm 1.3\%$
Chess	0	$86.2 \pm 1.9\%$	$86.2 \pm 1.9\%$
	1	$93.9 \pm 1.3\%$	$93.8 \pm 1.4\%$
	2	$95.1 \pm 1.2\%$	$95.5 \pm 1.6\%$
	3	$94.9 \pm 1.1\%$	$95.3 \pm 1.2\%$
DNA	0	$94.0 \pm 0.9\%$	$94.0 \pm 0.9\%$
	1	$94.0 \pm 1.6\%$	$94.1 \pm 1.1\%$
	2	$95.3 \pm 1.2\%$	$95.6 \pm 1.1\%$
	3	$93.3 \pm 0.9\%$	$95.5 \pm 1.8\%$
Vote	0	$90.2 \pm 3.8\%$	$90.2 \pm 3.8\%$
	1	$92.6 \pm 3.6\%$	$92.1 \pm 5.3\%$
	2	$92.3 \pm 3.5\%$	$93.5 \pm 4.1\%$
	3	$93.0 \pm 2.2\%$	$94.0 \pm 3.2\%$
Text	0	87.0%	87.0%
	1	87.9%	87.4%
	2	87.0%	88.3%
	3	86.8%	86.8%

Table 2: Classification accuracies for KDB.

Results

We tested KDB on five datasets from the UCI repository (Murphy & Aha 1995) as well as a text classification domain with many features (a small subset of the Reuters Text database (Reuters 1995)). These datasets are described in Table 1. Specifically, we wanted to measure if increasing the value of k above 0 would help the predictive accuracy of the induced models (i.e. compare the dependence modeling capabilities of KDB with Naive Bayes). Moreover, we wanted to see if we could uncover various levels of dependencies that we know exist in a few artificial domains by seeing how classification accuracy varied with the value of k. We also tested the modified KDB algorithm which employs a mutual information threshold, θ. In these trials we set $\theta = 0.03$, which was a heuristically determined value. The results of our experiments are given in Table 2 with KDB-orig refering to the original algorithm and KDB-θ refering to the variant using the mutual information threshold.

The two artificial domains, Corral and LED7, were selected because of known dependence properties. The Corral dataset represents the concept $(A \wedge B) \vee (C \wedge D)$ and thus is best modeled when a few feature dependencies are allowed, as is borne out in our experimental results (higher accuracies when $k > 0$). The LED7 dataset, on the other hand, contains no feature dependencies when conditioned on the class. Our algorithm helps discover these independencies, as reflected by the similar accuracy rates when $k = 0$ and $k > 0$.

In the real-world domains we find that modeling feature dependencies very often improves classification results. This is especially true for the KDB-θ algorithm, where classification accuracies when $k > 0$ are almost always greater than or equal the $k = 0$ (Naive Bayes) case. In the Chess ($k = 1, 2, 3$), Vote ($k = 2, 3$) and DNA ($k = 2, 3$) domains, these improvements are statistically significant (t-test with $p < 0.10$). Moreover, by noting how the classification accuracy changes with the value of k we get a notion of the degree of feature dependence in each domain. For example, in both Chess and DNA, we see large jumps in accuracy when going from $k = 0$ to $k = 2$ and that there is no gain when $k = 3$, thus indicating many low-order interactions in these domains.

It is important to note that the Boolean encoding of the Vote and DNA domains has introduced some feature dependencies into the data, but such represetational issues (which are often unknown to the end user of a data mining system) also argue in favor of methods that can model such dependencies when they happen to exist. Also worth noting is the fact that as k grows, we must estimate a larger probability space (more conditioning variables) with the same amount of data. This can cause our probability estimates to become more inaccurate and lead to an overall decrease in predictive accuracy, as is seen when going from $k = 2$ to $k = 3$ in many of the domains. The KDB-θ algorithm is less prone to this effect, but it is still not impervious. In many data mining domains, however, we may have the luxury of have a great deal of data, in which case this degradation effect will not be as severe. Nevertheless, these results indicate that we can model domains better in terms of classification accuracy and get an idea for the underlying dependencies in the domain, two critical applications of data mining.

In future work, we seek to automatically identify good values for k for a given domain (possibly through employing cross-validation) and better motivate the value of the θ threshold. Also, comparisons with other

Bayesian network learning methods are planned.

Acknowledgements We thank Moises Goldszmidt for his comments on an earlier version of this paper. This work was supported by ARPA/NASA/NSF under a grant to the Stanford Digital Libraries Project.

References

Buntine, W. 1994. Operations for learning with graphical models. *JAIR* 2:159–225.

Cooper, G. F., and Herskovits, E. 1992. A bayesian method for the induction of probabilistic networks from data. *Machine Learning* 9:309–347.

Cooper, G. F. 1987. Probabilistic inference using belief networks is NP-Hard. Technical Report KSL-87-27, Stanford Knowledge Systems Laboratory.

Ezawa, K. J., and Schuermann, T. 1995. Fraud/uncollectible debt detection using a bayesian network learning system. In *UAI-95*, 157–166.

Friedman, N., and Goldszmidt, M. 1996. Building classifiers using bayesian networks. In *AAAI-96*.

Geiger, D. 1992. An entropy-based learning algorithm of bayesian conditional trees. In *UAI-92*, 92–97.

Good, I. J. 1965. *The Estimation of Probabilities: An Essay on Modern Bayesian Methods.* M.I.T. Press.

Heckerman, D.; Geiger, D.; and Chickering, D. 1995. Learning bayesian networks: The combination of knowledge and statistical data. *Machine Learning* 20:197–243.

Koller, D., and Sahami, M. 1996. Toward optimal feature selection. In *Proceedings of the Thirteenth Int. Conference on Machine Learning.*

Kononenko, I. 1991. Semi-naive bayesian classifier. In *Proceedings of the Sixth European Working Session on Learning*, 206–219. Pitman.

Murphy, P. M., and Aha, D. W. 1995. UCI repository of machine learning databases. http://www.ics.uci.edu/~mlearn/MLRepository.html.

Pazzani, M. J. 1995. Searching for dependencies in bayesian classifiers. In *Proceedings of the Fifth Int. Workshop on AI and Statistics.*

Pearl, J. 1988. *Probabilistic Reasoning in Intelligent Systems: Networks of Plausible Inference.* Morgan-Kaufmann.

Reuters. 1995. Reuters document collection. ftp://ciir-ftp.cs.umass.edu/pub/reuters1.

Shachter, R. D. 1986. Evaluating influence diagrams. *Operations Research* 34(6):871–882.

RITIO - Rule Induction Two In One

David Urpani[†], Xindong Wu[‡], Jim Sykes[*]

[†] Division of Building, Construction & Engineering, CSIRO
Graham Road, Highett, VIC 3190, Australia

[‡] Department of Software Development
Monash University
900 Dandenong Road
Melbourne, VIC 3145, Australia

[*] School of Information Systems
Swinburne University of Technology
Hawthorn 3122
Melbourne, Australia

Abstract

The identification of relevant attributes is an important and difficult task in data mining applications where induction is used as the primary tool for knowledge extraction. This paper introduces a new rule induction algorithm, RITIO, which eliminates attributes in order of decreasing irrelevancy. The rules produced by RITIO are shown to be largely based on only the most relevant attributes. Experimental results, with and without feature selection preprocessing, confirm that RITIO achieves high levels of predictive accuracy.

Introduction

The pervasive use of sensor and information technology in all aspects of our life has resulted in the generation of vast amounts of digital data. Converting raw sensor data into useful information for human decision makers is one of the driving forces behind research into applications of data mining.

Inductive learning is the primary method for discovering new knowledge from a database by providing concept descriptions which are able to generalize. The two major forms of representation used in inductive learning are the decision tree (DT) and the rule structure. DTs are known to cause fragmentation of the database whenever a high-arity attribute is tested at a node (Pagllo & Haussler 1990) and also have a tendency to repeat subtrees when expressing disjunctive concepts. As a consequence of these two problems DTs tend to grow very large in most realistic problem domains, and they are usually decompiled into a set of rules. Rule-like structures are a more convenient form to express knowledge. Rules are similar to the way human experts express their expertise and human users are comfortable with this way of expressing newly extracted knowledge. Algorithms directly inducing a set of rules are therefore at a distinct advantage as they immediately create the rule set.

Hypothesis generation in induction involves searching through a vast (possibly infinite) space of concept descriptions. Practical systems constrain the search space through the use of bias (Utgoff 1986). One such bias, which has not been given much attention is to minimize the number of features in the concept description. We propose a rule induction algorithm, RITIO (Rule Induction Two In One), which prefers hypothesis spaces containing fewer attributes, generalizing by removing irrelevant attributes. We show that this form of attribute based induction can very efficiently provide syntactically simple concept descriptions with high generalizing powers even in noisy environments. We provide an empirical evaluation of RITIO with C4.5 (Quinlan 1993), C4.5rules and HCV (Wu 1995).

In the next section we describe the RITIO algorithm, and we follow this with the results of an empirical investigation. Two sets of results are presented. The first set is of RITIO without any feature selection (FS) preprocessing and the second set uses FS preprocessing. An algorithm called Classer, reported elsewhere (Urpani & Sykes 1995) is used for this purpose. Classer uses genetic search to identify a subset of features that result in identical or improved classification rates on a nearest neighbour classifier.

RITIO - Rule Induction, Two in One

RITIO carries out a data driven, specific-to-general search for a consistent set of rules which describes the different classes in the data. Like ID3-like algorithms, RITIO makes use of the entropy measure albeit in a different way as a means of constraining the hypothesis search space but unlike ID3-like algorithms the hypotheses language is the rule structure. ID3-like algorithms including ID3 and C4.5 need a decompiler (such as C4.5rules) to transform decision trees into rules, whereby RITIO carries out rule induction without decision tree construction.

Initially the rule set is a copy of the training set representing a set of maximally specific generalizations referred to as the rule matrix (RM). In the initial RM, which is the rule matrix at level $L = 0$, a rule exists for each training instance. Each level L refers to one stage in the induction process, with higher levels denoting increasing rule generalization. There are a maximum of $N - 1$ levels where N is the number of attributes in the database.

RITIO examines each attribute in the training set at each level L, and selects the least relevant. The heuristic used to identify relevancy is the information theoretic function designed by Shannon (Shannon & Weaver 1949) and popularized in Quinlan's ID3 (Quinlan 1986). In contrast to ID3 the heuristic used in RITIO selects the attribute providing the lowest information gain. The entropy of an attribute A, $E(A)$ is the information required to classify an instance based on the information in that attribute. It is defined as follows:

$$E(A) = \sum_{j=1}^{V} (RelFreq_j \times Inf_j)$$

where V is the total number of distinct values in attribute A, and

$$RelFreq_j = P_j/T$$

with P_j being the number of occurrences of value j in attribute A and T being the number of training instances,

$$Inf_j = -\sum_{k=0}^{C} [P_{j_k}/P_j \times log_2(P_{j_k}/P_j)],$$

with P_{j_k} being the number of occurrences of value j in attribute A belonging to class k and C the number of classes in the training set.

$E(A)$ is calculated for each attribute in the database. In ID3 the attribute with the minimum entropy is selected at a decision tree node to split the tree. RITIO chooses the attribute with the maximum entropy as the candidate for elimination from the RM. This guarantees that the least relevant attribute (according to information theory) is eliminated. The induction process will make a total of $N - 1$ entropy calculations.

On identifying the first least relevant attribute, RITIO checks against each training instance to see whether removal of that attribute results in an inconsistency. An inconsistency is here defined as the occurrence of the same example with different classifications after the removal of the least relevant attribute. An attribute whose removal from a rule causes no inconsistency anywhere in the training set is termed a 'removed' attribute.

After removal of the least relevant attribute from all instances where such removal does not cause an inconsistency, a new, more general RM results. The RM has now been partitioned into two distinct groups: one which still retains the full, initial dimensionality, N, the 'retain' group, and the other with a reduced dimensionality, $N - 1$, the 'remove' group. The RM is now at level 1.

In succeeding rounds of entropy calculations all previous 'least relevant' attributes are not considered. In this case the least relevant attribute from the remaining, $N - 1$ attributes across the two existing partitions is chosen as the next candidate for elimination.

Once this attribute has been chosen the next round in the RM generalization process commences. While checking for consistency the following rules henceforth apply when identifying members of the training set to be used in the checking process:

1. If checking a rule belonging to the 'retain' group all training instances are used. In some cases this means checking also against previously eliminated attributes.

2. If checking a rule belonging to the 'remove' group only training instances belonging to that group are used. As before, the current least relevant attribute is dropped form those rules which do not cause an inconsistency.

The RM at level $L = 2$ has now been partitioned into four groups (ie retain & retain, remove & retain, retain & remove and remove & remove groups). The process repeats itself iteratively $N - 1$ times with new entropy calculations, consistency checks and further partitioning of the RM. At any point in the induction process the RM will contain a maximum of 2^{L-1} partitions up to a final maximum of 2^{N-1} different partitions.

The final RM contains a set of maximally generalized rules guaranteed for consistency. The generalizing process results in a reduction in the number of rules from the original training set size. This manifests itself by repeating rules which are eliminated in the rule extraction process. Another effect of the generalizing process is a reduction in the average dimensionality of the RM as attributes are progressively eliminated. The rules are finally presented as an unordered list in conjunctive normal form.

Real world databases are often noisy, contradictory, incomplete and redundant. To be of any practical use RITIO needs to be able to generalize in the presence of noisy data. RITIO handles noise by a series of processes distributed throughout the induction process. These techniques are discussed in detail elsewhere (Urpani 1996).

Experimental Evaluation

In this section we present the results of an empirical investigation into the performance of RITIO (with and without feature selection preprocessing), using Classer) and compare the results obtained by RITIO with those using C4.5, C4.5rules and HCV.

Throughout the experiments the same default conditions were used for all the databases. Obviously fine tuning different parameters in RITIO would have achieved higher accuracy rates. This however would have been at the expense of a loss in generality and applicability of the conclusions. The default conditions used in RITIO were as follows:

1. The induced rule set was pruned by eliminating those rules which had the same class coverage of less than 5.0%.

2. The maximum number of mismatches allowed during deduction is the number of attributes minus one.

Similarly default conditions were adopted for the three other programs C4.5, C4.5rules and HCV as recommended by the respective authors.

All databases used were divided randomly into training and testing partitions by a 70/30 split of the instances. This was carried out 10 times to obtain 10-fold cross-validation trials.

The Data

The data used in our experiments (see Table 1) can be divided into three groups. The first group is made up of data with 100% nominal attributes. The second group contains data of mixed nominal and continuous attributes. Most of these two groups of data were obtained from (Murphy & Aha 1995), and are available from the HCV software data suite (Wu 1995). The third group of data originates from an aluminium smelter. Further information on all data sets can be found in (Urpani 1996).

Rule Accuracy

Tables 2 shows the accuracy results obtained by the four programs, HCV (Version 2.0), C4.5, RITIO and C4.5rules. The best result for each problem is highlighted with **boldface** font in the table. Results for C4.5 are the pruned ones. The RITIO results are the average of ten fold cross-validated results on unseen test cases. Also included for RITIO is the 95% confidence interval estimate of the mean of the accuracy results. This estimate shows the variance associated with the results and is a good indication of the stability of the algorithm over different databases. For 8 databases out of 10 in the first group in Table 2, RITIO

(with FS) obtained the best results. RITIO (without FS) performed just as well relative to the other data sets, however its accuracy was nearly always lower than that from Classer+RITIO.

Out of the 4 databases with continuous data in the second group, RITIO obtained the best results on 2 of them. RITIO produced a particularly good result on the water treatment plant database WTP which is a notoriously difficult real world database, significantly exceeding the next best. FS preprocessing did not seem to particularly improve RITIO's performance on these data sets.

With the industrial databases shown in the last group, RITIO again obtained the best accuracy results for 5 out of the 7 databases. Furthermore in 4 out of 7 cases FS preprocessing obtained a better result than when using RITIO without preprocessing. In several cases such as the 'Temperature' and 'Prediction 3' databases RITIO obtained a very significant improvement over the next best result.

Conclusion

We have presented a new induction algorithm, RITIO, which uses the information theoretic function in a novel way to induce directly a set of rules. It is similar to HCV (Version 2.0) in its approach of using matrices but has stronger noise handling capabilities by eliminating attributes, starting with the least relevant attribute. This is in direct contrast to the DT inducer in C4.5 which uses the most relevant attribute first to branch on. Results also indicate that RITIO's induction accuracy can in many cases be improved through the use of a FS preprocessing procedure.

The algorithm has been shown in the experiments carried out on a wide variety of databases to produce concept descriptions of consistently high accuracy which perform better in most cases than C4.5, C4.5rules or HCV. Future work involves looking at different evaluation functions to employ when selecting attributes for elimination. The consistency check procedure will also be modified to take a 'softer' fuzzy approach (Wu & Måhlén 1995). This ability to tolerate different levels of inconsistency should add to the already good noise tolerance of the RITIO algorithm.

References

Murphy, P.M. & Aha, D.W., UCI Repository of Machine Learning Databases, Machine-Readable Data Repository, Irvine, CA, University of California, Department of Information and Computer Science, 1995.

Pagllo, G. & Haussler, D., Boolean feature discovery in empirical learning, *Machine Learning*, **5**(1990): 71-99.

Table 1: Databases Characteristics

Database	# of Instances	Attributes	Classes	Majority Class (%)	Continuous Attributes (%)	Avg # of Values per Attributes	Unknown Values (%)
Hayes-Roth	160	4	3	40.60	0.00	4.00	0.00
Monk1	556	6	2	50.00	0.00	2.80	0.00
Monk2	601	6	2	65.70	0.00	2.80	0.00
Monk3	554	6	2	52.00	0.00	2.80	0.00
Tic-tac-toe	958	9	2	65.30	0.00	3.00	0.00
Soybean	683	35	19	13.50	0.00	2.80	12.00
Vote	435	16	2	61.40	0.00	3.00	5.00
Breast Cancer	286	9	2	70.3	0.00	5.80	0.00
Lymphography	148	18	4	54.7	0.00	3.30	0.00
Primary Tumor	339	17	21	24.8	0.00	2.20	3.00
Aus-Credit	690	15	2	56.00	40.00	4.56	0.65
Lab Neg	56	16	2	65.00	50.00	2.62	35.75
Wine	178	13	3	40.00	100.00	n/a	0.00
WTP	523	38	13	52.18	100.00	n/a	2.95
Pot Noise	542	22	2	50.00	100.00	n/a	0.00
UFT	407	20	2	50.00	100.00	n/a	0.00
Temperature	321	22	3	33.33	100.00	n/a	0.00
Pot Difference	195	22	2	50.00	100.00	n/a	0.00
Prediction 1	721	56	2	50.00	100.00	n/a	0.00
Prediction 2	721	68	2	50.00	100.00	n/a	0.00
Prediction 3	616	68	2	50.00	100.00	n/a	0.00

Table 2: Accuracy (%) Results on Discrete Data

Database	HCV (Version 2.0)	C4.5	RITIO	95% Estimate	C4.5rules	Classer+RITIO
Hayes-Roth	85.70	85.60	87.92	4.14	71.4	90.4
Monk1	100.00	83.30	97.37	5.96	100.0	100.00
Monk2	85.20	69.70	94.97	3.39	65.3	94.97
Monk3	98.10	97.20	99.45	0.61	96.3	100.00
Tic-tac-toe	88.00	94.30	98.32	1.11	100.0	94.37
Soybean	80.20	82.4	96.80	0.68	80.6	97.10
Vote	97.80	97.00	98.97	1.10	93.6	99.96
Breast Cancer	72.3	72.8	91.26	7.19	73.5	92.11
Lymphography	74.30	69.00	84.90	6.35	72.4	93.10
Primary Tumor	38.2	34.00	75.67	5.81	33.80	73.10
Aus-Credit	82.50	91.0	93.22	2.38	90.0	89.00
Lab Neg	76.50	88.2	77.16	5.37	88.2	80.5
Wine	90.40	98.1	92.37	2.16	98.1	92.70
WTP	58.62	60.90	94.77	0.83	59.2	94.77
Pot Noise	94.48	97.80	96.00	1.47	97.2	94.33
UFT	70.37	69.60	89.11	4.46	72.1	84.40
Temperature	48.57	61.90	82.71	4.60	67.6	81.96
Pot Difference	89.23	96.90	93.38	3.40	96.90	99.23
Prediction 1	74.90	68.60	89.58	5.58	75.3	91.60
Prediction 2	67.78	57.9	83.71	2.13	57.5	85.70
Prediction 3	60.50	53.80	86.63	2.35	54.6	87.20

Quinlan, J.R., Induction of decision trees, *Machine Learning*, 1(1986).

Quinlan, J.R., *C4.5: Programs for Machine Learning*, CA: Morgan Kaufmann, 1993.

Shannon, C.E. & Weaver, W., *The Mathematical Theory of Communications*, The University of Illinois Press, Urbana, IL, 1949.

Urpani, D., Knowledge acquisition from real-world data, *PhD Thesis*, School of Information Systems, Swinburne University of Technology, Australia, 1996.

Urpani, D, & Sykes, J., Facilitating knowledge acquisition from industrial process data by automating feature selection, *Proc. of the 8th Intl. Conf. on Industrial and Engg. Applications of Arti. Intelligence and Expert Systems*, Melbourne, Australia, June 6-8, 1995, 161–170.

Utgoff P.E., Shift of Bias for Inductive Concept Learning, *Machine Learning: An AI Approach*, Volume 2, Chapter 5, Morgan Kaufmann Pub., 1986, 107–148.

Wu, X., *Knowledge Acquisition from Databases*, Ablex Publishing Corp., U.S.A., 1995.

Wu, X., and Måhlén, P., Fuzzy interpretation of induction results, *Proc. of the 1995 International Conference on Knowledge Discovery and Data Mining (KDD-95)*, Montreal, Canada, August 20-21, 1995, 325–330.

Mining Associations in Text
in the Presence of Background Knowledge

Ronen Feldman

Mathematics and Computer Science Department
Bar-Ilan University
Ramat-Gan, ISRAEL 52900
feldman@bimacs.cs.biu.ac.il

Haym Hirsh

Department of Computer Science
Rutgers University
Piscataway, NJ USA 08855
hirsh@cs.rutgers.edu

Abstract

This paper describes the FACT system for knowledge discovery from text. It discovers associations – patterns of co-occurrence – amongst keywords labeling the items in a collection of textual documents. In addition, FACT is able to use background knowledge about the keywords labeling the documents in its discovery process. FACT takes a query-centered view of knowledge discovery, in which a discovery request is viewed as a query over the implicit set of possible results supported by a collection of documents, and where background knowledge is used to specify constraints on the desired results of this query process. Execution of a knowledge-discovery query is structured so that these background-knowledge constraints can be exploited in the search for possible results. Finally, rather than requiring a user to specify an explicit query expression in the knowledge-discovery query language, FACT presents the user with a simple-to-use graphical interface to the query language, with the language providing a well-defined semantics for the discovery actions performed by a user through the interface.

Introduction

Suppose someone comes along and gives you a large collection of textual documents – newswire stories, internal business memos, netnews articles, email messages, or even WWW pages – and asks you to find something interesting in the collection. We have previously labeled this problem "Knowledge Discovery from Text" (KDT) [Feldman and Dagan, 1995; Dagan et al., 1996].

This paper describes FACT (Finding Associations in Collections of Text), a tool for discovering associations in collections of textual documents given background knowledge about the topics of documents in the collection. Central to this work is a query-centered view of the discovery process [Imielinski, 1995]. Given a collection of data, there is a corresponding implicit collection of possible results supported by the data. FACT provides a query language for the discovery process in which a user can specify queries over this implicit collection of possible results supported by the data. However, rather than requiring the specifica-

tion of an explicit query expression in this language, FACT presents the user with a simple-to-use graphical interface in which a user's various discovery tasks are specified, with the underlying query language providing a well-defined semantics for the discovery actions performed by the user through the interface. As part of this interface a user can specify constraints over the set of desired results in terms of background knowledge about the topics of the documents, with FACT exploiting such constraints in how it structures its search for possible results.

We begin the paper with an overview of the FACT system. We then describe the general problem of finding associations, our association-discovery query language, and our algorithms for executing queries in this language. Finally, we discuss the use of FACT on a collection of Reuters newswire stories using background knowledge automatically extracted from the CIA World Factbook.

The FACT System Architecture

FACT takes as input three sources of information. The First is a collection of textual data on which the discovery process takes place. Since our approach begins with the assumption borrowed from the Information Retrieval literature that each document is labeled with a set of keywords representing the topics of the document, the input text collections must either already be labeled with such keywords (as is the case for the Reuters data discussed in Section 6), or must be fed through a text categorization system that annotates documents with such keywords.

In addition to that, FACT also takes as input background knowledge for its discovery process. To be usable by FACT such knowledge must define unary and binary predicates over the keywords labeling the documents, representing properties of the entities represented by each keyword and relationships between them. Thus for the Reuters newswire data, for example, FACT is told for each country-keyword the organizations of which that country is a member, thereby defining a set of unary predicates over the country-keywords (one per organization). FACT is also given information about which countries neighbor one another, defining a set of binary predicates over the country-keywords. Since such information is rarely available in the precise form needed by the FACT system, it will usually be necessary to develop tools that understand the format of an information source and can translate into the necessary format for FACT. For example, the background knowledge used in our Reuters newswire experiments comes from the CIA World Factbook, a structured textual document with information about the various countries of the world. To make it possible for FACT to use this knowledge we had to develop a tool that parses the Factbook's well-structured text and converts it into the format used by FACT.

Finally, FACT is provided with the user's specification of a knowledge-discovery task, which is acquired from the user via a simple graphical user interface. The interface knows about the various keywords that can label a document, as well as the various unary and binary predicates defined by the background knowledge that can be applied to these keywords, and allows the user to specify a query using this keyword and predicate vocabulary via a collection of menus.

The results of this discovery process are then passed on to a tool, that can effectively present the results and allow the user to browse them. This component of FACT filters out redundant results [Feldman et al., 1996], sorts results in decreasing order of confidence, and enables the user to access and browse those documents that support each of the individual results that it presents to the user.

The Query Language

To execute an association-discovery task a user specifies a query in FACT's association query language – the association-discovery process should only return results that satisfy the query . Each association-discovery query has three parts. The first part specifies what types of keywords are desired in the left-hand and right-hand sides of any found associations, as well as what support and confidence the association should have. Thus, for example, a user can express an interest in associations that relate a set of countries labeling a document to a person also labeling the document, as long as the association has sufficient support and confidence in the collection.

The second (possibly empty) part of a query specifies constraints – in terms of the predicates defined by the background knowledge – that the user wants any found association to satisfy. There are two types of background knowledge that can be used in queries. The first are unary predi-

cates over keywords. In specifying a query, each unary predicate is viewed as a class of keywords, specifying the set of keywords for which it is true. Thus, for example, the unary predicate EC that is true if a keyword is the name of a country that is a member of the European Community is viewed as a class whose members are those keywords that are European-Community countries. A user can request that a unary predicate be true of some keyword in an association by specifying that the keyword be a member of the class defined by the unary predicate.

The second type of background knowledge that can be used in queries are binary predicates, which define relationships between keywords. Thus, for example, the background knowledge might define the binary predicate Nationality, which is true whenever the first argument is the name of some person whose nationality is the country appearing as the second argument of the predicate. For the query language each binary predicate is viewed as a function: given the value of the first argument, it returns the set of values for the second argument that would make the predicate true. The predicate Nationality, for example, would be viewed as a function that takes a person's name as input and returns the country that is that person's nationality; the predicate ExportCommodity becomes the function Export-Commodities that takes a country keyword as input and outputs the keywords representing that country's export commodities. Further, whenever a function is applied to a set of keywords, the function returns all second arguments that make the predicate true for any element in the input set of keywords. A user can request that a binary predicate be true of some keywords in an association by specifying that one keyword be amongst the values returned by the function when it is applied to some other keyword in the association.

Finally, the third (also possibly empty) part of a query specifies constraints on the size of the various components of the association. Thus, for example, a user can request associations that have only one keyword on their right-hand side, or that mention at most 5 country keywords.

Figure 1 gives a BNF grammar of our association-discovery query language, , where nonterminals are written in angle brackets, "(0,1]" represents the set of reals between 0 (noninclusive) and 1 (inclusive), and <CategoryType> is defined as appropriate for a given domain, dividing the keywords labeling the documents into subclasses (such as "country", "person", etc., in the Reuters newswire data). Any expansion for "<Arg>" to "<Var>" must a variable that was previously defined in "<Pattern>" for that query (i.e., this is a context-sensitive portion of the language that cannot be represented in BNF).

```
<Query> ::= Find (<support>/<confidence>) Pattern
    Where: <BackgroundConstraint>*
        <KeywordConstraint>*


<support> ::= <integer>
<confidence> ::= (0,1]
<Pattern> ::= <VarList> ⇒ <VarList>
<VarList> ::= <VarExp> | <VarExp>, <VarList>
<VarExp> ::= <Var> : <TypeExp>
<TypeExp> ::= <CategoryType> | <CategoryType>+


<BackgroundConstraint> ::= <Arg> <Operator> <Arg>
<Operator> ::= ∈ | ∉ | ⊆ | ⊄ | = | ≠
<Arg> ::= <Var> | <Keyword> | <Class> | <BgExpression>
| LHS | RHS | All
<BgExpression> ::= <BackgroundFunction>(<Arglist>)
<Arglist> ::= <Arg> | <Arg>,<Arglist>


<KeywordConstraint>   ::=   <#Exp>   <CompOperator>
<#Exp>
<#Exp> ::= <numeric constant> | #(<category>) | #(LHS) |
#(RHS) | #(All)


<CompOperator> ::= > | ≥ | < | ≤ | = | ≠
```

Figure 1 - BNF grammar of the Query language of FACT

For example, the query "*Find*: (10/0.2) c:country+ ⇒
p:person, *Where*: Nationality(p) ∉ c, #(LHS) ≤ 3" (taken
from the Reuters newswire domain) requests associations
where, at least 20% of the time, whenever some set of at
most three countries labels a document it is also labeled
with some person whose nationality is not one of those
countries, and this occurs at least 10 times in the collection.

Query Execution

Our algorithms for executing association-discovery queries
in the presence of background knowledge are based on
those described by Agrawal and Srikant [1994] and Mannila et al. [1994]. Once a collection of all σ-covers (X is
called a σ-cover if |[X]| ≥ σ) has been found, the traditional
association-discovery process attempts to find all subsets B
for each σ-cover X for which X\B ⇒ B holds with the desired confidence γ. To limit the search to those associations satisfying the constraints we use the σ-cover algorithm in a slightly different fashion, so as to use the constraints to reduce the search space and make the association
generation process more efficient.

To do this, we divide the constraints on possible associations into two classes. The first class contains those
"simple" constraints that refer to only one side of the association, such as LHS ⊆ Arab League, or Iran ∈ RHS, as

well as those constraints that require some property to hold
on the whole association, such as #(All) < 5. The second
class contains those "complex" constraints that require
some relationship to hold between elements of the two side
of the association, such as RHS ⊆ LandBoundaries(LHS).
We use both classes of constraints to reduce the space of
possible σ-covers that must be considered.

Figure 2 gives an outline of this algorithm for finding associations in the presence of such constraints. It takes as input
the collection of documents, Ds; K(D) is used to refer to
the collection of keywords labeling document D. The algorithm finds all possible LHS candidates, only searching
through those that satisfy the simple constraints on the
LHS. For each such result the algorithm considers which
other keywords could appear as the RHS of the association,
constrained according to whatever additional constraints
are present. At the end of the process it determines which
associations satisfy the support and confidence from those
that were created satisfying the given constraints.

```
Use the σ-cover algorithm to create Ls, the set of all left-
hand sides that could satisfy the association-discovery
query, constrained to only consider those keywords satis-
fying the simple constraints on the LHS.
For all D ∈ Ds
    For all X ∈ Ls do
        if X ⊆ K(D) then
            B = The keywords in K(D)\X that satisfy the con-
            straints on RHS (either simple constraints or com-
            posite constraints) and that appear with the required
            support.
            Update co-occurrence counters for X and all subsets
            of B
        end if
    end do
end do
Form associations based on the accumulated co-occurrence
counters. Remove those associations that do not satisfy the
required support and confidence.
```

Figure 2 - Query evaluation algorithm

Applying FACT to Newswire Data

To investigate the use of FACT to find associations in text
we used it on the Reuters-22173 newswire data often used
in research in Information Retrieval. Our goal is not just
the discovery of associations in text, but doing so in the
presence of background knowledge of the domain. To investigate the role of background knowledge in association
discovery for the Reuters-22173 collection we used background knowledge extracted from the 1995 CIA World
FactBook, a structured textual document containing information about each of the countries in the world. The information about each country is divided to 6 sections: Geog-

raphy, People, Government, Economy, Communications, and Defense Forces.

As a crude measure of the efficiency of our algorithms, we ran a series of queries using FACT and compared the cpu time (on a 486/50) and the number of associations found for each query. Each query was created by instantiating one of two query templates. The first template (T1) includes a background-knowledge constraint that requires the right-hand side of any found association to be in the Land-Boundaries of the left-hand side: "*Find:* (5/0.1) c1:country+ $\Rightarrow$ c2:country+ *Where:* c1 $\subseteq$ **CountryGroup**, c2 $\subseteq$ LandBoundaries(c1)". To generate a query **CountryGroup** is replaced in this template by some country organizations defined in the background knowledge. The second query is generated in the same way from an identical template (T2), only without the LandBoundaries constraint: "*Find:* (5/0.1) c1:country+ $\Rightarrow$ c2:country+ *Where:* c1 $\subseteq$ **CountryGroup**."

Figure 3 shows a graph giving the cpu time it took FACT for evaluating each of the queries for those country organizations whose queries generated from template T2 produced at least 25 associations (the execution time for those giving fewer associations was negligible, and was excluded to avoid a cluttered graph with many nearly-zero values). Figure 4 gives a graph that shows for each country organization the number of associations produced for that query. (Organizations listed on the X axis are ordered identically for both graphs, according to the number of results generated for its instantiation of template T2.) These results show that rather than slowing down the association-discovery process, the specification of background-knowledge constraints actually provides information that is exploited by our discovery algorithms, speeding up the association-discovery process.

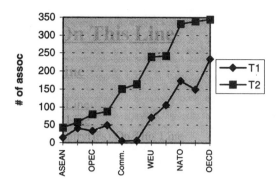

Figure 4 - # of associations found for two sets of queries

Summary

This paper has described the FACT system for knowledge discovery in collections of textual documents, which finds associations amongst the keywords labeling the documents given background knowledge about the keywords and relationships between them. Rather than forcing the user to specify an explicit query expression in some arcane knowledge-discovery query language, FACT presents the user with an easy-to-use graphical interface in which discovery tasks can be specified, with the language providing a well-defined semantics for the discovery actions performed by a user via the interface.

References

[Agrawal and Srikant, 1994] Agrawal A. and Srikant R. Fast algorithms for mining association rules. In *Proceedings of the VLDB Conference*, Santiago, Chile.

[Dagan et al., 1996] Dagan I., Feldman R., and Hirsh H. , Keyword-Based Browsing and Analysis of Large Document Sets. To appear, In *Proceedings of SDAIR96*, Las Vegas, Nevada, April 1996.

[Feldman et al., 1996] Feldman R., Dagan I., and Kloesgen W. Efficient Algorithms for Mining and Manipulating Associations in Texts. To appear, In *Proceedings of EMCSR96*, Vienna, Austria, April 1996.

[Feldman and Dagan, 1995] Feldman R. and Dagan I. KDT - knowledge discovery in texts. In *Proceedings of the First International Conference on Knowledge Discovery(KDD-95)*, August 1995.

[Imielinski, 1995] T. Imielinski. Invited talk. *The First International Conference on Knowledge Discovery(KDD-95)*.

[Mannila et al., 1994] Mannila H., Toivonen H., and Verkamo A. Efficient Algorithms for Discovering association rules. In *Proceedings of KDD-94*, pages 181-192.

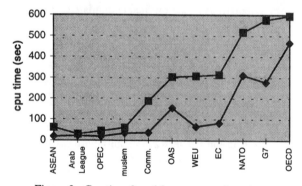

Figure 3 - Cpu time found for two sets of queries

Extraction of Spatial Proximity Patterns by Concept Generalization

Edwin M. Knorr and **Raymond T. Ng**
Department of Computer Science
University of British Columbia
Vancouver, B.C., V6T 1Z4, Canada
{knorr,rng}@cs.ubc.ca

Abstract

We study the spatial data mining problem of how to extract a special type of proximity relationship—namely that of distinguishing two *clusters* of points based on the types of their neighbouring *features*. The points in the clusters may represent houses on a map, and the features may represent spatial entities such as schools, parks, golf courses, etc. Classes of features are organized into concept hierarchies. We develop algorithm GenDis which uses concept generalization to identify the distinguishing features or concepts which serve as discriminators. Furthermore, we study the issue of which discriminators are "better" than others by introducing the notion of maximal discriminators, and by using a ranking system to quantitatively weigh maximal discriminators from different concept hierarchies.

Introduction

In recent years, there has been considerable research in detecting patterns hidden in data (Agrawal *et al.* 1992; Agrawal, Imielinski, & Swami 1993; Borgida & Brachman 1993). A reasonable and rather popular approach to spatial data mining is the use of clustering techniques to analyze the spatial distribution of data (Ng & Han 1994; Ester, Kriegel, & Xu 1995; Zhang, Ramakrishnan, & Livny 1996). While such techniques are effective and efficient in identifying spatial clusters, they do not support further analysis and discovery of the properties of the clusters. To this end, we have developed an approximate, but efficient, algorithm (Knorr 1995) to discover knowledge about the clusters by analyzing the features that are in close proximity to the clusters. More specifically, given a spatial cluster Cl, the algorithm finds the top-k features that are closest to Cl in an aggregate sense. An aggregate notion of proximity is needed because the distribution of points in a cluster may not be uniform. For example, a particular golf course may appear in a cluster's top-10 list if the golf course is relatively close

to many of the houses in the cluster. On the other hand, a particular shopping centre which is actually closer to the cluster (in terms of feature boundary to cluster boundary distance) may not appear in the top-10 list if few houses are relatively close to the shopping centre.

It is also important to identify common *classes* of features which are in close proximity to most (or all) of the input clusters (Knorr & Ng 1996). This notion of *commonality extraction* is important because, for example, it is often unlikely that one particular golf course is close to every cluster, even though each cluster may have *some* golf course close to it—though not necessarily the same one. If such is the case, then a generalized statement can be made concerning the fact that the clusters tend to be near golf courses. Such statements can be useful in terms of knowledge discovery because they describe generic types of features common to multiple clusters.

While aggregate proximity relationships and commonality extraction can be quite valuable, we are also interested in determining the distinguishing features (or classes of features) between two clusters. For example, if an expensive housing cluster and a poor housing cluster are given as input, we may find that concepts such as "golf courses", "private schools", and "social services centres" are discriminators, in which the expensive housing cluster is close to a golf course or a private school, but the poor housing cluster is not; and, the poor housing cluster is close to a social services centre, whereas the expensive housing cluster is not.

In this paper, we describe an algorithm called GenDis, which finds "discriminating" classes of features that serve to distinguish one cluster from another. We use concept generalization to extract the discriminators. Attribute-oriented concept generalization (Han, Cai, & Cercone 1992; Lu, Han, & Ooi 1993) has been shown to be quite useful in guiding the discovery of general patterns. The work in this paper differs from the attribute-oriented approach in a number of

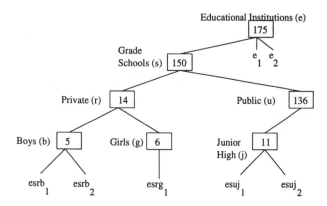

Figure 1: Educational Institutions Concept Hierarchy

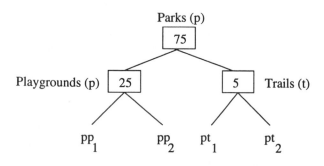

Figure 2: Parks Concept Hierarchy

ways. First, to identify discriminating patterns, we do not use set differences and thresholds. Second, our notion of maximal discriminators is unique. Finally, we introduce a way of ranking the discriminating concepts.

Concept Hierarchies

In a GIS context, we define a feature as a natural or man-made place of interest. Natural features may include mountains, lakes, islands, etc., and man-made features may be schools, parks, golf courses, shopping centres, etc. We define a *concept* to be a class of features. Each concept is part of some hierarchy. The trees shown in Figures 1 and 2 are two concept hierarchies, to which we will refer throughout this paper. In the educational institutions hierarchy, one subclass of educational institutions (shorthand "e") is grade schools ("s"). Grade schools in turn are classified into private ("r") and public ("u") schools, which can be further sub-classified into less general concepts. Specific instances of schools appear at the leaf level. The leaves are considered to be trivial concepts. We use shorthand notation to identify any node in a tree. For example, in Figure 1, the feature $esrb_1$ is a boys' private grade school, and the feature e_1 is an educational institution that is not a grade school (e.g., art school, university, technical college). The cardinalities of the

concepts are also listed. In our example, there are 175 educational institutions, 150 of which are grade schools. Of those 150 grade schools, 14 are private grade schools—and of those 14, 5 are exclusively for boys, 6 are exclusively for girls, and 3 are co-ed (not shown). For simplicity, only those concepts that are relevant to our discussion are shown—namely those concepts relating to specific features which appear in at least one of the original top-k lists. Recall that a top-k list for a given cluster contains the k features "nearest" the cluster—nearest in an aggregate sense.

Algorithm GenDis: Extraction of Maximal Discriminators

Motivation and Definition

Due to limited space, we limit our discussion to the extraction of patterns for "dissimilar" clusters. More specifically, given two clusters as input, we aim to find discriminating features, or simply *discriminators*, that distinguish one cluster from the other.

A natural way of detecting discriminators is to use set differences on the two lists. (This is the underlying principle used in the attribute-oriented approach.) Consider the concept hierarchies in Figures 1 and 2, and:

- suppose the top-k list associated with an expensive housing cluster Cl_e contains $esrb_1$, $esrg_1$, and pp_1 (plus a number of features that are found in the top-k list of a poor housing cluster Cl_p)

- suppose the top-k list associated with Cl_p contains pt_1 and $esuj_2$ (plus a number of features common to Cl_e)

Set differences on these two lists yield all 5 mentioned features as discriminators. The presence of $esrb_1$, $esrg_1$, or pp_1 distinguishes Cl_e from Cl_p—and the presence of pt_1 or $esuj_2$ distinguishes Cl_p from Cl_e. While this approach of using set differences is easy to compute, drawing distinctions based solely on individual features can be somewhat limiting. For example, closer scrutiny of these 5 features and the clusters to which they belong reveals that private schools are close to the expensive cluster, but not to the poor cluster; and that a public school is close to the poor cluster, but not to the expensive cluster. Thus, while $esrb_1$ and $esuj_2$ are both educational institutions, and pp_1 and pt_1 are both parks, a key question is: *how different* is $esrb_1$ from $esuj_2$, and pp_1 from pt_1? This question motivates our study of maximal discriminators, defined below.

Concept generalization can help answer the "how different" question by highlighting the differences between features. For example, the difference between

$esuj_2$ and $esrb_1$ is that the former is a junior high public school, whereas the latter is a boys' private school. This observation can be obtained by generalizing $esuj_2$ to $esuj$, and by generalizing $esrb_1$ to $esrb$. This leads to two questions. First, in ascending the concept hierarchy, how many levels of generalization are most appropriate? We defer the answer to the next paragraph. Second, is this kind of highlighting by generalization always possible? To answer this question, suppose in our example that $esuj_2$ were $esrb_2$ instead. Although $esrb_1$ and $esrb_2$ are distinct entities, generalizing both features yields the same class of boys' private schools. In effect, rather than highlighting the differences, generalization in this case underscores the similarities or the lack of differences between the features. Thus, in evaluating the differences between features, concept generalization is useful in both highlighting the differences and identifying the lack of differences, whatever the case may be.

To capture the essence of the above discussion, and to determine the appropriate number of levels of generalization, we use the notion of the *smallest common ancestor* of a set of nodes in a tree. More formally, if $F_1, \ldots, F_u$ are all features in the same concept hierarchy, the smallest common ancestor of $F_1, \ldots, F_u$, denoted by $sca(\{F_1, \ldots, F_u\})$, is the root of the smallest subtree containing $F_1, \ldots, F_u$. Now, suppose F and G are two sets of features from the same concept hierarchy. We define the *maximal discriminator* of F and G, denoted by $md(F, G)$, as follows:

- If the subtree rooted at $sca(F)$ contains $sca(G)$, or if the subtree rooted at $sca(G)$ contains $sca(F)$, then $md(F, G)$ is NULL.

- Otherwise, let F' be the child of $sca(F \cup G)$ such that the subtree rooted at that child contains $sca(F)$, and let G' be the child of $sca(F \cup G)$ such that the subtree rooted at that child contains $sca(G)$. Then, $md(F, G)$ is the pair $\langle F', G' \rangle$.

For example, consider Figure 1 and the sets $F = \{esrb_1, esrg_1\}$ and $G = \{esuj_1, esuj_2\}$. By definition, $sca(F)$ is esr, $sca(G)$ is $esuj$, and $sca(F \cup G)$ is es. Furthermore, F' is esr and G' is esu. Thus, the maximal discriminator is $\langle esr, esu \rangle$, which corresponds to private schools and public schools—the observation we want, as discussed above.

Consider $md(\{esrb_1\}, \{esuj_1, esrb_2\})$ as another example. This time $sca(\{esuj_1, esrb_2\})$ is es, whose subtree contains $esrb_1 = sca(\{esrb_1\})$. Thus, the maximal discriminator in this case is NULL, indicating that the sets $\{esrb_1\}$ and $\{esuj_1, esrb_2\}$ are not considered to be sufficiently different.

```
1          Initialize answer set S to empty set
2          For each concept hierarchy
2.1          Let F be the set of features from
                this hierarchy for one cluster
2.2          Let G be the set of features from
                this hierarchy for the other cluster
2.3          If both F and G are empty
2.3.1            goto 2.6
2.4          If either F or G is empty
2.4.1            add <C,nil> to S, where C is
                    the root of the concept hierarchy
2.5          else
2.5.1            compute md(F,G) as defined
2.5.2            if md(F,G) is not null
2.5.2.1              add md(F,G) to S
2.6          End-for
3          Compute and report the final rankings of
              the discriminators in S
```

Figure 3: Algorithm GenDis for Extracting Maximal Discriminators

One may wonder what the word "maximal" in maximal discriminator means. It is used to describe the situation in which the sets F and G are generalized to the fullest possible extent. Any further generalization will render the sets identical (corresponding to $sca(F \cup G)$). Thus, the maximal discriminator reports the broadest difference between two sets. In our first example, the broadest difference is simply the distinction between private and public schools—as indicated by $md(F, G) = \langle esr, esu \rangle$.

A useful by-product of the notion of smallest common ancestors and maximal discriminators is the ability to report more specific information. In general, by following the path from F' to $sca(F)$, and by following the path from G' to $sca(G)$, we get more specific levels of distinction. The most specific level of distinction occurs with the pair $\langle sca(F), sca(G) \rangle$; however, in practice, if $sca(F)$ (or $sca(G)$) is a leaf, then it may make more sense to report the parent of the leaf. For example, suppose $F = \{esrb_1\}$ and $G = \{esuj_2\}$, and suppose "St. George's School" is the name of feature $esrb_1$ and "Pierre Elliot Trudeau School" is the name of feature $esuj_2$. A user who is unfamiliar with these feature names may prefer to see a more general level of distinction—namely, the distinction of a boys' private school versus a junior high public school. We leave the desired level of distinction as an application issue, but mention it for completeness.

Algorithm GenDis

Figure 3 presents the outline of Algorithm GenDis for extracting maximal discriminators for two clusters, using multiple concept hierarchies. Let us apply the algorithm on clusters $Cl_e = \{esrb_1, esrg_1, pp_1\}$ and $Cl_p = \{pt_1, esuj_2\}$. Suppose the first iteration of the for-loop considers the educational institutions hierarchy, in which $F = \{esrb_1, esrg_1\}$ and $G = \{esuj_2\}$. In Step 2.5.2.1, $md(F, G)$ is the pair $\langle esr, esu \rangle$, which is added to the answer set S. The pair corresponds to private schools and public schools, which highlight the distinction (in terms of kinds of features) between the two clusters. In the next iteration, the parks hierarchy is used, in which $F = \{pp_1\}$ and $G = \{pt_1\}$. From Figure 2, $md(F, G)$ is the pair $\langle pp, pt \rangle$, which corresponds to playgrounds and trails. Thus, $\langle pp, pt \rangle$ is added to S, yielding a second discriminating class of features.

Like the situation for identifying and quantifying commonalities (Knorr & Ng 1996), maximal discriminators from different concept hierarchies should be ranked (i) to give an idea of how strong the discriminators are, and (ii) to take into account the varying cardinalities of different concepts and hierarchies. This can be done as follows. Given the pair $\langle F', G' \rangle$ as a maximal discriminator, the score is defined by the maximum of the cardinalities of F' and G', normalized by the total cardinality of the concept hierarchy. These scores are then ranked. For example, from Figures 1 and 2, we see that the score for $\langle esr, esu \rangle$ is $136/175$ (approximately 0.78), and the score for $\langle pp, pt \rangle$ is $25/75$ (approximately 0.33). Although the scores depend on the cardinalities and granularities of the various concept hierarchies, smaller scores are generally favoured since they often reflect the fact that different types of discriminating features having relatively low probabilities of occurrence appear in both clusters.

The score for $\langle C, nil \rangle$, where C is the root of a concept hierarchy (e.g., $\langle e, nil \rangle$) is 1 because, as shown in Step 2.4.1 of Algorithm GenDis, this corresponds to a situation where concepts from the hierarchy rooted at C appear in one of the two top-k lists, but not both. Of course, those cases where $md(F, G)$ is NULL are not included in the list of discriminators—and hence, the rankings—since F and G are not considered to be sufficiently different.

From a complexity standpoint, smallest common ancestors can be computed in $O(1)$ time, with $O(n)$ pre-processing time, where n is the total number of nodes (Harel & Tarjan 1984). It is easy to see that the complexity of computing maximal discriminators is equally low.

Future Work

In future work, we will investigate how to generalize the extraction of maximal discriminators from two clusters to n clusters, in an efficient manner. In other words, given n clusters and their n top-k lists, we aim to distinguish cluster Cl_i from the remaining $n - 1$ clusters, for all $i \in \{1, \ldots, n\}$.

Acknowledgments

This research has been partially sponsored by NSERC Grants OGP0138055 and STR0134419, IRIS-2 Grants HMI-5 and IC-5, and a CITR Grant on "Distributed Continuous-Media File Systems."

References

Agrawal, R.; Ghosh, S.; Imielinski, T.; Iyer, B.; and Swami, A. 1992. An interval classifier for database mining applications. In *Proc. 18th VLDB*, 560–573.

Agrawal, R.; Imielinski, T.; and Swami, A. 1993. Mining association rules between sets of items in large databases. In *Proc. ACM SIGMOD*, 207–216.

Borgida, A., and Brachman, R. 1993. Loading data into description reasoners. In *Proc. ACM SIGMOD*, 217–226.

Ester, M.; Kriegel, H.; and Xu, X. 1995. Knowledge discovery in large spatial databases: Focusing techniques for efficient class identification. In *Proc. 4th Int'l Symposium on Large Spatial Databases*, 67–82.

Han, J.; Cai, Y.; and Cercone, N. 1992. Knowledge discovery in databases: an attribute-oriented approach. In *Proc. 18th VLDB*, 547–559.

Harel, D., and Tarjan, R. 1984. Fast algorithms for finding nearest common ancestors. *SIAM Journal on Computing* 13:338–355.

Knorr, E. M., and Ng, R. T. 1996. Finding aggregate proximity relationships and commonalities in spatial data mining. *IEEE Transactions on Knowledge and Data Engineering (Special Issue on Database Mining)*. Forthcoming.

Knorr, E. M. 1995. Efficiently determining aggregate proximity relationships in spatial data mining. Master's thesis, Dept. of Computer Science, Univ. British Columbia.

Lu, W.; Han, J.; and Ooi, B. 1993. Discovery of general knowledge in large spatial databases. In *Proc. Far East Workshop on Geographic Information Systems*, 275–289.

Ng, R., and Han, J. 1994. Efficient and effective clustering methods for spatial data mining. In *Proc. 20th VLDB*, 144–155.

Zhang, T.; Ramakrishnan, R.; and Livny, M. 1996. Birch: An efficient data clustering method for very large databases. In *Proc. ACM SIGMOD*, Forthcoming.

Pattern Discovery in Temporal Databases: A Temporal Logic Approach[1]

Balaji Padmanabhan and Alexander Tuzhilin
Leonard N. Stern School of Business
New York University
{bpadmana, atuzhili}@stern.nyu.edu

Abstract

The work of Mannila et al. [4] of finding frequent episodes in sequences is extended to finding temporal logic patterns in temporal databases. It is argued that temporal logic provides an appropriate formalism for *expressing* temporal patterns defined over categorical data. It is also proposed to use Temporal Logic Programming as a mechanism for the *discovery* of frequent patterns expressible in temporal logic. It is explained in the paper how frequent temporal patterns can be discovered by constructing temporal logic programs.

Introduction

In this paper, we address the problem of finding interesting patterns in temporal databases [1,2] defined over categorical (symbolic) data. This is an important problem that frequently occurs in various applications such as molecular biology (finding patterns in genetic sequences), telecommunications (finding patterns in network behavior) and financial services (finding patterns in analysts' recommendations of stocks). To address this problem, a language for *expressing* temporal patterns has to be defined and mechanisms to *discover* patterns in temporal databases need to be developed. This is a broad problem, and it has been addressed before in such fields as speech recognition, signal processing, as well as in the KDD field itself. For example, Agrawal et al. [3] provide a *shape definition language*, SDL, for expressing shapes in sequences. In the context of categorical data, the problem has been addressed by Mannila et al. [4] and by the string matching research community [5].

Mannila et al [4] define temporal patterns in sequences of events with *episodes*, where episodes are defined as partially ordered sets of events that can be described by directed acyclic graphs. Given a class of such episodes they describe an efficient algorithm that finds all frequent episodes from that class. Their paper presents an interesting approach that was tested on telecommunications data. However, the episodes defined in [4] have a limited expressive power in specifying temporal patterns. For example, it is unclear how episodes can define such temporal patterns as "event A always occurs until event B occurs" or that "either event A or event B occurs at the same time." In addition, their approach works on sequences, and not on temporal databases (i.e. temporal *predicates* changing over time).

String matching researchers use regular expressions to define patterns on strings of alphabets and develop efficient string matching algorithms. Aho [5] presents a survey of such algorithms. Regular expressions are defined over an alphabet, and therefore this approach works well with strings of symbols but does not generalize to temporal databases, where *predicates* change over time.

In this paper we extend the work of Mannila et al. [4] (finding frequent patterns in temporal categorical data) and propose the use of first-order temporal logic (FOTL) [6] to express patterns in temporal databases (the propositional case constitutes a special case of the first-order case). As an example of how episodes can be expressed in Temporal Logic (TL), the partial order of symbols "A→B→C", defining a *serial* episode of [4], can be expressed as "A *Before* B *and* B *Before* C". In addition, TL can also be used to express patterns such "Hold(Stock) *Until* Bearish_Market_Sentiment", where Hold is a temporal predicate. Moreover, we propose to use TL for discovering temporal patterns by generating *temporal logic programs* (TLP) [7,8,9] for these patterns.

TL provides several important advantages as a mechanism for the specification and discovery of patterns in temporal databases. It is a well-studied, expressive and theoretically sound formalism that has been extensively used in various fields of computer science for dealing with temporal phenomena. TL can be used *both* for the specification of temporal patterns and for their discovery in temporal databases (using TLP techniques described below). Therefore, TL provides a sound framework for integrating the specification and discovery methods.

Preliminaries

We use FOTL [6,10] to express temporal patterns. The syntax of FOTL is obtained from first-order logic by adding temporal operators such as *Since, Until, Next* (o), and *Previous* (•) and some of the derived operators, such as *Always* (□), Future and Past *Sometimes* ($\Diamond$, $\blacklozenge$), *Before, After* and *While*. In addition, we consider *bounded* temporal operators [9,12] $Until_K$, $Since_K$ etc. For example, $A Until_K B$ is defined as:

$(D,t) \models A\ Until_K\ B$ iff $\exists m, t \leq m \leq t+k$, such that $(D,m) \models B$ and $\forall i, t \leq i < m, (D,i) \models A$

The semantics of FOTL is defined in terms of *temporal structures*, i.e., predicates changing over time [10]. We assume that time is discrete, linear and bounded, that temporal predicates define a *temporal database* [1,2], and that temporal relations are represented as *event tables* [13], i.e. tables with a single temporal attribute.

A *temporal pattern* is a ground FOTL formula, i.e. a FOTL formula containing only ground atoms and no

[1]This work was supported in part by the NSF under grant IRI-93-18773

variables and quantifiers. A *class* of temporal patterns is defined by a temporal formula, ψ, with one or more variables in it. An *instantiation* of all variables in ψ with specific ground values, defines a temporal pattern. In this paper we adopt the convention of using uppercase alphabet to represent variables in a temporal formula.

Temporal Logic Programming. A TLP program consists of a set of temporal rules of the form BODY → HEAD, where various TLP systems make different assumptions about the structure of BODY and HEAD. For example, a rule that "Employees who have been fired from a firm (worked there sometime in the past, but not now) cannot be hired by that firm in the future" can be expressed in an extension of TLP system, *Templog* [7] as:

♦EMPLOY(firm, person) ∧ ¬EMPLOY(firm, person)
→ □ ¬EMPLOY(firm, person)

Alternatively, as done in *Datalog$_{1S}$* [14], we can also express TLP programs in first-order logic using explicit references to time. For example, instead of using the temporal predicate EMPLOY(firm, person), we can use its FOL equivalent EMPLOY(firm, person, time) specifying the employment history of the person over time. Moreover, Templog and the corresponding FOL language Datalog$_{1S}$ are equivalent in their expressive power [8]. We will use an extension of Datalog$_{1S}$ to express TLP programs. Datalog$_{1S}$ will be extended by allowing negation both in the body and in the head of a rule, as done in doubly negated Datalog$^{¬}$* [15], and by allowing comparisons between temporal variables (e.g. $t_1 < t_2$) in the body of Datalog$_{1S}$ rules. We will call the resulting extension *eDatalog$_{1S}$*. We will adhere to the parallel inflationary semantics of Datalog$^{¬}$* [15] when we define semantics of eDatalog$_{1S}$. Intuitively, all the eDatalog$_{1S}$ rules are fired in parallel, and if there are conflicts in rules, program execution terminates, as done in Datalog$^{¬}$*.

Finding Frequent Temporal Patterns

In this paper we address the problem of finding *frequent* and *most frequent* patterns in temporal databases. For example, if D is a temporal database, then we may want to find all the frequent patterns in the class of temporal patterns, $ψ = X_1$ *Until$_K$* X_2, where X_1 and X_2 are second-order variables ranging over the predicates in the temporal database D. To do this, for any temporal pattern that belongs to the class ψ, we can count the number of time instances for which the pattern holds on D. The pattern is then frequent if it exceeds a threshold value c.

For example, assume that X_1 is associated with predicate p(X), X_2 with predicate q(X) in D, X is instantiated to a_0, and K=5. If a pattern "p(a_0)*Until$_5$* q(a_0)" occurs 90 times in D and c is 70, we conclude that the pattern occurs frequently in D. Alternatively, we could have searched for the *most frequent* patterns in D, i.e., the patterns having maximal frequency counts in comparison to other patterns in the given class.

In the unrestricted case, the problem of finding the most frequent patterns can be trivially non-interesting. If we consider the (infinite) class comprising of *all* TL

formulae, then an example of the most frequent pattern would be "p(a) ∨ ¬p(a)", where p(X) is a temporal predicate in a temporal database D. Therefore, we have to restrict our consideration to certain well-defined classes of temporal patterns for which the problem becomes non-trivial. For example, some classes of temporal patterns can be defined as follows:

1. A single FOTL formula, where the "variables" could be arguments of predicates, but cannot be of second-order, i.e. range over predicates.

2. A parameterized single FOTL formula defines a class of temporal patterns that may differ from each other by some parameters of the temporal operators. In the example discussed above, "K" is a parameter of *Until*.

3. The class of all the temporal patterns defined using only AND and NEXT operators.

Class Defined By A Single FOTL Formula

To illustrate the discovery methods described in this section, consider the following class of temporal patterns defined by the expression

$$ψ(X,Y,Z) = a(X,Y) \; Until \; b(Y,Z) \qquad (1)$$

where a and b are temporal predicates from the temporal database D. We want to find all possible instantiations for the variables X, Y and Z for which pattern (1) occurs frequently (its frequency is above a certain threshold). To find such instances, we construct a TLP that will identify all the occurrences of temporal patterns that belong to ψ.

Let a(X,Y,T), b(Y,Z,T), and ψ(X,Y,Z,T) be the temporal predicates that appear in (1), but with explicit references to time. Figure 1 illustrates a TLP program, written in eDatalog$_{1S}$, that computes ψ(X,Y,Z,T) using a distinguished predicate q(X,Y,Z,T).

(i)   simtime(0)
(ii) simtime(T) → simtime(T+1), ¬ simtime(T)
(iii) simtime(T), a(X,Y,T), ¬a(X,Y,T-1) →
        flag1(X,Y,T), flag2(X,Y,T)
(iv) simtime(T), a(X,Y,T), a(X,Y,T-1) → flag2(X,Y,T)
(v)   simtime(T), b(Y,Z,T), flag1(X,Y,T1), flag2(X,Y,T-1),
        (T1 ≤ T2 ≤ T) → q(X,Y,Z,T2)
(vi) simtime(T), ¬a(X,Y,T), flag1(X,Y,T1),flag2(X,Y,T-1),
        (T1 ≤ T2 ≤ T) → ¬flag2(X,Y,T2), ¬flag1(X,Y,T1)
(vii) b(Y,Z,T) → q(X,Y,Z,T)

Figure 1. TLP computing a(X,Y) *Until* b(Y,Z).

To simulate the forward movement in time, the program in Fig.1 uses predicate *simtime* that acts as a system clock, and Rule (ii) advances it forward on a tick-by-tick basis. Rule (iii) sets flag1 when the predicate a(X,Y) is true for the first time instant in a period of time when it holds continuously, and rule (iv) continues to set a new flag (flag2) for all time points in that period. Now when b(Y,Z) is encountered with flag1 and flag2 on, rule (v) sets the distinguished predicate, q(X,Y,Z) to be true for all instances of time from when flag1 was first set *until* the time when b(Y,Z) holds. Rule (vi) resets flags after the *end* of any continuous period of time when a(X,Y) holds.

To find frequent (or most frequent) patterns of the form (1), the program in Fig.1 can easily be extended to incorporate a counter of the number of instances when $q(X,Y,Z,T)$ is true. Note that the use of (first-order) variables in the program facilitates construction of a *single* TLP program to find all instances of temporal patterns in D that belong to the class ψ. We can generalize this example into the following theorem, the proof of which can be found in [11]:

Theorem. For any class of temporal patterns specified by a single FOTL formula φ defined on a temporal database D, there exists a TLP program PROG with the distinguished predicate q, such that for any finite instance of D, $q \cong \varphi$, i.e. q holds whenever φ holds and vice versa.

The proof of this theorem is by induction on the number of operators in the TL formula φ, and is *constructive*. Also, there is a notion of "safety" of FOTL expressions, without which TLP programs may not terminate. Our TLP programs can be shown to terminate if D is finite and the domains of the arguments in predicates are all finite.

Class of Patterns Consisting of AND and NEXT Operators

Here we consider the class of temporal patterns TL$\{\wedge,o\}$ consisting of $\wedge$ and o operators and study two problems of finding the *most* frequent and *all* frequent patterns.

Most Frequent Patterns. Because of the distributivity of $\wedge$ and o operators, any pattern from TL$\{\wedge,o\}$ depending on temporal predicates X_0, X_1, ..., X_n can be converted to the following canonical form (for clarity we omit arguments of the predicates) :

$$X_0 \wedge o^{k1} X_1 \wedge o^{k2} X_2 ... \wedge o^{kn} X_n \qquad (2)$$

where $1 \le k1 \le ... \le kn$ and for $i \ne j$, $X_i \ne X_j$ when $ki = kj$. The *most frequent* patterns in this case will be of the form:

$$\psi_{i,j}(K) = X_i \wedge o^K X_j \qquad (3)$$

The TLP that counts the occurrences of all the temporal patterns that belong to $\psi_{a,b}(X,Y,K) = a(X) \wedge o^k b(Y)$ is given in Figure 2, where predicate count$_{a,b}$ (X,Y,K,VAL) specifies how many times (VAL) the pattern $\psi_{a,b}$ (X,Y,K) occurred in the database.

(i) simtime(0)
(ii) simtime(T) $\rightarrow$ simtime(T+1)
(iii) simtime(T), a(X,T) , b(Y,T+K) , count$_{a,b}$ (X,Y,K,VAL), $\neg\psi_{a,b}$ (X,Y,K,T)$\rightarrow\psi_{a,b}$(X,Y,K,T),count$_{a,b}$(X,Y,K,VAL+1)

Figure 2. TLP program that simulates a $\wedge$ o^K b.

The program counting the most frequent occurrences of patterns belonging to (3) is obtained by combining the TLP programs presented in Fig. 2 for all possible pairs of predicates a and b and adding the "control" logic selecting the highest values (VAL) in predicate count$_{a,b}$ for various values of a, b, X, Y and K. We would like to point out that the program that finds the most frequent patterns of the form (3) (and hence (2)), does it in *one single* forward "sweep" in time during the execution of the program, and, thus, its complexity is linear in time.

Frequent Patterns. The starting point for finding frequent patterns from TL$\{\wedge,o\}$ is the canonical form (2) of these patterns. Since frequency of patterns is a monotonically decreasing function of n in (2), there is a value of n for which *no* temporal pattern given by (2) is frequent. Therefore, our goal is to find such maximal value of n (N) and also find *all* frequent patterns of the form (2) for n<N.

Unlike the case of the most frequent patterns, we cannot reduce (2) to a simplified expression and will be dealing with the general case of (2). A naive approach would be to find frequent patterns for (2) for successive values of n (until the next value of n does not generate any new frequent patterns) without using the outputs from previous iterations. However, we will use a more efficient algorithm that is based on the idea of generating larger candidate patterns from smaller ones. This method of generating candidate patterns was used effectively by Agrawal et al.[16] and by Mannila et al [4] to mine association rules and episodes respectively.

We will first start with finding frequent patterns for a single predicate p. In other words, the expression (2) is reduced to the case :

$$p(X) \wedge o^{k1} p(X) \wedge o^{k2} p(X) ... \wedge o^{kn} p(X) \wedge ... \qquad (4)$$

where X is a vector of the attributes of predicate p.

The algorithm, described in Fig 3, iteratively generates frequent patterns for successive values of n in (4) by utilizing the frequent patterns discovered in the previous iteration. T* is the largest value in the time domain (such value exists since the time domain is bounded), freq$_n$(X,K$_1$,..,K$_n$) is the class of all the frequent patterns found at stage n, count(X,K$_1$,..,K$_n$,VAL) is a predicate that tracks the frequency count, VAL, and c is the threshold frequency value. Predicate holds(T,X,K$_1$,...,K$_n$) is used in Rule (iii) to avoid double-counting. Initially, it is set to False for all of its values. The algorithm executes until the saturation point is reached, i.e. until freq$_n$ = ϕ.

n=1 and freq$_0$ = set of all frequent ground predicates p
repeat
       compute freq$_n$ with TLP program TLP$_n$;
       n=n+1;
until (freq$_n$ = ϕ);
print freq$_i$, i=1,2,...,n-1
       where the program TLP$_n$ is :
(i)   simtime(0)
(ii) simtime(T) ,T $\le$ T* $\rightarrow$ simtime(T+1)
(iii) simtime(T), p(X,T), p(X,T+K$_1$),...,p(X,T+K$_{n-1}$),
      freq$_{n-1}$ (X,K$_1$,...,K$_{n-1}$), p(X,T+K$_n$),
      count(X,K$_1$,..,K$_n$,VAL), $\neg$holds(T,X,K$_1$,...,K$_n$) $\rightarrow$
      holds (T,X,K$_1$,...,K$_n$), count(X,K$_1$,..,K$_n$, VAL +1)
(iv) simtime(T*+1), count(X,K$_1$,..,K$_n$, VAL), (VAL > c)
      $\rightarrow$ freq$_n$ (X,K$_1$,...,K$_n$)

Figure 3. Algorithm to find all frequent patterns of form (4)

Note that in rule (iii) in Figure 3, we add the predicate $\text{freq}_{n-1}(X,K_1,...,K_{n-1})$ to the body of the rule. This can improve efficiency if a smart rule evaluation strategy is used since, for all values of T, $\text{freq}_{n-1}(X,K_1,...,K_{n-1}) \Rightarrow p(X,T), p(X,T+K_1),...,p(X,T+K_{n-1})$. Thus, we have to evaluate $p(X,T), p(X,T+K_1),...,p(X,T+K_{n-1})$ only for the frequent values of $X,K_1,...,K_{n-1}$ in Rule (iii).

The generalization of the algorithm presented in Figure 3 to the class of patterns of the form (2) that are defined by multiple predicates is straightforward but notationally cumbersome and, thus, we omit it. Furthermore, it leads to the combinatorial explosion in the size of the TLP programs constructed by the algorithm (as a function of the number of predicates in the database). We would like to note that, in contrast to the "most frequent patterns" case, we construct *multiple* TLP programs (one program per iteration) in this algorithm. This means that the complexity of the algorithm is no longer linear in T*.

Experiments and Conclusion

We used TL to express patterns and implemented TLP programs in OPS5 for an application in which different financial analysts rate various stocks in terms of buying, selling, or holding recommendations. In this application, we wanted to find the most frequent recommendation change patterns made by various analysts and the correlation patterns of stock recommendations across different analysts (e.g. frequently, analyst A recommends "buy" for a stock until analyst B recommends "sell"). For example, a recommendation change pattern can be expressed as:

$$\text{Analyst\_Report}(\text{analyst,stock,recommendat}) \wedge$$
$$\neg \text{ o Analyst\_Report}(\text{analyst,stock,recommendat})$$

In this case we want to find the analysts that changed their recommendations most often for different stocks. The eDatalog$_{1S}$ program that finds such patterns is very similar to the one presented in Figure 2, and we simulated this program in OPS5 on a Sun Sparc20 using an artificially generated data set consisting of 3 analysts, 3 stocks, and 300 days (we assumed that the frequency of recommendations was one day). The performance as a function of the size of the data set is presented in Figure 4.

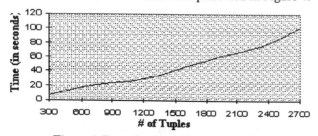

Figure 4. Execution Time Vs. Database Size

These preliminary results demonstrate that the performance of our implementation is quite slow. We attribute this to the following factors. Mainly, our version of OPS5 does not support arithmetic in the body of a rule.

Therefore, we simulated expressions of the form P(A,T+1) by creating new predicates and making the OPS5 program bigger and less efficient. Second, the OPS5 interpreter has the serial semantics (one tuple instantiation per recognize-act cycle), and this also slowed the execution of the TLP program. In summary, to make the TLP technology practical for the pattern discovery purposes, there is a need to develop efficient TLP interpreters that support such important features as pseudo-parallel execution of temporal rules and that would provide an efficient support for the temporal dimension.

References

[1] Tansel, A.U., Clifford, J., Gadia, S., Jajodia, S., Segev, A. and Snodgrass, R., 1993. In *Temporal Databases, Theory Design and Implementation.* Benjamin/Cummings.

[2] Clifford J., Tuzhilin A., 1995. *Recent Advances in Temporal Databases.* Springer-Verlag.

[3] Agrawal, R., Giuseppe, P., Edward, W.L., and Zait, M., 1995. Querying Shapes of Histories. In *Proceedings of the 21st VLDB Conference*, pp. 502-514.

[4] Mannila, H., Toivonen, H., and Verkamo, A.I., 1995. Discovering Frequent Episodes in Sequences. In *The First International Conf. on Knowledge Discovery in Databases (KDD-95)*, pp 210-215.

[5] Aho, A.V., 1990. Algorithms for Finding Patterns in Strings. In van Leeuwen, J., ed., *Handbook of Theoretical Comp. Sc., Vol A :Algorithms and Complexity.* Elsevier.

[6] Manna, Z., and Pnueli, A., 1992. Temporal Logic. In *The Temporal Logic of Reactive and Concurrent Systems.* Springer-Verlag.

[7] Abadi, M., and Manna, Z., 1989. Temporal Logic Programming. *J. of Symb. Computation* v8, pp. 277-295.

[8] Baudinet, M., Chomicki, J., and Wolper, P., 1993. Temporal Deductive Databases. Ch13 in [1].

[9] Tuzhilin, A., 1992. SimTL: A Simulation Language Based on Temporal Logic. *Transactions of the Society for Computer Simulation*, 9(2), pp. 87-100.

[10] Kroger, F., 1987. *Temporal Logic of Programs,* volume 8. Springer-Verlag.

[11] Padmanabhan, B., and Tuzhilin, A., 1996. Using Temporal Logic to Find Patterns in Temporal Databases. Working Paper #IS-96-2, Dept. of Info. Systems, NYU.

[12] Koymans, R.,1990. Specifying Real-Time Properties with Metric Temporal Logic. *J. of Real-Time Systems*, v2.

[13] Snodgrass, R.T., 1995. *The TSQL2 Temporal Query Language.* Kluwer.

[14] Chomicki, J., and Imielinski, T., 1988. Temporal Deductive Databases and Infinite Objects. *Proc of PODS.*

[15] Abiteboul, S., and Vianu, V., 1991. Datalog Extensions for Database Queries and Updates. *J. of Computer and System Sciences*, vol. 43, pp. 62-124.

[16] Agrawal, R., Mannila, H., Srikant, R., Toivonen, H. and Verkamo,A.I., 1995. Fast Discovery of Association Rules. In Fayyad, U.M., Piatetsky-Shapiro, G., Smyth, P., and Uthurusamy, R. eds., *Advances in Knowledge Discovery and Data Mining.* AAAI Press.

Exploiting Background Knowledge in Automated Discovery

John M. Aronis
Department of Computer Science
University of Pittsburgh
Pittsburgh, PA 15260
aronis@cs.pitt.edu

Foster J. Provost
NYNEX Science and Technology
400 Westchester Avenue
White Plains, NY 10604
foster@nynexst.com

Bruce G. Buchanan
Department of Computer Science
University of Pittsburgh
Pittsburgh, PA 15260
buchanan@cs.pitt.edu

Abstract

Prior work in automated scientific discovery has been successful in finding patterns in data, given that a reasonably small set of mostly relevant features is specified. The work described in this paper places data in the context of large bodies of background knowledge. Specifically, data items are connected to multiple databases of background knowledge represented as inheritance networks. The system has made a practical impact on botanical toxicology research, which required linking examples of cases of plant exposures to databases of botanical, geographical, and climate background knowledge.

Introduction

Discoveries made by computer programs have been characterized as human/computer discoveries because the discovery process is far from being completely automated (Valdes-Perez, 1995). One area where the human component has been vital is in guiding the discovery system based on background knowledge. In this paper we augment a standard inductive learning program by connecting data items to background knowledge represented as inheritance networks with role links and a limited form of non-monotonic inheritance, extending the ability of the program to make discoveries by using the semantics of the features describing the data items.

Representing Background Knowledge

Scientific domain knowledge takes on a rich, structured form. Prominent in any scientist's store of useful background knowledge are various taxonomies, categories, and relationships between concepts. To automate discovery using these forms of domain knowledge we must represent and reason about classes and relationships, and be able to bring the knowledge to bear on the discovery process. *Inheritance networks* are an efficient way to implement this kind of reasoning, because they can represent class structure and complex relational knowledge, yet can be navigated efficiently (Fahlman, 1979).

Figure 1 illustrates how some knowledge about plant families and their properties can be represented using standard inheritance network notation. A few records from a database of potentially toxic plant exposures and a small part of a botanical knowledge base are shown. Unlabeled arrows are *ISA links*, which can be interpreted as set inclusion. Thus, the link T. radicans → Toxicodendron means that every plant in the species T. radicans is also in the genus Toxicodendron. The link Toxicodendron → Anacardiaceae means that the genus Toxicodendron is a subset of the family Anacardiaceae. The *role link* Araceae $\overset{contains}{\rightarrow}$ Calcium-oxalate means that plants in the Araceae family contain calcium oxalate. Since calcium oxalate is present throughout the Araceae family we put the link at the family level, and let lower nodes *inherit* it. Calcium oxalate is specific to R. rhabarbarum (within its family), so the contains link is put directly on that species' node. These data are not in the primary database, but can be found in other databases.

Nodes and links can be used to form predicates. For instance, Toxicodendron(x) is true of everything in the genus Toxicodendron. Roles represent relations and can be multivalued; an exposure can have more than one substance link. We can use predicates to characterize sets of data items in terms of the knowledge base. For instance, Toxicodendron(substance(x)) characterizes the exposures 1-3. The more complicated predicate Calcium-oxalate(contains(substance(x))) characterizes exposures 4-5.

We note several advantages of this representation. First, inheritance networks provide a natural way to represent domain knowledge. For instance, our system allows a limited form of nonmonotonic inheritance to represent and reason about default and incomplete information. Second, since the representation does not duplicate domain knowledge for each database record there is a huge gain in both time and space efficiency. Third, inheritance networks are sufficient to represent multi-table relational databases, with role composition representing joins between tables. Finally, using inheritance networks for inductive learning connects automated discovery to work in knowledge representation.

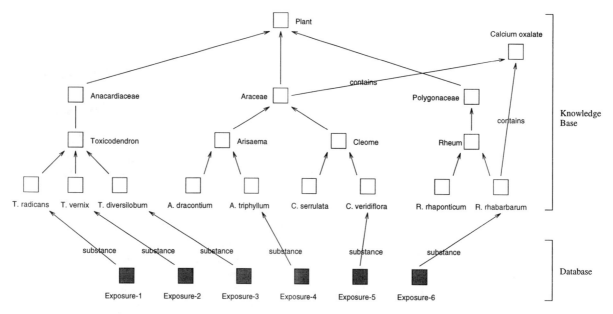

Figure 1: Linking Data to Botanical Knowledge.

An Illustrative Example

Consider the network in Figure 2. Six examples of Datura exposures are shown, connected to a database of geographical and climate knowledge. Datura exposures normally occur in August–October; here we are interested in characterizing an anomalous subset of toxic exposures that occur in May. The Knowledge-Based Rule Learner (KBRL) starts with general predicates and attempts to specialize them. The user defines criteria with which the system will judge a discovery to be interesting. For this example, we use the simple criteria: an interesting pattern is one that covers all of the May exposures, and none of the others.[1]

The search starts with the general predicate US(location(x)). Since testing reveals that this is an overly general characterization, its *specializations* are formed from relationships in the network, and are immediately tested:

Southeast(location(x))

Southwest(location(x))

The first predicate fails to cover any members of the concept class in the database, so the system rejects it. The second correctly excludes some of the complement of the concept class, while still covering the incidents we are interested in categorizing, so the system retains it. However, since this predicate still covers part of the complement, the system tests each of its specializations:

---

[1] Of course, discovering a pattern characterizing a concept is seldom this simple. Predicates have to be evaluated statistically, and the concept will usually be covered only partially or covered by a disjunction of predicates.

Nevada(location(x))

Arizona(location(x))

Neither of these have adequate coverage—they reject items in the concept class—so the system rejects them and looks for other ways to specialize the current hypothesis. The system cannot use the hierarchy of locations to refine its hypothesis any further, so it tries the zone link. Retaining the predicate already found, it forms the rule:

Southwest(location(x)) & AnyZone(zone(location(x)))

Again, the additional predicate is vacuous, so it is specialized to create the three hypotheses:

Southwest(location(x)) & Hot(zone(location(x)))

Southwest(location(x)) & Mild(zone(location(x)))

Southwest(location(x)) & Cold(zone(location(x)))

Checking each of these verifies that the first characterizes the May incidents perfectly, so it is retained as a characterization that satisfies the system's criteria for an interesting discovery.

Some Details of the Algorithm

KBRL, based on the RL learning program (Clearwater & Provost, 1990), performs a general-to-specific heuristic search for a set of conjunctive rules that satisfy user-defined *rule evaluation criteria*. At each stage of the search, KBRL *specializes* the currently most promising rules by either restricting their predicates, or adding new ones to the conjunction on the left-hand side of the rule. KBRL starts with the rule $T(x) \rightarrow C(x)$, where $T(x)$ is the most general concept in the knowledge base (true of everything), asserting that everything is a member of the concept C. KBRL performs

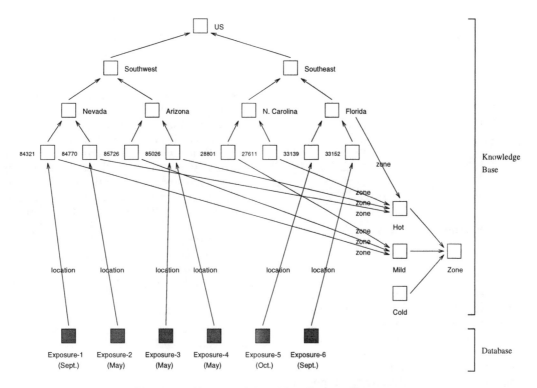

Figure 2: Characterizing May Datura Exposures.

an n-best search through the space of rules defined by the following *specialization* operators:

1. The rule $\dots P(f_n \dots f_1(x)) \dots \rightarrow C(x)$ can be specialized to the rule $\dots P(f_n \dots f_1(x)) \dots \& T(x) \rightarrow C(x)$.

2. Given a rule of the form $\dots P(f_n \dots f_1(x)) \dots \rightarrow C(x)$ and ISA links $P_1 \rightarrow P, \dots, P_n \rightarrow P$ in the network, the rules $\dots P_1(f_n \dots f_1(x)) \dots \rightarrow C(x)$ through $\dots P_n(f_n \dots f_1(x)) \dots \rightarrow C(x)$ are specializations.

3. If the node P has f role values which are restricted to P', the rule $\dots P(f_n \dots f_1(x)) \dots \rightarrow C(x)$ specializes to $\dots P(f_n \dots f_1(x)) \& P'(f_{n+1}f_n \dots f_1(x)) \dots \rightarrow C(x)$.

The first operator—*Add a Predicate*—allows us to add additional predicates to a rule. This allows us to form rules with several conjuncts. The second operator—*Specialize a Predicate*—searches downward through a network identifying classes of the concept. It is important to note that in some cases there will be several different classifications of items. In botany, for example, there are different hierarchies based on different approaches to classification. The KBRL search algorithm explores all of these, specializing predicates according to each hierarchy and using heuristics to guide the search down paths that make meaningful distinctions in the current context. The third operator—*Restrict a Role*—selects a set of items based on their

relationship to other parts of the knowledge base. Notice that the third operator is recursive, and we can restrict the predicate P(x) to P'(f(x)), P''(gf(x)), etc. Thus, we can talk about concepts such as "the average annual rainfall of the location of the exposure."

Membership in interesting classes may be determined by exceptional information, so it is important to incorporate and use some form of nonmonotonic information. We currently use a simple form of default inheritance that allows role values to be overridden by more specific information. Consider the diagram in Figure 3. The items in the concept, marked by "+", are characterized by the predicate $Q_2(f(X))$. This includes every item in P_2, which all have f's that default to Q_2, as well as I_3, which has an exceptional f value.

An Application to Botanical Toxicology

We have been working with botanical toxocologists to analyze a database of potentially toxic plant exposures (Krenzelok, et al., 1995a,b,c). KBRL was applied to these data linked to a knowledge base of geographic areas and their climates constructed from several sources on the World Wide Web.

As an example of the flexibility of learning with background knowledge represented as an inheritance hierarchy, consider the geographic knowledge base, which consists of approximately 1000 geographic regions. The smallest, most specific region is a "zip code area"—a geographically contiguous set of zip codes

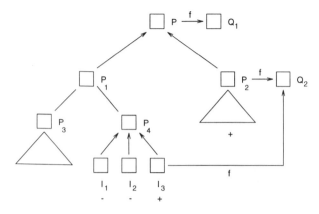

Figure 3: A Relation with an Exception.

Discussion

KBRL extends the notion of tree-structured attributes (Almuallim, Akiba & Kaneda, 1995) by allowing values to reference into multiple ISA hierarchies, complete with role relations and inheritance. However, the expressiveness of KBRL's language is currently limited to binary relational terms, and thus is not as expressive as some existing inductive logic programming systems (Muggleton, 1992). The design of KBRL purposely chose efficiency over expressiveness when it came to decisions about particularly expensive constructs, such as n-ary and recursive relational terms. On the other hand, because it was crucial for applications with incomplete data, KBRL incorporates default inheritance, which is difficult to deal with naturally in other relational systems. However, KBRL's form of nonmonotonic inheritance is limited, and will be difficult to extend since we want to allow multiple values and multiple ISA inheritance with negation.

Acknowledgements

This research was supported by National Science Foundation grants IRI-9412549, BES-9315428, and by the W. M. Keck Foundation.

References

Almuallim, H., Akiba, Yasuhiro, A., and Kaneda S. (1995). On Handling Tree-Structuree Attributes in Decision Tree Learning. In *Proceedings of the Twelfth International Conference on Machine Learning (ML-93)*. Morgan Kaufmann.

Clearwater, S. and Provost, F. (1990). RL4: A Tool for Knowledge-Based Induction. In *Proceedings of the Second International IEEE Conference on Tools for Artificial Intelligence*, 24–30. IEEE C.S. Press.

Fahlman, S. (1979). *NETL: A System for Representing and Using Real-World Knowledge*. MIT Press, Cambridge, MA.

Krenzelok, E.P., Jacobsen, T.D. and Aronis, J.M. (1995a). Mistletoe Exposures ... The Kiss of Death. To appear in *American Journal of Emergency Medicine*.

Krenzelok, E.P., Jacobsen, T.D. and Aronis, J.M. (1995b). Jimsonweed (Datura stramonium) Poisoning and Abuse ... An Analysis of 1,458 Cases. Submitted to *American Journal of Emergency Medicine*.

Krenzelok, E.P., F.J. Provost, Jacobsen, T.D., Aronis, J.M., and Buchanan, B.G. 1995c. Poinsettia (Euphorbia pulcherrima) Exposures Have Good Outcomes ... Just As We Thought. To appear in *American Journal of Emergency Medicine*.

Muggleton, S. (Editor) (1992). *Inductive Logic Programming*, Academic Press.

Valdes-Perez, R., (1995). Some Recent Human-Computer Discoveries in Science and What Accounts for Them. *AI Magazine*, 16(3), pp. 37–44.

that share the same first three digits. Zip code areas are arranged into a hierachy, with upper levels for states and geographic regions. Climate data, including rainfall, solarization, soil conditions, and temperatures, are linked to nodes in the geographic hierarchies by role links. In most cases, KBRL reasons about similarities in climate conditions by utilizing the exposure records' zip-code fields. However, some exposures are missing the zip code, but do have the telephone area code. Fortunately, KBRL can key into the geographic knowledge base at a less detailed level using the telephone area code.

The inheritance hierarchy allows the use of the most specific climatic information possible. The nodes at the lowest level do not all have complete information, so some information must be inherited from the state level. Although information at the state level is complete, it tends to be approximate. We also used a knowledge base of botanical species, genera, and families adapted from a U. S. Department of Agriculture database. Several small hierarchies of demographic factors, treatment patterns, etc., were also used.

One area of investigation in which KBRL took part was a study of exposures to Datura species. Many of the rules KBRL found refined the existing model of a seasonal spread of Datura exposures, but were not surprising to our botanical and toxicology collaborators. Rules showing that Datura exposures peak later in colder areas than in warm areas are a reflection of the fact that plants take longer to mature in colder climates. Other rules, such as a surprising degree of Datura abuse in some states, were unexpected but could have been found by other methods. A new rule was found that characterizes an unexpected set of May exposures in terms of basic enviromental conditions. This new rule was judged significant by our collaborators in botany and toxicology (Krenzelok, et al., 1995b).

Data Mining with Sparse and Simplified Interaction Selection

Gerald Fahner

International Computer Science Institute
1947 Center Street - Suite 600
Berkeley, CA 94704, U.S.A.
fahner@icsi.berkeley.edu

Abstract

We introduce a novel, greatly simplified classifier for
binarized data. The model contains a sparse, "digital"
hidden layer of **Parity** interactions, followed by a sig-
moidal output node. We propose priors for the cases:
a) input space obeys a metrics, b) inputs encode discrete attributes. Stochastic search for the hidden layer
allows capacity and smoothness of the approximation
to be controlled by two complexity parameters. Aggregation of classifiers improves predictions. Interpretable
results are obtained in some cases. We point out the
impact of our model on real-time systems, suitability
for sampling and aggregation techniques, and possible
contributions to nonstandard learning devices.

Introduction

For huge databases with many variables that interact
in complex ways, careful human selection of a feature
space can become unmanageable (Elder & Pregibon
1996). (Vapnik 1995) emphasizes a complementary approach to data modelling, namely to approximate the
unknown dependency by a "smart" linear combination
of "weak features". Any reasonable feature space may
be chosen; the predictive power arises entirely from
capacity control. Data mining tools operating accordingly must identify the relevant features or interactions
between variables. Here we focus on the issues

- **Sparseness**: how many interaction terms should a
  reasonable model include?

- **Preference**: can a *priori* preferences be assigned
  within a group of models of same size?

- **Simplicity**: are there reasonable feature sets that
  are particularly simple to compute?

The first issue is dealt with by applying Vapnik's Structural Risk Minimization. For the model family discussed in this paper, a nested set of models of increasing size is created and the optimum compromise between low training error and tight worst case bound
for the test error is determined.
We tackle the second issue by assigning preferences to
individual input features, speeding up the search process and improving performance over the worst case
bounds. Interactions that seem natural are given high
probability. Less obvious interactions are also explored
to allow discovery of unexpected dependencies. Without domain knowledge, general priors are used that

punish rapidly oscillating or high order interactions.
The third issue gains importance for mining huge
amounts of data, for recent computationally intensive
methods that sample in model space, for real-time data
analysis, and for possible use within future optical or
biomolecular hardware. Here we present a model with
greatly simplified interaction features, as compared to
"classic" neural networks.
In the following, we discuss heuristic methods for the
identification of models for binary data. In order to
discover knowledge we may estimate joint probabilities or perform soft classification of binary vectors
$\underline{x} \in \{-1, 1\}^N$.

Sparse Multinomial Logistic Model

We model a stochastic dependency between $\underline{x}$ and a
two-valued outcome variable $y \in \{0, 1\}$. The regression
$p(y = 1 \mid \underline{x})$ is estimated from a training database $\mathcal{T}$ of
labeled examples $(\underline{x}^i; y^i)_{i=1}^{\#\mathcal{T}}$. For approximation of the
regression, we use the logistic model

$$\hat{y} = \frac{1}{1 + \exp\{-f(\underline{x}, \underline{\theta})\}} \qquad (1)$$

with $f : \{-1, 1\}^N \to \mathbb{R}$:

$$
\begin{aligned}
f(\underline{x}, \underline{\theta}) =\ & \theta_0 + \theta_1 x_1 + ... + \theta_N x_N \\
+\ & \theta_{1,2} x_1 x_2 + ... + \theta_{N-1,N} x_{N-1} x_N \\
+\ & \theta_{1,2,3} x_1 x_2 x_3 + ... \\
+\ & ... \\
+\ & \theta_{1,2,...,N} x_1 x_2 ... x_N \qquad (2)
\end{aligned}
$$

subject to the constraint that

$$
\underline{\theta} = \begin{pmatrix} \theta_0 \\ \theta_1 \\ \vdots \\ \theta_{1,2} \\ \vdots \\ \theta_{1,2,...,N} \end{pmatrix}
$$

is a *sparse* vector of reals with an a *priori* fixed number
of non-vanishing components. Fixed size models are
fitted to the data by maximizing the log likelihood:

$$log\ lh = \sum_{i=1}^{\#\mathcal{T}} y^i\ log\ \hat{y}(\underline{x}^i, \underline{\theta}) + (1 - y^i)\ log\ (1 - \hat{y}(\underline{x}^i, \underline{\theta}))$$

Maximization is over all models of given size. This hard combinatorial problem can in general only be solved approximately.

The unconstrained expression (2) is known as "Walsh expansion" (Walsh 1923). The additive and higher order interactions form an orthogonal base (of dimension 2^N) for real valued functions over binary strings. Model (1) can thus approximate any regression function. In contrast, the sparse version has finite capacity. By enlarging the number of interactions sufficiently, any dichotomy over the input space can be approximated. Determination of a reasonable model size is crucial for obtaining low generalization error.

The second and higher order interaction terms can be considered as hidden nodes in a sparse network. Each node basically evaluates the Parity predicate (in the $(0, 1)$ representation) over some selected submask of input bits, which can be done in parallel. Heuristic supervised learning algorithms were proposed for problems of unknown order (Fahner and Eckmiller 1994).

Model Identification by Pruning and Replacement

The algorithm presented in the box below determines model size, selects a set of interaction terms, and simultaneously computes respective coefficients $\theta_{i,k,..}$.

---

1) chose model size within interval $[\frac{\#\mathcal{T}}{100}, \#\mathcal{T}]$
2) chose prior distribution $p(complexity; \mu)$ for individual interactions
3) initialize model with tentative interactions drawn according to $p(complexity; \mu)$
4) maximize $log\ lh\ (\underline{\theta}\,|\,\mathcal{T})$ and obtain weight vector $\underline{\theta}^*$
5) prune "brittle" interactions
6) install novel tentative interactions replacing the pruned ones
7) back to 4) until stopping criterium is met; output final sparse model

---

The maximization **4)** is over a fixed model structure, and the likelihood function possesses a single maximum. Fig.1 depicts the inner "Pruning and Replacement" loop (**4)** to **7)**). The stopping criterion of the algorithm varies with applications. For any preselected size and prior distribution, the algorithm outputs a sparse multinomial. Search for the best model (minimum validation error) is over the two-dimensional parameter plane spanned by model size and the single parameter μ, which determines the prior distribution for feature complexity (see explanation to Fig.2). We sample an ensemble of models from a reasonable region of the plane. We distribute the training of individual models over a network of workstations, which requires no communication.

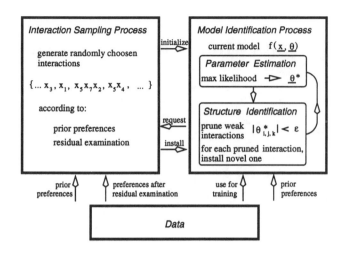

Figure 1: Stochastically driven interaction selection: Right module modifies the current model by iterative application of parameter estimation and structure modification. In the simplest case, an interaction is pruned if its weight is below some threshold ϵ. More advanced pruning mechanisms include prior preferences or statistical significance tests to reveal "brittle" interactions. For any interaction pruned, a request for a novel term is sent to the left module.

Left module generates several candidate terms according to prior preferences, and ranks them according to their correlation with residual misclassification error. Greedy selection installs the term with the highest correlation.

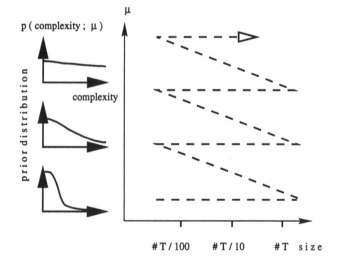

Figure 2: Capacity control plane: with increasing size, reduction of training error is possible at the expense of overfitting. μ parametrizes the form of a generic complexity prior distribution (as indicated qualitatively) for individual features. With increasing μ, complex interactions are more likely to be included in the model, thereby increasing the effective model space.

Complexity Measures for Interactions

For two types of input space semantics: a) binary representation of metrical input data, b) binary encodings of discrete attribute values, we propose respective complexity measures for individual interactions:

- **a) zero crossings**: maximum number of sign flips along straight line through input space

- **b) order**: number of multiplicative factors included in the interaction

Fig.3 illustrates case a) for a two-dimensional rectangular input space. Both continuous $\vec{a}$ and $\vec{b}$ axes are uniformly discretized into 4 intervals. For each dimension, the intervals are encoded by increasing binary numbers ($-$ stands for 0, $+$ for 1), preserving the order relation of the aligned intervals. Each box in the rectangular region is encoded as a 4-tuple $x_1x_2x_3x_4$ formed by the concatenation of the discretized and binarized coordinate values of the boxes. The given example generalizes to higher dimensions, to arbitrary binary resolutions individually chosen for each dimension and to nonuniform parcellings.

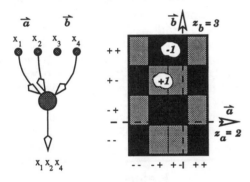

Figure 3: Behavior of the interaction term $x_1x_2x_4$ in two dimensions. The interaction term oscillates between -1's and 1's, undergoing zero crossings at some box borders. Along the two dashed arrows, the number of zero crossings z_a and z_b is counted separately for each of the coordinate axes. The maximum achievable number of zero crossings for an arbitrary direction linesweep is given by $z_a + z_b = 5$.

Simulation Results

We illustrate the working of the model for the **2-spirals** problem. In the original formulation (Lang and Witbrok 1988), the classifier has to separate two continuous point sets in $I\!R^2$ that belong to one or the other of intertwined spirals. The problem is formulated for binarized inputs as follows: each point in the plane is represented by some bitstring B_aB_b which is the concatenation of the truncated binary expansions for the points a- and b-coordinates. We chose 7 bit resolution for each coordinate, which is much more than required to distinguish between any two training examples. We use the "zero crossings" prior. A particular choice of coordinate axes breaks shift invariance and isotropy of the original problem, due to the invariance group properties of the Walsh functions. In order to restore the effect of broken symmetries, we apply the binarization for a transformation set (TS) of several randomly shifted and rotated (around coordinate center $(0,0)$, not around center of the spirals, since we assume no a *priori* knowledge) versions of the original input vectors. For each coordinate system, a separate model is trained on 335 examples per class. Size and prior complexity are constant over TS. The approximation over the discretized $[0,1)^2$ is computed by averaging over the estimates of all members of TS. Training is stopped as soon as all training examples are correctly classified or no further error reduction is achieved within a reasonable number of iterations. Fig.4 shows a result with adequately designed models.

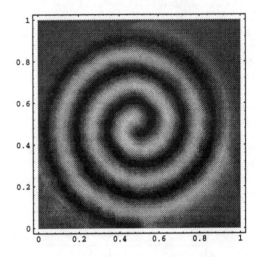

Figure 4: Approximation for models with size $= 50$, and with a prior that encourages a moderate number of zero crossings. TS contains 679 models, contributing to the apparent smoothness of the approximation.

The best models mainly use the 4 most significant bits of the binary encoded input vectors, and hardly contain interactions with more than 15 zero crossings. In contrast, models with a more flat zero crossings prior exhibit rich connectivity also to the least significant bits, thus overfitting the data. Using a well designed *single* model (instead of TS) yields approximations with an orthogonal axes bias, and a tendency of the approximation to undergo changes at fractions of low powers of two. But the concept of the two spirals is clearly learned by capacity controlled single models, proving the high flexibility of this model class.

The second task is the **Gene** benchmark (Nordewier, Towell and Shavlik 1991) for predicting splice-junctions. Problem description, data, and encoding conventions can be found and are adopted from the the *PROBEN1* collection in the Neural

Bench Archive at CMU (**ftp.cs.cmu.edu**, directory /afs/cs/project/connect/bench/contrib/prechelt). The problem provides 120 binary inputs, and 3175 data labeled according to three classes. Three models are trained separately to discriminate each class against the other classes. 900 patterns are used for training, 100 for crossvalidation, the rest for testing. Training is stopped when no further improvement can be achieved on the training set within a reasonable number of iterations. We use the "order" prior. We find models of size ≈ 60 with interactions up to second order to be superior. For prediction, we chose the label of the model with the maximum active output as class label. Test error is $7-8\%$, comparable to results from literature with MLPs, and superior to experiments with *ID3* and Nearest Neighbor (Murphy and Aha 1992, UCI Repository of machine learning databases, **ftp.ics.uci.edu**, University of California, Irvine, CA).

A drastic reduction of prediction error to slightly above 6% is achieved by aggregating 50 models for each class, starting with different seeds for the random number generator, and using majority voting for the class decision. Best voting results are achieved with models of size = 250, and interactions up to order 4 are found significant. Models trained on the same class exhibit a strong overlap of the more significant interaction terms, and high variability among the weaker interactions. We conclude that the improvement in prediction accuracy arises from less biased size constraints in conjunction with reduced variance of the aggregated classifier.

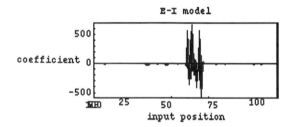

Figure 5: Structure histogram for an Exon-Intron boundary predictor aggregated from 50 models: Inputs are ordered along the horizontal axis. Vertical axis measures absolute weight coefficients of interactions. A peak indicates that the corresponding bit contributes (in an additive way or participating in some higher order interaction) to the classifier decision; the height of the peak measures the strength of this contribution.

Fig.5 reveals some gross information on the structure of interactions for the gene-splicing problem. A striking observation is that genes in the local neighborhood of the junction have the most impact on the type of junction, and that no significant long range interactions are present.

Discussion

The paper contributes original research to: integrated data and knowledge representation for numeric and categorical data, model simplicity and scalability issues, and distributed search for the best model. The computationally feasible automatic model identification determines relevant interactions between binary variables. It constitutes a much faster, less biased, and wider applicable modelling process than human feature selection. This makes our data mining tool a good candidate for real-time and high dimensional data analysis. A serious challenge for automatied search of wide model classes is the problem of overfitting. We overcome this difficulty by incorporating powerful novel regularization techniques for binary data formats. Our first simulation results hint that model aggregation further stabilizes predictions.

Simplifying the computation of feature sets becomes an important issue regarding explosive growth of data mines, shrinking time spans for data analysis and decision making, and state-of-the-art sampling and aggregation techniques. Our findings show that floating point multiplications can be avoided for some important data mining applications, speeding up the inference process significantly. A technological quantum jump may help to overcome severe scaling problems. The bit-interactions which make up the "atomic" knowledge entities of our model seem well suited for parallel distributed processing by novel computing technologies under development. It remains to be seen if models similar in spirit could simplify the implementation of statistical learning algorithms on future quantum computers for large scale, high-speed data mining.

References

Elder IV, J. F., and Pregibon, D. 1996. A statistical perspective on knowledge discovery in databases. In: *Advances in Knowledge Discovery and Data Mining.* U. M. Fayyad, G. Piatetsky-Shapiro, P. Smyth, R. Uthurusamy eds. Menlo Park, CA: The MIT Press.

Fahner G., and Eckmiller, R. 1994. Structural adaptation of parsimonious higher-order neural classifiers. *Neural Networks* 7(2):279-289.

Lang, K. J., and Witbrok M. 1988. Learning to tell two spirals apart. In: Proceedings of the 1988 Connectionists Model Summer School, 52-59. New York: Morgan Kaufmann Publishers.

Noordewier M. O., Towell G. G., and Shavlik J. W. 1991. Training knowledge-based neural networks to recognize genes in DNA sequences. In Advances in Neural Information Processing Systems 3:530-536. San Mateo, CA: Morgan Kaufmann.

Vapnik, V. N. 1995. *The Nature of Statistical Learning Theory.* New York: Springer.

Walsh, J. L. 1923. A closed set of orthogonal functions. *American Journal of Mathematics* 45:5-24.

Inferring Hierarchical Clustering Structures by Deterministic Annealing

Thomas Hofmann & Joachim M. Buhmann *
Rheinische Friedrich–Wilhelms–Universität
Institut für Informatik III, Römerstraße 164, D-53117 Bonn, Germany
email:{th,jb}@cs.uni-bonn.de, http://www-dbv.cs.uni-bonn.de

Abstract

The unsupervised detection of hierarchical structures is a major topic in unsupervised learning and one of the key questions in data analysis and representation. We propose a novel algorithm for the problem of learning decision trees for data clustering and related problems. In contrast to many other methods based on successive tree growing and pruning, we propose an objective function for tree evaluation and we derive a non–greedy technique for tree growing. Applying the principles of maximum entropy and minimum cross entropy, a deterministic annealing algorithm is derived in a meanfield approximation. This technique allows us to canonically superimpose tree structures and to fit parameters to averaged or 'fuzzified' trees.

Introduction

Clustering is one of the fundamental problems in exploratory data analysis. Data clustering problems occur in pattern recognition, statistics, unsupervised learning, neural networks, data mining, machine learning and many other scientific fields. The wide range of applications is explained by the fact that clustering procedures are important tools for an automated or interactive detection of structure in data sets. Especially for large data sets grouping data and extracting typical prototypes is important for a compact representation and is a precondition for further symbolic processing stages. In the context of data clustering the detection of hierarchical structures is an essential goal of data analysis. In this paper we consider binary trees with stochastic transition nodes, (Breiman *et al.* 1984) applied to vector–valued data.

We will formulate data clustering as a stochastic optimization problem to be addressed in the *maximum entropy framework*. Maximum entropy methods have been introduced as a stochastic optimization method, called *simulated annealing* in a seminal paper of Kirkpatrick et al. (Kirkpatrick, Gelatt, &

---
*Supported by the Federal Ministry for Science and Technology (BMBF) under grant # 01 M 3021 A/4. The LANDSAT data have been provided by D. Klaus.

Vecchi 1983). To overcome the computational burden of Monte Carlo sampling, efficient *deterministic annealing* variants have been derived for a number of important optimization problems (Yuille 1990; Kosowsky & Yuille 1994; Buhmann & Hofmann 1994; Gold & Rangarajan 1996), including unconstrained clustering and vector quantization. (Rose, Gurewitz, & Fox 1990; Buhmann & Kühnel 1993). Maximum entropy methods have recently been successfully applied to the case of tree–structured vector quantization in (Miller & Rose 1994; 1996). Similar methods have also been used in the context of regression (Jordan & Jacobs 1994) and for unsupervised learning problems (Dayan, Hinton, & Zemel 1995). The key idea in simulated and deterministic annealing is to reformulate a given combinatorial optimization problem as a stochastic optimization problem. A temperature parameter T is introduced to control the amplitude of the induced noise. In the zero temperature limit, $T \to 0$, the combinatorial problem is recovered, while for high temperatures the objective function is smoothened. Tracking solutions from high temperatures thus helps us to avoid unfavorable local minima.

The major novelty of our approach is an *explicit* treatment of the topology of binary trees in the maximum entropy framework, which results in a systematic and well–founded 'fuzzification' of binary tree topologies. At a finite computational temperature different trees are superimposed resulting in an average tree structure. An average tree is not a single tree but a tree mixture. The proposed algorithm optimizes the tree topology *jointly* with all other relevant parameters, e.g. data assignments to clusters and decision node parameters.

Unconstrained Data Clustering

We restrict our attention to the case of real–valued data vectors $\mathcal{X} = \{\mathbf{x}_i \in \mathbb{R}^d : 1 \le i \le N\}$, and a corresponding set of prototypes $\mathcal{Y} = \{\mathbf{y}_\nu \in \mathbb{R}^d : 1 \le \nu \le K\}$, $K \ll N$, $\mathbf{y}_\nu$ representing a group G_ν. To describe the mapping of data vectors to prototypes we introduce an indicator function representation by Boolean assignment matrices $M \in \{0,1\}^{N \times K}$ obeying the constraints $\sum_{\nu=1}^{K} M_{i\nu} = 1$, for all i. The objective function for unconstrained data clustering is usually stated as (Duda & Hart 1973)

$$\mathcal{H}(M, \mathcal{Y}|\mathcal{X}) = \sum_{i=1}^{N} \sum_{\nu=1}^{K} M_{i\nu} \, \mathcal{D}(\mathbf{x}_i, \mathbf{y}_\nu), \qquad (1)$$

where $\mathcal{D}$ is a problem dependent distortion measure, e.g. $\mathcal{D}(\mathbf{x}_i, \mathbf{y}_\nu) = \|\mathbf{x}_i - \mathbf{y}_\nu\|^2$. Applying the principle of maximum entropy, Boolean assignments are replaced by assignment probabilities $\langle M_{i\nu} \rangle$, maximizing the entropy $S = -\sum_{i=1}^{N} \sum_{\nu=1}^{K} \langle M_{i\nu} \rangle \log \langle M_{i\nu} \rangle$ subject to fixed expected costs $\langle \mathcal{H} \rangle$. For a given set of prototypes the assignment probability of vector $\mathbf{x}_i$ to group G_ν is the Gibbs distribution

$$\langle M_{i\nu} \rangle = \frac{\exp\left[-\mathcal{D}(\mathbf{x}_i, \mathbf{y}_\nu)/T_M\right]}{\sum_{\mu=1}^{K} \exp\left[-\mathcal{D}(\mathbf{x}_i, \mathbf{y}_\mu)/T_M\right]}, \qquad (2)$$

where T_M is the computational temperature. Minimization of the expected costs with respect to the prototype vectors results in an additional set of centroid equations,

$$\mathbf{y}_\nu = \sum_{i=1}^{N} \langle M_{i\nu} \rangle \mathbf{x}_i \Big/ \sum_{i=1}^{N} \langle M_{i\nu} \rangle, \qquad (3)$$

for the case of squared Euclidean distances. Eqs. (2) and (3) can be solved efficiently by an EM algorithms (Dempster, Laird, & Rubin 1977). In a more general situation additional prior assignment probabilities $\pi_{i\nu}$ are given. Applying the principle of minimum cross entropy this results in modified, 'tilted' assignment probabilities,

$$\langle M_{i\nu} \rangle^\pi = \frac{\pi_{i\nu} \exp\left[-\mathcal{D}(\mathbf{x}_i, \mathbf{y}_\nu)/T_M\right]}{\sum_{\mu=1}^{K} \pi_{i\mu} \exp\left[-\mathcal{D}(\mathbf{x}_i, \mathbf{y}_\mu)/T_M\right]}, \qquad (4)$$

which minimize the cross entropy to the prior for fixed costs $\langle \mathcal{H} \rangle$ ((Miller & Rose 1994)). For uniform priors, we recover Eq. (2) as expected. Tilted assignments will be used in the following section to model the influence of the cluster hierarchy on data assignments.

Decision Trees for Data Clustering

In this paper we consider stochastic binary decision trees with a given number of K leaves, representing the data clusters. We denote nodes of the tree by n_α, $0 \leq \alpha \leq 2K - 2$. Associated with each inner node n_α are two test vectors $\mathbf{y}_\alpha^l, \mathbf{y}_\alpha^r \in \mathbb{R}^d$ and a control parameter $\lambda_\alpha \in \mathbb{R}^+$. The test vectors determine transition probabilities $p_{i\alpha}^l(\mathbf{x})$ and $p_{i\alpha}^r(\mathbf{x})$ for a given vector $\mathbf{x}$ according to the formula

$$p_\alpha^{l/r}(\mathbf{x}) = \frac{\exp\left[-\lambda_\alpha \mathcal{D}(\mathbf{x}, \mathbf{y}_\alpha^{l/r})\right]}{\exp\left[-\lambda_\alpha \mathcal{D}(\mathbf{x}, \mathbf{y}_\alpha^l)\right] + \exp\left[-\lambda_\alpha \mathcal{D}(\mathbf{x}, \mathbf{y}_\alpha^r)\right]}. \quad (5)$$

$p_\alpha^l(\mathbf{x})$ and $p_\alpha^r(\mathbf{x})$ are the probability for vector $\mathbf{x}$ to continue its path with the left and right successor of

n_α, respectively. λ_α controls the stochasticity of the transition, hard decision boundaries are obtained for $\lambda_\alpha \to \infty$. The path probability $\pi_\gamma(\mathbf{x})$ of a data vector $\mathbf{x}$ from the root to a node n_γ is given by the product of all transition probabilities at inner nodes on that path. In the limit of all $\lambda_\alpha \to \infty$ the tree defines a unique partitioning of the data space. Following (Miller & Rose 1996) we optimize the tree in order to minimize the deviation of the decision tree data partitioning from an unconstrained clustering solution with assignment probabilities $\{\langle M_{i\nu} \rangle\}$. As a suitable measure of divergence between probabilities the cross-entropy or *Kullback–Leibler divergence* is employed,

$$\mathcal{I}(\{\langle M_{i\nu} \rangle\} \| \{\pi_{i\nu}\}) = \sum_{i=1}^{N} \sum_{\nu=1}^{K} \langle M_{i\nu} \rangle \log \frac{\langle M_{i\nu} \rangle}{\pi_{i\nu}}, \qquad (6)$$

where $\pi_{i\nu} = \pi_{\nu+K-2}(\mathbf{x}_i)$. The binary tree is optimized such that the leaf probabilities $\pi_{i\nu}$ approximate as closely as possible the target probabilities. Conversely, for a given tree the prototype vectors $\mathcal{Y}$ are selected to minimize the expected distortion $\mathcal{H}(\mathcal{Y}, \{\pi_{i\nu}\}) = \sum_{i=1}^{N} \sum_{\nu=1}^{K} \langle M_{i\nu} \rangle^\pi \, \mathcal{D}(\mathbf{x}_i, \mathbf{y}_\nu)$, where $\langle M_{i\nu} \rangle^\pi$ is the tilted distribution from Eq. (4). The path probabilities obtained from the tree take the role of a prior to impose structural constraints on the selection of prototypes.

Since our goal is to explicitly optimize the tree topology, we introduce an adjacency matrix representation for binary trees. Let $U^l, U^r \in \{0,1\}^{(K-1)\times(2K-1)}$ encode the successor relation between nodes in the tree. $U_{\alpha\gamma}^{l/r} = 1$ denotes that n_γ is the immediate left/right successor of inner node n_α. To avoid directed cycles we use the node numbering as a total order, where successing nodes are required to have a higher index. Furthermore every inner node has exactly one left and one right successor and all nodes except the root n_0 are required to have a unique predecessor. The path probabilities $\pi_\gamma(\mathbf{x})$ are related to the adjacency matrices by the formula,

$$\pi_\gamma(\mathbf{x}) = \sum_{\alpha=0}^{\gamma-1} \pi_\alpha(\mathbf{x}) \left[U_{\alpha\gamma}^l \, p_\alpha^l(\mathbf{x}) + U_{\alpha\gamma}^r \, p_\alpha^r(\mathbf{x}) \right], \quad (7)$$

with $\pi_0(\mathbf{x}) = 1$. Path probabilities are efficiently calculated by sequentially propagating the probabilities from the root to the leaf nodes. This results in a well-defined optimization problem with a single objective function for the tree topology encoded by U^l, U^r and all involved continuous decision node parameters.

Optimizing the Tree Topology

The problem of finding an optimal decision tree is computationally difficult for two reasons: (i) the number of binary trees grows exponentially with the number of leaves; (ii) evaluating the quality of a single topology requires to fit all continuous parameters for test vectors and prototypes. The maximum entropy method offers a stochastic framework which renders an average over tree topologies feasible. Parameters are fitted not to a single tree, but to a weighted superposition of structures which converges only in the zero temperature limit towards a uniquely determined topology. This results in a 'fuzzification' of structures at finite temperatures, which is gradually eliminated in an annealing process.

Consider an extension of the probabilistic partitioning model, such that not only the transitions are stochastic, but also the successors of n_α are randomly drawn from the set of nodes $\{n_\gamma, \gamma > \alpha\}$. This means the connection between n_α and n_γ, encoded by $U_{\alpha\gamma}^l, U_{\alpha\gamma}^r$ is a random variable, with expectations $q_{\alpha\gamma}^l = \langle U_{\alpha\gamma}^l \rangle$ and $q_{\alpha\gamma}^r = \langle U_{\alpha\gamma}^r \rangle$, respectively. The probabilities have to be chosen such that $\sum_{\gamma>\alpha} q_{\alpha\gamma}^l = \sum_{\gamma>\alpha} q_{\alpha\gamma}^r = 1$ in order to obtain a correct normalization. A class of probabilities which is of special interest in this context are *fair* probability distributions. A fair probability distribution possesses the additional property that every node except the root has the same average number of predecessor, i.e. $\sum_{\alpha=0}^{\gamma-1} \left(q_{\alpha\gamma}^l + q_{\alpha\gamma}^r \right) = 1$, for all $\gamma > 0$. Fair probability distribution have the advantage, that the constraints on U^l and U^r are at least fulfilled in the average. In the extended model we can calculate path probabilities for $\mathbf{x}$ simply by replacing the Boolean variables in Eq. (7) by their probabilities.

Applying the maximum entropy principle to the objective function in Eq. (6), we assign the Gibbs probabilities $P(U^l, U^r) = \frac{1}{\mathcal{Z}} \exp\left[-\mathcal{I}(U^l, U^r)/T_U\right]$ to every tree topology U^l, U^r. $\mathcal{Z}$ is a normalization constant and T_U a temperature (or Lagrange) parameter. Ideally, we would like to average tree topologies according to the Gibbs distribution, without performing a tedious Monte Carlo sampling of trees. A standard approximation technique to analytically calculate Gibbs averages is the *meanfield approximation*. In the meanfield approximation we restrict the set of admissible probability distributions to distributions Q which are *factorial* and *fair*. Within this restricted set we want to pick a Q^* which maximizes the entropy for fixed expected costs or equivalently minimizes the cross entropy to the true Gibbs distribution $\mathcal{I}(Q\|P)$.

Omitting the technical details, the link probabilities $q_{\alpha\gamma}^{l/r}$ of Q^* are 0 for $\alpha \geq \gamma$ and are otherwise given by

$$q_{\alpha\gamma}^{l/r} = \frac{\exp\left[-\left(h_{\alpha\gamma}^{l/r} + \rho_\gamma\right)\right]}{\sum_{\bar\gamma>\alpha} \exp\left[-\left(h_{\alpha\bar\gamma}^{l/r} + \rho_{\bar\gamma}\right)\right]}, \quad h_{\alpha\gamma}^{l/r} = \frac{\partial \mathcal{I}}{\partial q_{\alpha\gamma}^{l/r}}. \quad (8)$$

The above cross entropy minimization problem has been reduced to the problem of finding values for the Lagrange parameters ρ_γ, such that Q is fair. Standard methods from combinatorial optimization, developed in the context of matching problems, can be applied to find solutions for Eq. (8) if all $h_{\alpha\gamma}^{l/r}$ are kept fixed. In our simulations we used an iterative proce-

dure known as Sinkhorn's algorithm (Sinkhorn 1964; Kosowsky & Yuille 1994). To give the basic idea, the Lagrange parameter ρ_γ can be interpreted as the 'price' of linking n_γ to another node n_α. These prices have to be simultaneously adjusted, such that every node has in the average exactly one predecessors. To arrive at a final solution we recalculate the derivatives

$$\frac{\partial \mathcal{I}}{\partial q_{\alpha\gamma}^{l/r}} = -\sum_{i=1}^{N} \sum_{\nu=1}^{K} \frac{\langle M_{i\nu} \rangle}{\pi_{i\nu}} \frac{\partial \pi_{i\nu}}{\partial q_{\alpha\gamma}^{l/r}} \quad (9)$$

and insert into Eq. (8), until a stationary state is reached. This is similar to the application of Sinkhorn's algorithm for graph matching problems (Gold & Rangarajan 1996).

Fitting Continuous Tree Parameters

The continuous decision node parameters are chosen in order to minimize $\mathcal{I}$. Applying the chain rule in calculating derivatives yields the final formula

$$\frac{\partial \mathcal{I}}{\partial \mathbf{y}_\alpha^{l/r}} = -2\lambda_\alpha \left(\mathbf{x}_i - \mathbf{y}_\alpha^{l/r}\right) \Big[s_\alpha^{l/r}(\mathbf{x}_i)$$
$$-p_\alpha^{l/r}(\mathbf{x}_i) \left(s_\alpha^l(\mathbf{x}_i) + s_\alpha^r(\mathbf{x}_i) \right) \Big], \quad (10)$$

where $s_\alpha^{l/r}(\mathbf{x}_i)$ denotes up-propagated unconstrained leaf probabilities. The test vectors can be optimized by gradient methods, e.g. steepest descent or conjugate gradient techniques. The derivation of similar equations for the control parameters λ_α is straightforward.

The optimization of prototype vectors $\mathbf{y}_\nu$ proceeds according to the centroid condition in Eq. (3), with the unconstrained assignment probabilities replaced by the 'tilted' probabilities of Eq. (4). The only remaining variables are the temperature parameters T_M and T_U, which are iteratively decreased according to an appropriate annealing schedule.

```
┌─────────────────────────────────────────────────┐
│        Tree Clustering Algorithm (TCA)          │
│ INITIALIZATION                                   │
│    choose yν, yα^l/r, λα randomly                │
│    chose ⟨Miν⟩, ⟨Uαγ^l/r⟩ ∈ (0,1) randomly;      │
│    temperature TM ← T0, TU ← cTM;                │
│ WHILE TM > TFINAL                                │
│    REPEAT                                         │
│       estimate tilted assignm. {⟨Miν^π⟩}, Eq.(4) │
│       update prototypes {yν} with tilted assignm.│
│       calc. unconstr. assignm. {⟨Miν⟩}, Eq.(2)   │
│       adapt {yα^l/r} and {λα} by gradient descent│
│       apply Sinkhorn's algorithm to calc. {qαγ^l/r}│
│    UNTIL all {yν},{yα^l/r},{λα} are stationary    │
│    TM ← TM/2; TU ← cTM;                          │
└─────────────────────────────────────────────────┘
```

Results

The tree clustering algorithm can in principle be applied to any set of vector-valued data. As a test example we chose synthetic two-dimensional data and

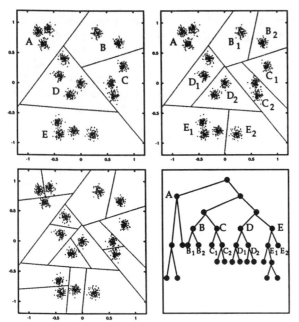

Figure 1: Hierarchical clustering of artificial two-dimensional data from 16 isotropic Gaussian modes. Displayed are partitionings with $K = 4, 9$ and $K = 16$ clusters.

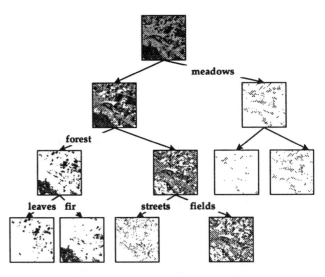

Figure 2: Hierarchical clustering of a LANDSAT multispectral image with 7 channels. Hierarchical clustering reveals the underlying relationship between regions. Only the top levels of the tree are displayed.

real world data from multispectral LANDSAT images with seven spectral channels. The results on the synthetic data at different levels are shown in Fig. 1, together with a representation of the final tree topology. The obtained hierarchical data partitioning retrieves the structure of the generating source. Fig. 2 shows the hierarchical split of the LANDSAT data. Regions which correspond to particular clusters are grey-scale coded and can be identified with the help of external information. The split between meadows and other areas occurs first in our example. Further down in the hierarchy, a separation of forest from urban areas can be observed. The hierarchy is stable for runs with different initial conditions.

References

Breiman, L.; Friedman, J. H.; Olshen, R. A.; and Stone, C. J. 1984. *Classification and Regression Trees*. Belmont, California: Wadsworth Intern. Group.

Buhmann, J., and Hofmann, T. 1994. A maximum entropy approach to pairwise data clustering. In *Proc. Intern. Conf. on Pattern Recognition, Jerusalem*, volume II, 207–212. IEEE Computer Society Press.

Buhmann, J., and Kühnel, H. 1993. Vector quantization with complexity costs. *IEEE Transactions on Information Theory* 39(4):1133–1145.

Dayan, P.; Hinton, G.; and Zemel, R. 1995. The Helmholtz machine. *Neural Computation* 7(5):889–904.

Dempster, A. P.; Laird, N. M.; and Rubin, D. B. 1977. Maximum likelihood from incomplete data via the em algorithm. *J. Royal Statist. Soc. Ser. B* 39:1–38.

Duda, R. O., and Hart, P. E. 1973. *Pattern Classification and Scene Analysis*. New York: Wiley.

Gold, S., and Rangarajan, A. 1996. A graduated assignment algorithm for graph matching. *IEEE PAMI*. in press.

Jordan, M., and Jacobs, R. 1994. Hierarchical mixtures of experts and the EM algorithm. *Neural Computation* 6(2):181–214.

Kirkpatrick, S.; Gelatt, C.; and Vecchi, M. 1983. Optimization by simulated annealing. *Science* 220:671–680.

Kosowsky, J., and Yuille, A. 1994. The invisble hand algorithm: Solving the assignment problem with statistical physics. *Neural Computation* 7(3):477–490.

Miller, D., and Rose, K. 1994. A non-greedy approach to tree-structured clustering. *Pattern Recognition Letters* 15(7):683–690.

Miller, D., and Rose, K. 1996. Hierarchical, unsupervised learning with growing via phase transitions. to appear.

Rose, K.; Gurewitz, E.; and Fox, G. 1990. Statistical mechanics and phase transition in clustering. *Phy. Rev. Lett.* 65:945–948.

Sinkhorn, R. 1964. A relationship between arbitrary positive matrices and doubly stochastic matrices. *Ann. Math. Statist.* 35:876–879.

Yuille, A. 1990. Generalized deformable models, statistical physics, and matching problems. *Neural Computation* 2(1):1–24.

Static Versus Dynamic Sampling for Data Mining

George H. John and **Pat Langley**
Computer Science Department
Stanford University
Stanford, CA 94305-9010
{gjohn,langley}@CS.Stanford.EDU
http://robotics.stanford.edu/~{gjohn,langley}/

Abstract

As data warehouses grow to the point where one hundred gigabytes is considered small, the computational efficiency of data-mining algorithms on large databases becomes increasingly important. Using a *sample* from the database can speed up the data-mining process, but this is only acceptable if it does not reduce the quality of the mined knowledge. To this end, we introduce the "Probably Close Enough" criterion to describe the desired properties of a sample. Sampling usually refers to the use of *static* statistical tests to decide whether a sample is sufficiently similar to the large database, in the absence of any knowledge of the tools the data miner intends to use. We discuss *dynamic* sampling methods, which take into account the mining tool being used and can thus give better samples. We describe dynamic schemes that observe a mining tool's performance on training samples of increasing size and use these results to determine when a sample is sufficiently large. We evaluate these sampling methods on data from the UCI repository and conclude that dynamic sampling is preferable.

Introduction

The current popularity of data mining, data warehousing, and decision support, as well as the tremendous decline in the cost of disk storage, has led to the proliferation of terabyte data warehouses. Mining a database of even a few gigabytes is an arduous task, and requires either advanced parallel hardware and parallelized data-mining algorithms, or the use of sampling to reduce the size of the database to be mined.

Data analysis and mining always take place within the context of solving some problem for a customer (domain expert or data owner), and thus many decisions must be made jointly by the customer and the data miner. The analyst's job is to present the sampling decision in a comprehensible form to the customer.

The PCE (Probably Close Enough) criterion we introduce is a criterion for evaluating sampling methods. If we believe that the performance of our data-mining algorithm on a sample is probably close to what it would be if we ran it on the entire database, then we should be satisfied with the sample. The question is how to quantify *close enough* and *probably*. For simplicity, we consider only accuracy in *supervised* classification methods, although the PCE framework is more general. This focus lets us leverage existing learning theory and make the discussion more concrete by defining *close* in terms of accuracy.

Dynamic sampling refers to the use of knowledge about the behavior of the mining algorithm in order to choose a sample size — its test of whether a sample is suitably representative of a database depends on how the sample will be used. In contrast, a *static* sampling method is ignorant of how a sample will be used, and instead applies some fixed criterion to the sample to determine if it is suitably representative of the original large database. Often, statistical hypothesis tests are used. We compare the static and dynamic approaches along quantitative (sample sizes and accuracy) and qualitative (customer-interface issues) dimensions, and conclude with reasons for preferring dynamic sampling.

Static Sampling Criteria

The aim of static sampling is to determine whether a sample is sufficiently similar to its parent database. The criteria are static in the sense that they are used independently of the following analysis to be performed on the sample. Practitioners of KDD sometimes speak of "statistically valid samples" and this section represents one attempt to make this precise. Our approach tests the hypotheses that each field in the sample comes from the same distribution as the original database.

For categorical fields, a χ^2 hypothesis test is used to test the hypothesis that the sample and the large database come from the same distribution. For numeric fields, a large-sample test (relying on the central limit theorem) is used to test the hypothesis that the sample and the large database have the same mean.

a)		B			b)		B		
		T	F				T	F	
A	T	50	50	100	A	T	10	0	10
	F	50	50	100		F	0	10	10
		100	100				10	10	

Table 1: a: Counts of a database containing 50 copies of records <TT>, <TF>, <FT>, <FF>. b: Sample containing 10 copies of records <TT>, <FF>. These both look *the same* to univariate static sampling.

Note that hypothesis tests are usually designed to minimize the probability of falsely claiming that two distributions are different (Casella & Berger 1990). For example, in a 95% level hypothesis test, assuming the two samples do come from the same distribution, there is a 5% chance that the test will incorrectly reject (type I error) the null hypothesis that the distributions are the same. However, for sampling we want to minimize the probability of falsely claiming they are the same (type II error). We used level 5% tests, which liberally reject the null hypothesis, and are thus conservative in claiming that the two distributions are the same. (Directly controlling Type II error is more desirable but complicated and requires extra assumptions.)

Given a sample, static sampling runs the appropriate hypothesis test on each of its fields. If it accepts all of the null hypotheses then it claims that the sample does indeed come from the same distribution as the original database, and it reports the current sample size as sufficient.

There are several shortcomings to the static sampling model. One minor problem is that, when running several hypothesis tests, the probability that at least one hypothesis is wrongly accepted increases with the number of tests. The Bonferroni correction can adjust for this problem. More important, the question "is this sample good enough?" can only be sensibly answered by first asking "what are we going to do with the sample?" Static sampling ignores the data-mining tool that will be used. The tests we describe are only univariate, which is problematic (see Table 1). One could as well run bivariate tests but then there is of course no guarantee that the three-way statistics will be correct. It is also unclear how the setting of the confidence levels will effect sample size and performance, so this is a poor framework to present to a customer.

Dynamic Sampling

Sampling a database is a scary prospect. It involves a decision about a tradeoff that many customers are rightfully hesitant to make. That decision is how much they are willing to give up in accuracy to obtain a decrease in running time of a data mining algorithm. Dynamic sampling and the PCE criterion address this decision directly, rather than indirectly looking at statistical properties of samples independent of how they will be used. Ultimately, the costs of building the model (disk space, cpu time, consultants' fees) must be amortized over the period of use of the model and balanced against the savings that result from its accuracy. This work is a step in that direction.

The PCE Criterion

The Probably Close Enough criterion is a way of evaluating a sampling strategy. The key is that the sampling decision should occur in the context of the data mining algorithm we plan to use. The PCE idea is to think about taking a sample that is probably good enough, meaning that there is only a small chance that the mining algorithm could do better by using the entire database instead. We would like the smallest sample size n such that

$$Pr(\text{acc}(N) - \text{acc}(n) > \epsilon) \leq \delta \ ,$$

where $\text{acc}(n)$ refers to the accuracy of our mining algorithm after seeing a sample of size n, $\text{acc}(N)$ refers to the accuracy after seeing all records in the database, ϵ is a parameter to be specified by a customer describing what "close enough" means, and δ is a parameter describing what "probably" means. PCE is similar to the the Probably Approximately Correct bound in computational learning theory.

Given the above framework, there are several different ways to attempt to design a dynamic sampling strategy to satisfy the criterion. Below we describe methods that rely on general properties of learning algorithms to estimate $\text{acc}(N) - \text{acc}(n)$. But first, in order to test the PCE framework, we must select a learning algorithm.

We chose the naive Bayesian classifier, which has a number of advantages over more sophisticated techniques for data mining, such as methods for decision-tree and rule induction. The algorithm runs in time linear with the number of attributes and training cases, which compares well with the $O(n \log n)$ time for basic decision-tree algorithms and at least $O(n^2)$ for methods that use post-pruning. Also, experimental studies suggest that naive Bayes tends to learn more rapidly, in terms of the number of training cases needed to achieve high accuracy, than most induction algorithms (Langley & Sage 1994). Theoretical analyses (Langley, Iba & Thompson 1992) point to similar conclusions about the naive Bayesian classifier's rate of learning. A third feature is that naive Bayes can be implemented in an incremental manner that is not subject to order effects.

Sampling through Cross Validation

Despite the inherent efficiency of naive Bayes, we would like to reduce its computational complexity even further by incorporating dynamic sampling. There are several problems to solve in deciding whether a sample meets the PCE criterion, but each of them is well-defined in terms of our goal. We examine samples of increasing larger size n, adding a constant number of records to our sample repeatedly until we believe the PCE condition is satisfied.

First, we must estimate $\text{acc}(n_i)$. In our algorithm, we used leave-one-out cross-validation on the sample as our estimate of $\text{acc}(n_i)$. Then we must estimate $\text{acc}(N)$. For a first attempt, we assume that whenever $\text{acc}(n_{i+1}) \leq \text{acc}(n_i)$, the derivative of accuracy with respect to training set size has become non-positive and will remain so for increasing sample sizes. Thus $\text{acc}(N) \leq \text{acc}(n_i)$ and we should accept the sample of size n.

In initial experiments on UCI databases we found that this method for putting a bound on $\text{acc}(N)$ is sensitive to variance in our estimates for $\text{acc}(n_i)$, and often stops too soon. On average, accuracy was reduced about 2% from the accuracy on the full database, while the sample size was always less than 20% of the size of the original database.

Extrapolation of Learning Curves

Perhaps this sensitivity could be overcome by the use of more information to determine $\text{acc}(N)$ rather than just the last two estimated accuracies. One method is to use all available data on the performance of the mining algorithm on varying-sized training sets, and use these to fit a parametric learning curve, an estimate of the algorithm's accuracy as a function of the size of the training sample. Extrapolation of Learning Curves (ELC) can predict the accuracy of the mining algorithm on the full database.

But first, we must estimate $\text{acc}(n)$. In our algorithm, when considering a sample of size n we take K more records from the large database and classify them and measure the resulting accuracy. This is our estimate of $\text{acc}(n)$. Then we must estimate $\text{acc}(N)$. We use the history of sample sizes (for earlier, smaller samples) and measured accuracies to estimate and extrapolate the learning curve. Theoretical work in learning, both computational and psychological, has shown that the power law provides a good fit to learning curve data:

$$\widehat{\text{acc}}(n) = a - bn^{-\alpha} \ .$$

The parameters a, b, α are fit to the observed accuracies using a simple function optimization method. We used

Dynamic Hill Climbing (Yuret 1994), which seems to work well.

We know N, the total size of the database. Given $\widehat{\text{acc}}(N)$ as our estimate for the accuracy of our data mining algorithm after seeing all N cases in the database, we can check the difference between this expected value and the current accuracy on our sample of size n, and if the difference is not greater than ϵ, we accept the sample as being representative.

If the difference is greater than ϵ, we reject the sample and add the additional K records (sampled previously, to get an estimate of the accuracy of our model) to our sample, updating the model built by our mining algorithm. For this to be efficient, the mining algorithm must be *incremental*, able to update itself given new data in time proportional to the amount of new data, not the total amount of data it has seen.

Experiments: ELC vs Static Sampling

Preliminary studies with ELC sampling for naive Bayes gave good results relative to the non-sampling version of this algorithm, which encouraged us to carry out a fuller comparison with the static approach to sampling. To this end, we selected 11 databases from the UCI repository that vary in the number of features and in the proportion of continuous to nominal features. Since our goal was to learn accurately from a small sample of a large database, and since the UCI databases are all quite small, we artificially inflated each database by making 100 copies of all records, inserting these into a new database, and shuffling (randomizing their order). Very large real databases also have high redundancy (Moller 1993), so we do believe the results of these experiments will be informative, although real large databases would obviously have been preferable.

For each new inflated database, we shuffled the records randomly and ran five-fold cross-validation — we partitioned it into five disjoint and equal-size parts, and repeatedly trained on four out of the five, while testing on the held-out part. For each training step, we first sampled the database using either no sampling (taking all records), static sampling, or dynamic sampling (ELC). We then recorded the number of samples used and the accuracy on the held-out piece. We repeated this entire procedure five times, getting a total of 25 runs of sampling and 25 estimates of accuracy.

We initialized both sampling algorithms with a sample of size 100. For the static scheme, we used a 5% confidence level test that each field had the same distribution as the large database. For dynamic sampling, we fit the learning curve and checked whether $\widehat{\text{acc}}(N) - \text{acc}(n) < 2\%$. In either case, if the sample

Table 2: Sample size (n) and accuracy for 25 runs.

Data set	Naive Acc.	Static Acc.	Static n	Dynamic Acc.	Dynamic n
Breast Cancer	95.9	95.9	300	95.9	300
Credit Card	77.7	77.0	500	77.2	1180
German	72.7	63.8	540	71.8	2180
Glass2	61.9	60.0	100	61.9	720
Heart Disease	85.1	83.2	180	85.1	900
Hepatitis	83.8	83.2	100	83.8	540
Horse Colic	76.6	76.1	240	76.6	640
Iris	96.0	96.0	100	96.0	560
Lymphography	69.1	67.1	100	68.5	600
Pima Diabetes	75.3	75.7	420	75.5	1080
Tic-tac-toe	69.7	69.2	620	71.1	620

was ruled insufficient we increased the size by 100 and repeated.

Table 2 shows the results on the 11 inflated databases from the UCI repository. Note that extrapolated learning curve sampling meets the PCE criterion with $\epsilon = .02$: in no case was the accuracy on the entire database more than .9% higher than the extrapolated sample accuracy. Static sampling, while approving much smaller samples, did worse at matching the accuracy on the entire database: in two cases, its accuracy was 1.9% worse than the accuracy on the entire database, and on one domain (German) its accuracy was nearly 10% lower.

Related and Future Work

Perhaps the best examples of dynamic sampling are the peepholing algorithm described by Catlett (1992) and the "races" of Moore & Lee (1994). In both approaches the authors identify decisions that the learning algorithm must make and propose statistical methods for estimating the utility of each choice rather than fully evaluating each.

The form of our parametric learning curve comes from Kohavi (1995), who discusses learning curve extrapolation during model selection. Kadie (1995) proposes a variety of methods for fitting learning curves.

In the future we intend to apply PCE to different data mining tools, such as Utgoff's (1994) incremental tree inducer. The tradeoffs effecting variance in the estimated learning curves should also be addressed.

Conclusion

Data mining is a collaboration between a customer (domain expert) and a data analyst. Decisions about how large of a sample to use (or whether to subsample at all) must be made rationally. The dynamic sampling algorithm proposed offers parameters that relate directly to the performance of the resulting model, rather than to a statistical criterion which is related in some unknown way to the desired performance. Because of the interpretability of the PCE criterion and because of the robust performance of dynamic sampling in our experiments, we recommend the general framework and encourage further study towards its computational realization using fewer or more well-founded approximations.

Acknowledgments

George John was supported by an NSF Graduate Research Fellowship, and Pat Langley was supported in part by Grant No. N00014-94-1-0746 from the Office of Naval Research.

References

Casella, G. & Berger, R. L. (1990), *Statistical Inference*, Wadsworth & Brooks/Cole.

Catlett, J. (1992), Peepholing: Choosing attributes efficiently for megainduction, in *Machine Learning: Proceedings of the Ninth International Workshop*, Morgan Kaufmann, pp. 49–54.

Kadie, C. (1995), SEER: Maximum likelihood regression for learning-speed curves, PhD thesis, Computer Science Department, University of Illinois at Urbana-Champaign.

Kohavi, R. (1995), Wrappers for performance enhancement and oblivious decision graphs, PhD thesis, Computer Science Department, Stanford University, Stanford, CA.

Langley, P. & Sage, S. (1994), Induction of selective Bayesian classifiers, in *Proceedings of the Tenth Conference on Uncertainty in Artificial Intelligence*, Morgan Kaufmann, Seattle, WA, pp. 399–406.

Langley, P., Iba, W. & Thompson, K. (1992), An analysis of Bayesian classifiers, in *Proceedings of the Tenth National Conference on Artificial Intelligence*, AAAI Press/MIT Press, pp. 223–228.

Moller, M. (1993), "Supervised learning on large redundant training sets", *International Journal of Neural Systems* **4**(1), March, 15–25.

Moore, A. & Lee, M. (1994), Efficient algorithms for minimizing cross-validation error, in *Machine Learning: Proceedings of the Eleventh International Conference*, Morgan Kaufmann, pp. 190–198.

Yuret, D. (1994), From genetic algorithms to efficient optimization, Master's thesis, Computer Science Department, Massachusetts Institute of Technology.

Efficient Search for Strong Partial Determinations

Stefan Kramer and **Bernhard Pfahringer**
Austrian Research Institute for Artificial Intelligence
Schottengasse 3
A-1010 Vienna, Austria
stefan@ai.univie.ac.at

Abstract

Our work offers both a solution to the problem of finding functional dependencies that are distorted by noise and to the open problem of efficiently finding strong (i.e., highly compressive) partial determinations per se. Briefly, we introduce a restricted form of search for partial determinations which is based on functional dependencies. Focusing attention on solely partial determinations derivable from overfitting functional dependencies enables efficient search for strong partial determinations. Furthermore, we generalize the compression-based measure for evaluating partial determinations to n-valued attributes.

Applications to real-world data suggest that the restricted search indeed retrieves a subset of strong partial determinations in much shorter runtimes, thus showing the feasibility and usefulness of our approach.

Introduction

Functional dependencies (Mannila & Räihä, 1994) are a fundamental form of knowledge to be discovered in databases. In real-world databases, however, we have to face the effects of noise on functional dependencies: dependencies among attributes that would have been functional without noise are likely to have exceptions. Consequently, algorithms for inferring functional dependencies would not return those dependencies which are distorted by noise. More precisely and in machine learning terms, they would overfit the data, meaning that these algorithms would find too specific functional dependencies instead of the ones we would like to find.

In contrast to functional dependencies, *partial determinations* ((Russell, 1989), (Pfahringer & Kramer, 1995)) or *approximate functional dependencies* allow for exceptions. (In this respect, they are similar to *association rules* (Agrawal & Srikant, 1994).) Partial determinations may reflect probabilistic dependencies among attributes, but they may also be "impure" functional dependencies, i.e. functional dependencies which are distorted by noise and have only a few exceptions. In this paper, as in (Pfahringer & Kramer, 1995), we deal with those partial determinations which

help to compress a given database as much as possible. These highly compressive partial determinations will be called *strong partial determinations*.

In the next section we summarize the ideas from (Pfahringer & Kramer, 1995). Subsequently, we define and explain a new compression-based measure for partial determinations ranging over n-valued attributes. Then we describe an efficient method to search for strong partial determinations. In section 5, we report on experimental results of our method in several "real-world" databases.

Compression-Based Evaluation of Partial Determinations

Partial determinations are expressions of the form $X \to_d Y$, where X is the set of *RHS* (right-hand side) attributes, and Y is the set of *LHS* (left-hand side) attributes. d is the *determination factor* $d(X, Y)$ (Russell, 1989), the probability that two randomly chosen tuples have the same values of Y, provided they have the same values of X. In the following, we will restrict ourselves to RHSs consisting of single attributes.

Given a relation r, we define a mapping that corresponds to the expression $X \to_d Y$: the mapping relates the values of X occurring in r to the most frequently co-occurring values of Y. The tuples in r with Y values other than those majority values are called exceptions to the mapping in r.

The basic decision is which partial determinations to search for in databases. If we are interested only in accuracy, we are likely to get overly complex partial determinations in the presence of noise: we will find partial determinations fitting the noise instead of the underlying dependencies. To avoid this, we also have to take into account how complex partial determinations are. Therefore, (Pfahringer & Kramer, 1995) proposes a compression-based measure based on the so-called *Minimum Description Length* (MDL) principle (Rissanen, 1978). The MDL principle tries to measure both the simplicity and the accuracy of a particular theory (in our setting: a partial determination) in a common currency, namely in terms of the number of bits needed for encoding both a theory and the data

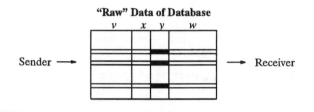

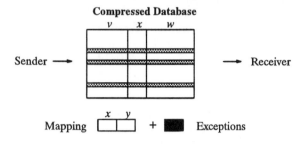

Figure 1: Transmission metaphor.

given that theory. The theory with the *minimal* total message length (the most compressive partial determination) is also the *most probable* theory explaining the data (Rissanen, 1978).

To illustrate the key idea of the measure for partial determinations proposed in (Pfahringer & Kramer, 1995), we consider the hypothetical task of transmitting a given database as efficiently as possible (see fig. 1). If we can find a good partial determination $X \rightarrow_d Y$ for a given attribute Y, transmitting the partial determination instead of the raw data may improve efficiency considerably: we just have to transmit the mapping (the *model*) and transmit the information to correct the values of Y for the exceptions to the mapping. Thus, we have to identify the exceptions (the "grey tuples" in figure 1) and transmit the corrections (the black box in figure 1). The values of Y need not be transmitted anymore. Thus we achieve some compression of the data, the degree of which is estimated by our measure based on the MDL principle.

The work reported in (Pfahringer & Kramer, 1995) has several limitations and problems: the paper only deals with partial determinations ranging over boolean attributes. Secondly, the problem of efficiently finding compressive partial determinations has not been solved. Thirdly, the method has not yet been applied to real-world databases. The following sections present extensions of our work that overcome these problems and limitations.

A New Compression-Based Measure for Multi-Valued Partial Determinations

In figure 2, we define the new compression-based measure for partial determinations ranging over multi-valued attributes. The total coding length (1) is the sum of the coding length of the mapping and the coding length of the corrections to be made. The coding length for a mapping (2) is the sum of the coding length

for specifying the LHS-attributes and of the coding length for the string of values for the RHS-attribute. The alphabet for this string is the domain of the RHS-attribute.

Exceptions to the mapping are encoded by (3). We have to identify the exceptions, and additionally encode a string of corrections for the identified exceptions to the mapping. Again, the alphabet of this string is the domain of the RHS-attribute.

The entropy-based bound of (Shannon & Weaver, 1949) is used as an estimate for the cost c_{choose} of encoding the selection of E elements out of N possible elements (4). Encoding a string over a multi-valued alphabet (5) is a straightforward generalization of (4). It can be thought of as a repeated binary selection encoding of what is the value occurring most frequently and which positions in the string are exceptions, i.e. have a different value. The resulting formula can be simplified to the definition (5) for c_{string}, which is just the sum of the entropy of the distribution of values in the string (6) and of an encoding of the values' identities sorted according to their frequencies (a kind of codebook for the particular string, 7).

Efficient Search for Strong Partial Determinations

Based on the view of partial determinations as functional dependencies which are distorted by noise, we propose an efficient search strategy to find strong partial determinations. Starting with overfitting functional dependencies, we propose to search for the best subset of left-hand side attributes according to our MDL-measure which avoids fitting the noise. In machine learning terminology again, we propose to *prune* the left-hand sides of overfitting functional dependencies. Pruning is achieved by a complete A*-like search over all subsets of LHS-attributes of the original functional dependency. In the following, we will refer to this two-level approach as *restricted search*. Limiting our attention to this highly interesting subset of partial determinations enables efficient search.

Even though both searching for functional dependencies and for partial determinations is exponential in the worst case, on average functional dependencies can be searched for much more efficiently due to much stronger pruning criteria. Additionally the evaluation function is much simpler: just counting the number of tuples in a projection vs. creating a mapping and computing its coding length for a projection. So in restricted search the expensive part has only to deal with a small number of attributes, namely those occurring in the left-hand side of the respective functional dependency. Furthermore, as a functional dependency is a partial determination with no exception, it also supplies an upper-bound on the coding length of possibly better partial determinations in the restricted search.

The next section will empirically show the effectiveness of restricted search in comparison to *full search*.

$$c(PD) = c(Mapping) + c(Exceptions) \tag{1}$$

$$c(Mapping) = c_{choose}(|UsedAttrs|, |AllAttrs|) + c_{string}(RHS\ Values\ Mapping) \tag{2}$$

$$c(Exceptions) = c_{choose}(|Exceptions|, |AllExamples|) + c_{string}(Corrections) \tag{3}$$

$$c_{choose}(E, N) = N * entropy(\{E, N - E\}) \tag{4}$$

$$c_{string}(String) = length(String) * entropy(char\_frequencies(String)) + c_{value\_order}(String) \tag{5}$$

$$entropy(\{F_1, \ldots, F_M\}) = -(\sum_{i=1}^{M} plog(F_i/N)),\ \text{where}\ N = \sum_{i=1}^{M} F_i \tag{6}$$

$$c_{value\_order}(String) = \sum_{i=0}^{j-1} log(M - i),\ \text{where}\ M\ \text{is the cardinality of the alphabet}, \tag{7}$$

and j is the number of different chars in *String*.

$$plog(P) = \begin{cases} 0 & \text{if P=0} \\ P * log_2(P) & \text{otherwise} \end{cases}$$

Figure 2: The definition of the coding length c of a partial determination.

Full search is implemented as an iterative-deepening best-first search for partial determinations. For pragmatic reasons, if the number of attributes is larger than 20, both search approaches must be limited to left-hand sides of a prespecified maximum length, which is usually 10 in our experiments.

Empirical Results

For a preliminary empirical comparison of both search strategies we have done experiments using various small to medium-sized "real-world" databases. **Breast cancer, Lymphography**, and **Mushroom** are taken from the UCI-repository. **Peace, Conflicts**, and **Attempts** are databases capturing mediation attempts in international conflicts and crises (Trappl et al., 1996). Table 1 gives the sizes (number of attributes and number of tuples) of these databases and summarizes the search results. For the restricted search approach (pruning of overfitting functional dependencies) we list the number of attributes, for which a partial determination was found and the determinations' average compression factor. This compression factor for a given attribute is defined as the ratio between the coding length of the raw data and the coding length of the respective partial determination. Next we list the average compression factor achieved by a full search for partial determinations for the same RHS-attributes as those for which the restricted search found compressive partial determinations. Additionally we list the number of attributes for which *only the full search* was able to find compressive partial determinations, and again include their average compression factor. We can summarize as follows: for a subset of all attributes restricted search seems to find partial determinations which are on average almost as strong or compressive as those found by full search. Partial determinations missed by restricted search are on average significantly weaker (with the exception of the

Conflicts database). We have not yet performed detailed runtime measurements, but even for the smallest database **Breast Cancer** the difference is already of two orders of magnitude (80 seconds vs. 1 hour). For the other domains the differences in the runtimes were even more drastic. Summing up, the restricted search indeed retrieves a subset of strong partial determinations in much shorter runtimes.

Inspecting the retrieved determinations for useful knowledge also provided a few insights. For instance the **Peace** database includes both a few raw numerical attributes and their respective discretizations. Clearly a discretization should be functionally dependent on the raw data, which was *not* the case in the actual database. These erroneous discretizations were discovered as partial determinations. Moreover, we found strong partial determinations reflecting the implicit structure of the database: originally structured knowledge had been converted into one large and flat table due to restrictions imposed by standard propositional machine learning algorithms.

Related Work

(Shen, 1991) describes an algorithm that searches for determinations and two other kinds of regularities in a large knowledge base. Since the algorithm is just looking for determinations having a single left-hand side attribute, there is no need to avoid overfitting the data.

(Schlimmer, 1993) proposes an algorithm that returns every "reliable" partial determination with a complexity lower than a user-defined threshold. Since the evaluation function does not have a penalty for overly complex dependencies, it does not avoid overfitting

(Russell, 1989) and (Kivinen & Mannila, 1995) propose to determine the accuracy of partial determinations (respectively approximate functional dependen-

Domain	# A.	# T.	Restr.Search # PDs	Restr.Search Compression μ (σ)	Full Search Compression μ (σ)	Full Search # Add. PDs	Full Search Add. PDs Compression
Br. Cancer	11	699	6	1.49 (0.78)	1.64 (0.73)	5	1.20 (0.07)
Lymph.	19	148	14	1.13 (0.09)	1.13 (0.09)	5	1.01 (0.01)
Mushroom	23	8124	7	95.16 (26.84)	100.03 (23.25)	15	5.49 (6.32)
Peace	50	1753	33	4.47 (2.76)	4.63 (2.70)	16	2.11 (0.85)
Conflicts	33	268	24	1.38 (0.47)	1.38 (0.47)	4	1.37 (0.24)
Attempts	17	1753	10	2.23 (1.00)	2.26 (0.99)	7	1.65 (0.48)

Table 1: Results in real-world domains: the meaning of columns is explained in section 5.

cies) through sampling. However, if the proposed measures of accuracy would be used in a search framework, the returned determinations would overfit the data.

Conclusion and Further Work

Our contribution is twofold: firstly, we offer a solution to the problem of finding functional dependencies that are distorted by noise. Secondly, we propose a solution to the open problem of efficiently finding strong (i.e., highly compressive) partial determinations. Focusing attention on partial determinations derivable from overfitting functional dependencies enables efficient search for strong partial determinations.

Furthermore, we have generalize the compression-based measure for evaluating partial determinations to n-valued attributes. Applications to real-world data suggest that the restricted search indeed retrieves a subset of strong partial determinations in much shorter runtimes, thus showing the feasibility and usefulness of our approach.

Our approach to searching for partial determinations has several limitations: clearly, we cannot find *all* partial determinations, but only a subset. However, experiments indicate that those partial determinations which are distorted functional dependencies are among the most compressive dependencies to be found. It is also important to note that this approach is based on assumptions about real-world data, namely that there are strict functional dependencies which are distorted by noise. Thirdly, if the noise level is too high, no functional dependency might exist at all. So the pruning approach would not find partial determinations in these situations.

We plan to extend our work along the following lines: our method could be used to restructure the database in order to minimize the required memory, similar to INDEX (Flach, 1993). Another application of the measure could be to distinguish between reliable functional dependencies and those which are due to chance. Finally, it would be interesting to compare and combine our approach with sampling techniques as proposed in (Kivinen & Mannila, 1995).

Acknowledgements This research is partly sponsored by the Austrian *Fonds zur Förderung der Wissenschaftlichen Forschung (FWF)* under grant number P10489-MAT. Financial support for the Austrian Research Institute for Artificial Intelligence is provided by the Austrian Federal Ministry of Science, Transport and the Arts. Both the lymphography and the breast cancer domain were obtained from the University Medical Centre, Institute of Oncology, Ljubljana, Slovenia. The mediation databases were obtained from the Department of Political Science at the University of Canterbury, Christchurch, N.Z. We would like to thank M. Zwitter, M. Soklic and J. Bercovitch for providing the data, and Gerhard Widmer for valuable discussions.

References

Agrawal R. and Srikant R.: Fast Algorithms for Mining Association Rules. *Proceedings of the 20th VLDB Conference*, Santiago, Chile, 1994.

Flach P.A.: Predicate Invention in Inductive Data Engineering, in Brazdil P.B.(ed.), *Machine Learning: ECML-93*, Springer, Berlin, pp.83-94, 1993.

Kivinen J., Mannila H.: Approximate dependency inference from relations, *Theoretical Computer Science*, 149(1):129-149, 1995.

Mannila H. and Räihä K.-J.: Algorithms for Inferring Functional Dependencies From Relations. *Data & Knowledge Engineering* 12 (1994) 83-99, 1994.

Pfahringer B., Kramer S.: Compression-Based Evaluation of Partial Determinations, *Proceedings of the First International Conference on Knowledge Discovery and Data Mining*, AAAI Press, 1995.

J. Rissanen: Modeling by Shortest Data Description. In: *Automatica*, 14:465-471, 1978.

Russell S.J.: *The Use of Knowledge in Analogy and Induction*. Pitman Publishing, London, 1989.

Schlimmer J.C.: Efficiently Inducing Determinations: A Complete and Systematic Search Algorithm that Uses Optimal Pruning. *Proceedings of the 10th International Conference on Machine Learning*, 1993.

Shannon C.E. and Weaver W.: *The Mathematical Theory of Communication*, University of Illinois Press, 1949.

Shen W.-M.: Discovering Regularities from Large Knowledge Bases. *Proceedings of the 8th International Workshop on Machine Learning*, 1991.

Trappl R., Fürnkranz J. and Petrak J.: Digging for Peace: Using Machine Learning Methods for Assessing International Conflict Databases. *Proceedings of the 12th European Conference on Artificial Intelligence (ECAI-96)*, pp. 453-457, 1996.

Reverse Engineering Databases for Knowledge Discovery

Stephen Mc Kearney
Department of Computing
Bournemouth University
Talbot Campus, Fern Barrow
Poole, Dorset, UK
smckearn@bournemouth.ac.uk

Huw Roberts
Data Mining Group
pp13, MLB1
BT Laboratories
Ipswich, Suffolk, UK
huw.roberts@bt-sys.bt.co.uk

Abstract

Many data mining tools cannot be used directly to analyze the complex sets of relations which are found in large database systems. In our experience, data miners rely on a well-defined data model, or the knowledge of a *data expert,* to isolate and extract candidate data sets prior to mining the data. For many databases, typically large legacy systems, a reliable data model is often unavailable and access to the data expert can be limited. In this paper we use *reverse engineering* techniques to infer a model of the database. Reverse engineering a database can be seen as knowledge discovery in its own right and the resulting data model may be made available to data mining tools as background knowledge. In addition, minable data sets can be produced from the inferred data model and analyzed using conventional data mining tools. Our approach reduces the data miner's reliance on a well-defined data model and the data expert.

Introduction

Our experience of data mining large, complex databases has highlighted the importance of the role of the *data expert* in the data mining process (Roberts & Totton, 1996). A data miner often uses knowledge from both a domain expert, who knows about the world the data represents, and a data expert, who knows about how the data is structured and stored. By combining knowledge from both sources the data miner arrives at a *focus of interest* in the database from which minable data sets can be constructed. This occurs before conventional data mining tools are used. Without a data expert, large databases can be hard to understand since an accurate data model is often unavailable. In addition, getting access to an appropriate data expert may be difficult.

In this paper we describe a reverse engineering technique which produces data models of existing databases. This technique reduces the reliance of the data miner on the knowledge of the data expert by extracting knowledge directly from the database. In addition to constructing minable data sets, the method described can

also extract useful *domain* knowledge. This can be seen as knowledge discovery in its own right or as a source of useful *background knowledge* usable by some data mining tools to guide their search.

While data mining has been used to support schema integration and reverse engineering in databases, there has been little or no investigation of using *reverse engineering to support data mining*. Specifically, we use reverse engineered data models to generate data sets which can be input to conventional data mining algorithms.

Overview

Data mining a large relational database might start by generating a single large table containing all the data. Alternatively, a set of attributes may be selected based on the advice of a data expert or because they 'feel' like an appropriate set to be mined. The resulting table will contain a lot of attributes which may or may not contribute something to the data mining process. The missing component in this procedure is a method of systematically generating models of the data from which plausible relationships between entities in the database can be identified.

(McKearney, 1992) describes a method of building models of a database by analyzing relationships in the data. The resulting *abstract objects* describe relationships between object classes inferred from the data. Each abstract object depicts a relationship as one particular view of the data. A view describes the database in terms of individual data entities, for example, a relationship between employees and projects may be viewed as either an employee working on one or more projects or a project with one or more employees working on it. This work is similar to other reverse engineering efforts (for example, Springsteel & Kou, 1992) which mapped one data model schema, for example, the network model, to an equivalent (newer) schema, for example, the relational model (Boulanger & March, 1989).

Each abstract object can be converted to one or more database queries from which a data set may be produced and then analyzed.

Method

The method has three stages: *dependency analysis*, *entity analysis*, and *object analysis*. Abstractions inferred during these stages can be mapped to a set of database queries which when executed generate minable data sets.

Dependency Analysis

Attributes in a database relation can either describe concepts, *descriptive attributes,* or structure concepts, *structural attributes*. Structural attributes, which contain identifying data values, contain very little semantic knowledge about a concept and so a good knowledge discovery data set contains only descriptive attributes. The descriptive attribute *employee salary*, for example, contains more knowledge about an employee than the structural attribute *employee number*. Hence, it is important to remove *structural attributes* when preparing a data set. Classifying each attribute as descriptive or structural is possible when the dependencies between the attributes are known.

(McKearney, 1992) discusses a method of measuring the degree to which one attribute determines another, call *informativeness*. Informativeness is a measure of the dependency between attributes and may be used to infer unique or near-unique attributes in the database. Highly informative attributes may be used to infer entities and simple relationships in a database. The informativeness of attribute set Y over attribute set Ω is defined as:

$$I(\Omega|Y) = \frac{\sum_{X_i \in \Omega} w(X_i) H(X_i|Y)}{\sum_{X_i \in \Omega} w(X_i) H(X_i)}$$

where $H(X_j)$ is the entropy of attribute set X_j and $H(X_j|Y)$ is the conditional entropy of attributes set X_j given attribute set Y_j. $w(X_j)$ is a domain dependent weighting for the attribute set X_j which is normally $1/n$, where n is the number of attributes in Ω.

Entity Analysis

The second stage in producing a model of the data is to group the database attributes into entities. Relationships between entities are represented by foreign keys between relations. We generalize the concept of a foreign key to that of a *reference* between relations. A reference from relation r_1 to relation r_2 is made by storing a highly informative attribute about r_2 in r_1. For example, a relation *car* references a relation *person* by storing *person-no* in each tuple of *car*, thus representing the fact that each person owns a car. Entities are inferred by analyzing these references.

Depending on the types of reference in which a relation participates, it can be classified as either an entity or a relationship (Batini et al, 1992). We use database design rules to classify each relation as either (i) an *entity*, when it is referenced via a highly informative attribute set, (ii) a *weak entity*, when it is referenced via part of a highly informative attribute set, or (iii) a *relationship*, when two or more relations reference it and the combination of the references are a highly informative attribute set. The present method assumes that references can be identified from the database schema.

Object Analysis

The references identified during the entity analysis are simple relationships between individual relations. More complex relationships, called *abstract objects,* can be inferred by using database design rules to analyse each reference. An abstract object is a description of the part, or *role*, played in a relationship by the entities in the database. Each abstract object is a high level description of a database region from which a minable data set can be produced.

For example, in an employee database, an abstract object *employee-and-dependants,* which describes the relationship between employees and their dependants, might consist of the classes *employee, employee with dependants, employee without dependants, a set of dependants* and a *dependant*. In this example the concept being represented is that of an *employee* who may or may not have *dependants*. During the object analysis each entity is treated as a class in the object model.

A single reference can consist of one or more classes, each playing one or more roles. There are three pairs of roles (Smith & Smith, 1977; Brodie, 1981):

- **Aggregate/Component** A class which relates two or more classes because of the relationship between them is an aggregate, for example, an aggregate class *car* relates the component classes *door, wheel,* and *engine*.
- **Superclass/Subclass** A class which describes the common properties of one or more classes is a superclass, for example, *vehicle* is a superclass of subclasses *car, bus* and *train*.
- **Set/Member** A class which groups a set of classes together is a set, for example, *car wheels* is a set of member class *wheel*.

Currently, object analysis uses database design rules derived from common methods of mapping an entity-relationship model to a set of relations (Elmasri & Navathe, 1989). For example, subclasses in the relational model are often represented as relations with common primary key attributes. Each rule consists of evidence describing an observation about the content of the database and a conclusion which can be inferred given the evidence. The following rule classifies two entities as subclasses of an *inferred* superclass ($e_j.a$ is the set of values in attribute a of e_j):

Evidence A reference exists between two informative attributes $e_1.a$ and $e_2.a$, and $\underline{e_1.a} \neq \underline{e_2.a}$.

Conclusion The entities e_1 and e_2 both play the role of disjoint subclasses of an inferred superclass e_3 which contains the common attributes of e_1 and e_2.

Example If data about skilled and unskilled workers is held in two relations, *skilled-worker* and *unskilled-worker,* and both relations are identified by the attribute *enumber* then a new class *employee* can be inferred whose instances are both a unskilled-worker and a skilled-worker.

In the relational model aggregates are represented by a foreign key in one relation referencing the primary key of another relation. Using this knowledge the following rule classifies an entity as an aggregate:

Evidence A reference exists between an uninformative attribute $e_1.a$ and an informative attribute $e_2.a$.

Conclusion .The entity e_1 is an aggregate with component e_2.

Example If an entity *employee* contains an attribute *car-reg* which is also an identifier for an entity *car* then an aggregate *employee*, with component *car*, can be inferred.

Analyzing all the references in a database will produce many different abstract objects. Therefore, each abstraction must be reviewed by the data miner and domain expert and a suitable set of abstractions selected for data mining. Our approach hides the complexities of data structuring by describing each relationship using higher level constructs.

Query Generation

Each role defined in an abstract object is mapped to one or more database queries. For example, the abstract object *employee*, a superclass consisting of two subclasses, *unskilled-worker* and *skilled-worker*, maps to a data set composed of those attributes which are common to both *unskilled-worker* and *skilled-worker* and which, therefore, are properties of the *employee* concept. Discoveries generated from the *employee* data set are true for both *unskilled-workers* and *skilled-workers*.

Inferred classes, which consist of structural attributes and no descriptive attributes, are used to label instances of the classes from which they were inferred. For example, assume that two subclasses of *car, employee-car* and *company-car*, are inferred from a reference between *employee* and *car*. The instances of *employee-car* and *company-car* are contained in *car*. Therefore, a new

attribute, *type*, can be added to *car* which classifies each instance as either 'employee owned' or 'company owned'. This additional information can be used during the data mining search.

Data sets can be generated for each pair of roles:
* **Aggregate/Component** An aggregate data set is generated by joining the relations making up its components.
* **Superclass/Subclass** A superclass data set is generated from the union and projection of the shared attributes of its subclass relations.
* **Set/Member** A set is more complex as it describes the properties of a group of instances. Two methods can be used to analyse such data. First, summary data may be calculated for each instance of the set. Second, each set instance may be generated as a distinct data set.

Example

Consider the following relation schemas:
> **employee** (fname, minit, lname, ssn, address, sex, salary, superssn, dno)
> **dependant** (ssn, dependant-name, sex, relationship)
> **works-on** (ssn, pno, hours)
> **project** (pname, pno, plocation, dno)
> **department** (dname, dno, mgrssn).

A dependency analysis of the *employee* relation in produces three potential keys *fname, lname* and *ssn*. Of these keys only one takes part in a reference to other relations in the database, *ssn*. It is assumed to be the primary key. A dependency analysis of the remaining relations identifies the attributes *(ssn, pno)* and *pno* as keys in the relations *works_on* and *project*, respectively. Three entities, *employee, works_on* and *project,* are inferred from these findings. An abstract object consisting of an aggregate class *works_on* and components *employee* and *project* is inferred using the rule:

Evidence A reference exists between an informative attribute $e_1.a$ and attribute $e_2.a_1$, and a reference exists between an informative attribute $e_3.a$ and attribute $e_2.a_2$. The attribute set $(e_2.a_1, e_2.a_2)$ is informative.

Conclusion Entity e_2 is an aggregate class with component classes e_1 and e_3.

This object produces the relational schema:
> **emp-proj** (fname, minit, lname, address, sex, salary, superssn, dno, pname, pno, plocation, dno)

The corresponding SQL query is:
```
SELECT fname, minit, lname, ssn,
address, sex, salary, superssn, dno,
hours, pname, pno, plocation, dno
FROM employee, works_on, project
```

```
WHERE employee.ssn = works_on.ssn AND
works_on.pno = project.pno
```

The result of running this query is a data set consisting of examples of the relationship between employees and projects. The data set can be analyzed using traditional data mining tools.

Related Work

There has been little published work on reverse engineering relational databases as part of the knowledge discovery process. (Goldberg & Senator, 1995) introduce two new database operations, consolidation and link formation, which re-structure the database for knowledge discovery. Several data mining tools have been developed to analyse complex data structures. In the KATE system, (Manago & Kodratoff, 1991) apply an ID3-style algorithm to analyse frame-based data structures. This algorithm assumes the existence of a frame-based representation of the data. The abstract objects inferred in our approach may be used as the input to the KATE system.

(Ribeiro et al, 1995) propose a method of analyzing individual relations and combining the results using knowledge of the primary and foreign keys. Other algorithms make use of concept hierarchies which impose structure on otherwise simple data sets, for example: attribute oriented induction (Cai et al, 1991). (Ketterlin et al, 1995) have extended the COBWEB algorithm to discover useful clusters in structured databases. Their algorithm also analyses entity instances, but does not induce structure; instead it relies on a pre-defined entity-relationship model of the data. Ketterlin argues that databases are designed using entity-relationship models and that the analysis of these systems should be performed at this level of abstraction.

Conclusion

There is a need to apply data mining to real databases which are characterized by complex data structures. We have presented a method of generating minable data sets from real databases. Our approach differs from other approaches by using database reverse engineering techniques to infer models of the data contained in the database. Database design heuristics have been used to analyse relationships in the data. Abstract descriptions of the data, called *abstract objects*, are inferred from these relationships and these are used to produce data sets which are minable by conventional data mining tools. We are currently studying the application of this technique in an operational environment.

Data mining real databases remains a complex problem and our approach raises some issues which we hope to investigate in the future. These include selecting the most suitable abstract objects using criteria specified by the data miner and using the abstract object descriptions as input to more complex data mining algorithms.

Acknowledgment

This work was funded by BT Laboratories.

References

Batini, C., Ceri, S., Navathe, S. B., 1992. *Conceptual Database Design*. Benjamin/Cummings.

Boulanger, D., March, S. T., 1989. An Approach to Analyzing the Information Content of Existing Databases. *Database* (Summer issue), 1-8.

Brodie, M. L., 1981. Association: A Database Abstraction for Semantic Modeling. In *Entity-Relationship Approach to Information Modeling and Analysis*, Chen, P. P. (ed.), North-Holland, 577-602.

Cai, Y., Cercone, N., Han, J., 1991. Attribute-Oriented Induction In Relational Databases. In *Knowledge Discovery in Databases*, G. Piatetsky-Shapiro and W. J. Frawley (eds.), AAAI Press, 213-228.

Elmasri, R., Navathe, S. B., 1989. *Fundamentals of Database Systems*, Benjamin/Cummings.

Goldberg, H. G., Senator, T. E., 1995. Restructuring Databases for Knowledge Discovery by Consolidation and Link Formation. In *KDD-95: Proc. of the 1st Int'l Conf. on Knowledge Discovery and Data Mining*, 136-141. AAAI Press.

Manago, M, Kodratoff, Y., 1991. Induction of Decision Trees From Complex Structured Data. In *Knowledge Discovery in Databases*, G. Piatetsky-Shapiro and W. J. Frawley (eds.), AAAI Press, 289-308.

McKearney, S., 1992. Inferring Object Schemas from a Database Instance. DPhil Thesis, University of Ulster.

McKearney, S., Bell, D., Hickey, R. J., 1991. Inferring Abstract Objects in a Database. In *CIKM-92: Proc. of the 1st Int'l Conf. on Information and Knowledge Management*.

Ribeiro, J. S., Kaufmann, K. A., Kerschberg, L., 1995. Knowledge Discovery from Multiple Databases. In *KDD-95: Proc. of the 1st Int'l Conf. on Knowledge Discovery and Data Mining*, 240-245. AAAI Press.

Roberts, H., Totton, K., 1996. Data Mining in BT. In *Proc. of Data Mining 96*, Unicom Seminar, London.

Smith, J. M., Smith, D. C. P., 'Database Abstractions: Aggregation and Generalization', in *Readings in AI*, Mylopoulos, J., Brodie, M. L. (eds.), Morgan-Kaufmann, 1989, pp138-145.

Springsteel, F., Kou, C.,1992. Reverse Data Engineering Technology for Visual Database Design. *Information and Technology*, 34 (2), 97-105.

Performing Effective Feature Selection by Investigating the Deep Structure of the Data

Marco Richeldi and **Pier Luca Lanzi**[†]

CSELT
Centro Studi E Laboratori Telecomunicazioni S.p.A.
Via G. Reiss Romoli 274 - Torino, ITALY
(Marco.Richeldi@cselt.stet.it Lanzi@elet.polimi.it)

Abstract

This paper introduces ADHOC (Automatic Discoverer of Higher-Order Correlation), an algorithm that combines the advantages of both filter and feedback models to enhance the understanding of the given data and to increase the efficiency of the feature selection process. ADHOC partitions the observed features into a number of groups, called factors, that reflect the major dimensions of the phenomenon under consideration. The set of learned factors define the starting point of the search of the best performing feature subset. A genetic algorithm is used to explore the feature space originated by the factors and to determine the set of most informative feature configurations. The feature subset evaluation function is the performance of the induction algorithm. This approach offers three main advantages: (i) the likelihood of selecting good performing features grows; (ii) the complexity of search diminishes consistently; (iii) the possibility of selecting a bad feature subset due to overfitting problems decreases. Extensive experiments on real-world data have been conducted to demonstrate the effectiveness of ADHOC as data reduction technique as well as feature selection method.

Introduction

Feature selection plays a central role in the data analysis process since irrelevant features often degrade the performance of algorithms devoted to data characterization, extraction of rules from data, and construction of predictive models, both in speed and in predictive accuracy. The interest in the feature selection problem is intensifying because of the pressing need of mining volume data warehouses, which usually contain a large number of features (for example, in finance, marketing, and product development applications). Indeed, it is quite a hard task to filter irrelevant features out during the warehouse construction process.

Feature selection algorithms that have appeared in the literature can be categorized in two classes, according to the type of information extracted from the training data and the induction algorithm (John, Kohavi, & Pfleger 1994) Feature selection may be accomplished independently of the performance of the learning algorithm used in the knowledge extraction stage. Optimal feature selection is achieved by maximizing or minimizing a criterion function. Such approach may be referred to as the *filter feature selection model*. Conversely, the effectiveness of the *feedback feature selection model* is directly related to the performance of the concept discovery algorithm, usually in terms of its predictive accuracy. (John, Kohavi, & Pfleger 1994) argued that feedback models are preferable for feature selection algorithms and supported their claims with empirical evidence. However, the literature do not address some important issues. First of all, it is not clear which is the best starting point for the search of a good subset of features. Starting the search on the whole set of original features usually turns out to be unfeasible due to combinatorial explosion when the number of features is not limited. An alternative might be start with the features used by a decision tree algorithm. Second, current feature selection algorithm do not help to answer a basic question that arises in a number of data analysis tasks, that is whether there exist some fundamental dimensions which underlie the given set of observed features. This is a major drawback in marketing applications, for example, in which gaining an insight of the deep structure of the data is as important as achieving a good generalization performance.

The attempt to address these open issues are the basis of our research work. In this paper we introduce a statistical algorithm, called ADHOC (Automatic Discoverer of Higher-Order Correlations), that combines the advantages of both filter and feedback feature selection models to enhance the understanding of the given data and increase

---

[†] Current address: Politecnico di Milano, Milano, Italy

the efficiency of the feature selection process. Two empirical analysis on real-world data have been conducted to demonstrate the effectiveness of ADHOC as data reduction technique as well as feature selection method. Experimental results are presented and discussed in the last section of the paper.

Data reduction in ADHOC

Factor Analysis (FA), Principal Component Analysis (PCA) and Cluster Analysis (hereafter designated as Statistical Data Reduction Techniques or SDRTs) are well established procedures that are effective in many domains. But the set of mathematical assumptions on which they rely diminish their applicability in a number of machine learning and data mining applications. This is mainly due to the following factors: SDRTs fit a linear model to the data; are suitable to handle numeric features only; are often fooled by spurious or masked correlation; the outcome of SDRTs is rarely easy to interpret.

Current statistical techniques may not represent an optimal solution to the data reduction issue in the data mining framework. The ADHOC algorithm provides a different approach to data reduction that overcomes some of the problems which degrade the performance of pure statistical techniques. ADHOC accomplishes data reduction in four stages: (i) Detection of linear and non-linear direct associations among the original features, (ii) Detection of indirect associations among features by investigating higher-order correlations, (iii) Clustering of related features to discover the hierarchy of concepts underlying the data, (iv) Selection of the most informative partition of the features.

Analysis of direct association between features. Input of the algorithm is a training set of feature-valued examples. In the first stage, ADHOC measures direct pairwise association between features by comparing the outcome of two non-parametric (distribution-free) statistical analysis, namely, correlation analysis and chi-square analysis. Measurement of the (linear or non-linear) dependence between any pair of features are normalized in the range [-1, 1] and collected in a matrix called the *first order dependence matrix*. Unlike SDRTs, ADHOC can handle both numeric and symbolic features. Numeric features are automatically discretized with the algorithm described in (Richeldi & Rossotto 1995) if they need to be compared with symbolic features to estimate possible dependence. ADHOC selects the most appropriate test from a set of available statistics for any given pair of features automatically. For example, correlation between a real-valued feature and an ordinal discrete-valued feature is estimated by applying a Stuart's Tau c test.

Analysis of indirect association between features. ADHOC identifies groups of features that are equivalent measures of some factor. It can be regarded, therefore, as a clustering technique. However, the mechanism underlying the formation of clusters is very different from the one employed by cluster analysis of features.

SDRTs rely on the analysis of direct correlation between features to perform data summarization. Their goal is to obtain factors that help to explain the correlation matrix of the features. But correlation may not provide a reliable measure of the association between two features, as it does not take effects of other features into account. Spurios correlations may occur, or correlations may be imposed artificially or masked by other features. In this case, indirect relationships between features need to be investigated, since direct associations, which are measured by correlation, do not convey enough information to discover the deep structure of the data.

ADHOC search for indirect association is based on the concept of feature *profile*. The profile of a feature F denotes which features F is related to and which ones F is not related to. For example, let A, B, C, D, E, and F be six features that characterize a given data set. Also, let 0.2, 0.1, -0.8, 0.3, and 0.9, be estimates of the direct relationships between F and A, B, C, D, and E, respectively. F's profile is defined as the vector <0.2, 0.1, -0.8, 0.3, 0.9, 1.0>. Features which have similar profiles provide different measurement of the same concept (data dimension) for they are equally related (unrelated) to the rest of the features. If the converse were true, two concepts would be related in two contrasting ways at the same time, a very much unlikely situation in nature. Comparing feature profiles may yield more reliable an estimate of true association than a direct measure of association, such as correlation, provided the cardinality of the feature profile is not too small (at least 4). Since components of the profile vector express correlations, comparing feature profiles may be viewed as correlating correlations. The result of the comparison has been named *2nd-order correlation* in (Doyle 1992), to stress out the double application of correlation. Accordingly, standard Pearson's correlation coefficient is named *1-st order correlation*. A statistical test, called R_{sim}, was designed to estimate profile similarity. Higher-order correlations between features are computed by recursive application of the R_{sim} statistics. Nth-order correlations result in a matrix called the *Nth-order dependence matrix*. By examining the Nth-order dependence matrix, one can determine the strength of relationship between features, and group those features that appear to be related. The recursive process halts when the profile similarity of features in each cluster goes over a predefined threshold or a given number of iterations have been done. Predictor variables may be partitioned into four different categories of clusters. They are called *Positive_Concept, Negative_Concept, Undefined*, and *Unrelated_Features*, respectively, and reflect the different typology and strength of dependences that may exist between a set of features. Features that share very similar profiles, i.e., that appear to contribute to the same dimension of the phenomenon, are grouped into a cluster of type Positive_Concept. Features related by a negative association to other features are assigned to a Negative_Concept-type cluster. Features which appear not to influence or to be influenced significantly by the rest of the features form the Unrelated_Features cluster. The Undefined cluster contains all the remaining features which can not be assigned to one of the other three types of clusters.

The analysis can then be repeated on each group of features in turn. The aim is refining the classification, as for the Positive_Concept clusters, or identifying relationships that could be masked by other features, as for the Undefined cluster. Cluster refinement is terminated when cluster cardinality goes below to a predefined value.

As a result, ADHOC returns a hierarchy of clusters which would resemble the hierarchy of concepts that characterize the observed phenomenon. A test of homogeneity of content is then applied to every level of the hierarchy to determine a good factorization of features.

Selection of the best feature subset

The problem of feature selection involves finding a good subset of features under some objective function, such as generalization performance or minimal use of input features. In our opinion, a feature subset cannot be truly informative and, consequently, good performing on unseen cases, unless it contains at least one feature which contribute to define every dimension underlying the data. Moreover, if there exist n important concepts that contribute to the target concept, and a feedback model identifies a feature subset with less than n features which achieves the best predictive performance, it is very likely that the subset overfit the data. On the other hand, in the very unlikely case in which data has no structure, every feature can be regarded as reflecting a single concept and the search would start from the entire set of features. The search for the best feature subset in ADHOC is based on the above considerations. The second step of the algorithm consists of selecting at most one feature from each of the factor, i.e., dimension of the data, that has been discovered in the data reduction step. As a consequence, feature subsets that reflect all the problem dimensions are formed, and search efficiency strongly increases. We investigated several search heuristics to select the smallest number of features from each factor (group of features which reflect the same data dimension). Among the others, genetic algorithms (GAs) turned out to be an excellent fit to this task (Vafai & De Jong 1992). Experimental studies were conducted by forcing the GA to select at most one feature from each factor, in order to focus the search on the best performing, least-sized feature subset which covers all the data dimensions. The feature subset evaluation function was the generalization performance of the induction algorithm C4.5. To fairly estimate the prediction accuracy of the learning algorithm, a k-fold cross-validation technique was applied. The training data set was broken into k equally sized partitions. The learning algorithm was run k times; in each run k-1 partitions were used as training set and the other one as test set. The generalization accuracy was estimated by averaging the error rate on the test set over all the k runs. Results, which are summarized and discussed in the next section, confirmed the intuition that GAs are able to find highly predictive, in many cases nearly-optimal, feature subsets.

Experimental results

We carried out an extensive empirical analysis in order to evaluate the effectiveness of ADHOC. We selected 14 real-world datasets featuring different types of problematic features, i.e., interacting, redundant and irrelevant features in different measures. Some of the datasets were drawn from the U. C. Irvine Repository (Murphy & Aha 1994), others from the StatLog Repository (Michie, Spieghalter, & Taylor 1994) and the COCOMO data set from (Bohem 1981). The experiments were carried out as follows. Real-valued features were discretized using the algorithm described in (Richeldi & Rossotto 1995) when necessary. The selection of the best number of data dimensions was left to the algorithm. The second step of ADHOC was performed by running C4.5 as induction algorithm and using the pruned trees. As a consequence, C4.5 was also used as term of comparison for the accuracy of the resulting feature subsets. To estimate the generalization performance of feature subsets, 10-fold cross-validation was used. ADHOC was first run on the training data; then the test set was used to evaluate the performance of the best feature subset learned by GA. The tables in this section report the average over the 10 runs.

Table 1 shows that the performance of feature subsets discovered by ADHOC improves C4.5 on 11 out of 14 domains. In particular, five times the improvement is significant at the 95% confidence level and twice at the 90% confidence level. ADHOC's performance is worse than C4.5's on the remaining three domains, in one of which, namely Segment, the degradation was significant at the 95% confidence level. Table 1 reports also the cardinality of the output feature subsets. Lack of space makes it impossible to list the factors as were discovered by ADHOC in the data reduction step for each dataset. However, we refer the interested reader to (Richeldi & Rossotto 1996) for a description of the results which were attained for two of the most interesting domains, namely German and COCOMO.

A second empirical analysis was conducted to evaluate the performance of the data reduction algorithm that was introduced above, hereafter designated ADHOC-DR. The test was made by comparison with the performance of factor analysis (FA) and cluster analysis (CA) of features. Basically, we run ADHOC on the same domains employed in the previous analysis two more times. The first step of ADHOC was modified to replace ADHOC-DR with FA and CA in turn. The second step of ADHOC was left unchanged, so that the discovered set of factors were used as starting point for the search of feature subsets carried out by the GA. Of course, since FA and CA cannot handle symbolic features, we had them to work on the same input correlation matrix that was used to feed ADHOC-DR. This was the best way to make a fair comparison among the three methods. Moreover, we run FA by using different factor extraction and rotation methods, then reporting the best performance result in case more alternative factor sets were discovered.

Table 2 summarizes comparison results. It can be noticed that both FA and CA could not process 6 out of the 14 datasets due to multicollinearity among the features. ADHOC-DR outperformed statistical data reduction techniques in all the remaining domains. The improvement was significant over the 95% confidence level in 3 out of 8 domains. Further analysis showed that each of the three datasets is characterized by quadratic relationships among features which cannot be discovered by statistical methods based on linear models. These results support the claim that investigating higher-order correlation may well overcome some of the problem of statistical techniques devoted to data reduction.

References

John, G. H.; Kohavi, R.; and Pfleger, K. 1994. Irrelevant Features and the Subset Selection Problem. In Procedings of the 11th Int. Conf. on Machine Learning.

Doyle, J. 1992. MCC-Multiple Correlation Clustering. *Int. Journal of Man-Machine Studies* 37, 751-765.

Vafai, H. and De Jong, K. 1992. Genetic algorithms as a tool for features selection in machine learning. In Proceedings of the 4th International Conference on Tools with Artificial Intelligence, 200-203.

Bohem, B. W. 1981. *Software Engineering Economics.* Prentice Hall.

Richeldi, M. and Rossotto, M. 1995. Class-Driven Statistical Discretization of Continuous Attributes. In Proceedings. of the 8th European Conf. of Machine Learning. Springer & Verlag.

Murphy, P. M. and Aha, D. W. 1994. UCI repository of machine learning databases.

Michie, D.; Spieghalter, D. J. and Taylor, C. C. eds. 1994. Machine Learning, Neural and Statistical Classification. Ellis Horwood Publ.

Richeldi, M. and Rossotto, M. 1996. Combining Statistical Techniques and Search Heuristic to Perform Effective Feature Selection. To appear in *Machine Learning and Statistics: the Interface.* Taylor, C., and Nakhaeizadeh, R., eds. John Wiley & Sons.

Dataset	C4.5		ADHOC		p-value	Dataset Size	Source
	%acc ± σ	*	%acc ± σ	**			
Anneal	95.6±1.6	19	95.0±2.3	8	0.292	798	UCI
Australian	84.2±4.0	14	86.7±2.8	5	0.014	690	STATLOG
Cocomo	73.8±21.2	18	77.2±21.8	7	0.420	63	BOHEM
CRX	85.0±4.0	15	85.1±6.1	7	0.941	690	UCI
Diabetes	69.6±5.4	8	71.2±5.5	3	0.404	768	STATLOG
German	69.5±5.2	20	74.2±2.5	7	0.018	1000	STATLOG
Glass	66.3±11.6	9	70.5±7.8	4	0.064	214	UCI
Heart	74.8±5.5	13	80.8±6.5	5	0.011	270	STATLOG
Pima	69.6±5.4	8	73.2±3.8	3	0.112	768	UCI
Satimage	85.5±1.3	35	86.6±1.1	6	0.040	6435	STATLOG
Segment	96.4±0.8	19	95.4±1.0	7	0.022	2310	STATLOG
Sonar	60.7±7.2	60	76.0±9.0	16	0.000	312	UCI
Vehicle	70.3±3.3	18	69.6±6.1	7	0.761	846	STATLOG
Vote	95.0±4.0	16	95.7±3.5	5	0.081	435	UCI

Table 1. C4.5 and of ADHOC's predictive accuracy on all the features and on the best feature subset, respectively. * column: no. of original features; ** column: size of the best feature subset. St. dev. given after the ± sign. P-values computed using a two-tailed T test.

Dataset	ADHOC		Factor Analysis		p-value	Cluster Analysis		p-value
	%acc ± σ	No Att.	%acc ± σ	No Att.		%acc ± σ	No Att.	
German	74.2±2.5	7	72.9±3.8	7	0.454	73.3±3.8	7	0.553
Glass	70.5±7.8	4	67.2±10.8	4	0.271	66.3±8.9	4	0.242
Pima	73.2±3.8	3	72.3±4.4	3	0.427	72.0±3.9	3	0.405
Satimage	86.6±1.1	6	85.5±1.4	6	0.021	85.4±1.4	6	0.021
Segment	95.4±1.0	7	94.4±1.2	7	0.045	82.7±2.6	7	0.000
Sonar	76.0±9.0	16	71.2±10.4	13	0.001	69.8±10.8	13	0.005
Vehicle	69.6±6.1	7	66.2±3.8	7	0.142	69.0±3.6	7	0.816
Vote	95.7±3.5	5	95.4±3.4	5	0.343	95.4±3.4	5	0.343

Table 2. Percentage predictive accuracy of ADHOC, Factor Analysis and Cluster analysis. St. dev. given after the ± sign. "No.Att" columns indicate the size of the best performing feature subsets. P-values were computed using a two-tailed T test.

Invited Papers

Harnessing the Human in Knowledge Discovery

Georges G. Grinstein

University of Massachusetts at Lowell
Institute for Visualization and Perception Research
Lowell MA
and
The MITRE Corporation
Bedford MA
ggg@mitre.org or grinstein@cs.uml.edu

Knowledge discovery is the process of discovering interesting, non-trivial patterns in data [1]. In the sub-field called knowledge discovery in databases (KDD) the discovery process targets data repositories, and often includes metrics on the results it has achieved, measuring how good the discoveries are with respect to, for example, non-trivialness, novelty, or extent.

Knowledge, the primary goal of data analysis and exploration, is most often discovered by generating information (structure) from data, and then abstracting non-trivial patterns (rules or associations for example) from the information. The discovery process can be done using numerous means that share the same goal: visualization, data mining, statistics, neural networks, or mathematical modeling and simulation [2].

Visualization Approaches

Visualization is different from the rest, however, in that it is also the actual mechanism by which the analyses and their results can be presented to the user. Visualization, in other words, harnesses the perceptual and cognitive capabilities of the human user, who is still the most powerful pattern recognizer and inference engine.

Visualizations can be divided into three classes [3, 4]]: exploratory, confirmatory or production. Exploratory visualization is dynamic and relatively unpredictable. The user typically does not know what to look for, or has minimal direction. The emphasis is on organizing, testing, developing concepts, looking for trends, and defining hypotheses.

In confirmatory visualization, on the other hand, the user has some sense of a goal, or some hypothesis to be confirmed. The visualization process is more stable and predictable. The user often selects predetermined system parameters, and typically is looking to confirm or refute hypotheses.

Production visualization is the most stable and predictable of the visualization approaches. Typically the user already has a validated hypothesis, and is looking to, for example, display data to emphasize a particular point. System parameters are set, but require fine tuning, perhaps using color map selections or layout formats.

Just as there are three classes of visualizations, there are three steps to the knowledge discovery process. The user initially defines concepts of interest and uses them to define domain structure in the data. Then one invokes algorithms that use the concepts to mine the data for non-trivial patterns. Finally the results are presented to the user, and the process is iterated.

Visualization in Knowledge Discovery

Where and how, in these three steps of knowledge discovery, can visualization be used?

In the first step, preliminary concepts or initial key points that need to be defined are typically presented as text files for the user to select and refine. In this initial part of the process today's user has few visualizations or presentations to call upon. This is therefore an open field for exploration. How might we visually represent concepts in the early selection stage, or visually have users define such concepts for interaction?

identify structures, patterns, anomalies, trends...
(databases, simulations, sensors, decision systems
data archives, communication systems ...)

Successful presentations at this stage will help the user formalize concepts, and will make it easier to focus the analytic tools.

In the second and third steps of knowledge discovery, the user ideally interacts continually with the selected information-setting parameters, fine-tuning, sub-selecting, and so on-based on examination of the preliminary information presented or visualized by the analytic tools. This iterative activity is fundamental to the discovery process, whether in KDD, or statistics, or modeling and simulation. And it offers further opportunities for innovative visualization technique. While many tools today summarize information visually, few offer the kind of intermediary visualizations that could reduce the number of iterations necessary to reach a result. We have to ask ourselves, then, how one can visually present the resulting datasets and summaries.

Visualization of databases, and more generally datasets, is in its infancy. Best known are statistical representations of data, such as statistical computations plotted in a variety of ways: histograms, time series, scatterplots. Modern approaches have extended the scatterplot concept. Whereas the pixel is a visual object whose representation on the screen is driven by three values (RGB or HLS, for example), an icon may be driven by an arbitrary number of values, permitting presentation of icons en masse on the screen [5]. Such generalizations enable us to display larger, higher-dimensional datasets.

It is interactive displays of this kind that will provide the mechanism, in effect the breakthrough necessary, to harness our human perceptual and cognitive capabilities. The user will then finally be able to interact visually with the information, and thus more fully participate with all the numerous components and steps of the knowledge discovery process.

Presentation

We will present a brief history of alternative visualizations and how they have been applied to various data visualization problems. The emphasis will be on how visualization, in particular exploratory visualization, can support the knowledge discovery process, including concept development for database management, database visualizations, and minimally structured dataset visualizations.

References

[1] Frawley, W.J., Piatetsky-Shapiro, G. and Matheus, C.J., 1991, Knowledge Discovery in Databases: An Overview. In Knowledge Discovery in Databases, Piatetsky-Shapiro and Frawley, W.J., Editors, AAAI/MIT Press, Vol 19, pp 1-27.

[2] Fayyad, U.M., Piatetsky-Shapiro, G., Smyth, P., and Uthurusamy, R., 1996, Editors, Advances in Knowledge Discovery and Data Mining, AAAI Press.

[3] Grinstein, G., and John P. Lee, 1996, Describing Visual Interactions to the Database: Closing the Loop Between Users and Data, Proceedings of the Second SPIE'96 Visual Data Exploration and Analysis Conference, San Jose, pp 93-103.

[4] Lee, J.P. and Grinstein, G., 1995, An Architecture for Retaining and Analyzing Visual Explorations of Databases, 1995 IEEE Visualization Conference Proceedings, Nielson and Silver (Editors), pp 101-108.

[5] Erbacher, R., Grinstein, G., Levkowitz, H., Masterman, L., Pickett, R. , Smith, S., 1995, Exploratory Visualization Research at the University of Massachusetts at Lowell, Computers and Graphics Journal, Special Issue on Visual Computing, Vol 19, No 1, pp 131-139.

Visualization ≠ graphics
Visualization = interaction with users
(exploring, steering...)

"tsher not face"
for data representation

Efficient Implementation of Data Cubes Via Materialized Views

Jeffrey D. Ullman

Department of Computer Science
Stanford University
Stanford CA 94305
ullman@cs.stanford.edu
http://db.stanford.edu/~ullman

Abstract

Data cubes are specialized database management systems designed to support multidimensional data for such purposes as decision support and data mining. For a given mix of queries, we can optimize the implementation of a data cube by materializing some projections of the cube. A greedy approach turns out to be very effective; it is both polynomial-time as a function of the number of possible views to materialize and guaranteed to come close to the optimum choice of views. The work reported here is a summary of results appearing in the following two papers:

V. Harinarayan, A. Rajaraman, and J. D. Ullman, "Implementing data cubes efficiently." To appear in 1996 SIGMOD. An extended version is available by anonymous ftp from db.stanford.edu as pub/harinarayan/1995/cube.ps.

H. Gupta, V. Harinarayan, A. Rajaraman, and J. D. Ullman, "Index selection for OLAP." Available by anonymous ftp from db.stanford.edu as pub/hgupta/1996/CubeIndex.ps.

Data Cubes

- Special-purpose DBMS for storing multidimensional data and handling queries that aggregate over some dimensions.

Example 1: Consider information about sales at a chain store. Dimensions might include day of sale, item sold, store at which sold, color of item, etc. Figure 1 suggests a 4-dimensional cube.

- One *critical* attribute represents the quantity to be analyzed, e.g. dollar amount of sale.

Views

The natural choice of views to materialize is a subset of the views of the form

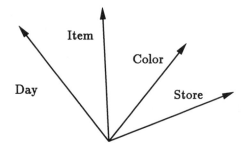

Fig. 1. A 4-dimensional data cube.

```
SELECT <grouped attributes>,
    SUM(<critical attribute>)
FROM <the data cube relation>
GROUP BY <some attributes>
```

- That is, a view is a projection of the cube onto some of its dimensions. Example:

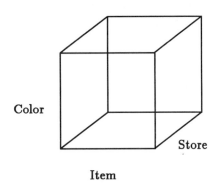

Queries

Typically group by some dimensions, select particular values for some other dimensions, and aggregate (sum the critial attribute) over the other dimensions.

```
SELECT <grouped attributes>,
    SUM(<critical attribute>)
FROM <the data cube relation>
WHERE <some attributes equated
    to particular values>
GROUP BY <some other attributes>
```

Example 2: The "shirts" plane of the Item-Color-Store cube represents the query "list the sales of shirts by color and store."

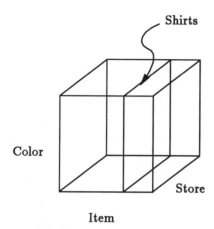

Relationship Between Queries and Views

Each query has a natural view from which it is most easily answered. However, it can be answered from views that group by more attributes; those views are larger and require additional cost. Most extreme: the raw data is a view (the *top view*) from which any query can be answered at great cost.

A (Slightly) More General Model

The *pure-or* model of view definitions:

- A collection of views (not necessarily projections of a data cube).
  - ✦ Each view can be constructed from any (perhaps none) of a set of "larger" views.
  - ✦ One view is the *top view*. It cannot be constructed from any view, and all views can be constructed from it.
- A collection of queries.
  - ✦ Each query has a weight, representing the likelihood of its being asked.
- For each query-view pair, there is a cost of answering the query from that view (may be ∞ if the view is unsuitable).
  - ✦ If query Q can be answered from view V, and V can be constructed from view W, then Q can be answered from W, and the cost is no greater than the cost of constructing V from W and then answering Q from V.
  - ✦ Each query can be answered from the top view at some large, fixed cost.

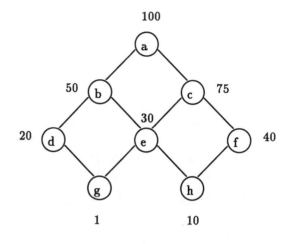

Fig. 2. Lattice of views to materialize.

Relationship to Data Cube

- Views form a hypercube.

- A view can be constructed from any view "above," i.e., a view that groups on a superset of attributes.

- A query has a natural "best" view, which groups by the same set of attributes.

- But a query can be answered from any view above its best view, at a cost equal to the size of that view (or some fraction if the appropriate indexes are available).

The Greedy Algorithm

- Assume the top view is materialed.

- Select additional views to materialize, one at a time, until some total cost of selected views is reached.

- At each step, select that unmaterialized view with the greatest *benefit*, i.e., the view that most reduces the average cost of answering a query, per unit space.

Example 3: In Fig. 2 is a lattice of views and their query costs.

- We shall assume that the queries each ask to see one of these views.

- *a* is the top view, already assumed materialized.

- *Simplifying assumptions*:
  - ✦ All views have unit cost of materialization.
  - ✦ All queries (= views) are equally likely.

- Want to select the 3 views that most improve the average query cost.

	First Choice	Second Choice	Third Choice
b	$50 \times 5 = 250$		
c	$25 \times 5 = 125$	$25 \times 2 = 50$	$25 \times 1 = 25$
d	$80 \times 2 = 160$	$30 \times 2 = 60$	$30 \times 2 = 60$
e	$70 \times 3 = 210$	$20 \times 3 = 60$	$20 + 20 + 10 = 50$
f	$60 \times 2 = 120$	$60 + 10 = 70$	
g	$99 \times 1 = 99$	$49 \times 1 = 49$	$49 \times 1 = 49$
h	$90 \times 1 = 90$	$40 \times 1 = 40$	$30 \times 1 = 30$

Analysis of Greedy Algorithm

Theorem (Harinarayan, Rajaraman, and Ullman): The benefit of the greedy algorithm can never be less than $(e-1)/e = 0.63$ times the benefit of the optimum choice of materialized views.

- *Oddity*: Frequently, after looking at the selection made by the greedy algorithm, we can deduce a much tighter bound. In particular, if either all chosen views contribute the same benefit, or the last view chosen contributes negligible benefit, then the greedy solution is optimal.

- A similar proof of the 0.63 bound appears in a different context by Cornujols, Fisher, and Nemhauser, "Location of bank accounts to optimize float," *Management Science* **23**, pp. 789–810, 1977.

- There is no tighter bound possible for the greedy algorithm, in general. Figure 3 is a counterexample.

- A recent result of C. Chekuri shows that *no* polynomial time whatsoever can have a worst-case bound better than the 0.63 that the greedy algorithm achieves.

More Complex Warehouses

The reason greedy is so successful is that the benefit function is *monotone*; that is, materializing a view never increases the benefit of some other view.

- If the costs of queries and views are nonmonotone, then greedy can be arbitrarily bad.

Views and Indexes

When queries involve specification of particular values for some attributes, e.g., "give the total sales of red items at the Des Moines store by month," indexes on materialized views can help. But there is no benefit to

Optimum = 1

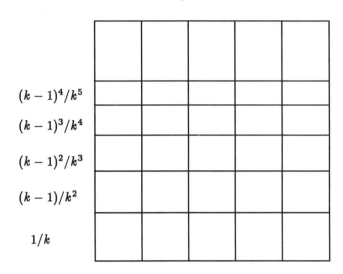

Greedy
$$= 1 - \left(\frac{k-1}{k}\right)^k$$

Fig. 3. Why greedy cannot do better than 63%.

choosing an index without first choosing a view upon which it is an index.

- Thus, if we treat views and indexes equally as things to materialize, there is nonmonotonicity, and greedy can be arbitrarily bad.

A Greedy Algorithm for Views and Indexes

For any view, its *tail* of indexes is chosen by greedily adding one index at a time, until the benefit per unit space of the view and the chosen indexes can no longer be increased.

The full algorithm is to repeatedly choose either

1. An index for a previously selected view, or
2. A view plus its tail of indexes that has the maximum benefit per unit space

until all available space is consumed.

Theorem (H. Gupta, V. Harinarayan, A. Rajaraman, J. D. Ullman): The above algorithm runs in time polynomial in the number of views and indexes and never performs worse than 47% of the optimal solution.

- The actual constant is $1 - 1/e^{0.63}$.

Acknowledgements

This work was supported by NSF grant IRI–92–23405, ARO grant DAAH04–95–1–0192, and USAF contract F33615–93–1–1339.

Index

Abdulghani, Amin, 256

Adriaans, Pieter W., 311

Agrawal, Rakesh, 164, 244, 287

Analysing Binary Associations, 311

application of mathematical theories, *see* mathematical theories, application of

applications, *see* data mining applications
  see also data mining and its applications: a general overview

Arning, Andreas, 164, 244

Aronis, John M., 355

Automated Discovery of Active Motifs in Multiple RNA Secondary Structures, 70

Automated Discovery of Medical Expert System Rules from Clinical Databases Based on Rough Sets, 63

Automated Pattern Mining with a Scale Dimension, 158

Bodek, Haim, 323

Bollinger, Toni, 244

Brachman, Ron, 89

Buchanan, Bruce G., 355

Buhmann, Joachim M., 363

Cercone, Nick, 271

Chan, Philip K., 2

Chang, Chia-Yo, 70

Cherkauer, Kevin J., 315

Cheung, David W., 307

Chew, Philip C., 134

Chiang, Jenny, 250

Ciesielski, Victor, 38

Clustering Using Monte Carlo Cross-Validation, 126

combining data mining and machine learning, 2-37

Combining Data Mining and Machine Learning for Effective User Profiling, 8

Comparison of Approaches for Maximizing Business Payoff of Prediction Models, A, 195

Czyzewski, Andrzej, 220

data mining
  applications, 38-81
  see also data mining and its applications: a general overview, 82-95

integration and application, 287-298
  techniques, *see* special data mining techniques

DataMine: Application Programming Interface and Query Language for Database Mining, 256

Data Mining and Model Simplicity: A Case Study in Diagnosis, 57

Data Mining and Tree-Based Optimization, 323

Data Mining with Sparse and Simplified Interaction Selection, 359

DBMiner: A System for Mining Knowledge in Large Relational Databases, 250

Dean, Christopher, 208

Debuse, J. C. W., 44

decision-tree, *see* decision-tree and rule induction

decision-tree and rule induction, 96-119

decision tree induction, *see* rule induction and decision tree induction

de la Iglesia, B., 44

Density-Based Algorithm for Discovering Clusters in Large Spatial Databases with Noise, A, 226

Deriving Queries from Results Using Genetic Programming, 303

Detecting Early Indicator Cars in an Automotive Database: A Multi-Strategy Approach, 76

Developing Tightly-Coupled Data Mining Applications on a Relational Database System, 287

deviation, *see* prediction and deviation

Discovering Classification Knowledge in Databases Using Rough Sets, 271

Discovering Generalized Episodes Using Minimal Occurrences, 146

Discovering Knowledge in Commercial Databases Using Modern Heuristic Techniques, 44

Discovery of Relevant New Features by Generating Non-Linear Decision Trees, 108

Domingos, Pedro, 96, 319

Efficient Implementation of Data Cubes Via Materialized Views, 386

Efficient Search for Strong Partial Determinations, 371

Efficient Specific-to-General Rule Induction, 319

Eick, Christoph F., 303

Elkan, Charles P., 267

Emde, Werner, 214

Empirical Test of the Weighted Effect Approach to Generalized Prediction Using Recursive Neural Nets, An, 183

Engels, Robert, 170

Error-Based and Entropy-Based Discretization of Continuous Features, 114

Ester, Martin, 226

Evaluating the Interestingness of Characteristic Rules, 263

Exceptional Knowledge Discovery in Databases Based on Information Theory, 275

Exploiting Background Knowledge in Automated Discovery, 355

Extensibility in Data Mining Systems, 214

extensibility of data mining systems, *see* scalability and extensibility of data mining systems

Extraction of Spatial Proximity Patterns by Concept Generalization, 347

Fahner, Gerald, 359

Fawcett, Tom, 8

Fayyad, Usama, 50, 82

Feelders, A. J., 102

Feldman, Ronen, 343

Field Matching Problem: Algorithms and Applications, The, 267

Flockhart, Ian W., 299

Fu, Yongjian, 250

Fulton, Truxton, 14

Ganesh, M., 291

general overview of data mining, *see* data mining and its applications: a general overview

Genetic Algorithm-Based Approach to Data Mining, A, 299

genetic algorithms, 299-306

Goldman, Robert, 140

Gong, Wan, 250

graphical models, *see* learning, probability, and graphical models

Grinstein, Georges G., 384

Grossman, Robert, 323

Growing Simpler Decision Trees to Facilitate Knowledge Discovery, 315

Hamilton, Howard J., 271

Han, Jiawei, 250

Harnessing Graphical Structure in Markov Chain Monte Carlo Learning, 134

Harnessing the Human in Knowledge Discovery, 384

Harp, Steven A., 140

Haussler, David, 50

Hirsh, Haym, 343

Hofacker, Ivo L., 20

Hofmann, Thomas, 363

Honkela, Timo, 238

Huynen, Martijn A., 20

Imielinski, Tomasz, 256

Imputation of Missing Data Using Machine Learning Techniques, 140

Induction of Condensed Determinations, 327

Inferring Hierarchical Clustering Structures by Deterministic Annealing, 363

Interactive Knowledge Discovery from Marketing Questionnaire Using Simulated Breeding and Inductive Learning Methods, 279

invited papers, 383-388

Ishino, Yoko, 279

Ittner, Andreas, 108

John, George H., 367

Kamber, Micheline, 263

Kasif, Simon, 14

Kaski, Samuel, 238

Kaufman, Kenneth A., 232

KDD for Science Data Analysis: Issues and Examples, 50

Khabaza, Tom, 89

Kloesgen, Willi, 89

Knobbe, Arno J., 311

Knorr, Edwin M., 347

Knowledge Discovery and Data Mining: Towards a Unifying Framework, 82

Knowledge Discovery in RNA Sequence Families of HIV Using Scalable Computers, 20

Kohavi, Ron, 114, 202

Kohonen, Teuvo, 238

Kontkanen, Petri, 176

Koperski, Krzysztof, 250

Kramer, Stefan, 371

Kriegel, Hans-Peter, 226

Lagus, Krista, 238

Lakshminarayan, Kamakshi, 140

Lange, Rense, 183

Langley, Pat, 327, 367

Lanzi, Pier Luca, 379

large databases, *see* systems for mining large databases

learning, *see* learning, probability, and graphical models

Learning from Biased Data Using Mixture Models, 102

Learning Limited Dependence Bayesian Classifiers, 335

learning, probability, and graphical models, 120-139

Leng, Bing, 152

Li, Deyi, 250

Linear Method for Deviation Detection in Large Databases, A, 164

Linear-Time Rule Induction, 96

Local Induction of Decision Trees: Towards Interactive Data Mining, 14

Lu, Yijun, 250

machine learning, *see* combining data mining and machine learning

Maintenance of Discovered Knowledge: A Case in Multi-Level Association Rules, 307

Mannila, Heikki, 146, 189

Masand, Brij, 195

mathematical theories, application of, 263-286

Mc Kearney, Stephen, 375

Mehta, Manish, 244

Mesrobian, Edmond, 32

Metapattern Generation for Integrated Data Mining, 152

Method for Reasoning with Structured and Continuous Attributes in the INLEN-2 Multistrategy Knowledge Discovery System, A, 232

Michalski, Ryszard S., 232

mining association rules, 307-314

Mining Associations in Text in the Presence of Background Knowledge, 343

Mining Entity-Identification Rules for Database Integration, 291

Mining Knowledge in Noisy Audio Data, 220

mining with noise and missing data, 140-151

missing data, *see* mining with noise and missing data

Monge, Alvaro E., 267

multimedia data mining, *see* spatial, temporal, and multimedia data mining
see also spatial, text and multimedia data mining

Multiple Uses of Frequent Sets and Condensed Representations: Extended Abstract, 189

Muntz, Richard R., 32

Musick, Ron, 120

Myllymäki, Petri, 176

Ng, Kenneth, 32

Ng, Raymond T., 347

Ng, Vincent T., 307

noise, *see* mining with noise and missing data

Northcutt, Dave, 323

Overview of Issues in Developing Industrial Data Mining and Knowledge Discovery Applications, An, 89

overview of data mining, *see* data mining and its applications: a general overview

Padmanabhan, Balaji, 351

Palstra, Gregory, 38

Parallel Halo Finding in N-body Cosmology Simulations, 26

Pattern Discovery in Temporal Databases: A Temporal Logic Approach, 351

Pattern-Oriented Data Mining, 152

Performing Effective Feature Selection by Investigating the Deep Structure of the Data, 379

Pfahringer, Bernhard, 371

Pfitzner, David W., 26

Piatetsky-Shapiro, Gregory, 82, 89, 195

Planning Tasks for Knowledge Discovery in Databases: Performing Task-Oriented User-Guidance, 170

Poor, Vince, 323

prediction, *see* prediction and deviation

prediction and deviation, 164-201

Predictive Data Mining with Finite Mixtures, 176

probability, *see* learning, probability, and graphical models

Provan, Gregory M., 57

Provost, Foster J., 8, 355

Quakefinder: A Scalable Data Mining System for Detecting Earthquakes from Space, 208

Quest Data Mining System, The, 244

Radcliffe, Nicholas J., 299
Raghavan, Prabhakar, 164
Rajan, Amynmohamed, 250
Rayward-Smth, V. J., 44
Reinartz, Thomas P., 76
Representing Discovered Patterns Using Attributed Hypergraph, 283
Rethinking the Learning of Belief Network Probabilities, 120
Reverse Engineering Databases for Knowledge Discovery, 375
Richardson, Travis, 291
Richeldi, Marco, 379
RITIO - Rule Induction Two In One, 339
Roberts, Huw, 375
rule induction and decision tree induction, 315-342
    see also decision-tree and rule induction
Rymon, Ron, 331
Ryu, Tae-Wan, 303

Sahami, Mehran, 114, 335
Salmon, John K., 26
Salzberg, Steven, 14
Samad, Tariq, 140
Sander, Jörg, 226
scalability and extensibility of data mining systems, 202-219
Scalable Exploratory Data Mining of Distributed Geoscientific Data, 32
Scaling Up the Accuracy of Naive-Bayes Classifiers: A Decision-Tree Hybrid, 202
Schlosser, Michael, 108
SE-Trees Outperform Decision Trees in Noisy Domains, 331
Self-Organizing Maps of Document Collections: A New Approach to Interactive Exploration, 238
Shafer, John, 244
Shan, Ning, 271
Shapiro, Bruce A., 70
Sharing Learned Models among Remote Database Partitions by Local Meta-Learning, 2
Shasha, Dennis, 70
Shavlik, Jude W. 315
Shek, Eddie C., 32
Shen, Wei-Min, 152
Shim, Kyuseok, 287
Shimura, Masamichi, 275
Shinghal, Rajjan, 263
Simoudis, Evangelos, 89
Singh, Moninder, 57
Smalheiser, Neil R., 295

Smyth, Padhraic, 82, 126
Sommer, Edgar, 214
spatial data mining *see* spatial, temporal, and multimedia data mining
spatial, temporal, and multimedia data mining, 343-354
spatial, text and multimedia data mining, 220-243
special data mining techniques, 355-382
Srikant, Ramakrishnan, 244
Srivastava, Jaideep, 291
Stadler, Peter F., 20
Static Versus Dynamic Sampling for Data Mining, 367
Stefanovic, Nebojsa, 250
Stolfo, Salvatore J., 2
Stolorz, Paul E., 20, 50, 134, 208
Suzuki, Einoshin, 275
Swanson, Don R., 295
Sykes, Jim, 339
systems for mining large databases, 244-261

Tam, Benjamin W., 307
Tanaka, Hiroshi, 63
technology spotlight (concise) papers, 262-382
temporal data mining, *see* spatial, temporal, and multimedia data mining
Terano, Takao, 279
text data mining, *see* spatial, text and multimedia data mining
Tirri, Henry, 176
Toivonen, Hannu, 146, 189
Tsumoto, Shusaku, 63
Tuzhilin, Alexander, 351

Ullman, Jeffrey D., 386
Undiscovered Public Knowledge: A Ten-Year Update, 295
Urpani, David, 339
Using a Hybrid Neural/Expert System for Data Base Mining in Market Survey Data, 38

Virmani, Aashu, 256

Waltz, David, 14
Wang, Jason T. L., 70
Wang, Wei, 250
Wang, Yang, 283
Wettschereck, Dietrich, 214
Wirth, Ruediger, 76
Wong, Andrew K. C., 283
Wrobel, Stefan, 214
Wu, Xindong, 339

Xia, Betty, 250
Xu, Xiaowei, 226

Zaiane, Osmar R., 250
Zembowicz, Robert, 158
Zhang, Kaizhong, 70
Ziarko, Wojciech, 271
Zytkow, Jan M., 158